The Purchasing & Supply Yearbook

2000 Edition

The Purchasing & Supply Yearbook
2000 Edition

Edited by
John A. Woods and the
National Association of
Purchasing Management

McGraw-Hill
New York San Francisco Washington, D.C. Auckland Bogotá
Caracas Lisbon London Madrid Mexico City Milan
Montreal New Delhi Paris San Juan Singapore
Sydney Tokyo Toronto

McGraw-Hill

A Division of The **McGraw·Hill** *Companies*

1 2 3 4 5 6 7 8 9 0 AGM/AGM 9 0 9 8 7 6 5 4 3 2 1 0 9

ISBN: 0-07-135860-9

The sponsoring editor for this book is Catherine Schwent. Design and Production services were provided by CWL Publishing Enterprises, Madison, WI, www.execpc.com/cwlpubent.

Printed and bound by Quebecor Printing

Contents

Preface

Welcome to the first edition of *The Purchasing & Supply Yearbook*, a resource designed to help you stay current with this rapidly emerging area of management practices. This book was developed for two fundamental reasons:

1. To provide *on an annual basis current information* on the most useful ideas, techniques, and case studies in the field of purchasing and supply management.
2. To serve as an *annually updated and revised reference* tool on publications, Web sites, organizations, and other information that will help you to apply purchasing and supply management practices efficiently and effectively.

We set four goals for ourselves in developing this book. While no single volume could substitute for your knowledge and experience, we wanted a book that would provide fast access to sources of information that would help you be more effective. To do that, we concluded that we had to deal with four requirements.

Create a Clearinghouse. There is much coming out in this field, and with the advent of electronic commerce, it is rapidly changing. So the National Association of Purchasing Management and McGraw-Hill saw the need for an accessible "clearinghouse" to which people with various roles and responsibilities in very different organizations could turn as a starting place to deepen their knowledge about this field and keep up with new material. We designed *The Purchasing & Supply Yearbook* to be that clearinghouse. It brings together in one place a wide selection of articles from magazines and journals directly or indirectly related to this field. We wanted to save you the time of finding what might be useful to you in performing your job and in applying purchasing and supply management practices, so we put these publications in one convenient compendium.

Emphasize New Practices. For much of the past, purchasing has been too limited in scope, seen as a staff position to service line departments. It's been an expense, not an investment. It's focused on transactions rather than relationships. That's all changing now, and one of the purposes of this book is to help you better understand how this field is evolving. To that end, we have sought articles that give a good sense of the array of practices that now fall under the responsibility of purchasing and supply management.

Develop an Authoritative Review. Yet another goal for *The Purchasing & Supply Yearbook* is to contribute to clearer thinking about the nature and application of purchasing and supply management such that we can bridge theory and practice. The field of supply chain management is broadly defined and takes in many different strategic thrusts. It remains in a state of ongoing definition and development. We hope to help provide food for thought for the people who are doing the defining and developing—practitioners in the field. By including the latest discussions of principles and applications, we hope to provide a way to systematize and standardize how you think about and keep up with modern purchasing practices. We will succeed if you believe this book is a resource that you use confidently, knowing it is current, reliable, and authoritative.

Create a Resource of Lasting Value. Because it is revised annually, *The Purchasing & Supply Yearbook* focuses on what has appeared in the year immediately preceding its publication. While currency is one of its strengths in a rapidly evolving field, we also intend for each edition to have lasting value. You will find material throughout the book that will continue to be applicable for many years as you go about applying purchasing and supply management practices in your daily work. You should be able to look at your collection of yearbooks each year and realize that you are building a library of the best practices in the field of purchasing/supply management. A value of the new edition each year is that it also updates you on all the key areas of purchasing, including new topics that reflect the latest developments in the field. In short, we have succeeded if this is the first source you go to for information on purchasing and supply management.

Organization

To make it easy to find material, we have divided this yearbook into six content parts and one reference part. Here's a brief overview of what you'll find.

Part One, Supply Management Concepts, includes a variety of articles on the conceptual foundation of purchasing/supply management, providing a perspective on the breadth and nature of this field. As a representaive article, see: "The Evolution of Purchasing to Supply Chain Management" by Richard Pinkerton.

Part Two, Supply Management Techniques, looks to apply the concepts in Part One, presenting a number of specific techniques you can use to manage the supply process better. One representative article: "Effectively Selecting Suppliers Using Total Cost of Ownership" by Zeger Degraeve and Filip Roodhooft.

Part Three, Supplier Management and Development, focuses on the relationship with suppliers. The articles here describe a variety of tried practices for creating win-win relationships with the companies that provide your organization with goods and services. A representative article: "Are Supplier Awards Really Worth It?" by Elizabeth Baatz.

Part Four, Electronic Commerce, includes a selection of articles that look at the many different facets of this important method of transacting business today. If you want to know more about e-procurement, spend time in this section. Here's a representative article: "The New 'Dot.com' World of Electronic Purchasing" by Terri Tracey of NAPM.

Part Five, Supply Management's Legal Environment, looks at the different laws affecting the purchasing process. We've selected articles that look at the many different legal aspects of purchasing that you should be aware of. A representative piece: "Purchasing and Law: What's the Connection?" by Martin J. Carrara and Ernest G. Gabbard.

Part Six, Industry Practices, includes a variety of articles emphasizing case studies and current practices in the field. Read here how leading companies are using purchasing and supply chain management to improve quality, better satisfy customers, and increase profits. One example of what's here: "Anatomy of a Purchasing Revolution: Wellman's Story" by Erv Lewis.

Part Seven, Purchasing and Supply Management References and Resources, includes three detailed annotated directories of Internet sites, publications, and organizations, and a calendar of major events, meetings, and conferences taking place in 2000.

Criteria for Selection of Articles

We applied three criteria for selecting articles for *The Purchasing & Supply Yearbook*:

1. **They must be current**. Because this is an annual publication, part of its value comes from the timeliness of its content. Therefore, all articles included were published in late 1998 or 1999.
2. **They must be practical.** We wanted articles that would help you solve problems and exploit modern purchasing and supply management practices efficiently and effectively. Articles selected represent the best thinking about how to make the most of purchasing and supply management techniques. We want you to use this book, not just keep it on your shelf.
3. **They must be authoritative**. There are a lot of articles in this field. We've tried to choose articles that represent the best in their class, providing you with a standard for reading and judging other materials.

Using *The Purchasing & Supply Yearbook*

This book is not meant to be read cover to cover. Peruse the table of contents and read those articles of most interest and relevance to your specific situation. Go back to it from time to time for more ideas and examples. Here are some examples of how this yearbook might be used:

- A **purchasing manager** who wants to keep up with the field will find this a useful summary of the latest practices. It's particularly useful for those who are working toward certification.
- An **executive** who wants to increase his or her awareness of the role of purchasing in organizational success will find this a useful resource.

- A **consultant** might use it for keeping up with the latest thinking in the area of supply chain management.
- A **student** who is entering this field or is working toward certification will find this a valuable resource for better understanding this growing field and learning about sources for additional study.

Our Vision for the Book

We envision *The Purchasing & Supply Yearbook* as the first source to use whenever you have a question or problem that involves issues surrounding purchasing and supply management. We want this to be a problem-solving, practical resource for you. If you can't find a possible solution here, we intend for it to guide you to other sources where you can find help. We've developed this book to serve as an evolving documentation of changes in the field of purchasing management, so it will change over time as the field evolves. However, we designed it to help people to understand and even shape these changes.

Feedback from You

We want this book to meet your need for sound, current information on purchasing and supply management tools and techniques. What do you think of it? How can we improve it next year? We invite your feedback. There are three ways to contact us:

Write to us c/o McGraw-Hill, 1333 Burr Ridge Parkway, Burr Ridge, IL 60521
Write directly to Holly Johnson at hjohnson@napm.org
Write directly to John Woods at jwoods@execpc.com

We look forward to hearing what you have to say and to serving your needs for many editions to come.

Acknowledgments

This book was a major undertaking and would not have been possible without the help and support of many people. At McGraw-Hill, **Catherine Schwent** and **Jeffrey Krames** came up with the idea of the yearbook and provided the support needed to complete it in a timely manner.

We are especially grateful to the professionals who contributed original articles to this edition of the Yearbook: **Ray Bacanskas** and **Jack Wagner** (Part Two), **Jon Stegner** (Part Three), **Terri Tracey** (Part Four), **Ernest G. Gabbard** (Part Five), and **Carla Lallatin** (Part Six). Their articles lead off each of these parts, and we urge you to read them for the current perspectives in each of these areas.

Robert Magnan and **Nancy Woods** of CWL Publishing Enterprises have been a crucial part of our team in completing this book.

Finally, we want to thank you who have purchased this book. We hope that it lives up to your expectations and that you will take the time to give us feedback so that we can continue to make it useful to you in future editions.

John Woods and the NAPM Staff

About the National Association of Purchasing Management

The National Association of Purchasing Management (NAPM) is a not-for-profit educational association that provides national and international leadership in purchasing and supply management research and education. Since 1915, NAPM has served purchasing and supply management professionals from around the world. From its national office in Tempe, Arizona, NAPM works with approximately 182 affiliated associations around the country to continually keep its members and the profession well informed, and on top of the latest trends and developments in the field.

NAPM's award winning Web site, www.napm.org, features general information on the association as well as educational products and seminars, publications, purchasing and supply resources, and opportunities to enhance the purchasing and supply management professionals' skills through online courses and discussion forums.

NAPM's monthly *Manufacturing and Non-Manufacturing NAPM Report On Business*®, including the *Purchasing Managers' Index* (PMI) in the manufacturing survey, continues to serve as one of the key economic indicators available today. NAPM members receive this valuable report free in the pages of *Purchasing Today*® magazine, one of the many benefits of membership.

Members also enjoy discounts on a wide variety of educational products and services, along with reduced enrollment fees for more than 100 educational seminars held throughout the country each year. Topics cover the entire purchasing and supply management spectrum, from an introduction to purchasing to advanced purchasing and supply strategies. Programs are available for senior executives as well as beginning professionals and are delivered via a variety of mediums to suit individual learning styles such as self-study workbooks, seminars, workshops, conferences, online courses, and satellite seminars.

For individuals interested in professional certification, NAPM administers the Certified Purchasing Manager (C.P.M.) and Accredited Purchasing Practitioner (A.P.P.) programs, enabling thousands of purchasing and supply professionals to continually test their abilities and keep their skills well honed. Members receive discounts on preparation materials and exam fees.

NAPM also publishes *The Journal of Supply Chain Management*, a one-of-a-kind publication designed especially for experienced purchasing and supply management professionals. Authored exclusively by accomplished practitioners and academicians, this quarterly publication targets purchasing and supply management issues, leading-edge research, long-term strategic developments, emerging trends, and more.

To continue to develop the purchasing and supply body of knowledge the Center for Advanced Purchasing Studies conducts key research projects and benchmarks that contribute to healthy business growth and advance the strategic level of the purchasing and supply function.

To provide a forum for educational enhancement and networking, NAPM holds the Annual International Purchasing Conference and Educational Exhibit in various locations throughout the United States each spring. Many of the top leaders in the purchasing and supply management field look forward to this unique opportunity for members and non-members alike to learn from each other and share success strategies.

To learn more about NAPM or to join online, visit NAPM on the Web at www.napm.org. In addition to general information, the site features a vast database of purchasing and supply management information, much of which is available solely to members. The site includes a listing of general purchasing and supply management references, an extensive article database, listings of products and seminars available, links to purchasing and supply related Web sites, periodicals listing, other purchasing and supply organizations, and contact information for NAPM affiliates around the country.

For more information or to apply for membership via telephone, please call NAPM customer service at 800/888-6276 or 480/752-6276, extension 401. See the following pages for a membership application that you can copy and use.

National Association of Purchasing Management®

Membership Application
National Association of Purchasing Management, Inc.

Members are encouraged to join a local affiliated association. To obtain information on the affiliated association closest to you and dues information, please call NAPM customer service at 800/888-6276 or 480/752-6276, extension 401. Applications can also be submitted via the Internet at www.napm.org.

Please check the appropriate box:
❏ New Member ❏ Past Member   NAPM ID Number (if known) _____

❏ I am replacing the following current member in my company (If replacing a current member, send completed application to the affiliate.)

Member Name _____   NAPM ID# _____

Dr. Mr. Mrs. Ms. Miss _____
  (please circle)   First Name   MI   Last Name

Title _____   Company Name _____
Please check the preferred mailing address:
❏ BUSINESS   ❏ HOME

_____   _____

City _____ State ___ ZIP Code ___   City _____ State ___ ZIP Code ___

Country _____ Postal Code _____   Country _____ Postal Code _____

E-Mail _____   E-Mail _____
( ) _____   ( ) _____   ( ) _____
  Business Phone Number**   Fax Number**   Home Phone Number **
                  **For international numbers, please include country and city codes.

Date of Birth (optional): ____/____/____

Industry Code (Choose a 3-digit code from the list provided on the back of this application): ___ ___ ___

Number of employees at your location (Please check one) ❏ under 100   ❏ 100-249   ❏ 250-499   ❏ 500-999   ❏ 1000+

Education (Check highest level completed): ❏ High School   ❏ Associate's   ❏ Bachelor's   ❏ Master's   ❏ Other _____
                                   ❏ Student (estimated graduation date): _____

Are you a C.P.M.? ❏ Yes ❏ No   Are you an A.P.P.? ❏ Yes ❏ No

Do you hold other professional designations? If so, please list: _____

Would you like to serve on a committee? ❏ Yes ❏ No

Are you involved in sales? If so, explain: _____

Option I

❏ **Regular Membership** (see back for details) I choose to become a member through (please provide affiliate name): _____

For dues information and District/Affiliate code, contact NAPM Customer Service at 800/888-6276 or 480/752-6276, extension 401.

District/Affiliate Code
(Code provided by NAPM): ___ ___ / ___ ___ ___

Annual NAPM/Affiliate Dues:	$_____
Administrative Fee:	$_____ 20.00
Affiliate Initiation Fee:	$_____
Other:	$_____
TOTAL:	$_____

Option II

❏ **Direct National Membership** (see back for details) NAPM Dues (does not include affiliate benefits) $_____ 270.00

Option III

Regular Membership — Volume Discount Program (see back for details)

Method of payment (U.S. Funds Only):

❏ Personal Check   ❏ Company Check   ❏ VISA
❏ MasterCard   ❏ American Express   ❏ Diners Club

Charge Card# _____

Exp. Date __/__ Amount to be Charged $_____

Cardholder Signature _____

NAPM members receive *Purchasing Today®* magazine as a $12 portion and *NAPM InfoEdge* as a $12 portion of the national membership fee. I agree to abide by the *NAPM Bylaws*, *Principles and Standards of Purchasing Practice*, and *Statement of Antitrust Policy*, as stated on the back of this application. A copy of the *NAPM Bylaws* may be obtained by writing or calling NAPM Customer Service at the address and telephone number listed below.

Signature _____

RETURN TO:	APPROVALS FOR AFFILIATE/NAPM USE ONLY	
	NAPM _____ Date _____	**PSY 51**
	Affiliate _____ Date _____	
	Other _____ Date _____	

NAPM Use Only

Amount $_____   Approval # _____   Date Entered_____   Initials _____

NAPM, P.O. Box 22160, Tempe, AZ 85285-2160 • 800/888-6276 or 480/752-6276, extension 401 • Fax 480/752-2299

OPTION I
Regular Membership

Regular Membership is when an individual chooses to join an Affiliated Association and National. Each Affiliated Association will set the annual dues for their local membership, which will include National dues.

Any individual that chooses this type of membership will receive discounts on both national and affiliate levels.

OPTION II
Direct National Membership

Direct National Membership is when an individual chooses to join the National level of NAPM only. The annual dues are $270.

This membership allows for discounts on the National level of products and services only.

OPTION III
Volume Discount Membership

With NAPM's new Volume Discount Membership, companies with 50 or more purchasing employees nationwide can save substantially on their membership dues. This category is available to corporations as well as governmental entities of every level and type.

The discount schedule is as follows:

Number of Members (nationwide)	Discount on Dues (without meals)
50-99	10%
100-249	20%
250 and over	30%

Volume Discount Membership is arranged through your company or government entity. Volume Discount members and all necessary information will be provided to NAPM headquarters by one individual from each company/entity. NAPM will invoice your company/entity for the correct amount of dues, and forward the affiliate portion to the affiliate. Any individual with Volume Discount Membership will

receive the benefits of belonging to an affiliate and the National Association.

For more information contact NAPM at 800/888-6276 or 480/752-6276, extension 3111.

Principles and Standards of Purchasing Practice

LOYALTY TO YOUR COMPANY,
JUSTICE TO THOSE WITH WHOM YOU DEAL,
FAITH IN YOUR PROFESSION

From these principles are derived the NAPM Standards of Purchasing Practice.

1. Avoid the intent and appearance of unethical or compromising practice in relationships, actions, and communications.

2. Demonstrate loyalty to the employer by diligently following the lawful instructions of the employer, using reasonable care, and only authority granted.

3. Refrain from any private business or professional activity that would create a conflict between personal interests and the interests of the employer.

4. Refrain from soliciting or accepting money, loans, credits, or prejudicial discounts, and the acceptance of gifts, entertainment, favors, or services from present or potential suppliers that might influence, or appear to influence, purchasing decisions.

5. Handle confidential or proprietary information belonging to employers or suppliers with due care and proper consideration of ethical and legal ramifications and governmental regulations.

6. Promote positive supplier relationships through courtesy and impartiality in all phases of the purchasing cycle.

7. Refrain from reciprocal agreements that restrain competition.

8. Know and obey the letter and spirit of laws governing the purchasing function and remain alert to the legal ramifications of purchasing decisions.

9. Encourage all segments of society to participate by demonstrating support of small, disadvantaged, and minority-owned businesses.

10. Discourage purchasing's involvement in employer-sponsored programs of personal purchases that are not business related.

11. Enhance the proficiency and stature of the purchasing profession by acquiring and maintaining current technical knowledge and the highest standards of ethical behavior.

12. Conduct international purchasing in accordance with the laws, customs, and practices of foreign countries, consistent with United States laws, your organizational policies, and these Ethical Standards and Guidelines.

NAPM Antitrust Policy

It is the express policy and intention of NAPM to comply at all times with all existing laws, including the antitrust laws, and in furtherance of this policy, no activity or program will be sponsored or conducted by or within NAPM or any association affiliated with NAPM which in any matter whatsoever will represent or be deemed a violation of any existing law, including the antitrust laws. This statement of policy will be implemented by the publication of the "Principles for Antitrust Compliance," "Standards for NAPM Activities," "Standards for Membership and Professional Self-Regulation," and "Standards for Conduct & Use of Surveys" which are available to all members of the association upon request.

Dues, contributions, or gifts to this organization are not tax deductible charitable contributions for income tax purposes. Dues may, however, be deductible as a business expense.

Return to local affiliate association or:
NAPM
P.O. Box 22160
Tempe, AZ 85285-2160
Or fax application to 480/752-2299

STANDARD INDUSTRY CODES (SIC) — If you have responsibility for more than one industry, please use only the one three-digit code representing the major activity of the company, division, or plant for which you work. (Write the three-digit code on the reverse side of this form in the appropriate space.)

AGRICULTURE, FORESTRY, AND FISHERIES
010 Agricultural production - crops
020 Agricultural production - livestock
070 Agricultural services
080 Forestry
090 Fishing, hunting, trapping
MINING
100 Metal mining
120 Bituminous coal/lignite mining
130 Oil and gas extraction
140 Nonmetallic minerals, except fuels
CONTRACT CONSTRUCTION
150 General building contractors
160 Heavy construction contractors
170 Special trade contractors
MANUFACTURING
200 Food and kindred products
210 Tobacco manufacturers
220 Textile mill products
230 Apparel/other textile products
240 Lumber and wood products
250 Furniture and fixtures
260 Paper and allied products
270 Printing and publishing
280 Chemicals and allied products
290 Petroleum and coal products
300 Rubber and miscellaneous plastic products
310 Leather and leather products
320 Stone, clay, and glass products
330 Primary metal industries
340 Fabricated metal products
350 Machinery, except electrical

360 Electric/electronic equipment
370 Transportation equipment
380 Instruments and related products
390 Miscellaneous manufacturing industries
TRANSPORTATION, COMMUNICATION, AND UTILITY SERVICES
400 Railroad transportation
410 Local/interurban mass transit
420 Trucking and warehousing
430 U.S. Postal Service
440 Water transportation
450 Transportation by air
460 Pipelines, except natural gas
470 Transportation services
480 Communication
490 Electric, gas, and sanitary services
WHOLESALE AND RETAIL TRADE
500 Wholesale trade - durable goods
510 Wholesale trade - nondurable goods
520 Building materials/garden supplies
530 General merchandise stores
540 Food stores
550 Automotive dealers/service stations
560 Apparel and accessory stores
570 Furniture/home furnishings stores
580 Eating and drinking places
590 Miscellaneous retail
FINANCE, INSURANCE, AND REAL ESTATE
600 Banking
610 Credit agencies, except banks
620 Security commodity brokers/services
630 Insurance carriers

640 Insurance agents, brokers/services
650 Real estate
670 Holding/other investment offices
SERVICES
700 Hotel/other lodging places
720 Personal services
730 Business services
750 Auto repair, services/garages
760 Miscellaneous repair services
780 Motion pictures
790 Amusement/recreation services
800 Health services
810 Legal services
820 Educational services
830 Social services
840 Museums/botanical, zoological gardens
860 Membership organizations
870 Engineering/accounting/related services
880 Private households
890 Miscellaneous services
GOVERNMENT
910 Executive, legislative/general
920 Justice, public order, and safety
930 Finance, taxation, and monetary policy
940 Administration of human resources
950 Environmental quality/housing
960 Administration of economic programs
970 National security/international affairs
NONCLASSIFIABLE
999 Nonclassifiable establishments

Part One

Supply Management Concepts

There was a time when purchasing was just that—purchasing. The purchasing manager fulfilled requests for supplies from various departments in an organization and dealt with suppliers to get the best prices possible. That's not how it works anymore. Purchasing is at the heart of making the organization's processes run smoothly while keeping costs down and quality up. In fact, while the title purchasing manager remains, the function is much more one of *supply chain management*. Making sure that the supply chain functions in a way that keeps inventory low yet allows line managers and employees to always have the inputs they need when they need them is at the heart of the purchasing job description.

Purchasing and supply professionals view many key suppliers as partners and work with them to build mutually beneficial relationships. Organizations and their suppliers are adopting procedures that allow for continuous improvement of the supplier's processes, the organization's processes, and the ways in which they work together.

Part One of *The Purchasing & Supply Yearbook* is about better understanding the changes that have been taking place in the field of purchasing/supply chain management. You'll find eleven articles in this part carefully selected to provide overviews of the different facets of procurement today. In making these choices, we sought articles from many sources, some relatively short, some more detailed, but all with a decidedly practical and educational bent.

We begin with an article by Professor Richard Pinkerton, "The Evolution of Purchasing to Supply Chain Management." This documents in a systematic way the new role of purchasing and supply professionals and includes a variety of references that you may find useful to learn more. This is followed by a piece from *APICS—The Performance Advantage* designed to explain what supply chain management is all about—"Understanding Supply Chain Management" by William Walker and Karen Alber.

Another article that should prove interesting and useful is "Making ERP Succeed: Turning Fear into Promise" from Booz-Allen & Hamilton's journal *Strategy & Business*. It provides a very complete overview of enterprise resource planning, where people go wrong and how to make it work. We've included two different articles from *Purchasing Today*® that highlight the role of supply chain management principles and practices in nonmanufacturing settings: "Supply Chain Management: Who's Doing It and How?" by Carolyn Pye, and "A Tale of Two Chains" by Roberta J. Duffy.

Purchasing and supply chain management takes in many activities. The articles mentioned above plus the others in this part of the yearbook and the other parts should help you keep current and learn techniques you can use in your business.

The Evolution of Purchasing to Supply Chain Management

Richard Pinkerton, Ph.D., C.P.M.

We include this article because it provides a good introduction to how purchasing has gone from procurement of supplies to managing the supply chain. It provides a context for many of the other articles that are in this yearbook and a good overview of what supply chain management is all about. Finally, it includes around 30 references, many of which may be useful to you in learning more about the current and future directions of purchasing and supply chain management.

Introduction

The term "supply chain management" has become a popular buzzword, probably first used by consultants in the late 1980s and then analyzed by the academic community in the 1990s. How and why did this concept develop; what are its prerequisites; and how does an organization implement what can be a very vague philosophy? It is the purpose of this article first to trace the evolution and the development from a passive-reactive purchasing function focused on paper trails and inward orientation to the proactive strategic supply chain concept which integrates the supply functions over an entire channel of distribution. We must learn the history to appreciate and understand the enormous change from purchasing as a cost center to supply management as a "value adder."

The analysis then moves to the necessary prerequisites for establishing both the philosophy and practice of an integrated supply system as part of the firm's strategic planning as against a purely tactical orientation. It is the author's experience that, while the term "supply chain management" is in vogue, only the *Fortune* 500-level firms (and not all of them at that) have, or are actually implementing, this concept. Certainly, the typical purchasing manager is still internally focused and rather reactive as he/she tries to implement the concept while operating under reactive organizational structures, policies and procedures. To state that one embraces supply chain management is one thing; to actually do it is quite another.

Finally, a blueprint for change will be addressed that, hopefully, will give direction to those organizations which are serious about making what is a drastic change in procurement thinking and action. Indeed, many large firms have had to bring in an entirely new management team to effect this massive reorientation and execution. The definition of "supply chain management" will be given in the next section, where it is most appropriate.

Evolution: From Paper to Profits

The first real new broader view of purchasing was the materials management concept. Undoubtedly, this movement was accelerated by the Second World War (WWII), the rapid growth of aerospace firms and the influence of military logistics. The military always embraced a broad view of "supply" and the large manufacturing firms of WWII were influenced by, and clearly in many cases directed by, the War Department (and later by the Defense Department) to organize their defense contracting activities to reassemble their military customers. By the mid-1950s, articles were appearing on materials management and the first textbook on the subject of this broader view of supply appeared in 1962.[1]

It is also thought that the rapid post-WWII expansion of the marketing concept, which also grouped similar activities together, stimulated a similar addition in other functional areas. For example, by 1974, traffic and transportation activities gradually expanded into a definition using the term "logistics" defined as a combination of materials management and physical distribution management.[2] The reader should be warned that both movements encountered serious opposition as both advocates were viewed as taking over "my authority and responsibility." Marketing directors felt that finished goods distribution was their responsibility and production managers felt that production control and in-plant materials movement was their function. More will be written on this conflict later in the paper, as the dispute continues.

Although there are many different definitions of materials management, most experts seem to include the following sub-functions:[3]

1. inventory control, or "how many" parts, pieces, components, raw material and finished goods;
2. production control, or "when" including shop floor control-scheduling along with the materials handling, storage and movement necessary to reach work-assembly stations. As any production manager knows, this is the key to his or her control over operations and few want to give up this activity for obvious reasons;
3. subcontracting, or "what systems do we buy?"—this is a very misused word but in its purest form, it is a form of make/buy/outsourcing decision-making based on a prime contract held by the manufacturer. The best original examples are from defense contractors who could not possibly possess all the technology, time, ability or capacity to produce all the subsystems of a final weapons system such as an aircraft, tank or warship. This concept is even more popular today as the emphasis to concentrate on core competencies continues, a focus which began in a major way during WWII. The key distinction here is buying a system of multiple assembled parts as against one component at a time;
4. stores, or "work station storage and supporting or indirect materials";
5. purchasing-procurement, or "buying" pieces, pounds, gallons, tons of raw material and maintenance, repair and operating supplies—in a few firms, this included capital equipment but purchases of this magnitude were (and still are) seldom the decision-making responsibility of purchasing;

6. transportation, or "incoming and finished goods freight movement"; and
7. salvage, or "disposing of surplus and scrap."

The advent of materials management and computer tools that came with it as Materials Requirement Planning (MRP) and Material Resource Planning (MRP II), pioneered by Oliver Wight, forced the organization—for the first time—to look at the entire flow of both incoming materials and the outgoing finished goods as a system.[4] This integration greatly improved internal production communication but did not bring about much improvement in external communication with suppliers or internal communication on the determination of specifications.

It also forced trade-off analysis. In theory, and in practice for many firms, one materials vice president or director and their staff would now look at the "big picture" and resolve the inherent conflict among accounting-finance, production and marketing managers. For example, accounting-finance wants zero inventory, production wants lots of safety stock "just-in-case" and marketing wants warehouses filled with finished products to satisfy the unrealistic due dates they promised customers. Purchasing was caught in the middle with constantly changing delivery dates and/or quantities ordered from suppliers who have shaky quality and little, if any, long-range knowledge of the buyer's requirements. Again, design engineering continued to act on its own initiatives.

Ammer (1969) was the first academic, and Pooler (1964) was the first practitioner, to write books and articles stressing the need to view purchasing as a potential profit centre.[5] Both authors used the materials management concept to demonstrate that material savings directly improve profits as a higher leverage factor than merely increasing sales. However, Pooler still emphasised that purchasing could accomplish the same result on its own and he was the first to coin the term "proactive procurement."[6]

Materials management had a large following in the period from 1960 to 1985. During these years, the well-known, ever-intensifying competition from Japan, with its growing reputation for high quality products and a different management style, started to panic US executives at huge firms. They started to lose market share and, in some cases, total markets. Included in the analysis of Japanese methods, aside from the well-known Total Quality Management (TMQ) process, was a growing awareness that they had also a totally different management chain system. One of the first, if not *the* first, observer of this change in procurement operation was Burt (1984) and his Integrated Procurement Systems or "IPS" as he called it. Burt defines IPS:

> The procurement of material and services is a process that cuts across organizational boundaries. The process includes activities in marketing, engineering, operations, production, planning, quality assurance, inventory control, purchasing and finance. Integration of the procurement activities performed by these departments results in a synergism, a situation where the whole is greater than the sum of its parts.[7]

Thus Burt recognized and developed the cross-functional team approach which builds on the synergy advantages of the materials management but expands it to include suppliers at the planning and design stage in a partnership atmosphere. He emphasised total ownership costs and the fact that component-material price is merely one, and usually not the key, cost driver as is poor quality, improper specifications, late delivery, rework and other critical cost drivers identified by the Japanese. Burt's book represents a major bridge from materials management to supply chain management. Although little read, this first major work by Burt deserves to be a procurement classic.

Another important author and an outstanding production manager/analyst at IBM is Witt. In 1986, Witt wrote a small trade book which may have triggered the "chain" aspect of a total logistics process.[8] He may be the first production manager to analyze the entire channel of distribution including the identification of total inventory in the pipeline from raw materials to finished goods. Like Burt's book, Witt's was little read but it was another big step in the march to supply chain management. Perhaps we should call him the father of Logistics Early Involvement or "LEI."

Building on the ideas and writings of Burt and Witt, although never quoting either, Leenders and Blenkhorn have written a very popular trade book with a fascinating title, *Reverse Marketing* (1988).[9] The principal contribution of this book is the 11-step process purchasing can use proactively to approach suppliers. In other words, purchasing takes the initiative to obtain supplier support and involvement in a variety of projects to reduce procurement cost and improve performance. This concept is a form of purchasing research, a subject developed by Harold E. Fearon, a key academic leader in purchasing circles.[10] The significant value of the work by Leenders and Blenkhorn is that the book sold well, thereby helping to promote the ideas and concepts of Ammer, Burt, Witt, Fearon and others who pioneered the movement to supply chain management.

During the period from 1984 to 1997, we see a proliferation of books and articles with slightly different versions, more examples and clever titles but all focused on proactive strategic procurement, supply chain management based on a number of prerequisites which will be developed in the next section. However, a few key developments and works of this period must be cited.

As American industry continued its fascination with Japanese manufacturing systems and management with particular focus on just-in-time (JIT) production and supply, a method only made possible by TQM, the improvement of transportation networks and cycle time reduction became mandatory. With suppliers far more dispersed than in Japan, any JIT system to decrease inventory required a new emphasis to reduce time to produce, ship and use. Deregulation of the transportation industry and the development of ever lower cost microprocessing computers and special software programs would promote integrated logistics, the first real "chain" concept.

One of the logistics pioneers is William C. Copacino, a managing partner at Andersen Consulting and former consultant at Arthur D. Little, Inc. Copacino is a frequent writer for *Transportation Management* magazine and, from 1986 to the present, wrote extensively on integrated logistics and the supply chain management concept.

His 1986 definition is a good start at understanding how the word "chain" is used to link all the related activities first identified by Ammer's materials management concept.[11] Copacino writes:

The total cost concept of logistics is based on the interrelationship of supply, manufacturing and distribution costs. Put in another way, ordering, inventory, transportation, production set up, warehousing, customer service and other logistics costs are interdependent.

Copacino reinforces the concept of trade-offs which are only possible when inventory, supply, production and transportation decisions are analyzed simultaneously. This helps to avoid cost reductions of, say, 10% in one area, which in reality inflate costs by 15% in another. This is the same theme argued by Burt in his 1984 book, that is, the IPS system, and Witt in his 1986 book. As Copacino observes, "For example, this full system view will quickly identify the cost, service and velocity impact of any poorly conceived practices such as the tendency among buyers to procure large order quantities and generate bloated inventories because they are measured solely on the purchase price."[12]

The early General Motors (GM) experiment with JIT and TQM and supply chain management at the Buick plant in Flint, Michigan, was only a partial success as the auto giant learned that "Buick City," as it was called, was far more complicated than imagined.[13] One does not make such massive changes overnight even with gigantic resources. However, Buick City provided GM with many important chain management lessons, including how to make high quality cars before being scheduled to close by the end of 1999.[14]

Other logistics "chain" pioneers include Martin (1990) and Harmon (1993). Martin's book, *Distribution Resource Planning,* talks about "total marketing channel integration" and how the term "logistics" is replacing the term "distribution." Martin develops his version of Quick Response/Continuous Replenishment (QR/CR) which is an adaptation of MRP and MRPII.[15]

Harmon talks about "links" and "demand update chain" and, like Martin, stresses the need to eliminate the middleman with what he calls strategy No. 1. "The first step [in establishing a network-wide system] is for the company to implement the system in its own distribution and production facilities, with linkage to the first tier vendors a second priority. Later phases would add additional supply network tiers to the already operational system."[16] The ultimate goal is to have inventory continuously moving in a pipeline and never in storage.

Martin, Harmon, Copacino, Bowersox and other logistics visionaries seem to concentrate (understandably) their analysis on the huge retail channel systems to "link" or integrate the supply chain from raw material to the producer to the retail outlet to the final customer. The heart of this integration is the realtime computer data systems which share rather long-term demand schedules and release dates with all members of the channel. Such systems obviously require long-term partnerships—contracts with the trust so necessary to the sharing of sensitive information. In addition, the actual shipment orders are perpetually released, usually on a daily basis by electronic means.

Many of the manufacturers of consumer goods are now using "third party" service providers, such as integrated logistics firms, to run the continuous pipeline. The other requirements include the very latest material handling and bar coding equipment.[17] All these developments have promoted the rapid growth of distribution centres and the concept of "cross docking" or incoming shipments from the suppliers being immediately transferred to outbound trucks, i.e., boxes in and boxes out in a continuous operation being controlled by bar coding computer information systems. Thus, the goal of modern logistics is a network chain of continuous replenishment flow with zero, or minimum, storage at any distribution stage.

The best example of an integrated supply chain is Wal-Mart. A recent *Fortune* article summarizes the Wal-Mart supply chain story well.[18]

Part of the genius of Wal-Mart's ecosystem was also its unprecedented involvement and entanglement in the affairs of its suppliers. By 1984, Wal-Mart, which had become a very powerful channel to customers, began exerting heavy pressure on their suppliers like P&G to keep their prices down. Moreover, Wal-Mart compelled its customers to set up cross company information systems to attain maximum manufacturing and distribution efficiency. For example, Wal-Mart and P&G reached an unprecedented partnership that involved extensive electronic ordering and information between the companies.

Quite clearly these developments drastically changed the way purchasing had traditionally operated with suppliers. The focus is now on a long-term relationship with fewer suppliers based on trust or "win-win" negotiation philosophy and the sharing of confidential information. Purchasing would have to be proactive, strategic and move from "exchange" thinking (purchase order to purchase order) to a long-term relationship. Most purchasing personnel still have real difficulty with this change given their paranoia and fascination with extensive legal (usually one-way) protection. If one needs a 100-page contract filled with penalty clauses, the two parties obviously do not have a partnership. This is not to suggest that tough negotiation is inappropriate, but it does indicate that straight competitive bidding, with its focus on price versus cost, is obsolete for strategic sourcing.

Perhaps Harmon summarises the evolution very well when he writes:

Purchase, customer and factory orders will become obsolete for use with repetitive demand items and will be replaced by electronic interchange of schedules between customer and supplier. Thus, all suppliers in the distribution network will have a time-phased schedule of all their customers' actual orders and future forecasts. Hence they will be better able to plan future operations based on the most timely and accurate information available.[19]

Carlisle and Parker (1989) made very important contributions in the area of buyer/seller relationship and trust development.[20] Their writings and consulting activities directed at changing the historic adversarial relationship between buyers and sellers are to be admired. The mutual suspicions are very ingrained on both sides even in the fairly young. Buyers are convinced they are not getting the best price (they still have trouble understanding total cost) and suppliers, with historical justification, feel buyers will dump them for the first competitor who offers even a slightly lower price. Buyers still tell professors and consultants that top management and even some engineers only understand unit price and focus on short-term savings "to look good and inflate dividends." There is truth in both arguments but, until both sides change their view of thinking, supply chain management will never be successful for the average organization. We can only hope more executives read *Zero Base Pricing* by Burt, Norquist and Anklesaria, with its emphasis on all costs.[21]

Jordan D. Lewis (1990) also deserves a mention. His observations on alliances, partnerships and relationships are very astute. As Lewis writes:

> A senior executive of a major American auto company compared an experience of his firm with that of a Japanese rival. Yet the Americans gained only 4% of the reduction obtained by the Japanese. The main reason, says this executive, was the Japanese firms had long-term relationships with their suppliers. They were willing to take more risks; the firms had helped each other in the past and knew that they could count on each other in the future.[22]

Another important contribution was made by Burt and Doyle in their 1993 book.[23] This fine work actually blueprints how to move from reactive purchasing to strategic supply chain management and what they call "value chain management." Burt's co-author, Michael F. Doyle, and a former Ford procurement executive also teamed with Robert C. Parker, another ex-Ford executive, as a consulting and speaking team extolling the virtues of supply chain management. They may be the first (along with Burt) to talk about tier one to tier N suppliers and the extended enterprise, i.e., managing raw materials from mother earth to disposal.[24]

In yet another and very recent book, Burt and Pinkerton (1996) take the purchasing responsibilities in supply chain management and blueprint the actual philosophy, strategy, tactics, policies and procedures to insure proactive procurement.[25] Burt and Pinkerton revise and update Burt's earlier 1984 IPS and document the savings achieved in actual case histories. Their focus, on the new product-service development process, is rather unique within procurement literature.

Finally, it is interesting to examine how the leading textbook in the field of purchasing defines supply chain management. Dobler and Burt (1996) define the supply chain in this way:

> This chain is the upstream of the organization's value chain and is responsible for ensuring that the right materials, services and technology are purchased from the right source, at the right time, in the right quality. The value chain is a series of organizations extending all the way back to firms which extract materials from mother earth, perform a series of value-adding activities and fabricate the finished good or service purchased by the ultimate customer.[26]

If one wants a simpler definition, supply chain management links all the organizations in an integrated communications system to manage in the most effective and efficient manner. In very plain terms it means the buyer of tungsten for laser lamp manufacturing must have a long-term relationship with the tungsten processor and also ensure that the processor has a strategic plan to procure the raw tungsten, i.e. monitor the supplier of each supplier to some manageable number of levels.

The textbook definition along with purchasing professionals in general seem to under-play the importance of transportation logistics and overplay the role of purchasing. They would be well advised to spend more thought, time and effort on the entire field of channels of distribution-logistics and thereby grasp the bigger picture of the entire system and how they interact with other players as advocated by Pinkerton and Marien.[27] Bowersox and Closs (1996) as logistics writers do have the bigger picture but also underplay the role of purchasing and critical tasks of sourcing, negotiating and contracting.[28] Perhaps some-day, production, engineering, purchasing, materials and logistics people will really talk to each other as opposed to themselves and their own empires.

Supply chain management requires a balanced emphasis. This total systems view is extremely difficult to translate into actual operation. As Burt and a few others cited in the article have so long argued, tear down these departmental, functional walls and think macro. Plan strategically, then act locally with the proper integrated tactics.

Prerequisites for Supply Chain Management

The short history description outlined above reveals, at least in my opinion, how the build-ing blocks created this age of system "chain" channel integration. The materials manage-ment concept started the synergistic management awareness, the American development of micro computers and software facilitated it and the competition from the Japanese forced it.[29] Top management must (some do) realize that a supply chain is much bigger than procurement and logistics: it is an entirely new way of thinking and organizing the total lifecycle from raw materials to use of a final product or service by an ultimate user.

There is no chance of implementing the chain concept unless the following is in place or at least detailed plans set out to accomplish the following:

- *Top management understanding and commitment*—while this may be an old cliché for all new programmes, chain management starts at the top, the bottom layers will never force it.
- *The quest for excellence*—the only organizations which will make this change are those which will provide at all levels the desire and ability to embrace lifelong con-tinuous improvement in quality, service and personal effort.
- *Effective and efficient communications*—realtime electronic communications with shared information at all levels is an absolute must. Firms must do a much better job of forecasting, which requires a mix of maths modelling and industry experi-ence-judgement. The entire chain operation starts with demand forecasting and, if marketing managers really understand their role, they must dramatically improve their forecasting ability and accuracy.

- *Relationships instead of exchanges*—most people understand that partnerships, whether in marriage or business, require trust and long-term commitment.

  Purchasing personnel have a long history of being aversive because they were seldom rewarded (no one knows how to do it) for creative efforts and severely punished for mistakes. The price buyer is so well known it hardly needs any explanation. Many negotiation seminars still preach intimidation and almost childish tricks. The legal seminars are still extremely popular in purchasing circles. The heart of any good relationship is open communication and trust, not a legal document.

  Conversely, the production, engineering and logistics personnel must understand that sourcing is not the simple process they assume it is. Finding the right source and having fewer sources in long-term contracts makes sourcing even more critical. The Internet provides a list of possible candidates and what they make; it does not evaluate a potential partner for a long-term relationship nor can it possibly iron out the details of the performance requirements. While you buy generic products by computer, would you select a mate that way?

- *Cross-functional teams*—while most of us have been on a wide variety of teams, athletic, military and some business projects, most business members carry over to the team all the bad habits of committees which are merely temporary collections of people representing some other department or function. We all know most committee meetings are terribly dysfunctional, i.e., they either represent a speech forum for the boss or an opportunity for the members to protect vested interests. Team formation, training, operation and rewards require enormous maturity, patience and interpersonal skills. Ask any coach; many people simply cannot function on teams and that is why there are so few really great teams, even though many teams have a number of great individual performers.

- *The special philosophy-reality of teams, partnerships and alliances*—this may seem repetitious to previous comments but this prerequisite actually builds on earlier observations. Few teams/partnerships and especially alliances start based on complete harmony and trust; it must grow into this relationship based on experience, revisions and constant practice.

  Top management must provide constant support, guidance and training to resolve the expected conflict. Impatience and the wrong kind of pressure have caused many a coach and their team or partnership to fail. WWII and Gulf War allied forces were marked by contentious behaviour, yet both were magnificently successful with world issues at stake.[30] Unfortunately, many organizations have formed teams, partnerships and alliances based on lip service with no real commitment evident on either side.

  Long-term relationships, partnerships and alliances can only be achieved by reducing the number of suppliers, i.e., an organization does not need, nor does it have the time and money to manage a large number of relationships. The analogy to personal friendships is the same; one does not have the time to sustain a large number of close friends. This means purchases must be consolidated, standardised and simplified in order to increase the value or importance of the relationship.

How Does One Start to Link the Chain?

A rather detailed plan must be completed as opposed to the traditional audit. The traditional management audits, so popular with the giant firms from 1945 to 1985, were, for the most part, merely verifications that the corporate policies and procedures were being followed. As one might expect, they were, and still are, control programmes heavily, if not totally, run by the accounting departments. Audits almost always guarantee a continuation of the *status quo*; after all the corporate manual is law.[31]

Thus, the good old-fashioned planning process must be followed. It includes four formal stages: the situation phase; the objective phase and the creative or new action steps (the new plan or original plan in most cases); and the final phase, the implementation or execution phase.

The Situation Phase

The situation phase is actually the fact-finding activity to determine where the firm is at any given time. It documents the actual activities and results of all the relevant players. The best place to start is with an analysis of the contracting record of key suppliers and then work backwards. The organization is spending the big bucks with the critical suppliers, who, if there is failure or inefficiency, could shut down or damage corporate performance. With modern computer material data banks, the task is not very difficult. Count the number of requisitions and purchase orders per supplier which usually reveals far too much repetitive paperwork with far too many suppliers. This data will start to reveal the supply links in the chain and the costs to operate it.

The Objective Phase

This is where we want to go or be in the future in order to be more efficient and effective. We could call it the strategy phase. If we assume that the key managers understand the huge benefits of good supply management then what we should do is a natural progression from "where we are." This assumes that the firm has or will have all the prerequisites. Failure to have, or want to have, these foundations will almost certainly produce inaction and failure.

The Creative or New Plan

This phase takes the objectives, mission and vision developed and agreed upon in the second stage into the action steps, or "how," "when," "who," and "where" we accomplish the mission goal. The why part is articulated in the situation and objective phases. This stage is the operational time-phased marching orders, i.e., the flight plan to reach our destination. It is the failure to translate strategy into tactics and planning based on the wrong assumptions that produces analysis paralysis. At this stage, any hesitation on the part of top management is deadly as any organization has its people desperately trying to avoid change. These are the managers who find reasons not to take action and they are usually protecting their own sub-corporate empires.

At this or a prior stage, the organization must issue a policy statement endorsing the new plan and it must be in writing and given to all the workers, not just the managers. It should be announced in a series of corporate meetings by the president who blesses the plan.

Training, training, training—the three important activities prior to implementation. People cannot simply read the new policy or procedures. They have questions that need answering and they need confidence-building skill preparation such as is implicit in the objective: "how to be a productive team member." Teams need team building and negotiation training and lots of it.

The Execution Phase

The implementation act is the execution phase and we must monitor this mission progression. Anticipate the need for revision and/or restart. Retraining is absolutely mandatory. We so often hear "we did that last year," as if everybody learned it, did it right or even remembered it. Can anyone imagine getting on an airline knowing the crew never practised a form of continuous improvement? Almost nothing is ever learned well in one step and yet I have heard executives say that a good afternoon session on TQM is enough; who is kidding whom?

Conclusion and Outlook for the 21st Century

The case to adopt supply chain management is well made with many documented success stories. The aphorism that it still does "take money to make money" is still appropriate, so an organization must be willing to go through what will usually be a two/three year conversion period. How do you stop an operation long enough to change a new one? With difficulty is the answer. If your people are already overburdened, even with non-value activities, like checking requisites as just one minor example, an added team will probably be needed to extract them from one process while they change to another. After the planning, it is the actual starting with all its unknowns and anticipated problems that can grind a new plan to a halt. A company-wide task force, including consultants, is one answer but whatever you choose, the pay off of supply chain management is enormous.

It must be remembered that the supply chain concept is a product of recent evolution. The full adoption and implementation will take place in the 21st century as world markets become even more dominated by multinational corporations operating in the three great trading areas: the EU, the North American Free Trade Association (NAFTA) and the Asian Informal Alliance.

Notes

1. D.S. Ammer, *Materials Management and Purchasing,* 4th Ed. (Homewood, IL: Richard D. Irwin, Inc. 1980) See also L.J. De Rose, "The Role of Purchasing in Materials Management," *Purchasing Magazine,* March 1956, p. 115.

2. D.J. Bowersox, *Logistical Management: A Systems Integration of Physical Distribution, Materials Management and Logistical Co-ordination* (New York: Macmillan Publishing Co., Inc., 1974) pp. 14–25.

3. G.J. Zenz, "Materials Management and Purchasing: Projections for the 1980s," *Journal of Purchasing and Materials Management,* Vol. 17, No. 1, Spring 1981, p. 18.

4. O. Wight, *Manufacturing Resource Planning: MRP II: Unlocking America's Productivity Potential* (Essex Junction, VT: Oliver Wight Publications, Inc., 1984).

5. D.S. Ammer, "Materials Management as a Profit Center," *Harvard Business Review,* Vol. 47, No. 1, January–February 1969, pp 72–82, and Victor H. Pooler, Jr., *The Purchasing Man and His Job,* (New York: The American Management Association, 1964), pp. 19–22.

6. Victor H. Pooler, Jr. op. cit., pp. 239–246 and for the "Proactive" citation, see Victor H. Pooler, Jr. and D.J. Porter, "Purchasing's Elusive Conceptual Home," *Journal of Purchasing and Materials Management,* Summer 1981, p. 16.

7. D.N. Burt, *Proactive Procurement: The Key to Increased Profits, Productivity and Quality* (Englewood Cliffs, NJ: Prentice-Hall, Inc. 1984) p. ix.

8. P.R. Witt, *Cost Competitive Products: Managing Product Concept to Marketplace Reality* (Reston, VA: Reston Publishing, 1986).

9. M.R. Leenders and D.L. Blenkhorn, *Reverse Marketing: The New Buyer-Supplier Relationship* (New York: The Free Press, 1988) pp. 36–73.

10. H.E. Fearon, *Purchasing Research: Concepts and Current Practices* (New York: The American Management Association, 1976).

11. W.C. Copacino, *Supply Chain Management: The Basics and Beyond* (Boca Raton: FL: St. Lucie Press/APICS Series on Resource Management, 1997) p. 8, Quoting from his December 1986 article in *Transportation Management.*

12. *Ibid.,* p. 13. From his 1986 article in *Transportation Management.*

13. D.D. Buss, "GM Gears Up Buick City in its Biggest Effort to Cut Costs, Boost Efficiency at Older Site," *The Wall Street Journal,* February 21, 1985, p. 4. Also see Kevin R. Fitzgerald, "Buick City Heralds a New Era in Auto Making," *Modern Materials Handling,* November 1985, pp. 59–62 and R.L. Pinkerton, "Buick City: The History and Analysis of the General Motors Corporation's Just-in-Time Manufacturing System in Flint, Michigan," California State University, Fresno, The Sid Craig School of Business, University Business Center, working paper series, No. 101, 1991.

14. G. Gardner, "Buick City's Demise," *Ward's Auto World,* June 1997, pp. 23–29.

15. A.J. Martin, *Distribution Resource Planning: The Gateway to True Quick Response and Continuous Replenishment,* 2nd Ed., Essex Junction, VT: Oliver Wight Publications, 1993).

16. R.L. Harmon, *Reinventing the Warehouse: World Class Distribution Logistics*, foreword by William C. Copacino (New York: The Free Press, 1993) p. 18. Another good reference is John W. Schorr, *Purchasing in the 21st Century* (Essex Junction, VT: Oliver Wight Publications, 1992).

17. P. Quinn, "Tale of a Tiger: Tiger Accessories Earns Its EDI Stripes with Bar Coding Order Processing," *ID Systems*, August 1997, pp. 24–30.

18. J. Moore, "The Death of Competition," *Fortune*, April 15, 1996, p. 144.

19. Harmon, *op. cit.*, p. 157.

20. J.A. Carlisle and R.C. Parker, *Beyond Negotiation: Redeeming Customer-Supplier Relationships* (New York: John Wiley & Sons, 1989).

21. D.N. Burt, W.E. Norquist and J. Anklesaria, *Zero Base Pricing: Achieving World Class Competitiveness Through Reduced All-In Costs* (Chicago: Probus Publishing, 1990).

22. J.D. Lewis, *Partnerships for Profit: Structuring and Managing Strategic Alliances* (New York: The Free Press, 1990) p. 19.

23. D.N. Burt and M.P. Doyle, *The American Keiretsu: A Strategic Weapon for Global Competitiveness* (Homewood, IL: Business One Irwin, 1993).

24. R.C. Parker and M.F. Doyle, "The Future of Supply-Chain Management," *81st Annual International Purchasing Conference Proceedings,* 1996, pp. 181–186, published by the National Association of Purchasing Management,

25. D.N. Burt and R.L. Pinkerton, *A Purchasing Manager's Guide to Strategic Proactive Procurement* (New York: Amacom Division of the American Management Association, 1996).

26. D.W. Dobler and D.N. Burt, *Purchasing and Supply Management: Text and Cases*, 6th ed. (New York: McGraw-Hill, 1996) p. 13.

27. R.L. Pinkerton and E.J. Marien, "The Fundamentals of Inbound Transportation," *NAPM InfoEdge*, Vol. 2, No. 8, April 1997, The National Association of Purchasing Management, Tempe, AZ.

28. D.J. Bowersox and D.J. Closs, *Logistical Management: The Integrated Supply Chain Process* (New York: McGraw-Hill, 1996).

29. See the books and articles by R.J. Schonberger on the theme of Japanese management methods and philosophies. For example, one of his early works is "Just-in-Time Purchasing: A Challenge for U.S. Industry" with J.P. Gilbert, *California Management Review*, Vol. 26, No. 1, Fall 1983, pp. 54–68. Also consult the classic works of W. Edwards Deming, J.M. Juran, Philip B. Crosby, and the other quality pioneers.

30. L.R. Clayton, "Trust Should Grow Over Time," *Purchasing Today®*, May 1997, p. 29. Also see "Trust Should Be Immediate," by Blaine Vortman on p. 28 of the same issue.

31. R.L. Pinkerton and K.A. Pettis, "From Reactive to Proactive Procurement: A Case Study," *The 82nd Annual International Purchasing Conference Proceedings*, 1997, pp. 169–172, published by the National Associaton of Purchasing Management.

Richard Pinkerton has been a Professor of Marketing and Logistics at the Sid Craig School of Business at California State University, Fresno, since 1986. In 1996, he was elected Chair of the department. His industrial experience includes several years as Senior Marketing Research Analyst for the Harris Corporation of Melbourne, Florida, and Manager of the Sales Department at the Webb-Triax Company of Cleveland, Ohio. He is a specialist in price-cost analysis within the field of supply management. He has served as Chair of the Academic Planning Committee of the National Association of Purchasing Management (NAPM) and chaired the NAPM Research Symposium in 1992. Professor Pinkerton received his Ph.D. in marketing from the University of Wisconsin.

Understanding Supply Chain Management

William T. Walker, CFPIM, CIRM and Karen L. Alber, CFPIM

Want some help explaining supply chain management to others in your organiza-tion in terms they'll understand and appreciate? This article is designed to help you do that. In an era where purchasing goes far beyond procurement of supplies, it's useful to be able to articulate the value of effectively managing the supply chain to reduce costs, improve efficiency, and more effectively please customers. How does this happen? This article can help you answer that question as well.

D id you ever try to define supply chain management for your boss? About the time you were positioning it against logistics management or materials management, his or her eyes probably glazed over. When asked to skip the definition and just explain the ben-efit, you then got tangled up in the repetitive twang of ERP, DRP, MRP, and CRP.

The truth is, a two-minute sound bite cannot convey the whole message. But to help you out the next time you need to explain the essentials, here's an overview of the four broad prin-ciples that guide supply chain management. Though the concept may never be easy to grasp in water-cooler conversations, it will make better sense and be easier to implement when you look at it in these terms.

A Few Easy Definitions

Let's start with a quick glossary. First things first: *A supply chain* is the global network used to deliver products and services from raw materials to end customers through an engineered flow of information, physical distribution, and cash.

To expand on this definition, let's call a single company *the firm*, and let's call the firm's main line of business *the enterprise*. Most business enterprises today depend on the collective efforts of a group of trading partners to stretch a supply chain around the world, from the raw material supplier to the end customer. *A trading partner* is any organization outside the firm that plays an integral role within the enterprise and whose business fortunes depend on the success of the enterprise. Examples of trading partners are suppliers, contract manufacturers, subassembly plants, factories, distribution centers, wholesalers, retailers, carriers, freight for-warders, customs broker services, international procurement organizations, and value-added-network services.

Supply chain management oversees the enterprise relationships in order to get the information necessary to run the business, to get product delivered through the business, and to get the cash that generates profits for the business. Supply chain management looks at the enterprise as a whole. It includes not only relationships with other functions within the firm but also with all trading partner relationships outside the firm.

The objective of competitive supply chain design is to weave each of the trading partners into a seamless fabric of information flow, physical distribution flow, and cash flow for the benefit of the end customer. The trading partners achieve their profit, or loss, through their ability to work together while recognizing that each organization is largely dependent on the other. By leveraging the resources of its trading partners, the firm can gain access to a larger market, and win a larger market share, with a smaller investment of its own assets. Supply chain management increases customer service while increasing return on investment.

Even though companies have been in supply chain relationships for years, they have not formalized a set of principles to make the optimum profit across the entire enterprise. (One possible explanation: It's only recently that computer hardware and software of the type needed to run enterprise resource planning (ERP) have become powerful enough to extend beyond the boundaries of a single firm.)

But having such principles can do much to clarify how to turn concept into reality. Thus, you can use the following four principles to guide your firm's supply chain management.

PRINCIPLE A: Build a Competitive Infrastructure

Here we're using the word *infrastructure* to mean the set of business processes that define ordering, delivery, inventory replenishment, returns, accounts payable, and accounts receivable.

How do you make such processes competitive? By focusing on the customer. Every customer interacts with a supply chain in terms of ordering a product, taking delivery of the product, returning a defective or unwanted product, and paying for the product.

A process map is a useful device for describing the customer-to-customer closed loop that defines each type of interaction. For example, customer ordering information might flow to an order-processing organization, where it is matched with finished-goods-picking information for the warehouse.

The warehouse organization might then arrange a logistics connection to forward the physical product to the customer. As the goods are picked in distribution, a replenishment order is sent to the factory to make more product. The customer might be asked for a credit card number at the time of the order. The revenue cash flow originating from the customer's MasterCard or Visa account might then be directed as a payment cash flow to the supplier of the raw materials.

A firm makes its infrastructure more competitive when it simplifies business processes, reduces the number of parties who touch a process, and speeds up the velocity of information. For example, the personal computer industry sat complacently on two tiers of wholesale and reseller distribution until Dell Computer created the virtual store, complete with direct Internet ordering, door-to-door delivery, and personal credit card payment. The change rocked the industry and, in the process, made computer sales and distribution much more competitive.

Keep in mind, though, that when trading partners first connect into a supply chain network, their infrastructure performance will be limited by the least common denominator of hardware technology and of applications software. For example, customers who want to order books through Amazon.com must not only have an Internet connection but also Netscape or Explorer Web browser software. Without these basic requirements, customers cannot easily do business with Amazon.com.

PRINCIPLE B: Leverage the Worldwide Logistics Network

To streamline logistics, you must know where the market demand and the supply base are located geographically. You engineer a supply chain network by connecting all the origins of supply to all the destinations of demand, and to each trading partner in between. There is both a forward logistics path and a hidden, reverse logistics path. The reverse path is for product returns, product repairs and calibration, and the environmentally responsible disposal of packaging materials.

Once you understand the totality of the logistics network, you can analyze freight volumes to determine strategic routings and modes of transportation. Logistics works to optimize cost vs. time by developing and managing relationships with a small number of preferred forwarders, carriers, and customs brokers. The total supply chain may involve some import and export if there's a cost advantage in product manufacturing. In this case, import duty classification, country of origin documentation, and export licensing are essential to maintaining a reliable supply chain.

Logistics leverage can provide an important competitive advantage. Compared to the thin profit margins posted on many income statements, lowering the costs of freight, duty, and warehousing has the potential to offer significant savings. Reducing the total number of supply chain nodes can slash logistics costs by consolidating freight volumes and reducing the total number of routings. Capturing accurate, high-velocity information at the point of sale can replace the need to keep every stock keeping unit (SKU) in inventory at every warehouse.

For example, M&M Mars, the candy manufacturer, invested in sophisticated technology that uses a single bar-coded badge to track the SKU by SKU breakdown of full container loads. The company also employs a satellite with global positioning capabilities to pinpoint the location of tractor-trailers on the move. In effect, the company substitutes information for inventory.

Hewlett-Packard does the same by shipping generic DeskJet printers to regional postponement centers, where the product is completed to order. Workers at these centers customize each printer with a country-specific power supply, power cord, and local language documentation.

PRINCIPLE C: Synchronize Supply to Demand

A capable supply chain matches the rate of supply with the rate of demand at each node. It synchronizes the product mix that's in production with the product mix that customers order. A firm maximizes the end-to-end throughput of a supply chain when each trading partner in the chain adjusts its throughput to match actual market demand. When one link in the chain overproduces relative to the market demand, inventory is accumulated. But when one link in the chain underproduces, the end-to-end throughput of the whole supply chain suffers. In such a case, one of the trading partners will be the system constraint. The supply chain achieves its best throughput performance when each of the trading partners exactly matches the throughput of this system constraint.

Supply chain synchronization is the secret to improving customer service without increasing inventory investment. Production only builds, and the logistics channel only moves, what the firm has sold. Actual customer demand pulls the SKU mix through the channel.

But again, the system depends on the accuracy and velocity of the information every trading partner provides. For example, let's say Quaker Oats creates promotional packaging tied to a current sporting event. The entire supply chain—including the retail channel distribution center (DC), the wholesaler DC, the Quaker DC, the Quaker plant, and all the logistics connections—must be capable of surge capacity and must be synchronized to match the promotion's timing. Otherwise, Quaker Oats will experience a surge in hidden supply chain costs for overtime, expedited freight, and premium stocking space. This could result in diminished customer service and lost profits.

PRINCIPLE D: Measure Performance Globally

An enterprise-wide supply chain transcends the local department, the cross-functional team, the divisional structure, the corporate business climate, and even the country culture. Yet, too often, performance measures continue to be strictly defined in terms that optimize local operations and reward individual performance.

Measurement drives behavior. So for a set of trading partners to bring their operations into close alignment for a high-performance supply chain, all parties must agree upon the right global performance measures. This is the Achilles' heel of supply chain management. It requires that you engender enduring trust among the partners and put forth great effort in relationship management across different company and country cultures.

Earlier programs like Efficient Consumer Response (ECR) in the grocery industry and Quick Response (QR) in the textile and apparel industry wrestled with these issues. The textile and apparel industry has also been a leader in efforts to apply the Theory of Constraints to the issue of defining workable supply chain performance measures. More recently, the Supply Chain Council established a long-term goal to benchmark cross-industry best practices based on a generally accepted Supply Chain Operational Reference (SCOR) model.

For the future, these questions remain: How can multiple trading partners work together to identify and eliminate supply chain inefficiencies, information delays, and hidden operating costs? And how will these same trading partners agree to split the profits from such an effort?

Understanding ERP

The production and inventory management (P&IM) professional in a single-firm environment manages inventory using the time-proven concepts of material and capacity planning and control. Before such professionals can optimize the planning and control necessary to achieve superior customer service at a competitive advantage, they need to capture a significant amount of information in a single cross-functional database. P&IM professionals use the financial feeds with the database to link accounts-receivable and accounts-payable cash flows with the general ledger.

Computer-aided tools such as Materials Resource Planning (MRP II), and advanced manufacturing philosophies such as the Theory of Constraints (TOC), have enabled the single firm to achieve breakthrough performance.

Now imagine this firm as a middle link in a supply chain of worldwide trading partners. The partners deal in information, physical product, and cash. The growth of revenues and profits is directly tied to the end-to-end throughput the supply chain can sustain. Optimized production and inventory management through material and capacity planning and control moves beyond the single firm to encompass the entire enterprise. This is the realm of enterprise resource planning (ERP).

Conceptually, ERP is the information hookup along the supply chain that replaces the single database of information that's essential to the single firm. ERP combines a single information platform with enterprise-wide material and capacity planning and control relevant to all of the trading partners. But for an ERP installation to develop its maximum competitive advantage, every trading partner must learn and embrace the A, B, C, and D principles of supply chain management described above. The partners must also keep in mind the following tenets that are particularly important to them.

1. The number of nodes that define the supply chain should be minimized. The business processes that define customer interaction with the supply chain for ordering, product delivery, returns, and payment should be simplified and streamlined.
2. The forward and reverse logistics network should be built around relationships with a small number of preferred forwarders and carriers. Wherever possible, logistics volume should be maximized along certain routings.
3. Every trading partner should agree to plan and control in a manner that synchronizes supply to actual customer demand. Every trading partner should understand how the performance of the system constraint will set the ultimate throughput of the supply chain at the same time that performance depends upon the accuracy and velocity of information from each trading partner.
4. Finally, the trading partners should agree to a set of global performance measures defined from the customer's perspective. Everyone involved must remember that ERP, like MRP II, is but a tool that rests upon a set of fundamental resource management principles.

When understood well, and put to work correctly, supply chain management recognizes this basic fact: The fortunes of the firm, which is but one link in the chain, depend upon the sustained performance of the other trading partners in the enterprise.

William T. Walker, CFPIM, CIRM, is the architect of supply chain management for Hewlett-Packard's Power Products Division and president of the APICS Educational & Research Foundation.

Karen L. Alber, CFPIM, is industry segment manager-consumer products for SAP America and president of the Chicago Chapter of APICS. They are the authors of Supply Chain Management: Principles and Techniques for the Practitioner, *published in 1998 by the APICS E&R Foundation.*

The State of Supply Chain Strategy

Donald A. Hicks

Supply chain issues can be very confusing and the decisions are often difficult. The author of this article explains the confusion and difficulty in terms of two paradigms, raises some basic questions about strategic supply chain planning, and then outlines four steps to making big decisions about operational strategy. He admits, however, that "operational supply chain strategy remains the toughest link in the market" and adds, "My predictions for the post-2000 marketplace are huge improvements, more powerful solutions, and continued chaos."

Two years after the publication of my series on supply chain issues in *IIE Solutions* ("The Manager's Guide to Supply Chain Planning Tools and Techniques," September, October, and November 1997), things remain as confusing as ever. It's a challenge even for the supply chain planning gurus to sort through the marketing hype and ambiguity that surround supply chain products to arrive at a coherent framework for integrating the technologies available today.

So let's just forge ahead once again and examine the major paradigms in supply chain technology improvement. We will also look at the historical causes for the confusion and project future developments in this dynamic industry.

We'll begin by exploring the current state of supply chain planning and improvement thinking. What are the strategic supply chain planning questions? What are the main approaches used by consultants to answer these questions? How are process-based and operational-based approaches different?

Next, we will discuss a methodology for integrating the most advanced problem-solving tools in this area that pertain to strategic decision making. Supply chain strategic planning questions often require the use of multiple techniques to get the best answer, so we'll dive into some detail about how these tools work, what they do, and what they don't do.

Before we begin, a disclosure: the company I work for is one of the vendors with tools cited in this article. But this story is not a sales promotion; rather, it is an educational piece that attempts to clarify and elucidate.

Supply Chain Strategic Planning Problems

Every company that manufactures, distributes, transports, or stores inventory is subject to many decisions about how its operations will run. An office products company, for example, must decide each day what will be produced in Plant 1 on Line 2. How much of each product will be made and in what sequence? Another company is grappling every day with determinations about the number of widgets to pull out of inventory and put on the truck to Cleveland. These decisions are made by the millions every day. They are important, but they assume that very little in the overall situation can change. This makes them operational decisions.

Other, higher-level decisions don't rely on the same kind of assumptions. If you allow the inventory target for SKU AG001011 to be variable, for example, or if you can select to ship from one of several warehouses by different modes of shipment, then you are dealing with tactical decisions. For tactical decisions, you assume that core structural components of the network, such as products and sites, are fixed, but how the components interact and the rules for interaction are allowed to change.

In addition, for strategic planning decisions, anything can be changed—except, of course, the external market demand. The goal of strategic planning is to arrive at the most efficient, highly profitable supply chain system that serves customers in a market.

Of the three types of decisions (all of which overlap), supply chain strategic decisions involve the largest capital expenditures, the biggest risks, and the most potential for dire results. Strategic supply chain decisions often pose such significant questions as:

- How many plants and warehouses should I own?
- Should I close any of them?
- Should I stock inventory? For which products? In which locations?
- Should I outsource the task of transporting goods throughout my network?
- Should I make the key subassemblies or purchase them? From where?

From strategic decisions all else flows. Can you optimize the production schedule at the Detroit plant if you don't even know whether you should manufacture product in the United States? Can you seek optimal safety stock levels while deciding whether inventory should exist?

It's a little—no, a lot—like making sure the crew is moving your boat as fast as possible without bothering to check which direction the boat is going.

Two Paradigms

Technology suppliers make the situation more difficult. Promises to optimize and improve your supply chain without a prior analysis and understanding of your supply chain's complexities and dynamics rely, at best, on chance.

Do a Web search on "supply chain optimization." You will find IBM promising supply chain optimization by Web-enabling your enterprise; a book from CSC Consulting on supply chain optimization; i2 and Manugistics offering "solutions" that optimize your supply chain. Is everyone even speaking the same language?

No, they're not. These and the many other companies that lay claim to supply chain optimization are offering a spectrum of solutions and tools. Most of them do what they do well and can help improve various aspects of supply chain performance.

To understand where all these companies are coming from, you must understand where they have been. Over the last few years, supply chain supplierss and supply chain ideas have evolved into two camps, each with its own focus: information technology and logistics.

Rick Hendershot, manager of supply chain operations for Delphi Automotive, points out that "To understand why these are separate camps, you need only to read the recent CSC Consulting survey of CIOs, which identified alignment between IT and corporate strategy as their No. 1 concern worldwide. IT and process groups just don't communicate well."

The larger camp is the IT group. Followers of this paradigm believe that information is the key to supply chain improvement. They focus on collaborative planning, sharing information, and getting companies synchronized with suppliers and customers. They also focus on synchronizing internal departments and divisions so that they can be centrally controlled and coordinated. This camp is incredibly good at marketing.

The smaller camp is comprised of logistics followers. This group, rooted in a more traditional supply chain paradigm, focuses on applying high-powered numerical analysis to large data sets in order to solve huge planning problems through analysis and optimization. This group has been around for several decades and knows a lot about things like industrial engineering, logistics, and operations research, but not much about marketing.

Both camps are right in their core theses; both have a lot to offer the modern enterprise. I find it useful to differentiate between the two camps by the way they orient their focus with regard to the enterprise. The IT camp has an external focus, keying in on enterprise interactions with other enterprises. The logistics camp has an internal focus, homing in on operations within the enterprise itself.

The two paradigms of supply chain improvement are both essential and complementary. A company that is looking for improvement by coordinating its production schedules with those of its customers will likely find savings. A company that is seeking to trim monetary outlays by increasing manufacturing flexibility and optimizing its distribution network cost structure will probably be able to do so. The most powerful approach, and the approach that will be the standard in the future, is to leverage the external and the internal efforts to make the paradigms work together.

Strategic Decision Making

Now that we understand the differing paradigms, let's focus on strategic planning. We've looked at supply chain strategic planning problems and noted that they are the most important, biggest-dollar (and hence highest-risk) problems facing companies. We also discussed the different approaches to solving them. An important implication, which I want to state explicitly, is that strategic planning problems are also the most difficult to analyze and solve rationally.

It is often the case that high-level discussions of supply chain strategy are completely void of facts. High-level decisions about how to organize company operations and logistics can end up being a forum for political gaming and salesmanship, with outcomes decided by personal charisma and volume rather than rationality and science.

No wonder supply chain strategy often boils down to who has the biggest gun. Supply chain strategic problems have been nearly impossible to model and analyze rationally. The problems involve huge data sets with complex data interrelationships and a great deal of uncertainty. There is no single computational way to "solve" a strategic planning problem, which leaves a void. Non-quantitative or "'soft" arguments can win on the gray battlefield of murky logic and guesswork.

Drawing on his own past experiences and observations, Rick Hendershot notes that "This, by the way, is the primary reason that re-engineering has fallen from favor and acquired a bad name. People were assigned to teams, often in concert with installation of a software package, and told to re-engineer business processes. Often, these people had experience or knowledge only marginally related to the area being re-engineered. Since there was no way to quantitatively evaluate what-ifs, discussions often degenerated into interpersonal debates, endless discussions, and tests of will or political strength. In other words, there were only qualitative ways of discussing options."

The Next Generation

This problem is common to many companies, across many industries, reflecting a need for tools and technologies that can help move the discussion into a fact-based approach. The tools and techniques that perform this function are, in fact, the next generation of supply chain software applications. These tools will leverage the data provided by IT but will use powerful engineering and operations research algorithms to move supply chain strategic planning decisions into an orientation I call operational supply chain strategy.

Increasingly, the IT camp will pose supply chain strategy questions that must be answered using operational strategy approaches. Take the case of a global merger between two large companies. The wizards in the CFO's office determine that the merger is good business and makes sense financially. IT is brought in to "integrate the supply chains."

Historically, the result would be a fixation on linking ERP systems, a project to align and combine corporate databases, with little or no thought given to how the actual supply chain operations of the new combined company can be improved. Simply linking IT systems will not provide the cost-cutting measures or efficiency improvements that the CFO is seeking and the CEO and chairman are expecting. The architects of the merger must analyze and arrive at an operational strategy for the new company based on the physical reality of the business.

There are many reasons why operational strategy and real operational improvement are not part of the typical IT re-engineering effort or ERP implementation. One is the issue of different paradigms raised earlier. Another is the fact that these IT-based projects are so complex, sweeping, and expensive that an attitude prevails that "We should just get the system in place, then we'll figure what to do with it." In other words, the project becomes timetable-driven instead of supply chain performance-driven. While this attitude is understandable, the problem is that it is the operational changes that will provide the return on investment promised by the IT project in the first place. This is why many companies that implement ERP or supply chain planning software packages are looking for an ROI that never materializes.

Automating a process doesn't improve it; it just makes it automated. Real improvement comes from making a change in the way business gets done from a process standpoint, an operational standpoint, and a supply chain structure perspective.

Introduction to Operational Strategy

The operational strategy to supply chain strategic planning can be understood from a macro level as a four-step process. Remember that in strategic planning, almost anything goes; therefore, we have to start from the few things that can't be changed. The most important thing, of course, is customer demand.

After considering customer demand, we need to go through four different steps to make the big decisions: network optimization, network simulation, policy optimization, and design for robustness.

Network optimization. The basic structure of the network should be determined by looking at customer demand. Out of the hundreds of possible network site locations that could be included, which ones should be used? What is the fundamental network configuration that will minimize the total cost of servicing the demand? The task of structural design means being able to evaluate millions of potential structures and selecting the least-cost network.

This is exactly what network optimization models do very well. Utilizing huge math models and highly advanced solution-finding technologies, network optimization tools have been used widely for strategic planning. Leading suppliers have been Insight, Intertrans (now part of i2), and Caps Logistics (now part of Baan).

Network simulation. The problem with network optimization is that, in order to evaluate millions of models, each model is greatly simplified and cost-focused. When it comes to finalizing the proposed design or selecting which network design is best out of three or four alternatives, we need to predict how each design will operate in the real world with all its variability. For this we use network simulation, which uses a detailed and complicated model to determine how well a proposed supply chain will run (although not how it can be changed to make it better).

There are many suppliers providing general discrete-event simulation modeling tools that can be used to build these complicated models. However, these complicated models require a considerable amount of time to construct. A new class of supply chain simulator tools is emerging that will speed model construction and analysis of alternatives. These simulators are specific to supply chain problems and are usually based on existing modeling platforms. Although Llama-Soft offers the only such off-the-shelf tool at present, look for several more to be released soon.

Policy optimization. Once a network design is finalized, the task is to come up with the best operating rules—policies—for the supply chain structural objects to follow. Policies include rules about whether or not inventory should be kept for various products: for example, if full truckload shipments suffice or if LTL shipments are needed to achieve the necessary customer service; if the company should make or buy components for each product and main sub-assembly.

Policy optimization is a difficult task, and there are no tools that are both detailed enough to predict network performance and intelligent enough to prescribe policies. There are two main technologies available that come close. First, there are network optimization models that apply multi-time period analysis or more detailed production planning constraints. Second, and more promising, are tools that apply optimization or goal-seeking methods to simulation models that attempt to prescribe how the simulation model can be improved. Eventually, even higher-level intelligent design tools will apply combinations of simulation and optimization models in tandem to design how networks should be designed and how they should operate.

Design for robustness. For the first three phases of operational strategic planning, we have focused our efforts to design the best supply chain based on what we expect to happen. In design for robustness, we attempt to evaluate if there are things that *might* happen. This will ensure that the network doesn't perform poorly under other-than-expected conditions.

This is a difficult concept. Think of it this way: the goal of supply chain management is not just to be profitable; there is an implicit goal to avoid extremely bad performance even under conditions that are unlikely but possible. Optimal supply chain designs, arrived at through the first three phases, often tell us to close warehouses, move plants, or make other big-ticket changes. What if we were wrong about demand? What if the cost of supply doubles? What seemed like a good idea given forecasted conditions may kill the company under other conditions.

It leads us to a paradox: optimal answers are not necessarily the best answers. Our job is not only to succeed but also to avoid failure. This fourth step is the most difficult to grasp because it forces us to consider unpleasant possibilities and unplanned events. However, it is exactly a robustly designed supply chain that will ensure your company's survival under nearly any circumstance.

One final note on the four-step methodology. Rarely will a company go from phase to phase completely because most companies have a network structure that they wish to modify; they are not starting with a blank slate. Sometimes many of the policies are fixed, but we want to do contingency planning. Perhaps we need to identify whether our current structure can handle what we expect to happen. But if an other-than-expected thing happens, how should the new optimal structure change? Strategic planning, at its core, cannot simply be automated. Since the context and the problem are so completely intertwined, you can never take the human out of the loop, and that is exactly what makes strategic decision making so difficult.

Final Observations

Clearly, the task of supply chain strategic planning is a big one, and we have only scratched the surface. We are only at the beginning of a new stage of development in supply strategy improvements. Operational supply chain strategy remains the toughest link in the market, mainly due to the degree of difficulty in using sophisticated models and complicated algorithms.

In the future, we will see the most powerful technologies applied and integrated to produce a whole new class of more complete supply chain strategic planning suites. Even while these suites become integrated with tactical and operational planning suites, supply chain planning itself will grow and merge with IT-based demand planning focused solutions.

My predictions for the post-2000 marketplace are huge improvements, more powerful solutions, and continued chaos. It will be another 10 years before the IT and logistics camps complete their merging and integration, but customers and industrial companies ultimately will be the beneficiaries of the new world order.

Donald A. Hicks is the chairman and founder of Llama-Soft, a company that makes simulation-based business applications. Prior to founding the company, Hicks was the senior vice president of development for ProModel Corp. He was the designer and developer of the first simulation-optimization software package. He has a B.S. in systems engineering from the U.S. Military Academy and an M.B.A. from the University of Michigan.

Making ERP Succeed: Turning Fear into Promise

Scott Buckhout, Edward Frey, and Joseph Nemec Jr., Ph.D.

You want to know more about ERP—enterprise resource planning? This article from Booz-Allen & Hamilton's journal Strategy & Business *explains ERP and how to make it work for you. It's not easy to do, but the results can be worth the effort. As you'll see, however, though many companies subscribe to the idea of ERP, they don't always do a good job of implementing it, and they don't get the results they expect. These authors give you ideas on how to do it right.*

The FoxMeyer Corporation used to be one of the largest wholesale drug distribution companies in the United States, with more than $5 billion in annual revenues. Attempting to improve its competitive position and prepare for growth, the company decided to use a popular enterprise resource planning (ERP) system, a group of software programs designed to tie together disparate company functions to create more efficient operations in areas such as the assembly or delivery of products.

FoxMeyer became an early believer in the potential merits of ERP systems and installed one with the help of one of the most reputable system integrators. Yet, by 1997, after FoxMeyer had invested two and a half years of effort and more than $100 million, the company could only process 2.4 percent of the overnight orders that it had with ancient legacy systems—and even that small percentage suffered from information errors. The company fell into bankruptcy and was acquired for a mere $80 million. Its trustees are now suing its system suppliers, blaming the ERP implementation for its business failure.

Is this an extreme case? Clearly. Is this unusual? Sadly, no.

Implementations of ERP systems are struggling throughout the world. They take too long, cost too much and fail to deliver the promised benefits of competitive advantage and cost reduction. Despite the promise and the high investment required to implement ERP systems, statistics show that more than 70 percent of ERP implementations, whether self-created or designed by established ERP software vendors, fail to achieve their corporate goals.

In a landmark study, the Standish Group, a market research company specializing in software and electronic commerce, looked at implementations in companies with more than $500 million in revenues. The study found that the average cost overrun was 178 percent, the average schedule overrun was 230 percent of original expectations, and the average slide in functional improvements was an astonishing 59 percent deficit. (See Exhibit 1.)

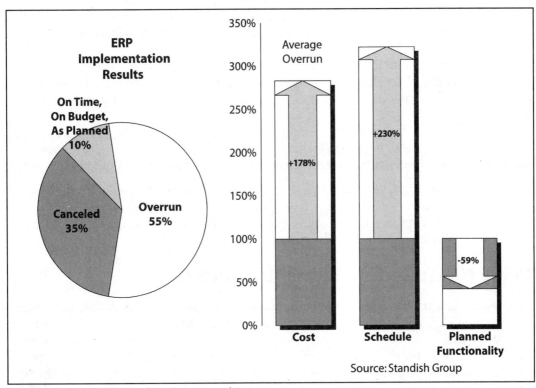

Exhibit 1. Few ERP implementations hit targets

·Still, such aggregate statistics hide real, and specific, horror stories about companies such as FoxMeyer Drug and the Dell Computer Corporation that have tried the systems. Dell publicly canceled its ERP system after two grueling years and an expenditure that exceeded $200 million. The company could tell it would not get the results for which it had paid so dearly and switched to a combined system/process solution that has redefined the industry.

Despite the horror stories, more than 20,000 companies worldwide paid in excess of $10 billion to adopt ERP systems in 1997 alone. Why do companies persist in trying? Some believe ERP systems will reduce the complexity inherent with using multiple data sources and systems that plague growth in global enterprises. Others hope ERP systems will solve the problem of legacy systems that inhibit re-engineering projects or the unknown difficulties that will arrive on Jan.1, 2000. Still others consider ERP systems the strategic weapons of the 21st century.

In fact, ERP systems have delivered for some companies. For example, use of such a system helped the Chevron Corporation cut purchasing costs by 15 percent and promises an additional 10 percent in the near future. International Business Machines Storage

Products reduced the time required to update pricing data from as much as 80 days to five minutes. Autodesk Inc. saved enough from inventory reductions alone to pay for the entire implementation.

So what is the problem with ERP systems? Is it a question, as some academic observers suggest, of poor corporate organization? Or is it, as some technicians believe, due to a real corporate inability to make the tough decisions necessary for a profitable implementation?

After more than five years of helping chief executive officers and general managers implement ERP systems, we believe neither of these reasons explains the gap between corporate expectations and results. Our experience shows ERP difficulties stem from two issues:

- The company has not made the strategic choices needed to configure the systems and processes.
- The implementation process spins out of business control naturally. This is inherent in the ERP implementation process.

ISSUE NO. 1: Getting Strategic Choices Made

ERP systems integrate key data and communications on planning, scheduling, purchasing, forecasting and finance for companies across regions, products, divisions and functions. Popular extensions can broaden this reach to sales, marketing, human resources and other functions. Many of the examples we will use will draw from the core ERP functionality, but the issue of strategic choices becomes even more important for a more comprehensive system. The system can provide management detailed insight into the operations of the business. For example, for a manufacturing company, an ERP system can show how much raw-material inventory is on hand, how much it costs to manufacture each product, and where each order is on the shop floor.

While an ERP system can provide this information, the key question is, should it?

Stepping back from the ERP system—looking at the information, communication and control functions it can provide—it becomes clear that the amount of control over a company's operations that needs to be provided by the ERP system depends on the design of the flow of products and services in the company.

A complex flow requires much system control. A well-designed value chain (e.g., "Product-Aligned Flow," in which the product flows using visual signals and well-defined routes) can embed many of the controls and other functions in the business process simply and far less expensively than the ERP system possibly could. (See Exhibit 2.)

The legacy processes that are being replaced, by necessity, embedded much of the communication and control in the business processes, and years of learning made this set of business processes very efficient and effective. Most implementations do not recognize and therefore do not capture this organizational efficiency.

Another celebrated version of the information, communications and control choices that companies miss is exemplified by the famous Japanese lean production systems. In these,

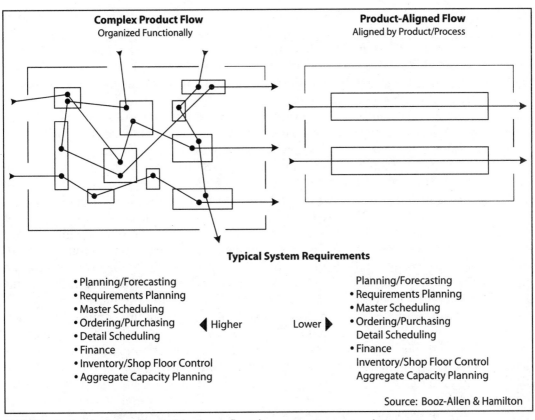

Exhibit 2. A product-aligned process flow lowers system requirements

much of the communication and control are designed right into the production system—and the computer has a very small role. (A Japanese visitor, after thoroughly examining a new ERP system in a United States automobile company, said, "This is a very impressive system. Of course, we'd have one too if we needed one.")

Lean production systems deliver low cost, low overhead, highly effective communication and control. How? For example, when a production process using Japanese kanban visual signals needs more raw material from a supplier, production workers pull a card and send it to the supplier. No computers, no orders, no overhead needed. The communication and control are built into the process design. Yet United States companies that are implementing ERP and lean production techniques often put a firewall between the two, not recognizing that this undermines both. The right answer is to recognize the decision the company is facing and make the decision explicit for all the company's efforts.

What can go wrong? At one company, the implementation team installed the detailed capacity-planning module of the ERP system, assuming that the company needed to understand and control capacity in detail (for example, per shift). In the legacy environment, detailed capacity planning had not been an option because the system was incapable of delivering it, so shop management got by with aggregate capacity planning as needed for staffing and capital decisions (which were made annually or quarterly). When implemented, the detailed capacity planning processes added overhead costs to do work no one had needed before. Tragically, the level of granularity required in the data (e.g., detailed, accurate setup and run times, scrap factors, machine downtimes) to develop the detailed capacity estimates accurately was impossible to achieve, so the capacity profiles created were useless. Nobody bothered to ask if the company in fact needed detailed capacity planning, and senior management saw the decision only when it was too late.

Judy Johnson, program director for the Integrated Systems Solutions Company, a subsidiary of the International Business Machines Corporation, put it this way: "This [is] not a decision to simply buy an I.T. tool—it [is] a decision on how to shape [the] business."

The reality is that an ERP system locks in the operating principles and processes for the corporation. Once the ERP system is installed, the odds of being able or willing to pay for modifications are close to zero. The cost, complexity, and investment of time and staff, and the implications and politics of untangling such an expensive investment prohibit most companies from tackling this issue. Consequently, it is important that ERP systems be implemented in a business-driven, cost-effective fashion from the start.

Management needs to translate the business strategy/key future competitive advantages into factors for the implementation. This often requires non-system actions to develop the physical or business resources to support the simpler system needs. For example, in a manufacturing company, lean manufacturing or alternative supplier relationship initiatives may be needed to eliminate the system-ordering functionality that adds so much cost and complexity. The result, of course, is a more efficient overall delivery process as the production or other delivery process embeds low cost communication and control.

Fortunately, only a limited number of critical business decisions require continuing top-management ownership. For example, in a manufacturing environment, senior management only has to focus on eight key areas to determine what actions should be inside or outside the system. (See Exhibit 3.)

ERP systems often provide a backbone of information, communication and control for a company, but managers seldom ask: "Which information? What communication? Where should control reside?" Even if they do ask and answer these questions, it is sometimes difficult to keep the decisions intact because the implementation process takes over and the decisions get recast on the basis of the system, not the business.

ISSUE NO. 2: How to Keep the Implementation Process from Spinning Out of Control—Put the C.E.O. in Charge

The new ERP commandment for senior management is "Put the chief executive officer in charge." We hasten to add that we are not referring to the usual "first commandment" of getting support from the top. Putting the chief executive officer in charge defines a different level of involvement in the implementation process.

	Business-Critical ERP Decisions	
Typical ERP Approach	**Critical Business Issue**	**Alternative**

• Frequently run Manufacturing Resource Planning (MRP) to generate planned production orders
  –Explode multiple layers in the Bill of Material
  –Schedule with detailed multistep routing for end part number
	• How will we know which parts to build and when?	• Build to rate for basic and stable parts
		• Cycle schedule for "Option" oriented parts

• Print work instructions every time an order is produced	• How will the mechanics know how to build each part?	• Use resident work instructions that leverage process stability in part families
• Run Capacity Requirement Planning module to build up capacity for each machine based on individual part setup and run time	• How will capacity requirements be estimated?	• Estimate capacity requirements based on aggregate demand on the bottleneck machine
• "Wand" each operation "complete" in the system for every order as it is moved between machines on the shop flow–indicating the exact location of every order	• How will we know the location of each order on the shop floor?	• Co-locate machines in cells; minimize work in progress; track orders with visual controls
• Run MRP system to generate start time for every operation on every order • Sort through queue in front of each machine to find next "hottest" job	• How will each mechanic know which order to work next?	• Work orders on a "first-in-first-worked" basis–no system information required
• "Wand" orders into system, which generates specific location in warehouse for every order received. • Use system to allocate raw material to specific production orders and "debti" from available stock	• How will we know where to store raw material and how much is available?	• Store inventory in a dedicated "static" location • Replenish inventory when level reaches visual reorder point
• Run MRP to generate purchase orders based on reorder lead times • Create individual purchase orders for every required shipment for raw material • Close every purchase order for each shipment received and pay upon delivery	• How will we know when to order raw material when it has been received?	• "Blanket" purchase orders that cover multiple shipments • Base shipments on cycle schedules or production rates • Base periodic payment on production rates (payment adjusted for exceptions)

• Use system to build up overall cost from each order
  (1) setup and run time for each required operation
  (2) Actual material consumption based on inventory allocations to each production order
	• How will we compute product costs?	• Periodically compute costs based on aggregate production (by part family) and aggregate resources consumed

Defaults to "Just-in-Case" Most Complex Solution	**Focuse on Business Needs**	**Opens Up Simpler Alternatives**

Source: Booz-Allen & Hamilton

Exhibit 3. Focus on key business decisions

The business case for implementing an ERP system is invariably built around significant cost reductions and improved capabilities. The cost savings are based on reduced legacy information technology costs as well as decreased indirect labor, direct labor and inventory costs. Improved capabilities often include world-class processes, tighter control and reduced cycle time.

Once the business case is closed, companies often focus on software and not business objectives—with an implicit assumption that the benefits will follow. At this time, senior executives typically relegate too much responsibility to technical experts. They mistakenly view the endeavor as an information-technology project, not a business project. Once management abdicates its responsibility for control, the working team is forced to make critical decisions by default.

Under this scenario, it is not long before the implementation begins to go off track. Well-intentioned people add "nice to have" functionality that can exponentially increase the level of complexity. Just getting to system cutover is a major accomplishment. Further complications are inevitable; it is common for an implementation to extend months beyond cutover because of unexpected problems such as missing data, slow response times or poorly trained staff. Jim Johnson, chairman of the Standish Group, estimates that at least 90 percent of ERP implementations end up late, over budget or both. "Once you hit $10 million, the chances of a project coming in on time and on budget are statistically zero."

Project managers sensing that budgets and schedules will soon far exceed original estimates try to get back on track by eliminating the redesign of certain business and physical processes. Implementation teams frantically tailor the new software to fit existing business practices. This rarely works.

As a result, the organization, having lost sight of any business objective, implements a crippled system, or one that is overloaded with unnecessary functionality. Whether the ERP system does not have enough capability or has too much, the company now has a system that needs to be fixed. The process of upgrading or reworking is not only expensive; it is also almost too complicated to implement.

Given the investment required to implement ERP systems, why are senior managers not more involved? Our experience suggests that chief executive officers and top managers are simply unsure of the role they should play. Top executives and senior managers focus on objectives and issues, while systems experts focus on processes. Neither side can ask the right questions of the other.

On a typical job, the chief executive might say, "ERP costs me half a billion dollars—give me some status, some sense of the results." The experts, always beyond budget and behind schedule, overwhelm senior managers with technical detail. Senior executives realize they cannot manage what they do not really understand and/or cannot translate into outcomes. As a result, they withdraw into pre-project boundaries, announcing that—despite the experience with systems implementation over the past 20 years—they will control the ERP installation with budgets and schedules.

Only when management realizes that an ERP implementation is a complex undertaking can management set out to make the right choices about what the company's ERP system should do and what it should not. Then, it can create a process of planning and implementation that will be effective. When the technologists make the technological decisions and senior management makes the strategic and business ones, the implementation meets its objectives, budgets and schedules.

Involvement by the chief executive officer on a small set of issues will greatly improve the likelihood of an implementation that is on budget and on schedule and that has the capabilities that support the corporate vision. The chief executive should get involved in three ways: by clearly outlining the organization's strategic priorities, by involving the organization at the appropriate level, and by linking management controls and incentives to project success.

C.E.O. ACTION ITEM NO. 1: Outline Strategic Priorities

The C.E.O. must take charge of the planning step for the ERP system. It becomes the most important and the most neglected step in making sure that the ERP system does what it is supposed to do. Without a strategic connection, the ERP system does what the technicians believe it should do—and not what is necessarily best for the company.

The key is to translate the company's vision, and the strategy that results from that vision, into concrete priorities, and then decide exactly how the ERP implementation will help the company deliver some, but not all, of these priorities.

What are the top priorities? How do they fit in with the industry's evolution? How do they resolve competitive issues? Which measures of operating performance are expected to improve and at what rate?

This front-end process is time-consuming and, in some respects, irritating to most managers who want to get on with the implementation. Yet, without it, no ERP system will work. Some senior executives counter this argument by saying, "We did articulate strategic goals, yet the ERP implementation is still a nightmare." When questioned more closely, we find that these goals, such as "improve customer service" or "standardize our processes," are too generic. With such objectives, middle management and staff do not have a framework for making decisions, and they generally allow the technologists to make them. As a result, system priorities remain out of line with corporate vision and senior managers complain that their ERP system has unnecessary capabilities, locked-in complexity and no strategic value.

In a very successful ERP implementation, Bay Networks developed four strategic objectives to communicate to its organization and implementation team:

- Growth: Future business growth will not be hindered by information-system capacity.
- Global Order Administration: Accept customer orders from any location into one system, assign shipment dates to available products in real time, schedule future ship dates for products not in stock, and check order status at any time.
- Financial Reporting: Have the ability to run profit and loss queries at any time on any day.
- Process Redesign: Focus re-engineering efforts on processes in which Bay derives its competitive advantage. The key here is to focus on priorities.

In two other very successful ERP implementations (at Owens Corning and the Compaq Computer Corporation) senior managers made the decision to modify the basic ERP software to match strategic goals. Both companies devoted significant time and expense to embed in the software key capabilities that were considered competitive advantages. Owens Corning, for example, needed to incorporate individualized distribution costs in their quotes. Compaq changed its manufacturing strategy from "build-to-stock," which calls for manufacturing to keep warehouses full, to "build-to-order," which runs plants only to fill consumers' orders. Compaq adapted its production processes and modified the generic ERP software to make that shift happen.

By creating this framework of strategic priorities, the chief executive focuses the implementation on exactly what is critical to the company's vision. In essence, this narrows the scope and prioritizes the business objectives within that scope; it creates absolute necessities. This alone simplifies the implementation and increases the likelihood of success. The chief executive, who has the required strategic insight and vision, is the only person who can take control at this level. Chief executives understand the industry's evolution, the company's competitive position and the next levers for growth.

C.E.O. ACTION ITEM NO. 2: Get the Organization Involved

Certainly, no one expects a chief executive to design data entry screens, or a software developer to determine how the company should face the market. Yet, in a way, most companies' current approach to ERP implementation seems to require both. Companies need to establish guidelines for involvement—or "rules of engagement" for different levels in the organization—so team members understand how and where their skills will be utilized and, more importantly, what issues they should resolve and what issues they need to raise to the next level of management. In most ERP implementations, these rules are not clearly defined. As a result, key strategic decisions are often made by the implementation team, those least equipped to make business decisions. A well-constructed implementation allows the people who best understand the issue to make the decision.

The chief executive manages the inevitable trade-offs among strategic priorities. Top operating management is accountable for the operational/tactical trade-offs. The first-line managers and implementation teams make the detailed design and execution trade-offs.

In one company with multiple divisions making different airplane subsystems, a corporate growth strategy was to extend past the traditional, original equipment manufacturer customers and serve new markets in service and maintenance. This would require that the divisions work together in new ways to provide one face to the new airline customer. The ERP "go" decision had been a division-level call, but the chief executive recognized that local division ERP implementations would complicate the servicing of new markets. He mandated that ERP implementation for these aviation subsystem divisions be done in concert with the new service strategy. This left the top operating management to make operational/tactical trade-offs and the implementation teams to focus on designing screens, data structures and detail steps.

In our approach, various levels of the organization engage in a series of dialogues, which help move the process along while aligning it with key strategic and operating priorities. The company translates the various choices that must be made during the implementation into the right language so dialogue can occur throughout the organization. Fortunately, setting up the process of dialogue is not difficult. Unfortunately, most ERP methodologies never mention it.

A meaningful series of ongoing discussions has to start at the top, with the chief executive and top management. The conversation should focus on implementation issues that affect the achievement of strategic goals. The chief executive always keeps in mind the alignment between the implementation and the strategic vision, making certain that the top management team understands the strategic priorities in a very concrete way. They discuss the short- and long-term impact of each trade-off, and continually monitor how each will affect the way the company meets its priorities. This will only include the small set of critical issues.

Armed with a better understanding of the company's vision, top operating management then makes the tactical and operating decisions that will align the processes and the ERP system with these goals. In the same way operating management has an ongoing dialogue with the chief executive, it conducts discussions with the implementation teams, focusing on operational and tactical alternatives. The goal is to balance physical and business processes, as well as system roles. These decisions often drive where a new process or control will reside—inside or outside the system.

For example, the management of raw-material inventory can either be embedded in processes or designed into the system. If it is embedded in the physical process, visual cues such as empty bins can signal a need for more material. If it is controlled by ERP, the system tracks total available inventory. When the inventory levels reach the reorder point in the system, a purchase order is generated. The first alternative provides lower cost with control at an aggregate level, while the second provides detailed control, albeit at higher cost.

The pros and cons of each alternative must be weighed against the priorities of the business, and top managers are best informed to make these trade-offs. They understand both the operational details of a particular business unit and the strategic priorities of the business. For example, if minimizing raw-material inventory is a strategic priority or if inventory costs must be tightly monitored because of fluctuating commodity prices, then the detailed control may be worth the higher cost. The cost/benefit trade is made specifically by those best qualified to make the decision, not by low-level systems implementers.

Within this overarching framework, the implementation teams and technologists make the detailed design decisions. Because they understand the system's technical aspects in great detail, as well as each unit's operating characteristics, they can design an optimal system. In a recent ERP implementation at Autodesk, for example, senior management decided that a rapidly changing business environment could make some of the ERP benefits disappear. As a result, management made speedy implementation a top priority. Aware of this goal, the implementation team focused solely on the core functionality the company needed, ignoring other "nice to have" features. The result was an implementation completed in just six months at the same time the company re-engineered 25 of its 40 business processes.

C.E.O. ACTION ITEM NO. 3: Link Management Controls, Incentives to Project Success

The chief executive can control the implementation by expressly linking key controls systems, performance measures and incentives to strategic priorities. In this way, the company:

- Prevents false declarations of success (the specific criteria are set up in advance).
- Helps implementation teams resist "scope creep" and focus on delivering results.
- Balances systems against business and physical processes, helping the company optimize overall business performance.

Following the successful Autodesk implementation, for example, Bill Kredel, the company's chief information officer, said, "Developing specific metrics to gauge project success and then tying those metrics directly to each executive's compensation played a major role in our success. Ten percent of the executive management's bonus and 20 percent of the implementation team's salary was tied to the success of the project." In a different approach, Bay Networks formed a risk-sharing partnership with the systems integrator, paying the integrator on the basis of the system's success.

How to Know if You Are on Track

Once a company commits to an ERP investment, it spends a great deal of time and effort determining if the implementation is working. We have found that, even with our approach, a large-scale implementation has to take some senior management attention away from the business for a time. Problems always arise and organizational infighting can get out of hand.

Keeping the following in mind can assist in determining whether the implementation will succeed:

- Does top management understand the connection between the system implementation and the achievement of strategic goals well enough to describe the system's priorities in strategic terms?
- Is the implementation plan coherent, comprehensive and linked to corporate objectives and non-system-related capabilities?
- Does the process include dialogue and discussion about the hard choices necessary between the systems and other sources of control?
- Does the company buzz indicate the organization buys into the link between strategy and system implementation?

These are key indicators that will help determine whether an ERP system will create a delivery system that runs like a dream, or a nightmare such as that faced by FoxMeyer.

Next Steps for ERP

The fundamental issue facing senior management is to insure that high—and in certain cases, very high—ERP investments generate full business benefits. The promise of the first wave of ERP installations has largely not been fulfilled. This is due not only to the problems in implementation described in this article, but also to the fact that many ERP installations were driven by the need to solve "year 2000" (or Y2K) compliance problems and/or were focused on fundamental financial applications.

Both of these areas of focus are by definition not going to generate major business benefits. One of the drivers of ERP investments has been the necessity to modernize systems due to Y2K. Obviously, the Y2K problem will either be resolved or systems will crash soon after Jan. 1, 2000. Thus, many installations were pressed by the Y2K schedule, and priorities were as simple as possible: a Y2K fix without the time to fundamentally rethink business processes to achieve step changes.

In the case of the financially focused applications, the installation of an ERP does not by itself generate much business value. Business value in financial areas is generated mainly by moving to shared server operations, which have been shown to generate savings of 30 percent to 40 percent.

So what is the next ERP opportunity? Simply stated, it lies in fundamental change in business operations focused on the "guts" of an enterprise: channel management, supply chain optimization, demand forecasting and other operations that can maximize customer service levels, minimize inventory levels and control other costs. These "guts" applications can be dramatically changed by examining overall business processes: Rethink organizational authority and responsibilities, and select and implement appropriate ERP applications to focus on these areas.

The challenges facing senior management are concentrated in the development of the strategic vision, say for the supply chain of an aerospace component subsystem supplier serving multiple end-users (original equipment manufacturers, repair depots, airlines, etc.) from decentralized profit-and-loss-based business units where the supply chain must be managed above the P.&L. sites. This example illustrates the key business decisions and change issues. Once the business vision has been developed and agreed to, the next challenge is to select the most appropriate ERP modules and/or best of breed bolt-on applications (e.g., for supply-chain management or decision support).

When these decisions have been made, the challenges of ERP implementation remain. The approaches described in the above article apply.

The end result of successful next-step ERP applications in the "guts" of a business have been shown to generate very significant benefits, such as a 40 percent reduction in inventory with a 30 percent improvement in customer service levels.

These central or "gut" ERP applications represent the real business value yet to be realized from the larger ERP system investments.

Scott Buckhout is a senior associate at Booz-Allen & Hamilton based in San Francisco. He specializes in helping companies develop business strategies and improve production capabilities. Mr. Buckhout earned his B.S. in aerospace engineering from Texas A&M University. He also holds an M.B.A. from the J.L. Kellogg Graduate School of Management at Northwestern University.

Edward Frey is a vice president of Booz-Allen based in San Francisco. He specializes in improving innovation and production capabilities for clients making aerospace and other highly engineered products. Mr. Frey earned his B.S. and M.S. in materials science from the Massachusetts Institute of Technology. He also holds an M.B.A. from Harvard University.

Joseph Nemec Jr. is a senior vice president of Booz-Allen and the leader of its global information technology group. During his 29 years with Booz-Allen, he has focused on helping Fortune 20 multinationals develop strategy and manage changes in organization, processes, culture and systems. Dr. Nemec earned his B.S., M.S. and Ph.D. from the Massachusetts Institute of Technology and is a member of the 81st Advanced Management Program at Harvard Business School.

Integrated Supply Basics and Benefits

Drew Curtis, C.P.M., CPIM and J. Don Etheridge, P.E., C.P.M.

Integrated supply is all about the development of long-term relationships between purchasers and suppliers with the goal of optimizing the costs of acquiring the products and services a company requires for its operations. This article provides an overview of integrated supply, including its use in nonmanufacturing firms, and describes the advantages of this approach to purchasing management.

Today's environment of competitive business strategies requires all aspects of an organization to improve efficiencies, validate costs, and optimize the supply chain. The purchasing and supply function is no exception. In their role of managing suppliers and the goods and services necessary to meet organization objectives, purchasing and supply managers must strive to establish a working model with suppliers that makes the most of that relationship. Integrated supply strategies are coming into play as a means to add value.

Integration, in terms of purchasing organizations and suppliers, has taken the form of various models, and can range from blanket system contracts to outsourcing entire functions. But, no matter the size or orientation of the organization, all integrated supply strategies involve shifting some of the responsibilities normally held by the purchasing organization to the supplier.

The aspects that a supplier can direct include:

- Physically warehousing inventory at the purchaser's site or nearby
- Carrying costs of inventory
- Forecasting material levels and requirements
- Ordering goods to meet requirements
- Servicing internal customers directly
- Working directly with multiple suppliers to service a single purchasing organization

The possibilities associated with integrated supply are broad, so it is difficult to determine general trends that encompass all aspects.

However, certain elements and their frequencies have been documented. For example, a 1997 study by the Manufacturers Alliance defines "insourcing" as transferring work

Integrated Supply Defined

A special type of partnering arrangement usually developed between a purchaser and a distributor on an intermediate to long-term basis. The objective of an integrated supply relationship is to optimize, for both buyer and supplier, the labor and expense involved in the acquisition and possession of MRO products—items that are repetitive, generic, high-transaction cost, and have a low unit cost.

Source: *Glossary of Key Purchasing Terms*, second edition

This definition can be expanded beyond MRO purchases to include the application of other supplies and services. Today's integrated supply agreements are much broader and cover the likes of long-term relations with original equipment manufacturers (OEM) suppliers and service suppliers, such as temporary labor agencies, printing and mailroom suppliers, and other service representatives.

done in-house to a supplier who performs the work at your location. This method of integrated supply is on the rise, according to the study, "Outsourcing + Insourcing = Best Sourcing." Eighty-five percent of participants responding as buyers indicated that the dollar value of their organizations' insourcing was higher than it was five years ago. Of the suppliers in the same survey, 87 percent reported the same increase.

Products and services that are non-value added or have a low strategic value are prime candidates for integrated supply relationships. When the low-value added functions are handled by a third party, purchasing and supply professionals can devote their time to more strategic activities. In the recent study, "The Future of Purchasing and Supply: A Five- and Ten-Year Forecast," completed by NAPM and the Center for Advanced Purchasing Studies (CAPS), A.T. Kearney, Arizona State University, and Michigan State University, several findings point to opportunities for integrated supply.

1. The study reports that tactical purchasing will become more automated and consortia and third-party purchasing will become more prevalent.
2. Third-party purchasing of nonstrategic items will increase, but will still be heavily managed by purchasing and supply professionals.
3. Strategic sourcing will require that the purchasing and supply function be tightly integrated with its suppliers. For those situations where integrated suppliers handle nonstrategic goods and services, the management of the supplier can be considered strategic sourcing, even if the actual transactions are not considered as such.

For each of these trends, the implications for purchasing and supply professionals are much more far-reaching. Not only will they play a strategic role in the management of these suppliers, but since the day-to-day transactions of such purchases are shifted, new responsibilities take their place. In the September 1998 issue of *NAPM InfoEdge*, "Skill Sets: Take Inventory, Take Action," the following skill sets were identified as relevant to the trends listed above, and thus potentially related to integrated supply models:

Strategic thinking: The purchasing and supply professional involved will need to determine the overall, broad consequences of bringing a supplier into an integrated relationship.

Technical knowledge: Integrated supply strategies can include involving a supplier on new product development or new process designs. Technical knowledge of products and processes is required in order to make improvements or changes.

Communication: This may include daily conversations about inventory, performance, internal users, and requirements. Purchasing and supply will also need to convince upper management of the merits of integrated supply.

Change management: Unless an organization already has an integrated supply model in place, the changes that accompany it may be unsettling for some. If internal users are now required to deal directly with an on-site supplier, they will need direction. If lead times and cycle times are targeted areas of integrated supply, there will be changes in forecasting methods which must be managed.

Risk management/risk assessment: Integrated supply strategies often involve sharing resources with a supplier that are not shared in a typical purchasing environment. For example, for a supplier to schedule services appropriately, he or she might require expected sales figures. A purchasing and supply professional's risk management expertise is necessary to determine how this information is best conveyed and what safeguards must be in place before doing so.

Is It Right for You?

Integrated supply strategies and the relationships that develop should be part of the organization's strategic plan. Purchasing organizations should not enter into these relationships until they have completed a process flow map of their materials and services to define their current situation. It is imperative to understand the current processes in order to ensure that the supplier has the ability to meet the needs of your particular business. Assign costs to each of the steps in the process so that suppliers' "total cost" added value solutions can be compared.

Once a thorough evaluation of the process has been completed it will not be difficult to determine if your company will prosper in this type of relationship. As a general rule, if the "total cost" of the product and management to support the program does not increase and the supplier meets all your qualitative criteria, it will be beneficial to engage in these programs.

Benefits of Integrated Supply

Organizations successful in utilizing integrated supply programs have achieved many benefits including:

Integrated Supply for Non-Manufacturing Organizations

Although integrated supply is often thought of solely as a procurement method for manufacturing organizations, the benefits of such arrangements can apply to non-manufacturing firms as well as service-oriented organizations. Although a firm may not need products related directly to the manufacture of products, they could benefit from the improved relationship and long-term commitment that comes with integrated supply relationships in some of the following areas:

Janitorial Products and Services—Cleaning products make up a large portion of any janitorial contract. Unfortunately, many janitorial service providers are small and are not able to leverage their size or develop cost-saving relationships with suppliers. A buyer may be able to develop an integrated supply relationship with a janitorial products supply for cost savings and better service. The buyer gains more purchasing power if they can leverage the purchases from several locations.

Office Machines—Buyers can negotiate integrated supply relationships where the supplier provides all copiers, facsimile machines and printers to the buyer under a complete service agreement. This relationship can be escalated by having the supplier provide on-site personnel to operate a copy center and mail room.

Temporary Labor—By carefully selecting and establishing a long-term agreement with a labor agency, the buying firm can establish savings by leveraging its labor costs by dealing with a single supplier. In addition to cost savings, simplification of the labor supplier base can speed screening and selection of potential candidates.

Office Supplies—Selection of a single office supply provider can improve costs and service for any firm. Many office supply firms make buying easy through Internet ordering and next-day delivery.

- materials availability
- inventory reductions
- space utilization
- employee productivity
- minimization of non-value added planning/purchasing administration
- payment efficiencies
- improved supplier relations
- receiving benefits
- cost knowledge
- improved time to market

Materials Availability

Perhaps the most important benefit achieved is the uninterrupted supply of materials which can be increased at a moment's notice. This inventory position allows manufacturing organizations to be flexible in meeting customer demands. This is not to imply that materials issues do not arise in integrated supply situations. Problems, if they do occur, are kept to a manageable minimum in successful programs.

Often, a supplier can improve the reliability of supply for critical items or items with long or unreliable leadtimes using a guaranteed stocking program. This is basically an assurance by the supplier that the required product will be delivered to the purchaser in a given period of time, usually 24 hours.

Inventory Reductions

Integrated supply can bring dramatic results in inventory reduction efforts. The supplier has many tools available to keep the buying organization's inventory low as well as improve the reliability of deliveries. Inventory reductions and all associated inventory-carrying costs can range from 20 to 40 percent of the average inventory on hand.

The supplier's value to inventory reduction will be especially noticeable in the early stages of an integrated supply relationship, because the supplier will be able to purge duplicates, errors, and inconsistencies in the current supply base. For example, particularly in MRO purchases, there may be 12 different ways to identify a particular office product, depending on which internal user you ask. An integrated supplier will not only consolidate those duplicates, which may result in volume discounts, but will also communicate directly with users to standardize requisitions and orders.

As the relationship progresses, the purchasing organization and the supplier should share schedules so that both parties can improve the planning function with increased efficiencies in production and logistics.

The benefits of inventory reduction may be achieved in several other ways as well. Here are some common models that can result in inventory reduction:

Consignment—Many suppliers are willing to maintain inventory at the purchaser's site. The purchaser pays for the goods only when they are drawn from stock.

Just-in-Time (JIT)—The basic JIT concept is an operations management philosophy whose dual objectives are to reduce waste and to increase productivity. Operationally, JIT minimizes inventory at all levels; materials are purchased, transported, and processed just in time for their use in a subsequent stage of the manufacturing process. Rather than a tool used to specifically lower inventory, this is a broad philosophy, of which lower inventories are just one result.

Buy Backs—The supplier buys back parts from the purchaser's organization and sells them back to the manufacturer, to another integrated supplier, or to another purchaser.

This is financially more attractive than salvaging excess parts. The price obtained for the items can vary according to the type of product being returned, the age of the product, and buy back terms negotiated into the integrated supply agreement. The cost of buy back services can be negotiated a variety of ways. The integrated supplier may absorb the cost of these services into its overhead, charge the purchaser a variable or fixed fee or buy the product back at a discounted price and sell it for a profit.

Return Policies—Integrated suppliers often can extend liberal return policies to purchasers. An example of this is with electrical parts and conduit. These items are often bought in excess for a project. When complete, the unused items can be returned to the supplier for a full refund. The purchaser may receive the full price for the bought back items or pay a restocking fee. The amount of restocking fee, or lack thereof, should be negotiated into the integrated supply agreement. The purchaser must keep in mind, however, that the savings gained by negotiating lenient fees may be offset by the supplier's added overhead costs.

Space Utilization

Space is at a premium in many parts of the country and the most efficient use of this space is necessary. Integrated supply programs that eliminate excess warehouse space enable organizations to use this space in other ways, thus saving the organizations a great deal of money. This is one of the major drawbacks of the in-plant store. Companies would benefit by employing point-of-use auto-replenishment inventory programs and eliminating secondary warehouse space whenever possible.

For example, a school district might have a central warehouse that stores various supplies. However, it also has schools spread over a wide geographical region. An integrated supplier who is charged with managing this inventory could allocate appropriate places to store supplies, not only freeing up space in the main warehouse, but also making supplies more accessible to the remote locations.

Employee Productivity

Employee productivity is increased through the elimination of non-value added administrative activities. Purchasing personnel can be more involved in managing suppliers' processes rather than suppliers' products. Organizations that have integrated supply strategies also experience smoother transitions between purchasers.

Efficiencies in Purchasing Administration

Although relationships with integrated suppliers usually mean lower prices for the purchaser, most of the savings come through increased efficiencies in the procurement process. By linking with suppliers, many costly process steps can be reduced or eliminated. This results

---

Comparison of Buy Back and Non-Buy Back Situations

Example: A supplier has 100 $3.00 motor bearings that are excess inventory. The responsible purchaser must eliminate this from inventory.

Without Integrated Supply—The purchaser must call around to potential users and salvage dealers to find a source for the bearings. Most distributors will be indifferent to buying the bearings because they may not have a perceived need and may not be willing to assume risk. Eventually, the purchaser finds a salvage company willing to buy the bearings for 35 percent of original value. The purchaser becomes responsible for getting a purchase order from the salvage company, shipping the items, and sending an invoice. This process takes an enormous amount of the purchaser's time.

With Integrated Supply—The purchaser calls the integrated supplier. They check their inventory, the manufacturer, and other potential buyers and find they can return the item to stock for a 10 percent restocking fee. The supplier comes to the purchaser's site and picks up the bearings. To pay for the bearings, the supplier issues a credit to the purchasing organization. The integrated supplier performs the majority of the work and allows the purchaser time to focus on more added value activities.

---

in lower operating costs to the buying organization. This aspect often goes unappreciated because it is not as tangible as an inventory reduction or purchase price decrease. Many organizations that do not use activity-based costing are not aware of the actual costs incurred to support material planning and purchasing programs. They understand that they will benefit from eliminating many routine purchasing activities, such as purchase orders, reschedules, and routine planning activities, and grow their purchase part database without adding personnel but have trouble putting a dollar amount to that benefit. Administrative benefits become much more important in the management of low-dollar line items because of the alternate uses of personnel for sourcing and negotiating contracts for premium materials.

There are fundamental steps in planning and procuring materials for production regardless of what system is being employed. Once a master schedule has been exploded, materials must be planned, purchased, expedited, many times rescheduled, cancelled, received, inspected, stocked, and sent to production. A basic integrated supply program can eliminate the material planning, purchasing, expediting, rescheduling, and canceling of repetitive parts that are on the agreement. Dock to stock certification programs can eliminate the need for inspection, sending the product directly to stock or a point of use location on the production floor.

Through means such as consolidated purchase requisitions and billing, the number of transactions can be reduced dramatically. Consolidated billing, for example, has provided many organizations dramatic savings in processing invoices. Only one invoice is forwarded to the purchaser for payment each month. This requires only one check to be drafted.

Payment Efficiencies

In addition to consolidated monthly billing, integrated suppliers and purchasers can use other methods to simplify the payment process.

Electronic Data Interchange (EDI)—EDI is the sharing of purchase order and invoicing information electronically. Despite typically high startup costs, this system is effective where there are a high number of daily transactions and part numbers and information can be easily shared. The method of exchanging this information does not have to be complicated. Many organizations have found that a simple fax transmission is more economical than EDI and equally efficient.

Self-Billing and Self-Invoicing—Many purchasers are now finding that the value in closely tracking orders through the two-way match (order/invoice) and three-way match (order/receipt/invoice) systems is outweighed by the administrative costs of maintaining such a system. Many have now moved to self-billing, a process in which the supplier provides billing for goods or services provided and the purchaser pays it without question. This requires a great deal of trust between supplier and purchaser, as well as a pre-negotiated contract.

Taking things one step further, some purchasing organizations have opted for a self-invoicing system. Since the purchaser and seller have negotiated the cost of a given item or service, the purchaser would generate the seller's invoice automatically upon receipt, allowing for the automatic generation of electronic payment. This system is truly paperless and, again, relies heavily on trust and pre-negotiated terms.

Electronic Payments—Electronic payments are money transfers from the purchaser's bank to the supplier's bank once an invoice has been approved for payment.

Procurement Cards—Many suppliers are not equipped to use procurement cards in daily transactions. By establishing a long-term relationship, suppliers have more interest in establishing payment terms and systems that facilitate a purchaser's use of procurement cards. The procurement card can lower transaction costs when used as a settlement option. Oftentimes, the purchasing organization's card provider will assist in establishing the supplier's ability to accept the card as payment, as well as train people and provide resources.

Telephone Transactions—An integrated supplier may not require an electronic, paper, or faxed purchase requisition but may use verbal transactions instead. This eliminates any administrative burdens on the buying organization and ensures that the purchaser's request is directly received by the supplier without any miscommunication.

Improved Supplier Relations

One Versus Many. By developing a relationship with an integrated supplier, the purchaser has made the decision to limit his or her supply base. One of the major advantages is

---

Case Study: Internet to Integrate

With a long-term relationship in effect, the supplier and purchaser can work together to build systems that enhance productivity. For example, Boise Cascade, a national supplier of office products, provides Corning Incorporated with all its daily stationery requirements. In lieu of traditional purchase orders, Corning employees are able to use the Internet to order supplies via the Boise Cascade Web site. Since a relationship already exists, requisitioners use passwords to enter orders, without any other approvals, directly to the Boise Cascade Web page. Once the order is submitted over the Internet, Boise Cascade processes and delivers it to the requisitioner the next day. At the end of the month, Boise Cascade provides Corning with one consolidated invoice for payment.

---

that it will reduce the effort required to manage the supply base. In other words, it is easier to manage one supplier than one hundred. Granted, not all suppliers have the capacity to provide every product and service required, but an effectively managed integrated supply program can significantly reduce the number of suppliers that must be actively managed; few is better than many. This will often result in higher exposure for the procurement organization since it is actively managing the supplier base and not dealing with problems associated with various selected suppliers.

For example, instead of trying to manage several different printing suppliers, because every department in the organization used their own printer, an integrated supply strategy might mean that a single printer's representative is located within the organization, on a part-time basis, to field quotes, requests, and job orders from internal customers. The purchasing and supply professional still manages the broad relationship with the printer, but now becomes a strategic component in improving that one relationship instead of merely being a transactional agent between several different printing companies.

Focus on the Long Term. Relationships with integrated suppliers tend to be long term. Thus, neither supplier nor purchaser can consider short-term gains but rather must focus on long-term gains. When the futures of the two organizations become intertwined and problems arise, the root cause is repaired more quickly since the purchaser's success is linked to that of the supplier.

The focus on the long term also benefits communications. The supplier has the opportunity to know many members of the buying organization. Relationships are established and it is easy for ideas and concerns to be communicated.

Communication may become difficult between the procurement organization and the integrated supplier in both centralized and decentralized environments. Since there are many customers using a single integrated supplier's services, different requirements and messages may become communicated to the supplier. In order to eliminate miscommunication, local and organizational chains of communication must be established. At the local level, the customers (e.g., maintenance personnel, inventory control) need daily access to the integrated supplier's local representative. They can communicate daily issues and ensure that all low-value, tactical activities are carried out in an efficient and timely manner. At the strategic level, contacts should be established between the integrated supplier's corporate organization and the purchaser's organization. The buyer should provide a senior purchasing contact to manage the overall relationship. In a centralized environment, this could be someone from the corporate organization. In a decentralized system, a lead individual should be assigned from the group that has the highest interaction, usually the most purchases, with that supplier.

Receiving Function

With an understanding of the purchaser's requirements, integrated suppliers can take steps to improve the productivity of the receiving organization. Suppliers can package goods to minimize handling requirements. For example, the supplier can break down pallet deliveries for purchasers unable to accept large pallet size deliveries.

By communicating with the purchaser's receivers, the integrated supplier can also tailor labels and shipping forms to facilitate streamlined processing of receipts. For example, many integrated suppliers now ship items with the purchaser's inventory-specific part number. This speeds receipts and minimizes the likelihood of losing material in transit. Many integrated suppliers have the technology to bar code all shipping forms and labels. Prior to shipment, all information pertaining to the shipment can be sent electronically to the receiving organization. Once the goods arrive at their destination, they are checked in quickly and effortlessly with a single scan.

For example, a hospital might receive a box of bandages of varying sizes. On the outside of the box, a label is encoded with the specific item numbers and corresponding quantities. Instead of manually checking the new inventory against a packing slip and then entering information into the computer or merely "accepting" the electronic transmission of the inventory, a bar-code scanner moves the bandages into the hospital's electronic possession. Obviously, in this scenario, reliance on the supplier's accuracy is required. How can you be certain that the box labeled "100 bandages" actually contains 100 bandages and not 99? Similar to other quality issues, spot checking and other controls can be put in place to verify accuracy. These potential inaccuracies must also be balanced with the potential inaccuracies of the employee who manually transmits information.

Cost Knowledge

Procurement professionals seek to ensure the goods and services they are purchasing are competitively priced. To determine fair pricing and ensure that the supplier is not needlessly adding to suppliers' costs by requesting non-value added work, the purchaser must have an understanding of the suppliers' margins and cost structures.

Obtaining pricing information or cost structure from suppliers may be a difficult, if not impossible, task. To many suppliers, there is no trust or long-term relationship that warrants the active sharing of this information. Fortunately, because most integrated supplier relationships are thoroughly negotiated and finalized with a contract, margins and pricing methods are agreed upon. In addition, many contracts provide a way to assure the purchaser that pricing continues within the contract terms. This is typically done through random audits of invoices.

Time to Market

In addition to aiding the buyer for routine purchases for existing products and services, the integrated supplier can aid in bringing new products to market. Since the supplier already has an understanding of the customer's needs and has developed relationships with members of the buyer's organization, they can easily integrate into a product development effort. The supplier can provide needed information on pricing, specifications, and delivery for items which may be required in the development effort. They are also positioned to provide any additional services to the buyer, such as JIT and consignment inventories with a minimum of negotiation and leadtime.

Drew Curtis, C.P.M., CPIM, is manager of strategic sourcing programs for Northeastern United States and Eastern Canada for TTI, Inc., at their regional office in Tewksbury, Mass. He has over 20 years experience in material/purchasing management in high-tech industries and has held positions at Cabletron Systems, Nashua Corporation, MKS Instruments.

J. Don Etheridge, P.E., C.P.M., is a commodity manager with NCR in Atlanta, Ga. He has worked in engineering and procurement positions for Corning, Carolina Power & Light, and the U.S. Navy's Nuclear Power Program.

Why Your Supply Chain Doesn't Work

Jim Thomas

Nearly all businesses rate supply chain management strategy as important, yet very few companies have an effective strategy in place. Companies may have ERP software, but things aren't working well because there's no plan in place, according to this article. Most of the other reasons why companies aren't doing a good job with supply chain management won't be surprising. The point of all this is that it takes commitment across the organization to make it work.

Ninety-one percent of North American manufacturers rank supply chain management as very important or critical to their company's success, according to a recent Deloitte Consulting survey. Yet only 2 percent of the manufacturers in the same survey rank their supply chains as world class. What's the problem?

In a word, strategy, answers Jim Kilpatrick, senior manager in Deloitte Consulting's Supply Chain Results Practice. Almost 50 percent of the companies surveyed have no formal supply chain strategy.

"Companies don't get it," says Kilpatrick. "Strategy involves more than managing the warehouse or transportation. It's also production, marketing, sales, and planning—the management of materials, information, and funds from the raw-materials supplier to the ultimate consumer."

The absence of a plan often explains why enterprise resource planning (ERP) software and other information technology initiatives fail, Kilpatrick continues. "Companies implemented ERP systems because it was the thing to do or because the competition did it," he says. "But the underlying business assumptions were not correct. The integration of timely general-ledger information is not enough. If you want to reduce inventory, it may imply SKU (stock-keeping unit) rationalization, which changes marketing and sales plans. You have to apply math to statistics if you wish to reduce safety stock or centralize the distribution of slower-moving products."

ERP systems initially worked because they were applied to back-office functions. "The systems generated savings that were driven by headcount reduction," says Kilpatrick. "But we are talking about getting money into the bank quicker. We need ERP systems to provide timely information that characterizes the pulse of the business."

Survival Strategies

Experts agree that a formal supply chain strategy will be critical for survival in any industry. Across the globe, companies are reducing their supplier bases by 40 to 70 percent, says Jonathan L.S. Byrnes, a senior lecturer at the Massachusetts Institute of Technology. He says the common denominator among the survivors is "supply chain excellence."

Byrnes, who specializes in strategy, says supply chain executives falter on strategic issues because their expertise and mindset generally revolve around tactical issues, such as cutting costs and improving operating efficiency. "I liken it to mowing the lawn around Stonehenge," he says. "Supply chain executives don't ask why these enormous stones have been placed in their path, but they are very good at mowing around them."

Kilpatrick agrees. "Distribution and operating managers generally are promoted to supply chain executive positions," he says. "They often do not know how to leverage technology, finance, and strategy."

This reliance on the tactical can only lead to short-term solutions, adds Kilpatrick. "Corporations go for the quick win, like lower transportation costs," he says. "But they do not knit transportation and inventory together to achieve long-term results."

Dissatisfied with internal solutions, companies often hire third-party logistics providers (3PLs) to come up with strategic solutions. Yet that rarely succeeds, says Byrnes. (See sidebar at the end of this article.) "3PLs rarely find themselves at the front-end of a major innovation," he says. "They usually don't enter the picture until a company develops its RFP (the 'request for proposal' companies use to solicit bids from 3PLs). By then, the customer has mapped out a strategy."

As a result, the third-party providers end up providing service improvements in an operational context only. "They take out a warehouse, reduce the size of a truck fleet, or remove a union, and save a company 10 percent," says Byrnes. "So the customer expects the 3PL to continue to take cost out of the system year after year. Sooner or later, those opportunities run out, but the 3PL still must live up to an unrealistic expectation because it could not articulate a supply chain strategy."

Failure to Communicate

Many times, executives fail to frame supply chain issues in terms top management can understand. This problem often is compounded by chief executive officers who do not fully comprehend the importance of supply chain issues. "Very few CEOs possess a supply chain background," says Byrnes. "These leaders have extensive experience in marketing or finance because 10 to 15 years ago, those were critical areas along the CEO career path. Supply chain management was not."

But it is critical today, and many innovations will take place in the supply chain over the next 10 years, says Byrnes. This period will be crucial for companies seeking to develop their supply chain strategies. It is the supply chain manager's window of opportunity, a time to drive supply chain strategy to the forefront of boardroom issues. Kilpatrick suggests supply chain managers start by addressing an issue that is important to everyone in the boardroom: customer service.

"Companies need to focus on what adds value to the customer," he says. "In supply chain management, that is an elusive challenge. For example, customers of office-furniture manufacturers may expect a seven-day order-to-delivery cycle. Some of these manufacturers may focus on rapid customer response and reduce their delivery cycle from seven to two days. But the customer is prepared for a seven-day cycle, so the reduction does not add value."

A strategy also must account for a diverse customer base that demands different levels of service. "Auto-parts distributors serve original equipment manufacturers with 100-percent fill rates," says Kilpatrick. "But do Sears and Pep Boys need that level of service? And do mom-and-pop shops need the same level as Sears?"

"The only way to find out critical information about your customers is to ask them," says Byrnes. "Prepare a survey or talk to purchasing or operations managers to learn what they need."

With such survey results in hand, the supply chain executive may define customer value. Chances are, the survey will include functions other than logistics, including sales, marketing, customer service, or finance. "No manager will be expert in everything, but the supply chain organization as a whole should," says Kilpatrick.

For that reason, the supply chain executive must team up with other top executives to create a supply chain organization and develop a plan. This involves selling a vision to other managers, who usually do not possess a supply chain background. Supply chain executives then must take the sales process forward and educate senior management as to the value of such a vision.

Unfortunately, these steps rarely happen, says Byrnes. "The supply chain executive dismisses opportunities by saying 'That's a marketing problem,' or 'No one asked me,'" he says.

The argument becomes circular: The supply chain executive did not offer his strategic plan to senior management because senior management did not ask for it. Meanwhile, senior management did not ask for a strategic plan because the supply chain executive never offered it.

Supply chain executives must get around this impasse by taking the initiative, Byrnes says. "The organization should generate its strategy through the supply chain executive," he says. "After all, the supply chain executive has the greatest understanding of how a change—say, in the mix of customers or customer order patterns—affects changes across the entire organization."

Without the initiative of an executive, supply chain management will produce average results, at best, says Kilpatrick. "Ninety percent of the companies we surveyed said supply chain management would become more important in the future. If that's true, average is not a good place to be."

Strategy and the Third Party

If companies fail in their own attempts at supply chain management, can third-party logistics providers (3PLs) provide a better solution? Observers answer with a qualified no.

Strategic roadblocks exist between third parties and customers, says Bruce R. Abels, president of Saddle Creek Corp., a Lakeland, Fla.-based 3PL. In a presentation called "Ethics and Protocols of Third-Party Relationships" at the Warehousing Education & Resource Council's annual conference, Abels said problems begin in the "pre-selection phase" where both parties exhibit self-destructive behaviors and seldom address strategic issues. Here, third parties oversell and under-listen, they inflate capabilities, they may lack knowledge in specific areas, and they don't ask hard questions.

On the other side of the table, customers "put the bid cart before the horse" by demanding a price quote without regard to the 3PL's capabilities. They often don't pre-qualify third parties, and they prepare bid packages that are incomplete. In addition, they ask for unreasonable leadtimes.

Abels advises 3PLs and customers to approach pre-selection as a "collaborative process." "Unfortunately, our industry compounds the problem by responding to bids," he says. As a result, the customer establishes the perception that the 3PL is a vendor, not a strategic partner, before the contract is signed. The perception continues as the relationship progresses through selection, preparation, and startup. By the time the 3PL begins operations, it often has become defensive about rates and margins. The customer "lets the 3PL handle problem issues," says Abels. Costs, not value, become the critical issue.

In a positive relationship, the third party and the customer share strategic components, including company mission, business objectives, logistics mission, and logistics objectives. And, just as important, Abels says, "both parties operate as equals."

Jim Thomas is executive editor of Logistics Management & Distribution Report.

How Purchasing Can Reduce Supply Chain Costs

Mark S. Miller, C.P.M., CIRM and Thomas M. Graddy

> *Throughout this book you will find articles on the role of purchasing and supply management in improving efficiency and reducing costs, while also improving quality and organizational results. This is one such article. It looks at six principles you can adopt to make your supply chain management system function better.*

Purchasing can play a major role in reducing supply chain costs. Our company has made the pursuit of improving our supply chain one of its top priorities. Supply chain management (SCM) is a composite of all the processes required to flow products from the supplier to the ultimate customer. To reduce costs in the supply chain requires the cooperation of many functional areas, including purchasing, to work together to improve the flow of materials and reduce the investment in inventory throughout the supply chain. Some of the actions that can be taken by a buyer to reduce the costs to flow product from the supplier to the ultimate customer are: 1) improve SCM information flow, 2) make supplier arrangements to reduce assets, 3) reduce cycle times, 4) outsource non-core functions, 5) improve customer service and 6) make supplier selection based on supply chain capability. Below we will discuss further these six cost reduction action items and the role purchasing plays in improving them.

Action #1: Improve SCM information flow. A key to improving the management of products in the supply chain is working with timely and accurate information. Purchasing typically is concerned with the flow of information from the customer to the supplier. The challenge is to expand the information flow throughout the supply chain, from customer to manufacturing to supplier. There are two areas that purchasing and supply can take lead roles to improve the information flow:

- *Expand EDI links with suppliers.* Electronic Data Interchange is a tool that allows current information to be passed quickly up the chain. Supply chain management requires the electronic links be built with customers, dealers, warehouses, transportation, manufacturing and suppliers. Purchasing needs to work with suppliers to expand the use of EDI. Traditional EDI involves communication to the supplier and often EDI is not compatible with current retail systems. SCM requires communications from the customer back to the supplier. Purchasing needs to work with the suppliers, retail stores, and systems to develop retail tracking. Purchasing needs to work with the supplier to react quickly to retail demand and ship directly to the dealers when stock is needed. Wal-Mart and other large retailers have been very successful in using retail demand to reduce supply chain costs.

- *Supplier personnel in the chain.* Another way purchasing can help improve communication in the supply chain is to locate supplier personnel at different levels in your supply chain. To make these strategies effective, the supplier needs to be involved in non-traditional ways with your supply chain. The supplier should have:
  - Personnel in-house in your office to expedite and manage schedules
  - Supplier systems personnel working with your retail locations to capture retail sales
  - Sales personnel helping to train and promote products to increase sales.

Purchasing's challenge is to persuade the suppliers to furnish resources at different levels of your supply chain to reduce supply chain costs.

Action #2: Make supplier arrangements to reduce assets. Once the supply chain is analyzed it is usually found that there are duplicate assets at different levels in the supply chain. The goal of SCM is to identify duplicate inventory and reduce it by reducing cycle times and improving the flow of information. Safety stock or just in case inventory is often being carried by: the supplier, the manufacturer, the warehouse, the dealer and the customer. Each entity is unaware of the level of inventory carried by the other. The challenge for purchasing is to work with the supplier to establish new methods to reduce the inventory, without jeopardizing customer service.

The goal is not to push the inventory to the supplier, but to reduce the redundant assets in the supply chain. There have been many supplier arrangements that have been established to reduce inventory including:

- Just in time
- Consignment supplier stocking
- Supplier managed inventory
- Quick response

The key is to recruit the supplier as part of your team to reduce the inventory in the supply chain.

Action #3: Reduce cycle times. The shorter the cycle time, the more responsive the supply chain will be and the less backup inventory that needs to be carried. Purchasing plays a key role in reducing supplier lead times that are a part of the SCM cycle times. The following are three key steps purchasing can take to reduce supplier lead times:

- *Track and measure supplier lead times.* Do you measure and track supplier lead times? This is the first step in reducing supplier lead times. Recognize which sup-

pliers and which commodities have the longest lead times and start with these. Set a goal with each buyer to negotiate lower lead times. This concept holds for each level in the supply chain, not just supplier lead times. Measure how long it takes for:
- Inbound transportation
- Transport time to customer
- Manufacturing lead times
- Distribution cycle time

If you do not measure it, you will not improve it.

- *Negotiate lower lead times.* The buyer should challenge supplier lead times. Ask for a breakdown of the components of supplier lead times. Compare one supplier lead time to others. When the lead time components are reviewed it is often found that most of the lead time is "waiting time" and little of the lead time is actual "processing" time. Challenge the supplier to reduce the waiting time. Other options to reduce supplier lead times include:
  - Utilizing distributors
  - Guaranteed volume commitments
  - Investing in new tooling

- *Understand the tradeoffs.* Inventory costs are reduced when supplier lead times are reduced. Be aware of the tradeoffs between lead time and inventory carrying costs and give buyers cost reduction credits for reducing lead times. We credit buyers with 11% of the value of the inventory reduced as cost savings. There are many other pieces of cycle time in the supply change that purchasing can help to reduce. Included in these are:
  - Reduce transportation cycle times.
  - Reduce manufacturing cycle times by reducing the bottleneck areas.
  - Receive product quicker through the use of bar codes.

Action #4: Outsource non-core functions. Another tactic to improve the supply chain is to outsource non-core functions and services. Outsourcing can reduce cycle times, reduce costs, plus give you more flexibility in managing changes in demand. We have outsourced many components and service functions in the past few years: machining, warehousing, cabs, hydraulic cylinders, packaging and printing, just to name a few. These are the major responsibilities that purchasing has in the outsourcing of non-core functions.

- *Select and negotiate with suppliers.* Purchasing needs to find, select, establish and manage the relationship with suppliers who will perform the outsourced function. Most buyers are more experienced in outsourcing direct material. Many of the items we have outsourced have been services such as:
  - Transportation services
  - Warehousing
  - Incoming inspection

- Mailroom
- Security

When establishing the outsourcing agreement for service items these are two key items to include:
- PERFORMANCE AND QUALITY MEASUREMENTS. It is difficult to establish performance and quality measurements for services, but these are needed to effectively measure the outsourced supplier performance. Several of our early service outsourcing agreements did not define well our performance expectations and we learned quickly that was a mistake.
- CLEAR DEFINITION OF CHARGES. It is also important to establish what the charges are for performing the service. Is the billing rate based on hours worked, services performed, or each job completed?

- *Manage the transfer process.* I have witnessed many disasters in the past few years that were caused by poor execution of outsourcing. Purchasing needs to help with the planning and implementation of the outsource to avoid a problem. You should negotiate so the old supplier builds a bridge quantity to protect the customer during the transition. The buyer also must arrange to transfer all the knowledge possible to the new supplier (tooling, specifications, quality requirements, forecasts).

Action #5: Improve customer service. We need to refocus our organizations on the customer. There is a tendency to concentrate on re-engineering the processes and forgetting the needs of the customer. The test of the effectiveness of the new process should be gauged by the impact to the customer. Purchasing should ask each day: How can we get the product to the customer on time? How can we reduce transport time? How can we improve communications with our customer? Establish objectives for the supply chain targeted on serving the customer better. Some measurements we have used include:

- Backorders
- Lost sales
- Fill levels
- Late shipments

Action #6: Select a supplier based on supply chain capability. Another key action needed to improve the supply chain is to establish a closer link with the suppliers who can help reduce supply chain costs. Purchasing should take the lead in establishing a sourcing strategy project for each purchased commodity. In the past at our company, we have had purchasing and engineering at each plant selecting suppliers focusing on low quotations and supplier reduction. The goal of our new project (which we are calling "strategic sourcing") is to establish corporate-wide preferred suppliers for each commodity that will reduce cost throughout the entire supply chain. The traits that will be critical to being designated a preferred supplier are also the factors that will improve supply chain management including:

- Communicate electronically to the entire supply
- Reduce lead times,
- Help reduce cycle times,
- Help reduce assets
- Improve customer service

Summary

Purchasing has a major role to play in reducing costs in the supply chain. Make sure you understand your role in SCM and prepare yourself so you can help make it more effective. These are some actions you should consider taking to reduce supply chain costs:

- Work on process improvement teams.
- Measure supply chain performance.
- Expand EDI with suppliers in the entire supply chain.
- Locate supplier personnel throughout the supply chain.
- Work to reduce supplier lead times.
- Help reduce the total supply chain cycle times.
- Understand the tradeoff between inventory and lead times.
- Make the supplier a member of your process team to reduce inventory.
- Claim inventory reductions as cost savings.
- Select and manage relationships with outsourced suppliers.
- Include performance and quality measurements in outsourcing agreements.
- Manage the transfer process to outsourced suppliers.
- Make sure you keep the customer as the focus of the supply chain.
- Strategically select suppliers who can help reduce supply chain costs.

Mark S. Miller, C.P.M., CIRM, is purchasing manager for Case Corporation, Racine, WI 53405, 414 636-6565, mmiller@casecorp.com.

Thomas M. Graddy, C.P.M., CIRM, is logistics and supply chain management manager for Case Corporation, Racine, WI 53405, 414 636-7975, tgraddy@casecorp.com.

Strengthening Internal Relationships

Eberhard E. Scheuing, Ph.D., C.P.M., A.P.P.

> *A value chain depends on relationships, on meeting the expectations and percep-*
> *tions of customers, whether external or internal. This article looks at how the chief*
> *purchasing officer of an insurance company used ServQual to determine internal*
> *customer satisfaction with the service performance of his department.*

Feeling somewhat isolated from the mainstream activities of this firm, the Chief Procurement Officer (CPO) of Major Insurance Company wanted to gain more coop- eration from the management and his fellow employees throughout the many divi- sions and locations of his vast international firm. He believed in the importance of the value chain (shown in Figure 1) where all links need to cooperate closely to add value to the prod- uct for the benefit of the external customer.

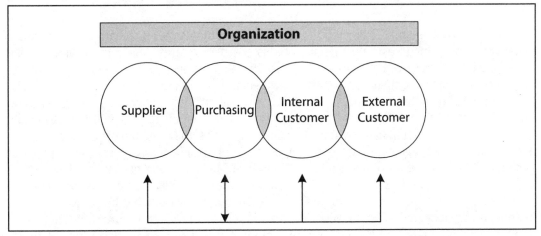

Figure 1. Links in the value chain

Being in a highly competitive service industry, he felt that his company's success in the marketplace depended significantly upon extent and nature of the cooperation between his purchasing team and its internal customers. Because any chain is only as strong as its weak- est link, he set out to strengthen his team's working relationships with internal customers.

Understanding Relationships

The CPO realized that these relationships were based on a set of expectations and perceptions that internal customers held about the performance of his team and drew a diagram to illustrate potential interaction patterns between these variables (see Figure 2).

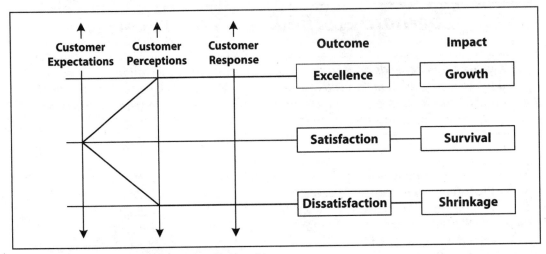

Figure 2. Factors driving customer behavior

He defined customer expectations as the performance levels customers anticipate receiving and defined customer perceptions as the performance levels his customers felt they had actually received. Customer response can then be seen as the behavior customers carry out as a result of their comparison of expectations and perceptions.

Figure 2 shows three potential patterns. If internal customers have reasonable expectations but perceived performance falls short of this level, the customers will be dissatisfied and might resort to doing their own purchasing. Worse yet, they will tell other potential customers and discourage them from involving the purchasing team in their procurement actions. This could result in a shrinkage of purchasing's role in the organization.

On the other hand, if customers' expectations are met, they will be satisfied and the purchasing team will continue to play a role in major Insurance's business activities. Although this appeared to be a desirable state of affairs, it occurred to him that this kind of outcome merely preserved the status quo temporarily and offered no assurance of future success. After all, the only difference between customer dissatisfaction and satisfaction was the absence of complaints. Stated differently, customers had no reason to continue to do business with the purchasing team other than that its performance was O.K. This state of customer responsiveness generally leads to complacency on the part of purchasing personnel and the beginning of value chain decline.

It quickly became evident to him that his team needed to *exceed* customer expectations in order to expand its role in the corporation. If his team delighted customers by going beyond their expectations, its contributions to corporate performance would be valued and sought out by others.

Measuring Internal Customer Satisfaction

Realizing that his team needed to walk before it could run, he searched for a proven approach to determining internal customer satisfaction with his team's current service performance levels. He found it in *ServQual**, a powerful tool developed and refined by a team of researchers based at Texas A & M University, Drs. Leonard Berry, A. Parasuraman, and Valarie Zeithaml.

Some of the benefits of *ServQual* include:

- asking customers to spell out their performance expectations
- comparing perceived performances with these expectations
- identifying differences between expected and perceived performances as service quality gaps
- prioritizing which service dimensions are more important than others from the customers' point of view

It uses a survey instrument to obtain these measurements from purchasing's internal customers. A *ServQual* survey usually consists of the following components:

- paired customer expectation and perception statements
- weights to reflect the relative importance of specific service dimensions
- overall evaluation of purchasing's perceived performance

This structure enables purchasing to identify and reduce service quality gaps, match the allocation of purchasing resources with the importance placed by its customers on specific performance dimensions, and track their overall performance evaluation.

Because his team needed to become familiar and comfortable with the new tool, Major's CPO selected photocopier repair services as the subject of the initial inquiry. Purchasing contracted with outside providers for this service and was thus judged based on the behavior and competence of these external repairpersons. He invited representatives from various divisions to participate in focus group sessions to determine their expectations of photocopier repair services. Focus group participants were asked to identify five key factors in evaluating the performance of repairpersons and thus, indirectly, of the purchasing team. Their input was used in designing the survey and formulating paired expectation and perception statements. Examples from the survey are:

- The repairperson *should arrive* on time.
- The repairperson *arrived* on time.
- Copier repairs *should be completed* during the first visit.
- Copier repairs *were completed* during the first visit.

Survey respondents were asked to indicate their level of agreement with each of the statements, using a seven-point scale, ranging from 1 for strongly disagree to 7 for strongly agree. They were also asked to provide weights for the five dimensions by allocating 100 points among them, and to offer a summary evaluation of the service received.

The results from this survey were tabulated. The reasons and remedies for shortfalls were discussed and agreed upon with selected internal customers. Having gained experience from this initial evaluation of specific external service providers, Major's CPO proceeded to broaden the scope of inquiry to include other supplier categories and—most importantly—the perceived performance of the purchasing team itself. In the process, he found that the five dimensions identified by *ServQual* were quite applicable to his organization.

The five *ServQual* dimensions are:

- *Tangibles*—the appearance of physical facilities, equipment, personnel, and communication materials, such as forms or reports.
- *Reliability*—consistency of performance and dependability; performing the service right the first time and honoring promises.
- *Responsiveness*—providing prompt service and callbacks.
- *Assurance*—possession of the required skills and knowledge; trustworthiness, believability, and honesty; keeping customers informed about the status of their requests.
- *Empathy*—respect and friendliness; ease of contact; caring concern for customers and their needs.

Applying this framework and a modified list of 22 *ServQual* statement pairs to measuring his purchasing team's performance, Major's CPO found out that there was room for improvement in the eyes of internal customers. Figure 3 illustrates a weighted gap analysis that measures the differences between expectation and perception scores and multiplies them with their respective weights. With an average difference of -.84, perceived performance has fallen short of expectations by almost a full point on all dimensions.

Dimension	Average Expectation Score	Average Perception Score	Difference	Relative Importance Score	Average Weighted Difference
Tangibles	6.8	6.2	-.6	.13	-.08
Reliability	6.8	5.3	-1.5	.32	-.48
Responsiveness	6.7	6.1	-.6	.25	-.15
Assurance	6.5	5.8	-.7	.18	-.13
Empathy	6.6	5.8	-.8	.12	-.10
Totals			-4.2		-.94
Average Difference			-.84		

Figure 3. Weighted gap analysis

With regard to the *tangibles* dimension, positive gap scores were produced by three statement pairs:

- The purchasing department's physical facilities should be visually appealing. Gap: +.24
- The purchasing department's staff should be well dressed and appear neat. Gap: +.42
- The appearance of the physical facilities of the purchasing department should be in keeping with the type of services provided. Gap: +.37

But these instances of perceived performance exceeding expectations were outweighed by a strong negative gap on statement pair:

- The purchasing department should have up-to-date systems support. Gap: -1.80.

This resulted in an overall difference of -.6 on the tangibles dimension.

The critical leverage point is, however, clearly the team's perceived lack of *reliability*. With a shortfall of -1.5 points and a relative importance of .32 or 32%, it alone constitutes more than half of the average weighted difference. Contributing to this overall difference were the negative gap scores resulting from the internal customers' responses to the following statement pairs:

- The purchasing department should keep its records accurately. Gap: -1.46
- The purchasing department should be dependable. Gap: -1.37
- The purchasing department should provide its services at the time it promises to do so. Gap: -1.39
- When the purchasing department promises to do something by a certain time, it should do so. Gap: -1.52

These negative scores are significant in both their gap sizes and the fact that customers feel that the reliability dimension is the most critical of all service-related dimensions. Therefore, much strategic as well as tactical attention is needed in addressing such customer concerns. The team met with its internal customers to discuss reasons for these discrepancies and agree on ways to improve their working relationships.

Improving Internal Cooperation

ServQual proved to be a valuable tool for Major's CPO in aligning his team's activities with its internal customers' concerns and priorities. Accordingly, its use was expanded to include a variety of services, such as overnight delivery, personal computer maintenance, in-house reprographics, mail, printing, and the procurement function itself. The dialog that was initiated through the focus group sessions and surveys opened up lines of communication between purchasing and internal customers. Survey results were shared with internal customers and external suppliers. In meetings, solutions to problems and further performance improvements were collectively identified and agreed upon. This enabled external service providers to improve their performance by understanding and focusing on specific customer expectations. It also became evident to colleagues from other parts of Major Insurance that purchasing professionals were able and eager to help them improve their own performance and thus add value to internal processes.

The lessons learned by Major's CPO from measuring internal customer satisfaction on a continuing basis with the use of *ServQual* include:

- Key value-added services include cost reduction programs and bringing new ideas to internal customers.
- Effective systems support was the number one concern of his team's internal customers.
- Purchasing team members must participate in their internal customers' strategic planning processes and vice versa.
- To strengthen internal working relationships, it is essential to understand and meet internal customers' expected service levels.

As the scope of inquiry broadened to the whole gamut of services provided by the purchasing team and the dialogue intensified, it was only natural for internal customers to start asking what they, in turn, could do to make purchasing's job easier and more rewarding. The purchasing team was thus able to communicate a wish list and suggestions on how their cooperation could be enhanced for greater mutual benefit. And purchasing was invited to participate in new service development projects, bringing selected suppliers into the process as appropriate.

Major's CPO and his team have been quite pleased with the strengthened internal working relationships and have learned a great deal in the process on how they can proactively bring greater value to the corporation. They found two axioms to be quite true: You can only manage what you can measure, and anything that is measured, improves.

*To learn more about *ServQual* read *Delivering Quality Service: Balancing Customer Perceptions and Expectations,* Detroit Free Press, 1990.

Eberhard E. Scheuing, Ph.D., C.P.M., A.P.P., is the NAPM Professor of Purchasing and Supply Leadership at St. John's University in New York. Dr. Scheuing is a member of IPSERA and an academic member of NAPM—New York, NAPM—Seven Countries, NAPM—New Jersey, and NAPM—Rochester, as well as an honorary member and honorary board member of NAPM—Long Island. He has also served as a member of the Board of Trustees of the Center for Advanced Purchasing Studies. Dr. Scheuing is the founder and president of the International Service Quality Association and co-editor of The Service Quality Handbook. *He has published more than 500 articles on various business subjects and 26 books, including several books on purchasing management, including* The Power of Strategic Partnering *(1994) and* Value-Added Purchasing: Partnering for World-Class Performance *(1998).*

A Tale of Two Chains

Roberta J. Duffy

Supply chain management is relevant in every type of business. In this article we learn how McDonald's and the American RedCross Blood Services have found the principles of supply chain management integral to their successful operation. You'll learn how in this article. It demonstrates the vitality of these principles regardless of the industry. Whether you're in manufacturing, services, retailing of some other category of organization, you may pick up some ideas that will help you as well.

When was the last time you drove by a hamburger restaurant? A hospital? Chances are it was recently, since there are over 300,000 fast food restaurants and over 6,500 hospitals nationwide. They're not what you think of when imagining prime models of supply chain management—they do not fit the same mold as America's traditional manufacturing industries, right?

But these and other non-manufacturing organizations all over the globe are implementing SCM. They're showing that a successful output of service is dependent on establishing long-term relationships with suppliers, playing a role in all aspects of the service chain process, and monitoring products and services to the final customer.

These two organizations are thinking in terms of their supply chains and they're doing it to feed us fast food and give the gift of life.

McDonald's Corporation

Business: Fast food restaurant chain
Suppliers: Food and packaging suppliers
Customers: Owners, consumers

Gone are the days of McDonald's employees living at potato plants to perform inspection functions. Instead of harvesting vegetables themselves, purchasing and supply management professionals at McDonald's are harvesting relationships with suppliers that are so solid and long-lasting, that they leave little room for anything but quality returns.

The McDonald's practice of supply chain management is not based so much on the presumption that they have direct contact with the initial supplier/end user, although in

69

some cases they do. Rather, it's based more on the fact that because they have established strong relationships and clearly communicated expectations with their suppliers, their influence and expectations are carried throughout the supply chain.

"We really think of our system as a three-legged stool," says Ken Koziol, director of supply chain management for the U.S. "One leg consists of the corporation, another the franchises, and the third leg the suppliers. Each member is part of our family. We treat them that way and expect them to behave in the best interests of the family."

Of course, it doesn't hurt that many of McDonald's suppliers are exclusive, meaning that McDonald's is the only organization they sell to. For example, there are eight meat plants that distribute solely to almost 13,000 U.S. McDonald's restaurants. Although they are entirely separate, independent business entities, by making them such an embedded part of the family, McDonald's has ensured that they will strive for the same goals, bringing quality in at a good value. This commitment does not come merely because their livelihoods depend on it, but from the energy McDonald's has put into supplier development.

Cultivate Your Suppliers

McDonald's communicates clear expectations for suppliers, starting with common values and a commitment to a strong working relationship and quality procedures and processes. A quality procedure might focus on an acceptable lean-to-fat ratio for a Quarter Pounder. The process controls would involve analyzing and optimizing a supplier's process of making that ground beef patty. Six supplier attributes are defined: assured supply of product, low cost/best value, technical competencies, system player, shared values, and management excellence. To maintain these relationships, McDonald's does several things, including supplier counsels, annual business reviews for suppliers, and formal supplier development. The focus concentrates on improvements rather than blame.

"We use supplier development quite extensively," says Koziol. "We also have a supplier expectations program that is really a two-way street. We can say, 'Here's what we expect of you. What do you expect of us?'" Over an intensive two-day process, they measure gaps in performance and draw up an action plan—for both parties concerned. For example, based on supplier response, McDonald's has improved their forecasting system, relative to sales during heaving advertising or promotional periods.

"As the focus shifts toward a long-term commitment, the focus of our decisions are on long-lasting improvements," says Koziol. While McDonald's will address an individual action by a supplier, they're more concerned with how capable suppliers are to improve their processes over time. "We're not going to point fingers while discussing a single batch of fries. However, we might discuss upgrading a plant that is growing obsolete."

Build Alliances at All Layers

Managing their resources as an entire supply chain, and not as individual components, means that each link in the chain could be involved at any stage. McDonald's suppliers are encouraged to be creative and bring ideas forward, whether it be about improving processes they're involved in or even new product development.

When Chicken McNuggets were introduced in 1983, one of the players most influential to bringing the product to life was an existing McDonald's supplier—a fish supplier, no less. Bud Sweeney, who provided fish for the fish sandwich, developed the Chicken McNugget idea into a marketable menu item.

"The point is, there was nothing in it for him; he did not set out to reap the rewards of this idea," says Koziol. "He just felt comfortable in his role as a team member—making contributions."

Reaching Down the Chain, Out to Customers

McDonald's direct impact on 35 million daily customers is not limited to mealtime transactions. The same strategic principals that are practiced up the chain with suppliers extend down as well to the franchise level. Suppliers are approved at the corporate level and chosen at the franchise level. But to ensure quality, compliance, and to ease the burden on the franchises, freeing them up to deliver to the final customer, McDonald's has developed purchasing committees. These committees, located locally to serve franchises, are comprised of corporate employees and franchises, who serve as a liaison between suppliers and the restaurants.

"One way the restaurants benefit is that the committees help take the guesswork out of ordering," says Ken Clement, owner of eight McDonald's restaurants in the Phoenix-metropolitan area. The purchasing committees work closely with the distribution centers and the restaurants, for example, advising them on predicted sales during a Big Mac promotion. The committees also strive to improve processes between distribution centers and restaurants. For Gary Kory, owner of two Chicago-area McDonald's, that meant adjusting a delivery schedule that better suited the restaurants and lowered the cost for the supplier. "The goal is to make things as simple as possible for everyone involved," says Kory.

"That's one of the benefits of a customized supply chain; the people on the front line don't have to deal with things coming in the back door, but can look to the front door— at their customers," says Koziol.

Create a Virtual Presence

McDonald's manages indirect suppliers through the relationships established with their first-tier suppliers. Whatever values and expectations originate at McDonald's are expected to be passed along to suppliers' suppliers as well. This is not to say McDonald's does not have any contact with the raw materials suppliers. For example, with potatoes, McDonald's will contract, through its suppliers, with the potato farmer for a specific acreage or pound of crop. The farmer at that level is aware of McDonald's specifications in terms of size, shape, specific gravity, defect levels, and more. The farmer will be paid on overall performance of his or her crop or fields for that year. Potatoes are purchased by a processor and then put into storage for various lengths of time. The McDonald's standards and expectations are in tact through all the links.

SCM = Relationships

"We believe relationships are made not only between companies, but also between individuals," says Koziol. For McDonald's, the key to their supply chain management model is those relationships. Through clearly stated expectations and open communication, the corporation and its suppliers enjoy a family-style alliance that leaves plenty of room for several businesses to succeed and little room for surprises. "If you're going to have a long-term relationship, you can't be surprising your business partner. We believe this type of strategic relationship is a competitive advantage not easily duplicated in a more transactional model," says Koziol.

American Red Cross Blood Services

Business: Blood donation/distribution
Suppliers: Donors, volunteer workers
Customers: Hospitals, patient recipients

Imagine that today you donated blood. Your donation became one of the nearly 6 million donations that the American Red Cross receives each year. But what happens to that pint of blood after it leaves your body? The process that follows, born out of the delicate nature of the products, requires effective communication and strategic logistics. Blood, as a product, must be managed properly at the American Red Cross, where healthy links are not only key to the success of this non-profit, non-manufacturing organization, but also vital to the lives of the 4 million patients who receive blood donations each year.

The first step is actually removing the blood from your arm. But even before this process starts, the Red Cross has begun to manage their potential product. As a donor you are given educational materials to read about risk factors to help you determine whether or not you should donate. This is followed by a personal interview with a trained Red Cross employee, again, to determine eligibility. If you are in poor health, or for any reason do not meet the standards, you will not be able to donate. If after leaving the donation site, any donor begins to feel poorly, they have the opportunity to contact the Red Cross after their donation and request that their blood be used. The Red Cross ensures a safe product and service by beginning with the proper suppliers.

"Donors come in all varieties, from all over the country," says Niall Conway, vice president of manufacturing for the country's largest blood collection and distribution agency. "We are unique in that we have a dual character. We are very embedded in local communities, but must have a national focus."

The community side of the process is most evident in the form of volunteers. A volunteer probably fed you juice and cookies after your blood donation, and might have been one of 1.5 million Red Cross volunteers nationwide. This link in the supply chain is absolutecrucial, as the ratio of Red Cross volunteers to Red Cross paid staff is 43 to one. "The volunteers are so crucial to the process," says Conway. "There's a group in Oklahoma of retired veterans that use their own vehicles and communicate 24 hours a day to coordinate blood delivery."

And, of course, the donors themselves are all volunteers, meaning the blood supply base in this product's chain is not necessarily purchased but rather recruited. However, sourcing for these volunteers still requires strategic planning. For example, certain rare types of blood occur more often in people of a particular race or ethnic background. Because the ideal blood match is from a donor of similar genetic make-up, the Red Cross targets recruiting in particular racial and ethnic communities.

Although the product is acquired through different means, once you have performed your duties as a donor, the path to the final recipient requires logistics to take top priority.

According to Conway, it's the biggest challenge they face. Managing the data and the blood itself is facilitated through eight national testing laboratories and a complex software system that will track the product through the remaining links. A sample of each blood donation is sent via overnight delivery to one of the laboratories, where each component is put through eight different tests for safety. This information is downloaded in the computer and by the following morning, the Red Cross has results on roughly 24,000 donations.

"Flights, airports, testing labs, and testing schedules are all laid out strategically so that samples can be flown in one day and get tested by the next," says Conway. The testing laboratories are located geographically for easy, efficient ground or air transportation of blood throughout the region each laboratory supports.

Once your blood has been tested, it becomes part of what Conway calls a national hub. The information is in the computer, but the blood may still be located near where it was originally donated, ready to be shipped where it is needed, or processed into various components and blood products. Accurate monitoring and management of hospitals' blood supplies is critical. The Red Cross may move rare blood types to needy locations or ship to areas where donations are expected to be low, for example, due to poor weather. "It's all about allocation," says Conway. "If we anticipate a hurricane in Puerto Rico, we're ready to ship."

With such a fragile product, time is of the essence. Depending on how it is stored, the shelf life of various blood products ranges from a few days to several months. The Red Cross is currently engaged in a large study with consultants to determine logistics and warehousing issues and seek out new solutions. The project is expected to be completed sometime this year.

Your blood is now in one of the 38 blood regions' storage sites, but that doesn't end the Red Cross' role. The product is ready to be administered to a recipient, but the information collected on the blood, such as donor health history, blood type, and an identification label, stays within the Red Cross field of management. By maintaining these tracking procedures, the Red Cross is able to trace a unit of blood to the hospital or recipient if there is any reason they decide the blood should not be used. In that instance, the Red Cross must take action and track down the recipient. Conway admits there are times when they've had to play detective in their realm of supply chain management.

Sometimes the route from donor to recipient is predesignated. One service offered by the Red Cross is autologous donation. This gives patients who anticipate the need for blood, for example, prior to surgery, the ability to donate their blood and actually receive it back themselves when needed. Similar to many organizations with a formalized supply chain management philosophy, the end goal is to get the best product to the most appropriate final user.

They say donating blood is giving the gift of life. It also means giving the gift of the American Red Cross, all its volunteers, its research facilities, and all other aspects of its supply chain. The blood you donated today, after going through carefully managed steps, may reach a recipient tomorrow in desperate need. But neither you nor they need think about the suppliers, logistics, or safety standards—the Red Cross has done it for you.

When Crisis Strikes

They say a chain is only as strong as its weakest link. So what happens to a non-manufacturing organization when a critical link fails to perform? Last August, thousands of organizations got a taste of that situation when United Parcel Service (UPS), the world's largest package distribution company, went on strike, bringing delivery services to a standstill.

At the time of the strike, Alan Green was director of distribution services at Alpha Shirt Company, a distributor of imprintable sportswear, which handled over 3,000 orders and 6,000 cartons a day by UPS. "We had to get very creative in our methods, very quickly," says Green. They were forced to examine options that weren't even considered before. They used the U.S. Postal Service, regional carriers they hadn't previously investigated, and even went as far as to find ways around the package limits set by operating carriers.

Green doesn't believe there was anything his company could have done in the way of managing UPS as a supplier to prevent the implications of the strike, but does feel that having a relationship with other suppliers might have been a factor.

Because of their high volume, Green feels they might have had some pull with UPS on their limited delivery, but there were other delivery services not accepting packages from anyone with whom they did not have an established relationship. "You can't put all your eggs in one basket. You have to have several options to protect yourself."

The most long-lasting effects of the strike will probably be felt on the other end of the supply chain. Positive dynamics emerged as a result of open and honest communication with their customers.

"We told them right from the beginning what we'd be able to provide and what we wouldn't," said Green. Seeing that they all had to work together as a chain, customers were honest with them, too. "They were able to concede some total shipments, for the sake of getting a partial shipment out with high priority."

Alpha Shirt Company and their customers helped fill the gap of the missing link. "We had our own trucks and drivers going places they'd never been before. In some cases they were meeting our customers on the highway, at gas stations and trucks stops, exchanging goods to keep the flow," says Green.

After the strike, Alpha Shirt Company continued to use UPS, but for Green the lessons learned from managing the weak link have caused some broader philosophy changes. "The biggest thing is to remain flexible. Be open to new ideas and new methods, even before you need to use them."

Roberta J. Duffy is a writer for Purchasing Today®.

Supply Chain Management: Who's Doing It and How?

Carolyn Pye

"According to CSC Healthcare' report, billions of dollars of cost-saving opportunities exist for the healthcare profession by implementing more effective [supply chain management] practices." This quote captures the message of this article that shows how supply chain management (SCM) practices can make a big impact on costs in healthcare. As in the article that precedes this one, learn more about the value of SCM practices no matter what the industry.

You're a purchasing and supply manager for a mid-sized non-manufacturing organization that's just starting to evaluate supply chain management and its feasibility for your organization. Or, you oversee purchasing and supply for a large manufacturing firm, and you've been practicing supply chain management for a while.

Wherever you are in regard to supply chain management, you may start to wonder how other industries and organizations are doing and whether there are any lessons to be learned. This article profiles the healthcare and distribution industries and their roles in supply chain management.

SCM: A Cure for Healthcare?

For supply chain guidance, healthcare professionals are looking to the Efficient Healthcare Consumer Response (EHCR) initiative and the report, "Improving the Efficiency of the Healthcare Supply Chain" compiled by El Segundo, California-based Computer Sciences Corporation. The EHCR initiative was launched in fall 1996 by a consortium of healthcare industry associations and healthcare supply chain participants. As a first step, the consortium enlisted CSC to study the current state of the healthcare industry, identify areas for potential cost savings, and develop a new model of a more efficient healthcare supply chain. To compile its report, CSC Healthcare interviewed medical manufacturers, distributors, providers, and academic and healthcare trade associations, looking for cost-reduction and efficiency opportunities that would cut the cost of providing healthcare without adversely affecting patients.

According to CSC's report, billions of dollars of cost-saving opportunity exists for the healthcare profession by implementing more effective practices.

The study also contains information on how providers, distributors, and manufacturers can help meet these goals. Recommendations of the study cover efficiency improvments across the breadth of the healthcare supply chain, including inventory control systems, continuous replenishment systems, electronic data interchange (EDI), automated data capture, electronic product information and ordering, activity-based costing, and strategic alliances.

What does this mean for purchasing and supply managers in the healthcare industry? Gary L. Bird, C.P.M., A.P.P., CPHM, logistics manager with DePuy Orthopaedic, Inc., envisions high-level information exchange among all the links in the healthcare supply chain.

DePuy makes orthopaedic knee, hip, shoulder, and spinal implants. The company also produces fracture fixation devices, complementary products and instruments for the operating room. DePuy's primary or first-tier customers are hospitals or physicians' offices, and DePuy's ultimate customer is the patient. Bird hopes to get to the point where, upon "care or use" of an implant, the doctor's office or hospital would instantly send the information electronically to DePuy. "DePuy would then be letting that information pass on to suppliers, 'We just sold a knee,'" for example.

"We want to know what has actually happened, so that as soon as one item is sold, we start forecasting another," Bird says, adding that retail giant Wal-Mart's method — instantaneously communicating sales data to suppliers at the moment of sale so suppliers begin work on the item's replacement—can be used as a model for the medical industry, as well as for ECHR goals.

DePuy Orthopaedic, Inc. spent the last several months implementing EDI. Once they get fully comfortable with EDI, DePuy's hope is that doctors will communicate their surgical schedules electronically and DePuy will communicate back with the procedure products requested to meet the schedule. DePuy currently deals with 530 hospitals, doing purchase orders, purchase order acknowledgements, price/catalog information, invoicing, and payments/remittance electronically, Bird says. Only a handful of hospitals have the capability to send their surgical schedule electronically, he adds, while the rest communicate their schedule manually.

Where will DePuy Orthopaedic, Inc. and the ECHR initiative go from here? "The ECHR needs leaders to step up from different parts of the healthcare industry," Bird says. "DePuy is trying to be a leader in the orthopaedic market."

This summer, participants in the EHCR initiative will likely begin meeting and looking for consultants to assist in cost-cutting activities. DePuy is on the replenishment and inventory committee. Proposals will be sent out and healthcare providers will put together stratgies, but the time line for implementing EHCR goals is uncertain.

"ECHR looks at costs in manageable size and how to address cost issues in all areas of the supply chain," Bird says. "Traditionally, whatever the clinical staff needed, they got. Now, value analysis teams exist within the hospital to determine the best product for the procedure. There's also been a reluctance to sharing information. Now, hospital purchasing and supply management needs to be more of a resource of what's available, providing details on the aggregate cost of the products."

One of DePuy's main challenges will be the ability of healthcare facilities to standardize its products, Bird says. "There are eight to 10 major players in orthopaedics. If a hospital could standardize and use one manufacturer for many products, the supply chain would feel the effects of better efficiencies."

Barbara Friedman, FASHMM-CPHM, director of materials at Kingsbrook Jewish Medical center in Brooklyn, says many hospitals, especially in the New York area, may still need to come up to speed in order to implement EHCR and supply chain management initiatives. Friedman is president of the New York chapter of the American Society for Healthcare Materials Management.

"There's frequently a struggle of politics versus money," she says. How do you turn away suppliers who have come to your facility for 50 years and have allowed the hospital extended payments?" Those hospital purchasing and supply managers who do succeed are those who present supply chain management and cost-reduction opportunities with an understanding of the culture and politics of an institution, she added.

Friedman's own goals for her hospital are to have agreements with primary suppliers and to follow the framework of the goals of the EHCR; one of her goals is hospital supply cost reductions in major clinical departments, i.e., operating room.

How are suppliers to the healthcare industry affected? Major suppliers and supplier networks may take the lead in providing automated stocking, ordering, and payment systems, and large networks may require all suppliers to automate the purchase process and bar-code their items. However, all suppliers, even smaller niche suppliers, will likely be affected in some way, says Jerry Cirino, president of Cleveland, Ohio-based Picker Health Care Products, the largest distributor of medical imaging supplies.

Hospitals frequently target larger-volume suppliers than his organization for supply chain management. "We're a classic niche distributor," he says, and they traditionally focus only on imaging needs. Picker distributes X-ray film, developing chemistry, trays, aprons, and other supplies for medical imaging to hospitals, clinics, and doctors' offices.

"As a niche supplier, the number and dollar value of our products is not extensive compared to major suppliers," Cirino says. "Supply chain management involves integration of business processes. Our processes are much simpler and fewer in nature." However, EHCR and other supply chain management movements will affect them, Cirino says. The EHCR and the Supply Chain Council have invited Picker to participate in supply chain management discussions.

Until about five years ago, hospital purchasing and supply departments didn't usually become involved in radiology purchase decisions. "Hospitals are now looking at cost control more," Cirino says. "The decision today includes the materials management perspective, as well as the user department. Today, salespeople call on teams instead of individual users. Supply chain management is here, and we are involved in helping them meet their goals."

Distributors Become Logistics Providers in Supply Chain

What role do distributors play in supply chain management? In some cases, they're making a business out of logistics services, providing a function that customers are glad to hand over. According to the National Electronic Distributors Association, most of the top distributors now offer some form of logistics services.

For example, Avnet, Inc. launched its Chandler, Arizona-based Integrated Material Services (IMS) division in December 1996 in response to customers' supply chain needs. The world's second-largest electronic components distributor, Avnet began focusing on logistics in 1990. But it wasn't until 1996 that customers began asking for logistics services.

Prior to launching IMS, Avnet spent three days meeting with 12 of its customers who were most advanced in supply chain management, along with three of Avnet's largest suppliers. Avnet asked these participants what their vision was in regards to supply chain management, and also asked them to identify Avnet's place in their supply chains.

"The first thing they told us is that Avnet is positioned between 300 suppliers and their end customers, and those suppliers and customers don't talk to one another," says Greg Frazier, IMS executive vice president. "They wanted us to be at the center of this information exchange—24 hours a day, seven days a week, anywhere in the world. They also wanted to be able to do their requirements planning on Avnet's automated system."

This information was a real eye-opener to Avnet. "We thought we were there to manage their parts," says Tom Brunell, Avnet IMS' vice president, materials management. "They told us, 'No, we need you to manage the information.' With good information, they need less inventory. So our customers started sharing more information with us." Today, Avnet's IMS division has 500 customers, and overall, Avnet's different divisions have a total of 70,000 customers.

Previously, the items on a purchase order received by Avnet would frequently change up to five times, Frazier says. "Now, customers share their MRP requirements every week —some share it every day—and we plan the material pipeline. That way, we have the best information available and we're working from the standpoint of demand planning." Avnet's customers send their orders on a weekly or even daily basis via EDI. Some customers transmit their information every four hours, Frazier says, and he expects this to become more common.

"Inventory flexibility is key to supply chain management," Frazier says. "When there's obsolescence, someone absorbs it in the supply chain. But if any one of our customers has excess inventory, we have 70,000 others who might need those parts. Avnet also has a half-billion dollar buffer stock. Now, people can focus on supply chain management instead of ordering parts."

And Avnet expects their customers' requests relating to supply chain management to continue to get more and more sophisticated. "In 1996, our customers told us they wanted us to manage information," Frazier says. "In 1997, that didn't change except that the word 'global' came up. We didn't deal with that before." In response, Avnet has opened several European and Asian operations and plans to use the same information systems operations there.

Brad Wallace, director of operations for Sonoma Systems, says his organization started using Avnet's Hamilton Hallmark division about seven years ago, and started using Avnet's IMS division last summer. This helped his organization shift its focus from in-house manufacturing to product development, Wallace says. "Sonoma Systems' core competency is to develop broad-based access devices. [Avnet's] core competencies are procurement and supply chain management. They bill me for an item when I ship to the customer. I have zero inventory and zero cash out-of-pocket."

Distributors such as Avnet are carving their niches in supply chain management based on customer needs. So whether it's surgical supplies or high-tech components, different players in numerous industries are identifying their roles in supply chain management.

Carolyn Pye is a writer for Purchasing Today®.

The Role of the Distributor

Jim Nelles

This article explores some of the major issues facing distributors today. These issues include the role of alliances and consortia, distributors' relationships with manufacturers, integrated supply, and electronic commerce. It includes a good review of the implications of changes in distribution for purchasing and supply management.

Ask five different people to explain the relationship between distributors, manufacturers, and purchasing, and you will probably receive five very different answers. Are distributors so complex that they defy definition? No, it is simply that a distributor can be many different things to different people. Whether you are watching your favorite television rerun, shopping for a new car, or buying a gross of screws, you are probably interacting with a distributor. In a very general sense, unless you are buying direct from the factory, or a factory outlet store, you are buying from a distributor.

Distributors come in all shapes and sizes and sell a wide array of products. For simplicity, the focus will be on wholesale and industrial distributors; however, the information should be transferable to all types of distributor networks, with the possible exception of distributors in the entertainment industry such as movie, music, and television program distributors. See the sidebar on the next page for some possible examples of how various industries and organizations can use distributors.

What Is a Distributor?

Simply stated, any organization that purchases a product and resells that product could be defined as a distributor. The distributor may buy direct from the manufacturer, a manufacturer's representative, or even another distributor. Distributors then (traditionally) hold the product until an order is received from a customer. In an attempt to justify higher prices for the products it sells, a distributor may offer to perform any number of value-added services for its customers. These services will be discussed in detail below.

According to the U.S. Department of Commerce, the distribution industry topped $4 trillion in sales in 1997. The Distribution Research and Education Foundation (DREF) estimates that the merchant wholesaler-distributor industry is the largest segment of wholesale trade, with 1997 sales of $2.5 trillion. In 1997, merchant wholesaler-distributors employed more than 5.1 million people.

Different Distributors	
Organization	**Distributor Possibilities**
Manufacturer	Pumps, bearings, janitorial supplies
Retailer	Janitorial supplies, office supplies
Bank	Office supplies, computer software
Public Institution	Office supplies, office furniture
Hospital	Medical supplies, cafeteria supplies
Television Network	Syndicated programs such as game shows or "sit-coms"
Airline	Hardware, computer terminals, forms
Not-for-Profit	Office supplies
Professional Sports Team	Tickets, medical equipment, office supplies
Distributors	Office supplies, forms, janitorial supplies

Challenges Facing Distributors

Centuries ago, the Phoenicians served among the first documented distributors. They used their superior navigation skills to sail the seas and buy rare and precious goods that they would then sell or trade to those who could not obtain the products locally. This continued uninterrupted for generations, until the Phoenician Empire collapsed.

Today's distributors are facing many key challenges across several fronts, including changes in customer requirements, increased competition on multiple fronts, the requirement to do business on an international, if not global, scale, and the increasingly important role of technology. How distributors respond to these challenges will determine their success.

We will review distributors' efforts to compete more effectively under four general categories: the use of alliances, relationships with manufacturers, integrated supply, and technology/electronic commerce.

Alliances, Consortia, and Consolidation

Changes in the world of distribution have forced many distributors to look for new ways to survive. One way distributors are seeking to prolong their lives is through alliance relationships, by which distributors pool their resources to create a separate organization to meet customer needs and improve sales, profitability, or geographic reach. According to an article by Adam Fein of Pembroke Consulting, distributors are joining alliances to manage various challenges such as:

- Increasing competition from larger consolidators
- Accelerating consolidation among traditional customers of distribution
- Customer requirements for integrated supply agreements and national accounts
- Growing interest in electronic commerce channels that (may) bypass distribution

The MRO (maintenance, repair, and operation) segment of the industry formed the first distribution alliances, reacting to changing customer requirements that included a desire to reduce the supplier base, reduce transaction costs, and have an outside party manage the entire MRO function. This was a direct result of a push by purchasing organizations to focus on their core competencies, and outsource "non-core" functions.

An alliance functions as a network in which member distributors have individual business objectives, yet operate within a formal or semiformal organization to achieve more encompassing goals. The formality of the various types of alliances runs the gamut from handshake deals to full-blown equity partnerships.

At their most basic level, alliances serve as a means to expand a distributor's geographic reach and customer base. For example, a distributor of wooden stepladders on the East Coast may partner with a distributor of wooden extension ladders in Chicago. Each distributor offers the other's product as a complementary, noncompeting line. Another example would be an office supplies distributor teaming with a distributor of janitorial or safety supplies. Together, the two distributors increase their customer base, and offer their customers a more complete solution. Obviously, this type of arrangement works best when the distributors' products are not substitutes.

Another, more formal alliance is a group purchasing organization, where distributors combine their individual purchases into one larger buy in an attempt to capitalize on volume discounts. In this type of arrangement, one of the distributors coordinates buys with suppliers, receives supplier shipments, and performs a "cross-dock" function, sending material to other distributors in the organization. In other arrangements, the supplier will drop ship directly to all participating distributors' locations.

At the other extreme, distributors may come together through an equity ownership arrangement in which the functions of two or more distributors become fully integrated. This type of alliance is usually long term and much more formalized in nature. An example of this type of relationship would entail a group of distributors coming together to form an organization to provide an offshore-based customer with integrated supply-type services.

Strategic alliances, particularly as they pertain to the purchasing and supply function, will become more prevalent in the future, according to a 1998 study by NAPM, the Center for Advanced Purchasing Studies (CAPS), A.T. Kearney, Arizona State University, and Michigan State University. "The Future of Purchasing and Supply: A Five- and Ten-Year Forecast" reports that these alliances will be necessary because of increasing competition and higher performance expectations. Alliances can provide their members with powerful growth opportunities, and pose considerable challenges to those not participating. The alliances forming today should be interesting to monitor, for many are being formed merely as a reaction to other alliances. This "I've gotta be in one" mentality could cause the success rate of alliances to fall even further as organizations follow a "me too" approach to alliances, failing to perform diligent research on potential alliance partners or to even fully consider the impact of joining/forming an alliance.

Consortia

Having the power of a national chain while remaining an independent and agile entity have long been key reasons why small and mid-sized distributors join consortia. Consortium members usually benefit from the collective buying power, marketing efforts, and rebate programs arranged with preferred suppliers. By pooling together in consortia, smaller distributors have been able to compete against major supply houses to win national contracts and integrated supply deals. The results include improved margins (resulting from combined volume), better supplier loyalty, and the ability to leverage sophisticated services for end users. For the customer, the increased competition usually means lower prices, improved service levels, and a reduced cost of acquisition.

An example of a consortium is the IMARK Group, an affiliation of 175 independent electrical distributors, which refers to itself as a "member-owned marketing group." IMARK's stated mission is to provide its members and manufacturers with value-added services to accomplish the following goals:

- Maximize profitability
- Increase market share
- Strengthen business relationships
- Network with other distributors

IMARK achieves its mission by offering financial, marketing, networking, and educational opportunities to its members and manufacturers. One interesting fact about IMARK is that it allows its members to offer their customers the Buying Power Credit Card. The card is designed to make credit convenient for customers, while providing a means to ensure that member distributors are paid within 24 hours of recognizing a sale. This service solves cash-flow problems that hound many smaller distributors.

Implications for Purchasing

Alliances and consortia are generally beneficial to the purchasing organizations they serve. As mentioned, alliances and consortia are formed, among other reasons, to allow smaller distributors to compete with larger, more diversified organizations. This pooling of resources leads to improved service, more diverse and creative value-added program options, and, in most cases, reduced costs. A strong alliance or consortium could place enough competitive pressure on large distributors to cause the larger organizations to reduce prices and improve service options in order to remain competitive.

There is a moderate concern for purchasing organizations as alliances and consortia grow in number and power. Potentially, members of an alliance or consortium could "corner the market" for a set of highly proprietary products, such as medical devices. This could lead to price fixing and service reductions, as distributors attempt to capitalize on their position of power. This position, however, is not sustainable over the long run.

Economic theory predicts that either the manufacturers of these products or one of the distributors will break from the alliance, reducing the price in attempt to capture the lion's share of the market. Over time, this will lead to the weakening of alliances, and their potential collapse.

Today, there are new issues that consortia must address if they are to remain a viable option for distributors. Consolidation and public roll-ups are challenging the consortium paradigm. "Buying groups did—and we thought they would—(become) an interim step toward a higher degree of consolidation," says Gary Buffington, executive director of the Industrial Distribution Association. "In one sense, the acquirers and major buying groups are now competing for the same types of companies and, given that, the buying group members are being acquired. So, I think fairly soon you will see buying groups left with a void in certain markets."

Conversely, some believe that the recent trend in consolidation is actually driving more distributors to participate in marketing cooperatives. According to Dave Gordon, vice president of marketing for the IMARK Group; "More and more distributors see now as the time to take advantage of benefits and join a group. They see the additional services are key, not just incremental profitability .... They look at their business in its entirety."

Consolidation

As mentioned above, consolidation also appears to be a route some distributors are taking as they struggle to compete in today's marketplace. A recent report by the Distribution Research and Education Foundation, *Facing the Forces of Change, Four Trends Reshaping Wholesale Distribution*, predicts that consolidation will continue over the next decade, particularly in highly fragmented segments such as electrical suppliers, power transmission, safety equipment, hose and accessories, and sanitary suppliers.

Many distributors say they welcome acquisition offers because they believe it will bolster their market share and help improve their management skills. Among companies with sales under $10 million that have either merged or been acquired, many said consolidation benefited them by lowering costs and increasing their market share, according to *Industrial Distribution's* 52nd annual survey of distributor operations.

Relationships with Manufacturers

Manufacturers use distributors as a means to sell a large volume of product to relatively few customers. This reduces costs to the manufacturer in the areas of sales, distribution, and relationship management, among others. Given that distributors are manufacturers' customers and that distributors perform a valuable marketing function for manufacturers, the relationship a manufacturer has with a distributor should be friendly, right? Interestingly, the relationship between manufacturers and distributors is often cantankerous, and sometimes even adversarial. This tension stems from the fact that a distributor wants to offer its customers as wide a variety of products from which to choose as possible. Conversely, a manufacturer wants the distributor to carry more of its products and less of any competing manufacturer's products. Traditionally, the desire on the part of manufacturers to secure distribution channels for their products and to freeze out their competition has led some manufacturers to offer distributors the "exclusive right" to sell the manufacturer's product within a given region. In return, the distributor agrees not to offer a competing manufacturer's product.

More progressive manufacturers are partnering with their distributors, creating opportunities for themselves by providing value-added services to the distributor. Thomas & Betts (T&B), a supplier of electrical components, has definitely raised the bar by creating a new level of partnering for use with its distributors. This program, known as distributor-manufacturer integration (DMI), takes the concept of supplier-managed inventory to the next level, and beyond. For examples of the services provided, see the sidebar, "Checklist."

Participants in early pilot programs reported a 45 percent drop in the average inventory levels carried for T&B products.

Distributors make three major commitments in order to participate in the DMI program:

- 75 percent of T&B-comparable items in their stock must be T&B.
- Stock balances reported each evening to the T&B computer must be accurate.
- The T&B planner must be told in advance of future conditions that would not show up in an analysis of past sales whenever the distributor has such information.

This type of distributor-manufacturer relationship offers many of the same potential benefits to the purchasing organization as alliances and consortia, including improved service and reduced costs. However, the downside potential may be greater. As larger, more powerful manufacturers solidify relationships with multiple distributors, they will potentially be able to block the product lines of other, less powerful manufacturers, reducing the options that a purchasing organization has with any one distributor. This, in turn, could lead to higher prices and reduced service options. Again, economic theory tells us that this is not a sustainable position. As less powerful manufacturers find themselves locked out of certain distributors, they will form alliances with competing distributors. These newly aligned groups will have to offer lower prices and better service than their larger, more powerful competitors. As purchasing organizations evaluate the product-price-service tradeoff and shift business to the newer, less powerful groups, the larger groups will have to reduce prices and improve service in order to remain viable.

Other Approaches

There are other, less formal approaches that distributors and manufacturers can, and have, taken in an effort to work more closely to increase channel efficiency and to combat shrinking margins and intensifying end-user demands. Some manufacturers and distributors are forming advisory councils in an effort to work toward their common goals.

Checklist

As part of its DMI Signature Service, Thomas & Betts (T&B) will perform the following for its distributors:

- T&B and the distributor remove any slow-moving T&B products.
- T&B takes over the job of deciding when and how much material to ship to a distributor. The distributor must transmit to T&B the end-of-day stock status on each program item. This is done via standard EDI transactions or through a personal computer provided by T&B.
- There are no minimum order requirements. For large distributors, T&B ships twice a week; for smaller distributors, once a week.
- T&B pays the freight on all shipments.
- On pre-designated "superstock" items, T&B guarantees to ship within 48 hours of determining a need.
- Every item is packaged separately, printing the distributor's warehouse location on each carton.
- Distributors record the receipt of a shipment, not individual items. All items and quantities are automatically received into stock.
- If a shortage or other error is discovered, T&B accepts the distributor's word and immediately adjusts the invoice. T&B delays the invoicing step until the system shows that all items were properly and accurately received. A distributor has 5 days to report any errors.
- The invoice is posted directly to the distributor's accounts payable system. T&B invoices all DMI shipments just once a month. Distributors have reported as much as an 80 percent savings in accounts payable activity with DMI items.
- Material can be returned four times a year, with no prior approval from a T&B representative, and credit is issued at current replacement cost, if the product is still salable. The distributor does pay freight, but there no restocking charge.

Originally, advisory councils were formed so distributors could have their voice heard by manufacturers. However, as the councils have become more refined, they have grown to offer all members the opportunity to share ideas, seek solutions to common problems, and network in a non-threatening atmosphere. Bostik, a Massachusetts manufacturer of adhesives and sealant, formed a distributor advisory council with the goal of tapping its distributors for new product ideas. According to Rich D'Autilio, Bostik's director of sales and marketing, with time Bostik realized that the council would be best utilized by focusing on business issues, such as improving customer service and generating new business.

The distributors sitting on advisory councils bring a multitude of overlapping purposes, one of which is to affect the sponsoring manufacturer's decision making. Councils give distributors an opportunity to input into manufacturers' channels management strategies, price structure strategies, and marketing strategies, among others. In addition, distributors have the opportunity to learn from one another in a noncompetitive environment. Manufacturers use the councils not only to mine distributors for new product ideas, but also to focus on and understand customer service and growth issues.

Though distributor advisory councils are more prevalent in the market than supplier advisory councils, Cameron & Barkley, a regional industrial distribution company in Charleston, South Carolina, is an example of a supplier council that works. Cameron & Barkley has three main purposes for its supplier advisory council:

- Update manufacturers on the state of the business and recent changes within the council
- Delve into specific business issues
- Provide time for social interaction, which works to build relationships

"We get some of the best minds in the industry to deal with issues as we perceive them," says Bob McQuillan, Cameron & Barkley's vice president, corporate/materials manager. "We present the issues the way we think they are and then, through facilitation and dialogue, we're able to determine whether there is value in our thought processes. That's almost impossible to do on an individual basis. Group dynamics speak very loudly to us."

The most typical members of a supplier council are mid- to upper-level managers from manufacturers, distributors, and purchasing organizations. However, as the councils have become more prevalent, their membership has expanded to include purchasing agents, sales representatives, and virtually anyone else who can provide industry insight and fresh, creative ideas.

Integrated Supply

The concept of integrated supply has become extremely popular as more and more of distributors' customers focus on their core competencies. Integrated supply is designed to allow a lead supplier, or "integrator," to take over all procurement, materials management, sourcing, and materials forecasting for its customer. To date, the vast majority of integrated supply customers has been large manufacturers. As a result, integrators must have a broad product offering and a wide geographic scope, or be able to form a consortium with those characteristics.

The traditional models of integrated supply established the integrator as the single point of contact for the customer. A consortium of manufacturers and distributors supported the integrator with material outside of the integrator's product base. As with most programs, this method has advantages and disadvantages for both the customer and the integrator.

Advantages

Customer advantages include decreased holding costs, since the integrator held the inventory, and reduced procurement costs, due to the customer now having a single point of contact. In addition, the integrator's expertise in inventory management led to less waste in the system. In many cases, the integrator's purchasing skills also created better deals with manufacturers, further reducing the product price. The advantages for the integrator are long-term contracts, significantly higher volume, a more secure relationship with the customer, and increased information flow for forecasting.

Disadvantages

A major disadvantage for the customer is that the lack of a competitive bidding process, once initial contracts were established, could lead to complacency on the part of the integrator. Customers can combat the complacency tendency with an integrated supply contract that requires an annual review of pricing, and allows for questionable prices to be challenged on the open market. The disadvantages for the integrator/distributor result directly from the advantages. The long-term contracts and secure relationships are often viewed by customers as "guaranteed business" that should be rewarded with reductions in product or service pricing. Distributors involved in integrated supply arrangements sometimes find themselves in the awkward situation of explaining to potential customers that not only are discounts unavailable under integrated supply, but that they must also compensate the integrator for services formerly regarded as free.

Integration

Distributors involved in integrated supply fall into one of two major categories: integrator or second-tier distributor. To be a successful integrator, the distributor must have established certain characteristics, including breadth and depth of product, geographic scope, and technological competency.

Product breadth and depth means that the integrator has a major portion of the products called for in the integrated supply relationship. The wider and deeper the integrator's offering, the less dependent it is on relationships with second-tier distributors.

Geographic scope addresses another major integrated supply driver: customer alliances. Customers are forming alliances at a rapid pace, many of which are national, if not global, in nature. With the exception of major catalog houses such as the McMaster-Carrs and the Graingers of the world, most distributors are regional at best. Third-party logistics companies such as FedEx have used their global presence in an effort to move into integrated supply. As this trend continues, watch for even further consolidation among distributors as they attempt to reach scale economies on both a national and global level.

Again, these changes should prove to be beneficial to purchasing and supply organizations. These new entrants are responding to the needs of purchasing organizations. The increased competition will force weaker distributors to improve their performance or it will drive them from the industry.

Technology

Finally, technology can often be the distinguishing factor between a successful integrator and an "also ran." The large manufacturing customers associated with integrated supply are technologically savvy, using EDI, the Internet, and other electronic commerce programs to conduct business. The expanded use of technology should help to make all people involved in the integrated supply function more efficient and profitable. As will be discussed in the next section, the use of Internet tools will allow services such as real-time order tracking, inventory management, bill upon receipt, and electronic funds transfer to become commonplace. All of these advances will drive cost out of the system, allowing for increased margins for the distributor and manufacturer, and lower prices for the end customer. This technology is available today for those willing to invest. Distributors that make the technology investment now will be able to compete in the next millennium; those that wait, will not.

Electronic Commerce

No innovation has created such a mix of excitement, fear, and misunderstanding as electronic commerce (e-commerce). The use of the Internet and other e-commerce solutions has the potential to revolutionize the distribution industry. The Internet is less expensive to manage and utilize than private EDI networks managed by third-party organizations. The use of a Web site allows a distributor to utilize an "electronic sales force" that operates 24 hours a day, seven days a week, doesn't take vacations, and never leaves the organization—taking clients with him or her. The value-added aspects of Internet-based electronic commerce are limitless, and include real-time order tracking, online product availability monitoring, and electronic funds transfer. In fact, a savvy distributor could even establish a system by which customers receive e-mails reminding them that it may be time to order a particular product.

Internet

Ron Schreivman, director of the National Association of Wholesaler-Distributors' Research and Education Foundation, says that asking if the Internet is good or bad for distributors is like asking if personal computers are good or bad for business. "The Internet is a pipeline," he says. "What matters is how you use this tool. Potentially, the Internet can take tremendous costs from the distribution channel."

Online Catalogs

While most distributors use the Web as a marketing tool to attract customers, e-commerce via the Internet is becoming increasingly popular. As an example, W.W. Grainger has invested heavily in its online shopping capabilities, including an agreement with Perot Systems to set up an Internet department store where customers can buy a range of MRO and non-MRO products. For Grainger, and other catalog houses, the use of the Internet has the potential to generate additional savings, as these distributors send fewer and fewer catalogs via traditional "snail" mail. Forrester Research estimates that business-to-business Internet commerce will grow from 1998 levels of approximately $17 billion to $327 billion by 2002. That is a compounded annual growth rate of more than 100 percent! General Electric expects to save $500 million over the next three years through online purchasing. By 2002, GE plans to spend $5 billion electronically.

The Internet allows small, local, and regional distributors to compete for customers on a national and even international level. The absence of geographic boundaries will create more competition. However, it will also create new problems for distributors. First, territorial agreements may become impossible to enforce in the world of electronic commerce. For example, if distributor A is licensed to sell manufacturer Z's products east of the Mississippi River, and distributor B is licensed to sell manufacturer Z's products west of the Mississippi, should distributor A be expected to refuse an order received via its Internet site from a customer in California? On a more devious level, unscrupulous distributors may target customers outside of their geographic region. Second, both small and large distributors will have to take steps to learn to profitably conduct business on a global scale. They will have to understand import/ export regulations and requirements, and establish relationships with international freight forwarders. In addition, distributors will have to reexamine their pricing structures to ensure that they are meeting their costs on any exporting they may do.

While the Web and other e-commerce outlets will enable many smaller distributors to compete with larger players, price, and perhaps margins, are bound to suffer as customers shop for both MRO and non-MRO products on the Web. Currently, there are several Web sites that allow customers to seek out the lowest priced airfare between two cities or the lowest priced hotel room in a given town. Can a site that generates a global search for the lowest priced hammer, pump, or valve be that far off? The Web will make it easier for customers who want to buy on price to do so.

The Internet will likely force margins down, but distributors should be able to maintain bottom-line profitability, because distributors on the Internet should have to spend less to make their margins. But selling on price is not a sustainable competitive advantage. Distributors will need to continue to work to differentiate themselves through value-added services, such as extended warranties, inventory management programs, and electronic funds transfer, to name a few. They will then need to work to market these services in such a way that even price-sensitive customers will be willing to pay extra for them.

Too Much Technology?

One of the biggest fears for distributors rising out of the Internet frenzy is that manufacturers will begin selling direct to mid-sized and small-end users, or that purchasers from distributors' traditional customer base will use the Internet to buy directly from manufacturers. Gary Buffington, executive vice president of the Atlanta-based Industrial Distribution Association, says that industrial distributors do not feel threatened by the possibility of purchasers using the Internet to buy directly from manufacturers. Most purchasers of industrial supplies aren't looking to buy these items on the Internet because the time required to do so would not usually be worth it to the purchaser, Buffington says. "An industrial buyer who bought direct would need links with hundreds of suppliers. An industrial distributor represents hundreds or thousands of suppliers. The Internet can only enhance this. If the distributor already adds value, the Internet won't affect that. The Internet is not going to cause purchasers to bypass channels except for some limited range of commodity products or for spot purchases."

On the manufacturer's side, it simply would not be profitable to manage thousands of small-dollar orders that would result from circumventing the distributor. Manufacturers may find a middle ground by which they allow customers to place orders on their Web site and then forward these orders on to distributors who would manage the order fulfillment process. This would be an automatic process, blind to customer and manufacturer alike, accomplished through an automated e-mail system. Manufacturers would then charge their distributors a "finder's fee" for any orders received in this manner. While issues such as invoicing would have to be addressed, this type of arrangement could become very popular.

Committed to Success

In the September 1998 issue of *PRAXIS* (now titled *PRACTIX*), the Center for Advanced Purchasing Studies (CAPS) identified an example of one organization's efforts in working with distributors. This designer and assembler of high-technology medical monitoring devices has had an onsite distributor presence for over 10 years. It uses three major distributors to supply most of its electronic component requirements and the parties involved believe they have a "best-in-class" relationship. To continue success as they face future challenges, the following agenda outlines evaluation criteria for the purchasing organization and the distributors.

Purchasing organization to judge distributors on:
- Top management support and commitment
- Inventory support against provided forecasts
- Shortage impact
- Cost models/competitiveness
- Availability and quality of engineering support
- Evidence of multi-facility support
- Global presence
- Organization-wide accessibility to onsite distributor store management
- Value-added contribution to manufacturing and business process

Distributors to judge purchasing organization on:
- Clearly communicated goals

- Growth opportunities provided
- How well support is facilitated
- Forecast accuracy
- Honesty and fairness in the business relationship

Source: *Praxis*, The Center for Advanced Purchasing Studies, September 1998.

Jim Nelles is an associate in the Chicago office of Mitchell Madison Group, a global management consulting firm. He has worked in the purchasing, procurement, and sourcing field for more than five years as a buyer, product manager, and consultant.

Part Two

Supply Management Techniques

A ll the articles in this book are in one way or another about supply management techniques, but this part is designed to give you some specific pointers for how to maximize your management of suppliers and the supply chain. It features an original article by Ray Bacanskas, and W. Jack Wagner, "Two-Way Performance Report Cards: A Supplier's Tool to Identify World-Class Customers," where you'll learn about a tool for working more closely with suppliers. While it's not so unusual for organizations to rate their suppliers, this approach suggests establishing relationships with suppliers, where they rate the quality of their customers. Such a two-way rating system facilitates continuously improving that relationship.

How do you select suppliers? Is it the ones who offer the lowest price? In the article "Effectively Selecting Suppliers Using Total Cost of Ownership" by Zeger Degraeve and Filip Roodhooft, learn how to make decisions based not just on price but all the other costs—as well as benefits—that come from the company you choose as a supplier. To accompany this concept, also see the article "Target Costing" by Lisa Ellram. This is a concept for bringing together purchasing, design, manufacturing, and often suppliers to determine the overall cost for an item and then figure ways to assure that costs meet rather than exceed targets.

You'll also find a fine piece from the journal *Business Horizons*, "The Use and Abuse of Power in Supply Chains," by Charles Munson, Meir Rosenblatt, and Zehava Rosenblatt. Did you ever encounter "channel bullies?" Learn how to deal with them and much more in this article.

Another important part of supply chain management is inventory control. This is what a *Purchasing Today*® article "Come Out, Come Out, Wherever You Are," is all about. Like the advice of others whose articles appear in this book, you'll find one of the keys to keeping costs and inventory down is your alliance with suppliers. You'll see that working closely with suppliers, along with creating cooperation among the different departments within the organization, is key to creating an efficient and smooth-running supply chain.

One way to view purchasing is as a supplier to other departments in the organization. How do you manage that supplier-customer relationship? That's what the article by Thomas Bassett, "Purchasing and Supply Interacts with Internal Customers" addresses. In this detailed piece, learn how to make sure the purchasing and supply department's customers are satisfied and how to continuously improve how purchasing serves those customers.

This is just a sampling of what you'll find in Part Two. It is an eclectic collection, but we think you'll find the best of current thinking among the articles we've selected.

Two-Way Performance Report Cards: A Tool to Identify World-Class Suppliers and Customers

Ray Bacanskas, C.P.M., P.E.
and William J. "Jack" Wagner, C.P.M.

This original article lays out a tool purchasing and supply managers can use in relation to suppliers—the two-way report card. This allows buyers to rate sellers and sellers to also rate buyers. The point is that only with two-way reporting can both parties improve the way they interact with each other to make the purchase and delivery of supplies as trouble-free as possible. Learn more about this tool here.

Introduction

Price, quality, and delivery have been the fundamental parameters buyers use to evaluate suppliers and make supplier/product selections. In this context, buyers were perceived, correctly or incorrectly, to have leverage over their suppliers. Recently however, as purchasing has evolved into supply chain management, individual firms in a chain find themselves simultaneously measuring suppliers and being measured by their customers, or the next firm in their supply chain. In addition, measurements can jump tiers or links in the supply chain. For example, a tier-two firm might measure a key factor of a supplier in tier four. As both physical and electronic integration bring suppliers and customers closer together, measurements grow in importance.

This article describes two-way report cards—buyers to sellers and sellers to buyers—and uses this information as a baseline for discussing how world-class buyers and sellers can use this report card tool as a means to gain competitive advantages in the marketplace.

What are the characteristics of a world-class supplier?[1]
- Assists in product development
- Delivers error free products
- Has a production system that delivers product on time and the knowledge to assist customers in reducing time-to-market
- Creates and sustains relationships with all members of the supply chain to achieve superior results

- Has an organization that continues to learn and quickly adapt to a rapidly changing world
- Attains a return on investment that contributes to the success of all members of the supply chain

What are the characteristics of a world-class customer?
- Delivers products that anticipate consumer needs and market trends
- Delights its customers by providing products with unique or unexpected benefits
- Markets products that are conscientiously built and have zero defects
- Builds and maintains a strong and an effective relationship with its entire supply chain
- Promotes learning/adapting and profits from its supply-chain-wide vision

In a more recent effort, some firms are developing a profile of a world-class customer and instituting a strategy to link world-class customers with world-class suppliers.[2] Firms that represent different industries are developing strategies around the premise that they need to be a better customer to attract world-class sellers. While a consensus on the characteristics has not been reached there are eight broad characteristics.

- *Total commitment.* Top down support from the entire organization within the buyer's firm
- *Communication.* Open and consistent communication with suppliers.
- *Price.* A world-class customer qualifies suppliers who best fulfill current and future delivery and quality requirements and then negotiates with them.
- *Long-term commitment to suppliers.* A world-class customer sets long-term goals and works with the supplier to achieve those goals.
- *Cost concepts.* Top customers have a detailed understanding of total cost concepts.
- *Measurement.* World-class customers are aiming their measurement systems at determining which suppliers have the potential to become the best all-around suppliers in the field.
- *Training.* For a growing number of suppliers, the mark of a world-class customer is their commitment to supplier training.
- *Can-do attitude.* World-class customers demonstrate a willingness to implement programs to track progress, knowing that the learning curve will be time consuming and difficult.

Two-Way Report Cards

Measurement followed by an effort to improve is what drives improvement. Report cards provide the facts to substantiate performance. The two-way report card is a new concept that takes performance monitoring and process improvement to a new dimension. Those who are directly involved with various aspects of quality and process improvement are familiar with one-way report cards, where buyers measure sellers' performance. Much less familiar is a concept that deserves a lot more attention but unfortunately is practiced by perhaps a handful of companies.

This concept is the two-way report card, where buyers measure sellers and sellers measure buyers. Perhaps it sounds a little out of the ordinary and novel, but it certainly deserves a second look, for it has merits that go beyond those that can be obtained from one-way report cards. Along with the benefits of heightened levels of awareness and improvement that report cards bring, they give buyers an opportunity to become world-class customers and perhaps even an opportunity for sellers to be more selective in the buyers they choose as partners for developing long-term relationships.

Report Card Development/Administration/Format

Report card development and administration is best suited for either the supply chain management (SCM) or the quality assurance organization (QA). SCM is centrally situated and is in the best position to interface with suppliers and internal line and staff organizations. The QA organization is often similarly situated. Regardless of who takes the lead role, the other should be actively involved in the report card process.

The report card format refers to the output document(s). Using a spreadsheet is a good way to present the measures, results, and grades in a convenient and structured format. The report card results can be filled out monthly, quarterly or whatever measurement period makes the most sense. Using this format, buyers and sellers can easily monitor results for improvement (see Figure 1). Similarly, it is also convenient to set up a corresponding text document in table format that contains the same set of measures, specific objectives, the grading criteria along with any descriptive/clarification information (see Figure 2.).

Establishing Buyer/Seller Measures

The measures selected should be those that provide the best gauge of product/service and relationship performance. As a general rule, there should be eight to ten buyer measures and the same amount of seller measures, although the final number is based on importance and the availability of supporting data. Buyers and sellers should have input into each other's measures and at least half of the buyer/seller measures should be dependent. This way, both the buyer and the seller have a stake in each other's performance and must work together to improve individually and collectively. For example, on-time delivery and lead time are two likely choices for dependent buyer/seller measures.

Once the measures are established, they can be changed based on mutual agreement. Different phases of the relationship may require a change in buyer and seller measures, which could involve what is measured, the number of measures, or both. For instance, a new buyer/supplier relationship may involve measures that are different from the measures in a mature relationship, such as on-time delivery and promptness of communication when there are problems. The bottomline: both buyer and seller must be flexible and be willing to accept change. However, when to change requires judgment and insight.

TWO-WAY REPORT CARD					
PERFORMANCE INDICATORS	2Q RESULT	2Q GRADE	3Q RESULT	3Q GRADE	ETC.
SUPPLIER REPORT CARD					
Timely Product Delivery					
Order Fill Accuracy					
Percent Product Returns					
Billing Accuracy					
System Availability					
Customer Satisfaction Survey					
OVERALL REPORT CARD GRADE					
BUYER REPORT CARD					
Order Lead Time					
Order Accuracy					
Percent Product Returns					
Timely Invoice Payment					
Average Requisition Size					
Average Requisition Size ($)					
Buyer Satisfaction Survey					
OVERALL REPORT CARD GRADE					

Figure 1. An example of a two-way report card

Setting Performance Objectives

The buyer and the seller set the performance objectives individually, although both have input into each other's objectives. Generally, the objectives could be based on industry, company, departmental, contract, or any combination of these. As with the measures, objectives are subject to change. When objective levels are consistently exceeded, it may be appropriate to raise the bar and set higher targets. Again, as with measures, both parties should exercise flexibility and good judgment.

Establishing the Grading Criteria

The grading criteria are a measure of how well buyers and sellers performance results meet their respective performance objectives. From experience, the most convenient grading

SELLER REPORT CARD	OBJECTIVES	GRADING CRITERIA
Timely Product Delivery	Based on Customer Requested Due Date (CRDD)	A for exceeding CRDD B for meeting CRDD C for missing CRDD by 10% Etc.
Order Fill Accuracy The Accuracy % is calculated as: (Lines processed - Sales & Warehouse Errors) ÷ Lines Processed	At least 90% of line items processed accurately	A = 95% to 100% B = 90.0 to 94.9% Etc.
Etc.	Etc.	Etc.
BUYER REPORT CARD	**OBJECTIVES**	**GRADING CRITERIA**
Order Lead Time	At least 30 days	A for < 25 days B for < 30 days C for < 35 days Etc.
Order Accuracy Accuracy % is calculated as: (Lines ordered - errors) ÷ Lines processed	At least 90% of line items ordered accurately	A = 95% to 100% B = 90.0 to 94.9% Etc.
Etc.	Etc.	Etc.

Figure 2. Accompanying text document with descriptive information

method to use is the familiar point grade system. As an example, assume the following: On-time delivery is a measure and the objective is delivery within 30 days. The grading scale could be set up as follows: A for less than 30 days, B for 30-35 days, C for 36-40 days, and so on. It is good practice to set meeting an objective as a B grade and exceeding the objective as an A grade. This provides some room for improvement. Again, as with measures and objectives, both parties should exercise flexibility and good judgment.

Quality Action Teams (QAT)

A QAT meeting is an excellent forum to review buyer and seller report card results and to address issues in general. Members of the QAT should address substandard performance and decide on corrective action steps to be taken by either the buyer, the seller, or both. The proceedings of the meeting should be well documented, including issues, responsible parties, and agreed upon dates for resolving the issues. The number of QAT members should be kept to a minimum and only involve those who are in a position to make decisions, recommendations or to take a problem to higher authorities when there is an impasse.

Benefits Summary

In summary, two-way report cards:

- Provide input into the decision process when selecting strategic relationship buyers and sellers
- Foster an honest and open relationship
- Build world-class customers and suppliers
- Optimize performance
- Produce tangible cost benefits

Key Success Factors

As with any new undertaking, especially one that could possibly "go against the grain" of any given culture or organization, the concept and benefits of two-way report cards must be clearly understood and supported by upper management. After all, it may be difficult for suppliers to rate buyers and it also may be difficult for buyers to publicize the fact that they are less than perfect. In summary, these are the key two-way report card success factors:

- Requires strong upper management support
- Must be included as part of departmental/individual commitments
- Supporting data must be accurate
- Supplier must be willing to participate and to rate the buyer honestly
- Supplier willingness to accpet ratings and commit to improvement
- Buyer must be willing to accept criticism without retribution

Conclusion

There can be many customers and suppliers in a given supply chain. Going through the supply chain, a product may be touched by many hands before it gets to its final destination, the consumer. The only way to assure that the consumer gets the absolute best in terms of quality, value, and price is to make sure that all the links in the chain do their best to maximize both process efficiency and the quality of outputs. A chain made up of world-class suppliers and world-class customers can produce exceptional results. While that may be difficult, implementing the right processes, including the two-way measures is a great start to producing world-class suppliers and customers as well as world-class products and services.

Interactions Between Buyers and Sellers

There are four possibilities of interaction between buyers and sellers who are either world-class or non-world-class. Figure 3 describes each of the four and provides some of the issues that buyers or sellers could use as a competitive advantage. It also provides answers to several questions that are a natural outcome of this topic.

- How would a world-class seller interact with a non-world-class customer?
- How would a world-class customer interact with a non-world-class seller?
- What type of competitive advantage exists?

Buyer	Supplier	Generally ...
World-Class Buyer	Non-World-Class Supplier	A non-world-class supplier is selected because the number of suppliers supplying a particular product/service is limited. The seller report card can be used to improve seller performance. If performance does not improve, buyer always has the option of selecting new suppliers when a given market opens up. The seller can use the world-class buyer as a model for attaining supplier world-class status. Buyer report card advised as a tool/vehicle to assure that buyer world-class status is maintained.
Non-World-Class Buyer	Non-World-Class Supplier	A non-world-class supplier selected because the number of suppliers supplying a particular product/service is limited or insufficient pre-selection supplier evaluation was performed. Seller report card can be used to improve seller performance and help Seller attain world-class status. Buyer and seller relationship can be expected to be inefficient and significantly increase the cost of goods sold. Finger pointing is the norm rather than the exception. Buyer is encouraged to participate in the two-way report card process to attain world-class status. Non-world-class supplier status may be at least partially caused by "poor" buyer performance.
Non-World-Class Buyer	World-Class Supplier	World-class supplier supplies many buyers. Non-world-class buyers may be at a risk in maintaining their supply stream. World -class suppliers can select the buyers that keep their cost of goods sold to a minimum. The two-way report card should be used as a tool for the buyer to enhance its status and in so doing minimize risks which could jeopardize supplier world-class status.
World-Class Buyer	World-Class Supplier	Optimum situations where both will benefit from two-way report card as tool to maintain their status.

Figure 3. Different relationships between buyers and sellers

Notes

1. Graham, Robert C., Rochester Institute of Technology's Center for Integrated Manufacturing Studies, 1996.
2. Morgan, James P., "Just How Good a Customer Are You? It Takes a World-Class Customer to Know and Use World-Class Suppliers," *Purchasing*, November 19,1998.

Ray Bacanskas, C.P.M., P.E., is senior consultant, supply chain management with BellSouth Telecommunications. His career in purchasing started in 1984, where he has had various assignments involving contracting and project management. At BellSouth's supply chain management organization, he assists various departments develop two-way performance report cards with special focus on outsourced functions. He was responsible for developing the initial performance report cards for BellSouth's three major switch suppliers. He has been a guest speaker on two-way report cards at national purchasing conferences and other forums. His work on report cards has also been published in national magazines.

William J. "Jack" Wagner, C.P.M., was a senior consultant in supply chain management with BellSouth Telecommunications. He has been active in NAPM for many years and has served as Chairman of the International Committee, President of NAPM-Georgia, Shipman Award Committee, and Program Chair for the 1994 International Conference in Atlanta. He has contributed articles on several topics to Purchasing Today *as well as other publications. He Chaired the NAPM Ethical Standards Committee from 1994-97. He was recently elected as NAPM's Senior Delegate to the International Federation of Purchasing & Materials Management. He is the NAPM instructor for Acquisition Ethics for the Procurement Division of the State of California.*

Effectively Selecting Suppliers Using Total Cost of Ownership

Zeger Degraeve, Ph.D. and Filip Roodhooft, Ph.D.

Cost management is an important strategic weapon. External purchases of products and services generally account for more than 50% of total costs, so it's important to select suppliers effectively and determine optimal order quantities. This article presents a rigorous decision support system using total cost of ownership information to compare purchasing and supply policies and achieve substantial cost savings. The system uses a dynamic mathematical programming model that derives a purchasing and supply strategy by minimizing the total costs, taking into account the relevant constraints.

Introduction

In almost every organization, the accounting system is an important source of information for both the external parties concerned (financial accounting) and the internal decision makers (management accounting). The aim of management accounting is to generate information enabling decision makers to structure the organization effectively and efficiently, in view of the organization's objectives. A well developed management accounting system provides managers with a better knowledge of their own business and ensures that the organization's objectives are pursued at every level.

The importance, in a highly competitive environment, of possessing a thorough knowledge of one's own activities and processes, together with the latest developments in information technology, have prompted many organizations to improve existing management accounting information systems. New concepts such as activity-based costing and management, target costing, life cycle costing, benchmarking, management charts, and operating indicators are examples of this. In the present business world, which is characterized by intense global competition, good information is undoubtedly a vital strategic weapon.

It is remarkable that the information originating from management accounting systems is mainly used to make internal improvements. However, in many lines of business, the cost of externally purchased goods and services also represents a substantial part of the total cost. Therefore, significant savings can also be made for purchased goods and services. It is, however, essential to gain an insight into the total cost generated by external purchasing, which involves several other factors in addition to the price. After all, the suppliers offering the most attractive prices would not necessarily be the cheapest if one were to take into account all the additional costs incurred by the supplier in the organization's chain of values.

This article presents a method which uses information from management accounting to select suppliers in such a way that an organization can improve its strategic positioning. Decisions relevant to the selection of suppliers include choosing suppliers and defining order quantities and delivery terms. This article describes the decision model for this problem using activity-based costing. The essential function of the model entails converting available information into usable knowledge. Specifically, it leads to a management decision support system which calculates the total cost of ownership and thus achieves objectivity in the selection process.

This article is structured as follows. The next section describes the implementation of management accounting information in the purchasing process. It deals specifically with how suppliers can be assessed and selected. The argument is made that the calculation of the total cost of ownership by means of activity-based costing provides interesting cost saving information with respect to the purchasing process. The third section describes the model for selecting suppliers based on information about the total cost of ownership. This model makes it possible to convert newly generated information into knowledge and, therefore, to optimize the choice of suppliers, the definition of market shares, and the timing of purchases. The possible uses for this model are described in the fourth section. The fifth section presents the results of two product groups at Cockerill Sambre, for which the required information was collected and the selection of suppliers took place on the basis of this model. The sixth section concludes this article.

Implementation of Management Accounting in the Purchasing Process

One of the most important tasks of the purchasing department is the selection of suitable suppliers for the various components to be purchased externally. Traditionally, the evaluation and selection of suppliers are often based on the price criterion. The cheapest supplier is usually selected without taking into consideration additional costs this supplier may introduce in the value chain of the purchasing organization. Thus, the costs related to unreliable delivery, limited quality of goods supplied, and poor communication are not involved in the selection process. If factors other than the price are taken into consideration at all, this usually occurs in a subjective manner (Weber and Current 1991). People in charge of purchasing, quality, production, and sales all express their opinions about the suppliers' performance on the basis of criteria which are important to them. Together, they will try to reach a point where the supplier will be regarded as either good or bad. This method is quite simple, it is not supported by objective criteria, and it rarely leads to performance improvements. Another simple, but widely used, method is the weighted point plan, which determines a global evaluation figure to assess a supplier's performance. A weighting factor is attributed to the different criteria reflecting the fact that each of the criteria has a different importance in the overall assessment. The supplier's total score is equal to the weighted average of the partial scores for the criteria considered. This score can be compared to a set minimum or to the total score of other suppliers. This system is also subjective. Both the weighting factors and the partial scores must be predetermined. Nonetheless, several variations on this system are widely used in practice.

This article suggests using the total cost of ownership for the assessment and selection of suppliers. Total cost of ownership attempts to quantify all of the costs related to the purchase of a given quantity of products or services from a given supplier (Bennett 1996; Carr and Ittner 1992; Cavinato 1992; Ellram and Siferd 1993; Ellram 1995b). The price is an initial important component. Optimum use of all discounts available can lead to substantial savings. In addition to the price component, other cost factors also play an important role, including the costs associated with quality shortcomings, a supplier's unreliable delivery service, transport costs, ordering costs, reception costs, and inspection costs. Suppliers with the most attractive prices are not always the cheapest if one takes into account all the additional expenses associated with the supplier.

Recent developments in management accounting make it possible to quantify costs related to the purchasing process and to establish a distinction between different suppliers. Activity-based costing is a management accounting technique which attempts to assign costs to cost generating activities within a business. This technique uses activity analysis, which defines the various activities performed by an organization. However, it is striking that most existing activity-based costing systems focus chiefly on activities related to products, services, departments, and, to a lesser extent, customers (customer profitability analysis). Such a system is seldom set up for the purpose of selecting suppliers and defining an organization's purchasing policy. This would require far more detailed information pertaining to the purchase of goods and services than envisaged in most activity-based costing systems. As such, all activities and related costs generated by external purchasing must be taken into consideration.

The philosophy of total cost ownership determined on the grounds of activity-based costing can be summarized as follows (Ellram 1995a; Roehm, Critchfield, and Castellano 1992; Roodhooft and Konings 1997). The first step is to define all the activities related to external purchasing. These are specific to every enterprise and should be expressed through the activity analysis. Obvious examples include negotiations with suppliers, placing orders, and reception of incoming goods. Subsequently, costs must be assigned to the different activities. This is a traditional step in every activity-based costing system. The next step is to define factors which raise the cost of a given activity (cost drivers). Finally, one must identify which activities are generated in the purchasing organization by each individual supplier.

Purchasing activities can be divided into three hierarchic levels (Degraeve and Roodhooft 1996). These levels will be essential for the formulation, at a later stage, of the decision model for the selection of suppliers. The first level is the supplier level. Activities are only performed at this level if a given supplier is being used. Costs at the supplier level could include, for example, the cost of a quality audit, the salary of a purchasing and supply manager who may manage the relationship with the supplier on a part-time basis, and, possibly, additional research and development costs incurred by the purchasing organization through the use of products from a specific supplier. Activities at the ordering level—the second hierarchic level—have to be performed each time an order is placed with a given supplier. Costs at this level could include, for example, receiving costs, invoicing costs, and transport costs. Activities at the unit level—the third hierarchic level—are performed for a unit product in a specific order. These could include, for example, the additional costs of a production shutdown caused by a fault in a product purchased from a supplier. Another example would be the cost arising from a product failure that was caused by a component purchased from a supplier. Inventory holding costs will also be allocated to the third level. Because the decision model takes several consecutive periods into account, an optimum ordering policy that compares ordering costs against inventory holding costs must be defined.

An understanding of the various components of the total cost of ownership can be used by a company to rationalize activities linked to the external purchase of products and services. The central issue in this article is to identify the point at which a quantity of products should be purchased and from which supplier. A decision model which implements the management accounting information described above makes it possible to achieve substantial savings in this context.

Decision Model for Selection of Suppliers Based on Management Accounting

The issue of the selection of suppliers is essentially a problem of selecting the most suitable suppliers for different parts or components. The objective is to select the ideal combination of suppliers, given the criteria that are important for the purchasing decision under a number of secondary conditions. Mathematical programming can be used to solve this sort of problem. However, in the existing literature, few models were developed for that purpose. The existing models chiefly focus on the price component. If other criteria are included in the model, this usually occurs in the secondary conditions (Akinc 1993; Benton and Park 1996; Chaudry, Forst, and Zydiac 1993; Rosenthal, Zydiac, and Chaudry 1995). Weber and Current (1993) use an objective function in which price, quality, and reliable delivery are weighed using multi-objective programming. Finally, Sadrian and Yoon (1994) incorporate a limited amount of cost data in their model. Typically, all the above models cover only one period.

This article presents a mathematical programming model (Degraeve and Roodhooft 1996) that takes account of different products to be purchased from different suppliers at different times. The dynamic nature of the purchasing process and stock policy are thus incorporated into the decision model. The length of time depends on the usual ordering frequency and can be a month, week, day, or even shorter interval.

In the objective function of the model, the aim is to minimize the total cost of ownership so as to meet the demand for a given product group over the period under consideration. As explained in the previous section, this consists of costs at supplier level, ordering level, and unit level. This implies that the price and all other costs generated in the purchasing organization's value chain by the suppliers are involved in the analysis. This approach indeed makes it possible to weigh different criteria against one another by using management accounting information.

Various constraints must be taken into account in the purchasing decision. First of all, the demand must be satisfied. Data pertaining to the demand can be derived from the MRP system or other information sources. The decision model then determines what quantities must be ordered to meet the demand, possibly for several consecutive periods, taking into consideration the initial stocks present and the desired end stocks. A safety period is often included if supplier delivery is unreliable. Obviously, late delivery can also generate additional expenses such as replanning, adjustments, reception, and invoicing, which will also have to be processed in the target function. Conditions may also exist regarding the minimum and maximum purchasing quantities from specific suppliers, which can be fixed either by the supplier or by the purchasing organization. For instance, the supplier may have capacity limitations which would make it impossible to produce and deliver more than a given quantity over a given period. Similarly, in order to maintain a certain level of independence, the purchasing organization may want to work with a minimum number of suppliers. A maximum number could also be set if too many suppliers would lead to management problems. Discounts must also be accurately modeled. For example, suppliers often give a percentage discount on the total purchase price of a set of different components, independently of the combination of products. In this case, every supplier specifies a given number of discount intervals, with minimum and maximum quantity limits and a discount percentage valid within the two associated limits.

The purchase decision may also be heavily dependent on specific local conditions. For example, a regulation may specify that a given percentage of a product's components must be manufactured locally. Another interesting example concerns perishable goods, for which the maximum stock may not exceed the total demand of a few periods. This decision model may be adapted to such additional conditions.

The decision model as it is described above results in a mixed integer linear program which can be solved using specialized optimization software such as LINGO (Cunningham and Schrage 1995) on any IBM 486 compatible or higher personal computer. Typical calculation times are a few minutes. The model will then propose a purchasing policy for a given time span consisting of a given number of periods.

Instead of implementing this policy for the entire time span, the model can be used with a dynamic, "rolling horizon." In this way, only the purchasing policy for the current period is implemented. When that period is over, the model is used again to calculate a new policy for the entire time span by including the changes which have occurred over the previous period. The new purchasing policy is thus only implemented for the first period. In this way, as time passes, the model is constantly recalculated using adjusted information concerning costs and stocks, reflecting the current situation in the system. A policy will always be calculated for the whole time span but will only actually be implemented for the first period.

Using the model in this way offers several advantages. First, it restricts the uncertainty in the model. Second, dynamically resolving the model using adjusted data enables the purchaser to take into account the change in performance of both the suppliers and his or her own business. Third, as a consequence of the "rolling horizon" principle, the purchaser is able to provide suppliers with accurate feedback concerning the impact of their performance changes on the purchasing strategy of the organization over time. (The mathematical specification of the decision model is available from the authors.)

Use of the Decision Model

The proposed decision model uses total cost of ownership information to define the purchasing policy of a business for a given product group in a dynamic way. The knowledge acquired through this model can be used for many different purposes.

First, it is possible to achieve substantial cost savings compared to the current purchasing policy. Indeed, it is striking that the selection of suppliers in many organizations is based on simple rules of thumb, past habits, or subjective impressions. Furthermore, it enables the purchaser to compare alternative purchasing strategies on objective grounds, based on the mutually analytical and rigid structure.

The model can also be used to assess alternative performance changes both by suppliers and internally within the purchaser's organization. In particular, the decision model can identify the specific improvements a supplier could make to ensure future purchases. In addition, the data can be used to rationalize internal activities related to purchasing. An insight into activities, costs, and cost drivers enables active cost management to be implemented. Generally speaking, the model provides a sound basis for answering "what if" questions that arise with respect to the purchasing function.

Subsequently, the information generated by the model can be used to negotiate with suppliers. If one is able to make suppliers aware of the additional costs and the causes, it will become easier for the suppliers to adjust to the purchasing organization's needs. Suppliers with high purchase prices and outstanding quality can be compared with the so-called "low price" suppliers, who may not perform as well when it comes to the additional costs. If the results of these comparisons are shared with suppliers, then a significant improvement could be achieved. In this way, the purchasing organization uses comparative information to motivate the supplier to perform better.

The understanding gained from the model can be used to make better "make or buy" decisions, a major issue in the present day business environment. A correct evaluation of the relevant cash flows is fundamental for such decisions. The additional costs generated by external purchases are rarely included in such analyses at present, but could be, using the cost information in the model.

Finally, the long-term relationship between the purchasing organization and its suppliers undoubtedly improves if the needs of both parties are taken into consideration. Assessment of suppliers and the discussion of results can lead to cost control beyond the boundaries of individual organizations. This form of interorganizational cost control can ensure that the traditional hierarchy between a purchasing organization and its suppliers is transformed into supplier partnerships.

Results at Cockerill Sambre

This section contains the results of two practical studies conducted at Cockerill Sambre, a large multinational Belgian steel producer with annual purchases of over $1.5 billion. The decision model described in this article was tested with two product groups with clearly different features. For this business, external purchases constitute the majority of total costs. Cockerill Sambre is in contact with over 4,000 suppliers. At present, its management is engrossed in a serious effort to improve the efficiency of the purchasing process. The purchasing strategies for the different product groups are subjected to in-depth analysis. The period examined covers one year and is divided into six sub-periods of two months each.

The results for heating elements are described first (Degraeve and Roodhooft 1999). A certain type of heating element exists for which the purchasing department of Cockerill Sambre had singled out three possible suppliers based on several criteria. First, there is a substantial difference in price. In addition, one of the suppliers takes back used elements and pays a certain amount for them. That supplier recycles those elements for the production of new ones. This is an additional yield which was contractually laid down as a fixed percentage on the purchase price. Second, there are significant differences in quality between the three suppliers. These differences mainly depend on the life of the heating element. A used element must be replaced by a new one, which requires a setup. The cost of the setup can be determined using the activity-based costing system. Another difference between the suppliers is the imposed use of the batches. If a supplier delivers only larger batches, the purchasing organization's flexibility is reduced. On the other hand, it also keeps reception costs down, since these do not depend on batch size. A further difference is the term of payment. A longer term of payment yields additional profit for the purchasing organization. The last criterion is the amount of time the individual in charge of the purchase spends with the supplier. This seemed to vary between the three suppliers.

For this product group, the costs at the supplier level consist of the cost of the purchasers. At the ordering level the costs include ordering, invoicing, and payment. As a result of the fact that every batch must be stocked separately, a batch level must be included in the analysis of this product group. The costs arising at this level are the reception costs for the batches. Finally, at the unit level, there are quality costs, purchase prices, inventory holding costs, and additional profits from the resale of the used heating elements.

The present purchasing strategy is based on a subjective consideration of the above criteria. Cockerill Sambre relies on three possible suppliers for this product group. The optimum solution produced by the decision model, however, uses only one supplier. Costs are reduced at all levels and the savings amount to 10 percent. At the supplier and ordering levels, the savings are achieved through a reduction of the number of suppliers and the number of orders placed. The selected supplier works with larger batches, so costs fall at this level. Finally, at the unit level, quality costs and purchasing costs fall, inventory holding costs rise, and additional profit is generated from the resale of the used heating elements, which the selected supplier takes back. However, for strategic reasons, Cockerill Sambre chooses not to be dependent on only one supplier: at least two suppliers are used for this product group. Furthermore, no more than 80 percent of turnover may be granted to the main supplier. When these secondary conditions are incorporated into the model, it still generates a cost savings of 8 percent compared to the present purchasing strategy. (The mathematical decision model for the heating element problem is available from the authors.)

The second product group examined concerns ball bearings (Degraeve and Roodhooft 1997). Various types of ball bearings exist, for which purchase decisions must be made. There are six possible suppliers. At present, two are actively used by Cockerill Sambre, while tests are being performed on the ball bearings of a third supplier. The following differences between the potential suppliers should be stressed. First, not all suppliers are able to supply all types of ball bearings. In addition, significant differences in price exist between the various suppliers for the distinct types. However, none of the suppliers is consistently cheaper for all types of bearings. Furthermore, certain suppliers offer a better service than others. These services mainly include technical support, training, and maintenance. When suppliers do not offer these services, additional costs are generated in the value chain of Cockerill Sambre. In addition, communication with some of the suppliers takes place via electronic data interchange (EDI), while others still manually process orders, invoices, and payments. Finally, differences also exist between terms of payment.

Costs at the supplier level consist of the costs of the purchasers who deal specifically with these suppliers and the additional costs generated by suppliers through a lack of service. At the ordering level, there are ordering, invoice processing, and payment costs. At the unit level, purchasing costs, inventory holding costs, savings through deferred payment, and additional profit generated by the resale of used ball bearings must all be included. The latter, however, does not differ from one supplier to another.

The present purchasing policy developed historically. The selected suppliers offer good service, use EDI, and have the lowest price for a (limited) number of ball bearing types. Based on the established components of the total cost of ownership, the decision model was used to define the optimum purchasing policy. The use of four suppliers minimizes the total costs associated with the purchase of ball bearings. One of the current suppliers no longer occurs in the solution while a second loses a significant market share. Compared to the present policy, the costs are reduced by 11.5 percent. These savings are achieved at the level of the purchasing costs. By contrast, the costs at the supplier level and the ordering level increase due to the use of more suppliers, the more limited service provided by the suppliers selected, and the manual processing of orders, invoices, and payments. (The mathematical decision model for the ball bearing problem is available from the authors.)

Conclusion

Recent developments in management accounting, combined with intensive computerization of the business environment, make it possible for organizations to collect a wealth of internal information. This article outlines how it is possible to use some of this information to achieve higher efficiency in the selection of suppliers. This selection should be based on several criteria. Price, quality, reliability with respect to delivery terms, service, and geographical location are a number of important examples. A decision model was presented which, based on the philosophy of the total cost of ownership, attempts to minimize the total costs involved in external purchasing. This approach enables substantial cost savings to be achieved and, at the same time, allows various purchasing policies to be compared with one another. For the practical cases studied, the model generated savings of approximately 10 percent compared to the existing total cost of ownership.

References

Akinc, U., "Selecting a Set of Vendors in a Manufacturing Environment," *Journal of Operations Management*, vol. 11 (1993), pp. 107-122.

Bennett, P., "ABM and the Procurement Cost Model," *Management Accounting*, March 1996, pp. 28-32.

Benton, W.C., and S. Park, "A Classification of Literature on Determining the Lot Size Under Quantity Discounts," *European Journal of Operational Research*, vol. 92 (1996), pp. 219-238.

Carr, L.P., and C.D. Ittner, "Measuring the Cost of Ownership," *Journal of Cost Management*, vol. 6, no. 3 (1992), pp. 7-13.

Cavinato, J.L., "A Total Cost/Value Model for Supply Chain Competitiveness," *Journal of Business Logistics*, vol. 13, no. 2 (1992), pp. 285-301.

Chaudry, S.S., F.G. Forst, and L. Zydiac, "Vendor Selection with Price Breaks," *European Journal of Operational Research*, vol. 70 (1993), pp. 52-66.

Cunningham, K., and L. Schrage, *LINGO: The Modeling Language and Optimizer*, LINDO Systems, Chicago, Illinois, 1995.

Degraeve, Z., and F. Roodhooft, "A Mathematical Programming Approach for Supplier Selection Using Activity Based Costing," Research Report 9659, Katholieke Universiteit Leuven, Department of Applied Economics, 1996.

Degraeve, Z., and F. Roodhooft, "Improving the Efficiency of the Purchasing Process Using Total Cost of Ownership Information: The Case of Heating Electrodes at Cockerill Sambre S.A.," *European Journal of Operational Research*, vol. 112 (1) (1999) pp. 42-53.

Degraeve, Z., and F. Roodhooft, "Determining Sourcing Strategies: A Decision Model Based on Activity and Cost Driver Information," Research Report 9718, Katholieke Universiteit Leuven, Department of Applied Economics, 1997.

Ellram, L.M., "Activity Based Costing and Total Cost of Ownership: A Critical Linkage," *Journal of Cost Management*, vol. 8, no. 4 (1995a), pp. 22-30.

Ellram, L.M., "Total Cost of Ownership: An Analysis Approach for Purchasing," *International Journal of Physical Distribution and Logistics*, vol. 25, no. 8 (1995b), pp. 4-23.

Ellram, L.M., and S.P. Siferd, "Purchasing: The Cornerstone of the Total Cost of Ownership Concept," *Journal of Business Logistics*, vol. 14, no. 1 (1993), pp. 163-184.

Roehm, H.A., M.A. Critchfield, and J.F. Castellano, "Yes, ABC Works with Purchasing, Too," *Journal of Accountancy*, November (1992), pp. 58-62.

Roodhooft, F., and J. Konings, "Vendor Selection and Evaluation: An Activity Based Costing Approach," *European Journal of Operational Research*, vol. 96 (1997), pp. 97-102.

Rosenthal, E.C., J.L. Zydiac, and S.S. Chaudry, "Vendor Selection with Bundling," *Decision Sciences*, vol. 26 (1995), pp. 35-48.

Sadrian, A.A., and Y.S. Yoon, "A Procurement Decision Support System in Business Volume Discount Environments." *Operations Research*, vol. 42 (1994), pp. 179-197.

Weber, C.A., and J.R. Current, "Vendor Selection Criteria and Methods," *European Journal of Operational Research*, vol. 50 (1991), pp. 2-18.

Weber, C.A., and J.R. Current, "A Multi-Objective Approach to Vendor Selection," *European Journal of Operational Research*, vol. 68 (1993), pp. 173-184.

The authors would like to thank Stéphane Verdood, Managing Partner, Arthur Andersen Business Consulting Belgium, for establishing the contacts with Cockerill Sambre S.A., and Camille Goossens, Consultant, Arthur Andersen Business Consulting Belgium, for the data collection.

Zeger Degraeve is Professor of Management Science at Katholieke Universiteit Leuven in Belgium. He earned his Ph.D. degree from the University of Chicago. Dr. Degraeve's research interests include operations management and production scheduling theory and applications.

Filip Roodhooft is Professor of Management Accounting at Katholieke Universiteit Leuven in Belgium. He earned his Ph.D. degree from the University of Antwerp. Dr. Roodhooft's research interests include the application of case study research and experimental research in cost and management accounting and the use of financial accounting databases of small and medium-sized companies in business economics.

The Use and Abuse of Power in Supply Chains

Charles L. Munson, Meir J. Rosenblatt, and Zehava Rosenblatt

The value of a supply chain depends on the relationships that link the partners and the balance between individual advantages and collective advantages. What happens when there's an imbalance, when power is abused? That's a key question. This article explores how business partners have used power to their advantage to the detriment of the relationship. The authors show how to deal with "channel bullies" through cooperative measures that can strengthen a supply chain and benefit all of its partners.

The ability of groups of companies to perform the spectrum of supply functions more efficiently than one company alone has given rise to supply chains. As with any other type of multi-organizational network, the effectiveness of a supply chain depends to a large extent on the relationships among its members. But often one company in a chain may attempt to influence other members in order to achieve its own goals and promote its own interests.

The *organizational power* theoretical framework we use to investigate such power-wielding has gained importance and relevance in research as interdependence among firms grows, caused in part by the tendency of some to shrink and become less integrated. As companies become smaller, they are more likely to externalize tasks, including supply functions (as exemplified by the increasing prevalence of outsourcing). This trend toward externalization increases interunit and interfirm dependence.

Organizational studies have recognized the effect such interdependence has on network forms. In the case of supply chains, increased externalization results not only in dependence but also in a structural imbalance in the network position of individual members. Although firms in a supply chain depend on each other and work together for mutual benefit, the relationships among them are rarely symmetrical. Supply chains often have channel leaders or "channel captains" that may exert tremendous influence on the other firms in the chain. These strong companies have numerous opportunities to exploit their relative advantages, and their choices can have significant long-term consequences on the overall health of the supply chain.

Organizational power is defined most simply as "potential force." It is the ability to get things done, to achieve desired goals and outcomes. Power is exercised through corporate politics by using various tactics or political games, such as "alliance building," that influence opponents and build power bases.

Early studies on the sources of power explored personal attributes (such as expert and referent power) and positional attributes (such as reward, coercive, and legitimate power). These notions of power were originally applied to key decision makers and were later adopted to the organizational level of analysis. In a supply chain, for example, a company has *expert power* if it maintains sole ownership of knowledge and expertise in the relevant content domain; it has *referent power* if other decision makers in the chain perceive its management as prestigious enough to publicly identify themselves with. A firm has *reward power* if its management can help other channel members achieve their goals; with *coercive power*, it can threaten other channel members. And a company with *legitimate power* has a handle on a formal leverage, such as a monopoly on producing or selling a popular product.

According to Pfeffer (1992), a supply chain member is powerful if (1) other members of the chain depend on it for their essential needs, (2) it has control over financial resources, (3) it plays a central role in the chain, (4) it is not substitutable, or (5) it has the ability to reduce critical uncertainty. However, dependent members of the supply chain can also resort to using power. When under pressure, they can try to influence stronger members by using various retaliatory measures.

The use of information is a major determinant of power for both strong and weak participants in a power "game." When a party withholds or distorts information, its power base may be increased, at least in the short run. Alternatively, the receiving party may be empowered when information is shared (or leaked). Under certain circumstances, this may prove costly to the sharing party. More often, however, information sharing increases trust and cooperation, to the benefit of both parties.

The way in which power is used can lead to ethical problems, created when an action taken by one company causes harm to others. Even when a company's tactics are legal, they can be ethically controversial when motivated by narrow interests or a one-sided set of values while ignoring the rights and interests of others. Power, then, may be not only used, but also abused. Armed with these notions, we shall examine the power-oriented interrelationships among supply chain members, focusing on five areas of interaction: (1) pricing control, (2) inventory control, (3) operations control, (4) channel structure control, and (5) information control.

Pricing Control

Using the power derived from their market centrality and dominance, large companies expect and demand lower prices or quantity discounts from their suppliers. The media have recently focused on Wal-Mart as a notorious "hardball" player demanding "rock bottom" prices from its suppliers. Wal-Mart uses its position as the world's largest retailer to full advantage, aware that many suppliers simply cannot afford *not* to sell to its huge customer base. The world's largest automobile manufacturer, General Motors, has also begun squeezing margins from its suppliers in recent years. Moreover, by purchasing in bulk and using only one or two suppliers for a given medical condition, HMOs have been able to garner discounts as high as 60 percent from pharmaceutical companies.

Not all beneficiaries of reduced prices or quantity discounts must be large corporations. A small firm may still be a major customer for some of its suppliers. Alternatively, a small supplier may possess unique knowledge and expertise, leading to an expert power base. In addition, small companies can gain buying power by joining formal or informal purchasing coalitions. Hospitals and pharmacies commonly form purchasing groups, especially with other parties that are not seen as a competitive threat.

Manufacturers are interested not only in the wholesale prices they set but also in the retail prices charged to consumers. Retail price may greatly affect the perceived quality of the product. Makers of designer clothing often do not want their products selling at discount store prices. Even though it is generally illegal in the U.S. for manufacturers to stipulate retail prices, powerful manufacturers do try to influence the final price to better manage consumer demand, respond to competition, and send the appropriate quality signal. Books, snacks, and greeting cards have prices printed on them, thus representing the legitimate power of the manufacturers.

Simply changing wholesale pricing habits can upset members of the channel. Partly in response to companies like Wal-Mart, Procter & Gamble has angered certain retailers by eliminating many of its trade discounts in exchange for "lower everyday prices." Retailers can no longer offer as many specials on popular P&G products as a marketing tool to draw customers into their stores.

Sometimes middlemen have pricing power, particularly in certain foreign countries. Poor craftsmen in the Mixtec region of Mexico receive little pay for their work. Their lack of power is due to the distance to final markets, lack of transportation infrastructure, limited knowledge of market needs, and absence of information about prices. Taking advantage of these conditions, middlemen set prices in both markets and boycott producers that try to circumvent the distribution channel.

In Japan, strong manufacturers dominate channels, discourage price-based competition, and impose suggested retail prices. Historically, the Japanese *keiretsu* system has made it difficult for small foreign and domestic firms to enter the market. And if these firms upset the harmony of the *keiretsu* with negative or comparative advertising or price wars, they may find themselves dropped altogether.

Example 1 illustrates a pricing inefficiency that develops when individual members of a supply chain maximize their own profits instead of cooperating to maximize the total supply chain profits. Specifically, the retailer sets a higher price than the wholesaler desires, stifling demand. The relative power of the firms may dictate how they can eliminate this inefficiency.

Inventory Control and JIT

Just-In-Time (JIT) production policies have had a big impact on the inventory levels of some companies. The concept revolves around reducing inventory levels by only receiving orders

Example 1.

Using Power to Eliminate a Pricing Inefficiency in the Supply Chain[1]

Consider a wholesaler that sells a product through an exclusive retailer. For the sake of simplicity, assume that the product has a short life, so inventory effects can be ignored. The demand curve facing the retailer can be written as $P - 500 - 2D$, where P is the retail price and D is demand. The wholesaler's marginal cost per unit is $80, and the retailer's (exclusive of the wholesale price) is $20. In this case, the wholesaler maximizes profits by setting a wholesale price of $280.[2] With this wholesale price, the retailer maximizes profits by setting the retail price equal to $400, creating a demand of 50 units. The wholesaler earns $10,000, the retailer $5,000. The total channel profits that result from this sequential, individual decision-making equal $15,000.

However, if the two firms are considered as one organization, then the retail price should be set at $300, inducing a demand of 100 units and resulting in total channel profits of $20,000 (see table below). In other words, the channel is losing $5,000 through individual optimization. Either firm could try different methods to obtain the extra $5,000 for itself.

The wholesaler could cause the retailer to set P equal to $300 by setting the wholesale price equal to $80. But then the wholesaler would have zero profit and the retailer would garner the entire $20,000. So the wholesaler must use some technique other than simply changing the wholesale price to create the level of demand that maximizes channel profits by creating an additional $5,000 of available profit. Depending on the wholesaler's power, it could try (1) a suggested list price of $300 or (2) keeping the original wholesale price of $280 but offering an all-units quantity discount of $50 per unit for purchases of 100 units. With the quantity discount option, the retailer would be indifferent to purchasing 50 units for $280 each or 100 units for $230 each. Thus, by accepting the quantity discount, the retailer's profit would remain $5,000, but the wholesaler's profit would increase to $15,000 (extracting the rest of the $20,000 of potential channel profits).

On the other hand, depending on the retailer's power, it could try to (1) demand a lower wholesale price or (2) accept the original wholesale price of $280 but demand an all-units quantity discount of $100 per unit for purchases of 100 units. With the quantity discount option, the wholesaler's profit would remain $10,000, while the retailer's profit would increase to $10,000.

Wholesale Price	Retail Price	Resulting Demand	PROFITS		
			Retailer	Wholesaler	Total System
$80	$300	100	$20,000	0	$20,000
$100	$310	95	$18,050	$1,900	$19,950
$200	$360	70	$9,800	$8,400	$18,200
$280	$400	50	$5,000	$10,000	$15,000
$300	$410	45	$4,050	$9,900	$13,950
$400	$460	20	$800	$6,400	$7,200
$480	$500	0	0	0	0

This table shows profits for Example 1 under individual optimization for selected wholesale prices in which the wholesaler first sets the wholesale price and the retailer then sets the retail price to maximize its own profits. Because the wholesaler acts first, it will choose a price of $280 to maximize its own profits, resulting in a demand of 50 units. However, the total system profits are maximized when demand equals 100 units.

[1]*See Jeuland and Shugan (1983) for a generalized version of this problem.*
[2]*Let W represent the wholesale price. The retailer will want to create the demand that sets its marginal revenue equal to its marginal cost, or 500-4D = 20 + W, i.e., W - 480 - 4D. This equation describes the wholesaler's demand curve. The wholesaler's profit function then equals (480 - 4D) D - 80D, resulting in a profit-maximizing demand of 50 units and a wholesale price of $280.*

just before they are needed in the production process. The introduction of JIT also obligates suppliers to deliver smaller orders more frequently. Depending on the relative power of the companies, a manufacturer may be able to demand JIT delivery or it may have to pay a surcharge to receive it. Rainbird Inc. pays Connor Formed Metal Products Co. an additional 2¢ per unit for JIT delivery of springs. In return, Rainbird has been able to halve its inventory costs for springs. JIT delivery may be impossible in some cases. Allen-Edmonds Shoe Corp., a small manufacturer, had trouble implementing such a system because its suppliers would not cooperate.

The Japanese were the first to use JIT on a wide scale. However, we usually only hear about the positive results that occur when strong manufacturers such as Toyota insist on JIT delivery from suppliers. Small firms have no choice but to offer it in order to keep their customers, despite potential added costs and inventory levels. JIT delivery requirements have also been a barrier to foreign firms that otherwise would like to enter the Japanese market.

Some retailers request that manufacturers ship goods on consignment. The goods remain the property of the manufacturer until sold, even though they are physically located with the retailer. Consignment allows retailers to return unsold goods, which places additional risks on manufacturers. Uncertainty of demand frequently determines the existence of consignment. Jewelry distributors often sell on consignment because of the seasonality and faddish nature of jewelry. Power position may also determine consignment agreements above and beyond market factors. Kmart has asked many of its toy suppliers to sell on consignment. Some have complied for fear of losing such a large customer.

For packaging efficiency, some firms deliver only in preferred container sizes and refuse to sell single units. On the other hand, purchasing firms sometimes request or demand customized packaging. This is particularly true with warehouse clubs such as Costco. In either case, restricting container sizes may place inventory control burdens on other parties in the chain.

Example 2 illustrates a lot-sizing inefficiency that develops when individual members minimize their own costs instead of cooperating to minimize the total supply chain costs. Specifically, the size of the retailer's orders causes the manufacturer to spend too much money on setup costs. Again, the firms' relative power may dictate how this inefficiency can be eliminated.

Example 2

Using Power to Eliminate a Lot-Sizing Inefficiency in the Supply Chain*

Consider a retailer that purchases a product from a manufacturer. Demand occurs at a constant and uniform rate of 40,500 units per year, and the retailer's annual holding cost per unit is $9. The setup costs are $40 and $320 for the retailer and manufacturer, respectively. Suppose the manufacturer has a "make-to-order" (lot-for-lot) production policy and an (essentially) infinite production rate. This implies that the manufacturer effectively carries no finished goods inventory and practices JIT production. With these parameters, the retailer's economic order quantity (EOQ) is $[2(40)(40,500) / 9]^{1/2} = 600$ units. In other words, the retailer minimizes its average annual setup and holding costs (at $5,400) by purchasing 600 units. But with this order size the manufacturer must have an average of 67.5 setups per year, implying annual setup costs of $21,600. The total channel holding and setup costs as a result of the retailer ordering its own EOQ come to $27,000.

However, if the two firms are considered as one organization, then the order quantity that would minimize total channel holding and setup costs equals $[2(40 + 320)(40,500) / 9]^{1/2} = 1,800$ units (see table). With this order size, the retailer's costs increase to $9,000 but the manufacturer's costs fall to $7,200, and the total channel costs become $16,200. In other words, the channel is "wasting" $10,800 because the members are not coordinating their efforts. Either firm could try different methods to obtain the extra $10,800 for itself.

Depending on the manufacturer's power, it could try to (1) impose a minimum purchase requirement of 1,800 units or (2) offer the retailer a quantity discount of 9¢ per unit for orders of 1,800 units. The quantity discount would more than compensate the retailer for its higher holding and setup costs, while reducing the manufacturer's total costs (net of quantity discount) by $10,755. Theoretically, the retailer should be willing to cooperate because its financial situation would not worsen. On the other hand, the retailer could request (demand) a quantity discount from the supplier of 35¢ per unit for orders of 1,800 units. This would transfer almost all the manufacturer's $14,400 savings from lower setup costs to the retailer, more than compensating the latter for its additional setup and holding costs of $3,600. Theoretically, the manufacturer should be willing to cooperate because its financial situation would not worsen. The relative power of the two firms would likely dictate the final size of the discount in the range between 9¢ and 35¢.

This table shows costs for Example 2 for selected retailer order quantities. Acting in its own interest, the retailer will choose an order quantity of 600 units to minimize its own costs. However, the total system costs are minimized when the order quantity equals 1,800 units.

*See Monahan (1984) and Lee and Rosenblatt (1986) for generalized versions of this problem.

| Retailer's Order | SETUP AND HOLDING COSTS | | |
Quantity	Retailer	Manufacturer	Total System
300	$6,750	$43,200	$49,950
500	$5,490	$25,920	$31,410
600	$5,400	$21,600	$27,000
1,200	$6,750	$10,800	$17,550
1,800	$9,000	$7,200	$16,200
2,400	$11,475	$5,400	$16,875
3,000	$14,040	$4,320	$18,360

Operations Control

The Japanese are known for their emphasis on quality, and suppliers of strong manufacturers like Toyota must meet stringent quality standards. Powerful U.S. manufacturers have imposed similar requirements on operations practices. As they continue to slash their supplier bases, strong companies are demanding quality improvements from suppliers. In many cases, they will use only suppliers that have passed the expensive and time-consuming ISO 9000 certification. In a survey of 126 mid-sized firms, Grant Thornton discovered that 76 percent had eliminated suppliers that could not or would not adopt higher quality control standards (Emshwiller 1991). Quality standards have become formalized in many cases, as shown by Ford's Q1 award bestowed on high-performing suppliers.

Suppliers are not the only supply chain members that get pressured by production companies. Manufacturers also place requirements on their dealers. Michelin Tires bypassed its dealers by selling a line of tires only through warehouse clubs, while still expecting the dealers to service the tires. Fanning (1988) reports that Snap-On Tools regularly sends its dealers unordered shipments of promotional tools, which must be paid for within a week or returned for credit up to one month later. One dealer complained that Snap-On allegedly pressured him to extend credit to certain customers he felt were a bad credit risk.

Strong retailers also impose operations requirements on other supply chain members. They exert power through slotting allowances, shelf space allocation, and private label competition. In the 1980s, retailers forced manufacturers to provide UPC symbols on packages to allow for electronic scanning at the checkout line. Electronics suppliers complain nowadays that big retailers are accepting returns for electronics too easily and sending them back as defective. Consumer fraud significantly drives up the costs for these manufacturers. Large retailers are dictating to their suppliers what should be made, in what colors and sizes, and how much to ship and when, threatening to drop suppliers that do not comply. A Duracell manager explains his position as a supplier: "With customers of Wal-Mart's size, we will package, distribute, and serve in a customized fashion to meet their needs" (Gillis 1996).

As the world's largest retailer, Wal-Mart has received considerable attention recently over its strong-arm tactics: demanding discounts, telling producers what to make and how to act, requiring customized marketing plans, bypassing middlemen. Suppliers comply because the potential customer base is too important. But Wal-Mart is taking advantage of its size and market centrality to gain a competitive edge and promote its interests to the exclusion of smaller members' interests.

Channel conflict also occurs in marketing arrangements. Retailers routinely demand cooperative advertising allowances from suppliers, as well as assistance in the form of in-store selling, stockkeeping, and reimbursement for the cost of fixtures to help the stores promote the suppliers' merchandise. In large distribution networks, such as Subway Sandwich Shops and auto dealerships, the franchisors and manufacturers desire mostly national advertising, whereas the franchisees and dealers want advertising dollars spent locally.

The carriers of advertising exert their power as well. Television networks screen ads for content and refuse to air those that fail to conform to certain standards of decency. Recently, cable TV companies in Latin America threatened to discontinue carrying networks that were advertising direct satellite systems during their programming (because satellite systems are substitutes for cable TV). Most networks eliminated the satellite advertising because their only pipeline into most homes was through the local cable companies.

Control over the Channel Structure

Franchisors or manufacturers distributing through dealer networks face the challenging task of allocating sales areas to their distributors. Adding distributors increases the potential customer base but may reduce the number of customers allocated to individual distributors, which must sell enough to stay in business. The distributors bear most of the risk of oversaturation of distribution outlets. Subway Sandwich Shops has alienated franchisees by opening them very close together. In one case, reports Marsh (1992), Subway allegedly pressured a store owner to buy a new planned shop less than a mile away, implying that it would be sold to a different owner if he didn't. In another instance, says Fanning, Snap-On Tools allegedly pressured a dealer to split its territory with another. Taco Bell pulled customers away from current franchisees when it acquired and converted 66 Pup 'N' Taco restaurants into company-owned Taco Bells.

Beyond opening similar outlets, companies sometimes alienate distributors by opening new channels of distribution. Kentucky Fried Chicken has placed outlets in nontraditional locations, such as Sears stores. Levi Strauss upset small retailers when it began selling jeans to large stores. After Taco Bell opened low-cost burger chains, sales and profit margins at its Mexican restaurants dropped.

Channel structure may become destabilized when companies bypass links in the supply chain altogether. Retailers such as Wal-Mart, Cataloger-Fingerhut, and Builder's Square have refused to deal with manufacturers' representatives, desiring direct contact with the manufacturers themselves. On the other hand, in an effort to reduce idle capacity, reach new customers, and improve profit margins, some manufacturers are undercutting retailers by opening factory outlet malls. Lens Express sells replacement contact lenses directly through the mail.

ATK, a rebuilder of Japanese car engines, originally entered the U.S. market by exporting its products through U.S. engine rebuilders. Eventually, however, it began to sell directly to wholesalers (the U.S. rebuilders' main customers) and even to individual mechanics and installers, eliminating exclusive territory rights. As a result, fierce competition sprang up between ATK and its original customers.

Sometimes manufacturers go so far as to try to limit competition by "monopolizing" their retailers. Bovée et al. (1995) reports that Hallmark Cards has allegedly pressured retailers not to sell the products of a competitor, Blue Mountain Arts. John Deere and Company, says Rose (1992), has also tried to restrict the freedom of its dealers to sell products from other companies. Conversely, strong retailers have an incentive to limit the number of competitors that sell their suppliers' products. In May 1996, the Federal Trade Commission filed a suit against Toys R-Us, alleging that the toy retailer was inflating prices and constraining competition by refusing to purchase toys from manufacturers that sold identical items to discount stores and warehouse clubs.

Ultimately, companies can control the channel structure through vertical integration. In Examples 1 and 2 presented earlier, each firm could explore vertical integration in an effort to eliminate the inefficiencies resulting from the current lack of coordination between the companies.

Information Control

Companies can gain power by obtaining information, and strong ones can obtain information by using their power. Economists have studied asymmetric information models (such as "principal-agent" models) that illustrate the resulting consequences when parties interact but their levels of knowledge differ. Supply chains may be viewed as consisting of networks of principal-agent relationships.

One form of information exchange that has prevailed in recent years is electronic data interchange (EDI). Firms have eliminated paperwork by transmitting standard business documents via EDI. Northern Telecom reports reductions in purchase order processing costs due to EDI by as much as 47 percent. Despite international standards for EDI, companies develop their own interpretation of the standards, and smaller firms must customize their EDI systems for each of their large trading partners. Worse yet, some EDI requirements differ not just between firms but between different plants within the same firm.

Often, the costliest element when initiating EDI is recruiting partners with which to share information. Many small firms are reluctant to undertake EDI because of the significant costs of training, testing, changing accounting procedures, purchasing or developing software, establishing network access, and so on. The recruitment process is easier for powerful firms that can demand EDI compliance. According to Davis (1995), a 1994 survey by the EDI Group reported that 55 percent of respondents started using EDI because their principal customer or supplier forced them to do so. In 1990, Wal-Mart and Kmart set deadlines for their suppliers to have EDI capability, with the threat of lost business as a penalty for noncompliance. Even more far-reaching than that, reports Davis, Ford told all of its first-tier suppliers in 1995 that they must be performing EDI with their own suppliers by January 1997.

Suppliers that perform vendor-managed inventory (VMI) manage the inventory levels of their products at their customers' locations. VMI shifts power to the suppliers because the suppliers have more decision-making responsibility and can obtain cost and inventory information about their customers without necessarily offering their own in return. In fact, VMI failures can occur when the suppliers are not given enough information. The VMI program at Spartan Stores, a Midwestern regional grocery distributor, failed partly because the firm was not providing its suppliers with information on upcoming promotions, so the vendors' forecasts did not accurately reflect the effect of the promotions.

Like VMI programs, other information links can shift power to suppliers. A firm that requires computer-aided design (CAD) equipment from its major suppliers to link directly with its own CAD installation greatly increases its own switching costs and its dependency on those suppliers.

Companies can use information systems as powerful marketing tools because other firms want access to those systems. Once those firms are "hooked," the switching costs can be substantial. American Hospital Supply quickly dominated its market with the help of its electronic ordering system, which included inventory management software for its customers. Hospitals enjoyed the easy purchasing procedures; once they became accustomed to the American Hospital Supply system, they didn't want to learn other systems. In addition, the company gained negotiating power with its suppliers because its system provided more information about the hospital supply market than the suppliers could obtain.

Diagnosing Supply Chain Power

The diagnostic questionnaire on pages 123-124 can help managers quantify the impact of other chain members on their own firms. Based on the framework and examples we have described here, the questionnaire can be modified to reflect company-specific situations.

Retaliatory Measures

Companies cannot expect to wield their channel power without meeting resistance. Abused firms can retaliate in many ways: boycotting, competing directly, increasing the dependence of channel leaders, forming coalitions with other firms in the same position, and seeking legal solutions.

A powerful but potentially costly way to fight against the demands of a strong firm is to boycott by ending part or all of the relationship with it. After Procter & Gamble eliminated many of its trade discounts in exchange for everyday low pricing, a number of retailers retaliated by dropping certain sizes and types of P&G products. Others added surcharges to the remaining products or reduced their promotion of P&G's brands. After Goodyear started selling its tires through Sears, hundreds of independent dealers adopted additional (especially private label) brands. In response to manufacturers opening factory outlet stores, JCPenney and Saks Fifth Avenue have threatened to cancel orders when the same items appear at outlets, and Yaring's and Gold's have boycotted producers with outlets. Retaliatory measures such as

Diagnosing the Power Impact of Your Supply Chain Partners

Instructions. Identify those companies that are major players in your supply chain. For each one identified, evaluate its strategic *importance* and *power* relative to your firm with respect to the five major areas presented below. To help guide your assessments, we have identified some attributes for rating within each area. Other attributes specific to your situation can, of course, be added. Each area, and the attributes within it, require two assessments through the following scales (if not applicable, just ignore that item or assign a zero value to its importance):

	Very low			Moderate			Very high
• Strategic importance to your firm:	1	2	3	4	5	6	7
• Power relative to your firm:	Very low			Moderate			Very high
	1	2	3	4	5	6	7

The product of these two factors provides a comprehensive understanding of the overall potential impact on your firm by the organization being rated. Rate each of the attributes using the scale above according to their degree of importance (from very low to very high) and degree of power (from very low to very high) with respect to your firm. If you prefer, you can undertake this rating process for a specific division or product line within the organization.

Area and Attributes	Importance (I) 1......7	Power (P) 1......7	(I) x (P)
1. *Pricing Control*			
Demands lower prices.	_____	_____	_____
Demands quantity discounts.	_____	_____	_____
Influences retail prices.	_____	_____	_____
Other.	_____	_____	_____
2. *Inventory Control*			
Demands just-in-time production process.	_____	_____	_____
Demands goods on consignment.	_____	_____	_____
Demands preferred containers/packaging.	_____	_____	_____
Demands unique lot sizes.	_____	_____	_____
Other.	_____	_____	_____
3. *Operations Control*			
Demands quality improvements and/or ISO certification.	_____	_____	_____
Demands special service.	_____	_____	_____
Demands easy return policies.	_____	_____	_____
Demands unique forms of customization.			
Demands special marketing/advertising allowances.	_____	_____	_____
Other.	_____	_____	_____

	Importance (I) 1......7	Power (P) 1......7	(I) x (P)
4. *Control over the Channel Structure*			
Uses or threatens allocation of sales areas.	_____	_____	_____
Uses or threatens new channels of distribution.	_____	_____	_____
Uses or threatens direct customer contact.	_____	_____	_____
Demands exclusive relationship with your firm.	_____	_____	_____
Uses or threatens vertical integration.	_____	_____	_____
Other.	_____	_____	_____
5. *Information Control*			
Uses asymmetric information.	_____	_____	_____
Demands electronic data exchange.	_____	_____	_____
Demands the use of CAD systems resulting in increasing costs.	_____	_____	_____
Other.	_____	_____	_____

Scoring: Multiply the *importance* (I) *and power* (P) scores together for each row (resulting in numbers between 1 and 49). Considerable information with respect to the power game can be garnered by analyzing each item independently. Nevertheless, if an aggregate score is desired, one way to obtain it is as follows. For each of the five areas, add over all of the rows and divide this sum by the number of rows in that area (excluding rows with "zero" importance). Add over the "averages" of all five areas and divide by 5. Take the square root of this result (which will be a number between 1 and 7). The closer the value is to 7 (or 1), the more (or less) impact this company has on your own firm.

---

these may reframe the relationships among supply chain members.

Large discount retailers often annoy manufacturers by slashing the retail prices of their goods, such as when using them as "loss leaders." Price is one signal of quality, and manufacturers want some control over the retail prices of their products. Some manufacturers, like BrenCon Energy Products Inc. and Sashco Sealants, boycott by refusing to sell to mass merchandisers. Others, such as the lawn care products maker Scotts Co., sell certain items exclusively to independent lawn and garden stores. Wal-Mart has used toys as "loss leaders" in the past, so Step 2 Corp. does not sell to Wal-Mart or warehouse clubs. Step 2 has agreements with its retailers not to use its products as "loss leaders."

Sometimes damaged companies not only boycott but fight back by selling competitors' products. In response to factory outlet malls, Macy's, Saks, Wal-Mart, Bloomingdale's, and other retailers have opened their own retail outlets containing damaged, outdated, unsold, or overstocked goods that often sell for deeper discounts than those at the factory outlets. When

Kroy Inc., a small office equipment company, dropped its 1,000 dealers in favor of direct selling, the dealers began selling competitors' products. When Kroy cut back on its direct selling and tried to retain the dealers again, only about half of them accepted Kroy back.

Because channel influence often depends on relative power, one way to gain influence is to increase one's power by increasing the dependence of channel leaders. In Japan, manufacturers have historically dominated channels; however, large supermarkets have recently begun to challenge the manufacturers' power by controlling new information technologies, which allows them to perform such channel functions as risk handling and inventory planning. The Japanese manufacturers have also lost power because the supermarkets have successfully sold private label products and imports. In another example, small suppliers create dependence (hence retaliatory power) when they become JIT suppliers, because any disruption in the supply process can be pervasive, immediate, and costly. JIT also entails relative difficulty in substituting the actors in the production process (especially if sole suppliers are being used).

Joining trade associations represents another way to increase power. The National Sporting Goods Association and the National Shoe Association have urged boycotts against manufacturers with factory outlet stores. According to Ruffenach (1992), the 3,000 members of the Association of Kentucky Fried Chicken Franchisees threatened to sue the franchiser when it announced its decision to open outlets in nontraditional locations. Nationwide Insurance abandoned its plan to sell through banks after the Independent Insurance Agents' Association of Ohio applied pressure. And several New York apparel vendors share strategies on how to cope with retailers' demands.

Legal action is a powerful retaliation tactic for fighting channel bullies. Not only can companies sue; they can also lobby legislators. Lawrence (1992) reports that the Manufacturers' Agents National Association lobbied the FTC to investigate Wal-Mart after the retailer announced that it would negotiate with a manufacturer's agent only after speaking with a principal of the manufacturing firm.

Recent events in the travel industry have prompted a combination of retaliatory measures from travel agents. By early 1995, most of the major airlines had imposed a limit on payments to travel agents of $25 and $50 for a domestic one-way and round-trip ticket, respectively. The previous policy had been an unbounded 10 percent commission on the ticket price. In response, a group of travel agents and associations, including the American Society of Travel Agents (ASTA), filed collusion charges against the participating airlines (which had adopted their caps within days of each other). As a result, ASTA convinced TWA to eliminate its caps in return for dropping the lawsuit against the company and a promise to increase bookings compared to the other airlines. Travel agents agreed to try to divert as many sales as possible away from any airlines that continued imposing commission limits.

All these various retaliatory tactics represent mostly hostile responses that add little to the joint effectiveness of the supply chain. They exacerbate conflicts and sharpen differences in interests and goals among channel members. In other words, they follow a "win-lose" pattern of conflict resolution rather than a "win-win" pattern. An alternative approach, cooperation, can be far more satisfactory for all supply chain members.

Cooperation: The Long-Term Alternative

The Japanese *keiretsu* philosophy emphasizes long-term relationships between channel members. The philosophy, however, does not necessarily eliminate the abuse of channel power. To avoid potential retaliatory measures or ethical problems, strong companies should consider more cooperative approaches based on trust for achieving their goals.

Trust between channel members can entail tangible benefits to the parties, as illustrated in a 1996 study of a major manufacturer of automobile parts and 429 of its retailers (Kumar 1996). Using a "holistic" set of evaluative questions to measure performance, the investigators determined that, when compared to low-trusting retailers, the retailers with a high level of trust in the manufacturer (1) generated 78 percent more sales for the manufacturer, (2) were 12 percent more likely to carry the manufacturer's products in the future, (3) were 22 percent less likely to have developed alternative sources of supply, and (4) "performed" 11 percent better.

Strong firms can often maintain solid channel relationships by including other channel members in the decision-making process and/or providing concessions to eliminate potential losses from new directives. Individual car dealers have consociated to have a voice in the advertising policies of the automakers. When Rubbermaid increased its number of distribution outlets by 67 percent, it simultaneously improved cooperative advertising plans and increased channel members' margins. Kentucky Fried Chicken introduced a "pass-through" royalty to franchisees equal to 2 percent of sales from new outlets opening near them. Meanwhile, some large firms have subsidized the EDI start-up costs for their small trading partners.

Companies can often benefit by broadening the perspective of their competitive environment. In many cases, they should consider their own supply chain members as allies in competing against other supply chains. Information sharing can play a crucial role in this context. The "Beer Game," which is played by students in many business and engineering schools, is a production simulation game in which a retailer, a wholesaler, a distributor, and a factory make decisions based on incoming orders but without knowing what the other supply chain members are doing. Despite a relatively stable demand pattern, the game often results in large inventory and/or large back-order levels, which could be slashed if the players shared information.

The apparel industry provides two recent examples of information sharing in the supply chain. First, a fiber producer (Du Pont), a textile mill (Milliken & Co.), an apparel manufacturer (Robinson Mfg.), and a retailer (JCPenney) formed an alliance to jointly identify market needs and develop a brand new product line. The unprecedented relationship included almost daily communication among the parties. Second, more than 1,500 retail stores of The Limited, Inc. have partnered with the major credit bureaus to develop an electronic information-sharing system that offers a 29-second approval procedure—pared down from eight minutes—for customers who wish to establish credit at the stores. This new procedure has increased the stores' business and provided the credit bureaus with a new product to market.

Cooperative efforts can be particularly valuable when the new policies would increase channel profits as a whole. Companies that share data through EDI or other means improve forecasts and eliminate paperwork throughout the channel. Hewlett-Packard uses a mathematical program to determine inventory levels for some products at dealer stores as well as for its distribution centers, thereby minimizing inventory levels at all locations while maintaining target customer service levels. Federated Department Stores asked suppliers to upgrade the hangers on which they shipped clothes so it would not have to change hangers in its stores. Suppliers' costs increased by a nickel per unit, but Federated saved a dime. The retailer was willing to compensate the suppliers for their increased expenses, and the channel as a whole saved five cents per unit.

The numerical examples presented earlier can be treated in the same way. In both cases, total channel profits would increase if the two firms made decisions as though they were one combined company. In Example 1, a wholesale price of $280 and a quantity discount of $75 per unit for purchases of 100 units would maximize channel profits and evenly split the increased profits between the two companies. Table 1 shows the after-discount profits for both parties under various discount amounts. The discount ultimately used may depend on the comparative power of the parties; nevertheless, any discount between $50 and $100 will improve the financial position of both parties—a win-win situation.

Per-Unit Quantity Discount	PROFITS (net of discount)		
	Retailer	Wholesaler	Total System
$50	$5,000	$15,000	$20,000
$60	$6,000	$14,000	$20,000
$75	$7,500	$12,500	$20,000
$90	$9,000	$11,000	$20,000
$100	$10,000	$10,000	$20,000

Table 1. After-discount profits from Example 1 (The wholesale price is $280 and the selected quantity discounts offered from the wholesaler to the retailer apply to orders of 100 units.)

The wholesale price is $280 and the selected quantity discounts offered from the wholesaler to the retailer apply to orders of 100 units.

In Example 2, a quantity discount of 22 cents per unit for orders of 1,800 units would (approximately) split the $10,800 of decreased channel costs equally between the two firms. Table 2 shows the after-discount costs for both parties under various discount amounts. Any discount between 9 and 35 cents creates a win-win situation. Interestingly, the manufacturer can still improve its position even after providing a quantity discount larger than the retailer's total current annual setup and holding costs.

Costs are for selected quantity discounts offered from the manufacturer to the retailer for ordering 1,800 units per order.

In both examples, the quantity discounts would more likely be offered and accepted if the two firms shared information, cooperated in the development of the discount schedules, and agreed to split the increased profits/cost savings equitably.

Per-Unit Quantity Discount	SETUP AND HOLDING COSTS (net of discount)		
	Retailer	Wholesaler	Total System
9¢	$5,355	$10,845	$16,200
16¢	$2,520	$13,680	$16,200
22¢	$90	$16,110	$16,200
28¢	–$2,340	$18,540	$16,200
35¢	–$5,175	$21,375	$16,200

Table 2. After-discount costs from Example 2 (Costs are selected quantity discounts offered from the manufacturer to the retailer for ordering 1,800 units per order.)

Beyond legal restrictions, companies do not have to follow any rules of fair play when dealing with other members of their supply chains. As a consequence, ethical problems arise, such as the question of whether weaker members in a chain are pushed to act against their own interests, or whether achieving the goals of the more powerful members defeats those of the less powerful. Strong firms can (and do) make decisions that can be detrimental to other channel members. The injured parties can (and do) take actions, legal or otherwise, to fight back.

The extent of conflicting versus cooperative actions by strong firms likely mirrors their respective time horizon orientations. Those with a short-term perspective may indeed benefit from the use of coercive power tactics because weaker supply chain members may have no immediate means of redress. In the long term, though, conflict-generating actions prove inefficient and damage trust, lessening the chain's total effectiveness and competitiveness. Long-term stability is founded on the profitability of the entire chain, even though one partner can exact premiums in the short run.

Scholars have argued that U.S. firms in the 1970s and 1980s lost industry leadership positions to foreign companies because their short-term emphasis on profits precluded them from making long-term investments. World-class companies today recognize that developing strong supply chain partnerships should also be considered a long-term investment. Supply chain interrelationships are based on power. And when power is used cooperatively, it promotes, rather than hinders, the general utility of the chain. Cooperative measures may reduce the level of power abuse and create a stronger supply chain, engendering rewards that can be shared by all members.

References

"Aerospace and Air Transport: Major Airlines," in *Standard & Poor's Industry Surveys*, Vol. 1 (New York: Standard & Poor's, July 1996): A40-A43.

A.F. Borthick and H.P. Roth, "EDI for Reengineering Business Processes," *Management Accounting*, 75, 4 (1993): 32-37.

C.L. Bovée, M.J. Houston, and J.V. Thill, *Marketing*, 2nd ed. (New York: McGraw-Hill, 1995).

E.K. Clemons and F.W. McFarlan, "Telecom: Hook Up or Lose Up," *Harvard Business Review,* July-August 1986, pp. 91-97.

E.R. Corey, "The Role of Information and Communications Technology in Industrial Distribution," in R.D. Buzzell (ed.), *Marketing in an Electronic Age* (Boston: Harvard Business School Press, 1985): Ch. 2.

D. Davis, "Evolution in EDI," *Manufacturing Systems* (supplement), August 1995, pp. 22-28.

C. Duff, "Nation's Retailers Ask Vendors to Help Share Expenses," *Wall Street Journal,* August 4, 1993, p. B4.

"Eli Lilly and Company: The Flexible Facility Decision," Harvard Business School Case #9-694-074, 1993.

J.R. Emshwiller, "Suppliers Struggle to Improve Quality as Big Firms Slash Their Vendor Rolls," *Wall Street Journal*, August 16, 1991, pp. B1-B2.

D. Fanning, "Monkey Wrench at Snap-On Tools," *Forbes,* June 27, 1988, pp. 126, 128.

K. Fitzgerald, "Antitrust Case Threatens the Image of Toys R-Us," *Advertising Age, 67,* 22 (1996): 6.

J.R.P. French and B.H. Raven, "The Bases of Social Power," in D. Cartwright and A. Zander (eds.), *Group Dynamics: Research and Theory,* 3rd ed. (New York: Harper & Row, 1968): 150-167.

C. Gillis, "Duracell's Logistics Power...," *American Shipper, 38,* 3 (1996): 62.

A. Goldman, "Evaluating the Performance of the Japanese Distribution System," *Journal of Retailing, 68,* 1 (1992): 11-39.

A. Grandori and G. Soda, "Inter-Firm Networks: Antecedents, Mechanisms and Forms," *Organization Studies, 16,* 2 (1995): 183-214.

M. Grimm, "Taco Bell Franchisees Want It Hot 'n Later," *Brandweek, 33,* 33 (1992): 3.

K.G. Hardy and A.J. Magrath, "Ten Ways for Manufacturers to Improve Distribution Management," *Business Horizons*, November-December 1988, pp. 65-69.

K. Helliker, "Thriving Factory Outlets Anger Retailers as Store Suppliers Turn into Competitors," in McCarthy and Perreault, *op. cit.* (1992): 116-117.

J. de la Paz Hernandez Giron and M.L. Hernandez Giron, "Structuring Favorable Market Opportunities for the Mixtec Region of Oaxaca, Mexico," *Journal of Macromarketing, 13,* 2 (1993): 22-31.

L.T. Hosmer, "Strategic Planning as if Ethics Mattered," *Strategic Management Journal,* Summer 1994, pp. 17-34.

A.P. Jeuland and S.M. Shugan, "Managing Channel Profits," *Marketing Science, 2,* 3 (1983): 239-272.

C.C. Johns, "Credit Bureaus and Limited Credit Services Partner to Provide Customers Truly Quick Credit," *Credit World, 84,* 2 (1995): 21-22.

N. Kumar, "The Power of Trust in Manufacturer-Retailer Relationships," *Harvard Business Review,* November-December 1996, pp. 92-106.

A.A. Lappen, "The $29 Million Lesson," *Forbes, 137,*4 (1986): 64, 68.

E. Lawler III, *High Involvement Management* (San Francisco: Jossey-Bass, 1986).

J. Lawrence, "Wal-Mart Draws Fire," *Advertising Age, 63,* 2 (1992): 3, 43.

H.L. Lee and C. Billington, "The Evolution of Supply-Chain-Management Models and Practices at Hewlett-Packard," *Interfaces, 25,* 5 (1995): 42-63.

H.L. Lee and M.J. Rosenblatt, "A Generalized Quantity Discount Pricing Model to Increase Supplier's Profits," *Management Science, 32,* 9 (1986): 1,177-1,185.

A.J. Magrath and K.G. Hardy, "Avoiding the Pitfalls in Managing Distribution Channels," *Business Horizons,* September-October 1987, pp. 29-33.

B. Marsh, "Franchise Realities: Sandwich-Shop Chain Surges, But to Run One Can Take a Heroic Effort," *Wall Street Journal,* September 16, 1992, p. A6.

R. Mathews, "Spartan Pulls the Plug on VMI," *Progressive Grocer, 74,* 11 (1995): 64-65.

E.J. McCarthy and W.D. Perreault, Jr. (eds.), *Applications in Basic Marketing: Clippings from the Popular Business Press, 1992-1993 Edition* (Homewood, IL: Richard D. Irwin Inc., 1992).

D. Milbank, "Independent Goodyear Dealers Rebelling Against Goodyear," *Wall Street Journal,* July 8, 1992, p. B2.

H. Mintzberg, "The Organization as Political Arena," *Journal of Management Studies, 22,* 2 (1985): 133-154.

H. Mintzberg, *Power in and Around Organizations* (Englewood Cliffs, NJ: Prentice-Hall, 1983).

J.P. Monahan, "A Quantity Discount Pricing Model to Increase Vendor Profits," *Management Science, 30,* 6 (1984): 720-726.

E. Norton, "Last of the U.S. Tire Makers Ride Out Foreign Invasion," *Wall Street Journal,* February 4, 1993, p. B6.

W.D. Perreault, Jr. and E.J. McCarthy (eds.), *Applications in Basic Marketing: Clippings from the Popular Business Press, 1995-1996 Edition* (Homewood, IL: Richard D. Irwin Inc., 1995).

J. Pfeffer, *Power in Organizations* (Boston: Harvard Business School Press, 1992).

V. Reitman, "Manufacturers Start to Spurn Big Discounters," *Wall Street Journal,* November 30, 1993, p. B1.

V. Reitman, "Retail Resistance: Eliminated Discounts on P&G Goods Annoy Many Who Sell Them," *Wall Street Journal,* August 11, 1992, p. A1.

R.L. Rose, "Deere, Dealers Cross Swords Over Plows," in McCarthy and Perreault, *op. cit.* (1992): 112.

C. Ross and J. Pollack, "Riney Stuck in Subway Ad Fight," *Advertising Age, 67,* 27 (1996): 1, 26.

G. Ruffenach, "Chicken Chain's Strategy Ruffles Franchisees' Feathers," in McCarthy and Perreault, *op. cit.* (1992): 110-111.

Z. Schiller, "GM Tightens the Screws: Only the Fittest of Its Suppliers Will Survive," *Business Week,* June 22, 1992, pp. 30-31.

M. Thornton, "Tomorrow's Blueprint," *Apparel Industry Magazine, 56,*3 (1995): QR10-QR14.

A.H. Walle, "The Japanese in the Automotive Aftermarket: Rethinking Business-to-Business Marketing Strategies," *Management Decision, 32,* 7 (1994): 60-63.

J.D. Zbar, "L. America Cable Systems Squelch Ads for DirecTV," *Advertising Age,* July 8, 1996, p. 8.

Charles L. Munson is an assistant professor of management and decision sciences at Washington State University, Pullman, Washington.

Meir J. Rosenblatt is the Myron Northrop Professor at the John M. Olin School of Business, Washington University, St. Louis, Missouri, and a professor at the Davidson Faculty of Industrial Engineering and Management, Technion-Israel Institute of Technology, Haifa, Israel.

Zehava Rosenblatt is a lecturer at the Faculty of Education, University of Haifa, Israel.

Target Costing

Lisa Ellram, Ph.D., C.P.M., C.P.A., C.M.A.

Target costing—a process that brings together purchasing, design, manufacturing, and often suppliers to determine a cost for an item—can significantly help strengthen profit margins. This article presents a case study of a company that has learned the value of target costing. It outlines the process and summarizes the benefits.

What Is Target Costing?

In the strictest definition, target costing is a process whereby purchasing, design, manufacturing, and often suppliers work together to achieve a specified cost for an item. Traditionally, each department would work independently, throwing information about design, cost and product features "over the wall" to the other. This latter approach is a sequential process, whereas, with target costing, all parties work concurrently. The overall target cost is determined by subtracting the desired profit from the estimated selling price.

In Carsrun Company's (CRC) new product development process, each new model has a dedicated team to manage and execute development. This team includes representatives from marketing, manufacturing, research and development, and purchasing and is responsible for the entire model, from inception to introduction. This cross-disciplinary team is supported by functional teams that support new product development.

In an effort to meet target profit margins, representatives from research and development and procurement have shared accountability for the overall target costing process since the mid-1990s. Research and development's contribution to the process focuses on target design activities and includes all aspects of value engineering.

Those in research and development have a high level of expertise in the design process. They generally have years of experience and have worked on a variety of car models, so they are familiar with cross-model issues. Before CRC had established clearly who was responsible for determining cost, it was difficult to hold anyone accountable for not achieving target costs. Did CRC pay too much for components due to poorly designed products, flaws in the purchasing and supply network, or poor research and development? Now, the company can plan the most efficient way to purchase parts and easily track flaws in the process.

Procurement and research and development professionals develop cost models based on their knowledge of the industry, historical costs, and supplier input. Purchasing professionals use these models to establish target costs. They compare the resulting models to supplier costs to determine accuracy. If the results are acceptable, the model is used as a common language for discussing cost issues.

CRC's target costing and cost modeling form a synchronized system that covers a high percentage of the components used to manufacture automobiles.

Designers clarify specifications as they relate to the target cost. This information is very useful in negotiations. Purchasing and design personnel work together to develop ways to work with suppliers and to find areas of opportunity in the negotiation process.

The use of detailed cost analysis to support target costing is more effective when purchasing fabricated parts than high technology. However, the market is very competitive in those "black box" areas. The key to controlling costs in "black box" areas is to have effective strategies with suppliers: establish strong relationships and dual sourcing.

CRC has a procurement group organized around each of the company's major processes: plastics, stamping, electrical, machinery, and components. There is a cost expert in each of the five procurement groups. A goal of the cost expert is to provide education and training to the other members in that group, so that all become skilled in managing and evaluating costs. Each expert also helps manage cost issues for new model development, thereby coordinating activities for the entire group.

CRC sales determines the selling price of an automobile, also called the target price. The targeted selling price, minus desired profit, yields the total amount of the target cost necessary to produce an automobile. This is based on the profit objectives for CRC. This cost is divided broadly into manufacturing costs and materials/components, also known as "car set target cost."

Each of the five major categories—engine, interior, chassis, electrical and body—receives a share of the cost based on historical models and any known major changes affecting those models. All of the parts within a category are exploded, as in a bill of materials.

The individual part target costs are then established before the drawing is authorized. Design and purchasing personnel aim to meet or beat that cost when designing the new part. Thus, the target cost and design are based on what CRC can afford to budget. This is based on what CRC surmises the market will bear, as well as on historic prices and on potential design changes.

CRC will create a target cost for almost every purchased component in an automobile. The source of the data supporting those targets varies: from CRC's detailed cost estimations, market data, competitive quotations, pricing on similar models, to pricing in the global market.

CRC also uses target costing in its manufacturing operations as a way to estimate overhead and to determine the cost per car of various manufacturing processes.

CRC's entire target costing process is based on the phrase, "plan, do, check, action," which is often used in CRC's other management processes. The "plan" is concept development, "do" is detailed cost development and attainment, "check" involves top management reviews, and "action" requires implementing the directives from the review process.

Monitoring Target Costing Before and After New Model Introduction

With the huge number of parts involved in assembling a product, CRC has developed a detailed tracking system to monitor the costs of individual parts. The procurement group is responsible for this cost-tracking model.

The procurement cost group is divided into a new-model group and a mass-production group. The new model-group uses the tracking system to manage ongoing price negotiations for each part, from the beginning of the new product development process.

This system tracks reasons why variances occur between target costs and supplier quotes. These reasons include: specification issues, volume changes, process differences, and other factors. The system tracks how each of these variances changes through the negotiation process.

The system also can focus on a particular reason (e.g., total variance due to volume change) so that the new-model team can understand major issues that need to be addressed.

The team also picks several key models, such as popular configurations of an automobile, and develops a target cost for those based on the target costs of individual components in the bill of materials. These are compared to the latest supplier price quotations. This can be done throughout the development process and is an important part of the feedback loop for the ongoing management of costs.

Based on the variances, the new-model cost group sets schedules and priorities for the procurement professionals who are negotiating prices for new parts.

These variances are reviewed as part of a formal process—the management philosophy of "plan, do, check, action." The result is an action plan directing the buyer to what he or she should do next.

At the new-model review meeting, staff present problems, ask for guidance and support, or present a plan to solve the problem.

These reviews ensure that all staff members know about variances, so everyone can work together to minimize or eliminate them.

CRC continues to give target costing high visibility even after a new model is introduced. The company simply hands off responsibility for target costing from the new-model group to the mass-production group.

The real test of how actual costs compare to target costs occurs when the new model is rolled out. This comparison is a good measure of how a model meets the overall target. It also helps staff pinpoint cost variances. The variances are documented for all items in the bill of materials, just as they were during the development process.

The associate who buys an item with an unfavorable variance is accountable for explaining the variance and working with the supplier to achieve the target. Performance is also monitored and reported monthly, with staff working with suppliers to continually improve purchasing power. This is no small task, given that CRC purchases thousands of different parts.

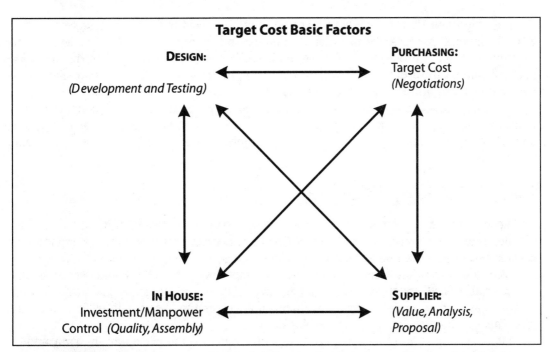

Target Cost Basic Factors

DESIGN:
(Development and Testing)

PURCHASING:
Target Cost
(Negotiations)

IN HOUSE:
Investment/Manpower
Control *(Quality, Assembly)*

SUPPLIER:
(Value, Analysis, Proposal)

Figure 1. Target costing is not an exclusive purchasing job. It requires synchronized effort from all areas.

Key Success Factors in Target Costing

There are a number of reasons target costing is successful at CRC. First, CRC committed adequate resources to the task. The company put in place a focused group of procurement professionals to identify and select suppliers for new-model development and for component changes.

This selection is based on suppliers' performance history, design recommendations, and other relevant factors. These purchasing professionals do not get involved in day-to-day buying and supply issues. That is handled by another group in purchasing.

Top management support is key to the success of this entire process, especially because of the many resources allocated to new product development.

Second, the company is very concerned about costs associated with the entire new-model development process. This, and the high visibility given the process, gives the procurement staff the skills to develop accurate and detailed part costs.

Target costing also is very visible in the mass production stage. This ongoing piece of the "plan, do, check, and action" process helps close the target cost loop.

CRC has institutionalized the philosophy of target costing. The company has the tools to develop, monitor, track and report on the entire process. This is important to ensure the accuracy of and accountability for the data.

It is important that teams share responsibility and accountability for target costing at CRC. Teamwork is necessary in order to identify and incorporate all key issues into the development and introduction of new models. There is an overlap of responsibilities between purchasing and research and development, but this is viewed positively. This overlap ensures that nothing falls through the cracks.

Finally, target costing is successful because CRC believes in cultivating long-term relationships with suppliers. They know the company wants to retain them as viable suppliers and reduce underlying costs, not just prices. Suppliers are more willing to cooperate and share data.

Benefits of Target Costing

The benefits of target costing are numerous. Target costing has helped CRC better meet its planned profit per vehicle. It also helps CRC control investments in tooling, as amortizable costs of production are integral elements of the process.

From idea inception, target costing creates a high level of visibility and accountability for materials costs throughout the product life cycle. Teams prepare feasibility studies before drawings are set, so target costing identifies variances as they occur and ensures that the problems causing the variances are resolved.

Target costing is an excellent way for procurement staff to develop an in-depth understanding of the product it is buying. Because most of the procurement staff have business rather than technical degrees, this product knowledge enables them to communicate with engineers and suppliers, and increases their credibility.

Target costing helps identify which gaps are soft (the supplier wants more profit) versus hard (there is a genuine inability to meet the target). This helps determine when alternatives to negotiation are needed to improve the price of parts. Alternatives include supplier development, a feature trade-off or redesigning the model.

Conclusion

Target costing is a cooperative, team-based effort at CRC. It is a dynamic process that has evolved with the market and is based on proven methods. Target costing is an integral part of CRC's new-product development process and ongoing cost-management system.

Lisa Ellram, Ph.D., C.P.M., C.P.A., C.M.A., is an associate professor in the Department of Supply Chain Management at Arizona State University. She is co-author of four books, Strategic Supplier Partnering: An International Study *(1993),* Purchasing for Bottom Line Impact: Improving the Organization Through Strategic Procurement *(1995),* Outsourcing: Implications for Supply Management *(1997), and* Fundamentals of Logistics Management *(1998), and has published articles in a variety of journals. She has also authored or co-authored four research projects funded by the Center for Advanced Purchasing Studies (CAPS).*

Come Out, Come Out, Wherever You Are

Nandita Ravulur

Purchasing and supply professionals in the future will continue to work at reducing total supply chain costs, primarily through greater efficiency in managing inventory. A recent study of the future of purchasing and supply stresses the need for negotiating strong, win-win relationships with suppliers. This article reports on trends that are helping make the inventory management process more efficient and reduce costs.

Minimize inventory. That's been the motto of purchasing and supply professionals as they constantly weigh the expense of holding inventory in a bid to trim carrying cost. Today's focus on shareholder value creation and return on net assets has only served to sharpen this focus.

Developing strategies to achieve continuing cost reductions contributes directly to shareholder value, according to "The Future of Purchasing and Supply: A Five-and Ten-Year Forecast." This joint research initiative, conducted by NAPM, the Center for Advanced Purchasing Studies (CAPS), A.T. Kearney, Inc., Arizona State University, and Michigan State University, suggests that "lean supply chains" will be a competitive strategy of purchasing and supply professionals. "Resources will be increasingly shared between highly independent firms that rely on each other as customer/supplier in the supply chain to maximize value-added contributions and reduce duplication of resources."

The study's discussion on strategic cost reduction confirms purchasing and supply managers' efforts to reduce inventory costs since it's considered an important area of cost savings. The study also confirms for many the value of investigating all aspects of total cost management (which includes inventory) and that ultimately contribute to shareholder value and return on net assets.

Current Status

The past practice of passing on inventory costs to suppliers has been a poor solution. "With today's view of the virtual supply chain, transferring costs to other elements of the supply chain (i.e., your suppliers) makes no more sense than transferring the cost within the four walls of your plant," says Bob O'Meara, vice president at A.T. Kearney in Chicago, Illinois. Costs, after all, need to be minimized, and not transferred.

According to the United States Department of Commerce, the U.S. economy deals with $1 trillion worth of inventory at any given point in time. Encouraging signs of reduced inventory levels in the system are evident. For starters, purchasing and supply managers have taken the basic steps to reduce inventory and the costs associated with managing inventory.

The NAPM Inventories Diffusion Index, a component of the *NAPM Report on Business*®, has been showing a faster rate of decrease in inventory since 1988. The rate of decrease has been in the 40 percent range since 1993. Attention to customer service also improved during this period as the supply chain has been able to deliver greater customer satisfaction—with less investment and lower inventory levels.

And what specific techniques have been used to reduce inventory? Purchasing and supply managers made considerable improvements in processes by using blanket orders, upgrading performance contracts, implementing liquidated damages clauses, and improving operating and transaction costs across the supply chain.

"The trick is to find other opportunities that also reduce operating and transaction costs, and, therefore, allow the supplier to provide his or her goods at a lower cost," says O'Meara.

Inventory's Supply Chain Goal

Total supply chain cost reduction will remain the goal of purchasing and supply professionals. To support this, supplier efficiency in managing inventory has taken center stage. Best-in-class inventory management suppliers process critical information that includes demand patterns, frequency, quantity of orders, leadtime, cycle time, and so on. As a result, inventory management suppliers really manage information, not inventory. In doing this, they help keep the supply chain moving.

Effective Strategies

Traditionally, purchasing and supply professionals attempted to achieve efficiency through better prices and improved delivery. Most organizations realize that their duty of controlling costs does not stop at the negotiation table, so they more often negotiate for better methods. Some of the sophisticated methods used include joint process improvements, global and strategic sourcing, supplier rationalization, specification changes, and integrated supply.

Purchasing and supply managers and suppliers are constantly looking for win-win relationships. "The Future of Purchasing and Supply: A Five-and Ten-Year Forecast" confirms that strong, win-win relationship building is a must in order to lower inventory costs and thus total cost. Following this concept, the study forecasts "negotiations will become more complex and sophisticated and rely less on emotions."

In addition to developing win-win relationships, purchasing and supply managers develop inventory control strategies with suppliers to manage inventory costs. William F. Given, executive director of procurement for Pacific Bell in San Ramon, California, says, "During the process of our negotiation, we try to increase our product and service efficiencies and tighten our deals." His organization insists on a split-up of the costs from the suppliers and an item-ized breakdown. "We also do reverse engineering to be sure that suppliers are not overcharg-ing us and check for hidden charges," he says. Some examples of hidden costs uncovered by Given's organization include freight cost, which constituted 3 percent of the price, and war-ranty cost, which constituted 6 percent of the cost.

Purchasing and supply managers should not forget the labor cost issue if they are look-ing at controlling total costs. Elliott Weiss, associate professor for the Darden School at the University of Virginia, says that assessment of relative labor rates for supply processes can also give a better understanding of suppliers' costs. For example, if labor costs in the sup-plier factory go up, the purchasing and supply manager might make significant savings by bringing in-house some of the processes.

Seeking Efficiencies

Supply chain efficiencies are critical to reduce large amounts of inventory; so is improving performance in the supply chain. Working with suppliers to remove uncertainty and com-pressing leadtimes are critical to reduce inventory in the supply chain.

Chicago-based Jose Morales, vice president of A.T. Kearney, says efficiencies are also influenced by the velocity at which the inventory is being moved through the supply chain to the customer. Purchasing and supply managers and suppliers focused on efficiency work together to reduce leadtimes and the root causes of uncertainty that lead to high levels of safety stock. "In most cases, they have done all they can working apart, and now, the next level of benefits will only be achieved when they work together," says Morales.

Working together will require organizations to concentrate on relationship management with suppliers and customers covering all areas of the shared business processes between the purchaser and the supplier. Several of the trends presented in "The Future of Purchasing and Supply" reflect the practices in the purchasing and supply profession today. "The focus on relationship management will require that all elements of relationship management, including trust building, communications, joint efforts, and planning and fostering interde-pendency, will be increasingly studied and managed to achieve competitive advantage."

The study reflects the efforts made by purchasers and suppliers to reduce costs and increase efficiencies in the inventory management process.

Suppliers Are Doing

So how are suppliers managing inventory? How are they working with stakeholders to reduce inventory costs?

Gary Clonts, president of Tech Pak, an Oklahoma City-based supplier of corrugated boxes to Macklanburg-Duncan, says his organization provides inventory management to purchasers as a service. "We offer inventory as a customer service and just charge for the floor space and add in the warehousing charge." Tech Pak manages inventory in such a way

Inventory Control Issues

Organizations analyze a variety of issues to effectively reduce inventory and cost in the total supply chain, say O'Meara and Morales. One needs to:

- Engage customer service
- Share information
- Determine the right amount of inventory at the right point
- Determine who holds inventory at what point in time
- Increase velocity and movement of inventory
- Develop electronic information sharing
- Involve other departments
- Conduct joint process improvements
- Develop value-added relationships with suppliers
- Constantly look for cost-reduction opportunities

that Macklanburg-Duncan never runs out of boxes, especially when there is a blanket purchase order. Other costs, like freight charges and labor, are included in the price of the box.

Most suppliers agree they need to pass on the inventory costs. George Krall, president of Mebane Packaging, based in Mebane, North Carolina, and Glaxo Wellcome's largest supplier of folding cartons, says that if purchasing managers are moving inventory to their suppliers, they are not doing anything to take cost out of the supply chain—they are merely transferring the cost. These costs eventually make their way to the price of the product. "Somebody still has to pay for the inventory. The only way to take the cost of out of the supply chain is to improve processes, have smaller quantities, and increase quality so as to take out activities such as redundant inspection costs," he says.

Glaxo Wellcome and Mebane Packaging developed a system where Glaxo shares forecasting information and production schedules with onsite employees from Mebane. "We improved order patterns and orders come in more effectively in terms of timing and production costs. This initiative led us to reduce costs by 13 percent and leadtimes by 20 percent," Krall says.

Sharing Information

Sharing projections, forecasts, and other information is critical to reducing inventory costs and making systems like Just-In-Time work efficiently. Many purchasing and supply professionals advocate sharing projections and forecasts with suppliers. Mitchell Millstein, CPIM, C.P.M., president of Supply Velocity, a consulting firm based in St. Louis, Missouri, says that if an organization wants to reduce order quantities and on-hand inventory, it must give suppliers forecast information and be responsible for the parts that suppliers build based on the forecast. "Any other method is sticking suppliers with inventory which has to be paid for sooner or later," he says. The key to reducing inventory in the entire supply chain is to integrate forecasting with scheduling. Successful organizations, for example, utilize a raw material forecasting mechanism to take customer orders.

Additionally, both parties in the relationship should develop world-class practices, develop a concept of shared cost rather than taking cost from one pocket and putting in the other, and share sensitive information without fear or concern, says O'Meara.

Arkansas-based Wal-Mart, for example, has been working with its suppliers to jointly minimize total costs and improve processes. At Wal-Mart, information technology is the key for efficiently sharing information.

Working Together

"Competition and the focus on shareholder value require organizations to be as aggressive in managing their inventory costs as they are with any other kind of cost," says O'Meara.

He states another client example related to specifications on board boxes. The client organization worked with suppliers to identify certain box sizes that were more efficient for their suppliers to produce while at the same time minimized wasted space. The organization reduced scrap cost, set-up times in their plants, and achieved longer production runs— all of which contributed to eliminating costs. This was achieved through joint process improvement.

O'Meara and Morales agree that reducing inventory and cost can be effectively achieved by working beyond cross-functional and organizational boundaries, involving people well outside of the traditional purchasing organization.

Organizations must repeatedly ask themselves, "How much inventory do we need to carry? Where should we put the inventory that we own? Can we work with our suppliers so that it costs us both less to meet the service requirements of our customers?" "The sophisticated information technology tools made available in the market directly support the decisions and analysis related to inventory management in an extended supply chain," says Morales.

Better Processes

Purchasing and supply managers say that it's critical for organizations to strive for the right amount of inventory at the right point in time in the supply chain. Sensing a need for better inventory management practices, suppliers are trying to adapt their processes to efficiently manage inventory. Organizations are even hiring outside services to take inventory out of the supply chain and manage it in the best possible manner.

Robert L. Kass, president of Choice Logistics, a New York City-based provider of inventory control and management solutions for the medical instrumentation and high technology industries, says that suppliers need to constantly improve their processes.

Kass' organization works with purchasers to cut down on the purchasing organization's storage locations, improve cycle time, and fine-tune inventory. "We practice reverse logistics where we keep track of where the parts are and how fast they need to come back so that purchasers need to store less inventory," he says.

Anthony A. Noe, C.P.M., director of purchasing at Macklanburg-Duncan, says that long-term relationships with suppliers helped his organization work out better processes with suppliers. Noe gives one example where suppliers ship products in rail tankers rather than in trucks. "This measure saved 2 cents per pound of raw material, resulting in an overall price reduction of about 5 percent. Our suppliers are much more conscientious and products are removed in accurate batches during shipment."

Organizations are realizing that suppliers are the best resource for ideas to cut inventory costs, decrease leadtimes, eliminate redundant processes, and incorporate technology to bring about efficiencies in the system. Suppliers know their business better than anyone else, and they know they are one of the best sources for identifying costs. A major consensus exists in the supply management profession that reducing inventory is the right thing to do, and the best way to achieve this is to shake hands with suppliers.

Nandita Ravulur was a writer for Purchasing Today®.

Culturally Effective Contracting: Modifying Contracting Practice for International Use

Dick Locke

Standard U.S. purchasing contracting practices can be not only ineffective, but also counterproductive when buyers use them in other countries. This article explains both the cultural and legal differences that cause this loss of effectiveness. It suggests specific changes in practices and provides examples of the right and wrong way to work with potential foreign suppliers.

Introduction

Like all countries' legal practices, the practices in the United States developed from both legal and cultural influences. Our practices have become unique, however, because our legal system developed from a legal basis that most of the rest of the world does not use, and because we buy and sell a small percentage of our gross domestic product compared to other industrialized countries. We are not as knowledgeable about normal ways of doing business internationally as people in other industrialized countries are.

This discussion will cover first the legal basis, and then the cultural underpinnings of our legal practices. It will then cover some practices that are unique and explain why people in other countries find the practices disturbing. Next, it will discuss the reasons why many (but not all) buying companies want contracts with their suppliers. Finally, it will show ways to meet (and not meet) the goals for contracting.

I should note here that I am not an attorney, and that you should check the applicability of any advice in this presentation with your attorney before making any significant decision.

Legal Differences

There are two major legal systems in the world. The system that 49 of the 50 United States use is called "common law." This legal system grew out of British law in the 12th century, and is found only in Britain and its former colonies. The basis of common law was originally that judges should strive for a just conclusion based on the facts of a particular case. When enough judges found the same way in the same circumstances, this became *de facto* law by precedent. The idea of creating law by precedent did not survive the industrial revolution, and our legal system now has a lot of legislative-written laws. However, there is still more room for precedent in our system than in the other legal system.

Contracts in a common-law system are almost infinitely negotiable. Almost everything has to be written down unless buyer and seller wish to rely on precedent or on the Uniform Commercial Code. This leads to very lengthy contracts. A "default" clause in an U.S. contract, for example, often defines default, specifies the remedies for default and defines the procedures by which those remedies will be attained. It's not unusual to see a 350-word default clause in an U.S. purchase contract.

The rest of the developed world uses "civil law." (This is also called "code law.") This grew out of Roman law, and was developed in continental Europe during the Renaissance. Under civil law, legislatures or other bodies write lengthy codes to cover as many situations as possible. Precedent has much less weight in influencing decisions. Contracts are usually much briefer because the parties expect to use the established codes that define terms, establish rights, provide remedies, and define the procedures for attaining them.

One company that had a 350-word default clause in its standard U.S. purchase contract had a nine-word clause in its German (civil) contract: "In the event of default, German law will apply." Parties contracting in Germany generally regard the default law as fair, and spend their negotiating time discussing business issues, not legal details.

Countries that had a choice of legal systems chose civil law. Most attorneys that are trained in civil law find common law difficult and troublesome. It seems too vague and too subject to the whims of a particular judge or jury.

Cultural Differences

A buyer must consider cultural differences as well as legal-system differences. There are many cultural differences between countries, but there are three major differences that affect purchase contracting.

The first difference is a different emphasis on "uncertainty avoidance," a term developed and explained by Geert Hofstede in his pioneering book *Culture's Consequences*. Simply put, it reflects differences in how sure people in a culture want to be of the future before they will proceed with something. France and Japan have high uncertainty avoidance scores. The U.S. has a fairly low score. This cultural characteristic affects lead time and flexibility more than it affects anything else.

In addition to different emphases on uncertainty avoidance, there are different mechanisms for coping with uncertainty. In the U.S., a legal contract is a major uncertainty avoidance mechanism. A normal American reaction to any potential difficulty is "put it in the contract." We even usually have a "complete agreement" clause, which states that the total understanding between the companies is in the contract. A contract reduces uncertainty by allowing a powerful third party, the courts, into a dispute.

In most Asian countries, even those with high uncertainty avoidance, contracts are much shorter and much vaguer. In those societies, the major uncertainty avoidance mechanism is to get to know potential business partners very well before entering into a business relationship.

This leads to the second major cultural difference, the importance of a personal relationship in business. The U.S. treats business rather impersonally compared to other countries. Fons Trompenaars, a Dutch researcher, illustrates this well. He runs multinational workshops in Europe where he asks for reactions to hypothetical situations. One question involves a car accident where your close friend is driving. The friend is speeding and injures a pedestrian. The friend's attorney comes to you and encourages you to lie in court to protect your friend. Trompenaars asks two questions: What right does the friend have to ask you to lie in court? Would you or would you not lie? Approximately 95% of Germans, Canadians and Americans answer either that the friend had no right to ask this or the friend had some right but they still wouldn't lie. Approximately 65% of Spanish and 25% of Koreans give these answers. While Trompenaars' book seems to treat this data as an "honesty graph," it's much more enlightening to consider it as a graph of the different importance and sense of obligation given to friendships in different countries.

Trompenaars specifically suggests not loading contracts with penalty clauses or strict requirements when dealing with cultures that get low scores on this exercise. These clauses will be seen as an accusation that the other party would cheat if the contract didn't forbid it, and a person whose integrity is challenged may react by acting with less integrity.

The third major cultural difference is the attitude toward contracts. Western cultures, and particularly the United States, tend to believe "a deal is a deal," and once a contract is signed everyone is expected to follow it without requesting changes. As a result, contracts are expected to cover everything that could happen and become very long. In most Asian countries there is a more flexible attitude. A contract is seen as more of a guideline, and life with its frequent changes is seen as too complex to capture all the possibilities in a written document. As a result, if something unexpected happens, either party is able to reopen negotiations. Both parties are assumed to be well intended and to take reasonable care of each other's interests.

Both of these attitudes toward contracts can be carried to counterproductive extremes. The best solution is somewhere in the middle.

U.S. Legal Practices

There are a few legal practices that are especially disturbing to sellers in other countries. We already mentioned one, which is that contracts become lengthy because too many items go into them. A second one is that they are wordy and written in a special type of English, legal English (more on correcting that later). A third common problem is that they are written one-sidedly and give the buyer a variety of rights and the seller as few rights as possible. Domestically, we recognize that the draft language is usually negotiable and the buyer often doesn't seriously intend to insist on it. Buyers routinely, and sometimes carelessly, send these draft documents to foreign sellers with an assumption that they will ask to have items changed if they find them distasteful. Some special caution is needed here. There have been academic studies that show that one of the biggest obstacles to a negotiated agreement that could have been win-win is the opening offer being seen as completely unreasonable to the other party. A seller faced with an unreasonable contract may draw back from the deal.

Purpose of Contracts

I see two major purposes for written, signed agreements between the buyer and seller. The first purpose is to get people to write down and agree (in some degree of detail) to the major responsibilities of the parties. I believe this is especially important when dealing with foreign suppliers. This exercise will bring most disagreements and misunderstandings into the open before business starts. It also creates a document that will survive personnel changes.

The second major purpose is to use a signed, legally enforceable agreement to get a party to do something they would not do otherwise. A strong third party, normally a court, enforces compliance. Achieving this goal is much more difficult when dealing internationally. The international legal system is slow and expensive. A legal cycle may be several times longer than a product life cycle. Many major companies do not try very hard to make an agreement that will be useful in court.

Preparing a Contract Draft

Here are six key steps to take in preparing a contract proposal for foreign suppliers. This is by no means an exhaustive list, but one designed to reduce problems due to legal and cultural differences.

1. *Remove all clauses from your standard contract that are applicable in the U.S. only.* Some of these are veterans' rights, EEO, and OSHA clauses. Even if a clause says "when applicable" take it out if it isn't applicable. One very common clause states in essence "Seller will follow all U.S. federal, state and local laws." A foreign supplier will have a difficult time even deciding which laws are applicable, if any. If there is a particular U.S. law or group of laws that you want the seller to follow, state it.

2. *Rewrite or eliminate all clauses that are too harsh or one-sided.* Carefully consider whether they are necessary, and if not, take them out. A clause stating that the supplier will not sell to anyone else at a lower price, for example, is a poor way to start a new relationship. If there is a clause that you would normally agree to make two-way during negotiation, make it two-way before the supplier sees it.

3. *Simplify the English.* Legal writing is often indefensibly hard to read. If one of the major

purposes of an agreement is to document expectations, then the contract should function as a communication tool. If you are working with an attorney, this is not a trivial problem. Many complex contract clauses have been passed on from attorney to attorney over the years with a comment that "this has worked in the past." To rewrite them into simple English will take time and thought. You might face resistance.

Fortunately, you have support. The Securities and Exchange Commission has drafted rules that require prospectuses to be written in plain English. Vice President Gore's Reinventing Government program is requiring all government communications to be written in plain English. Both organizations have published guidelines. Some key recommendations are:

- use active verbs
- use short sentences
- avoid legalese and jargon
- use bulleted lists and tables, rather than long lists of words separated by commas

A good test, and an enlightening exercise, is to use your word processor's grammar checker on your contract proposal. Often, the grammar checker will reject entire paragraphs. (Think of the effect of this style of writing on someone for whom English is a second language.) Pay attention to typography, white space and overall appearance of the document.

4. *Decide if you want to have the United Nations Convention on the International Sale of Goods (CISG) applicable to your contract or not.* The CISG is a UN treaty that the U.S. and several other countries have signed. If the buyer's and seller's countries have both signed it, it will be applicable to your contract unless you specifically exclude it. There are some aspects of the CISG that are unfavorable to buyers and some that are unfavorable to sellers, and it is not completely understood. Most companies exclude it. You will need to put specific exclusionary language in your agreement: "The United Nations Convention on the International Sale of Goods will not apply."

5. *Consider arbitration rather than courts to solve problems.* Arbitration will be faster and less costly in most cases. It also will tend to reach a compromise, rather than have one party prevail completely. It is a good solution for solving what both parties see as a temporary impasse in their relationship.

6. *Establish the courts and legal system under which disputes will be settled.* You need to pick a country and city. If the supplier has all of its assets in its home country, often the best choice is the supplier's home country. This works best if the buying company has a legal presence in the supplier's country and there is a stable, functioning legal system.

Summary

Cultural and legal differences make international contract negotiating challenging, but also often enlightening. Many of your assumptions will be challenged. You may discover excellent foreign practices that are also applicable to domestic contracting, and often you can improve your overall contracting processes. If there is one key lesson, it is that U.S.-style contracts are not the only way to achieve optimum supplier performance. Personal relationships, obligations to customers, and the ease with which a foreign supplier can do business with your company also can lead to success.

References

William Jefferson Clinton, "Presidential Memorandum on Plain Language," June 1, 1998, www.plainlanguage.gov/cites/memo.htm.

Geert Hofstede, *Culture's Consequences, International Differences in Work-Related Values*, abridged edition (Newbury Park, CA: Sage Publications, Inc., 1989).

Dick Locke, *Global Supply Management, A Guide to International Purchasing* (Burr Ridge, IL: Irwin Professional Publishing, 1996).

Securities and Exchange Commission, *A Plain English Handbook: How to Create Clear SEC Disclosure Documents* (Washington, DC: August 20, 1998, http://204.192.28.3/pdf/handbook.pdf.

Fons Trompenaars, *Riding the Waves of Culture* (Burr Ridge, IL: Irwin Professional Publishing, 1993).

Richard C. Wydick, *Plain English for Lawyers* (Durham, NC: Carolina Academic Press, 1979).

Dick Locke is President, Global Procurement Group (www.globalpg.com), San Francisco, CA 94114, 415 695-1673, dlocke@globalpg.com.

Beyond
Plan-Source-Make-Move

James Aaron Cooke

The supply chain can be seen as compartmentalized, with players having certain roles but without much sense of the interdependence of roles or the supply chain can be seen holistically. This latter model, as the author of this article states, "better conveys the synthesis of the numerous dynamic interactions that must occur among supply chain partners to fulfill consumer demand." In this article, Cooke explains the value of the holistic or organic model and, among other things, explains the role of the Internet in facilitating interactions among members of the supply chain.

Supply chains come in all sizes and shapes. Some have many links; others do not. Some chains emanate from manufacturing, while others are woven around marketing. They stretch across different industries and geographical boundaries. They handle different production requirements and move their products by different modes of transportation.

No matter the type of chain, the purpose of supply chain management is to focus on meeting customer demand while minimizing inventory of both raw materials and finished goods. Yet as companies work together in an extended enterprise, the chain itself tends to gain more links and become more complex to manage.

Such complexity requires a shift in corporate thinking. "An enterprise is no longer a single corporation; it's a loose collection of trading partners that could contract with manufacturers, logistics companies, [and] distribution organizations," says William T. Walker, a supply chain manager at Hewlett-Packard's power products division in Rockaway, N.J., and co-author of the book *Supply Chain Management Principles and Techniques for the Practitioner*. "The supply chain has to have a holistic, end-to-end enterprise point of view."

Organic Model

The Supply Chain Council, an organization that focuses on supply chain practices, has defined four processes common to all supply chains—plan, source, make, and move. Although that definition applies broadly, many consultants note that it best describes a single company rather than an extended enterprise. "Every company has multiple customers and multiple suppliers," says Charles R. Troyer, a partner in CSC Consulting's New York office, "and many of those suppliers are parts of other competing supply chains, which means my customers are dealing with my competitors."

The council's definition of a supply chain strikes many as too one-dimensional to describe the intricate cross-links that exist in a multi-company supply chain. "Plan-source-make-move is too linear," says Troyer. "As I focus on the end consumer, I also have to have an equal focus on the interests of my trading partners."

Given the numerous connections between supply chain partners, a more appropriate depiction of an extended enterprise would be an organic model. An organic representation better conveys the synthesis of the numerous dynamic interactions that must occur among supply chain partners to fulfill consumer demand. "We're seeing an evolution from plan, source, make, and move to a holistic view of how multiple enterprises are going to cooperate to make efficient use of resources to get a product delivered," says Steve Gold, a partner in the supply chain strategy practice at KPMG in Chicago.

Gold says a holistic view of the supply chain would have to encompass the entire community of participants. Take a supply chain for potato chips as an example. The KPMG consultant says it would include the farmer who grows the potatoes, the package manufacturer who supplies the bags, the actual maker of the potato chips, the food distributor who handles the product, the trucking company that performs store delivery, and the supermarket where the product is sold, to name just the prominent ones. "You've got 30 or 40 enterprises working together just to enable potato chips to be put on a shelf," Gold reports.

With so many companies involved, visibility becomes critical to the extended enterprise's success. Trading partners require visibility about activities throughout the pipeline in order to coordinate the supply chain. Even the farmer should have knowledge about potato-chip sales projections to plan his planting and harvesting of a potato crop. Likewise, the potato-chip maker should have information about crop conditions to plan his production schedule. "At any point in time, [supply chain members] should know both quantity and status of inventory," says Steve Nevill, a principal at the consulting firm Kurt Salmon Associates in Atlanta. For instance, Nevill contends that the manufacturer should be informed by the retailer the moment the product arrives at the store.

The Importance of Being Online

Information technology provides the means for trading partners to share intelligence to handle a complex supply chain. "Instead of supply chains being driven by physical flows, they will be driven by information flows," says Joe Martha, the Cleveland-based leader of the supply chain strategy practice for Mercer Management Consulting.

Business software can help an individual supply chain partner track product demand and forecast sales in an effort to synchronize production with consumer takeaway. "Most companies that do well have comprehensive systems that are proactive in terms of planning and forecasting," Nevill notes.

But success for all supply chain members won't be possible unless the trading partners themselves integrate their disparate computer systems and hardware. Gold, for one, sees trading partners connecting portfolios of IT applications. For instance, a supplier may connect his advance planning and scheduling system (APS) to a retailer's warehouse management system (WMS) in order to predict future production requirements more accurately. "The ability to assemble the correct portfolio of applications is really the next big step in technology advancement," says Gold.

Such systems and application integration, however, may be just the first step required. In the future, Gold predicts, each member of a supply chain community will have to build its own control center, which will act as an information repository for all data required to manage the flow of materials. Smaller trading partners in the community may even have to subcontract with third-party logistics providers or IT companies to obtain access to such data-control centers.

Gary Cross of the IBM Consulting Group foresees supply chain partners taking advantage of new Internet technologies to provide "just-in-time" information. In other words, when a customer gives a retailer an order, the retailer in turn would query its carrier on rates and delivery availability.

Cross contends that the deployment of Extensible Markup Language (XML) on the Internet will make such a scenario possible in the near future. XML is a more advanced language than the Hypertext Markup Language (HTML) that's currently used to exchange data on the Internet. XML allows for the use of special tags before a message that would allow a browser to identify the message. Through the use of those tags, the browser could immediately recognize whether a sequence of numbers—say, 1,2,3—refers to a purchase order or an advance shipment notice. "XML provides a way to describe the rest of the information following in the transmission," says Cross.

For an extended enterprise engaged in supply chain management, XML tags could be placed on such common messages as the purchase order or the advance shipment notice. A Web browser capable of decoding XML then would be able to ascertain quickly the nature of the messages from a supply chain partner. Furthermore, it would become possible for one member's computer system to respond automatically to information requests from another member's system.

XML thus could provide an alternative to electronic data interchange, which has been limited so far to big companies willing to make the investment in the requisite computer services and hardware. "We see XML as 'new age' EDI," says Cross.

How the Money Moves

Although software can help channel the information flow required to coordinate material movements, there's a third element that's often overlooked—fund flow between the trading partners. Peter Metz, deputy director of the Massachusetts Institute of Technology's Center for Transportation Studies in Cambridge, Mass., says that trading partners in the supply chain also need a clear picture of how money is moving. "The fund flow has not gotten the attention it needs," he notes.

Some companies are working to address that. Consultant James Morehouse of A.T.

Kearney Inc. in Chicago says several retailers are considering an experiment with a pay-on-scan arrangement. Under that plan, every trading partner in the supply chain would get paid when the consumer makes a purchase at the retail checkout counter. "When everybody ends up getting paid when the consumer pays," he says, "everybody [in the supply chain] has an incentive to keep [inventory levels] lean."

But a supply chain must do more than provide visibility over materials, information, and money. It also must offer enough flexibility that partners can change it to handle new products. For example, the members of the potato-chip supply chain might decide to produce potato sticks as an alternative snack food. "You can't have a supply chain that's just optimized for one mission," says Metz. "When the next mission comes along, the supply chain won't be able to handle it."

Consultant Kevin O'Laughlin in Ernst & Young LLP's Boston office says such flexibility may become more important in the future as manufacturers embrace configuration management. Such a strategy requires that a manufacturer customize a product for a particular set of clients. A shoe manufacturer, for instance, might tailor his production to produce footwear with a particular sole and style that appeals to a higher-income customer. O'Laughlin adds that an increasing number of manufacturers are becoming interested in configuration management.

Of course, someone in the supply chain has to decide what's best to make for the end consumer. Morehouse believes that in any given supply chain, someone has to take charge and orchestrate the process. "The captain of the supply chain should be like the captain of a team," says the A.T. Kearney consultant. "I have to select players and put the team together."

In some cases, Morehouse notes, the captain of the extended enterprise might be a powerful retailer. In others, it would be a strong manufacturer. "One organization tends to be the captain," he says, "And [the team] only stays together as long as everybody feels there is a benefit."

That unity will be taxed as supply chain partners make decisions and weigh the tradeoffs between inventory and production capability necessary for speedy throughput of product to the customer. To maintain the cooperation, companies will have to adopt a big-picture perspective on what's required from each partner. "You've got to take a complete supply chain view," says Cross, "as opposed to optimizing some components at the expense of others."

Supply Chain Diversity

When it comes to structuring a workable supply chain among trading partners, there's no one solution. Nor is there one piece of software on the market that will provide it. "People are looking for a silver bullet," says consultant Gold. "There's more to it than just [installing] an application."

Indeed, Gold thinks that companies will have to work harder than ever at constructing and managing the complex supply chains that will take shape during the 21st century. "We've gone through this period where people focused on taking costs out of the supply chain," he says. "But supply chains will become more complex as people sell through other channels like the 'Net or in other parts of the globe."

The extended enterprises operating these supply chains will face the enormous challenge of coordinating many activities simultaneously. Although that task appears daunting, leading companies today have shown that it can be done if they mind the details. "Attention to details is what does things better," observes Gene Tyndall, supply chain international director at Ernst & Young.

In the end, though, companies will not achieve a supply chain breakthrough until they realize that no company can run or build the chain itself. Instead, companies must work in collaboration and adopt a holistic view of the supply chain. "While technology is the driver, people will be a big component of the success of this thing," says Gold. "People have to shift their thinking about the supply chain, and a lot of organizations will have to do the same thing."

James Aaron Cooke is senior technology editor of Logistics.

Purchasing and Supply Interacts with Internal Customers

Thomas J. Bassett

Perhaps the most appropriate view of purchasing is that it serves line personnel who are carrying out the organization's mission to deliver valuable products and services to the organization's customers. These personnel are the purchasing and supply department's customers. What are the ways purchasing can most effectively work with and serve these customers? That is the question this article seeks to explore and answer. You may not have thought about your tasks in this way, but it provides insight into how you can more effectively add value for the organization and for those it serves.

Current estimations indicate that a majority of North American organizations spend anywhere from 50 to 60 percent of sales for direct materials purchased from local, regional, and global suppliers. As a result, it's no surprise that senior management is looking directly at purchasing and supply management to (1) source and add value-producing suppliers, and (2) build and maintain shareholder value. A.T. Kearney's *Catalyst*, a special supplement to *Chemical Week*, reports, "Although some old-style companies still write procurement off as a bureaucratic backwater, leaders are realizing that their total spending accounts for 50 percent of total revenue and represents a substantial opportunity for building and sustaining long-term value." Of course, the task of elevating purchasing and supply from a day-to-day administrative role to a strategic and value creating role requires a commitment from senior management.

Purchasing and supply has established its importance because of its potential to directly affect the bottom line. An experienced purchasing and supply department is able to work closely with supplier organizations to bring measurable value-adding processes to the buying organization. Certainly, as a purchasing department looks up the chain, it can easily identify its role impacting goods and services entering into the organization. Looking down the chain, a purchasing department's immediate link is typically to an internal business unit or department—its internal customers.

Within this context, the term "internal customer" will most likely mean the end-user department. However, keep in mind that some internal departments use purchasing and supply as a "pass-through" function to assist the end-user department.

While executing the organization's business plan, purchasing and supply must facilitate the day-to-day needs of each and every internal customer's wants by making sure he or she is receiving the specified goods and services at the right place, at the right time, at the right quantity, and, of course, at the right price. It does not hurt to keep this fundamental mission statement of the purchasing department's roles close at hand.

From a strategic standpoint, purchasing and supply is responsible for ensuring that suppliers respond to internal customers with the end result of these relationships producing an organization with distinct competitive advantages. It is mainly for this reason that many organizations now make the effort to include and consider purchasing and supply possibilities and limitations when formulating strategic organizational goals.

Creating Value

Purchasing receives input from internal customers, then processes or acts upon this input. This leads to additional feedback and interaction with internal customers, forming a continuous communication loop. Purchasing gains a unique vantage point from which to observe the entire organization and each function within it as strategic objectives are played out and accomplished. Looking to the side, purchasing and supply will find it easy to identify those internal customers not in sync with the organization's strategic goals.

For example, the most common situation encountered by a corporate purchasing department is that of finding out that distant plants, facilities, or locations are not releasing needed items from a national agreement set in place by corporate purchasing for all the facilities to use. While navigating the purchasing and supply function down the road, it's the corporate purchasing and supply department that has the best overall view of which internal processes are moving toward organizational goals and which are not.

Let's take a moment to define value. Within a mathematical framework, value can be computed as: worth ÷ cost.

If the value is greater than 1, a product and/or process contains necessary costs. Conversely, if the value is less than 1, a systematic approach, called value analysis, is conducted to find the unnecessary costs inherent in a product and/or process and, thus, the attempt is made to eliminate unnecessary costs. Value analysis is linked to another concept, product life cycle (PLC) costing, which urges the purchaser to look more closely at the overall costs of owning an asset beyond the initial purchase price of the asset. Sometimes referred to as cradle-to-grave costing, PLC costing will be discussed later.

Improving Efficiency

Listed under the primary objectives of purchasing and supply is the responsibility to improve the efficiency of operations and procedures for internal customers. The statement "an organization is only as good as its supply base" does indeed have *substantial* merit. As the buying organization, if input does not meet the specified standards, excessive transformation will increase costs. In this sense, excessive transformation is interpreted as being required to:

- reject product,
- repair product,
- rework product, or
- ship out product to another firm to "make-good" the product.

In terms of purchasing services it could mean having to supply more training to a contractor than originally estimated or having a project take longer than anticipated. In simple terms, the more efficient and dependable the supplier, the less costly it is to do business with that supplier. This scenario takes on more importance if you are purchasing finished goods from a multiple-product supply house. When buying from a multiple-product supply house, if product is unusable, the process of returning goods is usually double the work. Underlying this entire discussion is the importance of garnering senior management support and buy-in of the value analysis concept. As a purchasing professional, attempt to determine if senior management is beginning to recognize the critical relationships intertwined within your organization's supply chain. Many of these relationships are now commonly defined by their dependency on electronic networks.

See the sidebar, "Let Me Count the Ways," for other areas in which purchasing and supply can play a value-added role with the internal customer link.

Internal Customer Roles

How does the purchasing and supply management department look for internal customers deserving of such value analysis processes? Oftentimes directives are sent to purchasing and supply mandating that the supply chain be the target of the first investigation. Yet, this supplier-centered approach assumes that the initial opportunity to grow economic value lies strictly with the exploitation of the supply chain. The experience gained as purchasing and supply management professionals cautions us not to overlook the internal customer's processes; thus, value analysis can also be approached from a process-centered directive to aid in the identification of priorities.

This is not to say that just because the internal customer is satisfied that value analysis flies out the door. Constant change in technology brings about new ways to perform transformation of raw materials into finished goods. In order to identify or improve value, senior management needs to bestow the value analysis responsibility to purchasing and supply and grant it the authority to conduct such analyses.

As far as technology is concerned, A.T. Kearney's *Catalyst* estimated that over the next several years, some 90 percent of normal procurement transactions will be eliminated, and 99 percent of the remaining transactions will be completely automated. The supplement further states that transactions that do not add value will become extinct and, in comparison, those necessary transactions that do add value will integrate transparently into other business processes.

Hovering over the organization is this ever-expanding umbrella composed of external customers, the final consumers of your products or services. From a purchasing and supply

Let Me Count the Ways

In a 1996 CAPS study, "Executive Summary of Purchasing's Organizational Roles and Responsibilities," the following are functions that report to purchasing: scrap/surplus disposal, materials and purchasing research, inbound traffic, inventory control, material planning, stores/warehousing, receiving, and outbound traffic. In addition to overseeing these areas, and assisting them as internal customers, purchasing can offer value to all areas of an organization through several activities. Purchasing and supply can provide numerous other value-adding activities to internal customers.

1. Assist with budget preparation:
   a. The budget committee may require anticipated standard costs for materials in order to determine production costs to produce the targeted number of finished units.
   b. An internal customer may be given the objective to increase throughput by "x" percent, and, thus, require from purchasing and supply a commodity's price history and forecast.
2. Verify a supplier's quality control systems:
   a. Secure the supplier's quality mission statement and quality manual.
   b. Find out who is supplying the first-tier supplier.
3. Offer advice and assistance with quote preparation:
   a. Assure that the quotes being generated by internal customers properly define the needed specifications and, of course, make reference to those specifications.
   b. Help the internal customers pinpoint the strengths and weaknesses of each returned quote through the issuance of standard quotes.
   c. Provide all the selected bidders with a level playing field. One area that requires special attention is that of preventing end-user departments from accepting pre-bid technical assistance from a single supplier. This will result in a pre-bid advantage. Also, make sure that notifications of changes are presented to all bidders at the same time.
4. Gather information:
   a. Keep internal customers updated on any outside conditions that would affect their processes; for example, changes in technology, changes in labor contracts, changes in the applicable law, changes in industry standards, changes that come about due to mergers/acquisitions, changes in supplier's personnel, changes that arise due to natural disasters, and changes resulting from supplier plant shutdowns.
5. Formulate or join the supplier audit team to:
   a. Investigate the supplier's workflow or capacity.
   b. Analyze the condition of the supplier's equipment.
   c. Determine the morale and appearance of the supplier's workforce.
   d. Observe how the supplier's workforce operates equipment.
   e. Determine the degree of computer automation and technology.

6. Publish leadtimes for every incoming product used by internal customers:
   a. Define how leadtimes are calculated. Typically they will begin with purchase order creation and end with delivery, which should result in requisitions being prepared on time.
7. Publish a list that identifies the following items:
   a. Products, services, or commodities which are secured under present agreements.
   b. Dates which these products, services, or commodity contracts will be up for renegotiation or new bids.
   c. New products, services, or commodities that are under development and require supplier participation in the early product development stage.
   These lists can be communicated via intranet, newsletters, or period reports.
8. Involvement with cost reduction and cost avoidance:
   a. Standardization of incoming products and services can lead to lower material costs, lower production costs, lower future pricing, and lower usage of products or materials. Standardization is affectionately called "variety control." The closer the internal customer moves toward taking full ownership of the products, the less purchasing and supply might be involved directly with the transaction. The purchasing and supply management professional will play a more strategic role in the process by setting up contracts, investigating new sourcing opportunities, and working with suppliers to add more value to an existing relationship.
   b. Promote purchasing and supply as a crucial department to the point where corporate policy mandates that purchasing is to be included on new product development teams, capital projects, due diligence teams, and value analysis projects. Communicate to internal customers that the most effective way to take advantage of the purchasing department's skills, talents, and experiences is by early involvement. Purchasing and supply should be brought into the picture during the recognition and description stages of required materials and services to contact suppliers. Not only will this help facilitate alignment between internal customers' needs and suppliers' abilities, but it can result in purchasing and supply identifying cost saving opportunities based on its expertise with a given market or supplier.

management perspective, in addition to external customers, there are the various internal customers who rain down their needs upon purchasing and supply from distant plants, branches, and/or subsidiaries. It's the funneling of these needs directly to purchasing and supply that most often require open lines of communication with purchasing and supply management and various end-user departments. Those departments can include:

- accounting
- information systems
- quality control
- production
- warehousing

- engineering
- customer service
- maintenance and repair
- sales and marketing
- human resources
- senior management

Identifying Opportunities

How would purchasing and supply begin to identify internal customers, prioritize their needs, and decide which front to attack first?

Plans can set the pace. Naturally, a majority of the needs inherent to a particular internal customer are both defined and assigned by senior management via implementation of the business plan. For example, if the business plan calls for an increase in manufacturing output, the only way to achieve this is via plant expansion because every machine ran at a 98 percent or better capacity level last year. Hopefully, before the engineering study was done to determine the size of this addition, purchasing and supply was able to attend the capital budget approval meeting to determine material costs and labor rates and identify potential contractors. Coinciding with its role on the budget committee, and as soon as this capital budget is approved, purchasing and supply management must be presented with the budget so that each line item is deciphered one by one to determine the full impact upon the department. At this point, the increased workload may be assigned to an individual buyer based on his or her experience, the dollar value of the secondary projects within the main project, and or by the type of contracts that will need to be executed.

In the situation of purchasing services, the human resource element—hiring and staffing—will no doubt be the major contributor to cost for providing the service. In this instance, purchasing and supply can assist both sales and marketing and human resources in determining labor rates for that specific geographical area for bid preparation and assist in determining and negotiating the prices charged by media to attract these necessary employees.

Departmental divisions. Purchasing and supply, with its prescribed ability to perform internal investigations, can focus efforts to the internal customer issuing the most requisitions or requiring the most dollars in terms of revenue spent. Externally, an experienced purchasing and supply manager would examine the entire supply chain route that his or her goods take in order to identify possible bottlenecks and develop contingency plans for product or material interruption.

Teams. Purchasing and supply's participation in cross-functional teams is another method that would aid in the prioritization of internal customers. Designating purchasers to join the job rotation process with various departments is an excellent way to gather valuable information as to the future needs of internal customers and the timeframes in which those needs will be met. One technique is to shadow the process engineers, that is, follow the group performing the time studies, assessing the processes, and identifying the ways to increase capacity. Regardless of which method is used, the desired end result for purchasing and supply is to ascertain the internal customer's goals and timeframes.

Spend categories. Another technique to prioritize the needs of internal customers is to fragment the purchasing dollars spent into categories. For example, commodities, services, raw materials, MRO items, component parts, and utilities compose the major categories. Then, by linking the purchasing dollars spent to the appropriate internal customer, an individual procurement strategy can be tailored to meet that department's needs. However, an individual procurement strategy must not take precedence over purchasing and supply management's ability to capitalize on the opportunity to consolidate buys across different business segments to achieve lower economies of scale. Operating in this capacity will allow purchasing and supply to function as a mechanism that will lead the procurement strategy within the organization. This center-led approach will ensure that supplier management procedures are being used consistently throughout the organization and that best purchasing practices are being implemented. Performing this job will be easier if (1) individual plants function as their own cost centers, and (2) the finance department has established charge codes for material costs. One area that deserves special consideration is MRO. Inherent with MRO purchasing is the desire by the local plant to maintain these purchases locally. However, MRO purchasing is indeed an area where national supply agreements can be used to maintain the day-to-day operations while at the same time placing the organization in a strategic framework to share common parts or services among its various business units. If the luxury of having a central stocking facility exists, that's even more reason to place MRO items on a national agreement because leading the organization-wide procurement function from a central location will substantially decrease unauthorized buying. This, however, does not mean removing the local purchaser from his or her responsibility of obtaining the organizational-wide goals of purchasing at the least total cost, buying at the specified quality level, reducing the supplier base, ascertaining a high-degree of inventory turns, and enforcing the central purchasing policy at the local level.

How to Win Friends and Influence Internal Customers

Every internal customer fears losing control over processes. This is where the purchasing and supply professional hops the fence and becomes a sales professional. In order for a sales presentation to be effective it must be built on a solid proposal foundation. A full-blown sales proposal may not be necessary. Use a scaled down version, which the purchasing and supply professional can label an "insight proposal," that attempts to assess a current product or process. It should also provide comparisons of the current product or process to proposed changes by detailing the expected positive results in both quantitative and qualitative terms.

One tactic is to ask the internal user to co-author the proposal with purchasing and supply. Purchasing and supply will have to rely on the internal customer's labor pool to test the proposal. So, with this thought in mind, make a concentrated effort to emphasize to the internal customer that if the insight proposal is implemented, and costs savings result, purchasing and supply will allow the internal customer to take full credit for the cost savings realized. This is one of the fastest ways to gain acceptance from internal customers. See the sidebar, "Insight Proposal," for steps to conduct an insight proposal.

Insight Proposal

Here is a brief outline of the steps to conduct an insight proposal, which is an outline that assesses a current product or process and justifies proposed changes.

As we know, senior management's blessing is required in order to buy in to any value analysis project conducted by purchasing and supply.

1. Assess the current product and/or process.
2. Accurately and precisely describe the proposal objective a way that measurable results can be obtained.
3. List the expected results.
4. Measure the results and determine if the objective was achieved, and if not, explain and detail why it wasn't achieved.

Let's consider a simple example. It was brought to the attention of the purchasing department that one particular older copy machine was experiencing an average monthly repair bill of $300 for the past four months. Let's assume that this copier is paid for and there is no service agreement in place. As it turns out, a certain end-user department that requires two-sided copies has been using the machine out of convenience instead of walking down the hall to the larger duplexing copier. More copies are made than what is needed. This additional work load was placing much strain on the older copier, thus resulting in breakdowns. Not depending on any additional circumstances, purchasing can send a letter to that department manager clarifying the company policy for performing large copy jobs. From least costly to most costly contingent upon other vital circumstances, purchasing and supply can suggest to the user department that they

a. retrofit the old copier to handle the additional work load,
b. retrofit and negotiate a service agreement for the old copier, or
c. replace the old copier with a new machine with an optional service agreement.

An easy measurement would be to project the costs of doing nothing versus the costs of doing something compared on a cost-per-copy basis. That is, calculate the cost-per-copy using the old machine inclusive of the repair costs versus the cost-per-copy of purchasing a new machine. Total pay out, expected usage life, and cost of ownership all come into play and can serve as objectives to substantiate and measure the decision that was chosen.

Analyzing and Assessing

Suppose for a moment that the purchasing and supply management department has determined that the organization has received two different invoices from different suppliers who supply the same material but with a different density. At one time, the original written specification required only size and weight, but over the years, some internal customers have aligned themselves with their favorite supplier. Reasons given by the internal customers as to why each uses a different supplier vary from on-time delivery, to problem solving initiated by the supplier, to nonconforming product, to an actual difference in material composition. The problem is further compounded by the fact that the old specification was written for the internal customer who now uses the least amount of this material. Each internal user is reluctant to give up his or her favorite supplier. In addition, purchasing and supply has heard the following objections from internal customers:

- "We tried the other supplier once before and it didn't work out."
- "Quality will suffer."
- "We would have to build up inventory in the event of failure."
- "We would have to alter our process and we don't have the time or labor to do so."

With responses like these, it is evident that the value analysis team should be composed of individuals from engineering, information systems, cost accounting, and purchasing and supply. The response by the team is, of course, tailored to meet these objections one by one in order to consolidate this demand and produce economies of scale while avoiding the addition of downstream costs for one or all internal customers.

By itself, purchasing and supply should not attempt to source engineer-specified products, nor should it be held responsible for doing so. Purchasing and supply should be informed that a specific number of parts are needed and then be allowed the necessary time to inform the internal customer of the best way to obtain the parts.

In getting back to the supply dilemma between the two internal customers, suppose that the value analysis study determined that the internal customer who purchases at the higher initial price (not surprisingly, the one that the specification was originally written for) does a better job of managing the material throughout ownership of the material. And thus, this internal customer has lower overall operating and ownership costs. This idea was previously mentioned as product life cycle costing.

As a purchasing and supply management professional, the need to share such information is critical toward meeting the strategic goals of the organization. Now armed with this information, purchasing and supply can tailor this cost of ownership data according to the processes in place for that particular internal customer. Therefore, it must be explained to each of the internal customers involved in the conflict that the value analysis study evaluated the cost of ownership from both viewpoints and it was determined that the internal customer with the least amount of demand did a better job of controlling its total costs of ownership while in control of the material. Are the lower costs a result of the different processes or the different materials? Cost-benefit analysis will determine if it is less expensive to change the processes resulting from an alteration in material or if the organization will receive a lower total cost on the material purchased by undergoing this standardization. Subsequently, cost-benefit analysis will determine if a simple change in processing would be the best route to pursue. If so, each internal customer will keep his or her current supplier.

Total cost of ownership and standardization go hand in hand. Each internal customer, similar in the end product or service he or she produces, but located at different facilities, may require unique materials due to unique external customer demands. Again, a primary objective of purchasing and supply is to look for materials applicable to the standardization process. By structuring the value analysis procedure to include the review of operational costs (cost of maintenance, cost to keep the equipment in a state of operational readiness, damage and repair costs, and cost to rebuild) and not concentrate on the purchase price alone, lower supply costs will result from standardization. These savings can then be passed through to the external customer, making the organization more competitive.

Purchasing's Role: A Key Link

Purchasing and supply management has to take on the role of bonding agent to pull internal customers together and foster closer cooperation among user departments. This means that purchasers no longer function as a single decision making unit, but act as a member of a value analysis team which analyzes the costs and benefits of a decision. It's imperative that the purchaser take into consideration the overall strategic objectives of the organization and not limit his or her functions on one specific internal customer, business unit, or end-user department.

"The Future of Purchasing and Supply: A Five- and Ten-Year Forecast," a joint research initiative of NAPM, CAPS, A.T. Kearney, Arizona State University, and Michigan State University, isolated 18 initiatives that will shape the purchasing and supply function in the years to come. Many of these require cooperation among internal users. One initiative identified was strategic cost management. In a nutshell, purchasing and supply are tasked with linking critical commodity strategies to strategic supplier management strategies to produce internal buying expertise. See the diagram in Figure 1.

Purchasing as Trainer

One of the ongoing tasks of purchasing and supply is in the area of training internal customers to be better customers. Often, we solve a problem for one internal customer and then move on to the next fire. The probabilities are high that if the time was not taken to educate the internal customer as to why the supply problem occurred, the same problem will surface again.

Sharing value analysis data among internal customers is just as important as sharing purchasing objectives with suppliers. Again, standardization, with purchasing and supply

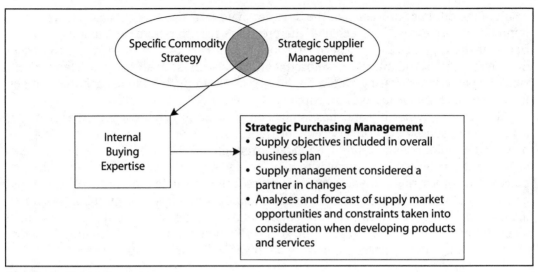

Figure 1. Strategic cost process

leading the way, is achievable by using internal electronic catalogs, and by front-end loading the current enterprise resource planning (ERP) system with third-party procurement software which can post material costs automatically to the general ledger. In addition, third-party software assures compliance with established purchasing and supply contracts, systems, and procedures. This combination of electronic catalogs, EDI, electronic commerce, and purchasing software management systems is what is known as eProcurement.

Putting It All Together

Just how would the purchasing and supply department match up the benefits they are able to offer with specific internal customers? On a generic basis, the question is often asked, is there a specific set of benefits that internal customers would like to experience from purchasing and supply? The answer is yes. In a study that outlined how to provide quality service to internal customers, Joyce Young, Ph.D., and Dale Varble, Ph.D., both assistant professors of marketing at Indiana State University, address this topic. "Purchasing's Performance as Seen by Its Internal Customers: A Study in a Service Organization" covered a questionnaire called SERVQUAL, developed by Parasuraman, Zeithaml, and Berry in which five service quality dimensions were identified to measure the gap between expectations and the perceived service provided. In a broad construct, the researchers combined the dimensions of service into the dimensions listed below:

1. Reliability—the ability of purchasing and supply to perform the promised service dependably and accurately.
2. Responsiveness—the willingness of purchasing and supply to help customers and provide prompt service.

3. Assurance—the knowledge and courtesy of purchasing and supply employees along with their ability to inspire trust and confidence.
4. Empathy—purchasing and supply should be caring and provide individualized attention.
5. Tangibles—purchasing and supply should keep up to standard the appearance of its physical facilities, equipment, personnel, and communications material.

The SERVQUAL questionnaire provides a way to obtain feedback from internal customers who listed their perceptions as to the "ideal" purchasing department. The dimensions above were ranked in order of importance—from most preferred to least preferred.

The Role of Procurement Cards

One tool that many organizations use to facilitate purchases is the procurement card. At this point in time, selling a procurement card program to senior management and internal customers should be quite easy. There are numerous successful testimonials that can be drawn upon for reference, benchmarked, and used as case builders for a proposal. Every senior management team is interested in eliminating processing costs. Many organizations that have a procurement card program in place derive the same data—around 80 percent of their total transactions accounted for only about 4 percent of the organization's expenditures. Of this 4 percent, the purchase order dollar value is under $1,000. The program advantages that purchasing and supply can highlight include:

- a reduction in paper
- a reduction in processing costs (labor, materials, and technology)
- a reduction in the supply base
- a reduction in unauthorized buying
- a reduction in one-time buys

In addition, a procurement card program assists purchasing and supply with supplier selection, contract consolidation, real-time data (in regard to expenditures by commodity) with higher-volume buys that can lead to more buying clout, and accurate measurements in regards to supplier performance.

Use of the procurement card has cut transaction costs for Union Camp (UC) on a company-wide basis by $7 million. Union Camp recently merged with International Paper to become the world's largest producer of forest products and distributor of paper, paperboard, and packaging supplies.

In 1997, UC achieved this $7 million mark with a 1997 end-of-year goal of $12 million. "We're only one year into coordinated buying, so we feel that the target is going to be achieved and exceeded," said Bill Stewart, vice president of purchasing and distribution. Use of procurement cards at UC has cut transaction costs from an average of $116 per transaction to $16 to $25 per transaction on more than 59,000 transactions in 1996. A cross-team value analysis team was formed and given the task of how to make the company's purchasing operation more cost effective. According to Stewart, the team identified nonvalue-added steps in the procurement process at Union Camp. Out of the 58 steps identified, the team determined that only eight or nine were essential. Stewart notes that buying teams are put together to determine the specifications, but once established, the package is given to one negotiator who runs with the show. Ongoing meetings, at least one every month, take place with all suppliers. The procurement cards are used by the end-user departments and not by the purchasing department. One end result produced a reduction of thousands of transactions per month into one bill.

Suppliers undergo a pre-qualification process which establishes specific levels of pricing. UC does not have to float as much credit because suppliers get paid on time and UC is able to take advantage of payment term discounts.

The procurement card program at UC has also reduced approval time. This is relevant because during research, UC found that the greater the number of signatures required on a requisition, the less any one individual felt responsible for it. And each approval was adding one extra day to the approval process. The rally cry at UC was "Death to all invoices!"

To reiterate, start by defining what percentage of purchase orders, under a certain dollar amount, make up half of all purchase orders issued. Before taking on such a project, make sure that each strategic business unit or cost center is well-defined from a financial standpoint and that the expenditures resulting from the procurement card transactions can be accurately charged to the proper general ledger account.

Control and Authority in One

It goes without saying that in order to accomplish the benefits of standardization via the procurement card, all suppliers are pre-qualified with negotiated buying discounts arranged up front. Once all the agreements are settled on paper, the card can be issued to the users. Or, if cards are already being used, but a new qualified supplier is being added, the card will be activated for that supplier once agreements are in place.

Empowerment to use the card must be the underlying mentality from top management on down or else the card will sit in the user's drawer. If you're going to trust the employee to operate a $300,000 piece of equipment, this same trust must carry over to the using of the p-card. The element of control is established by locking out nonqualified suppliers and implementing level III security features. Reports are generated that detail a failed attempt to purchase with those nonqualified suppliers. When a situation like this occurs, the end-user department who made the attempt to purchase from a nonqualified supplier can be reminded with whom the national supply agreements were made.

If executed properly, the procurement card program allows the end user to experience the freedom of purchasing at his or her convenience, perhaps from a choice of pre-qualified suppliers, while the purchasing and supply department maintains control by overseeing the program and activating or restricting certain suppliers.

The Approach to Take

The appropriate approach when working with internal customers should be set by a combination of senior management and the chief purchasing officer (CPO) relevant to organization policy and the purchasing policy. More than 10 years ago Harry Figgie, Jr. authored *Cutting Costs: An Executive's Guide to Increase Profits*. In his book, Figgie devoted two chapters to the function of purchasing and supply. One chapter is titled "Emphasis on Purchasing" and another is titled "ABC Inventory Control." And, not by coincidence, the following chapter is promptly titled "Product Redesign," with the text and explanations concentrating on standardization. In general, Figgie made the case that growth is expensive and it should be viewed as a cost-adding process, while on the other hand cost reduction costs nothing. Figgie states:

> The cost of materials can be reduced with existing personnel, and without additional investment. This is perhaps the most important message found anywhere in this text; material is almost always the area where the greatest savings can be realized, and the savings can be obtained by focusing on purchasing, aided by engineering and manufacturing.

Note how Figgie chose purchasing and supply as the front-runner to lead cost reduction, but right behind purchasing and supply Figgie identifies two internal customers of purchasing and supply: engineering and manufacturing. The book goes on to identify six specific purchasing techniques that a purchasing and supply manager could implement to add value to all operations, transcending all internal customers.

1. Use ABC product stratification.
2. Promote competition for every product/material and/or service purchased.
3. Avoid single-source items.
4. Standardize materials.
5. Negotiate effectively.
6. Insist on the highest integrity from the purchasing staff.

Figgie believed in job rotation, rotation within the department, and rotation with other user departments. Cross-functional training provides employees with the opportunity to gain a better and more complete understanding of how their own individual work affects internal customers. The tendency with engineering, Figgie notes, is the department's failure to specify "or equal" or "standard," the governing trend is to specify brand name along with designing custom parts. NIH, according to Figgie, stands for "not invented here," and is an acronym that purchasing and supply should uphold so that standardization will come about. Yet pride of authorship and design sometimes gets in the way.

Thomas J. Bassett is the corporate purchasing manager at International Total Services, Inc., which provides personnel service to the major airlines and personnel for commercial security. He is responsible for the development and administration of company purchasing policy.

The Rise of the "Chief Resource Officer"

Frank Casale

This article examines an emerging trend in the management of outsourcing and related sourcing strategies. Widespread transformation of product cycles, business processes, and management principles have given rise to outsourcing as a strategic tool, helping companies to succeed in a rapidly shifting business environment. With the advent of strategic outsourcing, a new role within the organization is developing—the Chief Resource Officer (CRO)—whose job is to manage outsourcing.

Over the past few years, outsourcing has moved up the food chain. It is no longer seen as a project-based tactical move or solely as a cost-cutting measure. Today, outsourcing is considered to be a premier management lever for achieving innovation. It provides the means to develop new businesses, products and technologies for a wide range of industries in a variety of operations, including information technology, real estate facilities, postal services and even business processes.

Driven by the rapid and significant embracing of outsourcing worldwide, companies at the forefront of this new wave are finding it necessary to assign an individual, or a team of individuals, to a dedicated role: overseeing outsourcing. After all, outsourcing deals can represent US$5 million or US$10 million a year, or even US$1 billion a year if you look at some of the latest megadeals at J.P. Morgan and DuPont.

In fact, the Outsourcing Institute (OI) estimates that, by 2001, US$319 billion of corporate resources will lie outside corporate boundaries in the U.S. alone. This represents a staggering number of services, contracts, relationships and overall risks and rewards that need to be actively managed by skilled leadership.

Companies rightfully need to take a look at who, within the organization, has the skills, characteristics and business knowledge necessary to operate at that level of authority. After careful consideration, they have discovered that they need a fresh breed of outsourcing manager, one whose functions are strategic and broad-based. This has resulted in the advent of the CRO—a new executive pioneer.

The CRO, when empowered as the focal point of all outsourcing strategy, implementation and relationship management, can ensure that all outsourcing relationships live up to expectations. The potential, where given the scope, lies in their pivotal role in organizational transformation, competitiveness, globalization, and ultimately the increase in shareholder value for their enterprise.

The Emerging CRO

Who is this new executive? It will be someone with the ability to a pull together all the varied elements of the internal organization, the external organization and the suppliers in order to work in a cohesive manner in, potentially, a virtual company.

CROs already exist, but they go by other names. Directors of external resources and vice presidents of outsourcing are some of the people whose skills, objectives and missions are to manage and deploy outsourcing to support the bottom line.

The OI has monitored, and is now spreading the word about, this powerful trend towards the CRO. As the leading source of non-biased information about outsourcing, we will help to recognize and empower this new breed of executive, particularly in the role of assessing and establishing new relationships, while also managing and monitoring existing ones.

Some of the characteristics and skills needed by a CRO have been documented. They include:

- managing different businesses,
- cost management,
- project management,
- contract negotiations,
- political and cultural consciousness,
- the ability to think out of the box, and
- being comfortable with change.

Based on information and interviews with members who function as CROs, the OI has found that the head of an outsourcing engagement team is really managing a myriad of resources at a company. Therefore, they often see themselves as internal consultants in a virtual organization.

One executive at a major entertainment company said: "We access the appropriate skills in the company, whatever skill sets we need in order to make a project happen. Because you need different people for an information technology outsource than you do for custodial or cafeteria food services, we try to access the appropriate skills in the company, bring them into a team environment, and let them work through the project."

CRO Benefits

Based on interviews with members and a recent industry forum held in conjunction with *Business Week*, the OI has chronicled some of the benefits to companies who have a CRO, or a person in that role. They include the following:

- intelligent outsourcing by way of business-add—the CRO is tasked with building value-add and is someone that has to be fully aware of, and measured on, bringing value-add deals to the table;
- more success in outsourcing—a good portion of outsourcing deals fail because the client was unclear as to what they needed, or their needs changed and the contract needed to be revised. If there are dedicated resources managing those relations, there is a greater chance of ensuring successful deliverables; and
- shorter cycles—what had been a 14-month cycle two years ago for buying and selling outsourcing is down to just under a year.

Our member executives report that one of the major success factors for outsourcing deals is ensuring that someone at the client company will monitor and maintain the contract as if it were a living entity. They say that a contract is good for establishing expectations, prices and service levels; but it is just a tool. If there is no one to use the tool effectively, the deal can get into trouble.

In addition, the new role of the CRO is to go out and find new partners and arrangements, based on the markets the company wants to enter. Companies are looking ahead at the resource content—at other organizations to resource with, what to resource and what to do on their own. The role of the individual thus becomes more important and different in terms of understanding the business, who the players are and the content is that they want to examine.

No matter which direction the wind is blowing, the potential is enormous for the CRO, as a top-level career executive, to change the way outsourcing is bought and sold. The CRO can help to enable organizational transformation, which will result in increased competitiveness, globalization and shareholder value. In short, the CRO can ensure ongoing business success.

Frank Casale is President of the Outsourcing Institute, responsible for the network of resources and programs. As co-founder of the institute, he monitors industry and business trends to identify new products and services and has been a leading advisor to many organizations in their efforts to secure internal and external resources. In addition, Mr. Casale is founder and president of Casale Management Services, Inc., a New York-based full-service provider of information technology consulting, training, networking and executive research. He is publisher of and regular contributor to The Source, *the Institute's quarterly management review and presents management conferences throughout North America and Europe.*

Part Three

Supplier Management and Development

This part of the book is about practical techniques you can employ to improve your relationship with suppliers and help assure that the quality, timing, and prices you receive from them will continuously improve. You'll find nine articles from a variety of sources, including an original piece written just for this book, all chosen to help you keep current on supplier development.

The original article is by Jon Stegner and is titled "The Long-Term Value of Supplier Training." Stegner is director of supply management planning at Deere & Company. He shares Deere's approach to setting up training programs for the many companies that actually do much of the work of producing the products Deere sells. Whether you outsource some or a lot of your work, this article provides insights into how to assure you will get the quality of inputs you expect and your customers require. You'll also find another article and perspective on the Deere approach to supplier development to conclude Part Three—"Deere on the Run" by Peter Golden.

What makes a superior supplier? The answer to that question according to a survey undertaken by *Purchasing* magazine is found in the article of the same title by Kevin Fitzgerald. Learn what your colleagues said in response to several questions about what they think of their suppliers. Use the ideas in this article to think about how to judge the traits of your suppliers and their ability to meet your needs.

An important concern for many suppliers has to do with dealing with minority suppliers. Learn more about this issue in the article "Minority Supplier Development: Supplier Consolidation Brings New Challenges" by Brian Milligan. He explores this subject from many different angles and concludes with suggestions on how to build and sustain your relationships with minority suppliers. You'll also find a number of examples of how different companies deal with minority suppliers.

Several times we've written of improving relationships with suppliers, but in the article "Critical Supplier Relationships: Generating Higher Performance" by Mary Siegfried Dozbaba you'll learn more about how to use suppliers to help you better satisfy your customers. The article includes guidelines for working with suppliers to achieve company success.

A seemingly controversial approach to supplier management is the use of awards. However, Elizabeth Baatz in the article "Are Supplier Awards Really Worth It?" demonstrates that, in fact, they are worth it. Citing research from the Georgia Institute of Technology, she shows why this is true. Those supplier companies that win awards not only do a better job of delivering the goods for their customers, they are more profitable at the same time. Learn more about supplier awards in this article, and whether they are something your company should consider.

This is a sampling of what you'll find in Part Three. Every article provides you with some useful techniques for working better with your suppliers.

The Long-Term Value of Supplier Training

Jon Stegner

In this original article, written especially for this yearbook, Jon Stegner, Director, Supply Management Planning, Deere & Company, describes the supplier training process at his company. This training is vital at Deere, which outsources up to 70% of its manufacturing. Managers have to be intimately involved with their suppliers to assure that the company gets the quality Deere—and its customers—require. How can you accomplish what Deere has? This article provides background to answer that question. And for more on Deere, see the final article in Part Three: "Deere on the Run."

Training is a powerful business tool that can help any organization meet customer needs, serve its markets, prepare for tough times, improve performance and profitability and continue to grow. And nowhere is talent and education more valuable than within the supply chain.

Let's face it: suppliers are playing an increasingly important role in the success of businesses everywhere. More and more companies are outsourcing parts and services that they once produced or provided internally. A supplier's ability to keep pace with your processes, practices and technology translates directly into quality, cost and customer satisfaction.

Deere & Company is a good example of an organization that relies on the ability of suppliers to level up to high standards and implement manufacturing best practices. We outsource about 70 percent of the manufacturing costs of our products. So great is our reliance on suppliers that we are investing significantly in supplier development, over the last year hiring more than 50 engineers to work full-time with the supply base.

This approach is based on a belief that long-term company-supplier relationships provide long-term benefits for Deere and its customers and shareholders. But long-term relationships are of no value unless both parties benefit in substantial ways, such as cost reduction and improved quality. Supplier development engineers provide technical support and know-how to suppliers, even going so far as to reside on site for weeks or months at a time if the resulting benefits for suppliers will reap significant benefits to Deere. The investment is substantial, but the expected payback is cost-downs of three to five times the additional salary and expense.

As we work with suppliers to improve their manufacturing processes, we—and they—often discover that the suppliers' employees do not have all the skills needed to effectively participate in improvement activities. For example, process mapping is a frequently-used tool that examines all of a supplier's operations from start to finish to find waste and eliminate it. It's a tool that any company can use internally to improve processes and efficiencies, yet a skill that many smaller suppliers lack. Training suppliers in process mapping gives them an important skill set by which they can continually examine internal processes and improve them.

The training that Deere makes available to suppliers is the same training that we provide in-house. So, as our supply management professionals improve their own skills, they are able to recommend to suppliers the courses that will benefit them most. In this way, training not only improves capabilities up and down the supply chain, but builds higher trust and longer-lasting, mutually beneficial relationships.

Deere & Company Training 1998-1999		
	Internal Supply Management	**Suppliers**
Attendees	2,515	5,152
Number of Classes	194	649

Consider fully the influence your suppliers have on the cost, quality and delivery of your finished products and the question changes from "Why should we invest in supplier training?" to "How could we consider not doing so?" Still, there are several things to consider before leaping headlong into a supplier training program.

Decision makers must understand the value if a program is ever to get off the ground. Supplier training is an investment of time and money, and most executives will want assurance of a significant payback.

Training must be carefully designed according to real needs—those of your company and your suppliers. Gap analyses—both within your own organization and the supply chain—can lead you to an understanding of where your time and efforts should be placed.

Cost considerations will influence the type and extent of training you offer, but there are ways to make training dollars go farther, including state-sponsored subsidies and grants.

You must be able to prove the value of the program year after year.

Where to Begin?

Supplier training begins with an understanding of the needs of your organization, the capabilities of your supplier and the gaps between the two. This understanding can emerge using structured "gap analysis" techniques that study what stakeholders want and need as well as overall organizational strategy that may or may not be reflected in any unit or departmental plan. Or, you may take a more unstructured approach that compares anecdotal and informal performance data with organizational strategy and operational plans.

One option is to conduct supplier visits and structured interviews to gather a deeper understanding of their needs and wants than is possible through a written survey alone. (See Supply Management Education Research—Questions at the end of this article.) It is important to meet with suppliers on their home "turf" to show commitment and gain the necessary understanding.

At the same time, it is important to talk with stakeholders in your company who interact with the specific supplier—for example, manufacturing, engineering, accounts payable, and others. These meetings provide an internal yardstick by which to evaluate supplier wants and needs. As gaps are uncovered, priorities can be set for supplier training courses that will most benefit both parties.

No matter how you approach gap analysis, course offerings should always result from an understanding of which supplier skills will have the most impact on your own business.

Determining the Scope of Your Training Program

If your organization is like most, there will be limits on your time, money and staff. You may need to carefully choose which suppliers are invited (or required) to participate in training.

For example, you may decide to tie the education and training program to your supplier evaluation and rating process. Or, you may focus training according to the strategic initiatives of your company. It's also important to consider the needs articulated by your own internal business units and the objectives they are trying to meet now and in the future.

John Deere has made the decision to extend formal supplier training opportunities to our "preferred" and "key" suppliers based on several rating categories. Selection of these suppliers often results from development of a commodity strategy that gives certain suppliers preference when new or increased business arises.

We focus our training resources on suppliers that:

- Share Deere's desire to be "best in class";
- Are willing to commit to an increased level of responsibility;
- Have a strong management team committed to working with Deere toward continuous improvements;
- Present a business opportunity significant enough that both Deere and the suppliers would commit resources to shared objectives;
- Are willing to share information relative to cost, technology and resources;
- Adhere to certain cost-management principles;
- Provide timely communication of process change and quality information and have a high quality rating;
- Have specific cost-reduction programs in place with costs to Deere lower than average for the commodity;

- Hold quarterly and biannual meetings with sales representatives and purchasing management as well as performance reviews by Deere.

Toward this end, we recently reorganized our own course descriptions according to the areas by which our suppliers are evaluated. Courses are now categorized under "organizational effectiveness," "cost," "delivery," "quality," "technical," and "wavelength (attitude)," allowing suppliers and Deere to more easily target specific courses to specific areas of need.

Cost Considerations

Cost is a consideration when determining the size and scope of your supplier training and education program, but it should not be the overriding one. It is possible to design supplier training programs that offer a long-term payback at a nominal cost to the supplier.

Deere offers some 60 courses each year, none with the intent of making a profit. When offered at cost, fees range from $200 per person for a course such as "Benchmarking the Best in Class" to $725 for "Win-Win Negotiations." However, there are ways to substantially reduce the cost to the supplier.

Depending on the state in which you do business, your training programs may be eligible for state assistance. Deere has received grants from the State of Illinois and works in consortiums with other companies in the states of Iowa and Wisconsin to apply state economic development funds as a partial offset to supplier tuition. Last year, Deere administered more than $1 million in state training grants for Deere and its OEM Consortium members.

The impact of state economic development funds can be maximized when companies band together to make training available to their suppliers. In Iowa and Wisconsin, for example, Deere instructors partner with their counterparts at other companies, nationally recognized training providers, regional and local subject matter experts, contract instructors and community college instructors. To maximize availability to a supplier's employees, the courses are offered throughout each state and on various dates, based on feedback and forecasts received from the targeted suppliers.

In Illinois, where Deere has obtained grants directly from the state, we've been able to substantially reduce the cost of participating in the courses we offer. As an example, the $725 cost of the "Win-Win Negotiations" course as subsidized in Illinois is as low as $335 per person.

Grants are far from corporate welfare. They improve the competitive climate in the state that offers the incentives. Deere has recently extended the Illinois program to selected Tier 2 suppliers. This training is often the only training available to smaller companies. They benefit from receiving proven programs, at less than full retail cost. Deere's Tier 1 suppliers benefit from their suppliers' new skills and efficiencies, and that value is ultimately passed along to Deere and its customers—a "win-win-win-win" proposition.

Tracking Results

If it's worth putting time and effort into designing and implementing a supplier training program, then it's worth the effort to track the results. Only by tracking performance improvements and supplier feedback can the program be honed and improved to best meet mutual needs.

If you participate in a state-subsidized training consortium, feedback mechanisms are likely built in. For example, the Iowa Business Council Supplier Training Consortium conducts a year-end survey of program participants that asks them the following questions:

- Have the training objectives of your company been met?
- Has your company made improvements in key areas (inventory reduction, scrap reduction, improved customer satisfaction, improved quality, reduced cycle time, etc.)?
- Describe the effects that training has had on those employees who participated in the training program.
- What training was most beneficial for your company and why?
- Describe the effects that training has had on your company.
- Has there been an effect on turnover rate?
- Has unit cost of items produced been affected?
- Has your sales market expanded?
- Have sales increased or decreased?
- Did wages/earnings of retrained employees increase as a direct result of participation?
- Were employee benefits affected as a result?
- Describe future training needs which your company has identified.
- What improvements could be made in future programs?
- Other comments, suggestions.

Deere uses responses to questions like these to gauge future demand for training programs and to fine-tune existing ones. Each year, we also send a curriculum projection survey to suppliers seeking to determine their course needs and projected participation. This is further refined through subsequent supplier focus group meetings that are designed to obtain a deeper understanding of supplier training needs. The results are used to develop the next year's curriculum.

It's also important to develop a course demand forecasting system that can be linked to a course completion tracking system. Our education tracking system provides summary data and information such as student participation, supplier participation, classes completed, and relevant costs.

Benefits to You and Your Company

Success, of course, is not universal. Not every supplier will learn what is taught and not every supplier will use what is learned. But in the overwhelming majority of cases at Deere, supplier training has proven well worth the investment.

Between 1995 and 1998, a tillage equipment supplier substantially improved on-time deliveries to all three Deere factories with which it does business, attributing the improvements to supplier development and training. At one factory alone, on-time deliveries rose to 99 percent last year from 20 percent four years earlier.

Another supplier expects a departmental decrease of 240 labor hours a week and backlog reduction savings of $40,000 to $70,000 per day—costs that would otherwise be passed along to Deere and our customers.

It is common for us to hear from suppliers who have participated in our training programs. That feedback provides valuable insights into what training and education can do for us and our suppliers. For example:

- "We are very proud of our accomplishments over the last four years and feel that it is not coincidental that our improvements started at the same time that our participation in the John Deere/State of Illinois Industrial Training Program did."
- "Improvements in production process and production quality are attributed to the company focusing on training and being committed to changing the culture."
- "The training that showed the greatest outcomes so far was the cycle time reduction training. We currently have three cycle time reduction teams working on identifying improvements in our process...."

For suppliers without formal training budgets—especially smaller suppliers who may pay for training out of the owner's wallet—evidence of true payback is of vital importance. For the sponsoring company, the payback is what justifies to key decision makers a continued investment of company resources in supplier training.

The combined results of supplier development on the shop floor and training in the classroom result in better quality, better delivery, reduced cycle times and reduced costs for both your company and the supplier.

To Find Out More

A number of resources are available to help get your supplier training program off the ground. For more information, consider contacting the following individuals:

Don DeDobbelaere
Administrator, Illinois Supplier Training Program
Deere & Company
309-765-5194

Carol Kulek
Industrial Training Program Manager
Illinois Dept. of Commerce & Community Affairs
217-785-6004

Mike Nance
Administrator, Iowa Supplier Training Program
Deere & Company
309-765-4599

Beth Balzer
Iowa Department of Economic Development
515-242-4754

Myrt Levin
Executive Director
Iowa Business Council
515-246-1700

Mike Bailey
Manager, Supply Management Training
Deere & Company
309-765-5631

Supply Management Education Research Questions

General Comments and Insights:

1. What is your training budget for the year?

2. What is your training goal for each employee? (Hrs/yr./employee)
   What "counts" as training? (Classes, Seminars, APICS/NAPM Dinner Mtgs., etc?)

3. Do you use individual "Training Plans" for the employees?

4. What is the role of the Illinois State Training Program\Deere & Co. for your company? (Broad-based classes, division-oriented, unit-oriented, individual person as target)

   What other training & education resources do you utilize?

   What value are you receiving from the Illinois Supplier Training Program?

   What are your expectations of the Illinois Supplier Training Program?

What went well?

What went wrong?

6. Do the course offerings meet your needs?
   What others would better serve you?

7. What prohibits or influences student enrollments from your company?

8. How do you perceive our current process? [Enabler, hindrance]
   What could be done to make it better?

9. Are the classes and training experiences making a difference on the job? How do you know?

10. How do YOU learn best? (Lecture, Hands-On, Interactive, with Follow-up, etc.)
    Describe YOUR best learning experience.

Other comments:

Jonathan (Jon) Stegner is Director of Supply Management Planning at Deere & Company, Moline, IL. Current responsibilities include strategic sourcing, cost management and supplier development for Deere's indirect materials, service and non-traditional purchases. He leads the supply management and supplier training group as well as the supply management workforce planning and development programs. Jon is a 20 year practitioner of supply management having worked for companies such as Honda, TRW, and Bush Industries.

What Makes a Superior Supplier?

Kevin R. Fitzgerald

How do companies rate their suppliers? What are companies doing to help their suppliers improve? These are just two of the questions raised in a recent survey of purchasing and supply professionals. This article presents the survey results and a few comments that provide insights into current trends in purchasing-supplier relationships.

Purchasing professionals have always wanted many things from their suppliers—high quality, on-time deliveries, strong technical support, quick response, just to name a few. But results of a recent *Purchasing* survey indicate that sophisticated purchasers now seek suppliers that not only can meet standard performance criteria, but also will:

- Work very closely with customers to raise performance levels, contain costs, and develop leading-edge technologies.
- Share data, resources, and people to overcome obstacles that stand in the way of mutually agreed-upon goals.
- Identify aspects of the buyer's operations that can be improved.
- Respond quickly to problems and emergencies.

According to the results of our survey, the vast majority of companies now track supplier performance, and more than half of these companies recognize superior performance with top-level supplier recognition, multiple-tier supplier ranking systems, or a combination of both. While only a few companies provide formal training for suppliers, most use supplier performance ratings and other data to spur continuous improvement in their supply base.

Survey results also show that it's not at all unusual for suppliers to lose top-level status due to inconsistent performance. And a good number of buyers report that distributors—especially of chemicals and electronic components—outperform the rest of the supply base. A lesser number say that metal fabricators are performing at a lower level than other types of suppliers.

	% of repondents
Do you track supply performance?	Yes = 84% No = 16%
Do you single out certain suppliers as "preferred"?	Yes = 55% No = 36% NA = 9%
Do you have multiple tiers for ranking suppliers?	Yes = 51% No = 40% NA = 9%

Beyond the Basics

We asked purchasing pros to identify common traits among suppliers that have achieved top-level status. After providing the "givens" of quality, on-time delivery, etc., many survey respondents elaborate eloquently on the type of relationship they seek most.

Top-level suppliers have the "ability to function as an extension of our facility," says one PM. "This means listening, being proactive, and having a knowledgeable sales, production, and research and development staff that can work as a team toward strengthening both our positions in the marketplace."

"Working together" and being "proactive" are constant refrains in survey responses. Purchasing pros don't want suppliers to sit around waiting for problems to happen. They expect them to anticipate potential problems and constantly prod buyers as to how they are performing, both positively and negatively.

When problems arise, purchasing pros want their suppliers to move quickly to find the cause of the problem and correct it, but buyers are willing to help. "We work closely with suppliers to solve any quality or delivery problems," says William Bailey, PM at FEMA Corp., a valve manufacturer.

Many purchasers are quite willing to share data, knowledge, and even in-depth financial information with their key suppliers. Harvey Miller of Trek Industries Inc., a producer of industrial cleaning systems, says his company opens the books for the best suppliers. "They are given everything they need to be successful," he says.

"We advise (suppliers) what is expected, tell them when they do a good job, show them where they have problems, and help them work to resolve them," says Foreman Rogers, PM at Unitron Inc., a manufacturer of AC power converters for the airline industry.

Purchasing pros also want regular visits from suppliers, and they're more than willing to send their own people out to help suppliers. "We inject our people into the supplier as required," says Jamie McDonald, PM at Square D Co.

What Gets Measured Gets Done

Sixteen percent of readers responding to our survey say they do not track supplier performance. This result is a significant improvement from the results of similar *Purchasing* surveys done in past years.

Also: Several buyers whose companies don't currently track performance indicate that they're in the process of creating systems to quantitatively measure performance. As expected, it's usually small companies with very few purchasing personnel that do not measure supplier performance.

Data from supplier rankings is used in a variety of ways, purchasing pros say. Performance data is used by many companies to reward top suppliers with annual awards, dinners, and other formal recognition programs. It's shared with other internal departments, and it's used to award new business to top-performing suppliers when possible.

No Substitute for Meeting Spec

Quality may be a "given" in some industries, but purchasing professionals continue to tell us that receiving product that meets specifications is the single most important trait in a top-level supplier, and that all too often suppliers still ship materials and parts that don't conform.

Our survey asked buyers two questions concerning most-desired supplier performance traits: What criteria are used to rank suppliers and what traits are characteristic of top-performing suppliers?

Forty-four percent of purchasing pros indicate that quality measures (conforming to spec) are used to determine supplier rankings, the highest figure of any performance measure. And 28% of respondents identify quality as a key trait in their top-performing suppliers, again the highest figure of any supplier attribute.

What specific criteria determine supplier ratings? (% of respondents)
Quality = 44%
On-time delivery = 36%
Price/total cost = 24%
Service/technical support = 19%
Technology = 6%
Others* = Less than 5%
*Innovation, problem solving, knowledgeable salesforce, communications, good management, correct paperwork

Traits of top-performing suppliers (% of respondents)
Quality = 28%
On-time delivery = 14%
Service = 12%
ISO 9000 certification = 8%
Good response/flexibility = 7%
Good management = 5%
Others* = Less than 5%
*Integrity, ethics, honesty, technology, product/market knowledge, good problem solving, customer focus

Other Key Supplier Traits

Delivery measures are used by more than one-third of survey respondents in their supplier-performance tracking systems. In past reader surveys, delivery problems were usually tagged as the most frequent problems by buyers. This survey was no exception—more buyers respond that late deliveries still occur more than any other problem.

Pricing issues continue to move down the list of most important criteria, albeit slowly. And nearly as many buyers indicate that "total cost," not price, is a trait of top-performing suppliers. As we've seen in the results of many other surveys, purchasing professionals continue to become more aware of the importance of total cost versus purchase price. They also continue to become more sophisticated at measuring total cost.

Service from suppliers also is highly valued. Many survey respondents indicate they place a great deal of emphasis on how well—and how quickly—suppliers respond to problems and emergency situations.

Also: A good number of purchasing professionals still place emphasis on having suppliers certified to ISO 9000 quality standards.

Lonely at the Top

Only a handful of suppliers in a company's total supply base reach top-level status, buyers say. It typically takes at least a year to achieve top-level status, though the range of responses to this question was very broad—three months to five years.

How long does it ususally take for suppliers to reach top-level status?
    Average = 1.6 years
    Range = 3 months - 5 years

Surprisingly, many suppliers don't stay at the top level too long. More than three-quarters of survey respondents report that suppliers have been removed from top-level status. Reasons for removing suppliers from the top level, of course, center around declining performance in many different areas. But, again, inconsistent delivery performance was mentioned by more survey respondents than anything else, followed by non-conforming parts and materials.

Have any suppliers attained and lost top-level status? (% of respondents)
    Yes = 77%
    No = 23%

One underlying reason for performance decline stands out clearly in survey results: management change at the supplier. Many survey respondents pinpoint supplier management changes—usually due to a merger or acquisition—as the reason that supplier performance tails off, and it usually happens very quickly after a merger or acquisition is finalized.

A typical response: "Management changed and service to our company dropped," according to Foreman Rogers from Unitron Inc. Another purchasing pro indicates that a change in management led to a change in a supplier's quality-control organization, and off-spec product was the immediate result. The supplier was subsequently dropped from top-level status.

More than a couple of survey respondents point out that small suppliers outperform larger ones. For example, Daniel Carrier, director of corporate purchasing at the Foxboro Co.—a manufacturer of controls and control systems—reported that "a small but quality-oriented company was bought out by a much larger company that has not yet reached certification level."

Other purchasing pros highlight the importance of good salespeople and a resultant decline in service when a good salesperson was replaced by an inferior one. Several buyers cite dishonest salespeople as the reason for dropping suppliers from top-level status.

Not a Lot of Training

To help suppliers raise their performance levels, the majority of purchasing professionals simply communicate needs, expectations, and problems to suppliers.

Only 13% of survey respondents indicate that they actually provide training to suppliers. But those that conduct training do it fairly extensively.

How do you help suppliers improve?
Communications (of expectations and problems) = 56%
Training = 13%
Plant visits/audits = 7%
Others* = Less than 5%
*Good forecasts, cost-meeting incentives

Examples: "We assist suppliers through training, both at their facilities and at our place of business," reports a purchasing manager for a company that makes equipment for the cement industry. Robert Wittel, material control manager at Aeroquip Inoac, a producer of exterior plastic automotive components, says, "We teach how to build quality into the process and remove variability from the process. We invite suppliers to internal training classes such as problem solving."

A good number of companies have recently created cost-cutting incentive programs with suppliers. Manufacturers in many industries have benchmarked win/win types of incentive programs like Chrysler's SCORE—supplier cost reduction efforts—in which cost savings are split with suppliers.

Many buyers report that they now include suppliers in design work and production planning much earlier than in the past. Generally, respondents indicate these early-involvement efforts are part of broader initiatives to work more closely with suppliers in all aspects of their business.

"We involve suppliers in program initiation, and we include them in the design process," says Clarice Johnson, manager, purchasing services at Akzo Nobel, a manufacturer of ethical pharmaceuticals. "We recognize and use their technology and expertise."

A good number of purchasing pros also report that, in an effort to help suppliers raise performance levels, they've worked hard to improve their own production scheduling and forecasts. These are areas that invariably are mentioned when suppliers are asked what they'd like their customers to improve.

Some Stand Out—Both Ways

Nearly half of survey respondents say that suppliers of certain types of products and services perform at a higher level than the rest of the supply base.

When asked what category of suppliers stood out, only one type of supplier is cited by more than a handful of survey respondents—distributors, especially chemical and electronics distributors. Survey respondents credit distributors with being very service-oriented and responding quickly to problems. Other types of suppliers that were noted for good performance included electronic parts manufacturers, fine-paper producers, and plastic-resin suppliers.

What buyers outsource (% of respondents)
  Cable assemblies   71%
  Subsystem boards   60%
  Motherboards   53%
  Subsystem assembly   42%
  Power supplies   40%
  Entire system build   16%

A lesser number—35% of survey respondents—indicate that certain types of suppliers perform significantly worse than the rest of the supply base. Several respondents indicate they're having problems with metal fabricating suppliers, which is not unusual during periods of strong economic growth due to capacity limitations and the current scarcity of experienced workers.

Are suppliers of certain products/services...
  better than the rest of the supply base? (% of respondents)
  Yes = 46%
  No = 54%
  worse than the rest of the supply base? (% of respondents)
  Yes = 35%
  No = 65%

Kevin R. Fitzgerald is editor-in-chief of Purchasing.

Competency Development in Supply Chain Management

Eberhard E. Scheuing, Ph.D., C.P.M., A.P.P.

This article presents a case study of a director of supply chain management who designed and implemented a process for developing the skills of her team. It outlines her systematic approach: assess the situation, identify core competencies, adopt strategies, decide on tactics, and establish metrics for measuring the results of the process.

Profiling the Purchasing Workforce 2000

Susan Parker was facing a significant challenge. As Director of Supply Chain Management at Biz Comm, she needed to ramp up the competency of her team to help her company retain and enhance its leadership position in a rapidly changing industry. As a provider of state-of-the-art business-to-business telecommunications services, Biz Comm had long prided itself on the professionalism of its purchasers. While Susan was justifiably proud of her team's contributions to corporate performance, she realized that she needed to transform her organization from a focus on transactions to a strategic sourcing perspective, and that new competencies were needed to successfully compete in a turbulent marketplace.

Designing the Process

To address the challenge, Susan assembled a competency development team, composed of key members of her organization. The team scoured the literature and searched the Internet for forward-looking supply chain competency models—to no avail. Susan called academic acquaintances as well as colleagues at other organizations. While all of her contacts agreed on the need for a significant reskilling of purchasing professionals, she was unable to find a ready-to-use solution.

Finding themselves in uncharted territory, Susan and her team set out to develop their own solution. After some discussion, they outlined and agreed to follow the process shown in Figure 1.

During the *assessment* phase, they examined three major dimensions:

- Organizational analysis—nature of the business, key capabilities

- Task analysis—essential tasks performed by supply management
- Individual analysis—abilities, skills, and knowledge of team members

Selected team members then visited their counterparts in several other companies and invited three professors to join them for a roundtable discussion of the purchasing organization of the future. In addition, they held a number of brainstorming sessions with other team members as well as internal customers and key suppliers. These meetings enabled them to identify a set of core *competencies* for supply chain management professionals and relate them to job levels in their organization. Key results of this effort are shown in Figure 2.

Not content with headline-type summary descriptions of the competencies needed for effective supply chain management at the beginning of the next millennium, they drilled deeper to pinpoint the skills necessary for implementation. For each of the competencies identified, they spelled out the set of skills required.

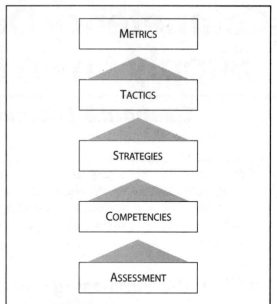

Figure 1. The competency development process at Biz Comm

Competency	Director	Leader	Manager	Buyer
Benchmarking Best Practices			✓	✓
Change Driver/Leader	✓	✓		
Coach and Developer	✓	✓		
Cross-Functional Leadership	✓		✓	
Customer/Suppler Focus	✓	✓	✓	✓
Job Knowledge	✓	✓		✓
Problem Solving	✓	✓		✓
Project Management			✓	✓
Supply Chain Analysis			✓	✓
Understands Customer Usage			✓	✓

Figure 2. Biz Comm's supply chain competency matrix (key components)

For instance, the competency "Coach and Developer" derives from varying combinations of the following skills:

A. Anticipates and strengthens individual and organizational capabilities,
B. Strengthens individual and organizational capabilities,
C. Anticipates emerging staff development needs,
D. Influences others, and
E. Pursues own professional development.

In this competency, the director needs to demonstrate skills "A" and "E" while leaders must display skills "B" through "E"; in contrast, managers and buyers are not expected to possess these skills.

Similarly, the competency "Supply Chain Analysis" was seen as involving the following skills:

A. Knows/applies analytic techniques (life cycle analysis, cost/value analysis),
B. Understands suppliers' financial conditions,
C. Analyzes manufacturing processes,
D. Applies quality analysis techniques,
E. Conducts life cycle analysis,
F. Applies cost/value analysis, and
G. Is knowledgeable about supply chain.

In this competency, managers require skills "A" to "D" while buyers need skills "B" to "G"; the director and leaders are not expected to practice this competency.

Implementing the New Approach

To put their competency development model into effect, Susan and her team adopted a number of *strategies*. First, they conducted a series of *briefings for leaders* within their own organization. To share their findings and plans with a wider audience, they also invited select human resource professionals and key customers to these briefings. As anticipated and hoped for, the briefings turned into lively discussion forums with many good questions and suggestions being presented by the participants. The results of the briefings enabled the team to further refine and sharpen its approach.

Second, recognizing that the transition from boss to coach is difficult at best, the team brought in an experienced facilitator to present several *coaching workshops*. While the emphasis in these workshops was on enabling the organization's supply chain leaders to develop these crucial skills, Susan demonstrated leadership in action by participating with them.

Third, the team invited all members of the supply chain management organization to participate in *assessment workshops*. While the team had conducted its own assessment and benchmarking effort in the process of developing Biz Comm's supply chain management competency model, it did not want to impose its own solution on the organization as a whole. Rather, drawing on its experience, its members guided their colleagues through an evaluation and discovery process that involved two major components:

- assessment of the organization as a whole by identifying its strengths, weaknesses, opportunities, and threats (SWOT analysis) and comparing them to best practices in other firms, to determine supply chain management competencies needed for the 21st century; and
- assessment of their personal competency profiles with regards to:
  - current competencies,
  - competencies needed in the new organization, and
  - personal development opportunities (competency gaps).

In the self-assessment portion of the workshops, participants were asked to spell out their own desired competency profiles with two perspectives in mind: performing more competently at their current levels and preparing for advancement to the next career level.

Having earned the designation Certified Purchasing Manager (C.P.M.) some time ago, Susan had made it clear to the members of her organization that she expected a strong commitment to continuing professional development from all of them. Accordingly, buyers were expected to earn and maintain accreditation as Accredited Purchasing Practitioners (A.P.P.s) while all other professionals needed to earn and maintain C.P.M. status. There simply was no room in Susan's organization for people who did not believe in continually improving their knowledge, skills, and performance.

Fourth, because all change is stressful, the team found it helpful to offer *competency model focus groups* as a vehicle for posing questions, airing concerns, offering answers and solutions, and generating creative suggestions for improvement. Its members were disappointed by the limited turnout at these sessions but found that the proposed changes actually received widespread support among their colleagues who welcomed the changes.

Fifth, to provide a source of reference, the team developed a *human resource guide* that offered competency comparison charts and development opportunities. This guide was released after obtaining input and approval from both the company's human resources and legal departments. It enabled all members of the supply chain management organization to verify their own current situation and plan their future development activities.

Making It Happen

To put this grand design into effect, the *tactics* the team suggested involved both the hiring of a Manager of Supply Chain Management Education and the use of a Success Factors Profile.

Having asked key members of her organization to serve on the competency development team in addition to their regular substantial duties, Susan was particularly pleased to hear them suggest the creation of the new position of *Manager of Education.* Inasmuch as her organization represents an intellectual resource of supply chain management experts to Biz Comm, its members could only stay on the cutting edge by having an individual totally dedicated to their continuing professional education. This manager would be responsible for designing and implementing professional development plans and programs for the supply chain management organization, based on an initial analysis of individual development needs. He/she would assist members of the organization in formulating personal development plans and carry out just-in-time interventions to help achieve professional development goals.

The Manager of Education would be aided in carrying out this responsibility by drawing on the *Success Factors Profile* formulated by the supply chain competency development team. The Profile was based on both its internal investigation into expert characteristics and its benchmarking visits to other firms. Combining an individual's self-assessment in the strategy phase with the assessments by his/her supervisor and peers, the Manager of Education would determine the specific factors driving success in specific supply chain management competencies and assist members of the organization in capitalizing on them.

Measuring Success

Susan and the members of her team recognized that they needed *metrics* to prove that the significant changes they had initiated were paying dividends. They instituted periodic reviews, based on key performance indicators as well as feedback from both internal customers and suppliers. At each milestone, they compared actual results to planned performance levels to capture shortfalls early and leverage growth opportunities.

A High Performance Team

What are the results of this substantial and very time-consuming effort? Susan has seen a real difference in her organization. While three members of her organization have chosen to move on, she has been besieged by inquiries and applications from Biz Comm employees in other parts of the firm who want to join her team. And on several occasions, having heard through the grapevine that exciting things were happening in Biz Comm's supply chain management organization, fellow professionals have approached her at meetings of her local NAPM affiliate to inquire about job opportunities.

Excitement is running high in her organization as its members upgrade their skills and see their efforts at self-improvement rewarded in their paychecks. So Biz Comm's supply chain management organization is right on target to meet its competency development goals at the threshold of the new millennium.

Eberhard E. Scheuing, Ph.D., C.P.M., A.P.P., is the NAPM Professor of Purchasing and Supply Leadership at St. John's University in New York. Dr. Scheuing is a member of IPSERA and an academic member of NAPM—New York, NAPM—Seven Counties, NAPM—New Jersey, and NAPM—Rochester, as well as an honorary member and honorary board member of NAPM Long Island. He has also served as a member of the Board of Trustees of the Center for Advanced Purchasing Studies. Dr. Scheuing is the founder and president of the International Service Quality Association and co-editor of The Service Quality Handbook. *He has published more than 500 articles on various business subjects and 26 books, including* The Power of Strategic Partnering *(1994) and* Value-Added Purchasing: Partnering for World-Class Performance *(1998).*

Minority Supplier Development: Supplier Consolidation Brings New Challenges

Brian Milligan

An important issue for purchasing and supply managers is understanding and working with minority suppliers. This is sometimes mandated and sometimes it just makes good business sense to do because such suppliers are the most competitive. Whatever the circumstances, this article provides a detailed review of the issues surrounding minority suppliers and will help you become current.

I t's time minority suppliers made like the phoenix, the mythical bird that emerges through fire stronger than it had been before. In order to survive in coming years, minority- and women-owned firms must band together for strength and seek out companies that want sustainable relationships with their suppliers. While they're at it, they also should consider convincing other, non-minority suppliers that they are not trying to alienate them or push them out the door.

That's the challenging dichotomy that minority- and women-owned suppliers face, according to long-term observers of minority supplier development. They must rise up to meet the changing supplier-base landscape. It's a landscape that can be fruitful if these suppliers approach it the right way.

"We have to run the gamut," says Reginald Williams, chief executive officer for Procurement Resources Inc. in Georgia and probably the best known consultant on minority business development. Procurement Resources develops and coordinates a variety of planning, research, and training programs on the subject of minority business enterprise.

There is good news for minority suppliers, as well as challenges. Across the nation, women- and minority-owned suppliers are succeeding in areas that they have never succeeded in before. They are breaking down barriers.

As these smaller suppliers continue to flourish in the automotive industry and others, they are steadily erasing the very stereotypes that once held them in check. As they flaunt their competitive spirit, the once-popular illusion that minority and women-owned suppliers provide poor-quality goods at high prices is disappearing.

Disappearing, too, is the notion that a company must hire minority- and women-owned suppliers simply because it is the "right thing to do." Each year, the social advantages of hiring such suppliers takes more and more of a back seat to the logical reasoning that the minority population is growing, and those who wish to keep a solid customer base clearly gain from using these suppliers. Essentially, the importance of social engineering in minority supplier development is being replaced by simple economic reasoning.

"It's important for our economy, and our company," says Lauren McGregor, manager of supplier diversity for the Connecticut-based United Technologies Corp., a conglomerate with an aggressive minority supplier development program. "It's like asking the question, 'Why is it a good thing to have minority employees?' It's not only the right thing to do, it's necessary to have a successful business."

Daunting Problems

But these suppliers are also running into daunting problems. Among them:

- The typically small minority- or women-owned businesses are falling by the wayside as newly merged mega-companies are drastically consolidating their supplier bases and looking for suppliers who can provide goods on a national or even global basis.
- Small suppliers, who may not be able to afford the latest in computer technology, are missing out on growing e-commerce activity.
- Minority-owned suppliers are falling prey to a kind of "white backlash," in which other suppliers resent their foothold in some markets and attribute their success to programs like affirmative action and not business expertise.

All of these things are taking place at a time when minorities are poised to become an ever-more important player in the supply chain. Minorities now represent an estimated 26% of the U.S. population. That population is expected to grow to nearly 50% during the next 50 years, according to the Milken Institute in California. The institute is a private, non-profit foundation established to support research on the detriments of economic growth. It predicts that by 2050, the U.S. population will have increased by 120 million, with 90% of the growth occurring in minority communities.

The effect of this population growth on the economy is undeniable, especially when one considers the fact that many minority communities are located in key population centers in the United States. These communities are in New York, Los Angeles, Chicago and Miami, the institute notes, resulting in concentrated areas with significant purchasing power and market demands. This translates into minority-owned businesses continuing to be one of the fastest growing segments of the U.S. economy.

But the institute notes that minorities are still underrepresented when it comes to the ranks of the self-employed. Of the total, Asians (4.4%), Blacks (6%), and Hispanics (6%) are all still behind the percent of non-minority males who own their own business. Still, the tide is turning.

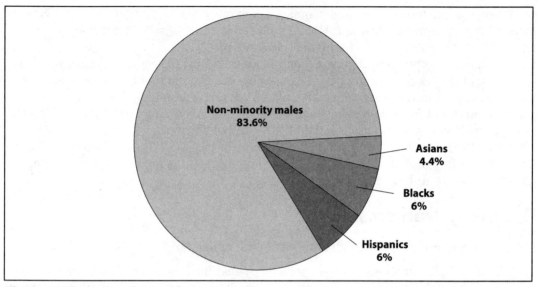

Figure 1. The ranks of the self-employed   Source: The Milken Institute

Strong Growth Rate

Trends show minority-owned businesses are growing at twice the rate of all existing firms in the U.S. Between 1987 and 1992, the number of these firms increased at a 4.7% annual rate while sales grew at a 10.75% annual rate, according to the Milken Institute.

According to the Office of Advocacy of the U.S. Small Business Administration, there were 3.25 million minority-owned businesses in 1997 alone, generating $495 billion in revenue and employing nearly 4 million workers.

By comparison, there were an estimated 8.5 million women-owned businesses in 1997, accounting for more than one-third of all businesses and generating $3.1 trillion in revenue. Their numbers, according to the office, have been increasing more rapidly than other small businesses in the economy, growing 89% during the last decade.

But any success these suppliers may be earning is coming at a price. It is the potential for hard feelings that has Williams the most worried. He says the push to bring minority suppliers on line in the 1980s led to a sort of backlash, one that caused some competitors to seethe in resentment. He notes how his company began to recognize heightened consternation among corporate clients who once believed wholeheartedly in the programs, which followed along the ideals of affirmative action. "Many on their staff had started to question whether or not such programs were necessary or even needed any longer," he says. "Many of my clients privately confided in me that they were unsure such programs were still necessary."

Some say this backlash is just an illusion. "I haven't seen it in the year and a half that I've been in business," says Scott Perkins, vice president of the Michigan-based minority supplier Trumark Steel & Processing. "I don't buy into that, and I don't believe anybody we do business with is making buying decisions solely on minority content. Because at the end of the day, it's performance that matters."

Others agree with Perkins' assessment. Representatives from prominent companies like Missouri-based Anheuser-Busch say performance is the final decision-maker when it comes to picking a supplier. Floyd Lewis, director of corporate affairs, says supplier choices are made based on a lot of factors. The most important ones, he says, are ability and resources.

"Anheuser-Busch has a philosophy and that is we want to support all communities with whom we do business," he says. "And we don't exclude any.

"Who we do business with and how much is based on a lot of factors," he continues. "One is the resources that the minority business has, that the willingness is there, and our ability to connect with those companies that can do business."

A Real Backlash

But others say the backlash is real. Some feel the icy complaints from competitors when the minority-owned businesses successfully land contacts.

"I do see it," says Specialized Packaging Group President Carlton Highsmith. "I see it in some of the medium-sized companies we attempt to sell to.

"People are a little bit uncomfortable or not accustomed to having companies of our size compete or bid for projects that we bid on," the president of the minority-owned supplier continues.

Some professionals feel more than a little bit prickled by this backlash. It harkens back, they say, to a time when women- and minority-owned companies were looked down upon simply because of the gender or color of their owners. "The assumption is that minority-owned businesses are not viable competitors," says Dorothy Brothers, national minority business development executive for Bank of America.

Complicating things further, some say the implied assumption that minority-owned companies have "arrived" and don't need special treatment is unfair and misguided. Some, like Springboard Technology Corp. President Anthony Dolphin, say minority-owned companies face a multitude of challenges that other suppliers simply would not face.

"I think for anyone to imply that minority companies have arrived is just an inappropriate way of thinking," says Dolphin, whose company is a minority-owned supplier. "The challenges for minority companies are enormous."

But this backlash is bound to exist in the competitive business world of supply chain management. Hard feelings and resentment are nothing new when companies are vying for a bid, and many representatives from a majority-owned supplier felt these feelings when another white-owned supplier made the grade.

The feelings are bound to be compounded in a landscape where companies are consolidating their supplier base. "When companies are reducing their supplier base, it knocks out not only women and minorities, but other businesses as well," says Phyllis McCarley, program director for the New York-based IBM Corp. "When a corporation has an initiative in place to make sure it has a diverse supplier base, I'm sure companies that are knocked out see it as not fair."

But sadly, Bank of America's Brothers says these feelings seem more pronounced when a minority-owned supplier is involved.

"One thing people forget is when minority-owned companies weren't part of the supply pool, there was always a majority-owned company that lost to another majority-owned company," she says. "That seems to not get as much attention."

Growth of Minority-Owned Businesses

- Hispanic-owned businesses were the most numerous minority-owned enterprises by 1997, accounting for 1.4 million of the 3.25 million total, followed by Asian-owned businesses (1.1 million) and black-owned businesses (880,000).
- The number of Hispanic-owned businesses increased more rapidly in the period of 1987-97 than did other types of minority-owned businesses: The Hispanic growth rate was 232%, compared with 180% for Asian-owned businesses, and 108% for black-owned businesses.
- Asian-owned businesses accounted for a majority ($275 billion or 56%) of the $495 billion all minority-owned businesses generated in 1997, followed by Hispanic-owned businesses ($184 billion or 37%) and black-owned businesses ($59 billion or 12%).
- From 1987 to 1997, revenues grew (after factoring out inflation) by an estimated 463% for Asian-owned businesses and 417% for Hispanic-owned businesses but only 109% for black-owned businesses.
- Asians are the most likely to have employees: nearly one-quarter of Asian-owned businesses in 1997 had employees, vs. one-seventh of Hispanic-owned businesses and one-tenth of black-owned businesses.

Source: Office of Advocacy of the U.S. Small Business Administration

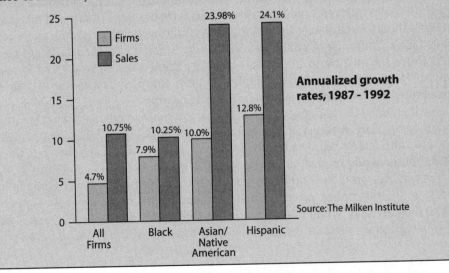

> ## Growth of Women-Owned Businesses
>
> - Over 23.7 million employees worked for women-owned firms, an increase of 262% from 1987 to 1997.
> - In 1997, there were more than 1.4 million women-owned businesses with employees who generated $2.8 trillion dollars in revenue. The number of women-owned businesses with employees grew by 46% from 1987 to 1997.
> - Revenue of women-owned business with employees grew 221% from 1987 to 1997, after adjusting for inflation.
> - There will be about 4.7 million self-employed women by 2005. This is an increase of 77% since 1983, compared to a 6% increase in the number of self-employed men.
>
> Source: Office of Advocacy of the U.S. Small Business Administration

Providing Information

Williams says Procurement Resources has begun to tackle this thought process not by challenging people, but by providing information. He says his concerns boil down to three unfortunate things:

- The majority of Americans believe incorrectly that programs in minority purchasing are designed to offer business opportunities for women and minorities regardless of the capabilities of the company.
- A large number of people believe these programs are no longer necessary, that minorities have "arrived" in the world of business.
- Many people still believe these programs unfairly take away competitive opportunities from white males who don't happen to fit into any of these protected classes or categories.

Highsmith believes one thing alone can help minority-owned companies fight the backlash. "It's going to take more companies that will compete on the basis of merit, on their excellence, and I think that is what will make it go away," he says. "We have to deliver all those things that companies are looking for."

Bringing companies around to the idea of minority supplier development remains an uphill battle, however. According to the U.S. Department of Commerce, 95% of the goods and services purchased by major corporations are still purchased from companies that are owned by white males. That means that less than 5% of the goods and services are being purchased from companies that are owned by women and minorities. "This is absolutely embarrassing," Procurement Resources' Williams says.

Consolidation Challenges

But even if some corporate players are divided on the perceived backlash, there is one area that virtually all agree on: The dramatic effort on the part of big companies to consolidate the supplier base is posing an undeniable challenge, one that won't be easily overcome by small suppliers.

If minority- and women-owned suppliers are to come out on top here, they will have to morph into something bigger.

Harriet Michel, president of the National Minority Supplier Development Council in New York, says consolidation remains the biggest problem facing minority suppliers today. The council is a constant advocate for minority suppliers.

Michel believes the minority-supplier landscape now stands at a crossroads. Five years from now, she says, the landscape will appear very different.

On the negative side, the ranks of minority suppliers could be seriously thinned during this time. On the positive side, a smaller, stronger number of joint minority-owned companies could survive.

"In the meantime, things could be very painful," she says. "But hopefully they will be coming out on the other end, and we'll have stronger companies that can compete."

Her prediction is coming true. As the corporate trend toward utilizing smaller supplier bases that provide larger supplies continues, small suppliers are falling by the wayside. This is bad news for the typically small women- and minority-owned suppliers.

Many minority suppliers are witnessing the consolidation trend now, but feel almost helpless to do anything about it. Large companies readily admit that smaller suppliers don't have access to the vast resources, and don't provide all the value-added services they need from a supplier. Their growth is limited not only in terms of resources, but also in terms of training and development.

"The supply bases are consolidating, and smaller businesses are typically not necessarily in the position to handle a national or global size contract because of the size of their business," says United Technologies' McGregor.

The National Minority Supplier Development Council's Michel sees a kind of corporate schizophrenia in this.

"They have a strong CEO statement that is committed to the small minority," she says. "But in reality, they are whacking the suppliers down."

The loss of minority suppliers can be widely felt, trickling on down from job loss to an impacted tax base. It's a situation that leaves many small suppliers feeling cheated, or at least unable to gainfully compete against larger operations.

"They are asking minority suppliers to compete with billion-dollar companies," says Frank Quintana, co-owner of Quintana Industrial Supply Inc. in Massachusetts.

The challenge is finding ways that small suppliers can become bigger, merging or otherwise forming joint ventures or strategic alliances. By joining forces, they can more competitively go after the contracts that will keep them afloat.

"The minority-owned businesses that are smaller or medium-sized are impacted by this, and they are forced to form alliances in order to go on," Brothers says. "That is the only way they are going to stay in the game long term."

Going Through the Fire

The smaller companies that do this successfully will find themselves acting like the phoenix, going through the fire and emerging stronger on the other side.

"They have to grow—through a joint venture with somebody, or creating strategic partners on a deal, or engaging in relationships that they didn't engage in before," says Courtland Cox, director of the Minority Business Development Agency in Washington.

But one thing is virtually a given: Not all of the businesses are going to make it through.

"There's going to be a shake-up," Brothers says. "I think some businesses will not exist. The smaller business will not exist.

"You will find more and more minority enterprises will in fact merge with other companies so that they can have (sufficient) capacity," she continues.

That is, in effect, what happened with Specialized Packaging Group.

Specialized Packaging Group has faced many of the challenges endemic to minority-owned suppliers. Among them were the practical problems of gaining access to decision makers in large corporations to try and coax them into buying their products. The company likewise has had difficulty gaining affordable capital for growth. But these challenges are miniscule when compared to the challenge of supply base consolidation.

To face the future with a show of strength, the team behind the Connecticut-based operation realized it would have to acquire other operations, and merge. By 1998, the company acquired the North American general folding carton business of Alusuisse Lonza Group Ltd. Now, with annual sales of more than $75 million, the company is the largest minority-owned manufacturer of folding cartons in the U.S.

To company president Highsmith, this was not just a way of acquiring more capital and power. It was a means of facing a growing world of companies that expected more and more from their suppliers. As they steadfastly consolidated their supplier base, they were looking for suppliers who could provide products and services on a national or even global level. Highsmith says Specialized Packaging Group had to become bigger in order to survive in this world. Today, the company supplies Procter & Gamble Co., Johnson & Johnson, and Colgate-Palmolive Co., to name a few.

"We are now poised to support most customers on a global basis," he says. "Through acquisition, we got to that point."

Spring Board Technology Corp. followed a similar route. The company acquired the Communication Products Repair Group from Compaq Computer Corp. in 1998. Today, the larger company finds that strategic alliances and joint ventures are liberating. These alliances allow the once-small companies to become more formidable players and seek out contracts they could only dream of getting before.

"There are suppliers who we strike strategic relationships with to go after initiatives together," company President Anthony Dolphin says. "I think it's a wonderful thing. If we are going to go after major business opportunities, I believe this is a must. Size is an issue."

But Highsmith is quick to point out that this is not as simple as it sounds. With every joint venture and acquisition, there is a risk, he says. Highsmith says suppliers that decide to go this route run the risk of joining with other firms that don't share the same values or philosophy. The unwary supplier here can also run the risk of losing control of their company in the long run.

"The disadvantage is you want to make sure you manage your growth, and make sure those you partner with share common values and philosophy of business," he says.

Cautious Ventures

But Highsmith believes Specialized Packaging has been cautious in its ventures, and the company is not done growing yet.

"Joint ventures are the most practical way to growth, especially in this environment of consolidation," he says. "We have not stopped with our acquisition. We are very much looking for additional people to acquire or do a joint venture with."

Michel says this story is one that will have to be repeated on many levels, if the small firms are going to survive. "The smaller the minority firm, the more pressure there will be for them to do just that," she says.

Michel says it would be a terrible loss if many minorities or women-owned suppliers did fold. And this loss would not be limited to having a lot of people become unemployed.

Because of their sheer nature—they are lean and hungry for contracts—these suppliers are able to offer companies long-range benefits. They offer new approaches and innovative suggestions on how to handle supply demand. "We can't believe only white people have all the good ideas," she says.

William Ender, director of the services group for the Pennsylvania-based Bethlehem Steel Corp., says he has seen this sort of innovation many times on the part of minority-owned suppliers. Bethlehem Steel developed an aggressive supplier diversity program after it was approached by representatives from the automobile industry. Today, the company actively seeks bids from minority suppliers and women-owned businesses.

Ender recalled how one such supplier, which provided paper products, saw an opportunity when Bethlehem Steel needed office supplies. The owner of the company teamed up with another company that could provide office supplies on a national scope, and soon became the office supplies supplier for the steel company. "That individual realized that if he wanted to grow, he would have to become something different," Ender says. "We see that a lot."

Michel warns that if you take away suppliers like these, you will take away their solutions as well.

"You just cut yourself off from a whole range of solutions," she says. "The process should be open so anybody can come in and make a contribution."

Michel says her organization once focused on trying to bring more and more minority suppliers to fruition. But with some 75,000 of them now teetering on the edge of extinction in the United States, the focus has shifted to keeping existing ones alive. "Now we have to pay attention to them," she says. "If you lose one, it takes a lot of time and effort to get another one up to that level."

But Michel says all is not lost. In fact, she says, some minority- and women-owned suppliers are becoming supply partners in corporations, becoming integral partners in the corporations' work. This is an important step, she asserts.

Bethlehem Steel, for example, nurtures its minority suppliers by providing mentoring programs. The programs give the suppliers a chance to meet with the company executives, scope out their needs and find places where they can grow. "It becomes Bethlehem's challenge to find out areas within these suppliers that need to be developed, provide what assistance we can, and give them an opportunity to meet with the community," says Bethlehem's Ender. "We try to find out how best to solve their needs, their need to grow, and put them in touch with people who have those areas of expertise."

But nurturing such companies is not always easy when it comes to state politics. Michel says at one time, states voluntarily created programs to assure participation by all races. But, she says, anti-affirmative action activists knocked such programs out of many states. Today, she says many states, including the city she works in—New York—don't buy into the theory of working to create minority suppliers. She believes this is a loss, putting women and minorities at an unfair disadvantage.

"If you have proof that white, male-owned businesses have 80% of the business, and they sue, it means they want 100%," she says. "I mean, what is enough?"

Overcoming Politics

But Williams says even state politics can be overcome. He says companies that have recognized this concern are trying to address it by dispelling the notion that the programs are designed as a gift for a particular racial group. Much of this effort was led by the National Minority Supplier Development Council.

But the most significant effort came from a broad-based national training program financed by corporate members of the council's chapter in Detroit. The chapter, called the Michigan Minority Business Development Council, designs and presents a series of large-scale seminars for corporate buyers. The seminars are held biannually in Detroit, and they focus solely on the business cases behind supplier diversity. They stress the business value of diverse business partnerships, instead of the government's regulatory and compliance requirements.

Perhaps because they stress these benefits, and avoid more forceful tactics, they meet with great success. Since 1991, the program brought in more new corporate members that have started minority purchasing programs than any other organization in the United States. In the long run, they launched their own supplier diversity program.

"That is significant," he says. "They commissioned us to present the program in an environment of trust, to add no more burdensome paperwork to the process and to accent the fact that each of these companies in some ways generates its revenues from a diverse consumer base who buy their products. The result has been nothing short of amazing."

Williams says in the past four years, his organization has witnessed a 19% increase in minority business utilization among the companies that participated in the program. One such company, the Michigan-based Johnson Controls Inc., became one of the world's leading suppliers of automotive parts.

Williams says the training successfully addressed the developing anxieties. It did this by appealing to all people, he says, and not just minorities. "It removes the stigma of 'us vs. them,'" he says.

Williams says there is an important, basic fact that his company is trying hard to get across. It's a motto developed by IBM. "We want our pool of suppliers to look just like the customer," he says. "In other words, if our pool of suppliers are all black, we have failed at supplier diversity. If they are all white, we have failed at supplier diversity."

Williams says minority- and women-owned suppliers today must continue to search for a way in which they can coalesce with other core suppliers and augment their strengths. By doing this, he says, they can strategically align themselves with larger partners who have stronger capabilities.

Those who don't want to play this game run the risk of not being used. Instead they are passed over, he says.

But while this may be true, he notes that many do not want to hear this advice. He says some suppliers fear he is trying to condemn the small supplier with this message.

"People don't like this message," he says. "It suggests that the little guy won't make it.

"I don't mean to say that," he continues. "But I've got to bring the real world into the process."

Developing Strategies

Once companies take these first important steps, Williams says it is important to develop them so that they become something more than one-time indulgences. Such strategic alliances foster relationships, he says, and enable both sides to develop supplier investment strategies. Williams says it is important to develop strategies, like mentor programs, that foster joint partnerships with suppliers to encourage volume increases and major service support requirements.

Williams uses the analogy of NASA, which he says is the perfect example of how a company can develop an efficient, beneficial relationship with a minority supplier. NASA, he notes, uses minority- and women-owned suppliers when it builds projects like the space station or the robot that was recently sent to Mars to collect soil samples. "NASA worked with them. And had they not done it, there would have been no minority firm that has that capability.

"Supplier diversity requires you to look at ways in which you can enhance the long-term capability of minorities in the broader marketplace," he says.

The key, Williams says, is for companies to seek out sustainable, long-lasting relationships as they try to develop supplier diversity. They must believe that these relationships will work to the good of the company.

"That term is critical," he says. "In this environment of mega-mergers, transactions and acquisitions, unless the corporate culture accepts supplier diversity as a value inherent to the corporate success and well-being, it will be relegated to being a flash in the pan. What that means is under any transition or reorganization, the program would be lost or even forgotten."

Williams uses the analogy of American Airlines to illustrate his point. It is a company, he says, that has learned how to put supplier diversity to its advantage.

American Airlines, Williams says, uses supplier diversity to enhance its marketing objective. "Certainly there is a social spillover, but the primary thrust of this initiative is to support the business objective of the company, not to provide business welfare for some individual," he says. "The unique thing this results in is a partnership that transcends race."

Michel agrees that this sort of symbiotic relationship is just what is needed. She says there is no doubt that minority suppliers will have to become stronger in order for them to survive. But for them to survive, corporations will have to work with them.

"They can't just be left in the corner by themselves," she says.

"We don't pretend for a minute that we can change market forces," she continues. "We honestly read the tea leaves and say, 'This is what it is and we have to prepare for the new world order.' What we can do is get people prepared."

Sustaining Relationships

While IBM's McCarley agrees that some things remain hopeful about the future, a strong effort is needed on the part of companies that utilize minority- and women-owned suppliers. She notes that many companies, like United Technologies, are stepping up to the fray by providing scholarships, management training programs, and quality supplier initiatives designed to help the smaller companies grow. But despite these commendable efforts, a company may be tempted to switch to a more sophisticated supplier who can provide more state-of-the-art service. This would be a mistake. McCarley says companies that stick with the smaller suppliers may be surprised at their veracity and eagerness to please in the long run.

"You have to go into these partnerships where both companies are working together so both of their goals and objectives are met," she says.

Cox believes this effort will escalate in the future. The issue will be forced, he says, by the very people who purchase the goods and services provided by companies that use minority- and women-owned suppliers. Simply put, those companies that underutilize or shun such suppliers will run the risk of being shunned by that population segment. "They (the minority community) are the final analysis," he says.

"I think things have to get better because the realities are, the minority business community will force it," he continues.

The Future

So what does the future hold for minority- and women-owned suppliers? One hope is that they will branch out, and reach into areas that they have typically not reached into before.

One such sector is manufacturing, a void that remains largely unfilled by minority suppliers. In fact, the void is so significant that it prompted Brothers to help create a furniture manufacturing company in North Carolina.

Brothers and others who watch minority supplier growth say there are opportunities across the board for suppliers in this area.

And while things are definitely improving in the high-tech industry, many still say this is a sector, along with biotech and other science-related fields, that tends to be avoided by minority- and women- owned suppliers.

Service, Education May Be the Key

Companies are consolidating their supplier bases. Contracts are harder to get, and the little guy is finding it harder and harder to compete on a national level. This makes today's supply environment very difficult for most minority suppliers.

But all is not lost. If there's a key to success for minority suppliers, it lies in their ability to find niches and provide excellent service.

It's simple advice, but it's what it's going to take for survival in a landscape where big companies are consolidating their supplier base. That's the one hidden card that Frank Quintana believes minority- and women-owned suppliers hold. It's the key, he says, that could help them gain a foothold in an increasingly challenging corporate landscape. "They can only compete if service is considered a factor," he says.

Quintana speaks from experience. His company, Quintana Industrial Supply Inc., an industrial supply company with warehouses in Massachusetts and Connecticut, watched as the corporations it regularly provided supplies for grew bigger and bigger—and harder to supply.

Quintana recalls how just a few years ago, his company had a contract with the Massachusetts-based Dynamics Research. But when the company suddenly sought a national bid for a supplier that could take care of all of its divisions, his company could not compete. Quintana says this probably cost Quintana Industrial Supply $100,000 per year in revenue. "That $100,000 is out the window, and there's nothing I can do in that situation," he says. "This happens more often than not these days."

Quintana says in theory, it should be easy for minority- and women-owned suppliers to make great gains as they compete for contracts. He says the typically smaller supplier has an edge, and can exploit this if it approaches things the right way. "Smaller suppliers can react more efficiently or quickly. They can do a lot of things much quicker than billion-dollar companies. In that way, we can outperform the Goliaths of industry."

"The key is to find areas where service levels have to be met," he continues.

To do this, he says smaller suppliers must go the extra mile. This means offering extra services to customers, such as an Internet purchasing system, distribution packages, or on-site supplier reps who manage customer inventory.

For example, Quintana notes that his company was able to impress the Connecticut-based United Technologies Corp. even after that corporation consolidated a portion of its supply base to 10 suppliers. He believes part of the reason for his success is Quintana Industrial Supply's proven promise of 24-hour delivery service.

But still, as companies continue to consolidate, Quintana says his company is finding it more and more of a challenge to drum up business. "I know when I approached other Fortune 50 companies that it's much more difficult than it was five years ago," he says. "Right now corporations are so fixed into cost-saving measures and into consolidating their supplier bases, they are all looking for more effective ways of doing business."

Scott Perkins, vice president of minority-owned supplier Trumark Steel & Processing in Michigan, agrees. "What should companies be doing better? I think they have to focus on what the customer really desires," Perkins says.

Perkins says so many companies—including those owned by women and minorities—fail to improve on basic management fundamentals as they run their business. They need to improve in small but important areas, like proper accounting, purchasing habits, or simple management. Failure to do so can hurt them as they try to break away from competitors.

In a time when supplier bases are being consolidated, Perkins says these companies can't afford the mistakes.

"You have to have the same strategies as a major company," he says. "I think in today's arena, service is the key driver. It makes the difference between an average supplier and an excellent supplier. Service is the one element that will break you away from the rest of the pack."

Dan McMackin, a spokesman for the Atlanta-based United Parcel Service, says minority- and women-owned suppliers often believe that lower prices will get them the job. But a lower price is not enough, he says.

McMackin gave the example of a Hispanic roofing company that worked for UPS. The company bid for the project, and offered something extra in the process. McMackin says the company offered to take a growing, local African American-owned roofing company under its wing and become its mentor. During this process, it would teach the other company how to acquire contracts with companies like UPS. In the end, it would provide UPS with yet another source for roofing work and supplies.

"At some point anyone can offer a lower price," he says. "You can cut your rates to the point where other companies do not think you are wise to. But if you want to differentiate yourself somehow, service is the way to do it."

It is the deeds—not the words—that grab the big company's eyes.

"Mr. Say is nothing. Mr. Do is the man," says Courtland Cox, director of the Minority Business Development Agency in Washington D.C. "People are saying a lot.

It's what they are doing that's the [important] thing."

Carlton Highsmith, president of the minority-owned supplier Specialized Packaging Group, says the owners of the typically smaller women- and minority-owned suppliers must strive to educate themselves. It is this very education that will help them gain headway in the marketplace, he says.

"They must make sure they understand the landscape," he says. "They must understand their market—what it is, what it takes to be successful—to deploy the discipline and expertise to meet those requirements, and to keep the customer's requirements as the focal point of their business."

Highsmith uses his own company as an example. The Connecticut-based Specialized Packaging Group, a manufacturer of printed folding cartons for the household, personal care, oral care, food and beverage industries, sported annual sales of $71,310,000 by May. The firm showed a 186.2% growth in revenues during 1998.

He says this sort of attitude will go a long way toward eliminating some people's perception that minority- and women-owned suppliers provide sub-par work and should be given the job for the good of society.

Brian Milligan is an editor with Purchasing.

Critical Supplier Relationships: Generating Higher Performance

Mary Siegfried Dozbaba

Relationships with suppliers have been changing—significantly. Price and quality are no longer enough. To be competitive, organizations are expecting their suppliers to do more to help satisfy customers and improve the bottom line. This article examines how companies are developing supplier relationships and the results they've been achieving.

In today's business world an increasingly large percentage of a product's value comes from suppliers, prompting business executives to realize the value in building and sustaining strategic relationships with critical suppliers. The traditional price-based relationship with key suppliers is changing, giving way to long-term relationships based on total cost, trust, flexibility, innovation, and quality. And these effective relationships with critical suppliers are helping organizations positively impact customer satisfaction, financial performance, innovation, and organizational growth.

In "The Future of Purchasing and Supply: A Five- and Ten-Year Forecast," supplier relationships were identified by CEOs as one of five "critically important" business drivers. "Supplier relationships have emerged as a priority and increasingly are viewed as an underutilized vehicle for enhancing overall performance," according to the 1998 study, a joint research project by NAPM, the Center for Advanced Purchasing Studies (CAPS), A.T. Kearney, Arizona State University, and Michigan State University. The study found that organizations will continue to outsource manufacturing, services, design, and other aspects of their business, and, therefore, "the success of many firms will depend on their ability to clearly establish external resources and competency needs and to develop two-way business and technical exchanges that benefit both parties."

A 10-year forecast included in the study predicts that:

- Strategic supplier alliances will grow in importance and number.
- Strategic supplier alliances will provide the basis for competitive advantage.
- Dominant supply chain players will increase sourcing influence at the design and development stage.

- Purchasers and suppliers will increasingly participate in joint planning and development activities.
- Organizations in the supply chain will increasingly share resources including intellectual properties, people, information, and other assets. This resource sharing will be driven by the focus on core competencies and the need to maintain flexibility.

Recognizing Its Importance

Many organizations today are realizing the importance of critical supplier relationships and looking to their purchasing and supply professionals to forge effective, strategic relationships. That was the situation recently at Delta Air Lines where a recent initiative created key relationships with critical suppliers.

At Delta, the purchasing department buys everything from airplanes to peanuts and has 105 critical suppliers—those who fall into a category where the airline is spending more than 80 percent of its purchasing dollars. Udo Rieder, former vice president of purchasing and now vice president of engineering and quality for Delta's technical operations division, says the organization decided to take a hard look at the 50 suppliers from which it bought parts on the surplus market.

"We had 50 suppliers with whom we had an arm's-length relationship that, after acceptable quality levels were met, was 100 percent price based. About a year ago, we had a change in policy where we decided to narrow those suppliers down to two," Rieder explains. He says it was a conscious decision to "consolidate buying through a strategic alliance." The suppliers chosen as critical suppliers had done business with Delta in the past. Rieder says that prior to the decision to create a strategic relationship with just two suppliers, there was an internal department at Delta "that bought those parts and it occupied most of their time." Now, he points out, "the suppliers provide on-site representatives and manage the parts that we purchase per our defined procedures and specifications. We have been able to increase savings by 50 percent for the operating unit while significantly reducing procurement process time."

Before choosing the suppliers, Delta used a supplier evaluation matrix to assess the suppliers' capabilities and made team visits to the supplier organizations. "The evaluation and visits were done not just by purchasing but all our internal customers as well. We stressed the point that this was a Delta Supplier Initiative, lead by procurement," says Rieder.

Rieder notes that a key ingredient in developing and sustaining critical supplier relationships is to have the support of senior management. "The concept happened here automatically because we have a management group that is from inside and outside the airline industry that understands the importance of strategic supply chain management. We have their absolute support. When developing relationships, it's important to get top-down buy in."

Evolving over the Years

At Rockwell Automation, a world leader in industrial automation based in Wisconsin, Mariann J. Anderson, CPIM, manager of procurement and scheduling at the packaged control products division, has seen how relationships with suppliers have evolved over the years. "Back in the 1970s, we had a traditional bidding relationship with our suppliers. It was based on who could give us the cheapest price. By the 1980s, we moved more toward single source suppliers and started having technical and business exchanges. In the 80s we also felt it necessary to have iron-clad contracts with our single-sourced suppliers. Now, in the 90s, we've developed a high level of trust. So instead of contracts we institute agreements with our critical, single-sourced suppliers. This was a natural progression in our long-term relationships. Some relationships have been in existence for as long as 20 years or more," says Anderson. "These are truly strategic partnerships."

Anderson explains that Rockwell continues to work on enhancing these relationships even further and actively look for ways to leverage suppliers in traditional and nontraditional ways. Recently, during a supplier meeting, one of the participants looked out the window and saw Rockwell adding an addition to its building. This supplier was doing the same in one of its plants. As a result, the two parties decided to look for ways to leverage construction purchases.

In another example, Anderson explains, "With our major sheet metal supplier, we are looking at ways to combine raw material purchases throughout the organization for increased leveraging power. This major supplier is Accutec, an organization that fabricates sheet metal for our products."

Anderson says sheet metal is such a strategic commodity for Rockwell that it made sense to establish and build a strategic relationship with Accutec. The relationship is a "win-win situation" for both organizations. By developing this strategic relationship, both organizations can work together to impact the bottomline and provide better customer satisfaction.

This relationship works in a couple of ways, Anderson notes. "We bring additional business to our suppliers by developing programs to help us gain market share. We can offer them larger volumes and they offer us better pricing," she says. "If we grow and expand, that in turn improves their business. It's the chicken and the egg scenario that needs to be balanced. Can we get more volume if we decrease the cost of the part, or do we need more volume before we can decrease the cost of the part?"

By creating a long-term relationship, suppliers also can better understand an organization's business and technical issues so they can directly participate in finding solutions. "You need to talk with your supplier and get them involved in your business. Let them know where you expect to grow your business and what markets you plan to explore because that's the most successful way for both of you to grow," Anderson says. "Our suppliers know our plans to expand the business globally. Through frequent meetings and strategic planning outlines, our suppliers understand the things that are important to our customers. We're looking to them for sheet metal expertise elsewhere in the world as we grow."

At Rockwell Automation, the organization solicits critical suppliers to participate in new product development. Rockwell's suppliers provide technical expertise, innovation, and product knowledge while working with their people to develop world-class products and services. The parties discuss marketing plans and supply requirements. Rockwell relies on its critical suppliers' input.

Anderson says her division labels all major suppliers as critical because they constitute "80 percent of our purchase dollars a year."

Of course, Anderson adds, critical supplier relationships don't happen overnight, but take "many, many meetings" and a commitment by both parties to work together. She believes the key issues in the relationship revolve around quality, price, inventory, customer service, technical expertise, flexibility, and delivery. "And despite good relationships, we never rest on our laurels; we are always looking for ways to do better."

For example, Anderson says Rockwell now wants to get more involved in Accutec's supply chain management and raw materials pricing. "Tough market conditions force us to look for new and creative ways to take the cost, but not the value, out of the product. Because of the relationship that's already been established, such a step is possible."

Taking cost out of a purchased part is one way to impact market growth; however, it's not the only way. "Through our relationship with Accutec, it became apparent that many of our resources were tied up working on quality or delivery issues," says Anderson. "Accutec now provides an on-site person who is an integral part of our factory floor. Providing this service enables Rockwell to use our resources more efficiently and provides Accutec with direct feedback on quality, delivery, and customer issues. Monthly reviews are conducted (and driven by Accutec) to measure performance in delivery, quality, inventory turns, communications, packaging, and count accuracies."

Anderson continues, "Accutec has really become an extension of our business. Our competitors have high volume sheet metal fabrication capabilities within their facilities, we don't. This situation could be a real competitive disadvantage. However, Accutec understands this element of our business and, through their increased flexibility and low cost products, we make this a competitive advantage. They have the expertise and capital to invest in this commodity. We rely on Accutec to provide this core competency, truly making our strategic partnership a win-win situation for us both."

Trust-Based Relationships

Relationships with critical suppliers are usually trust-based partnerships, according to Timothy Laseter, vice president for Booz-Allen & Hamilton and the author of *Balanced Sourcing*. The first step in developing a relationship is to understand the value of the relationship and what each side hopes to get out of it, Laseter says. "The problem with some organizations is they don't identify what they want to get out of a long-term relationship. The relationship is not the objective itself. The objectives are issues such as product development, supply chain integration, cost reduction, or streamlining delivery."

He also noted it's important to properly identify which supplier or suppliers an organization considers critical. A critical supplier normally is segmented around how much is purchased and the critical nature of the materials purchased from the supplier. However, that's not always the case.

For example, Laseter says, a mid-size steel stamping organization could view the steel mill from which it purchases steel as a critical supplier. But in reality, there is little chance of developing a strategic relationship with that supplier because the mid-size organization won't have much leverage with the large mill. A more important supplier would be a steel service center that buys steel in bulk and holds inventory for the mid-size organization. Laseter says the chance to develop a relationship is much better and that the supplier and the steel stamping organization should view the relationship building process as critical.

While trust is an important foundation for a strategic critical supplier relationship, Laseter notes that "translating trust into action requires three things: mutual dependence, goal congruence, and knowledge of competency." He points out that:

- Mutual dependency occurs when both parties understand that cooperation is necessary for each organization to succeed.
- Goal congruence occurs when common, aggressive goals drive both sides to achieve maximum benefit from the relationship.
- Assessment of supplier competency typically covers four broad areas: capabilities, cost structure, risk factors, and relationship potential.

Tapping into Supplier Knowledge

Once a critical supplier is identified and a relationship is forged, one of the key advantages to the relationship is the ability to tap into a supplier's expertise and get the supplier involved in innovation—a move that benefits both parties. Eddie Reynolds, director of corporate supply management for Sun Microsystems, Inc., in Palo Alto, California, says one of the most important aspects of a good supplier relationship is supplier involvement in new product development. "I think our critical suppliers are people who have more knowledge and expertise so we bring them in very, very early. We bring them in at the conceptual stage and they come with ideas about cost, product availability, and delivery time."

Reynolds says good relationships with Sun Microsystems' critical suppliers have resulted in suppliers providing "resident planners and engineers who live in our buildings. They have access badges and they sit down regularly with our designers." He estimates that there are about 23 resident planners and engineers from Sun Microsystems' critical suppliers throughout the organization.

Reynolds says that early supplier involvement and continuing participation in innovation are possible in effective supplier relationships. "The key is everyone needs to have a stake in the game. In a typical supplier situation without a good relationship, at the end of the day there is no sense of a long-term commitment."

Using critical suppliers' expertise has been an essential part of relationships forged with suppliers at Herman Miller Corp., an office furniture manufacturer. Blaine Vortman,

---

Trends to Watch

Professionals trying to obtain information on the future are always interested in trends. But what are the trends as they relate to supplier relationships? A few have been identified based on the interviews and research for this article.

- Executives are asking purchasing and supply professionals to influence customer satisfaction through supplier relationships.
- Since supplier training programs are effective at developing strategic partners, there appears to be an increase in establishing solid training programs for key suppliers.
- Part of a strategic supplier relationship involves offering critical suppliers larger volumes in return for better pricing.
- Technical exchanges and sharing expertise are key by-products of a critical supplier relationship.
- Organizations are paring down the number of suppliers in an effort to work on relationships that can benefit both parties.
- Before choosing critical suppliers, organizations are conducting thorough supplier assessments or audits.
- Performance-based contracts are being used with critical suppliers to enhance relationships and to make those relationships work better.

---

commodity manager for Herman Miller, says the role of one of its critical suppliers was integral when the organization was designing its Limerick Chair, a stackable chair whose design won awards at the Office Furniture Industry Trade Show. Vortman says the organization relied on the expertise of Metal Standard Corp., an organization that performs tube bending and stamping for chairs, to the extent that Metal Standard employees were meeting weekly with designers, engineers, manufacturing, and purchasing department representatives from Herman Miller. "They were involved in design and development," Vortman says. "They helped us to make sure the chair was manufacturable and their input was sought every step along the way. They helped us decide where to bend the chair and how to design brackets. They even invested in a robot welding unit for the chair program," he adds.

More than a year ago, Herman Miller rolled out Supply Net, a Web site for critical suppliers that provides information about demand, inventory, receiving, and invoicing. Vortman says that Bay View Industries, another Herman Miller critical supplier, is fully integrated into Supply Net and also was instrumental in helping the organization refine the site.

"They download demand figures, schedule parts on their manufacturing floor, and pull out receiving reports through Supply Net," Vortman explains. An auto-vouching portion of the program creates payments automatically for Bay View parts received at the end of each week. "The entire system has drastically reduced manual work and errors have gone away," Vortman says. Another important aspect of Supply Net is that it has shortened supplier leadtime from order to delivery from five to four days. "My division of Herman Miller has a short leadtime from order to shipping, two weeks maximum," Vortman explains. "Our goal is to reduce that time to five days, and I believe that will be possible with Bay View's help."

Some Basic Guidelines

One of the first steps in creating a relationship with a supplier is to define key business drivers—those aspects of your business that set your organization's direction. Business drivers for a hotel, for example, might be customer service, reducing expenses, or keeping employees happy. Once you determine your business drivers, the next step is to identify the critical suppliers that share your direction, and will actively help support you. In establishing a relationship, there are four key factors to consider:

- **Permanence**—This is not a one-time transaction; it's a mutually beneficial long-term relationship. It's not business today, but business for the future. Organizations today are moving away from a transactional to a relationship culture.
- **Participative**—In a relationship, suppliers will be participating in activities at your organization ranging from strategic planning to design to engineering to supplying materials for new products. There is a sense of belonging. It's alienation (looking at something from a distance) versus camaraderie ("I'm a part of this.").
- **Principled**—The relationship is built on trust and both parties are going in the same direction. What is important and determines success for one party similarly affects the other. Principles are shared. Both parties are aligned toward similar goals.
- **Partnering**—This relationship is a partnership; both sides can understand the other's viewpoint and can examine issues from each other's perspective. If it hurts one side, it will hurt the other sides.

Once the relationship is established on those key factors, there is an ongoing "Circle of Success" involving four steps:

- **Guidelines**—Develop guidelines and understand the needs of both sides. Have common objectives and create measurable expectations.
- **Maintenance**—Continually reinforce guidelines and look for additional opportunities to enhance the relationship. If there is a problem or concern, work together to make improvements. In most cases, it is better to work out problem areas than to change suppliers.
- **Feedback**—Establish on-going performance measures. Make it clear what will be measured and how it will be measured.
- **Learning and Improving**—Create a wheel that keeps on turning and getting better. Find out what is working and what is not working, and make needed changes.

Information provided by Ricardo R. Fernandez, C.P.M., A.P.P., managing principal for Advent Group Inc. in Miami, Florida.

Supplier Relationships and Customer Satisfaction: The Connection

Vortman adds that developing relationships with critical suppliers also directly affects customer satisfaction—one of its most important end results.

He explains that one of Herman Miller's customer satisfaction goals is to deliver goods quickly to its customers and that customer goal is well understood by its critical suppliers.

"We must have suppliers deliver fast to us to fulfill our promise to our customers. They understand the customer satisfaction goal. All our efforts toward shortened leadtimes relate directly to our efforts to fulfill promises to our end customers. Because of excellent relationships with suppliers we work together to keep customers satisfied," he explains.

Rockwell Automation's Anderson agrees that customer satisfaction is a key by-product of effective supplier relationships. The suppliers "understand the importance of our commitment to customer satisfaction and it becomes their commitment as well. We all exist because of the end customer."

In addition, Vortman believes it's important to respond quickly to critical supplier concerns and to focus on showing appreciation for a job well done. "A critical supplier with whom we have a relationship came through recently in a pinch. We needed some parts with lightning speed and they delivered for us. I called them later and hosted a pizza party at their organization," he says. It was a small gesture that went a long way to building on an important relationship, he adds.

Supplier relationships are becoming more important because about 50 percent of the cost of goods is in materials and an increasing number of these materials are coming from outside the organization, according to Michael W. Gozzo, president of Total Business Consulting Group, Inc. in Aptos, California. "The thrust in business involves concentrating on what an organization does best. There is a shift from performing certain activities in a business, so suppliers are playing a more important role. And the relationship with critical suppliers is key because those suppliers have a major impact on my business," he adds.

Before creating a relationship with a critical supplier, Gozzo says it's important to understand three basic principles—the need to do more today with fewer resources; the cost of doing business is affected by time; and quality affects the bottomline.

"Time is the primary element involved in purchasing. Time is the direct line to the bottomline," he says. "There is a correlation between improved availability and improved sales: shortened leadtimes affect sales and when time is reduced, all aspects of inventory are reduced."

Quality should be a primary principle with suppliers because it will affect the relationship, Gozzo adds. "There is a significant cost associated with poor quality. When something comes in wrong, someone has to do something to make it right and that involves extra time and extra costs."

Once these basic principles are understood, a relationship can be created with critical suppliers. Gozzo suggests some basic guidelines in developing a relationship:

Using Suppliers for Creativity

Once a relationship is established with a critical supplier, a major advantage for an organization is tapping into that supplier's expertise and getting him or her involved in new product development and innovation.

Some tips for making the most of supplier expertise include:

- Work with suppliers proactively. Let them know where you are now and where you want to make changes.
- Get the supplier involved early on in product development and design—even when you are just conceptualizing.
- Use the supplier's knowledge about the availability and cost of parts and supplies when designing a product.
- Invite supplier designers, engineers, and others to meet with your organization's employees to work together on innovation.
- Be up front with key suppliers and ask what they would do to improve processes, or even issues dealing with improved relationships.
- Reward your critical suppliers for being innovative. Establish a program that motivates critical suppliers to feed you innovative solutions.
- Never discount an idea. Even if the idea isn't practical, one idea can germinate creative thought in other directions, helping the group to eventually come up with solid solutions.

Information and insights provided by Michael W. Gozzo, president of the Total Business Consulting Group, Inc., in Aptos, California, and Timothy Laseter, vice president for Booz-Allen & Hamilton in New York.

- **Orientation**—Help suppliers understand the impact they have on your business and then understand the role they play.
- **Assessment of suppliers**—Conduct a thorough review or audit of what they do. Review with them what needs to be changed and help them make those changes.
- **Measurement**—Constantly measure critical areas such as time, quality, and on-going performance.
- **Continuous review**—Monitor and make changes throughout the relationship.

Endorse the Performance-Based Contract

Lorrie K. Mitchell, relationship manager for BellSouth Telecommunications, Inc., in Atlanta, Georgia, says she agrees with the idea of measuring and reviewing suppliers and is a strong believer in performance-based contracts with critical suppliers. "When you have a contract, that means you have a relationship. With performance-based contracts, there is tracking and a good deal of communication." Communication is one of the most important aspects in developing a relationship with suppliers—or, for that matter, anyone, she adds. "We should all be relationship managers. If you are doing more than a one-time transaction with a supplier it's worth it to invest in developing a relationship."

Relationships with critical suppliers mean you can "get to know what makes them tick, what makes them lose money, what makes them make money, and what are their margins," and that helps in creating performance-based contracts. In creating such a contract, Mitchell says, you start by sitting down with all parties involved and asking them what are the key areas to make all of us successful. She adds that the contract must look "at the big picture" and address five aspects to monitor: (1) customer satisfaction, (2) product or service quality, (3) end-user satisfaction, (4) process performance, and (5) unique issues related to your situation. Then the purchasing manager must decide how to measure the performance, how to document it, and how often performance will be measured and reviewed.

Mitchell says the contract is more than a score card; it's a vehicle for communication between the organization and the critical supplier. "If the score card shows that the five-day delivery period was only met 89 percent of the time instead of 95 percent of the time, that does nothing for me. I want it to lead to a discussion; let's find out why this is happening and how we can make changes. The important thing at this point is that you have a relationship with a supplier who wants to work with you," she says.

Once you have formed a strategic relationship with a supplier, Mitchell says, "you don't hit the streets with a request for proposal (RFP) every time you need something because you work that relationship and you immediately look to your supplier." She says a relationship allows "you to be an advocate for them and in turn the supplier looks for ways to make you successful."

Purchasing and supply professionals agree that their department plays a key role in developing and nurturing critical supplier relationships. Most say that purchasing should take the lead in driving the relationships but, once established, they should act only as a coordinator, allowing supplier engineers to talk with organization engineers and designers.

Total Business Consulting Group's Gozzo noted that sometimes when procurement takes the lead it forgets to integrate all other departments. "It's important to orient the entire organization to the principles involved in this relationship. The pitch should be that this is an organization program, not a materials management program. Once established, procurement then acts as an intermediary and a liaison, but always remember to continue to lead."

Take the Reins

If purchasing is not taking the reins in critical supplier relationships, they are creating an opportunity for future problems, says Alan L. Duckworth, director—product development, supplier evaluation, and management services for Dun & Bradstreet. "Purchasing needs to be forward-thinking in this process. Developing expanded relationships with the right key suppliers is of paramount importance. Developing the information to identify the best partner is the first crucial step. The question that has to be asked is 'Are you leading or following?'"

Duckworth says not only is it important for purchasing to lead the relationship, but also to demonstrate to upper management that such relationships have a positive affect on the bottomline. He says the purchasing department at Dun & Bradstreet went through a reengineering effort in the recent past. A large part of that effort involved selection of a few large dollar expenditure categories and created sole source relationships with suppliers in areas such as temporary agencies, travel services, and printing. "Those changes produced dramatic financial savings so we were able to quantify to our CEO a significant and tangible financial impact," he says. "In the first wave of restructuring, savings from these cost avoidance measures contributed about 3.5 cents earning per share which really put our purchasing department on the map for adding value to the corporation. The dollar amount saved in year one was $8.1 million."

Gozzo adds that there is a definite connection between cost of materials and services and the bottomline. "This has to continuously be in front of the CEO." He says it's the job of a strong purchasing and supply professional to make those issues known to the CEO or the chief financial officer.

To make relationships happen, and in turn let the CEO know how it affects the bottomline, develop a certain skill set, suggests Delta Air Line's Udo Rieder. "You absolutely have to have a skill set in your [purchasing] organization, otherwise these programs can fail. You need people with a comprehensive knowledge about how business works. A strong procurement person should have finance, technical, and analytical skills, and must be both a team member and a team leader."

Supplier Training: Not Just for Educating

Not only will a training program for suppliers assist in making the suppliers' business more efficient and better aligned to your organization's needs, but the program creates better working relationships and better understanding. Deere & Company, in Moline, Illinois, which has a longstanding training program for its employees, began focusing on supplier training seven years ago. Deere expanded supplier training programs to 65 course offerings and expects enrollment of 9,000 supplier students for 1999.

Deere offers supplier training programs to its supply base. Suppliers regard the programs as effective and cost efficient. Several states have recognized the importance of training for small suppliers and provide financial support that reduces supplier costs for training their employees. The annual assessment of supplier results continues to support the idea that these programs make suppliers more effective and more profitable.

In two states, Deere participates in a training consortium with other OEMs. Deere also partners with community colleges for skill-based classes such as computer training and blueprint reading.

Following are some aspects about Deere's supplier training program that can be followed by other organizations in establishing such a program:

- Partner with states and other organizations to help minimize costs and to take advantage of expertise.

- Leverage your organization's employee training programs and available public courses.
- Allow suppliers to define their needs and choose the appropriate courses. (Deere expects suppliers to use the Achieving Excellence program for supplier performance ratings as an important tool in identifying needs.)
- Initially, it may be difficult to define payback. Develop relevant, well-taught classes, however, and suppliers will recognize the payback and continue to participate.
- Minimize the administrative burden placed on suppliers. For many small suppliers, we are their main source for effective training.
- Conduct classes at supplier sites if possible—this is especially helpful to small businesses.
- Continually look for feedback and involve suppliers in defining how to improve the program.
- Establish a nomination process with the buying community for choosing suppliers who can participate.
- Offer a wide variety of courses to meet supplier needs and keep content fresh and forward-looking.
- Look for new ways to deliver programs.

An important outcome of supplier training programs is improved relationships, a better understanding of an organization's philosophy, and increased understanding of an organization's processes.

Information provided by Art Rowe, C.P.M., project manager for Deere & Company Supply Management Training Programs in Moline, Illinois.

Mary Siegfried Dozbaba is a freelance writer based in Chandler, Arizona.

Are Supplier Awards Really Worth It?

Elizabeth Baatz

The answer to the question in the title of this article, as you will quickly see, is "yes." Citing a comprehensive study undertaken by two professors at Georgia Tech, this article explains how those companies that measure and reward the quality of performance by suppliers reap substantial benefits over those companies that don't. Still, the award process is not a panacea, but one part of the process of facilitating greater quality and cooperation between companies and their suppliers.

Crystal sculptures, gold-plated trophies, and walls full of plaques proclaiming "Supplier of the Year" adorn the hallways and lobbies of more American corporations than ever. But does the pomp and circumstance that surrounds supplier awards produce real benefits? Or are the awards simply feel-good accolades aimed at producing "warm and fuzzy" feelings for winning suppliers?

According to top purchasing executives and award-program planners, supplier awards and the recognition banquets that come with them are far more than just an excuse to sponsor a fancy dinner and hand out a few trinkets to business associates. For many, a supplier awards dinner at the end of the year represents a final step in an intense journey that involves rigorous data collection under the TQM (total quality management) rubric as well as multitudes of meetings with suppliers and purchasing's internal customers. Top purchasers view their awards programs as integral parts of their overall efforts to improve total quality.

Listen to what Robert Rudzki, chief procurement officer at Bethlehem Steel in Bethlehem, Pa., has to say about supplier awards: "Our awards program [started in 1997] is simply part of a continuum in our strategic sourcing process that began a few years earlier." That process saved the company $100 million in costs from 1995 to 1998. "The entire emphasis in our strategic sourcing program is on continuous improvement, and the awards reflect this," Rudzki asserts.

Furthermore, as a three-time winner of General Motors' supplier award, Rudzki says folks at Bethlehem Steel didn't need a lot of convincing to understand the motivational pull that an awards program can provide.

Another example: At Intel in Santa Clara, where arguably one of the most rigorous and hotly contested corporate supplier awards program resides, the Supplier Continuous Quality

Improvement (SCQI) award has been won by only three companies since 1990. "Once a supplier enters the SCQI program [which entails a ISO 9000-type certification process, scorecard metrics, and a strategic improvement plan], they see systemic rewards," says Deirdre O'Connor, materials quality manager for corporate purchasing. So why have an award?

"Human nature requires recognition. When someone busts their hump, we want to recognize that," says O'Connor, who emphasizes that the top Intel award is very difficult to achieve.

GOOD Programs Pay Off

Using awards to provide recognition and motivate suppliers is all well and good, but bottom-line contribution is what separates value-added events from simple fun and games. According to a recent study of 600 publicly traded winners of corporate supplier awards and

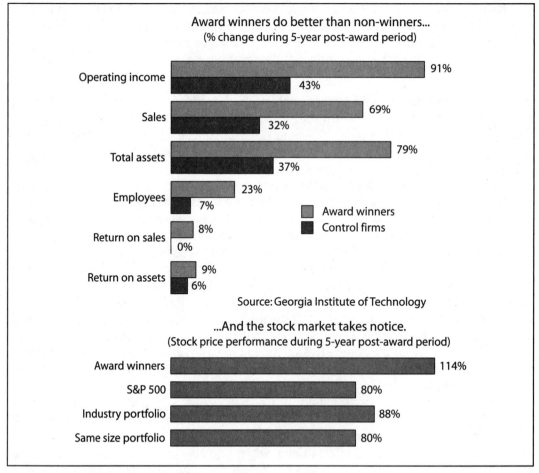

Figure 1. The benefits of winning awards

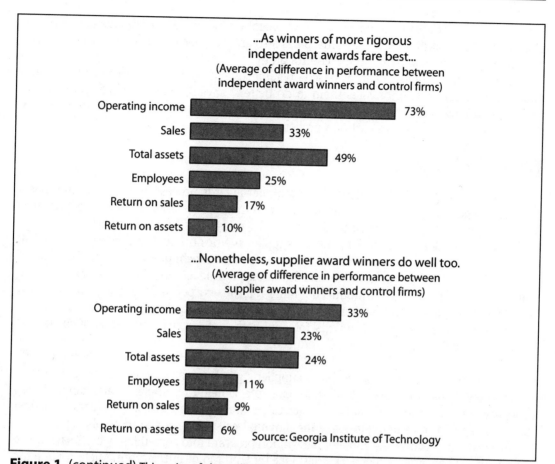

...As winners of more rigorous independent awards fare best...
(Average of difference in performance between independent award winners and control firms)

Operating income	73%
Sales	33%
Total assets	49%
Employees	25%
Return on sales	17%
Return on assets	10%

...Nonetheless, supplier award winners do well too.
(Average of difference in performance between supplier award winners and control firms)

Operating income	33%
Sales	23%
Total assets	24%
Employees	11%
Return on sales	9%
Return on assets	6%

Source: Georgia Institute of Technology

Figure 1. (continued) This series of charts illustrate some key results from a study entitled "Impact of Total Quality on Financial Performance: Evidence from Quality Award Winners" by Professors Kevin B. Hendricks and Vinod R. Singhal. The study, published in August 1998, may be obtained by contacting Professor Singhal at the Georgia Institute of Technology by e-mail at vinod.singhal@mgt.gatech.edu, by phone at (404) 894-4908, or by fax at (404) 894-6030.

independent quality awards such as the Baldrige Award and the Shingo Prize, award winners on average do garner measurable, statistically significant gains. In a five-year period after achieving an award, prize-winning companies clearly outperformed a control group of non-winners in a number of accounting measures. For example, operating income among the winners rose 91% while the control group's income rose only 43%. (See charts, Figure 1.)

Still, all award programs are not equal, cautions Vinod R. Singhal, a professor of management at the Georgia Institute of Technology and co-author of the award winners study. "Supplier awards are usually not as tough as the Baldrige," says Singhal. Even so, according to Singhal's analysis, winners of supplier awards outperform the control group by significant amounts, albeit winners of independent awards perform better than everyone. For example, winners of supplier awards managed to grow operating income 33 percentage points higher than companies that did not win awards. Sales also grew 23 percentage points faster for supplier award winners compared to the control group.

"Even when a supplier award is based on subjective analysis, the simple fact that a supplier is getting feedback motivates them to do better," says Singhal. "Initially very subjective in nature, over time you will find supplier awards programs become more objective. Supplier award programs are part of a process."

Works in Progress

Indeed, most companies characterize their supplier awards process as a journey that has a long way to go. That's so even in automotive manufacturing, where supplier awards have been a staple in the procurement toolbox since the mid-1980s or even earlier.

For example, General Motors maintains supplier metrics on quality, service, and price to determine its prize winners, and just this past year added a technology metric to the process.

Chrysler, which has awarded several hundred plant-level gold Pentastar awards each year for more than a decade, introduced a more rigorous corporate-level platinum Pentastar award five years ago. The tougher platinum award recognizes less than a dozen top performers. Corporate role model awards for suppliers that excel in one area, such as cost reduction or quality, are also being introduced.

At Honda of America Manufacturing, the supplier award metrics have been recently adjusted to account for the impact that a supplier's glitch might have on consumer satisfaction or safety. Thus a supplier of brakes, for example, is held to a stricter award standard than a supplier of radio knobs. And at Ford Motor the entire supplier recognition program has just undergone a major revamping to make the judging less subjective and more objective.

"We wanted to evolve the supplier recognition program into something better," says Gregg Sherrill, director of supplier technical assistance for Ford Motor in Dearborn, Mich. "When the award was not objective, then even internal people would wonder why a particular company won an award." As a result, Ford has worked to put in place a metrics program to drive an awards program that tracks key performance goals. To be considered for a top award, a supplier must qualify first at a "Q1" level of performance based on joint automotive quality standards similar to ISO 9000. Then the supplier must hit six target metrics which include a delivery rating, cost rating, and parts-per-million rejects of 60 or less.

The end result will be three levels of awards based on the number of targets that have been hit and other factors. "We haven't decided on names for the awards yet," says Sherrill. "But we expect the first of these to be handed out in March 1998."

Making the awards process more objective isn't for the faint of heart, however. Udo Rieder, vice president of purchasing for Delta Air Lines in Atlanta, says maintaining data integrity can be a big, big chore. For example, at Delta, supplier metrics track unit pricing this year versus a year ago. But if the color of the part changes, then the part number in the information-systems database changes too and tracking the price change suddenly gets dicey. "If there are enough problems like this, then we have to go in the system and manually fix the data, which can consume a good deal of the buyers' and managers' time," says Rieder. "We want to spend less time gathering data and more time on working to improve performance."

Delta just gave its first supplier awards on October 14, and already Rieder is talking about the challenge of meeting the next generation of cost metrics. "Instead of measuring unit costs, we want to measure total costs." So if a new jet engine blade costs more per unit, but saves the airline money over time via more efficient fuel consumption, "then the supplier should not be penalized in its award scores," says Rieder.

Metrics Based on Strategy

Devising the appropriate metrics upon which to base the supplier awards is where the rubber meets the road. "The data determine the winners," says Cesar Penaherrera, vice president for Honda of America Manufacturing in Marysville, Ohio. "And the data should coincide with your strategy," he says. "At Honda, the award mirrors our QCDDM process of sourcing. [QCDDM stands for quality, cost, delivery, development, management.] We have formalized this approach in the last three to four years."

Likewise, Delta's supplier awards program also mirrors its strategy of controlling costs and increasing productivity. "With 61% of our operating costs coming from purchased goods and services, and only 36% of the total costs flowing through purchasing," says Delta's Rieder, "we are trying to develop a performance-based culture under a foundation of solid metrics throughout the entire company." So every month, not just prior to an annual award dinner, all buyers in procurement, all internal customers, and vice presidents get a report with suppliers' scores.

Of course, in the information-systems driven awards programs, suppliers have access to their scores every month too. At Delta, suppliers see their own scores and also a ranking of where they fall relative to similar suppliers. At Ford Motor, many of the metrics used in the awards program are delivered continuously to suppliers through a confidential page on the Internet's World Wide Web.

Purchasing's demands for high quality and low cost may be communicated more quickly via the Web, but old fashioned face-to-face contact also remains a key intangible benefit of running an awards program. Most companies—Bethlehem Steel, Miller Brewing, and Honda to mention a few—make a point of delivering the awards not only to upper management at a fancy banquet, but also to the workers on the shop floor.

"It's one thing for the boss to say that quality is important, but another thing entirely for the customer to come out and say it," says Jerry Schiedt, corporate purchasing director for Miller Brewing Company in Milwaukee. "When we actually visit a plant to present an award to the folks who made the award possible, then we build a relationship with the company and the folks on the floor who do the work to ensure the quality of the products we buy." A little thank you can go a long way to successful partnerships. Adding in a speech and session of autograph signing by Miller Brewing Company spokesman Rusty Wallace, a famous race-car driver, doesn't hurt either, says Schiedt.

Investors See Value

Race-car drivers, however, won't convince another constituency that running a supplier awards program is a good idea. The key driver of the trend to corporate America's increasing demand for supplier recognition comes from upper management. And the ultimate driver of the trend for all public companies, of course, is Wall Street. Luckily, says Professor Singhal, Wall Street does recognize the positive link between winning awards and performance.

According to Signhal's study, companies that won awards enjoyed a 114% hike in their stock price over a five-year period. Meanwhile, the Standard and Poor's 500 index rose only 80% over the same period and a portfolio of stocks from industries that match the award winners' jumped only 88%.

Gathering upper-management support for a supplier awards program is a critical first step for anyone who wants to begin a supplier evaluation and awards program, says John MacLean, vice president of purchasing for American Airlines in Fort Worth, Texas. "I came from the automotive world, so I was accustomed to supplier performance measurement systems. The first thing we did: Built a business case for our Supplier Excellence 2000 program, went to 15 key officers of the company and had them sign a document stating that they saw a need for SE2000 and would support the program."

"After gathering management buy-in, we knew that creating a rigorous and meaningful supplier awards program would take time," says Irma Todd, manager of supplier quality for American Airlines. "We started down the road to a supplier award in 1993. The first report card wasn't issued until 1996 and the first awards weren't handed out until 1997."

Even after all the time and money has been invested in developing supplier performance metrics and meaningful awards, corporate supplier awards programs still need more work, says Jeff Trimmer, director of operations and strategy for procurement and supply at Chrysler. "The awards are nice and the supplier can get a big display case of these things," says Trimmer. "But what the supplier really wants to know is 'am I going to get more business from this award?'" Traditionally, the relationship between the amount of business won and the award won has been unclear, although companies like Miller Brewing, Chrysler, and Delta Air Lines make big efforts to advertise the winners.

But "a supplier should be able to track the relationship between its performance and its share of the business," says Trimmer. Maybe in the next generation of supplier awards, the link between the sculpture in the trophy case and the supplier's bottom line will become clearer. But then again, as long as Wall Street appreciates the award winners, then at least the public companies are getting the award that the chief executive really desires.

Elizabeth Baatz is an editor with Purchasing.

OEM Cycle Time Reduction Through Supplier Development

James L. Patterson, *Ph.D., C.P.M. and J. Dougal Nelson*

This case study examines the steps that a manufacturer took to decrease cycle time, reduce production costs, and improve the quality of its products. It describes how the company's Integrated Supplier Development team provided its suppliers with in-house resources and engineering expertise to help the suppliers make their work processes more efficient and cost-effective.

Background

Accent Equipment is a U.S.-based industrial equipment OEM with multiple manufacturing, assembly, and distribution facilities located throughout the world. A largely decentralized company, Accent is divided into several operating divisions, each focusing on a specific type of equipment.

Over the past several years, Accent has found it increasingly difficult to compete effectively in many of its market segments because of significant global competition. Several of its product lines are highly seasonal, meaning that the bulk of production takes place in a relatively narrow timeframe each year. After addressing internal production scheduling effectiveness and reducing manufacturing costs, Accent decided to evaluate the leadtimes of key suppliers. This analysis revealed component leadtimes that were often measured in terms of months and weeks instead of days and hours. Accent determined that these leadtimes were excessive and also recognized that they resulted in higher pipeline and work-in-process inventories, thereby increasing Accent's manufacturing costs.

In 1995 one of Accent's divisional engineering managers decided to approach several of the division's strategic suppliers and "sell" them on the advantages of utilizing the engineering and process management expertise to address cost and cycle time reduction. A pilot program involving 16 suppliers was approved by Accent's management. These targeted suppliers agreed to share any cost savings derived from the supplier development projects with Accent Equipment. Based on the success of the initial projects, a seven-member project team, the Integrated Supplier Development (ISD) group, was formed in 1997 to assist the division's key suppliers by providing in-house resources and engineering expertise in implementing manufacturing cost and cycle time improvement projects.

Accent's suppliers are typically closely or privately held businesses employing 100 to 300 workers. As such, any investment for process or manufacturing improvements reduces income or cash flow to the owners. In other words, these owners require an immediate return on their investment if they are going to participate in Accent's supplier development projects. The ISD group decided early on that the best way to approach the key suppliers would be to focus on cycle time reduction, knowing that incremental improvements in both cost and quality would be achieved in addition to reduced cycle time.

Time-Based Competition

Traditionally, OEMs have tried to reduce leadtimes by focusing on production efficiencies, keeping machines running at capacity, and concentrating on timely delivery. This traditional approach has been replaced with a strategy of time-based competition at Accent Equipment. Higher quality, greater responsiveness to customer demand, cost reduction, and the development of technologically advanced products are some of the external benefits enjoyed by manufacturers competing on time-based capabilities. Internal benefits include simplified organizational structures, shorter planning loops, faster reaction to changes in demand, and better communication, coordination, and cooperation between functional areas.

One of the major forces driving the search for more effective supply chain management practices has been the need to reduce the time required to provide customers with product. Reduction in cycle time can often be attained by adopting a quick response manufacturing strategy. This approach significantly reduces the time required to move goods and materials through members of the supply chain to the ultimate customer.

Effective use of quick response manufacturing (QRM) involves developing entirely new ways of fulfilling customer demand, with an emphasis on minimizing leadtimes throughout the supply chain. Managing time instead of cost requires major organizational restructuring of the production function. Restructuring for QRM typically involves three changes:

1. Movement from functional process-based factory layouts towards product-oriented layouts.
2. Use of simpler, local production scheduling procedures as opposed to complex, centralized scheduling systems.
3. A shift toward smaller batch sizes.

In helping to design product-oriented supplier plant layouts to achieve QRM objectives, Accent Equipment often recommends that the supplier implement cellular manufacturing. Cellular manufacturing is a process design that links together all necessary operations to manufacture product families, or groups of similar outputs. Thus, work flows smoothly within the cell by eliminating unnecessary physical movement around the shop floor. Using cells allows resources to be dedicated to specific products while being located in close proximity to the entire process. The net result is a reduction in set-up time and work flow time, thereby decreasing supplier leadtime.

Production scheduling also benefits from cellular manufacturing. In a traditional process-oriented layout, any given job may visit a number of different work centers. In order to schedule production, an individual work center would have to be told which job needed to be processed next. Due to the high level of process visibility experienced in cellular manufacturing, each cell is given the responsibility of scheduling its own production to meet delivery schedules, ordering materials, and coordinating activities between cells. This results in simplified planning and control through shorter leadtimes, reduced work-in-progress inventories, and shorter set-up times.

The final change in implementing cellular manufacturing focuses on the benefits of smaller batch sizes. When smaller lot sizes are processed, the manufacturer enjoys reduced work-in-process inventories and simplified material handling. Since each individual cell is completely responsible for a family of closely related products, the number of set-ups is minimized. Also, implementing cross-trained employee teams within the cell can attain additional improvements in productivity and cycle time reduction.

Supplier Development

Accent Equipment's divisional ISD group has implemented a number of supplier development/cycle time reduction projects. In managing these projects, ISD has identified several challenges that must be addressed to improve supply base performance. The first challenge is the need to adopt an attitude that the supplier is functionally the same as any internal department. Therefore, it should rate the same attention and focus on performance improvement of its operations.

Secondly, the ISD group had to develop in-house expertise in the effective use of process management tools such as process mapping and total cost analysis. Process mapping, as practiced by Accent Equipment, involves the use of a cross-functional team drawn from the targeted supplier to identify and suggest improvements to existing processes. The Accent ISD project manager functions as a supplier development consultant and facilitator.

This approach has achieved several benefits for Accent. One such benefit is the attainment of commitment by the supplier's management team. It is not an issue of "Hi! I'm from Accent Equipment, and I'm here to help you!" The supplier must be convinced of the direct benefit to its manufacturing operation and the potential return on investment. Also, having a variety of supplier functional personnel actively involved in the change process improves buy-in at the user level as well.

Keys to Cycle Time Reduction Through Supplier Development

Many of Accent Equipment's suppliers are small and medium-sized manufacturers, under significant competitive pressures to reduce overhead and trim operating costs. As part of that focus on cost reduction, they have reduced employee headcount to bare minimums, focusing only on day-to-day operations. Therefore, developing and implementing new strategies, such as QRM and cycle time reduction, are often beyond their capabilities and available expertise. As one ISD manager stated, "Traditionally, OEMs like Accent Equipment have communicated tactical performance expectations to suppliers and left them to their own means to achieve them. Only when acute purchased-part quality or delivery problems arose have OEMs tended to provide suppliers with technical or people resources, and then only grudgingly. More often than not the solutions ended up being short-term and viewed by suppliers as self-serving and beneficial only to the OEM customer."

Accent Equipment's approach to cycle time reduction via supplier development incorporates several phases. First, the Accent ISD project leader coordinates an in-depth analysis of the supplier to uncover manufacturing efficiency problems and their root cause. The ISD consultant then helps develop a comprehensive plan to fix the problem, not just address its symptoms. The final step involves assisting the supplier in implementing the plan.

Afterwards, the ISD leader co-evaluates the plan's execution to ensure that the problem has been successfully resolved. These development services are provided at no cost to the supplier and Accent and the supplier split any cost savings. If no cost savings result from an ISD project, then no price reduction from the supplier is expected.

Tips for successful Integrated Supplier Development (ISD):

- Do: Make sure the supplier agrees to the basics of the project.
- Don't: Be judgmental of supplier practices or processes.
- Do: Shoulder your fair share of the work.
- Don't: Focus on price as the primary project metric.

A major challenge regarding ISD projects concerns how project results are measured. According to Accent Equipment, supplier development metrics consist of three levels: cost-based price reductions, tangible benefits, and intangible benefits. Cost-based metrics are actual price reductions based on a given ISD project's "annual recurring savings," i.e., actual dollars saved through process and cycle time improvement. Although the savings recur over time, they are only counted once, in the first year, to assess ISD's performance.

Other than direct price reductions, measurable and tangible benefits accruing to Accent include improvements in other tactical supplier performance metrics such as higher quality, improved on-time delivery, and reduced overhead.

Tangible improvements available to the targeted supplier typically include the following:

1. reduced manufacturing cycle time
2. improved productivity
3. reduced indirect labor
4. reduced material handling
5. more productive use of floor space
6. improved material yield
7. reduced rework
8. less expediting time

9. less overtime
10. reduced overhead structure.

Accent also recognizes certain intangible benefits from their cycle time reduction/supplier development projects. These are more difficult to quantify but nonetheless provide long-term savings. These benefits include increased customer responsiveness, reduced supplier turnover, and longer-term buyer-supplier relationships built on trust and mutual understanding of needs.

Targeted suppliers also experience a variety of intangible benefits from completing cycle time reduction projects, such as:

1. increased flexible customer responsiveness
2. easier-to-manage shop operations
3. improved employee morale
4. fewer manpower constraints
5. development of a new culture focused on continuous improvement
6. long-term buyer-supplier relationships built on trust and mutual understanding

Results of Accent Equipment's Cycle Time Reduction Program

Accent Equipment has achieved phenomenal improvements in cost and leadtime reduction. At several key suppliers, leadtimes have declined more than 90 percent. Because of the attendant benefits involved with the ISD projects, Accent has received price reductions of up to 15 percent.

Supplier	Original Leadtime	Revised Leadtime	Percent Change	Annual Price Savings	Project Staff Days	Savings per Staff Day
A	13 days	2 days	87%	$164,000	80 days	$2,050
B	32 days	2 days	94%	$77,000	34 days	$2,279
C	19 days	5 days	74%	$122,000	47 days	$2,606
D	17 days	3 days	82%	$137,000	11 days	$12,495

Figure 1. Improvements in leadtime and annual return per project staff day

The return on investment for Accent Equipment is calculated by dividing the annual price reduction by the number of project staff days spent working with the supplier. The group's performance is measured by the initial (first year) incremental annual price savings generated, i.e., each year's price savings is offset against the current year's expenses. The ISD group's goals are as follows:

- Minimum goal: Offset the group's current annual operating budget of $1 million.
- Target goal: Save at least $1,000 per staff day per project.
- Stretch goal: Offset the group's current annual operating budget of $1 million by a factor of 5:1.

A typical ISD supplier development project addresses approximately one-third of the supplier's factory capacity with the first project requiring Accent to invest an average of 60 staff days. Due to learning curve effects, the second project typically takes only about 20 staff days from Accent, and the final project at a given supplier involves a minimal number of staff days because the supplier recognizes the benefits and takes ownership and initiative of the development process.

Other significant supplier performance improvements that have resulted from completed ISD projects are:

- PPM defects improved from 14,400 to 300
- On-time deliveries improved from 74% to 99%
- Effective capacity increased by 25%
- OSHA reportable accidents reduced by 90%
- Work-in-progress inventories reduced 67%
- Factory floor space reduced 45%
- Rework reduced 37%

In addition to reducing leadtimes by 75 to 95 percent while improving product quality and reducing costs, suppliers have noticed improvements in employee attitude and morale. As one supplier observed, "The voice of the customer is much more powerful when communicating expectations than the internal view. Our operators now feel that they are part of an exciting process and that their opinions have value." Employees became more involved and more effective. Union involvement in and acceptance of the development process also increased. Rather than having the process forced upon them in an adversarial fashion, union management decided to collaboratively implement the plan.

Cycle time reduction has been an important focus of the supplier development program at Accent Equipment. Price reductions, supplier leadtime reductions, and improved communication with strategic suppliers have all been achieved by helping its key suppliers to improve their manufacturing operations. Implementation of QRM techniques, such as cellular manufacturing, has been a key component of Accent's supplier development activities.

James L. Patterson, C.P.M., A.P.P., is an assistant professor in the Management Department at Western Illinois University. He spent nearly 20 years in manufacturing and logistics positions and has published articles in various publications, including the International Journal of Purchasing and Materials Management, *the* European Journal of Purchasing and Supply Management, *and* Purchasing Today®.

J. Dougal Nelson is a graduate of Western Illinois University in business management.

It's Time to Power Up

Ricardo R. Fernandez, C.P.M., P.E.

How often do you review your suppliers' agreements? How do you do it? The author of this article contends that a powerful tool for managing the performance of suppliers can be the performance contract, which "does for suppliers what a good performance management and measurement process does for internal processes." He offers a few tips for measuring and reworking those agreements into effective performance contracts.

Performance Agreements

Imagine this. An organization has set a goal to have 95 percent of its purchasing and supply professionals attend a class on advanced negotiation skills. When the organization achieves the target, it decides to celebrate. However, the purchasing management forgot one key element: to measure their true intent. What did they want to achieve? Is it enough to have the employees attend an educational course or a purchasing-related seminar, or should the department measure the level of application and new skills of all the purchasing managers that attended the course? The department expected purchasers to learn something new and implement their newly acquired skills, but they didn't establish an appropriate measurement up front to ensure that result.

For example, they could have measured the total life-cycle cost of new contracts versus old contracts, and they could attribute at least part of the improvement or deterioration to the skills learned in the negotiation course and applied on the job.

The same type of performance measurement you would apply internally to employees should be applied to your critical suppliers. One good example of this procedure involves a public utility that recently outsourced its information systems processing function. The utility developed a set of metrics that measured the supplier's performance against the utility's business goals. Rather than stating the supplier's standards of performance in terms of hours of user support or hours of maintenance support, they stated the need for all mainframe applications to be available more than 99.8 percent of the time, and that all nightly processing jobs be successfully completed at a rate of 99 percent. It was left to the supplier to determine the necessary resources to achieve those levels of performance. The value that one supplier brought to the table over another in this case was its experience and success with the information systems function; they were able to perform this function at a lower cost than the utility. These savings become a shared benefit for both parties.

Building Flexibility

One very powerful tool in the management of supplier performance is the performance contract. This tool does for suppliers what a good performance management and measurement process does for internal processes. In fact, when it's well linked with the key business drivers of the organization, it will help manage the supplier and also help the purchasing and supply manager achieve higher levels of internal performance. Performance contracts have been used by many purchasing departments to get a better handle on their most critical purchases and especially for their long-term supplier relationships. Now that these contracts are in place and in operation, managers find themselves needing to rework the contracts for various reasons. Either the contract performance has surpassed the original expectations, the original goals have changed, or the contract has failed miserably. In any case, the contract needs to be reworked to better represent the current expectations. Although this is sometimes difficult to do, performance contracts must be set up to facilitate this rework possibility if it presents itself in the life of the contract.

Performance contracting can help a purchaser develop performance measures that never existed, making it easier to manage their processes as well as serve the supplier. By providing the information that both parties need to make fact-based decisions, they form a basis for systematic mutual process improvement. If, for example, a purchaser helps a supplier improve his or her process and thereby provide better products and services to the purchaser, the supplier benefits too. Now the supplier has a process that can be marketed to other purchasers which, in turn, increases the supplier's sales, market share, and profits. This is another reason why it's important to be able to easily rework our performance contracts. The contracts need to be flexible enough to allow for growth in the purchaser/supplier relationship they helped to establish.

A performance contract does not need to be developed for every procurement transaction. It's most appropriate when outsourcing functions or for the procurement of mission-critical products or services. The question should be, "Does this product or service directly tie in to the corporate key business drivers and is it in need of improvement?" If the answer is "yes," then it's best to develop a performance-based contract in which the supplier understands the expectations and that the financial rewards are tied to his or her performance level.

Reworking Your Performance Contract

A performance contract needs to be a living and breathing document. It needs to take on a life of its own. As one prepares such a contract, one needs to consider the possible outcomes and the expected consequences. Once the contract has been implemented, purchasing professionals should conduct periodic reviews as shown in the next section. These reviews will lead to conclusions that imply a need to rework the contract:

- The original performance goals are being met or surpassed and new ones need to be or have recently been set.

- The purchaser's competition is performing better and the purchaser expects his or her supplier to improve performance and contribute to the organization's competitive advantage.
- Market or labor conditions have not allowed the supplier to perform according to plan even with the best willingness and efforts to do so.
- Industry benchmarks or index studies have proven that current performance expectations are not in line with industry standards.
- Specifications were too strict.

The above are only a small representation of the reasons why performance contracts may need to be reworked. One can take the following steps to ensure that the rework process goes well:

- Consider the needs of both parties and the responsibilities that were originally negotiated. Are they still realistic?
- Examine the measurements and the measurement process for accuracy, timeliness, and common understanding. Were they set to reasonable expectations and within the capabilities of the supplier and the purchaser?
- Look at the status and results of past agreed-upon corrective actions.
- Explain the need to rework the contract to the supplier.
- Request input from the supplier on the need to rework the contract.
- Discuss strategies that will eliminate the current problems with the existing contract.
- Make changes that are mutually agreeable and beneficial to both parties.

Before performance contracts are reworked, purchasers must develop accurate processes in the design stage of the performance contract. Purchasing and supply managers should then ensure that a periodic measurement process is in place.

Periodic Measurements

One must review the measurement process to effectively rework the contract. The process could be providing incorrect information. The design of the data collection system may not be capable of providing better information.

Design performance measures to easily determine any gaps between expected performance levels and actual levels. Use these measures periodically to identify the extent of gaps and their priority for improvement. Select the highest priorities, then analyze the underlying processes to improve them and consequently improve the performance measures.

Timely scorecard updates that measure the financial aspects of performance as well as the key drivers of the contract are essential. This is to ensure that the information available is current and actionable and will help prevent any problems. The measures should be upstream so that they can be leading indicators of the health of the process, thereby allowing for more timely prevention rather than reaction. Be prepared to make adjustments throughout the length of the contract for changing conditions.

Completing the Cycle

Following the steps mentioned above will help ensure a complete system, with feedback mechanisms, that will contribute to the growth and the strength of long-term relationships.

This will lead to improvements in the supplier's processes and the purchaser's processes, cost reduction, service levels, and product or service reliability. Ultimately, the end user will be more satisfied, thus increasing revenues for both the supplier and the purchaser. All of these factors support and improve trust, and create stronger ties between the supplier and the purchaser. Benefits derived from process improvements could be shared between the parties of the contract, further improving the partnership. The performance contract is the key tool that facilitates this relationship and creates an environment for the mutual benefit of the supplier and the purchaser.

Ricardo R. Fernandez, C.P.M., P.E., is managing principal for Advent Group Inc. in Miami, Florida.

Deere on the Run

Peter Golden

E-commerce and the Web may receive featured billing on the supply management strategy marquee these days, but John Deere's Horicon, Wisc., facility has another scenario for streamlining its supply chain. At this plant, Deere's managers have partnered with suppliers to re-engineer their manufacturing process and achieve dramatic results in the reduction of cycle time and costs. This article explains how Deere has worked with suppliers and internal teams to make these improvements.

D eere-Horicon is expanding its supply management program around a new and innovative win-win supplier development design. In the bargain, it's getting two thumbs up for shortened supplier order fulfillment times and consistent purchased part price reductions, with an extra star for enhanced quality.

So what's the payoff for suppliers whose program admission ticket includes the requirement that they reveal otherwise confidential information about manufacturing costs, capital investment, and production plans? They can expect reduced manufacturing cycle times, improved margins, and a better understanding of manufacturing operations. Armed with proof-of-concept metrics from Deere-Horicon's process mapping sessions, suppliers are able to re-engineer operations with confidence and clear expectations of potential payback.

The key to this apparently impossible-to-achieve scenario is an academic/industry/public sector cooperative effort. Quick response manufacturing (QRM), a new approach to manufacturing cycle-time reduction, is playing a starring role. Preliminary reviews and results are generally positive, with a knowledgeable, enthusiastic cadre of supporters applauding what may qualify as a new supply management paradigm.

Teeing Off on Delivery Times

The first scenes in this story focus on an ever-increasing appetite for the game of golf. In the early 1990s Deere-Horicon experienced a greater than anticipated leap in demand for its golf course fairway and greens mowers, in large part due to a sharp upward trend in golf course openings. But responding to new demand put extra pressure on suppliers who were at the time adjusting to revisions in Deere-Horicon's manufacturing strategy.

With Deere-Horicon placing even greater reliance on suppliers' just-in-time capabilities, the need to rethink supplier relations was accompanied by the pleasant, if not entirely unanticipated, realization that assisting them would bring new benefits to Deere-Horicon, too.

For bedknife manufacturer Fisher Barton, Deere-Horicon's offer to analyze and re-engineer operations in the name of flexible, more efficient order fulfillment was at first greeted with skepticism. Bedknives, which are precision, multi-edged grass-cutting blades, must be produced to substantially higher tolerances than their first cousins, lawn mower blades, in order to achieve the short, uniform turf heights required by golf course greens keepers.

To benefit from Deere-Horicon's program, Fisher Barton would have to break long-standing original equipment manufacturing (OEM) supplier taboos, among them opening its books and manufacturing methods to intense customer scrutiny—in this case the Deere-Horicon supplier development team.

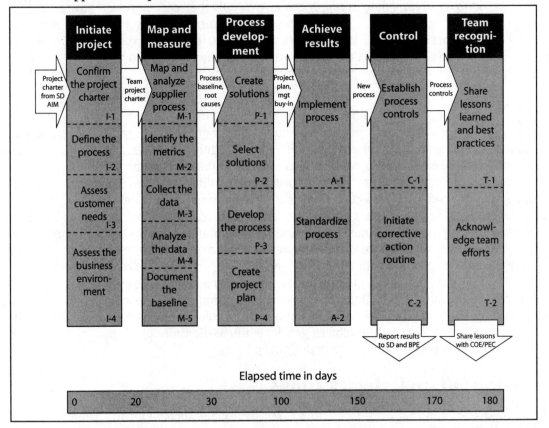

Figure 1. Implementation of Deere-Horicon's supplier development program relies on systematized approach to process re-engineering

QRM: Had Yours Today?

While the QRM acronym may conjure up notions of nutritional standards, quick response manufacturing in fact embodies a different regimen, one that promises better health for indus-

Queuing up for Quick Response Manufacturing

At first, there wasn't much to go on. Back in 1984, academic research suggested that a branch of algebra called queuing theory might have application in modeling manufacturing environments, but no one had actually tackled the demanding task of creating a robust, packaged program that would run on newly available PCs. Larry Ho, a senior Harvard faculty member and an internationally recognized authority on the mathematics of manufacturing systems, thought the approach worth pursuing; Rajan Suri, Ph.D., a collaborator and faculty colleague with a specialty in manufacturing systems engineering, took the first tentative steps to transform the academic literature into an analytical software package.

Working from an office just across the street from their classrooms in Harvard Yard, Ho and Suri founded Network Dynamics, Inc. and began to develop a PC-based application that would quickly convert inputs for critical manufacturing variables into outputs in the form of dynamic models of the manufacturing process.

Both men felt that issues such as lot-size planning, staff utilization, and machine availability were being swept under the rug by MRP and early ERP systems. Another type of manufacturing analysis, simulation, appeared to be too complex and lengthy to yield the rough-cut models they needed for quick and easy solutions to leadtime reduction.

But queuing theory, developed early in the century as a capacity management tool for the Stockholm telephone exchange, appeared to have real promise. Yielding just enough detail to make useful decisions from a relatively limited set of inputs, it quickly yielded the data needed for analyzing discrete manufacturing systems, especially those used to produce the highly configured assemblies associated with custom manufacturing.

While such an approach would not reveal the detail of simulation or create a control system with the breadth of ERP, it could identify quickly where constraints were creating bottlenecks in production and graphically represent shorter production scenarios. They termed this approach rapid modeling technology to distinguish their method from often-cumbersome simulation and MRP. Unlike other academics who left the classroom to exploit their technological breakthroughs, Ho and Suri recommitted themselves to teaching and publishing, with Ho continuing to make substantial contributions to manufacturing systems theory.

Suri, looking to confirm his ideas with working manufacturers while maintaining academic ties, took a professorship at the University of Wisconsin. His academic work and consulting increasingly focused on reducing leadtimes and the resultant benefits that could be obtained, an approach he began to characterize as quick response manufacturing.

To further test his ideas about leadtime reduction, he founded the Center for Quick Response Manufacturing at the University of Wisconsin's Madison campus. Suri also began work on a book manuscript based on both his industrial consulting experience and new lessons learned at the Center. Published by Productivity Press, *Quick Response Manufacturing* is now in its second printing.

Two associates from Harvard's doctoral program in applied mathematics have also joined Network Dynamics, which is now located in Burlington, Mass. Gregory Diehl,

Ph.D., became director of software development. Christos Cassandras, Ph.D., a professor of electrical and manufacturing engineering at Boston University, heads up special projects, including assignments with industry and government groups.

trial enterprises. Central to QRM is a relentless quest for flow time reduction. Deere-Horicon QRM practitioners use "manufacturing cycle time reduction" as a descriptor for this process. Within standard QRM terminology as developed by Rajan Suri, Ph.D., "leadtime reduction" is the terminology of choice. For practical purposes, both terms are functional equivalents.

At the University of Wisconsin's Center for Quick Response Manufacturing, IIE member Suri leads a consortium of roughly three dozen manufacturers intent on using new strategies to gain competitive advantage. There, Deere-Horicon has joined such diverse industrial organizations as Trek Bicycle, Ingersoll Cutting Tool, Alcoa, and others as a member of the Center. And while participants use QRM for a number of purposes—most notably manufacturing cycle-time reduction —none has implemented it so widely within a supply chain as Deere-Horicon.

As an easy-to-understand yet comprehensive approach to facilitating improvements in supplier operations, QRM is providing new insights into supply management strategy accompanied by tangible results in the form of sustainable benefits. Deere-Horicon calls this new method of working with suppliers "time-based supply management."

Strengthening the Supply Chain

Some years ago, John Deere realized that it had to focus on what the company does best: building farm, lawn, and construction equipment. During a major strategy realignment, the powers that be decided to rethink traditional notions of vertical integration and stop making many of the parts required for assembly of John Deere products. At the same time, supplier rolls were being cut in half. More parts from fewer suppliers meant fewer part-supply alternatives: Individual supplier delivery and quality performance would be critical.

But if Deere was to succeed in this new venture, it would need assurances that timely delivery, quality, and cost would match its own high standards (i.e., being able to work without costly pre-built inventory yet with heightened levels of process control to meet Deere's rigorous quality standards).

Paul Ericksen, supplier development manager at the Deere-Horicon facility, realized that the steep improvement curve defining his organization's expectations would present a challenge to vendors. Only a dramatic reconception of manufacturing strategy would equip them to meet new standards. An inventive supply management paradigm was needed, one combining the best of ERP, JIT, and continuous improvement. Beyond the doors of the Deere-Horicon facility, suppliers would need to adjust to new demands requiring both simplified approaches and standard applications for analyzing and solving a variety of unfamiliar problems.

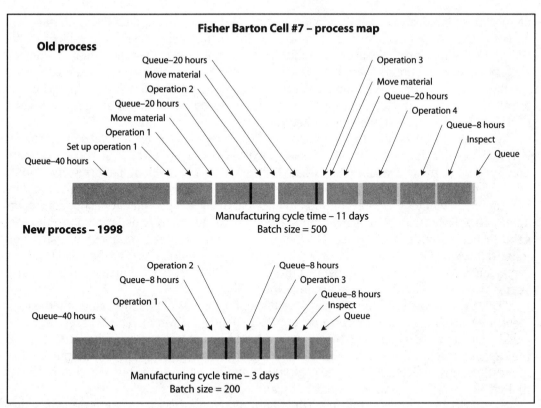

Figure 2. Working with the Deere-Horicon supplier development team, Fisher Barton was able to achieve dramatic results in cycle time

QRM, which recently had come to Ericksen's attention, seemed to fit Deere-Horicon's needs. Fortunately, assistance was readily available at the University of Wisconsin's Center for Quick Response Manufacturing. And a software package called MPX, developed by Suri specifically for manufacturing cycle time reduction, appeared useful as a way to help Deere-Horicon's suppliers create proof-of-concept justifications for actual manufacturing process modifications.

To ease the transition to new ways of thinking, Ericksen and his staffers attended a two-day professional development seminar taught by Suri. Deere-Horicon managers, engineers, and line employees learned the fundamentals of quick response manufacturing and MPX software.

Entering a Supplier's Inner Sanctum

Ask a supplier about margin information and production plans and chances are the response will be polite but not forthcoming. When initially confronted with Deere-Horicon's new supply management ideas, Dick Wilkey, president of Deere-Horicon supplier Fisher Barton, had an even stronger reaction. "I was more than a little concerned," says the president of the Watertown, Wisc., firm, about initial inquiries from one of his most important customers. "When someone mentions 'partnership' I get nervous; I know it's going to cost us money."

But Deere-Horicon buyer John Demeester would not be deterred: "We wanted to be able to call them on a moment's notice and tell them we needed 'X' amount of additional parts. If field demand increased, we still wanted delivery in a timely manner."

What convinced Wilkey to open the door all the way was Deere-Horicon's promise that it would not just focus on its own needs; a comprehensive gap analysis—process mapping—would be made available to evaluate Fisher Barton's entire manufacturing operations.

In seeking to improve supplier processing, Deere-Horicon offered a sincere *quid pro quo*: The company would do whatever it took to effect an overall improvement in suppliers' operations, effectively treating Fisher Barton like an internal John Deere department. In the bargain, Fisher Barton's trust would be compensated with genuine productivity gains and improved financials. Fisher Barton's goals, in turn, were ambitious. On the agenda was a campaign for faster order fulfillment, improved quality, enhanced employee pride, and a strengthened relationship with a very important client.

"QRM was a core objective for us," says Fisher Barton's Wilkey. "We had to build equipment, buy machinery, and move to becoming a cellular operation. The MPX system validated what we were going to do before we did it and assured us that the whole process had the capacity to produce to whatever the demand was at a given moment. We put a lot of money into this project and it's going to take a while to pay it off, but the bottom line is that we increased our production flexibility and lowered costs."

Says Ericksen, commenting on Fisher Barton's commitment to Deere-Horicon's program, "Supply management departments are feeling increasing pressure to deliver the goods while working to achieve cost-reduction goals with suppliers. But timeworn, positional supply management strategies produce only episodic results at best, which are difficult to maintain in the long run. The real trick is producing sustainable results. We think that's what we got at Fisher Barton. Supplier development represents a stand-alone supply management strategy, not just one of many supply management tools."

Relentless Quest for Speed

John Deere didn't get to be a *Fortune* 500 company and industry leader by sitting still. With a brand name that conveys the image of "best in the business," and retail relationships with merchandising powerhouses like Home Depot, John Deere knew that supplier programs are key to the company's long-term success.

But as Ericksen notes further, setting and publicizing goals and standards for supplier performance won't magically cause suppliers to meet Deere-Horicon's demanding manufacturing cycle time and cost reduction objectives efficiently. Says Ericksen, "OEMs who impose increased numbers of supplier performance measurement categories and set higher and higher threshold performance levels assume suppliers will quickly eliminate performance gaps.

"Contrary to expectation, new metrics often reinforce counterproductive supplier practices instead of gains in productivity," says Ericksen. "For instance, building to forecast and shipping from inventory to ensure on-time delivery may simply shift cost. Increased inspection activity to ensure acceptable as-delivered quality may be just another form of cost burden shifting. Although supplier personnel are working harder and longer than ever before, unless fundamental changes in manufacturing strategy are implemented, achieved supplier performance improvements may be marginal and short in duration."

What's needed, Ericksen suggests, is a fundamental change in supplier management strategy. The launch point for such an initiative? A process-based approach that, when fully understood by both management and engineering staffs, effects a change in the working culture of the supplier organization and the relationship between the supplier and the OEM customer.

"Time-based supply management brings substantial, sustainable improvement in supplier performance that yields improved financial results for both supplier organizations and OEMs," notes Ericksen. "Under time-based supply management, the order fulfillment effectiveness of a supplier is still the primary metric. Manufacturing cycle time reduction becomes the leading indicator of both the potential for cost reduction and the long-term viability of the supplier in achieving future positive results."

Sharing the Good News

Ericksen's interest in manufacturing-based economic development has led to his election to the presidency of the Wisconsin Manufacturing Extension Partnership. This public-private endeavor is associated with the National Institute of Standards and Technology and was established 10 years ago to provide support to America's small and medium-sized manufacturers.

Recently, process mapping, a way to identify areas for potential manufacturing cycle-time reduction, has been exported to Wisconsin MEP by Deere-Horicon's supplier development staff. Extension field agents working with small manufacturers are taking a cue from Deere-Horicon and also beginning to teach QRM and MPX as a way to attack problem areas.

At Deere-Horicon itself, supplier development work still goes on. When areas needing improvement are identified and documented via process mapping, Ericksen's teams teach supplier seminar participants the fundamentals of MPX as a shortcut to the benefits of quick response manufacturing. To make sure the underlying philosophy remains embedded at Deere-Horicon as well as its supplier network, QRM seminars are made available across the board to all management, engineering, and supplier personnel.

Both QRM seminar course material and the associated software have been licensed for distribution within Deere-Horicon and among its suppliers. Elsewhere, interest in QRM continues to grow. Suri's publishing and industrial consulting have led him to teach QRM seminars in locations as far afield as Germany, Finland, and Hong Kong.

The ABCs of QRM

As a widely admired professional football coach and mythic figure in Wisconsin sports lore once proclaimed, "Winning isn't everything, it's the only thing." An analogy to that famous dictum with regard to QRM might be, "Leadtime isn't everything, it's the only thing."

To grasp such a radical notion, take a look at how Deere-Horicon trainers Steve Addison and Aaron Armstrong handle a two-day supplier-development QRM seminar. Along with program colleagues, the two men typically work with groups of 12 to 20 employees from both suppliers and the Deere-Horicon facility.

"We seek participants representing a cross section of their companies, not just those directly involved in production," says Addison, who works with suppliers across the United States on behalf of Deere-Horicon. "Because QRM can affect an entire business, we like to work with accountants, buyers, and senior managers, as well as industrial and manufacturing engineers. With that kind of critical mass, we've got a good chance of getting sustainable positive results."

The course, which is licensed from MPX developer Network Dynamics, grew from the company's industrial consulting assignments and academic teaching module. Starting at Deere-Horicon with a train-the-trainer program taught by QRM originator Rajan Suri, Ph.D., the course begins with the basic principles of QRM. Application methods for using MPX software are interspersed with process mapping content specific to Deere-Horicon, which is the means the company uses to identify critical areas in which QRM and MPX can be brought into play.

"One of the really great things about the training is that every time we introduce it to a new group, we pick up more real-life examples to illustrate the basic points of QRM," says Addison. "Our supplier development community has created sophisticated approaches for using QRM, but our new students always bring unique experiences to the table.

"For example," Addison continues, "one MPX demonstration challenges members of a collaborative team to reduce manufacturing cycle time and work-in-process inventory. Even though the best solutions result from QRM ideas, no two are exactly the same."

According to Armstrong, "We want participants to recognize how MPX can be used to model their own factories, and look for opportunities to reduce manufacturing cycle time using the QRM approach." Training seminars help attendees challenge the status quo at their companies by using QRM to think outside of the box.

"Quick response manufacturing means focusing on manufacturing cycle time, a measurement that in the past has not been considered very important by many companies," says Addison. "Metrics like on-time delivery, defect rates, and cost have always gotten a lot of attention, but these are in many ways a consequence of manufacturing cycle time, making them secondary and dependent. If you are successful in reducing manufacturing cycle time, then cost, quality, and delivery should all improve."

As more and more trainees learn the ABCs of manufacturing cycle time reduction, both Deere-Horicon and its suppliers can point to an ever-growing body of positive evidence that QRM is a useful operating strategy.

Taking a strategic approach to creating sustainable improvements in supplier cost reduction requires corporate commitment and resources, but beyond its own operations Deere-Horicon is finding its supplier programs reflecting positively on regional economic development. Enhanced supplier financial health clearly has a positive impact on communities in which suppliers are located.

This represents an important change in the way a global enterprise such as John Deere relates to its suppliers. As a corporate citizen, Deere-Horicon is using its development program to strengthen both supplier relationships and the manufacturing economy of the state of Wisconsin. Overall, industry reviews of this innovative supply management strategy are favorable. By any measure, John Deere's Horicon facility has a hit on its hands.

For Further Reading

Suri, Rajan, *Quick Response Manufacturing: A Companywide Approach to Reducing Lead Times*, Productivity Press, 1998.

Peter Golden wrote this article with generous assistance from Deere & Company and Network Dynamics Inc. He is based in Brookline, Mass., where he has covered manufacturing systems since 1984. Golden can be reached at Petewrites@aol.com.

Part Four

Electronic Commerce

One of the most significant developments in the field of purchasing and supply chain management is the emergence of the Internet and its use to find and purchase supplies as well as interact with suppliers. The common term for this is "electronic commerce" or "e-commerce." In recognition of the importance of electronic commerce, we have devoted one part of this book to this subject.

We start off with an original article by Terri Tracey of NAPM that reviews current happenings in e-commerce in "The New 'Dot.com' World of Electronic Purchasing," and suggests directions for the future. This has the potential of enhancing the lines of communication among all the parties involved in the purchasing and supply process and facilitating just-in-time inventory control.

Following Tracey's article, you'll find a piece gleaned from Europe titled "Purchasing and the Information Age: Towards a Virtual Purchasing Organization" by Arjan van Weele. This documents the evolution of the use of information and communication technology in purchasing and supply chain management and helps you see what the European thinking is on this phenomenon.

From the journal *Management Accounting*, we've included the article "The Big E-Payback" by Steve Hornyak. It provides a special focus on how to use e-procurement on the purchases of items used in maintenance, repair, and operating activities that are repetitive purchases. By employing electronic technology, companies can better monitor and track these purchases, maintaining better control, helping to reduce costs in a variety of ways.

From the Gartner Group we have an article titled "The Fallacies of Web Commerce Fulfillment." It looks at things from the perspective of the seller, but it provides real food for thought on when it makes sense to use the Web and when it doesn't.

Another intriguing perspective on e-commerce comes from Weld Royal in his article "Death of Salesmen." He suggests that doing business over the Web may dramatically affect what traditional sales people do or if we'll even need them in the future.

Finally, we conclude with a series of short pieces gleaned from NAPM's *Purchasing Today®* magazine section titled "Tech Talk." We've included six of these articles, with topics ranging from "Information Body Guards" by Phillip Green to "E-Commerce Savings" by Torrey Byles. Each of these has practical tips to help you as you undertake e-procurement.

The New "Dot.com" World of Electronic Purchasing

Terri Tracey

What's going on in e-commerce today? Every article in this part is designed to answer that question, but this article in particular focuses on the latest changes, providing a review of 1999 and the latest developments in this rapidly evolving area of purchasing. You'll learn about "buy side" and "sell side" catalogs, for example. And you'll learn how certain companies with strong buying power are extending their purchasing clout to their customers. Read about these activities and more just below.

Electronic commerce is one of the fastest changing areas purchasing and supply management professionals have had to face this past year. Questions ranging from "Where do we start?" to "How do we integrate all our suppliers and internal/external systems?" are being dealt with. Many organizations have barely made a dent in entering this new "dot.com" world, while others have created brand new business models and taken advantage of opportunities never even thought of as little as three years ago.

Early 1999

Recent NAPM Survey Results. In a survey conducted by NAPM in March 1999, senior-level purchasing and supply professionals responsible for implementing electronic commerce initiatives within their organizations were asked how they managed twelve different aspects of electronic commerce. Respondents were grouped into "organization size" categories: Large = > $2 billion; Medium = $100 million to $2 billion; and Small = < $100 million. Additionally, the group was asked whether they handled each of the twelve functions via an internal only system, an Internet-based system, or integrated systems.

- *Internal Only System.* The application of "managing and administering contracts" is handled electronically by an internal-only system by more than 70 percent of the organizations, regardless of size. However, "transferring funds and managing payment" through internal systems is more prevalent in medium and small organizations (over 40 percent) than in larger organizations (19 percent).
- *Internet-Based Systems.* Most survey respondents use the Internet to look for suppliers. Some organizations (almost half in the large category) order through electronic catalogs; the same is true for purchasing products and services over the Internet. It

is interesting to note that a very small percentage, regardless of organization size, use EDI over the Internet.

- *Integrated Systems.* Electronic catalogs are the most common application used in an enterprise-wide system. It appears that about one-third of the large organizations use an enterprise system for most of their purchasing applications, while approximately 25 percent of the medium-sized organizations and 20 percent of the small organizations do.

Future Plans for Survey Respondents. Purchasing products and services is the activity most organizations will electronically-enable in the near future. Transmitting purchase orders and sending RFPs/RFQs are other functions that will soon be handled electronically by close to 70 percent of the organizations contacted. One of the activities that appears to be on the back-burner is managing and administering contracts; only one-third of the respondents is planning to digitize this process in their organizations.

ERP Systems. ERP (enterprise resource planning) system implementation had been continuing over the past few years, with actual system launches taking many more months and many more dollars than initially anticipated. The main reason for this was that businesses needed to change most of their internal processes and procedures to match the ERP software systems—from purchasing to logistics management to accounting; this was extremely difficult for many organizations. Alternatively, ERP software could be customized to specific business processes; however, this tactic also took additional time and resources—and would necessitate continued customization as software upgrades were delivered.

Middle 1999

Despite these survey results, which showed that many organizations were not EC-enabled early in the year, and the fact that ERP systems implementation was not going as smoothly as planned, most organizations began realizing that integrating their internal systems, tying into suppliers' internal systems through extranet or other technologies, and linking partners and tiers in the supply chain was critical to remaining competitive in the environment. ERP providers began creating alliances and partnerships with various electronic catalog suppliers and integrating the programs so they could offer more complete, seamless software packages to organizations.

Competitive Environments. Electronic commerce success stories were being touted throughout the media everywhere—Intel opening up a Web site and selling $4 million a day; Dell Computer finding huge success as an online computer retailer; and Cisco (another high-tech company) has enabled almost its entire supply chain so that members can not only sell over the Internet but also track parts and services from point of origin on to final customer delivery and payment. CEOs of organizations of all sizes and types began to take notice of this as well, and were pushing to get their own products and services out into, and onto, the World Wide Web.

However, business-to-business (B2B) electronic commerce involves much more than putting up a Web site and selling to an individual consumer sitting at their PC in their living room. Organizations were interested in EC-enabling both their internal systems (allowing staff outside the purchasing arena to place orders for MRO-type items) and their external systems (perhaps allowing their suppliers access to information such as expected delivery schedules, manufacturing planning timelines, etc., that would allow them to better plan and adjust their own schedules to meet delivery dates). In addition to researching and selecting new systems, installing and launching systems of this type was not limited to just the IS department, the purchasing department, or the accounting department. Major organization-wide decisions needed to be made regarding keeping, integrating, or doing away with existing legacy systems and processes; how to integrate existing EDI applications, if any existed with some or all suppliers; and if/how to change the way the organization has been conducting business for the past x number of years. In fact, EC-enabling the entire enterprise needed to be thought of not as one specific "system," but as a way to manage the business more effectively and efficiently using integrated computer systems/programs.

Electronic Catalogs. Organizations desiring to get into the EC arena decided to enter slowly. Many times, the first step taken was to look at internal spending—specifically non-production MRO (maintenance, repair, operations) items rather than items integral to production of the organization's major products. This could be handled in a number of different ways, but most focused on electronic catalog procurement. Three distinct models of electronic catalogs emerged:

- Purchaser-managed ("buy side") catalogs
- Supplier-managed ("sell side") catalogs
- Content aggregator-managed catalogs

Buy side catalogs have been around for a couple of years. Buying organizations (usually purchasers and IS) create all their own catalogs. The catalogs contain data such as pre-negotiated contract rates, and which items are approved for purchase by whom. The catalogs are generally housed on the buying organizations' intranet, are accessible by all employees, and allow streamlining of purchase requisition and order processes. A major downside to buyer-controlled catalogs is that the buying organization is responsible for keeping all suppliers' catalog data up to date; depending on the number of MRO suppliers the purchasing organization was dealing with, this could prove to be an almost impossible task. Find examples of such catalogs at **www.partnet.com**.

Sell side catalogs then began emerging as MRO suppliers started building their own Web sites and offering secure ordering access to their customers. One benefit to purchasers was that suppliers were responsible for keeping all their own content up to date. Downsides to this include purchasers now having to go to each Web site individually and likely deal with many different types of catalogs and layouts on the front end—some including graphics, others with no graphics; and some with pre-negotiated pricing while others provided only general public pricing. Purchasers then had to deal with all the individual suppliers' back-end systems, many of which did not allow for easy order tracking.

Basic *content aggregator models* came into the picture as an attempt to mitigate some of the downsides of the buyer- and seller-controlled electronic catalog models. Content aggregators acted as content intermediaries by aggregating content and contract information and hosting this on extranets. Individual buying and/or selling organizations did not have the investment in hardware or software that other models required. One benefit to suppliers is that they can access the content aggregator and update their catalog one time, and all their customers would see current information. Supply managers have access to pre-negotiated pricing and contract terms for all of their suppliers in one convenient location. Content aggregators may charge a one-time development fee to customize content to one organization, and may also charge a monthly and/or per transaction fee. See **www. mro.com** for an example of what this is about.

Benefits. Purchasing organizations benefit from electronic catalog technology by reducing cycle time and indirect materials costs. They also realize time savings from clerical activities, thus enabling them to focus on more strategic and value-added functions. Benefits to suppliers include reduced order entry costs—and errors, as well as more expedited tracking and payment. Selling organizations therefore pass on some of these savings to purchasing organizations.

Late 1999

Two key technologies and services emerged during the latter part of 1999—portal sites and online auctioning. Both of these technologies started as a consumer-to-consumer benefit, but businesses quickly began to see potential benefits and huge savings potential.

Online Auctions. As the year went on, almost no one was immune from hearing about all the great "success stories" of online auctioning. One company, eBay, was in the news almost daily for a while, illustrating that one individual (aka "supplier") sitting in one part of the world could post their item (aka "product") up on a Web site, and over a period of time various others around the world (aka "purchasers") would continually bid higher and higher prices for that product until the auction time was over. This example is obviously a consumer-to-consumer transaction. But, business-to-business auctioning was happening as well, with many organizations realizing millions of dollars in savings.

While electronic catalogs and many of the portals addressed MRO and non-production item acquisition, online auctions were tailor-made for purchasing standard "shop" items where the purchaser has a lot of choice in suppliers. Auctions also allow an organization to locate new suppliers in other parts of the world, and perhaps even focus on assisting a small, disadvantaged, or minority-owned business. Forrester Research estimates that B2B online auctions generated $8.7 billion in activity in 1998, and predicts explosive growth over the next three years—with over 80 percent of large companies trading online by 2002.

Value-Added Services. If the purchasing organization is interested in just one or two auctions, the company providing the auction service will certainly provide the infrastructure, processes, and procedures needed to conduct a successful auction. However, if the purchasing organization is interested in using online auctions for many large lots and many items, the auction service provider will partner with the purchasing organization to help identify potential suppliers and search for other / new sources. The buyer sets a reserve price (the lowest she/he will accept); this information is generally not provided to the bidding suppliers. Also important to consider is that the buyer is *not* pre-committed to take the lowest bid.

One of the first to enter the live, online auction/bidding marketplace was FreeMarkets OnLine, Inc. (**www.freemarkets.com**). It provides proprietary bidding technology and services to companies needing industrial components, agricultural products, and energy commodities. Companies ranging from Caterpillar to Westinghouse and Whirlpool have used this interactive, robust system to significantly drive down costs of purchased product. Several examples of savings achieved include:

- A major automotive manufacturer received bids 30 percent below previous paid prices on 288 different types of metal fasteners and consolidated its supply base from 200 to 8 suppliers. Approximately 16 percent of the contract up for bid was awarded to a minority-owned company.
- A major pharmaceuticals company received bids more than 60 percent below previous prices on promotional items using FreeMarkets. The company received 738 bids for the items in less than four hours.
- FreeMarkets helped a major aerospace concern source 600 different machined parts and consolidate its supply base from 30 suppliers to eight suppliers as a result of a six-hour online auction.

Portals, Hubs, Verticals...

Industry-, commodity-, and function-specific portals (or hubs) started to appear, combining buying and selling opportunities along with content and, for some, auctioning capabilities. Most hubs or portals specialize vertically along a specific industry or market, while others are now focusing more horizontally, or to address a specific function—such as purchasing.

Vertical Portals provide industry- or commodity-specific content and attempt to develop various types of relationships among the community. Successful verticals create a critical mass of key suppliers and purchasers, as well as master catalogs they can access. Examples of vertical portals include:

- **www.metalsite.net**—sourcing and auctioning services for the steel industry
- **www.fastparts.com**—OEMs, Contract Assemblers, Part Makers, and Distributors trade electronic components and equipment

- **www.band-x.com**—commodity auction site for telecom capacity
- **www.plasticsnet.com**—catalogs and auctions for resins and materials

Horizontal, or functional, portals focus on automating the same business process across different industries. Successful horizontals are usually built by professionals who have performed the function, and can therefore provide key process knowledge and workflow expertise. Examples of horizontal or functional portals include:

- **www.iMark.com**—surplus and capital equipment trading
- **www.usfreightways.com/processors/index.htm** (Processors Unlimited)—reverse logistics and surplus goods auction site (www.processorsauction.com).
- **http://in-site.bidcom.com/index.html**—construction projects
- **www.celarix.com**—real-time global logistics management

Hybrid Portals are now being created to either (1) combine vertical and horizontal needs, and/or (2) serve small businesses. One that has been around for a few years in this first category is **www.about.com** (formerly the Mining Company), a network comprised of hundreds of topic areas led by "human experts" in those various fields and industries. Each About.com site is devoted to a single topic, and includes with site reviews, feature articles and discussion areas. About.com does not foster electronic commerce within their communities.

Another market player is VerticalNet (**www.verticalnet.com**), which serves more than 40 different industries (or communities). VerticalNet's trade communities offer content, community, and commerce. Examples of the major communities are "food and packaging" and "manufacturing and metals." Each of these is then segmented into more narrowly-focused commodity- or industry-specific areas, such as (for "food and packaging") bakeries, beverages, food ingredients, and meat and poultry. Its business model allows it to spread its costs for auctioning and building its infrastructure over dozens of sites. Manufacturers pay a small annual fee to belong to one of the business communities; VerticalNet's new e-commerce center allows suppliers to complete orders online.

Other new players and business models address small businesses (**www.bizbuyer.com** and **www.buyerszone.com**), many offering services like personnel, mailroom, telecom, and marketing in addition to products such as office and computer equipment. Financial services and other large organizations are also beginning to realize they can provide their smaller suppliers and others with online services. For example, Wells Fargo & Co. currently allows up to 30,000 of its employees to order supplies and equipment from their desktops. However, it now plans to extend that system to its business customers. Merrill Lynch has also announced plans to offer this service to its customers. Extending their procurement systems to small and mid-size business customers allows these smaller organizations to take advantage of the leverage the larger organizations have with their suppliers and receive better pricing and reduce paperwork—and the smaller organizations do not have to incur the expense and expend the resources to purchase and implement their own internal systems.

This past year has seen electronic commerce boom, both on the business-to-consumer and the business-to-business angle. However, researchers and forecasters predict that B2B electronic commerce activities will range from over $200 billion next year to up to $1 trillion by 2003. With numbers like these floating around, most purchasing and supply professionals are recognizing they need to play a key role in implementing EC initiatives within their organizations—and will then be able to show a significant improvement in the bottom line.

Terri Tracey is the Vice President of Electronic Product Development for NAPM, and has been with the association since 1990. Her areas of responsibility include program content, product development, and management of NAPM's online products and programs including distance education courses, Web site, and electronic commerce programs.

Purchasing and the Information Age: Towards a Virtual Purchasing Organization?

Arjan J. van Weele, Ph.D.

Would you like to know more about how e-commerce has evolved over the past few years and the direction it's going, especially with regard to purchasing and supply chain management? This article provides a review of the role of information technology and the Internet and the changes this technology is bringing about in the purchasing function.

Purchasing structures in large companies nowadays are very different from what they were in the 1980s, and they will, without doubt, be different from today in the future. Two decades ago concepts such as purchasing portfolio management, total cost of ownership, supplier partnership, early supplier involvement and cross-functional buying teams were not known. Since then many new strategic and organizational concepts in the field of purchasing and supply (chain) management have been developed. The professional development of the purchasing and supply function in organizations can be analyzed from both an internal and an external standpoint. First, the internal role of purchasing changed from a mere operational role into a truly strategic role. From just handling orders, negotiating and contracting, purchasing in many organizations now focuses on initial purchasing aimed at developing order routines and support systems enabling users to order directly from suppliers, with whom systems contracts have been closed. Secondly, the interface between purchasing and its suppliers changed. From 'competitive bidding' and mere tendering, companies have tried to become more differentiated in their supplier strategies. This is reflected in attempts to apply supplier (portfolio) management, to integrate suppliers into product development and to go beyond the first tier of suppliers looking for opportunities to capture further cost benefits (supply chain optimization).

These changes are best illustrated by some major paradigm shifts that have taken place, reflected in the statements made by general managers and purchasing managers of some large manufacturing companies (see Box 1).

This article describes the background of these changes. Furthermore, we will discuss how companies try to cope with them. Finally, we present their implications for the role of purchasing and supply management. As we will show, purchasing managers increasingly need to assume responsibility for their information strategies and infrastructure.

Box 1: Major Paradigm Shifts in Purchasing

The changing role of purchasing and supply management can best be illustrated by the statements recently made by some general managers of some large manufacturing companies ...[1]

- "Purchasing in our organization is too important to leave it only to buyers..."
- "Purchasing in our company is moving into the line ... it is becoming more and more a line-responsibility..."
- "Going for sustainable cost savings in purchasing and supplier relationships requires cross-functional teamwork..."
- "If there is anything more important than purchasing in our company, it is a well kept secret..."[2]

Some interesting statements, which reflect the changing role and importance of suppliers, are the following:[3]

- "Suppliers should be considered as an essential part of our business; in fact they represent the external enterprise of our business..."
- "Suppliers need to be more involved in our future product development programmes in order to benefit from their specialist product and manufacturing expertise..."
- "Suppliers need to be online with us 24-hours per day. Those who do not have modern ICT will be excluded from our business..."

The Role of ICT in Purchasing

Traditionally, purchasing and supply management had a supply job to fulfil. The major task of this business function was to anticipate and meet the materials and service requirements of the organization. During the early 1980s many authors have argued that this role was too narrow. Since that time it has been stressed that the role of purchasing needed to go beyond this point. In order to manage the materials' flow effectively (and their corresponding purchasing processes) buyers needed to work much more 'upstream' and become more involved in product development policies, processes and projects (see among others Wijnstra (1998)). The debate among academics and practitioners was not only related to the internal role of purchasing and supply management. It was also stressed that this business function should focus much more on the active management of their supplier relationships. Hence, supplier management (management of the 'external resources' of the company) became a dominant issue in the boardroom of many companies. From that moment onwards both academics and practitioners became very creative in developing new strategic concepts (such as just-in-time scheduling, supplier quality assurance, early supplier involvement, supplier partnership, co-design and co-sourcing) in order to manage their supplier relationships more effectively.

As we see it, most companies still struggle to implement these new business concepts. As research has shown, partnership relationships are not providing companies with the results that they expect from it [see among others Lamming (1995) and Hendrick and Ellram (1994)]. Wijnstra's study on the role of purchasing in product development (1998) points out that companies experience many problems in fostering teamwork between development engineers and buyers on the one hand and between development teams and suppliers on the other hand. Of course, many reasons can be mentioned for these findings. One recurring one is the fact that most companies lack an effective communications and information infrastructure, which may support, enable and organize the highly complex and often rapidly changing interfaces among the disciplines and organizational entities involved in the purchasing process.

We therefore propose another role for academics and purchasing managers. This role is aimed at taking advantage of the new information and communications technology (ICT) in order to enable effective internal co-operation among the disciplines involved, to support effective management and control of supplier relationships and to enable an efficient information and materials flow from the internal user directly to the external supplier. As we see it this new role builds on the former ones; it does not stand on its own.

This logical evolution of the role of purchasing and supply management in organizations is illustrated in Box 2.

Why do purchasing managers need to assume this new role and responsibility? Why is this relevant and what needs to be expected from it?

Box 2: Evolution of Purchasing and Supply Management's Role in Organizations

1st Level: From traditional supply role: "anticipate and meet the materials and service requirements of our organization."

2nd Level: Via supplier management role: "effectively manage internal and external purchasing processes."

3rd Level: To purchasing and supply chain information management role: "effectively manage information infrastructure in order to enable business resource management."

Purchasing and Information Management: The Future Is Now!

Recent studies have pointed out that purchasing and supply management is lagging behind in computerization and information management. As Van Stekelenborg (1997) has demonstrated, the application of computer systems in purchasing is limited to the transactional part of the job. Order handling, expediting and accounts payable are now sufficiently supported by most standard enterprise resource planning (ERP) packages. However, most of these packages do not sufficiently support initial purchasing and are not capable of providing general management effectively with purchasing management information. Apart from vendor rating, these packages do not allow for effective contract management and monitoring in (multiplant) organizations, and adequate product-line management and supply base management. Early supplier involvement and supply chain management (keeping track of materials through the total supply chain) are not supported at all. Despite the good intentions of the large ERP-software houses (like SAP, Marcam and Baan) this type of solution will not be available within their new releases.

We question whether the solutions that we require need to come from these type of packages and suppliers. Given the fact that Internet and intranet technology is developing very fast, other solutions may be possible. Consider the following examples:

- Companies like Grasso, a medium-sized manufacturer of industrial cooling and heating equipment and part of a large German group with business units around the world, have installed a purchasing intranet within three months enabling exchange of product, supplier and contract information among all sites. Investment: less than US$35,000 for software (licenses) and three months' preparation. The system is based on Microsoft's Outlook software. Other manufacturing companies have built similar systems based on Lotus Notes software.

- A company like Wer Liefert Was (WLW) now has supplier addresses in eight EU countries available via its Web site, enabling buyers to conduct market surveys in a very short time. For commodities, long lists of potential suppliers may be developed in just a few minutes. Supplier information (with regard to product assortment, references and financial stability) may be asked for through WLW's extensive database and directly through e-mail from the supplier. Requests for quotations may be submitted through WLW's systems or directly through e-mailing the supplier concerned.

- Sony uses its purchasing Web site to attract new suppliers for certain commodities. Suppliers are requested to react to components that are in short supply. Suppliers may act through filling in the SQA-questionnaire and sending it through e-mail directly to Sony. In this way, the Internet is being used actively for 'reversed marketing.'

- Companies like FedEx, DHL Worldwide Express and UPS provide linkages through the Internet which enable companies to keep track of their deliveries. Some of these sites enable cost breakdowns per port of destination enabling buyers to find their most competitive source of supply.

- Although electronic payment is still troublesome, developments are going fast in this area. In the consumer goods business, some companies have posted impressive turnover figures and financial results (such as CD Direct, Amazon and DELL). Although legally not yet approved, it is expected that electronic commerce and payment will grow rapidly in the years to come.

Other examples can be added to this list. Box 3 provides an overview of how the Internet may be used in the purchasing area nowadays. It will already be clear from this list that the electronification of purchasing will develop very fast. New IT-supported tools will become available for the coming years, not only for buyers. However, the same tools will also be available to all other disciplines in the company (who, in general, are much better equipped with regards to computers than their counterparts in the purchasing organization). Of course, this raises the question for purchasing professionals as to what 'added value' they will provide to their companies.

In our view, this transition will outpace the capabilities of many purchasing professionals to adapt and to integrate them in the traditional purchasing structures and ways of working. It is our opinion that it will be much better to prepare for totally new purchasing (information and organizational) structures. The way these structures will look is the subject of the next paragraphs. (See Box 3.)

The Virtual Purchasing Organization

In some world-class companies, the workplace of the future, even in the field of purchasing and supply management, is already under construction (see Box 4). The walls in purchasing are coming down and the bridges are going up—the bridges consisting of up-to-date communication and information technologies and superior business and communications skills.

From the above, we expect that the traditional, functional purchasing organization will disappear. The speed of this process will be determined by the speed of adoption of the new information and communication technology. Apart from that, it will depend on the speed at which companies are willing and prepared to adapt to the new organizational paradigms. We expect this process of adaptation to differ among companies and, especially, among industries.

Earlier we stated that purchasing managers should provide added value to their company; otherwise their tasks, responsibilities and authorities will disappear into the line organization. It is imperative, therefore, simultaneously to increase functional expertise and develop economies of scale whilst enabling maximum flexibility at the business unit level. This could be done through the hard-core/ soft-core purchasing organization, which may serve as a model for future purchasing organizations.

Box 3: Internet and Intranet Applications

- *Purchasing market research and supplier selection.* Examples are Wer Liefert Was, Yellow Pages, Industrynet, all of which may be used to find (new) suppliers. Product descriptions may be derived from purchasing extranet. Supplier references may be checked from Dun & Bradstreet.
- *Sending requests for proposal.* This may be done through e-mail directly to the supplier. Bid information may also be exposed through specialized intermediaries such as BidCast or Tender Daily.
- *Virtual auctions.* Free Markets On-line provides software to organize auctions among suppliers for individual buyers. Some large retailers (such as Wehkamp in the Netherlands) have daily auctions for merchandise on sale.
- *Reversed marketing.* Some large subcontractors and manufacturers (such as NASA and Sony) have a special purchasing Web site on which they expose products for which they seek new suppliers. Initial screening is done through filling out a detailed questionnaire.
- *Commodity buying.* Some major commodities can now be traced on-line through the Internet enabling buyers to manage their commodity buyers from hour to hour enabling them to buy at the right moment.
- *Shipment tracking.* FedEx, DHL Worldwide Express and UPS have extensive Web sites where tariffs may be asked for express freight and shipments and deliveries may be tracked and traced.
- *Electronic payment.* Payment may be tied to credit cards or special purchasing cards, enabling paperless invoice handling.
- *Education and training.* Some universities and professional organizations have Web sites which present training and educational programs and virtual programs.

We envision in this (highly virtual) structure a small, highly specialized purchasing staff at the company's headquarters[4], responsible for: developing the corporate purchasing policy; building strategic alliances; (team-based) sourcing of key materials and services; supplier development programs; systems development; and professional development (training and education). This hard core will reside mainly at corporate headquarters and will be very small in size (less than 30 people for companies as large as IBM or Alcatel Alsthom). It will provide specialist product knowledge and superior purchasing process skills to the line-management of divisions and/or business units.

In this structure all division or business unit specific purchasing activities are conducted at lower levels within the organization. In addition, some specialist product expertise may be found within the purchasing organization. However, in the team-based purchasing processes, it will be the technology and product engineers that will predominantly bring in this knowledge. Hence, we feel that the purchasing professionals operating at these levels (divisional and business unit level) particularly will bring in process skills.

These process skills may be acquired fast through training and education and job rotation. However, this will require a superior educational profile of the buyers (project buyers or supplier managers) involved. These purchasing professionals in essence have a two-line way of reporting. First, they report to the team-leader of the teams they are represented in. Secondly, they report to the centre-led purchasing organization.

Apart from the product specialists, this part of the purchasing organization may have a soft core character. These purchasing 'specialists' may come and go, depending on the projects and needs of the company at a specific moment in time. We envisage that these soft core purchasing professionals may work within their own functional area (not necessarily being a purchasing department), which will mean that, in that situation, purchasing has moved into the line organization totally. The soft core purchasing specialists are the real on-the-spot purchasers, with the authority to make decisions on how one can best meet local supply needs. The hard core backs them up with sophisticated tools, such as cost models and state-of-the-art information systems, and product and market knowledge.

We expect that, for the buying of production materials (components), these purchasing specialists may move increasingly to research and development and product development. Ultimately, these specialists may be totally integrated into these activities. With regards to the buying of non-production materials, we expect the purchasing specialists to reside within the user departments. In all cases, a functional reporting relationship will exist to the centre-led corporate purchasing organization. Acceptance of this idea implies a totally new and different career perspective for the purchasing professionals involved.

Conclusions

New paradigms are changing the purchasing landscape. Over the past few years, many new business and organizational concepts have emerged in purchasing and supply management. However, at the same time, implementation is lagging behind and is often troublesome. The new ICT will provide companies and especially purchasing managers with unknown opportunities for market research, supplier management and contract management. We expect that the Internet technology will prove to be especially powerful in building purchasing synergy among different business units.[5] Product and supplier information and sensitive contract information may now be shared easily with colleagues in other business units and hence reinforce the negotiating position vis-a-vis the company's key suppliers. However, it must be recognized that this information will not be available to buyers only. As we see it, users will increasingly be involved in the buying process through direct information linkages into the purchasing and supplier information systems. This will change the role of buyers and purchasing managers even more drastically. We hypothesize that the purchasing profession may go the same way in terms of future development as disciplines like Quality Management, Marketing and Human Resources Management have gone. Purchasing management will probably move more and more into the line, the speed of this process being determined by the adoption of new ICT throughout the company.

> ### Box 4: Slashing Organizational Boundaries at IBM
>
> IBM is developing from a highly hierarchical organization into a flexible boundaryless organization in which teams can 'pop up' and dissolve, depending on the situation. For example, the European purchasing specialists, though they report to the Director of Procurement Europe through the line organization, are physically part of the marketing bid teams, working on customer projects and contributing to the development of solutions for these. Hence, buyers have a double role of forming close ties with their customer support teams and their suppliers. In fact, the old hierarchical structures are disintegrating as the effectiveness of cross-functional teams grows. The buyer is an integrated member of such customer-oriented teams and knows when to call in the industry-specific purchasing specialists, when complex components or services need to be acquired and contracted.
>
> In some projects, as many as 60 suppliers could be involved, including consultants, hardware specialists, software companies, financiers, facility management companies and others. It is unthinkable that sales representatives could commit themselves to a client solution and an agreement without the consent of his customer support team in which procurement has a significant contribution to make which generally would include assessment of supply risks, supplier capacity and nondisclosure of proprietary knowledge.
>
> *Source: Author's interviews, 1996 (adapted)*

Users will, beyond doubt, increasingly act as owners of the purchasing process, relying on buyers for specialist information, commercial support and supplier management.

Purchasing managers should assume a proactive role in developing and shaping their purchasing and supplier information systems. If not, they run the risk that software houses and new intermediaries on the Internet will take over these tasks, leaving purchasing managers and buyers empty handed!

Bibliography

1. J. van Empel, "New Entrepreneurs Bring New Dynamics in Dutch Economy," *NRC Handelsblad*, September 16, 1995 (Dutch text).

2. T. Hendrick and L. Ellram, *Strategic Supplier Partnerships* (Phoenix: Center for Advance Purchasing Studies study, 1994).

3. R. Lamming, "A Review of the Relationships Between Vehicle Manufacturers and Suppliers," *Research Report for Vehicles Division Department of Trade and Industry and the Society of Motor Manufacturers and Traders*, 1994.

4. Rosabeth Moss Kanter, "Constructing the Future," *Northern Telecom Annual Report*, 1995.

5. Tom Peters, *The Tom Peters Seminar* (New York: Vintage Books, 1994).

6. R.H.A. van Stekelenborg, *Information Technology for Purchasing*, Eindhoven University of Technology, Faculty of Technology Management (Ph.D. thesis), 1997.

7. Arjan J. van Weele and Frank A. Rozemeijer, *Revolution in Purchasing*, Philips Electronics/ Eindhoven University of Technology, 1996.

8. J.Y.F. Wijnstra, *The Role of Purchasing in Product Development*, Eindhoven University of Technology, Faculty of Technology Management, (Ph.D. thesis, 1998).

Notes

1. See, among other sources, "Purchasing's New Muscle," *Fortune*, 1996.
2. See William Marx, vice president Lucent Technologies in *The Conference Board*, 1996.
3. Author's interviews at Chrysler and Honda as described in *Revolution in Purchasing*, 1996.
4. ... or division-level, depending on the characteristics of the group.
5. This assumption is currently being verified in the research project conducted by Rozemeijer (1998). A major objective of this project is to find out how large companies in a variety of industries develop purchasing synergy among autonomous business units.

Arjan J. van Weele is Director of the Scientific Institute for Purchasing and Supply Development at Eindhoven University of Technology, the Netherlands. He is also part-time professor of purchasing and supply chain management at both Nyenrode, The Netherlands School of Business and Eindhoven University of Technology. He was a director at Holland Consulting Group (1989-1999), a specialized management consulting agency, where he was responsible for building a successful practice in purchasing and building resource management. From 1997 to 1999, he acted as Managing Director of the firm. Before this post, he was a management consultant at Coopers & Lybrand Management Consultants (1985-1989). Previously, he was associate professor of marketing at Nyenrode (1982-1985) and before that he worked as a research associate at Eindhoven University of Technology.

The Big E-Payback

Steve Hornyak

Here's another article that describes where things are going in e-procurement. Paying special attention to the maintenance, repair, and operating purchases that can take up as much as 30% of revenues, this article explains how e-commerce helps companies more intelligently buy the things they need and better track these costs, especially when they aren't made by the purchasing staff following normal rules. Learn how e-commerce can work for you.

It's one frantic afternoon. A division manager desperately needs her computer repaired. The sales team, late for a plane flight to a trade show in the next state, is clamoring for more presentation supplies and tabbed sales folders. Meanwhile, the human resources director says he needs a new cartridge for his laser printer, lunch for five employees visiting from a branch office, overnight shipping labels, and courier service to a sales office up the interstate. Do you want to be the one to tell them it may take up to a week to process their requests? In an Internet-savvy corporate environment where instant results are becoming standard business practice, you as accounting, finance, and purchasing professionals must re-examine ways to keep pace with the needs of modern business. Your company is depending on you.

The days of multiple purchase orders, manual purchase requisitions, and random expense purchases must end. Instead of wading through an alphabet soup of paper P.O.s and P.R.s (purchase orders and purchase requisitions) that can take days or weeks to process, employees will go to their computers and use a Web-based procurement system to summon a virtual shopping cart and order items they need right away. In fact, Web-based procurement systems actually transform employees into strategic buyers by granting them control over a subset of preapproved and budgeted items. No longer will they have to ask permission to order something. Based on the amount of purchasing power the company grants them, they can order at will and be alerted if their purchase isn't allowed or if they've reached their spending limit. The only constraint is that they must use approved vendors, but they'll have more choices than they realize.

Also, cash that previously had been lost in the shuffle of unregulated, inefficient purchasing will re-emerge on the bottom line. And the modern reengineered workplace will enjoy intelligent procurement systems that not only save money but provide significant savings in time and resources.

Goodbye, Conventional Purchasing

As a financial manager, how do you feel about sifting through reams of order requests? Wouldn't you like to see your time spent in a more value-added manner? Even though many companies have made great strides toward managing the purchasing habits of their employees, the procurement process for nonproduction goods and services such as computer, office, and facility supplies is often unpredictable and random. A company may deal with thousands of different suppliers ranging from couriers to caterers and from IT professionals to office supply companies. Without proper checks and balances on procurement spending in place, financial managers, controllers, and CFOs can't tell where the money is going or what they are getting for it.

And companies are spending—nearly $370 billion a year on nonproduction goods and services. These maintenance, repair, and operating (MRO) items can represent as much as 30% of a company's revenues. Because MRO purchases aren't made through normal company channels, it has been difficult for accounting and purchasing departments to keep tabs on these miscellaneous but vital supplies and services needed for doing day-to-day business.

Further, the labor-intensive process of handling purchase orders can cost corporations up to $200 per transaction. And with large companies generating hundreds of thousands of purchase orders each year, processing costs can be overwhelming. Not to mention that while waiting days or weeks for approvals, employees often grow frustrated that corporate service levels don't match their need for delivery of materials.

Hello, Web-Based Procure-to-Pay Solutions

Several temporary fixes have been introduced to solve the purchasing dilemma, including client/server purchasing and requisitioning modules, electronic data interchange (EDI) systems, and standalone procurement card solutions. Although these "point" systems have brought efficiency to the purchasing process, companies still haven't realized the collective benefit an integrated solution can provide, particularly in the area of MRO purchases. Even today's enterprise resource planning (ERP) systems have ignored the handling of MRO purchases.

But Web-based technology can provide the easy answers missing from many other solutions. For one, employees make their purchases within a familiar interactive medium. Using a shopping cart-style browser, employees examine items closely with full-color pictures and descriptions and select the goods and services they need. The Web interface offers a virtual glimpse at the product being purchased—not just a product number or a line item. Maneuvering quickly through the system on the Internet, users can pick and choose, point and click, and generally make the usual tedium of business purchasing into a fun experience. An e-procurement system ties together elements of other purchasing solutions to create an integrated procure-to-pay network in which high levels of purchasing controls and high levels of service to employees can co-exist harmoniously. Best of all, the Web is a real-time interface, so with one click of a mouse or push of a button, the transaction is made—and the appropriate monies are transferred.

If you were one of the more than a million new Internet shoppers this past year, you already have a mental picture of the procedure. Through the e-procurement system, employees have direct links to supplier Web pages so they can visually confirm technical specifications and view pictures, price points, or detailed descriptions. The system creates electronic requisitions for approval, routes them through the company's approval process, and submits them electronically to contracted suppliers. When the company receives the products, the system alerts Accounts Payable to pay the suppliers. All the pieces are online—status of requisitions, approvals, purchase receipts, and the complete history throughout the purchasing process.

E-procurement systems also streamline interactions with the supplier, resulting in faster delivery. Real-time technologies, attachment capabilities, and the ability for multiple sites or offices of the same company to share the same information enable secure, immediate order placement directly between a company and its product or service supplier. That means employees can be confident that if they place an order at 3 P.M. Monday, they will receive their supplies at 10 A.M. Tuesday.

In addition to shopping, employees can use the same system for responding to other procurement events such as making sure a new employee gets squared away. That means new employees can order supplies or business cards or they can enter data human resources needs to process.

How E-Procurement Impacts Your Bottom Line

How can you maximize your company's return on investment with e-procurement? First, e-procurement solutions simplify the purchasing process by reducing the number of times a request is handled and by restoring policy control. They also can reduce the overall cost of nonproduction MRO supplies, reduce processing costs by 70%, lower the volume of transactions, and decrease the total number of people involved in each purchase. Result: more efficient buying practices.

E-procurement also consolidates purchasing activities among multiple sites and the supplier base so a company can maximize bulk rates and corporate discounts. The more employees buy from contracted suppliers, the more strategic relationships purchasing agents can forge with those suppliers. Ultimately, buyers can use valuable purchasing data to measure supplier performance and increase purchasing from contracted suppliers, which results in negotiating better contracts and forming more strategic alliances with them.

Another advantage: Companies improve and reduce their inventory levels when they consolidate their supply base and shorten requisition and order fulfillment cycles. In addition, most e-procurement systems bypass additional transaction fees so a buyer won't be

Card Talk

As part of their electronic procurement systems, some companies are issuing special corporate purchasing cards, or "P-cards," that work like personal credit cards but in conjunction with e-procurement software. Employees can use them when they buy electonrically, over the phone, or in person.

P-cards are a purchasing tool designed to reduce the costs associated with authorizing, tracking, purchasing, and reconciling business purchases while allowing a company's central purchasing and accounting agents to maintain control over the big picture. The cards enable you as financial managers to streamline your purchasing process, reduce paperwork, enhance information availability, speed up acquisition cycle time, reduce chances of error, and free up management personnel to focus on more strategic issues.

Many P-cards on the market today have authorization controls that allow a purchasing department to assign cards to individuals or departments and know that purchasing will be carried out according to their instructions. The purchasing department can restrict how, where, and when employees use their cards by establishing preset limits such as dollars per month and per transaction, transactions per day and per month, or even types of suppliers.

To help management accountants and purchasing agents track use of and realtime expenditures charged on P-cards, special OLAP (online analytical processing) tools and integrated technologies can create comprehensive customized reports by individual user. According to the Aberdeen Group, P-cards are more popular than other available options such as reconciling care statements, electronic funds transfer, or electronic/digital cash.

Ultimately, P-cards help a company with timely electronic reporting and quick access to critical transaction data. Used as part of the new model for enterprise-wide electronic procurement, P-cards are another creative business solution to extend employees the flexibility and limited control over an allocated amount of money to buy critical goods and services when they need them.

surprised with tagged-on charges. In some cases, companies can even save on taxes, depending on the geographic chain of vendors they use to obtain a product. All these benefits help reduce the actual costs as well as the processing costs associated with purchasing MRO.

An e-procurement system also decreases the number of transactions and people involved in making each purchase as well as the actual processing time. Manual transactions usually take a week to process, including all the time spent exchanging paperwork and contacting suppliers to correct errors before anything is shipped. An e-procurement purchase takes as little as a day from the time an employee makes a request to the time the company receives the goods. In fact, using some of today's advanced systems, you can order a product in about 30 seconds.

One more advantage: E-procurement, like other procurement controls, puts an end to the accounting nightmare known as "maverick buying." This practice occurs when employees circumvent corporate purchasing policies by buying materials outside authorized channels—at retail prices—from noncontracted suppliers. For example, an employee disgruntled with the cumbersome paper trail required to buy a new shelf for the office might just walk to the store down the block rather than buying it from the company's authorized office supply source and getting reimbursed by the company. With e-procurement, the look and feel of the screen is closest to the real shopping experience. The maverick can buy the product online, choosing the exact product he or she wants, and can count on immediate delivery. The employee is happy, results are immediate, and all the transactions are tracked through company channels.

Choosing the Right Web-Based Purchasing System

Okay, so how do you choose the right system for your company? Critical areas you should analyze include the system's ability to handle content and manage catalogs effectively, its ease of integration with other systems in the company, and how well you think the employees will accept it.

Start with the ability to handle the key task of content and catalog management. Look at systems that can handle all sorts of suppliers who have a variety of catalog options rather than forcing suppliers to have transactional Web sites. After all, the catering service on your block may not have a Web-based catalog already built, but your executives may still want to purchase food for client meetings from this supplier. The software must allow users to search for a product quickly and easily. Employees should never be required to know the name of a subcontracted service supplier or the model number for a particular product. Instead, they should be able to make a request and be guided by a series of prompts, menus, or events they can figure out quickly.

Today's top e-procurement solutions also update catalog and other information already available on supplier Web sites without requiring specific action from suppliers, other than authorization. Look for these features because they allow companies to set up a virtual cost center for real-time monitoring of purchases and of employees who ordered supplies.

Here's something else to keep in mind. E-commerce must be a cooperative effort between customers and suppliers that benefits both parties. Let's look at an example. The underlying technology links products to the supplier's Web site so the customer can "thumb through" a virtual catalog and see a full description of the products and pricing a supplier offers. Then the same technology maps data from this supplier's site and pulls the information into the customer's product index. Having joint use of the same data results in more accurate ordering and fewer returns—a huge cost savings shared by a company and its suppliers.

For the Technophiles

For you technophiles, here's the way the technology should work for your company. An ideal e-procurement solution manages catalog and content management aggregation methods simultaneously. Types of content management options include OBI (Open Buying on the Internet) with links to preexisting supplier Web sites and content aggregation with a firm that is managing content for multiple suppliers for an annual fee. Other methods include local catalogs with data stored internally at an organization, proactive content that embeds artificial intelligence that will go to Web sites and pull data into the catalog, and a hybrid approach of a general index stored locally that links to online catalogs and noncatalogued items.

System integration also is a crucial component of an e-procurement system that's part of a procure-to-pay network. The ideal solution is an e-procurement system that seamlessly integrates a diverse set of resources including Web-enabled applications, application data streams, and legacy data files and reports with existing operational systems. Companies often have disparate systems within the same network, particularly if they have been acquired or have merged with another company. E-procurement solutions that use middleware to layer procure-to-pay functionality onto existing systems require no additional hard wiring for transactional workflow.

Another key feature to look for is event-based purchasing. Event-based purchasing refers to buying activities that correlate with a company, department, or personal event. Examples range from supplies for a new employee, catering services for a trade show or an annual meeting, to services required to change an employee's office location.

If the system has event-based purchasing, a new hire can click on a computer icon for a folder marked "new employee" and access a comprehensive personal supply and service tool kit. Then the employee can use the electronic folder to set up and buy computer and office supplies, summon services such as setting up phone lines and an Internet connection, and set up voice mail and e-mail accounts. Someone who receives a promotion might need new business cards, or someone attending an upcoming trade show might require travel arrangements, registration materials, booth supplies, and other items that are used consistently for a similar event. The technology for event-based purchasing helps companies account for supplies and services needed for recurring events and can expedite and control the related purchase requirements.

Making the Switch

By revamping the procurement process as a whole, rather than just simplifying the purchasing "event" between buyer and supplier, e-procurement enables companies to capitalize on the benefits of business-to-business e-commerce. Because it creates operational efficiencies using Internet and intranet technologies, e-procurement drives unnecessary costs out of simple transactions and frees up employees to focus on more strategic issues than completing an order.

Let's go one step further. Coupled with Web-based enterprise budgeting and planning, companies can use e-procurement to realize cost savings like never before. E-budgeting and e-procurement together can help the finance department plan directly for a system that significantly impacts the bottom line.

Enterprise-wide electronic procure-to-pay solutions deliver on the promise of the Internet to provide streamlined solutions for business. It's easier and less expensive to distribute information via the Web, and employees can connect from almost any remote location. Web technology provides a new way to buy critical goods and services, so everyone becomes a strategic buyer and helps the company experience savings almost immediately. This positive bottom line impact is the driving force behind one of the biggest e-paybacks companies are discovering this year.

Steve Hornyak is vice president, marketing, for Clarus Corporation (formerly SQL Financials International, Inc.) and has worked for the company since 1994. Prior to joining Clarus, he worked for Oracle Corporation and for Price Waterhouse LLP in its Management Consulting Services Group. He can be reached at 770 291-3900 or via e-mail at hornyak@ claruscorp.com.

'Net Gains

John S. McClenahen

E-commerce is coming. How much your company sells or buys via the Internet is still uncertain, but it will change how companies interact with their customers, according to this article. It will allow suppliers to service their customers more quickly. It will allow purchasers to more quickly be in touch with their suppliers. Indeed, it will facilitate and hasten the symbiotic relationship between companies and their suppliers with repercussions throughout the supply chain.

Don't spend a lot of time trying to figure out whether commerce on the Internet represents a global business revolution—or is merely another evolutionary step in the ways your company relates to its customers. The reality is that e-commerce, which Forrester Research Inc., Cambridge, Mass., figures could be generating sales reaching a staggering $3.2 trillion in the year 2003, is both revolutionary and evolutionary. And it's not limited to such headline-grabbing companies as Amazon.com Inc. and eBay Inc., whose Web sites are garnering huge numbers of hits. Or to the e-business unit of Avnet Inc.'s computer-marketing group in Phoenix, which has experienced growth averaging 30% per month since November 1997.

Among manufacturers, such companies as Dell Computer Corp., Oracle Corp., Gateway Inc., Cisco Systems Inc., and Hewlett-Packard Co. already are connecting in tiny fractions of a second tens of thousands of times a day to other businesses and to consumers. And such blue-chips as Dow Chemical Co., Boeing Co., AlliedSignal Corp., and General Electric Co. are installing sophisticated e-business systems. The marketing (and financial) message they and others are sending to firms that have yet to gain their first electronic customers is, *You can't afford to wait until the revolution/evolution debate is settled.*

Indeed, executives who fail to understand the Internet and bring it into their businesses will find that in five years their companies "will no longer be competitive," warns Julie Schoenfeld, president and CEO of Net Effect Systems Inc., a North Hollywood, Calif., provider of customer-support software.

Putting a positive spin on the same thought is Northbrook, Ill.-based Steven J. Johnson, codirector of Andersen Consulting's e-commerce practice. "There really don't appear to be too many limits to scale" for companies that use the Internet to do business with other companies, he observes. The "law of diminishing returns is quickly being replaced by what appears to be the law of increasing returns," he says.

Michael McLaughlin, a partner in Deloitte Consulting's business practice in Chicago, estimates there are a half dozen scenarios for the future of business on the Internet.

Nevertheless, his bottom line is the same: Business will be substantially different seven to 10 years from now. "The Internet and the use of digital networks will become so pervasive and so ubiquitous, particularly for manufacturers, that we won't understand how we lived without [them]," claims McLaughlin.

Forrester Research's year-2003 e-commerce sales projection of $3.2 trillion, a number only slightly smaller than Japan's entire GDP, translates to nearly 5% of all global sales.

Meanwhile, about 40% of the 802 CEOs participating in this year's Pricewaterhouse-Coopers(PwC)/World Economic Forum survey figure that electronic business will account for more than 10% of their companies' revenues during the next five years. And an impressive half of that 40% expect electronic business will exceed 20% of their total revenues. By comparison, 75% of the CEOs surveyed report 5% or less of total business now coming from the Internet.

But whether or not Internet-based commerce eventually accounts for 10%, 20%, or an even higher percentage of business-to-business and business-to-consumer sales, there's no doubt that during the next several years e-commerce will dramatically alter the way companies operate.

For example, Dow Chemical Co., which is taking an evolutionary and broad-based approach to business-to-business e-commerce, expects it to significantly increase customer options for dealing with the company. Customers may be able to go online to review product offerings, check orders and invoices, pay bills easier, collaborate real-time on product and part design, and integrate supply chains.

"I would define e-commerce as electronic touch of the customer," says Richard Payne, Dow's Midland, Mich.-based director of electronic commerce. "Dow is essentially composed of 14 different global businesses. And so what we've tried to do is to look at the needs of those businesses and see if there are tools that we can build that will be utilized across those business units."

CEOs responding to the PwC/World Economic Forum survey cite servicing customers more efficiently as their primary reason for expanding their electronic-commerce operations. Significantly, 50% of the CEOs say it's likely that nontraditional competitors will pose a competitive threat by using electronic business as a major channel to reach their customers.

"This is about velocity," stresses Net Effect's Schoenfeld. By allowing people to collaborate in ways never before possible, the Internet "creates an ability to come up with new ideas better and faster and [to] move the world ahead faster," she says. "Certain market share could be won before people even know it's at risk."

But for Don Tapscott the Internet is much more than a cusp-of-the-millennium, rich, robust, and high-in-bandwidth phenomenon accelerating the development of neat new sales and marketing tools. The Internet is revolutionizing company structure, contends the Toronto-based chairman of the Alliance for Converging Technologies, president of New Paradigm Learning Corp., editor of the just-released book *Creating Value in the Network Economy* (1999, Harvard Business School Press), and, not insignificantly, said to be the first person to apply the term *paradigm shift* to business and technology.

Those who believe the future of e-business is simply more buying and selling on the Internet are "fundamentally wrong," Tapscott asserts. "We're beginning to see the emergence of fundamentally new models of the firm and of how we create wealth [that] are as different from the old industrial corporation as it was from the feudal craft shop."

Highly integrated auto, chemical, and metals companies, for example, are on the way out as such things as disaggregation (and then reaggregation) of value creation, knowledge-rich and service-enhanced products, and something Tapscott dubs the internetworked "e-business community" are on the way in. "The notion of the virtual factory is actually becoming real," he says.

Cisco Systems, Tapscott suggests, is a company previewing the future. First, the Internet is the foundation for product design at Cisco. "These products are designed by the company in multiple locations," notes Tapscott. Second, the Internet is a manufacturing platform. "Cisco routers may be assembled in the Cisco plant. But that's a small piece of the overall value creation." Third, the Internet also is a platform for support, service, and sales—about 70% of Cisco's total sales are Internet sales.

Meanwhile, the heady pace at which e-commerce is advancing will put the pressure on railroads, motor carriers, and other asset-based transportation companies to respond to new buyer requirements and preferences, says William Rennicke, a vice president of Mercer Management Consulting, Lexington, Mass. With both consumers and business customers able to connect to suppliers via the Internet, traditional distribution channels are breaking up; the trend to smaller, quicker shipments is accelerating; and the demand for more information at every point in the supply chain is rising, says Rennicke.

"Transportation companies," he says, "need to be aware that the value migration now taking place—from assets to information—will be lasting and is going to necessitate developing new business designs that can capture profit and create shareholder value."

In 2010 jumbo jets, CAT scanners, and complex computer systems still probably won't be bought on the Internet. But a decade from now as much as 30% of all business-to-business buying could be through e-commerce, believes Philip Kotler, professor of marketing at Northwestern University's Kellogg Graduate School of Management in Evanston, Ill.

Kotler says that GE already uses e-commerce to buy commodity items and is saving 10% to 15% when compared with non-Internet purchasing. Citing competitiveness concerns, GE declines to confirm or deny the percentages. A company spokesperson, however, does confirm that something like $5 billion of GE's supply transactions could be conducted on the Internet by 2002.

By 2003, Forrester Research estimates, U.S. business-to-business trade on the Internet will total $1.3 trillion, 30 times the $43 billion transacted in 1998. And as business supply chains make more use of e-commerce during the next five years, the computing and electronics industries, today's leaders, will be supplanted by the aerospace and defense, petrochemical, motor-vehicle, and utility industries, the research firm forecasts.

Dow Chemical's Payne declines to put a dollar figure on the level of e-business his company may be doing three years from now. But he's sure that e-commerce won't be the only way Dow reaches customers and suppliers. For some, e-commerce will be their preferred way of doing business with Dow; for others it won't, he surmises. Payne also is convinced that e-commerce is going to go global. Although e-business has "a U.S. centricity" now, "I would tell you that other countries will likely follow the models that are set in North America. And I would guess that that movement will occur soon after the Y2K compliance issues are behind us."

Relatively easy access to PCs, relatively high levels of disposable income, and predominantly English-language content are three reasons e-commerce, especially business-to-consumer e-commerce, is mainly a North American phenomenon now, says Andersen's Johnson. In some of the world's other significant economies—such places as France, Germany, and Japan—language is holding back e-commerce growth. Nevertheless, "it will evolve, and it will evolve following a pattern of first [having] access and second [having] content that is useful," says Johnson.

"In working closely with our European counterparts, Latin America, and even Asia, [we find that] they're looking to ramp up extremely quickly," says Phyllis Brock, vice president of Nortel Networks' Web business organization, Santa Clara, Calif.

"In five years I [don't] see Europe being any different than the States," adds Nortel Networks' John Voglin, director of e-business and Internet systems. "I would say Latin America and Africa still are going to be significantly behind because they don't have the telecom infrastructure. And I don't think wireless is going to be at a point yet to support major business communications."

Singapore is not waiting for e-commerce to casually come its way. Last September its government launched a plan designed to develop the city/nation as a global e-commerce hub. It envisions US$2.35 billion worth of products and services being traded electronically through Singapore by 2003—and 50% of the country's businesses using some form of e-commerce by 2003.

With all the impressive projections of Internet business activity and expressions of high expectations for the future, it's easy to get caught up in e-business euphoria.

The reality, however, is that making "the transition from a physical-distribution model to the electronic-distribution or e-commerce model [is] not an easy thing to do," says Andersen's Johnson. Nor is it necessary (or advisable) for companies to run to embrace e-commerce and turn their backs on traditional business channels, he stresses. "What we are suggesting to our clients is to engage, to learn, and to understand how to use this channel and how to really effectively integrate it into [their] mix of business."

Nevertheless, if digital-economy guru Tapscott is correct, the growth of electronic commerce, at least in the short term, will in part be constrained by a lack of executive engagement. "There is a real urgency for senior management in manufacturing companies to wake up and get with it," he insists. "The first thing they have to do is to start using the technology personally. If you are not using this technology yourself, you have no hope of comprehending how it can change your business."

But e-business promises to be constrained, at least in the short term, by a couple of important and largely unpublicized nonexecutive issues.

The first is taxation. In the U.S. the federal government does not (yet) tax e-commerce. And for the next two years or so, state and local governments won't be able impose any new Internet levies—thanks to a 1998 law that also set up a study commission and gave it 18 months to analyze the taxation issue.

The e-commerce tax situation before last fall's moratorium was much like driving down a toll road and not knowing where the toll booths would be, how much the tolls were, and who had the authority to collect the tolls, observes Donald M. Griswold, national partner-technical services for state and local taxes at KPMG LLP, Washington. What's being reviewed right now is "how many times we have to tap the brakes."

Significantly, Griswold doesn't foresee the e-commerce car being stopped dead in its tracks by taxation. The moratorium allows time to develop some wise policy: "some certainty, some consistency, some fairness, and, hopefully, some administrative ease."

He ultimately may be right. But the tax commission hasn't exactly roared onto the e-commerce highway. Scheduling of its first meeting was delayed for months, caught in a dispute over who should be on the panel.

And the experience of a coalition being organized by Ernst & Young LLP to help U.S. companies deal with a complex e-commerce tax issue in the European Union (EU) isn't encouraging. At a San Francisco meeting on Jan. 29, seven international companies actively involved in e-commerce—with collective sales of more than $40 billion—expressed interest in joining the coalition. But that's as far as things went—even though formation of the group was prompted by a request from the European Commission, which manages day-to-day EU operations, for advice on how to apply Europe's widely used value-added tax to Internet trade between U.S. corporations and their EU customers.

The second issue constraining the growth of business on the Internet revolves around persistent concerns about security—the protection of information in transmission and storage, the protection of e-commerce users' identities, and the verification that Internet users are who they claim to be.

"There is still really no good security infrastructure in place," asserts David Osborne, senior vice president and chief technology officer of Micro Modeling Associates Inc., New York, a $48 million consulting firm heavily involved in business-to-business e-commerce. Smart cards and other sorts of authentication are needed, he says. "I think we're at least two years away, and until then people will Band-Aid it."

Significantly, security and the related issue of privacy, which includes the rules for disclosing information, are by no means only U.S. matters. Notably, the EU last Oct. 25 put into effect its comprehensive directive of data protection, which prohibits the transfer of identifiable personal data to countries that do not provide an "adequate" level of privacy protection. The U.S. and the EU differ on what constitutes "adequate" protection, in part because they take quite different approaches to privacy. The U.S. relies on a sectoral mix of regulation, legislation, and self-regulation; the EU fancies sweeping legislation.

"The EU privacy directive provides a laundry list of requirements for companies that exchange and transport data flows," states Larry Ponemon, the New York-based head of PwC's e-business privacy-and-security practice in the Americas. "The vast majority of the corporations in the United States are not even close to being in compliance. It's like a Y2K problem times a thousand. And so in theory the EU could prevent a lot of American companies from transacting business."

John McClenahen is a senior editor with Industry Week.

The Fallacies of Web Commerce Fulfillment

Gartner Group

The Web is a great tool for purchasing and supply managers and for those who want to sell to others, but don't make foolish assumptions that using the Web guarantees you'll be successful. The same business issues that apply to every other aspect of business apply to the Web as well. This article, which is mainly oriented toward sellers, rather than purchasers, still includes good advice for purchasers both from the perspective of buying and for making decisions about who to do business with over the Web.

Web commerce transactions are often unprofitable because companies fail to change their back-end fulfillment processes. Here are the major fallacies and how to avoid the traps they set.

Spurred by reports of $3.5 billion in 1998 Web holiday sales, many businesses are reevaluating and accelerating their time lines for selling over the Internet. But for many companies, especially those with brick-and-mortar operations, this can be a dangerous path. A little-discussed, not-so-pleasant fact is that many Web commerce transactions are unprofitable because of back-end fulfillment problems. Rather than rush headlong into Web commerce, companies that desire to sell physical goods over the Internet should first craft a strategy for efficient back-end fulfillment. Enterprises that fail to do so will have lower profitability and may permanently damage customer relationships. Here are the major fallacies to avoid:

Fallacy #1: We're selling over the Web, so we must be making money over the Web. Because most companies fail to capture the true costs of fulfillment, many delude themselves into thinking their Web commerce transactions are profitable. To understand the financial impact of Web commerce, companies must capture the additional back-end costs they may be incurring because of poor processes. These may include the cost of manually rekeying Web orders into traditional order management systems, back-order costs (particularly if multiple shipments are sent to fulfill a single order), cost of handling increased call center volume due to fulfillment problems, cost of handling Web returns, and added warehouse labor and inventory carrying costs. *Action item: Measure the true costs of Web fulfillment so that the company can put a plan in place to lower them.*

Fallacy #2: Our differentiation on the Web will come from our front-end processes. A front-end Web site is often the easiest and least differentiating section of an effective Web strategy. Posting product information on a Web site and taking electronic orders are activities almost any competitor can duplicate. E-commerce leaders are now looking to differentiate themselves through relationships with suppliers and optimizing the physical flow of goods—creating improved margins and better customer service. For instance, companies that wish to sell mass customized goods over the Web (e.g., following the Dell model) often must make fundamental changes to their procurement, manufacturing and distribution processes. These changes are less easily imitated by competitors and thus translate into more-sustainable competitive advantage. E-commerce leaders are also creating real-time visibility to inventory, capacity and transportation availability and are translating this into accurate order status and delivery date information for customers. Pioneers will take this a step further and create dynamic pricing, promotions and product mix optimization (e.g., Web cross-selling) based on real-time supply and demand data. *Action item: Seek to differentiate Web commerce activities through providing guaranteed delivery, mass customization and online order status information.*

Fallacy #3: We can always do back-end integration later. Horror stories abound about firms having to hire legions of temporary workers to rekey data from a Web ordering system into the traditional order management system, companies damaging customer relationships by accepting Web orders for out-of-stock or discontinued products, and Web customers receiving multiple shipments of the same order because a single order line was out of stock and the system could not handle exception conditions. These issues are symptoms of poorly integrated front- and back-end processes and lead to excessive costs and erosion of customer loyalty. (And bad "word of mouth" spreads much faster on the Web than it ever did in the brick-and-mortar world.) In some cases, these disconnects have forced companies to shut down their Web site. *Action item: Map the process flows and touch points between the Web commerce system and the back-end systems, and integrate them before launching a Web commerce initiative.*

Fallacy #4: Our logistics operations can handle Web commerce fulfillment. Companies with highly automated warehouses optimized for shipping full pallets in truckloads to wholesalers and retailers will find that their operations are ill-suited to picking and packing the much smaller orders typically purchased over the Web and shipping these by small parcel. Companies can choose either to outsource Web commerce fulfillment to third-party logistics (3PL) providers (incurring additional cost in both 3PL charges and inventory carrying costs) or to restructure their internal warehouse operations and systems (e.g., adding a small parcel transportation management system and reconfiguring their warehouse to support picking and packing of small order quantities). Companies with multiple warehouses must decide whether to reconfigure all their warehouses to support this activity or whether they should designate one warehouse as the Web commerce fulfillment center. Companies with seasonal spikes or frequent product shortages will also need to set clear business rules about how to prioritize existing channel relationships vs. Web orders or risk damaging both relationships. An efficient process will also need to be set up for handling returned goods. *Action item: Conduct an audit of physical processes and map out short- and long-range plans to handle the impact of Web commerce, accounting for rising Web commerce volume.*

Fallacy #5: Our existing supplier relations will support Web commerce. For retailers in particular, Web commerce will require a dramatic change in mindset toward suppliers. In the brick-and-mortar store world, retailers often squeeze suppliers and maintain adversarial relationships. In the Web commerce world, retailers must create a partnership with manufacturers to enable efficient fulfillment and to discourage manufacturers from selling direct, disintermediating the retailer. Retailers setting up a Web storefront must determine the optimal fulfillment strategy, and this may include having suppliers fulfill certain items (e.g., those with high transportation costs, high product value or sporadic demand) directly rather than fulfill them from a retail warehouse. *Action item: Rethink supplier relationships and sourcing and fulfillment strategies using network and capacity planning tools to determine the costs of different fulfillment scenarios and build a cost-optimized physical network to support Web commerce.*

Fallacy #6: Our order management system can handle Web commerce. Many order management systems were designed to support a small number of pre-defined customers. Selling over the Web requires these systems to be revamped to support transactions (including credit checks and billing) from vast numbers of previously unknown customers. Effective Web commerce also requires sharing internal information with customers. Web customers no longer find it acceptable for their orders to disappear into a black hole. They want Web access to information on product availability, delivery dates, and order status information; they want the ability to see past-order history, and they want to make incremental changes to the order until time of shipment. *Action item: Plan to extend the capabilities of the order management system, especially in the area of Web self-service. Also, conduct benchmarking tests to ensure that the system can handle the higher transaction volumes found with Web commerce. Start-up companies, in particular, need to understand that high-volume order management systems cost millions of dollars and they need to budget accordingly.*

Fallacy #7: We can now sell effectively to anyone around the globe. Most companies are excited about the increased global presence Web commerce will provide, while overlooking the fact that they have become de facto exporters. Companies' back-end systems are often ill-equipped to handle international trade deals. Companies that overlook the complexities inherent in shipping internationally will alienate customers by giving them unreliable information about lead times and total shipment costs, including import customs and excise duties. Furthermore, these companies are exposing themselves to increased risk of violating export compliance laws, resulting in fines and negative publicity. *Action Item: Examine export policies and processes to determine the overall level of exposure. Consider adding international trade content to hedge against risk and to provide a higher level of service to international customers.*

Bottom Line: Web commerce involves end-to-end business processes. Companies need to place just as much focus on the back-end processes as on the front-end processes. To prevent lost transaction profitability and diminished customer loyalty, make sure to include back-end fulfillment specialists on the Web commerce project team, and budget appropriately for back-end systems integration and enhancements.

For more information on the Gartner Group, visit www.gartner.com.

Death of Salesmen

Weld Royal

This article starts with the assertion "Internet-based commerce is threatening the traditional business patterns of distributors, dealers, and field sales staffs." It then goes on to document why this is in fact the case. The question becomes can these entities continue to add value in the age of the Internet? The answer to that question is not clear now, but this article provides food for thought on the directions the Internet is taking those who sell and those who purchase.

Chuck Holstrom faced an easy choice in this decision: conduct business over the Internet or lose customers. In February Boeing Co. executives warned the national account manager for international distributor Graybar Electric Inc., St. Louis, that suppliers without a Web presence probably would be eliminated shortly. Then in March he heard much the same message from Motorola Inc. "The head of Motorola's electronic-commerce department gave us a two-hour presentation and said anyone not making the change to Web-based commerce within the next year would probably be locked out of their business for good," Holstrom recalls.

Graybar, which put up its Web site in 1995 and introduced an extranet late last year, is ready just in time for the changes demanded by customers, but Holstrom remains awed by the speed and grip of Internet fever. "The implications of what's taking place are just immense," he asserts.

Internet-based commerce is threatening the traditional business patterns of distributors, dealers, and field sales staffs. Pioneering customers are forcing suppliers to restructure sales processes and requiring salespeople to develop expertise in specific industries and hone new skills. The technology has lowered barriers to market entry so that almost anyone with a good idea can open a Web site to sell goods as Jeff Bezos did four years ago when he launched Amazon.com Inc.

Traditional book sellers have been hit hard. Three years ago Encyclopaedia Britannica Inc. eliminated its 550-member North American sales force in favor of direct mail, television advertising, and its Web site. Last November a major U.S. book distributor, Ingram Book Group, was acquired by Barnes & Noble Inc., in no small part because of the online competition that had begun to shut Ingram out of markets.

Auto dealers also have been impacted. At Queensboro Toyota in New York, the company's own Web site, as well as general listings with online distributors such as AutoBytel, has helped generate leads outside the dealership's traditional field of coverage. But the Internet also has hurt business. Approximately 10% of Queensboro's car buyers come in "having kicked tires on the Internet. They've looked at what a car costs, and then they try to tell us what a fair price is without accepting the laws of supply and demand. It's un-American," complains Al Louzoun, the dealership's general manager.

Similarly, the financial-services industry is struggling to find its role in a world where e-commerce is encroaching into territory traditionally held by salespeople. When customers used to call brokerage firm Charles Schwab & Co. they would speak to a stockbroker who would buy or sell stocks on their behalf and earn a commission for doing so. Today customers can log onto *www.schwab.com* and complete the same transaction, but without human help, at a cheaper price. Business is booming.

To compete with Schwab and other online competitors, Merrill Lynch & Co. Inc. began offering online trading to a select group of customers in March. Like Graybar, the firm had little choice. "They had a quandary," points out a stockbroker at a rival firm. "They have this huge sales force and don't want the tail wagging the donkey, but on the other hand, they were concerned about losing business, because without an online option some of their clients would have gone elsewhere."

The giant brokerage had been trying to shift its 15,000 brokers from transaction-based business into fee-based money management for several years. The Internet is speeding up that move as it drives down the price of commissions. Merrill's army of brokers ultimately will be forced to pick up the new skills and behaviors associated with money management—or exit the business.

Additional industries in the throes of e-commerce-driven change include travel, computer hardware, steel, and other businesses selling products to well-informed buyers who know exactly what they want.

U.S. companies are the first to grapple with the Internet's jolt to direct sales and traditional distribution, but others are catching up. "In Europe, customer-relationship management is one to two years behind the U.S., and Asia's a little behind Europe," points out David L. Taylor, group vice president of Business Applications at Gartner Group Inc., a research firm in Stamford, Conn.

Laws, long-term relationships, the occasional reluctant customer, and even a backlash against e-commerce may stave off the technology's effect on traditional sales channels, but no industry is immune forever. Legal challenges—such as the now dismissed lawsuit by wine distributors in Massachusetts to stop Virtual Vineyards from shipping bottles to local residents—may shelter some industries temporarily. Traditional distributors may be able to prevent manufacturers from selling to tiny online upstarts—for a time. Some well-hyped e-commerce ventures will disappear during the next few years, doomed by unsuccessful business models, established companies with deeper pockets, or investors tired of sales without profits.

"The Internet is a bubble, and it will burst, but at the same time it is changing a lot of things," says Taylor.

For many people, the Web buying experience started out with a good book. Then consumers who began testing the waters of digital commerce at Amazon.com turned to the Internet for bridal gowns, airplane tickets, automobiles, even houses. Appreciating the Internet's 24-hour-a-day, seven-day-a-week access, and the opportunity it presented for price shopping, consumers brought their buying experiences to work.

The result? Business-to-business e-commerce is taking off. As the digital waves sweep through the workplace, salespeople are feeling their force. Distributors are restructuring their businesses from the core, finds Greg Girard, research director for supply-chain management at AMR Research Inc., Boston, who authored a report on the subject last November.

Companies that once bought product, stored it, and sold it when an order came in are adopting the Amazon.com model of "sell-source-ship." In this case, a distributor buys as little product as possible, and instead borrows it on consignment or tracks it down after receiving an order. "It's a sea change affecting practices with their vendors and customers," explains Girard. "Five years from now sell-source-ship will be the dominant model," he predicts.

Graybar salesman Holstrom still spends a majority of his time in face-to-face meetings, but his message has changed. Instead of just covering prices and benefits of a particular product, every request for proposal that crosses his desk demands information on Graybar's Internet strategy and how customers can order online. "I had some concerns about e-commerce, that we would be inundated with 25 million $25 orders, but that hasn't happened. Instead, my biggest customers are asking about broad capabilities, such as electronic data interchange," he says.

Similarly, at leading cherry-picker manufacturer JLG Industries Inc., McConnellsburg, Pa., salespeople now highlight everything the company has to offer—including its online access to inventory and 24-hour turnaround on warranty information—rather than just pitching product lines, explains Wade Jones, manager of parts marketing.

For companies that refuse to acknowledge the power of the Internet, the technology and the upstarts it spawns will nibble away at market share. Neil Rackham, who coauthored *Rethinking the Sales Force: Redefining Selling to Create and Capture Customer Value* (McGraw-Hill, 1999) offers an especially grim vision: "I have little doubt that the direct effect of e-commerce is to make more than half of sales jobs go away."

Victims will include middlemen and middlewomen who once thrived on information about supply and demand, selling to customers who knew less. Through search engines and Web sites, the Internet allows buyers to come up with the same information at a much lower cost. Rackham sees "cybermediaries"—third parties who help buyers and sellers come together—replacing face-to-face pitchmen.

Already cybermediaries populate certain online communities. In 1995 Internet computer and electronics company NECX Inc., Peabody, Mass., debuted its Office & Personal Technology Center Web site, billed as the hub of high-tech commerce. Today NECX offers buyers 60,000 products—everything from personal digital assistants to motherboards. It has no factories, no inventory, no company delivery trucks, and no field sales force. "In our world, the role of the salesperson is to assist and educate and help people be more effective online. In many ways, we look at ourselves as buyers' agents. Our goal is to help them find right product," relates Brian Marley, general manager for online channels.

The group most closely resembling a sales force at NECX is the company's "market makers," who perform a service function, looking at response time to e-mail inquiries, and how to fix "events" or mistakes occurring during a transaction. They also look for ways to attract new buyers such as plugging the NECX name in user groups online.

NECX's results show that buyers will spend a good deal more money online than just the cost of a best-selling paperback. Its products cost hundreds, even thousands of dollars. The company counts orders as high as $25,000 and a growing number of satisfied buyers. Repeat customers account for 75% of revenues in its Office & Personal Technology Center division. Overall corporate revenues in 1998 reached $430 million.

Ironically, although they advocate the virtual sales call over the face-to-face meeting, many executives running upstart cyber distributors have roots in traditional sales. Marley, for example, pitched Amway products door to door as a teenager. Later, he cold-called for Nynex, persuading companies to advertise in the Yellow Pages.

After 16 years at Dow Chemical Corp., Alf Sherk launched E-Chemicals in 1998, in part to take advantage of inefficiencies he saw as one of Dow's traditional account managers handling 30 to 50 customers. "You'd have a few strategic accounts that gave you a lot of business, but the ability of a fair number of smaller accounts to contribute to your growth relative to resources spent on them was marginal," he explains. "You wanted their business, but the cost of interacting, the demands placed on you, were too much."

At E-Chemicals, Ann Arbor, Mich., Sherk established a business model to supply the demands of those smaller accounts, but without devoting to them the kind of sales resources he did while at Dow. E-Chemicals lists standard chemicals and offers financing and competitive prices—yielding savings of as much as 30%—available because he does not employ a sales force.

He compares his approach to the auto industry. "Twenty-five years ago, a buyer would specify an option, which would be relayed back to the factory and put into the car. The industry realized that individual negotiation on options was ridiculous so they put all options on all cars and satisfied 75% of customers and eliminated all that administrative work."

Finding suppliers is not always easy for online newcomers such as E-Chemicals. Although Sherk buys from a number of blue-chip corporations such as DuPont & Co., in other cases he has been turned down by manufacturers concerned about alienating traditional distributors. "The fear of channel conflict is a real issue, but most chemical manufacturers have competitors that make duplicate product lines so we can usually turn elsewhere," he says. Over time, Sherk expects the voice of the customer demanding the option of buying online will force businesses to sell to Internet marketers despite objections raised by traditional distributors.

Channel conflict occurs not just between manufacturer and distributor. Corporate salespeople are affected when companies introduce Web-based commerce. In some cases, where a manufacturer's product is a standard commodity that can be listed in a catalog on the Web, Internet commerce proves a better way to distribute it than through an expensive field sales force.

Salespeople, however, remain masters of the complex highly engineered sale, where problems come up and new ideas and fresh insight help to solve them. Peter Burr sniffs out his prospects. He knows when he drives into a town that's home to a rubber manufacturer by the pungently sweet wafts of acetophenone, a compound used to cure rubber. A rotting-egg-like whiff points to a paper-pulp mill. "In the chemical industry, smell and sight become major tools," describes the worldwide marketing manager of rubber chemicals for Middlebury, Conn.-based Uniroyal Chemical Corp., a $1.2 billion subsidiary of Crompton & Knowles Corp.

Burr sees selling as an art. Calling on a customer means first looking for pallets by dumpsters and scraping off residue for a hint of what new products the company is making. It involves memorizing framed certificates in the office's entryway given out by trade groups for product quality or community awards for philanthropy. A good salesperson knows who won the bowling-league trophy that month and the golfer with the lowest handicap. He remembers the receptionist's first name and has time for a chat with anyone he bumps into in the hall. When customers visit him from out of town, he invites them to his house for dinner.

That kind of interaction builds a relationship, which Burr relies on to break down barriers and persuade customers to reveal problems and strategies. Such ties are especially important now that the chemical industry is locked in a price war, thanks to a glut of material. "Low cost doesn't solve problems, people do. They develop new products or environmentally friendly forms of chemicals or solve shipping problems," he believes.

His company's Web site offers detailed specification sheets and lists its sales offices around the world, complementing the face-to-face meeting, which Burr calls the backbone of his division's sales strategy. "Person to person, we can come up with solutions that benefit both the buyer and the seller. Computers [and the Internet] are great tools to give us more time to use our senses, but, hopefully, will never replace them," he says.

In fact, dismal consequences can emerge when a manufacturer's Internet strategy impinges on a salesperson's territory or relationships with customers. Similarly, trouble can occur when a corporation throws up a Web site like it would a billboard and then fails to respond to inquiries. "Companies have to tie their e-commerce channel into the rest of the business processes, and a high percentage haven't," says Frank Burkitt, a director in the Costa Mesa, Calif., office of technology consultant Pittiglio Rabin Todd & McGrath.

Cisco Systems Inc., San Jose, offers a model for integrating the Internet with other distribution channels. In 1994 the $8.5 billion data-networking giant started experimenting with the Web to serve customers when it introduced its online technical service, which included Web-based answers to frequently asked questions. Today 79% of all technical support is handled over the Internet.

In 1995 Cisco launched a system that permits customers to check the status of their shipments online. In the past, customers would call salespeople to check delivery. Salespeople would be forced to stay in the office trying to reach order administrators and then reporting product status back to customers. Delays returning calls or collecting information frustrated customers. Now all of that tracking is done by customers over the Internet on their own time. Salespeople spend fewer hours in the office.

Then, in 1996, Cisco began selling its products online. The idea was to free highly paid field sellers from as many transaction-oriented tasks as possible so they could act more as consultants and less like order takers. Picking out the right router or switch for a network can be complicated, and salespeople used to sift through orders listing detailed configurations, checking them for accuracy. Today that's all handled by a software program that allows buyers to select customized goods. If a Cisco product's specification doesn't match the customer's system, the software lets the buyer know.

"A salesperson is needed when the purchase is significant, complicated, and the decision is uncertain," says David Cichelli, senior vice president of sales consultancy at the Alexander Group, Scottsdale, Ariz. "At Cisco, that uncertainty occurs with the first sale or the new application. After that most purchasing is done over the Internet."

Weld Royal is a senior editor at Industry Week.

Looking Forward: Developing Laws for Electronic Commerce

Martin J. Carrara, J.D., C.P.M.
and Ernest G. Gabbard, J.D., C.P.M., CPCM

We have a legal section in this book, but we thought this article was better placed in this part of the book. E-procurement is here to stay, and there are certain changes in your contracts you need to consider. This article provides an overview of those changes and includes a sample agreement you can use as a starting point for contracting with suppliers over the Internet.

The use of electronic commerce for the purchase of goods and/or services is growing exponentially. Unfortunately, contract (purchasing) law has not kept pace with the speed of this growth. Therefore, the purchasing and supply professional must be aware of what laws apply and how terms and conditions are established in this electronic environment.

First, what constitutes "electronic commerce" for the purposes of this discussion? The term as discussed herein does not refer only to computer-to-computer electronic data interchange (EDI), but rather refers to all transactions for which there has been no traditional exchange of contractual documents, i.e., EDI, e-mail, fax transmissions, or even telephone orders. The reason for such a broad application in this context is that all such orders have a common denominator—they all lack the normal, written exchange which clearly establishes the terms and conditions that will govern the resulting transaction(s).

What Laws Apply?

Although the Uniform Commercial Code (UCC) is being revised to reflect modern commercial concepts, there is not yet a body of contracting law which applies specifically or exclusively to electronic commerce. Therefore, we must look to the existing body of contract law which governs all other contracts (purchase orders). These laws are the state commercial codes, most of which were patterned after the Uniform Commercial Code (UCC), and the court interpretations of those codes. Unfortunately, as previously noted, the UCC and most state commercial codes were developed 30 to 40 years ago, when computers and the concept of "electronic commerce" were inconceivable. The National

> ### *Staying Current*
>
> Many of the laws and guidelines affecting purchasing and supply professionals, in terms of electronic commerce, are being updated constantly or being addressed as issues arise. For current information, some resources are available:
>
> www.2BGuide.com
>
> This Web site offers background and drafting information about UCC Article 2B, pertaining to transactions in computer information.
>
> www.webcom.com/legaled/ETAForum/
>
> This Web site is a public forum on the proposed uniform electronic transactions act, for both lawyers and non-lawyers interested in following or participating in the drafting of the law.
>
> courses.ncsu.edu:8080/CSC379/readings/commerce/index.html
>
> This Web site offers many articles on electronic commerce, addressing security, legal, and business issues.

Conference of Commissioners on Uniform Laws (NCCUSL) and the American Law Institute (ALI) are in the process of drafting proposed UCC Article 2 revisions to deal with such modern issues; however, relief is not on the immediate horizon.

What Are the Issues?

While these codes/laws vary from state to state, they all have some common elements. Some of these elements create issues in the area of electronic commerce. The most problematic of these commonalties is the universal requirement for a "writing," contained in UCC 2-201, or your state's equivalent. Since current commercial law does not yet recognize electronic "bits and bytes" as a "writing," or as evidence of the existence of a contract, how can the contract manager or purchasing and supply professional establish a contract in this electronic environment?

What Is the Solution?

While there are many creative electronic contracting solutions being developed, they are not yet established, tested, or proven. Therefore, the most practical solution for the interim is to pre-establish the terms and conditions to govern your electronic commerce. This is accomplished by the utilization of an agreement between the parties, such as the "Electronic Commerce Agreement." See the box at the end of this article for a sample agreement. Certain issues of contract formation must be addressed for all electronic transactions, and these are covered in such a document. Other language therein will need to be revised and tailored to reflect the specific application for which it is to be used.

The sample agreement provides overriding and supplemental terms and conditions to deal with the contracting issues unique to this electronic environment. It clearly addresses the issue of the state law (or UCC) requirement for a "writing," as well as the requirement in some commercial codes for a "signature." The generally problematic issues inherent in this electronic environment are therefore addressed.

As may also be noted, the sample agreement refers to another set of contractual terms and conditions, labeled "Exhibit A." This set is needed to provide the terms and conditions unique to the electronic environment for such transactions (e.g., warranty). Such an approach will avoid the uncertainty created by the classic "battle of the forms" with which purchasers must frequently deal, even in traditional transactions. See the case study for a court decision that deals with this topic.

Case Study

The "battle of the forms" was one issue in a case between an engine manufacturer and a vehicle manufacturer [*Dresser Industries, Inc. v. The Gradall Co.*, 965 F.2d 1442 (7th Cir. 1992)]. The engine manufacturer, Dresser, and Gradall, the vehicle manufacturer who ordered engines, often conducted business through purchase orders. Typically, when Gradall sent a purchase order, it stated that the acceptance of the order would constitute an acceptance of all of Gradall's terms. Dresser then responded with an order acknowledgement which stated that it would accept Gradall's offer, but only on the condition that its (Dresser's) terms would govern the transaction. Needless to say, the two sets of terms were quite different. Without attempting to resolve this discrepancy, both parties acted as if a contract had been formed, with Dresser shipping the engines and Gradall paying for them. When problems arose, and the case went to court, one of the items debated was whether Dresser's terms or Gradall's terms applied. On this issue, the court said that the terms of the contract would be those on which their writings agreed, and "any other supplemental terms" provided by the UCC. Essentially, the case indicates that complete agreement on terms and conditions is not required, and that the UCC (in this case, Wisconsin's Uniform Commercial Code) will "fill in the blanks" when the parties fail to agree on specific terms and conditions.

Record Keeping

An ancillary issue, which is somewhat unique in this electronic environment, is that of satisfying the legal requirement of state and federal law for "records" of commercial transactions. The critical issue here is that the legal requirement for a "record" is not generally satisfied by an electronic format (disc, tape, or hard drive). The requirement for records varies considerably by statute/regulation; therefore, the purchasing and contracting professional may need to become more aware of the specific requirements. This may not be easy, since most purchasing professionals are unaware of what form of storage a "record" must take—even in the traditional purchasing transaction. Therefore, this is a subject which will need to be discussed with legal counsel, due to the diversity, complexity, and legal ramifications of such requirements.

As may be concluded, the electronic environment offers many benefits to commercial business, and it will undoubtedly increase significantly in the future. However, purchasing and contracting professionals must become familiar with very diverse state and federal requirements for creating a "writing," authenticating a "signature," and keeping appropriate "records" to satisfy many laws and regulations.

Sample Agreement

This document is an example of an electronic commerce agreement. It offers some sample contract language that would be appropriate in today's electronic commerce environment.

This Electronic Commerce Agreement is made by and between the following parties in order to facilitate their transacting business via electronic data interchange (EDI) or other method of electronic commerce.

Purchaser: Seller:

1. Parties Intend to be Bound by Electronic Data Transactions

Both parties to this agreement hereby evidence their intention to be bound by the electronic data interchanges as described herein and specifically agree as follows:

a) The parties agree that no separate "writing" shall be required in order to make their electronic transactions legally binding, notwithstanding any contrary requirement in any law.

b) To the maximum extent permitted by law, the parties hereby agree that the electronic data interchange procedures will be adequate to satisfy the requirement of any writing which may be imposed by any law.

c) The parties agree that no "signature" shall be required in order to have legally enforceable electronic transactions between them.

d) To the maximum extent permitted by law, the parties hereby agree that the confidential codes that they will be using in order to transmit information to each other will be adequate as any necessary "signature" which may be required by any law.

e) The parties hereby agree that neither will raise any defense of lack of writing or lack of signature or any other similar defense based upon a "Statute of Frauds" or similar rule in any dispute which may arise between them for any transaction entered into through electronic data interchange.

2. Offer and Acceptance

Electronic transmission of an order by Purchaser to Seller shall be effective as an offer when it is received on the Seller's terminal. Said offer shall be accepted by Seller in any one of the following ways:

  a) Via electronic transmission of an acknowledgment, acceptance, or receipt of the offer; or

  b) The shipment of the goods called for in the offer.

3. Terms of the Transaction(s)

The terms of any electronic transaction shall be those terms and conditions which may be contained in the electronic data transmissions, plus the terms and conditions attached hereto as Exhibit A. (*Note the requirement for general purchasing terms and conditions.*)

4. Miscellaneous

  a) The parties of this agreement may send and receive purchase and sale documents electronically themselves through direct interchange or through a third party network (TPN). If one party to this agreement selects a TPN to facilitate the electronic interchange, the party selecting that TPN shall bear responsibility for any mistakes of the TPN. If both parties jointly select a single TPN to facilitate their interchanges, responsibility for any mistakes or negligence of the TPN shall be borne equally.

  b) Nothing in this agreement shall be deemed to create any responsibility of either party to buy or sell any specific goods. This agreement is solely intended to facilitate the handling of electronic transactions between the parties. Neither party shall be entitled to or required to do any certain amount of business with the other, nor shall either party be required to do business with the other for any certain period of time.

  c) This agreement may be terminated by either party by giving ____ days written notice to the other. Such termination of this agreement shall not affect any transactions entered into before the effective date of the termination, even if the performance of such transactions is to take place after the effective date of termination.

  d) The parties agree that the documents to be exchanged electronically, the format to be used, and the products covered are those identified and mutually agreed upon by both parties. While it is the intent of both parties to use electronic transmission to the extent practical, this agreement does not preclude the exchange of documents by other methods when required by special circumstance.

  e) Each party shall adopt and maintain reasonable security procedures to ensure that (1) documents transmitted electronically are authorized, (2) its business records and data are protected from improper use, and (3) the security of access codes and electronic identification codes is maintained.

  f) Upon receipt of an electronic document, the receiving party shall promptly issue

> an acknowledgment to the sending party. Such acknowledgment is solely for the purpose of acknowledging receipt of electronic documents.
>
> g) This agreement shall be governed by the laws of the State of _____.
>
> Source: Ernest G. Gabbard, J.D., C.P.M., CPCM, 1998

Martin J. Carrara, J.D., C.P.M., is director of contract management in global procurement at Pharmacia & Upjohn Company. He is former president of NAPM—New York. He is an instructor of C.P.M. review and contract law seminars for various NAPM affiliates. He has authored several "Legal Briefs" columns for Purchasing Today®.

Ernest G. Gabbard, J.D., C.P.M., CPCM, is director of procurement and contracting for Allegheny Teledyne Inc. He is a frequent speaker on purchasing and contract law and management for NAPM and the National Contract Management Association and has taught these subjects for the University of California and California State University system.

Tech Talk: E-Commerce Hints and Techniques

Purchasing Today®

Every month, Purchasing Today® *includes a feature titled "Tech Talk." These are short articles that provide insight into some aspect of electronic procurement. We have compiled some of the best of the most current pieces from 1998 and 1999 in this part of the yearbook. Here's what you'll find here:*

- Digital Versus Digitized, Michelle Jolicoeur Bell
- Information "Body Guards," Phillip Green
- Saving Big Time, Robert D. Stoops
- Say Goodbye to Downtime, James T. Parker
- E-Commerce Savings, Torrey Byles
- E-Mail-Based RFP Management, Brian Caffrey

Digital Versus Digitized
Michelle Jolicoeur Bell

Web signatures are replacing wet signatures, and choosing an appropriate, secured technology is critical for your online transactions to be tamper proof.

You've just learned that you're short of critical supplies for your maintenance services division. You know that there is a quick way to remedy the situation, but you've never had to use it before. You logon on to the Web and place an order on your supplier's Web site. After placing the order, you authorize and process it by entering your password. But once you sign off, you wonder whether that was a wise thing to do. Can somebody access your purchase order and alter it in any way? Are you susceptible to fraud? Will this contract be valid in court?

More and more organizations are seeking to reengineer their business processes, particularly in the area of purchasing and supply, to take advantage of the ubiquity and cost effectiveness of the Internet. In this mass migration to the digital world, however, there exists much confusion over how to maintain the elements critical to any type of commerce:

- Proof of authenticity of the parties to the transaction.
- Proof of integrity of the transaction, documentation, and non-repudiation.
- The ability for the transaction to be upheld in the court of law.

Traditionally, these elements have been managed by securing the medium—either the paper the contract is printed on, or the private line over which the message is sent. With paper, we use the trusted, time-honored "wet" signature, and over leased lines, we use passwords. On the Internet, however, nothing is tamper proof, and passwords are easy prey for hackers. As a result, electronic signatures have been hailed as the solution to this dilemma, but just what is an electronic signature? Definitions vary, but there are two very distinct methods of electronically signing a document.

Digitized Signatures

The first and perhaps more familiar type of electronic signature is a digitized signature. Very simply, a digitized signature is a person's handwritten signature that has been reproduced in its identical form for use by a computer. This digitized version of the individual's signature can then be affixed to any electronic document.

In order to use digitized signatures, a purchaser or supplier must purchase a digitized signature software package. This package essentially consists of an electronic pad that is connected to your PC; an instrument that looks like a plastic pen, only without the ink; and a software program that must be loaded on each machine. The software program stores the digitized signature and allows it to be recalled and pasted onto different documents. Prices of these packages vary, and a thorough review of all available products should be conducted prior to purchase.

Digitized signatures work well in environments where the goal is to mimic the paper world by affixing a symbol that is meant to identify a particular individual as the source, or indicate that individual's approval, of the information conveyed in the document.

Until recently, digitized signatures offered nothing in terms of security. Anyone had the ability to alter the document, after the digitized signature had been put in place, making it impossible to verify the accuracy and legitimacy of the information. Furthermore, once a digitized signature was captured electronically, it was a simple matter to cut and paste it onto any other document, with or without the signer's consent.

However, accent improvements like password protection prevents unauthorized users from accessing and forging documents. There are also some products that claim to make it difficult to cut and paste signatures, and others that claim to detect alterations in a digitized signature document.

Digital Signatures

All these improvements in digitized signatures have been made in an effort to create security in something that is inherently insecure to the perils and potential sources of fraud in the electronic world. There is, however, a proven technology available in commercial off-the-shelf software that is infinitely more secure than digitized signatures. That technology is *digital signatures*.

Digital signatures are an actual transformation of an electronic message using public key cryptography. Through this process, the digital signature is actually bound to the document being signed, as well as to the signer, and therefore cannot be reproduced. The resulting signature is actually an extremely long string of alphanumeric characters. The alphanumeric characters have nothing to do with the physical representation of the signer's name, but are actually the unique result of a mathematical process involving the binary code of the message itself and the signer's private signing key (an extremely long primary number). Therefore, each time an individual digitally signs a different document, his or her digital signature will be unique to that document and hence extremely difficult to forge.

In order to implement digital signatures, purchasers and suppliers must obtain digital certificates, from a trusted third party that is willing to vouch for their identity, and their relationship to their signing keys. In the case of large organizations, this trusted third party may be the human resource department, or it may be an external entity, such as a financial institution, trusted by both the purchaser and the supplier, that issues certificates to both.

Digital certificates, or electronic IDs, are perhaps the biggest difference between digitized and digital signatures. These certificates allow you to rely on digital signatures with the assurance that someone you trust has verified the signer's identity and can vouch for its authenticity. This is somewhat analogous to signature guarantees and letters of credit offered by financial institutions. For digitized signatures to offer the same level of assurance, they would have to be analyzed by a handwriting expert and compared to a traditional handwritten signature kept on file.

Digital signatures, properly implemented and supported by an adequate public key and legal infrastructure, offer all the features necessary for secure electronic commerce including sender authenticity, message integrity, non-repudiation, and potential confidentiality.

Digital signatures are critical to the electronic conversion of any paper-based process that requires strong authentication of both the sender and the contents of the message, and/or nonrepudiation. It's absolutely imperative in placing or filling a large order that both parties to the transaction verify each other's identity and authority to place an order. In addition, there's a strong need to understand the volume for the order and the cost per unit. Thus, if something does go wrong, neither party can falsely deny the contents of the purchase order or their signature.

Legal Issues

It's important to review your state's laws before you choose between digital or digitized signatures. Some states have chosen to recognize only digital signature technology as legally binding, while others recognize that "electronic signatures shall not be denied legal effect, validity or enforceability." In other words, either type of electronic signature is legally binding and valid in a court of law.

Michelle Jolicoeur Bell is director of business development with the Digital Signature Trust Company in Salt Lake City, Utah.

Information "Body Guards"
Phillip Green, Ph.D.

The latest in high-tech identification promises to make the Internet a safe haven for business deals.

It's late Friday afternoon, and as you're checking over a critical electronic purchase order that will be processed over the weekend, you notice that the user specified the wrong product number. So you call the supplier—and begin to panic when all you get is a voice mail system. What can you do? Suddenly, you remember the supplier's new Internet ordering system has a new feature. Your mind races. Will you really be able to access and change your order?

At the supplier's Web site you enter the user name you were given when you enrolled in the new system months ago and are prompted to place your registered finger on the fingerprint scanner so the system will confirm your identity. You place your left index finger on the fingerprint-scanning device that has recently been connected to your computer. With relief you discover that you're able to access the supplier's database and that there is enough product to fill your order.

You click on the change-order option that you see on the screen. Within a few seconds, you've corrected the mistake, logged out of the supplier's Web site, and are on your way to a relaxing weekend with your family.

Sound like science fiction? It's not. In the near future, many of the purchasing systems we interact with on a daily basis will use some form of biometric identification for security.

"Eye" D Cards and More...

Biometric identification is a technique for identifying a person based on unique physiological or behavioral characteristics. The physiological characteristics used in biometric identification are relatively stable physical features, such as fingerprints, iris coloration, hand geometry, or facial features. The behavioral characteristics, such as voice, signature, and keystroke dynamics are also very stable but are influenced by the individual's personality. Depending on the nature of the system, biometric technology can be applied either for authentication—verifying that users are who they say they are, or authorization—granting access only to users who have the proper rights. This functionality acts much like using a password or personal identification number (PIN) to logon to your computer or network.

Despite the modern technologies, biometric identification is nothing new. In fact, biometric identification techniques have been around for more than 100 years, ever since law enforcement officers began to use fingerprints to place an individual at the scene of a crime. So what's new? Two factors have led to the emergence of biometrics as possible computer security alternatives today: the rapid increase in computer processing power and more sophisticated pattern-recognition algorithms. When these factors are combined with new, highly secure Internet technologies, the possibility of highly sophisticated business contracting over the Web can become a reality.

Choosing One

Which biometric technique is most suitable for a particular system (see box on Biometric Methods)? And which one will be best for you? There are many issues an organization must consider when answering these questions, but it's crucial to know that success or failure will depend largely on user acceptance, which is influenced mainly by ease-of-use, non-invasiveness, and proper functioning.

People will more readily accept intuitive and easy-to-use devices. Conversely, if they have a choice, they won't use a device that takes time and effort to operate properly unless they're highly motivated. This principle is fairly intuitive. Even though learning to drive a car is highly complicated, many people do it. In contrast, there are still people who have yet to set their VCR clocks correctly!

Ease-of-use, however, won't guarantee that your security measures will be accepted. The user must also believe that the device won't cause physical or emotional discomfort. Frequently, potential users voice concerns over using fingerprint scanners, due to the strong association between fingerprints and forensic science. Eye scanners also cause anxiety. People are protective of their eyes and may hesitate to present them for scanning. Aside from downright refusal, if people fear using a biometric device, they probably won't use the device properly—which will result in an unacceptably high failure rate for you.

Therefore, user concerns must be addressed completely by educating the users to alleviate their fears.

Cost Issues

Another important issue when implementing a biometric system is cost. Many of these techniques require specialized hardware, such as fingerprint scanners, while others require only software and use commonly available hardware (such as sound cards in speaker verification).

In the next two to five years, biometric identification devices will be a part of the security systems that we use to carry out business transactions. As future generations of purchasing systems are developed, organizations will need to consider the security needs of both the supplier and the purchaser, the cost of deploying the system, and the acceptance of the user population. From there, cost-benefit analysis will be essential for getting the most out of these important devices for your purchasing system's security.

Biometric Methods

Biometric Identifications

All people have numerous unique characteristics, but the few that have proven to be viable for biometric identification include:
- Fingerprint
- Iris Coloration
- Retinal Vein Patterns
- Signature Features and Dynamics
- Subcutaneous Vein Patterns
- Hand Geometry
- Facial Features
- Speaker Verification
- Keystroke Dynamics

Web Sites

The following Web sites contain more information on biometric identification devices:
- www.biometric.org/html/testcenter.html
- www.dss.state.ct.us/digital.htm
- www.bioapi.org

Phillip Green, Ph.D. is a senior technologist at Advanced User Interfaces Lab of the AMS Center for Advanced Technologies in Fairfax, Virginia.

Saving Big Time
Robert D. Stoops, CPIM

One organization effectively uses the Internet for its integrated supply process.

The Internet continues to revolutionize the purchasing and supply profession. Many are aware of the electronic commerce (EC) potential, and the press is touting the Internet as the next "Industrial Revolution." An organization can achieve enormous process improvements and cost saving possibilities by streamlining order processes, utilizing integrated supplier relationships, and applying EC tools.

Integrated supply is defined as a close relationship with a supplier where the purchase process steps are streamlined and redundancy is eliminated. By integrating the supplier and organization's processes, resources, and high performance, New Jersey-based Pharmacia & Upjohn maximizes mutual cost savings and shares information and procedural steps. Pharmacia & Upjohn's end users perform order entry of purchases they need and electronically send the information to the supplier. In turn, the supplier provides data entry (accounting) information to the organization thus eliminating, not transferring, work.

Fundamentals

At Pharmacia & Upjohn, a good deal of time is spent in developing an EC "trading partner" agreement (contract) which outlines the role and responsibilities of each party. The basics include the supplier relationship, mutual capabilities, ordering, delivery, billing logistics, standard contract terms, and the billing function.

The supplier's Web site is also critical to success of Pharmacia & Upjohn's electronic integrated supply system. Purchasing and supply investigates and questions the following: Is there an adequate investment in infrastructure resulting in adequate response time? Is the supplier's site easy to navigate? Can one find what is wanted quickly and easily? Is the order process easy to understand? How is the process managed? What types of security need to be in place?

For those looking to develop their own system, a supplier's site must be developed with all customers in mind. Therefore, it's critical that organizations not place specialized customization requirements on the supplier. The streamlined process means giving up some of the parochial perspectives in business-to-business EC.

Reaping the Benefits

Philosophies and process initiatives adopted by Pharmacia & Upjohn in implementing the electronic commerce initiative brought in substantial savings, and have only scratched the surface. The organization includes the cost of processing, the out-of-pocket cost of purchasing, receiving, and accounts payable when calculating purchase order costs. Traditional purchase orders cost $50 each in 1997, while procurement card processes accounted for about $18 an order and Internet orders averaged $3 an order. In addition, there are unsubstantiated savings for the supplier and reduced time for the requisitioner. In 1998, Pharmacia & Upjohn processed 26,000 orders for $2.8 million through its integrated supply/EC initiative. This translates into process savings of $1.3 million and the organization expects to double the saving figures in 1999.

Streamlined Order Processes

Change can be easy, and the senior management can be convinced once the purchasing and supply function identifies the savings opportunities for the senior management. For one, Internet ordering contributes to the elimination of process steps. Once integrated supply is implemented, there is no purchase order, no formal receiving function, and accounts payable receives invoices electronically from the supplier.

Second, payment is made to the supplier based on the invoice and there is no two- or three-way match performed. Pharmacia & Upjohn, for example, shares a unique trust-based relationship with the suppliers who bill only what is delivered. The bill is paid, no questions asked. Making the process work, achieving costs, and implementing trust with the organization (for the requisitioners) and with the supplier (for adequacy of the order process, delivery, and accuracy of the bill) are critical. Simply put, the process involves the customer (the requisitioner, not the traditional purchasing department) placing the order directly with the supplier through the Internet. The supplier delivers the goods and bills the purchasing organization electronically. Streamlining means the order placement lies with the end user while ordering functions, catalogs, order history, and billing are the responsibility of the supplier. The financial controls include control over the delivery location and the charges to the department within the budget and accounting reports.

Scale the Process to the Purchase

So the first steps in implementing Internet ordering don't start with "point and click," but rather by process redesign—and it has to be radical. Purchasing and supply organizations can no longer justify $50 to $100 plus orders for many maintenance, repair, and operations (MRO) commodities including office, industrial, laboratory, and maintenance supplies. Scaling the process to the purchase also reinforces the functionality and importance of other procurement processes. The traditional purchase order is still required for high-dollar and closely-managed purchases, including inventories.

Make the "End Result" Inevitable

One thing is certain: for the first time Pharmacia & Upjohn's purchasing organization can now put into the hands of customers an effective and efficient tool that allows them to place orders themselves. Customers can now have immediate confirmation of their orders and obtain an assurance on the delivery date.

Once the new processes are implemented, the purchasing organization can refocus efforts on adding value, planning, negotiating, and developing a superior supplier base. By shedding the high-volume, low-dollar transactions purchasing and supply can free itself to assist in meeting strategic organizational objectives. Ultimately, end users will order the correct material, from the preferred supplier at the lowest total cost. When the detail work with the supplier is set in place, the process flows smoothly. That does not mean the purchasing and supply manager's job is complete. Actually, working with the EC supplier requires a lot of attention, communication, and goal setting. What's changed? Rather than concentrate on transactions (the organization) or selling (the supplier), every purchasing and supply professional works for improvements, cost reductions, and problem elimination.

Common Challenges

Integrating supply purchasing processes requires a great deal of in-depth understanding from both the supplier and the buying organization. Individuals authorized to order approve delivery locations, track order information, and expedite billing (including the proper accounting information) and identify them early in the process. Though errors seem inevitable, Pharmacia & Upjohn has found the error rate (for accounting information) to be less than five percent.

As communication bandwidths expand and other technological improvements are made, response time will continue to speed up. This is only the beginning of the Information Revolution.

Robert D. Stoops, CPIM, is procurement and audit manager for Pharmacia & Upjohn Company in Kalamazoo, Michigan.

Say Goodbye to Downtime
James T. Parker, C.P.M., A.P.P.

Checkmark all the reliability issues including backup and clustering systems before you sign on the dotted line of your information technology contract.

The complexities associated with electronic commerce, Year 2000 software compliance, and increasing pressures to stay competitive have forced many organizations to replace aging hardware, software, and integrated systems with new technology. At the same time, organizations supplying these systems are racing to provide products with the latest innovations sometimes without the traditional quality control and debugging that is necessary to ensure a reliable product. What if your information technology (IT) hardware or software fails? Have you secured an effective backup system or negotiated a reliability clause in your contract?

Ensure System Viability

Contingency planning has become a mandatory aspect of IT purchases when forming electronic partnerships with suppliers. In many cases, businesses may rely on IT systems to perform the majority of their mission-critical functions. Disruptions in these functions could have devastating and costly effects on the organization. Not planning for disaster recovery and for other unforeseen problems potentially jeopardizes the flow of internal and external information.

Get a resource commitment from the supplier at the contract stage in case downtime is caused by the failure of the IT suppliers' equipment.

All organizations should have a disaster recovery plan in place for any unforeseen crises. When new IT systems are implemented there are additional considerations that must be included in planning for IT disruptions. Resolve the following areas with your IT suppliers to ensure that you have reliable systems.

- Draft a downtime contingency plan with your supplier prior to final contract execution. This plan should include a prioritized list of expectations that your organization has for the supplier in the event of disruption. This list should include response time-frames for bug fixes, crashes, and on-site support. All potential disruptions should be covered in this contingency plan along with expected response on the part of the IT supplier. For example, depending on your needs you may want to secure a backup system for the mainframe, client server, and intranet.

- IT suppliers will normally have a great deal of experience installing their systems and can provide a good perspective on potential problems that may occur. "Clustering" computer systems to allow redundancy can be an effective tool in forestalling problems. Clustering systems allow fault tolerance, disaster recovery, and provide business continuity data in addition to providing protection against loss of critical data due to fire, theft or any other disaster. Suppliers may be able to offer expertise unique to their own products where clustering is viable. For example, you can build redundancy into the systems through mirrored or "hot swappable" drives. Hot swappable drives have larger capacity to back up data against the traditional CD-ROM or jukebox systems.
- Establish clear communication and priority channels with the IT supplier. Knowing ahead of time how to deal with different types of problems and ensuring that both parties clearly understand what steps will be taken to resolve these problems will alleviate many disputes. For example, if your hard drive with critical and current purchase orders fails to respond, ascertain in advance that this is an urgent matter and that you may require prompt service 24 hours a day from your supplier. Categorize problem areas in advance and pre-establish the level of response expected from the supplier for each problem.
- Other considerations include establishing backup processing sites or "hotsites" that will enable the organization to operate during a major disruption. For example, if your business unit is in an earthquake zone, you may want to partner with your suppliers and arrange a system to back up your records at centers outside your facility. Give ample attention to costs associated with any disruptions caused by the supplier when negotiating contracts. While some suppliers will attempt to indemnify themselves for these types of disruptions, most will provide concessions for their own expenses related to repair and recovery.
- Finally, document the contingency plan and keep it flexible. Incorporate the plan into the contract and test the effectiveness of the plan with the supplier. Include provisions in the plan to cover security and how to handle security breaches.

Research All Viable Options

As with any major purchase, it's important to find out as much about technology purchases prior to committing resources and before negotiations begin. Examine the following issues before you enter into negotiations and sign a contract.

- Check the strength of the supplier's support systems: Sometimes the glitter of the package hides the true product within. With systems software purchases, there is seldom an easy solution. Once the system is purchased promises of technical support made by marketing and or sales often do not materialize. For this reason, prior to purchase, it's important to form a team of all key players including users, and information technology professionals within your organization who have a stake in the outcome. Even if the supplier's system is reputable, ask yourself, "Will the supplier's system and technical support work for your organization?"

- Include a maintenance clause: This is especially important, if your organization needs to depend on the supplier to install, maintain, and upgrade systems, and train personnel. Growth can also limit a supplier's ability to provide support in dealing with bugs and other problems as they start dealing with bigger issues. For example, to ensure a reliable backup system, you can have the supplier conduct twice a year mandatory backup and clustering tests.
- Do your groundwork: The most valuable tool in obtaining new technology is to carefully research what others have experienced in implementing a similar project. Time spent doing this research will pay major dividends later, if it assists in making the right choices. It's important to find other organizations who are willing to candidly share their experiences. The team should come up with a comprehensive list of questions that can be divided up into specialized areas for reference checking. Each team member will contact a counterpart at an organization with experience in installing the version of the IT system being considered. If possible, it's also important to find out what concessions were won in negotiations and what others paid for the product(s).

Ongoing Commitment

Salespeople move on to selling to other clients. It's important to get to know the technical support personnel and the installers prior to contract signing. Commitments must be made to support your IT system, especially during the implementation phase. Build a formal complaint process into the contract so that diplomatic and legal means can be utilized to minimize problems later. If a system fails to fulfill the requirements as promised by the supplier, the supplier must be held accountable and be willing to negotiate a refund, credit, or other suitable settlement. An IT supplier should be treated no differently than any other supplier you deal with.

The issues discussed should help you prepare for the unexpected. With today's competitive environment, organizations cannot afford technology failures. A straightforward plan of action can mean success and an assurance your organization will continue humming along.

James T. Parker, C.P.M., A.P.P., is director of purchasing at the University of Utah in Salt Lake City, Utah.

E-Commerce Savings
Torrey Byles

The costs of implementing e-commerce systems may pale in comparison to potential savings.

You've read about all the advantages of electronic commerce—the ease of working with suppliers, the time it will save the purchasing department and internal users. But how do the costs of such systems compare with the dollars they will save? These figures will be of interest not only to you, but also other stakeholders in the organization. When planning to implement new electronic commerce systems for purchasing, the first step is to prepare a business case or summary to upper management. The money invested for software licenses, consulting, training, and any recurring expenses associated with the new system must produce savings that exceed the money invested.

It's important to consider that streamlining procurement produces cost savings, not increased revenues. The cost savings of the new electronic commerce systems for purchasing are usually a result of lowered prices from strategic suppliers. The new systems allow the purchasing department to consolidate suppliers and then direct the organization's purchases to these few suppliers. In return for guaranteed volumes of business, the purchasing department can negotiate 5 to 20 percent price reductions with these suppliers.

This 5 to 20 percent in price reductions is the primary benefit of the new e-commerce systems and constitute the return on the invested money. Cost savings translate dollar-for-dollar to increases in an organization's profits whereas incremental revenue gains do not. When making the business case to upper management, purchasing managers should emphasize this difference. In fact, purchasing's impact on profits is fairly easy to calculate.

Show 'Em the Numbers

First, determine the dollar amount of annual purchases that the new electronic commerce system will impact. For organizations that already possess some kind an electronic data interchange (EDI), enterprise resource planning (ERP), automatic replenishment, or manufacturing requirements planning system, a new electronic commerce system may impact only a portion, not all, of an organization's purchasing. (The existing systems already handle the purchase of key production or resale items.)

Next, calculate the percentage of the organization's annual gross sales that purchasing represents (divide annual purchases by annual sales). In other words, if your organization had sales of $100 million in 1998, and it made purchases of $40 million, then the percent of sales that purchasing represented is 40 percent.

Next, divide this percent by the organization's profit margin, which itself is a percent. If your organization's margin is 10 percent, and purchased items represent 40 percent of sales, then 4 is the factor that you will use to determine the impact of the new system on profits.

The factor obtained by dividing the purchasing percent by the company's profit margin is multiplied by any net change in purchases that are enabled by the new e-commerce system. Remember, this is the amount you negotiated to reduce prices by when consolidating suppliers. If the system allows you to reduce purchase prices by 5 percent, then the impact on the organization's profits of this reduction is 4 times 5 percent, or 20 percent. In other words, a 5 percent reduction in spending results in a 20 percent gain in organization profits (all other factors being equal). See the box "Figuring Out the Savings" for the formula and some hypothetical examples.

Figuring Out the Savings

Here is a summary of the relationship between cost savings, profit margins, and profit contribution resulting from savings. The first example shows that a 5 percent savings in an organization's total spending can translate to a 20 percent gain in organization profits, given the specific assumptions regarding margins and proportion that supply expenditures represent of total sales. In this example, notice how much the percentage change in organization profits can increase as the percentage change in purchasing increases.

Purchasing's Multiplier on Profits (values are hypothetical)

(40%	/	10%)	X	5%	=	20%
(40%	/	10%)	X	10%	=	40%

Purchasing as a percent of revenues (calculated by dividing purchasing dollars by annual gross sales)	Profit margin	Percentage savings in spending new system allows	Percentage change in organization profits

Depending on the organization and industry, spending on MRO and other indirect items can be greater than direct production and resale items. Obviously, banks and government agencies spend much more on supplies than production goods. Yet even process manufacturers and utilities—companies with vast physical plants to maintain—actually will spend more on indirect maintenance items than direct production items (such as raw materials or fuels). This means, right from the start, that attention and systems that are applied to the indirect purchasing function can lead to greater absolute savings than attention and systems paid to direct purchasing.

Torrey Byles is president of Granada Research, an information technology consulting company in El Granada, California.

E-Mail-Based RFP Management
Brian Caffrey

If you recognize e-mail as a versatile electronic commerce tool that supports your purchasing and supply efforts, you might consider it as the medium for helping manage your RFP processes.

The majority of purchasing and supply professionals now have Internet access, yet very few are taking full advantage of its potential. The most popular online activities are interorganization e-mail, general information gathering, and some limited sourcing activity. Many organizations are developing strategies for expanded use of the medium and are exploring various commercial solutions that will facilitate their entry into the world of electronic commerce. Although this cautious approach is understandable, there are low-cost and low-risk ways to use existing technology to realize some of the benefits of electronic commerce now.

The Power of E-Mail

E-mail is one of the most powerful communication tools available and, in combination with standard desktop programs, can help purchasing and supply management professionals manage their bid solicitation process. Of course, to take advantage of this sourcing area through e-mail, suppliers must have suitably modern e-mail systems. It's wise to survey all of your suppliers prior to embarking. Ill-equipped suppliers should provide you with a timeline of their information technology upgrades.

Although the bid process is basically just a formalized communication, it's often a labor-intensive process with many non-value-added elements. The focus of the bid process automation approach presented here is on three non-value-added elements.

1. Mechanical aspects of bid document development
2. Bid document distribution
3. Compilation of bid responses

There are a few basic tools necessary to start automating the bid process:

- E-mail program
- "Public key" encryption program or digital certificates
- Database of supplier e-mail addresses and "public keys" (Current generation e-mail programs allow for both e-mail addresses and recipient public keys or digital certificates to be stored in their built-in address books.)
- Template RFP/RFQ documents
- Adobe PDF (Portable Document Format) document writer (Although this tool is optional, it allows for sharing of documents across multiple computer operating systems.)

After these basic tools are in place, you may proceed with the following supplier-related steps:

- Notify suppliers of your intention to move to e-mail as a primary communication tool and of the need to encrypt sensitive communications.
- Survey suppliers on e-mail servers, e-mail clients, maximum attachment size, desktop operating systems, and public key status.
- Provide suppliers with e-mail contact information and public keys for purchasing.
- Offer to educate suppliers on the usage of public keys and on how to obtain them.
- Solicit e-mail addresses and public keys from suppliers.
- Inquire about suppliers' other information technology capabilities.

Prepare to Distribute Your E-Mail-Based RFP

Once the foundation has been laid, the actual process of preparing and distributing bid solicitation packages is illustrated in the table "Distribution Cost Comparison."

The March 10, 1997, edition of *Forbes* reported on a commercially available automated bid process system. The article stated, "[The provider] claims cost savings of 10 to 15 percent, thanks to more and lower bids. It also claims a five-day savings in order time, thanks to the immediacy of the Internet." Of course, the actual benefits to be derived will vary by organization. Nevertheless, the potential for tangible returns is very real. Automating the process using readily available information technology tools promises to bring a number of benefits to purchasing's organization, including:

- Reduced cycle time
- Elimination of non-value-added activities
- Improved productivity
- Improved process quality
- Reduced process cost
- Potential for reduced product/service cost

Using e-mail to distribute bid solicitation packages in such a manner makes it as easy to send out 100 packages as it would be to send just one. In fact, if purchasing and supply distribute a large number of bid packages, the direct distribution cost savings alone could justify implementation.

North Carolina: "You've Got Mail!"

Whether or not e-mail-based RFP management is right for a particular purchasing and supply organization is up to those observing a need for automation in this area. You and your organization must be clear about your needs. Support from senior-level decision makers is critical to ensure success of an RFP management system.

On the public purchasing level, North Carolina is gradually moving toward an e-mail-based invitation-for-bids (IFB) management system. While not fully e-mail based, North Carolina's Division of Purchase and Contract spearheaded a new online supplier notification system. Called Vendor Link NC, registered suppliers receive overnight e-mails alerting them to posted solicitations for more than 250 of the state's major agencies (which include universities, community colleges, and various state departments). Suppliers fill out an online form telling Vendor Link NC what categories they want notification in. The e-mail alert pushes to potential suppliers information on specific solicitations and gives them an address to go to on the Internet to download the specification.

Until statutes change, state agencies cannot receive the supplier's proposal via encrypted e-mail. However, an e-commerce task force headed by North Carolina's secretary of state is working on legislation to enable use of a complete end-to-end electronic system.

The current benefits of the North Carolina system are many. One highlight is the fact that suppliers don't have to go to the many state agencies separately. In addition, both state agencies and suppliers can develop specific queries (sorting steps) that allow both groups to send to and receive from very specific audiences. The savings in time, postage, paper, and aggravation have already been dramatic. For example, since May of this year, an average of more than 10,000 e-mail notices per week have gone out versus the old paper method of alerting potential suppliers.

North Carolina's e-mail-based IFB management system is just one example of what is possible in today's technology driven environment. The state's efforts to improve on their current systems reflects the typical approach of organizations today to use technology to continuously improve their current practices.

Distribution Cost Comparison (two-pound package)	
Distribution Method	**Direct Cost/Recipient**
Overnight Delivery Service	+/ $10.00
USPS Priority Mail	$3.20
E-Mail	$0.00 (No cost)

Create Your Best First Effort

The best first effort of purchasing and supply professionals is to assess their own environment and determine if an e-mail-based RFP management system will enhance their processes.

In order to bring strategic value to its organizations, it's important that purchasing and supply be innovative and take the lead in business-to-business electronic commerce initiatives. As William Oncken says in the opening pages of his book, *Managing Management Time*, innovation is particularly vital to the success of any enterprise since "...without this the goals of the organization will fail to materialize."

Brian Caffrey is president of SOLCON in Jackson Heights, New York.

Part Five

Supply Management's Legal Environment

Legal issues aren't necessarily the most interesting part of the purchasing and supply process, but an understanding of them is, indeed, necessary. Helping you keep current on the legalities involved in making purchasing decisions for your organization is the focus of Part Five. We've sought to give you a good selection of pieces that will help you both understand these legal issues and some sense of where things are going with legalities in the future.

We start this part with an original article written by Ernest Gabbard, a regular contributor to NAPM publications. He explains how laws affect the purchasing process and takes us through these laws using a specific purchasing example. If you're looking for a quick primer on this field, read "The Legal Environment of Procurement."

For more background on the law and purchasing, we have included a variety of other articles. For example, "Got You Covered! The 21st Century Approach to Customer/Supplier Agreements" by Patrick S. Woods provides a review of items you should be sure are covered in agreements in the new millennium.

Also included is a guide to intellectual property for the purchasing manager: "Intellectual Property: What Is It? Why Is It Important to You?" by Leslie S. Marell. Here you'll learn about the importance of understanding intellectual property law when contracting with suppliers.

Then, because there are a number of laws you might not take into consideration when contracting with suppliers, we've included the article, "What's on the Books? Other Laws Affecting Purchasing and Supply." This gives you an overview of several different laws that you should know about, especially regarding international transactions.

We conclude this part of the yearbook with a series of articles similar to those in the "Tech Talk" section of Part Four. Here we have compiled a series of "Legal Briefs" pieces from *Purchasing Today*® dealing with a series of legal issues. These range from "Contract Clauses: Playing It Safe" to "The Statute of Frauds in Cyberspace" to "Do You, Purchaser, Take This Contract...." Each of these provides you with one or more legal points that will help you concur with the law, but more importantly, avoid problems that can occur because you didn't understand the legal implications of one type of purchasing decision or another.

The Legal Environment of Procurement

Ernest G. Gabbard, J.D., C.P.M., CPCM

In this original article by special contributor Ernest Gabbard, we learn some specifics of the legal environment that those in purchasing and supply must be aware of. There are many laws in this field as well as many precedents. Purchasing managers, through either ignorance or lack of concern, may pay a heavy price for not knowing about these laws. The author takes you through a number of purchasing scenarios and points out the legal ramifications of each one.

The modern procurement professional is more than just a purchaser of goods and services. An objective review of the activities of procurement professionals will reveal that their activities affect the legal rights and obligations of their employers in a multitude of ways. These rights and obligations can encompass the laws of contracts, intellectual property, antitrust, labor, environmental, and torts. It is therefore imperative that we have a clear understanding of the legal environment in which we function.

To illustrate this premise, let's analyze a typical purchasing transaction being conducted by a typical procurement professional on a typical business day. This may reveal the "legal" ramifications of such transactions.

Most procurement transactions begin with the receipt of a purchase requisition (P.R.) by the procurement department, which summarizes the requirement to procure a product or service. For this illustration, let's presume that the P.R. is for a specific electronic component utilized in the manufacture of the buyer company's product.

A review of the specification attached to the P.R. reveals that it was designed by the purchaser's company and that it contains proprietary information. Information such as trade secrets often provides the purchaser's company with its competitive edge. This circumstance is actually quite common, although not frequently recognized. Such information is governed by a body of intellectual property laws. The purchaser must protect such proprietary information from unauthorized disclosure or use. This protection is generally accomplished through a proprietary information non-disclosure agreement, which must be executed between the purchaser's company and any sellers to which this specification will be provided. I have personally observed considerable litigation and company failures that were a direct result of the inability to adequately protect intellectual property. There are numerous forms of intellectual property that must be protected, such as trade secrets, patents, copyrights, and trademarks.

The RFP Process

Once the purchaser has adequately protected the company's intellectual property, the purchaser will issue a request for proposal (RFP) to qualified suppliers. Such a request is not intended to create any contractual commitment for the purchaser's company; therefore, the purchaser must be cognizant of the aspects of contract law that deal with offer and acceptance. The wording of the RFP must clearly establish the purchaser's intent to *not* be obligated to make any purchase as a result of the exchange of correspondence at this stage. Many unwary purchasers have been surprised to receive an invoice for the seller's cost of preparing a proposal because the purchaser was not clear that he or she would not pay such costs. This can be avoided by careful wording of the RFP.

Let's look at an example. A short time after an RFP is issued, suppliers provide their proposals to supply electronic component(s). Let's presume that a review of these proposals reveals that all suppliers are charging nearly the same price. This may indicate potential collusive bidding. The purchaser must be able to recognize such patterns and be cognizant of the antitrust laws that govern competitive activities of buyers and sellers. Antitrust laws are complex and require legal counsel to interpret and deal with them. Purchasers must know when and how to involve their legal department, and therefore must recognize the "triggers" for antitrust law applicability.

If the purchaser determines that collusion is not an issue, he or she will move forward with a review of the proposals. This review must include a determination of whether the vendor has taken exception to any of the purchaser's contractual terms and conditions. The purchaser's knowledge of contract law is once again important at this stage. Consider the purchaser who receives a proposal that is replete with exceptions to the terms and conditions (T&C) contained in the purchaser's RFP. When evaluating such a proposal, a purchaser must be able to determine whether these exceptions are "deal killers." This may require involvement of the purchaser's legal department, but it is the purchaser's responsibility to know when to seek assistance and guidance. Purchasers should consider seller exceptions to T&C in the proposal a red flag, and such proposals should be carefully scrutinized before making a purchasing decision.

After a detailed analysis of all proposals, the purchaser will finally select one or more of the suppliers with whom to negotiate an agreement for the purchase of the electronic component. To prepare for negotiations, the purchaser must initially determine if there is any legal requirement to purchase from the lowest bidder. While there are generally no commercial laws that create such obligations for purchasers, those procurement professionals who work in public or government environments should be aware that there are many, varied, and sometimes complex laws and regulations which exist with respect to selection of suppliers. In this illustration, our purchaser is working for a commercial corporation and is free to commence negotiation with any responsible supplier who provided a responsive proposal.

The purchaser will now meet with company management to develop a negotiation strategy for establishing a contract with the supplier(s) who submitted the most advantageous proposal. For our illustration, the purchaser proposes to negotiate with two suppliers to create a "competitive" environment and obtain the lowest price from both suppliers. Purchasers must be sensitive to what laws might govern the conduct of such negotiations with suppliers. For example, are there any commercial laws that would prohibit purchasers from sharing the price received from supplier A with supplier B, for the purpose of negotiating a better price with supplier B? Alternatively, are there laws which would prohibit purchasers from misleading a supplier into believing that they must lower their price in order to beat their competitor's price, when that is not true?

To answer these questions, the purchaser must be sensitive to antitrust law in preparing for negotiations. The purchaser will find that there are very few legal limitations on sharing information from one supplier to another. However, most procurement professionals would agree that there are significant ethical issues regarding such practices. With additional research, the purchaser would also determine that the strategy of "misleading" a supplier in this manner is a violation of antitrust laws, and could subject the purchaser and the employer to significant penalties. Clearly, such a negotiating ploy should be avoided.

The Purchase Order as a Contract

After the negotiations are complete, the purchaser will issue a purchase order (P.O.) to the supplier(s) to satisfy the requirements contained in the P.R. that the purchaser received during the initial stage of the procurement process. Since the P.O. is a contract upon acceptance by the seller, the purchaser must be familiar with commercial contract law. This is a subject about which volumes are written and about which most purchasers will possess only a superficial understanding.

Purchasers do not generally represent their employers as attorneys; therefore, consultation with the purchaser's legal department will be necessary at certain stages of the procurement process. It is critical that purchasers have the ability to recognize the legal issues that can arise during this contract formation stage. Most purchasers will require a working knowledge of the Uniform Commercial Code (UCC) or of their state's version of the UCC in order to avoid the problems associated with either unintended contract formation or failure to form a contract when it was intended that one be formed. In this instance, purchasers should ensure that their P.O. is clearly the "offer" and that the supplier's response thereto becomes the "acceptance," pursuant to the applicable commercial code. The terms and conditions T&C contained in the purchaser's P.O. are critical to establish the respective contractual rights and obligations.

The supplier's acceptance of the purchaser's P.O. is frequently the stage at which substantial disagreement is encountered on what (T&C) will apply to an order. This is because suppliers frequently take exception to some or all of the purchaser's T&C. In such a case, will the T&C contained in the purchaser's P.O. govern, or will the T&C exceptions contained in the seller's acceptance govern? This is the so-called "battle of the forms" that has become so prevalent in the commercial contracting environment. The best defense in this "battle" is the language contained in the purchaser's P.O. It is therefore imperative that the purchaser comprehend the legal ramifications of this document and ensure that these T&C are clear, unambiguous, and undisputed.

At this point, let's presume that our purchaser has done a great job of establishing a contract with T&C which clearly outline the legal rights and obligations of both purchaser and seller in accordance with the aforementioned laws and regulations. What other laws could possibly affect the purchaser? Let's look at a few other issues that could arise in a "typical" business day.

E-Commerce Contracts

What about formation of a purchasing contract in the electronic-commerce environment? A review of the current contract laws in virtually all jurisdictions will reveal several significant issues with establishing a contract in "cyberspace." The purchaser will therefore need to recognize the additional requirements with which he or she must deal when conducting business electronically. For example, how does the purchaser satisfy the legal requirement for a "writing" that is contained in the commercial code of most states? The purchaser will generally want to establish an overriding agreement for electronic commerce whenever there may not be an exchange of traditional documents that could constitute a "contract."

Defective Products

What if our purchaser in this illustration receives a defective product from the supplier? This is not uncommon, and would require that the purchaser be familiar with the commercial law that deals with warranties, a warranty breach, a warranty disclaimer, and a waiver of warranty. Such a defective product could also cause a personal injury to an employee or third party; therefore, the purchaser could be exposed to tort law, which covers such circumstances. While injury claims are fairly rare, the rights and liabilities of the parties will become critical and will be significantly affected by the adequacy (or inadequacy) of the contract established.

Installation Issues

What if the contract required installation of purchased equipment or other services by the supplier on the premises of the purchaser's company? This raises many other legal ramifications that are governed by completely different bodies of law, such as labor law and tax law. Such transactions may even be governed by a different set of contract laws, since the UCC discussed above applies only to "the sale of goods." Whenever purchasers contract to bring supplier employees onto the purchaser's premises, the purchaser must be sensitive to the myriad of issues which exist in this area of the law.

Disputes

What if the purchaser and seller have a dispute about some contract term, such as price or delivery? The purchaser will need to recognize the potential of such a dispute resulting in litigation (lawsuit) and should understand the alternatives to litigation, such as mediation and arbitration, which are becoming increasingly popular for resolving commercial disputes. These are all governed by divergent laws and/or regulations that have a significant effect on purchasers rights and obligations. The potential for disputes should be considered when developing the contract during the formation stage, and appropriate clauses should be incorporated in the contract T&C to provide for alternatives to litigation.

Foreign Suppliers

This illustration has thus far been based upon procurement of electronic components from a domestic supplier. Would the legal requirements and ramifications change if the procurement were from a foreign source? In a word—*absolutely!* Laws of the seller's country and/or international laws would potentially supersede all of the bodies of law previously mentioned. This will often necessitate utilization of specialized international legal counsel. Some examples include:

- The UCC or state commercial code requirements may be replaced by a foreign law equivalent or by the United Nations Convention for International Sale of Goods (CISG).
- Intellectual property laws are considerably different or non-existent in many countries, so protection of the purchaser's intellectual property is substantially more difficult.
- Contract disputes potentially would not be subject to resolution in U.S. courts. Foreign courts are not generally a good alternative. Therefore, it is even more imperative that the T&C contain appropriate alternative dispute remedies.
- Tort laws are quite different from country to country. In fact, tort (civil) laws in some countries are tantamount to criminal laws in the U.S. It is therefore critical that purchasers be sensitive to the significant legal ramifications of foreign sourcing.

Conclusion

As you may conclude, what might seem like a complex transaction in the domestic U.S. market is exponentially more complex in the international legal environment.

It should be apparent that you will periodically need legal advice and counsel. However, the procurement professional must know when to seek assistance from the legal department. A functional understanding of these laws is therefore imperative in our modern commercial environment. Remember, ignorance of the law is not an excuse.

Ernest G. Gabbard, J.D., C.P.M., CPCM, is director of procurement and contracting for Allegheny Teledyne Inc. He is a frequent speaker on purchasing and contract law and management for NAPM and the National Contract Management Association and has taught these subjects for the University of California and California State University system.

Purchasing and Law: What's the Connection?

Martin J. Carrara, J.D., C.P.M.
and Ernest G. Gabbard, J.D., C.P.M., CPCM

> It's one thing to know the laws that affect what you do as a purchasing and supply manager; it's another to understand the source of those laws and why they are like they are. This article is designed to give you some background on things like the source and differences between common law and statutory law, the law of agency (appointing someone to act in another's behalf), and the relationship of all this to the purchasing and supply function.

W hy should purchasing and supply professionals be versed in purchasing and commerce laws? Every day, purchasers establish and manage business relationships with other commercial entities. The laws affecting these activities are complex, and include laws in the areas of contracts (which is the primary law affecting purchasing), agency (which is the source of legal authority for the purchaser), antitrust, intellectual property, labor and employment, and the environment, to name a few. Without a basic understanding of the legal aspects of purchasing, professional purchasers may encounter trouble. Purchasers who are uninformed concerning the legal aspects of purchasing may find themselves unintentionally or prematurely bound to a contract with a third party, or they may be surprised to find that they are unable to enforce an agreement they thought existed with a supplier. If a problem or dispute arises, they may find that the allowable remedies are less extensive than what was anticipated or they may be faced with unexpected liabilities. Violations could even potentially involve criminal penalties for the purchaser's organization or for the individual purchaser! However, when armed with some basic knowledge of the laws affecting purchasing, professional purchasers can proceed with confidence knowing that their rights will be protected and that they understand their obligations, risks, and liabilities. They will also be able to spot potential issues and know when to seek legal counsel to avoid or minimize their impact.

Sources of Law

Generally speaking, U.S. laws derive from two primary sources, "common law" and "statutory law."

Common Law

Common law originated in England and became the foundation of U.S. law in the original 13 colonies. It is not based on written rules of law, but rather is a body of legal principles based on historical customs, reason, and justice. Common law develops over time as courts make decisions on a case by case basis, developing what is known as "case law." In deciding cases, judges look to prior judicial decisions for established precedents, and make adaptations only to account for changing conditions and societal needs. Common law also includes a body of law known as "The Law Merchant." The Law Merchant was originally a separate body of law, as merchants trading around the Mediterranean Seas developed their own rules to govern their business transactions and resolve disputes, and it became part of the English common law in 1677.

Statutory Law

In contrast, statutory law consists of written rules of law enacted by legislative bodies at the federal, state, or local level. Statutes may override the rules of common law. Judges cannot change statutory laws, but they do interpret these laws as they apply to the facts of a particular case.

The United States Constitution prescribes the areas of law that are within the jurisdiction of the federal government, leaving the balance of law within the purview of the individual states. Much of commercial law, including contract law, is left to the states.

In the early years of U.S. history, as interstate commerce was spreading, it became increasingly difficult and confusing to conduct business due to the variations in commercial laws from state to state. In response, the National Conference of Commissioners on Uniform State Laws (NCCUSL) was formed to develop uniform laws that would be enacted by the various states. In 1896, NCCUSL completed its first such draft, the Uniform Negotiable Instruments Law, which was adopted by all of the states. This law applied to checks, drafts, and notes, but not to sales. The Uniform Sales Act, which was based on the English Sales Act, was approved by NCCUSL in 1906 and was adopted by 30 states. The Uniform Warehouse Receipts Act (1906) and the Uniform Bills of Lading Act (1909) followed shortly thereafter.

The Uniform Sales Act was viewed as not being comprehensive enough and thus still left too much variation between the states in the area of contract law. Additionally, there were no less than four proposed uniform codes governing commercial transactions (the Uniform Negotiable Instruments Law, the Uniform Sales Act, the Uniform Warehouse Receipts Act, and the Uniform Bills of Lading Act). As commerce in the United States grew rapidly, due primarily to the expanding transportation channels and communications network, it quickly outpaced these early attempts at uniform law. In 1942, the NCCUSL teamed up with the American Law Institute (ALI) in a major effort to develop a code that would alleviate these shortcomings. The first draft of the Uniform Commercial Code (UCC) was published in 1952 and was adopted by Pennsylvania in 1953. A substantially

The Role of Legal Counsel

What is the appropriate role for legal counsel in the purchasing and supply environment? All too often, purchasers may view the attorney, at best, as the one to resolve a problem that has already arisen or, at worst, as someone who attempts to prevent the purchaser from doing what he or she wants to do. Modern purchasing professionals view their legal counsel as a business partner. They know that by taking the appropriate steps, their attorney can help them to avoid many problems, to be prepared in the event that problems occur, and to develop the best possible solutions to accomplish their business objectives. Some organizations will have legal counsel in-house; others, particularly small organizations, will have an outside firm or individual with which they contract legal work. In either case, the purchasing and supply professional should have access to legal counsel as needed.

Purchasers should help to educate their legal counsel regarding their business operations. The more familiar the attorney is with the specifics of an operation, the better he or she will be able to help find the right solutions. Purchasers should form the habit of consulting with their counsel in advance of some planned business activity, rather than seeking assistance from legal after a problem or dispute has arisen. Additionally, purchasers should clearly outline all of the facts, rather than presenting the attorney with only a narrowly defined question or situation. Counsel's role is to know the laws governing a transaction and to apply them to the facts at hand, helping purchasers to understand the business risks and alternative solutions. In this way, the attorney does not simply tell individuals what to do, but rather helps clarify options and determine what action is in the purchaser's best interest. Finally, purchasers are well served by gaining a basic understanding of the legal aspects of purchasing, by attending seminars, and reading published works such as the articles in this book. This is not intended to transform the purchaser into an attorney so as to eliminate the need to seek counsel, but rather to help the purchaser spot potential legal issues and recognize the appropriate time to seek such counsel.

revised version was published in 1958 and it was this version that saw widespread adoption by the states.

It is important to understand that, although the UCC is a set of rules governing commercial transactions, the UCC itself is not law. The UCC as adapted (and sometimes modified) by the individual state legislatures is the statutory law that governs commercial transactions in that state. There may be variations in the UCC as adapted from state to state, and there may also be differences in the judicial interpretation of statutes in different states. Purchasing and supply professionals should check with legal counsel to understand the nuances in their particular state. In a dispute between contracting parties from different states, in the absence of an express provision providing which state's laws shall govern, the court hearing the dispute will make the determination of which laws apply based upon its own conflicts of laws rules.

Article 2 of the UCC applies to the sale of goods and replaces the Uniform Sales Act. In making decisions in cases involving the sale of goods, courts look first to the individual state's version of the UCC and then to case law when the UCC rules require interpretation or do not address the specific issue at hand. The UCC is not applicable to contracts for services, and courts primarily look to case law to resolve disputes in this area, although they may apply UCC rules by analogy. For an example see the case study at the end of this article. Where a contract is for a sale of both goods and services, courts may make a determination as to which—the goods or the services—is predominant. If the contract is predominantly for the sale of goods, the state commercial code (their adopted version of the UCC) will be applied. The common law will be applied where services comprise the predominant part of the contract. (In some cases the courts may apportion the contract, splitting it into one portion to which the state commercial code applies and another to which common law applies.)

The Law of Agency

Agency is a term used in law to describe the relationship that is created when one person (or entity) appoints another person (or entity) to act on his or her behalf in transactions involving third parties. Purchasing and contracting professionals generally perform their duties as agents of their employer, who is considered to be the principal in the agency relationship.

The extent of authority granted to the purchasing professional (as agent) will depend on the organization for whom he or she is acting. Government purchasing/contracting officers have very clear, express authority granted by statute and/or written certificates of appointment. The purchasing manager for a small company may simply operate under the implied authority inherent in his or her position or title. Purchasing professionals should recognize that performance of their function as an agent for their employer is considered to be "fiduciary," which requires that they exercise their authority with complete loyalty to their employer. The employee may, therefore, be held personally liable to either the employer or a third party for any improper actions.

Because of the significance of this agency relationship, the purchasing professional should have the terms of his or her authority expressed in a written agreement. However, the absence of such a written agreement does not obviate the existence of such authority, since purchasing personnel have been held to have implied authority to act on behalf of their employer. An employee may also be found to have apparent authority to act as an agent for his or her employer if it appears to a third party that he or she has such authority. This is often the case where a nonpurchasing person (e.g., engineers and project managers) makes a commitment for the employer and appeared to have authority to do so. This is why such interface between suppliers and nonpurchasing personnel should be restricted.

Case Study

The UCC gives a party to a contract for the sale of goods the right to demand adequate assurance of performance from the other party when there are reasonable grounds to believe that the other may commit a breach. UCC section 2-609(1) provides: "A contract for sale imposes an obligation on each party that the other's expectation of receiving due performance will not be impaired. When reasonable grounds for insecurity arise with respect to the performance of either party the other may demand in writing adequate assurance of due performance and until he or she receives such assurance may, if commercially reasonable, suspend any performance for which he or she has not already received the agreed return."

Does a party have a right to demand adequate assurance of future performance when reasonable grounds exist to believe that the other party will commit a breach, where the contract is not governed by the UCC? The New York Court of Appeals recently addressed this question in *Norcon Power Partners v. Niagara Mohawk Power Corp*, No. 172. In this case, Niagara Mohawk, a public utility provider, entered into a 25-year agreement in 1989 for the purchase of electricity from Norcon Power Partners, an independent power producer. In accordance with government regulatory policy, Niagara Mohawk would pay above-market rates during the initial years of the agreement, and would recoup these overpayments through reduced rates that would be phased in during the later years. In 1994, Niagara Mohawk anticipated that Norcon would be unable to fulfill its future repayment obligations and demanded assurance of performance. Norcon refused on the basis that Niagara Mohawk had no such right to demand assurance of performance under New York common law. In a decision issued on December 1, 1998, the New York Court of Appeals ruled in favor of Niagara Mohawk, importing the doctrine from UCC 2-609 into New York Common Law, saying, "This Court is now persuaded that the policies underlying the UCC 2-609 counterpart should apply with similar cogency for the resolution of this kind of controversy. A useful analogy can be drawn between the contract at issue and a contract for the sale of goods."

Martin J. Carrara, J.D., C.P.M., is director of contract management in global procurement at Pharmacia & Upjohn Company. He is former president of NAPM—New York. He is an instructor of C.P.M. review and contract law seminars for various NAPM affiliates. He has authored several "Legal Briefs" columns for Purchasing Today®.

Ernest G. Gabbard, J.D., C.P.M., CPCM, is director of procurement and contracting for Allegheny Teledyne Inc. He is a frequent speaker on purchasing and contract law and management for NAPM and the National Contract Management Association and has taught these subjects for the University of California and California State University system.

Got You Covered!
The 21st Century Approach to
Customer/Supplier Agreements

Patrick S. Woods, C.P.M., A.P.P., CPIM

Some companies have not even defined, much less, stated in writing, the expectations they have for their suppliers nor of themselves. On the other hand, some companies have strangled their suppliers with legalistic, cumbersome, and voluminous contracts that penalize their every move. This article moves us away from both extremes of the spectrum to more neutral territory by focusing on developing customer/supplier agreements that provide the purchaser with necessary and desired coverage but also benefit the supplier.

It has often been said in reference to any type of written agreement that it is normally designed to benefit the customer. This article will also focus on the major areas that should make up this agreement to maximize your coverage, but also develop a relationship with suppliers that is mutually beneficial. Focus areas of the agreement include term, formulas to effect price change, cost reduction goals, volume incentive rebates, technology and goals in respect to quality and delivery.

Note: The clauses explained in this paper make up what is commonly referred to as the Long Term Agreement (LTA). The LTA is different from a contract in that the LTA is a written summary of the goals to be achieved in the customer/supplier relationship. However, with a written notice (normally 30 days), either or both participant(s) can terminate this agreement. A contract implies a more "legalistic" document with termination being much more difficult and violations being subject to either litigation or arbitration. These recourses are not even addressed in the LTA. In association with the LTA, the purchase order is the contract.

Specific Clauses—Term of the Agreement

This is a very important element in that it establishes the tone of the relationship. In the clauses listed below, it is obvious that you are expecting a great deal from your supplier. They may question, "What's in it for me?" The term of the agreement states in writing that you are making a commitment to them for a certain period of time and at least within that period, you do not plan to resource the product and/or services covered to other supplier(s).

What should be the duration of the term? Agreements can certainly vary in term. Purchases that involve a lengthy start up or development time could be in longer duration than "on the shelf items." The agreements that I have been involved with are normally set for a term of three (3) years. In other cases, certain agreements may be "evergreen" in that they never expire unless one or both participant(s) choose(s) to terminate the agreement.

Sample language describing the term is as follows:

Term. The term of this agreement will be for a period of _____ years, commencing on _____ (the "Effective Date"). The term of this agreement will be extended automatically, in increments of one year, unless either party gives written notice of termination no less than 30 days prior to expiration of the then-current term. For purposes of this agreement, each reference to a "year" will refer to the applicable twelve-month period(s) beginning on the Effective Date of this agreement and/or subsequent anniversaries of the Effective Date.

Specific Clauses—Price Change

One of the key benefits of this agreement to you, the customer, is a written method for handling price changes. The days of the supplier walking into your office with their standard, annual 5% price increase are over. Prior to your development of this agreement, have a discussion (perhaps negotiation) with the supplier as to what is the primary driver of price change. My experience has been that the most inflationary element of the price of a product (services may be an exception) is the raw material.

Persuade the supplier to agree that the only factor that will effect price change will be the raw material (determine ahead of time what the raw material is) and then write this into the language. Thus far, we have titled this section "Price Change" as opposed to "Price Increase." The mutual benefit of using the former title is that as raw material experiences "inflation," the supplier will justly benefit but in the event the raw material experiences "deflation," then the customer will benefit. Yes, it is possible that per this agreement, the supplier may submit a price *decrease*. This is definitely a paradigm change and could represent 21st century thinking.

It's not as if you don't trust each other, but how will you and/or your supplier know whether the raw material has experienced inflation or deflation as well as the amount of the change? The key is to agree to an index, which will indicate the percentage of change. Most major materials including steel, plastic, corrugated, etc. will have an appropriate index. If neither you nor your supplier is familiar with such a factor, then you may wish to consult the supplier of the raw material who would probably be familiar with such an index. As an example, *Purchasing* magazine publishes its *Hotline of Transaction Prices*, which provides the quarterly price averages for various raw materials[1] comparing 1996 (prior) through 1999 (future).

Steel	10 indexes
Paper & Paperboard	10 indexes
Nonferrous Metals	25 indexes
Lumber	3 indexes
Precious Metals	5 indexes
Plywood	5 indexes
Energy	5 indexes
Plastics	13 indexes
Wood Pulp	6 indexes
Chemicals	20 indexes

Sample language describing price change is as follows:

Price Change. The LTA will list agreed to prices for each part number covered by the agreement. Such listing will also include raw material content for each product. Such prices will be fixed for the term of this agreement, except for the following adjustments:

Raw Material Price Changes. The price for each product may be adjusted in the event of a change in raw material price OR at the end of each three-month period after the Effective Date of this Agreement, the parties shall determine the "Quarterly Average Price" for that Quarter, which will equal the average price of _____ [raw material] per _____, as published in _____, during such Quarter. If any Quarterly Average Price is 5% greater or less than the Quarterly Average Price for the Quarter preceding the Effective Date of this Agreement, supplier will increase or decrease the price of each product containing raw material by an amount equal to (A) the difference between the two Quarterly Average Prices, multiplied by (B) the percentage of that product that is comprised of raw material. Such price increase or decrease will be effective for the next three-month period.

Specific Clauses—Cost Reduction

Supplier(s) that we want to establish relationships with are constantly striving for "continuous improvement" and are not simply resting on their laurels. One such area is cost reduction. The supplier who takes the attitude that we have drained "every drop of blood out of this turnip" does not fit the above description. One of the benefits of this agreement is that your supplier will agree to specific cost reduction goals. However, this carries a dual responsibility. We may expect our supplier to recommend opportunities to reduce cost, but as the customer, we have to provide the resources to receive and review those opportunities as well as to implement them, if feasible.

I have heard many a supplier voice a valid complaint that in the past they have suggested some very attractive cost reduction ideas but these ideas did not make it past the buyer's desk or even worse, his/her "File 13." To prevent this problem, as noted in the language below, it is recommended that you, the customer form a "steering committee" which is made up of 1 or 2 customer representatives as well as 1 or 2 supplier representatives (number of individuals depends on the complexity of the agreement). This committee would be responsible for meeting on a quarterly or semi-annual basis to review and/or generate cost reduction ideas.

The supplier benefits in that cost reductions in excess of the minimum percentage would be shared. Sample language describing cost reduction is as follows:

Cost Reduction Goals. Supplier agrees to provide customer with total annual cost reductions of ____% under this agreement. Cost reductions will be measured on the total value of products purchased under the agreement on an annual basis. If supplier does not provide the agreed cost reduction percentage in a given year, supplier will rebate the amount of the shortfall to the customer within 45 days after the applicable year. The parties will share cost reductions in excess of _____% equally, as described below.

Cost Reduction Calculations. Once a cost reduction program is implemented, the measurable cost reduction percentage will be tracked by the steering committee on a quarterly or semi-annual basis. For purposes of calculating the total annual cost reductions under this agreement, a specific cost reduction program will be counted for a period of no longer than 12 consecutive months. If a cost reduction program requires a capital expenditure by one or more parties, the party or parties making that expenditure will be entitled to the entire benefit of the resulting cost reductions until its or their capital expenditures have been recouped.

Cost Reduction Implementation and Administration. The steering committee will be responsible for creating, implementing, managing, and approving cost reduction programs. The customer will provide reasonable necessary support to the supplier to assist in creating cost reduction programs under this agreement. All proposed cost reduction projects will be submitted in writing to the steering committee. By _____ of each year during which the agreement is in force, beginning with the first full year covered by agreement, the steering committee will deliver the following to management:

- A proposal, including cost reduction targets, for the upcoming 12 month period to reduce costs under its agreement; and
- A report detailing its cost reduction efforts during the preceding 12 months, including the measurable cost reduction percentage achieved.

Specific Clauses—Volume Incentive Rebates

A further negotiation point with your supplier is a one-time rebate for business growth that your company is providing to them. This could be an area where you may have to test your *reverse marketing* skills. Reverse marketing is the process whereby the purchaser reverses roles with the supplier and sells him or her on an idea, program, or concept that at first may be perceived as unpopular or painfully expensive. You are requesting that your supplier give money back to you.

They may ask, "How is this justified?" I will admit that of all the clauses discussed in this paper, this is probably the most difficult. How could this be a plausible point with the supplier and put money back into your own pocket? Assuming that the increased business will be absorbed by their existing capacity, then their fixed costs will have been amortized into the initial/original business volume.

In pricing the additional business volume, the only costs that should be incurred by the supplier should be direct labor and materials. Fixed costs, therefore, should be irrelevant. However, if the increased business volume requires them to purchase new equipment, expand facilities, and/or incur additional fixed costs, then the additional portion would be relevant and the expected rebate should be reduced or not pursued.

Sample language describing volume incentive rebates is as follows:

Volume Incentive Rebates. The customer will be entitled to an annual volume incentive rebate based on the total dollar amount of purchases of products covered by the agreement. Based on the annual reports to be provided to the steering committee to customer management, management will calculate the volume incentive payable on account of such total purchases by multiplying total purchases by the incentive percentage indicated on the Volume Incentive Schedule set forth below.

Volume Incentive Schedule

Total Purchases	Rebate Percentage*
$0.1-6.0M	0%
$6.0-6.5M	3%
$6.5-7.0M	4%
$7.0-7.5M	5%
$8.0M +	6%

*At the start of this agreement, the annualized total purchases will become the starting base, and at the end of Year 1, business growth above this starting base and within the guidelines illustrated above will be subject to the rebate. The new total purchases, which include both the initial starting base and the business growth, will become the next year's starting base and business growth above this starting base and within the guidelines illustrated above will be subject to the rebate. However, in the event that total purchases drop or experience negative growth, then the next year's starting base remains the same as the previous year's starting base as opposed to the new amount.

Example: If the initial starting base is $6M and the total purchases at the end of Year 1 are $7M, then the business growth is $1M, which includes 3% of $500K + 4% of $500K - $35,000. The starting base for Year 2 would become $7M and rebates would apply to the schedule above for growth above $7M. Assuming that at the end of Year 2, the total purchases drop to $6M, then the Year 3 base would remain at $7M and rebates at the end of Year 3 would apply to the schedule above for growth above $7M as opposed to $6M.

Specific Clauses—Quality Goals

The key to an effective customer/supplier relationship is the supplier meeting and exceeding performance expectations. An important performance expectation is quality assurance. If you already have established a system for monitoring your supplier's quality (i.e. PPM, % shipment defective, % scrap, CpK, etc.) then this can be incorporated in the agreement language. If such a system does not exist, then you may wish to develop and then incorporate into the agreement. The agreement will also establish reporting requirements regarding the fulfillment of such quality goals and will provide penalties for their failure to meet such quality goals.

Sample language describing quality goals is as follows:

Quality Standards and Goals. Supplier agrees to achieve, during the term of this agreement, a quality measure of ____ PPM. On the products supplied, Supplier will maintain a ____ CpK or better for the customer defined critical key characteristics during this agreement.

Specific Clauses—Delivery Goals

Another key performance expectation is delivery. Again, if you already have established a system for monitoring your supplier's delivery, then this can be incorporated in the agreement language. If such a system does not exist, then you may wish to develop and then incorporate into the agreement.

Sample language describing delivery goals is as follows:

Delivery. The agreement will set a time period after the issuance of a purchase order in which an order will be deemed delivered "on-time." If a delivery is not expected to be made on-time, Supplier will notify the customer and will take all reasonable steps at its own cost to expedite delivery. If a delivery is not made on-time or if notice is given that a delivery is expected to be late, the customer may cancel the order immediately by delivering written notice of the cancellation to supplier. Absent such cancellation notice, supplier will deliver the order on an expedited basis at its own cost. Upon such cancellation, the customer will not have any further obligation with respect to such issue.

If a delivery is not on time and is canceled by the customer, the customer will be free to purchase the late products from a third party and deduct from payment of future invoice(s) from supplier for any difference between the third party purchase price and what the customer would have had to pay for such late products under the agreement.

Specific Clauses—Technology

Another key performance expectation is for the supplier to keep abreast and share with the customer in advancing technology.

Sample language describing technology is as follows:

Technology. As supplier is privy to new technology related to production, material and/or application, it will share this information with customer and incorporate into customer's products, per customer's product engineering approval. As requested by customer, supplier will provide prototype (timely) support to engineering cost reduction programs.

Parting Thoughts

Obviously there are additional clauses that you will want to incorporate into your LTA (i.e. warranty, indemnity, termination, force majeure, entirety, etc.) but these are primarily boilerplate and can be stated both in the LTA as well as in the Terms and Conditions section of the purchase order. In determining which suppliers and commodities should be covered by an agreement, I recommend the "80/20 Rule." The 20% suppliers/commodities that comprise 80% of your supply base (exact percentages may vary but the concept is applicable) should be the first focus for agreement coverage.

Keep in mind you can put anything you so desire into an LTA but the supplier has to agree as well. "Got You Covered! The 21st Century Approach to Customer/Supplier Agreements" should be viewed as a positive approach by both you, the customer, as well as your supplier. Good luck!

Notes

1. Patrick S. Woods, "Adding It Up: Performing Effective Supplier Price And Cost Analysis," *NAPM InfoEdge*, June 1998.

Patrick S. Woods, C.P.M., A.P.P., CPIM, is Commodity Manager for Emerson Electric/Fisher Controls, Sherman, TX 75091, 972 491-1394.

Intellectual Property: What Is It? Why Is It Important to You?

Leslie S. Marell, J.D.

> In contracting with suppliers, intellectual property issues often come into play. This article will help you understand the different forms of intellectual property, and how to deal with intellectual property when making purchasing contracts.

What Is Intellectual Property?

"Intellectual Property" is a generic term used to describe products of the human intellect that have economic value. Computer software is one of the many forms of intellectual property. Other examples include books, music, movies, artwork, designs and other works of authorship, names, logos, as well as certain inventions.

Intellectual property is "property" because a body of laws has been created that gives owners of such works legal rights similar in some respects to those given to owners of real estate or tangible personal property (such as cars). Intellectual property may be owned and bought and sold the same as other types of property. But in many important respects, ownership of intellectual property is very different from ownership of a house or a car.

Definitions

Basic definitions are required before we can deal with the real business world issues involving intellectual property law. The principal types of intellectual property legal protection are listed and defined below:

- Patent
- Copyright
- Trade Secret
- Trademark and Trade Name

Patent

Patent law protects inventions. Patent protection is available for any new and useful process, machine, method of manufacture, composition of matter, or any new, useful improvement. By filing for and obtaining a patent from the U.S. Patent and Trademark Office, an inventor is granted a monopoly on the use and commercial exploitation of an invention, for 20 years from the date of filing the application.

In the U.S. patents are awarded to the first to invent. When multiple inventors file applications to patent the same invention, the U.S. Patent Office must decide who was the first inventor. Therefore, it is important that the engineers maintain development records establishing the events surrounding the invention process in order to prove the date of invention. Invention records may also be useful to challenge the validity of another's patent.

Copyright

A copyright provides protection for a limited time to authors for their "original works of authorship fixed in any tangible medium of expression." Copyrights extend only to the expression of creations of the mind, not to the ideas themselves. The Federal law governing copyrights expressly excludes from copyright protection "any idea, procedure, process, system, method of operation, concept, principle or discovery." In other words, a pure idea, such as a plan to create an innovative software program, cannot be copyrighted, no matter how original or creative it is.

Copyright protection begins when the work is created. This means that there does not have to be a copyright notice, publication of the work or registration to secure the copyright. It is, of course, advisable to take these measures.

Ownership of Copyright. As a general rule, the creator of a work owns the copyright. The person who owns the copyright also automatically owns the exclusive rights to it and the rights to prevent others from copying, distributing, or preparing works based on the copyrighted materials.

Work for Hire: Employees and Independent Contractors. Work for hire is an important exception to the general rule that a person owns the copyright in a work he or she has created. If a work was created by an employee as part of his or her job, the law considers the product a work for hire, and the employer will own the copyright.

If the creator is an independent contractor, the work will be considered work for hire *only* if: (1) the parties have signed a written agreement stating that the work will be a work for hire; *and* (2) the work is commissioned as a contribution to a collective work, a supplementary work, an instructional text, answer material for a test, an atlas, motion picture, or an audiovisual work. *Thus, unless there is a contractual agreement to the contrary, and the work fits within one of the above categories the independent contractor owns the copyright.*

Creations by an Independent Contractor. The copyright developed by an independent contractor is owned by the independent contractor unless the contractor has signed an agreement to the contrary. The contract must state that the contractor conveys the copyright ownership in all works created under the contract to the engaging party.

Trade Secret

All that is necessary for something to be protectable as a trade secret is that (1) it gives the owner a competitive advantage; (2) it is treated as a secret by the owner; and (3) it is not generally known in the industry or business. A trade secret may be lost if the owner fails to identify it or take reasonable steps to protect it. Otherwise, trade secret protection is perpetual.

The fundamental question of trade secret law is, what is protectable? Clear examples are discoveries, ideas, designs, and specifications. However, even the way you use knowledge and information or the assembly of information itself may be a trade secret even if everything you consider important for your secret is publicly available information. An example of this is supplier and customer lists.

Trademark

Patent, copyright and trade secret laws do not protect names, titles or phrases. A trademark is any word, name, logo or other symbol adopted and used by a person, manufacturer or merchant group that identifies and distinguishes its goods from those manufactured or sold by others.

License vs. Sale

A license is an agreement between the owner of the intellectual property (the licensor) and a third party (the licensee) which gives permission to the licensee to use the technology in a manner that would otherwise be reserved exclusively to the licensor, as owner. For example, the licensor of the software program will convey a right to the licensee to use the program and reproduce the program under certain defined circumstances. The licensee is restricted in his or her use of the program and does not receive any ownership rights to the software. By contrast, a sale involves the transfer of an ownership interest in the property.

In the case of mass marketed shrink wrap software, the buyer is purchasing a copy of the copyrighted program. However, the buyer is not purchasing an ownership interest in the intellectual property itself. The buyer is restricted by copyright law from reproducing the software (except for backup copies) or making derivative works.

Practical Applications

With basic definitions in place, let us turn to some practical issues that arise in business with frequency and involve intellectual property law.

Independent Contractors: Who Owns the Intellectual Property?

Many companies turn to outside consultants to develop software, etc., whether alone or in combination with company employees. From a technical and business standpoint, this may be the most practical approach. But is can raise the important legal issue of who owns the intellectual property rights to the work created?

Since an independent contractor is not an employee, the copyright in the software created by the independent contractor does not automatically belong to the company, as it likely would under the "work for hire" principles applicable to employees. Instead of owning the copyright, the company would probably only be authorized to use a copy of the software and to modify it as necessary for operating its own business.

If your company expects to obtain ownership of the copyright to the software, it is imperative to have the consultant sign an agreement stating that all intellectual property rights in the software and related documentation he or she creates for the company belong to the company, either as a work made for hire or, alternatively, by assignment to the company under the agreement.

Contract Manufacturing: Outsourcing the Design or Manufacture of the Product

Outsourcing the Design. Outsourcing is becoming a more common way of doing business as companies streamline their operations and cut costs. If your company is outsourcing the design of a product, the discussion above relating to independent contractors is applicable. Your contract should clearly specify that the outsourcer will assign all its rights in the design to your company and your company will be the sole owner. If you do not have such a provision, the outsourcer will likely be the owner of the information it developed.

Manufacturing to Your Specifications. If the contract manufacturer will be building product to your company's specifications, your company will be handing over large amounts of confidential information and data to its supplier. This information may be in the form of software, databases, specifications, bills of material, statistics and memos and will all constitute trade secrets of the company. In order to protect the trade secret status of the information, it is imperative that two steps be taken: (1) The information be clearly marked that it is Confidential or Proprietary to the company; and (2) The supplier sign a non-disclosure agreement which requires the supplier to hold the information in confidence.

Keep in mind that in order for trade secrets to maintain their confidential status, the owner must take steps necessary to keep the information secret. Failure to identify the information as secret and to require a written agreement to maintain secrecy endangers the confidential information.

I.T. Outsourcers and Software Licenses

As companies increasingly rely on outsourcing vendors to perform computer-related functions, these outsourcers often require access to software licensed to their customers by third-party software licensors. Most software licenses restrict assignment (transfer) of the software to a third party without the consent of the licensor. The practical effect of this clause is to prevent giving outsourcers access to the licensed software. As a result, licensee must obtain consent from software licensors to allow outsourcers to use the software.

Licensors may be unwilling to provide consent and have, in some cases, insisted on payment of additional license fees.

To avoid such situations, it is advisable to include a clause in any new license agreement which extends the scope of permissible uses of the software to allow outsourcers to use the licensed software in the performance of outsourcing functions.

Sole Source Suppliers and Escrow

While a sole/single source alliance can benefit both the buyer and the supplier companies through the creation of a more solid business/partnering arrangement, the downside occurs if the supplier is unable to deliver.

In order to understand the full impact of this "downside," just be reminded of any recent problem you have had obtaining product from your sole source supplier.

What measures can be taken to protect our companies from these downside possibilities? While contracts are limited in their abilities to "solve" a problem, they can be helpful in addressing the issues to facilitate a solution.

Consider requiring that your supplier establish an escrow account in which the supplier deposits all designs, manufacturing data, processes, etc. necessary to manufacture and support the product. In addition, and if the bill of material for the product includes purchase of certain proprietary products, the supplier would deposit authorization that the buyer be able to purchase these proprietary products from third party suppliers. The contract would grant your company a license to use all the information in the escrow account if the supplier does not perform its contract obligations.

Keep in mind that in order to be able to effectively use this information, your company might likely first require technical understanding of the products. If that is the case, your contract will want to obligate the supplier to provide access to and training in the understanding and use of the information and data during the actual contract performance.

Employee Issues: Confidentiality, Ownership, Non-solicitation, Non-compete

Confidentiality. The issue of confidential information and the employee's responsibility is two pronged. The first prong relates to that confidential information which the employee either develops or learns in the course of his or her employment with the company.

In general, state laws provide that an employee may not, either during or after his employment, divulge or use trade secrets which were developed by him during his employment or divulged to him by his employer, even absent an express agreement. The rationale is that a employee is in a relationship of trust and confidence with the company. In addition, most companies require that their employees sign an agreement which acknowledges that the employee will maintain the confidentiality of the company's trade secret information both during and after employment.

The problematic aspect of this issue is raised when the employee wants to go to work for a competitor of the employer. The employee should be aware that under appropriate circumstances, the ex-employer may prevent the employee from going to work at a competitor if the following three factors are found to exist:

1. The former employee has knowledge of the first employer's trade secrets;
2. The employee's new job duties (and the products and technology he is working on) are so similar to those in the former position that it would be extremely difficult for him not to rely on or use the first employer's trade secrets; and
3. The former employee and the new employer cannot be depended upon to avoid using the trade secret information.

The second prong relates to that confidential information provided by a third party to the employee's company.

In those cases in which the employer signs a non-disclosure agreement to maintain the trade secrets of a third party, the employee—as an agent of the recipient company—is bound to the non-disclosure agreement and must abide by the confidentiality provisions. Failure to do so may subject both the company and the employee to damages.

Ownership of Intellectual Property. If a work was created by an employee as part of his or her job, the law considers the product a work for hire, and the employer will own the intellectual property rights to that work, as explained above. A work for hire is defined as "a work made by an employee within the scope of his or her employment".

In many instances, the courts have considered the intellectual property rights to a product developed by the employee to belong to the employer when the employee used company resources in developing the product, even if the employee's development was done outside working hours.

Non-Compete and Non-Solicitation Agreements. The non-compete clause prevents the ex-employee from working for a competitor or going into a business which competes with his or her ex-employer. The non-solicitation clause restricts the ex-employee from soliciting the business of the ex-employer's customers or suppliers.

The enforceability of these provisions varies by state. For example, in most employee/employer circumstances, California does not recognize the enforceability of a non-compete clause. Even in those states that do enforce non-compete provisions, the clauses must be narrowly written such that they are reasonable in time and geography limitations. The enforceability of the clause generally revolves around the underlying question of: Is there a legitimate business purpose for such restriction? In the absence of a sound business reason, the courts are reluctant to enforce a non-compete clause.

The non-solicitation clause will come under similar scrutiny in terms of reasonable time period and location, but is more often enforced by courts. A non-solicitation agreement may restrict the ex-employee from doing business with a supplier or customer of the ex-employer for a certain period of time.

Leslie S. Marell, Esq. has a law firm in Hermosa Beach, CA 90254, 310 372-8663, lsmarell@earthlink.net.

What's on the Books: Other Laws Affecting Purchasing and Supply

Martin J. Carrara, J.D., C.P.M.
and Ernest G. Gabbard, J.D., C.P.M., CPCM

You may think you need to be concerned mainly with the law of contracts as a purchasing manager, but there are many laws that affect the purchasing function. This article provides an overview of several you should know about, especially with regard to international transactions. You may be surprised to learn that there are even some criminal liability laws in some countries that you don't want to learn about after the fact! Continue reading to learn more.

Although the UCC might be the first body of work that comes to mind when you think of commercial purchases, it is by no means the only legal guideline to consider. There are many other laws, codes, and court interpretations' precedents that will apply to the purchasing and supply professional's work, including international issues, antitrust issues, and many others.

U.S. Laws Affecting Global Purchases

Today's global business economy has launched many purchasing professionals into international procurement. For many, this is a new "adventure," which stretches their experience and capabilities. The international legal environment can present some significant challenges even for the seasoned veteran. Considering space limitations, this publication will provide a summary of those laws which affect the international transaction, and outline how to establish those all-important terms and conditions for such transactions.

For purchasing and supply professionals, the international legal environment in which they conduct business with suppliers will be different for virtually every country. It is therefore appropriate to review the laws which will likely apply to transaction(s). The general bodies of law are:

- U.S. law
- the law of the country from which the purchase is being made

- international law

Interestingly, experience shows that the least obvious of these to the purchaser is U.S. law. When conducting a transaction abroad, there is often a misconception that such transactions are not subject to U.S. law. While there are many domestic U.S. laws that may not apply to our transaction, there are some which do apply, and with which professionals should be familiar. A partial list of the more substantive laws follows.

Anti-Boycotts Legislation

These pieces of legislation pertain to organizations doing business which might "cooperate" in the boycott of one nation against another. It is erroneously presumed to apply only to transactions occurring in the Middle East (the Arab-Israeli boycott). However, it also applies to "boycotts" in such other areas as India versus Pakistan and the People's Republic of China (mainland) versus Republic of China (Taiwan). The issues are often subtle, and frequently occur in such innocuous-looking documents as letters of credit. There is a requirement to "report" requests to participate in a boycott, which is very frequently overlooked, and results in the majority of violations by and prosecutions of purchasers and sellers.

Foreign Corrupt Practices Act

While this impacts the seller more frequently than the purchaser, it should not be overlooked. Essentially, it prohibits an organization or individual from making a payment that might benefit a foreign official. Purchasers should review it with legal counsel, so that they can recognize the issues which trigger its provisions.

Customs Laws

This is the body of law which governs the importation of goods into the United States. These laws will impact virtually all imported goods (and some services). They are quite complex, and will generally require the assistance of a customs broker or other import specialist.

Export Administration Act

Purchasers frequently overlook these laws, as they do not perceive themselves as "exporting." In reality, whenever a specification, drawing, or prototype is provided to a foreign person or entity, an "export" of technology occurs. While a majority of such exports are not restricted, some may be, and such controlled exports are not always obvious. As is the case with importation, the key here is to obtain advice and/or assistance from an "expert." This may often be someone other than the expert who is used for importation.

Foreign Laws to Consider

The above mentioned are only a few of the U.S. laws which may apply to international transactions. However, U.S. laws should not be a purchaser's only concern: these transactions will also be affected by the laws and regulations of the other country or countries from which goods or services are purchased. This is an area about which volumes are written, and is too complex to cover in this publication. This is particularly significant considering that each country will have its own unique laws and regulations which will apply only in certain circumstances. This is, therefore, an area that will require consultation with an attorney who is familiar with the local country's legal system. Relatively few U.S. attorneys possess such expertise, so be cautious who you engage for such advice. This may require engaging a foreign attorney, but this is not always the case. Some areas of foreign law which should be considered are:

Contract law. In some countries, certain contracts require approval of the local government. It would be important to know if this is a requirement.

Export control. Just as the United States Government controls exportation of certain commodities or services, foreign governments may prohibit or control export of the item(s) being procured.

Currency control. Not all countries allow transactions to be conducted in U.S. dollars or other non-local currencies. This may be a critical element to address in the terms and conditions.

Criminal law? Yes, your transaction could be "illegal" if structured in a certain manner. Criminal liability in some countries is a considerably different concept than in the United States with all of our due process protection of the individual. This is not something you want to find out the hard way.

International Laws

As if dealing with U.S. and foreign laws does not sufficiently complicate the transaction, such purchases will also be affected by international laws (not the laws of either purchaser's country or seller's country). Although there are several, too many to cover in detail, some of the obvious concern such international laws as maritime laws. These laws govern the rights and obligations of the parties for such issues as title and risk of loss of goods during air or surface transport. Consultants and/or legal counsel who are familiar with such laws will often need to be engaged.

There are other bodies of law such as this which ultimately should be considered by your attorney; however, it is not necessary (or possible) for the purchaser to be familiar with all such laws. Purchasing and supply professionals also need to be familiar with the following documents which are relevant to international transactions:

The United Nations Convention on Contracts for International Sale of Goods (CISG). This is a set of uniform "rules" which many countries (including the United States) have agreed to apply to their international transactions. If the two parties executing an agreement are from countries that are signatory members to the Convention, the CISG rules will be automatically applied, unless the contract specifically states that they do not apply. However, the parties may agree to not apply the CISG rules, even if they are from signatory countries. The CISG provisions parallel the UCC and are generally favorable to the purchaser. It should be noted that contracting parties have the option of applying: (a) the CISG, (b) the law of one of the parties, or (c) the law of some neutral forum. Therefore, the CISG also provides an excellent vehicle to resolve the often sticky issues of "applicable law" and "conflicts of law," when neither party wants to accept application of the laws of the other party. While the CISG does not contain the UCC requirement for a "writing," some U.S. courts have held that oral contracts may not be enforceable [*Deijing Metals v. American Business Center* (1995)]. Therefore, it is still appropriate to document the understanding of the parties in a written contract.

International Contracting Terms (INCOTERMS). These are standard "terms" for allocating the costs and risks of shipping goods in international trade. Domestic U.S. terms, such as "FOB origin" and "FOB destination," are inadequate in such transactions. Every purchaser and seller should have a set of the INCOTERMS to consult when establishing international terms and conditions. They are available from the International Chamber of Commerce in New York at a nominal cost. Some large commercial banks may also provide copies to their customers. A review thereof will reveal that these are significantly different than standard, domestic terms.

Terms and Conditions for International Purchases

As with establishing any contract, the purchasing and supply professional must: (1) understand the environment in which he or she is operating, (2) recognize the risks associated with the transaction in this environment, and (3) properly allocate these risks by clearly defining the rights and obligations in the contractual terms and conditions.

There should be no doubt that the environment for international purchases is considerably more complex. It follows that the terms and conditions for such transactions will be equally complex. The complexity will naturally be influenced by the following factors:

- the country with which you are contracting
- the size of the transaction
- the type and technical complexity of the goods or services being purchased
- any previous relationship between the parties
- consideration of the issues unique to the international transaction which are outlined above

Because of the multitude of transactionally unique issues to be addressed, there is no "standard" set of terms and conditions which are appropriate for all international transactions. Most organizations' "boiler-plate" approach to purchase order terms and conditions will be especially inappropriate for international transactions. This is an area that will require "customization" for each transaction. The best approach to the task of drafting such terms and conditions is to utilize a checklist to ensure that this multitude of issues is considered and addressed. Such checklists are available to the purchasing professional from many sources, such as Business Laws, Inc. in their *Legal Aspects of International Sourcing.* A list of "minimums" should also be developed to replace or supplement the purchaser's domestic purchase order or contract. There are many clauses which may be appropriate only for specific circumstances or transactions. Consequently, even the seasoned professional should use a checklist to ensure that all issues are considered and adequately addressed in the terms and conditions.

The complexity of laws applicable to the international purchasing environment offers professional challenges and rewards that are not available in the domestic market. However, with adequate preparation and research, it can be a valuable market!

Antitrust and Unfair Trade Practices

There are four principal federal laws which deal with antitrust and competitive practices:

- Sherman Antitrust Act (1898)
- Federal Trade Commission Act (1914)
- Clayton Antitrust Act (1914)
- Robinson-Patman Act (1936)

Each of these was intended to promote competition and to ensure that a fair and open marketplace exists in the U.S. economy. Many states have similar legislation, but such laws would generally apply only to transactions within that state. Most of the federal and state legislation is aimed at trade practices of sellers, although some provisions apply either directly or indirectly to purchasers. Volumes are written about each of these laws; however, the following discussion emphasizes and highlights the provisions which are relevant to the purchasing professional.

Sherman Antitrust Act

This legislation prohibits any action or conspiracy "in constraint of trade," and prohibits any "monopoly or attempt to monopolize." Most prosecutions under this act are for price fixing, bid rigging, or other forms of collusion among sellers. However, it also prohibits reciprocal dealings whereby a purchase of one product by a purchaser is conditioned upon the reciprocal purchase by the seller of a product from the purchaser's organization. The purchasing professional should be aware that such actions are prohibited by law, and should avoid any conduct which might be perceived as encouraging or condoning such activities.

Federal Trade Commission Act (FTCA)

The FTCA created the Federal Trade Commission (FTC), and provided the power for the FTC to interpret trade legislation such as the Sherman Act's "restraint of trade" provisions. It also prohibited "unfair competition" and "unfair or deceptive" trade practices. These prohibitions are clearly aimed at the seller's practices, and have very limited application to purchasers.

Clayton Antitrust Act

This legislation declared "price discrimination" to be illegal, and prohibited sellers from exclusive-dealing types of arrangements with purchasers and/or product distributors. Some of its provisions also govern corporate mergers or acquisitions that might create a monopoly. The Robinson-Patman Act significantly amended many of the substantive provisions of the Clayton Act, and is now the primary legislation to deal with these subjects.

Robinson-Patman Act

This legislation is the most familiar to purchasing professionals and is often used as an excuse by sellers to not provide lower prices to purchasers during aggressive negotiations. This Act specifically prohibits sellers from "price discrimination," where the effect of such discrimination may substantially limit competition or create a monopoly. While this is

Case Study

The 1971 case of *Kroger v. Federal Trade Commission* (438 F. 2nd 1372) established liability for the "lying buyer" which still exists today. In 1963, Kroger operated a chain of over 1400 retail grocery stores located in 19 states and which sold a variety of products, including milk and dairy products. Kroger decided to explore private label sales (selling products under a store brand name) in the hope that its own label might permit it to compete more profitably. They began to solicit bids from dairy and milk producers who would be interested in bottling the Kroger milk. On several occasions with one particular supplier, Beatrice, Kroger officials told Beatrice officials that the bids Beatrice was submitting were much higher than others they'd received and that they "might as well go back home" if that was all they had to offer. In fact, Kroger had not received quotations lower than what Beatrice was offering, but claims to have made those statements on the assumption that they would be receiving lower bids. Typically, for a purchaser to be held responsible for accepting discriminatory prices, the supplier must be held responsible for offering them. However, based on several such incidents as the conversation described above, the court said that the supplier was acting in good faith, trying to meet a third-party bid which the supplier had been told by the purchaser was lower, but the purchaser knew did not exist. So, the supplier's successful defense did not clear the purchaser from guilt.

obviously aimed at sellers, there is also a provision which prohibits purchasers from "knowingly inducing" a discriminatory price. It should be emphasized that the purchaser can be liable under these provisions only if the seller was guilty of price discrimination that had the stated adverse effect on competition in the marketplace. There are several defenses to liability contained in the Act, which make prosecution difficult. It is for this reason that there have been no Robinson-Patman Act cases filed by the FTC in the 1990s.

Where does this leave the purchasing professional? According to James Johnstone, in "The Robinson-Patman Act: No Barrier to Effective Purchasing," in *Purchasing Today*®, September 1996, the Robinson-Patman Act does not present a real barrier to effective, aggressive purchasing. The purchaser should not "knowingly induce" a discriminatory price; however, most price concessions are not "discriminatory." A few older cases of purchaser liability were based on a purchaser purposely misleading a seller to lower its prices based on a false assertion that the seller's competition had provided a lower price. While a seller may legally lower its price to "meet competition," the purchaser should not mislead a seller in negotiations.

These laws are complex, and this summary is intended to provide only general guidance on this subject. The purchasing and supply professional should consult with legal counsel whenever circumstances create a suspicion of prohibited conduct by the seller, or when purchaser's actions could conceivably violate such laws.

Other Significant Legislation

Although not inclusive, the following list includes other laws and issues relevant to purchasing and supply professionals.

Intellectual property laws: These would deal with issues of trademark, copyright, patents, and trade secrets of organizations. Purchasers who work with suppliers who have the intellectual rights to certain ideas, technologies, and products will have to be aware of what steps need to be taken to protect that information. Purchasers also need to ensure that they protect the intellectual property of their company when it is handled by a supplier.

Environmental laws: These can pertain to substances or materials that are potentially hazardous to the environment. Purchasing professionals must know their responsibilities in regard to transportation, storage, disposal, and use of potentially harmful substances. Some relative legislation includes: The Resource Conservation and Recovery Act (RCRA), the Comprehensive Environmental Response, Compensation and Liability Act (CERCLA), the Hazardous Materials Transportation Act, and Occupational Safety and Health Administration (OSHA) regulations.

Labor laws: These can pertain to using labor at fair prices and wages, and stipulating the appropriate definitions of contracted labor. They are primarily to protect contractors from excluding certain workers based on unfair pricing and purchasers should be aware of the implications. Relevant legislation includes: the Davis-Bacon Act, the Service Contract Act, and the Miller Act.

Facing the Future

Purchasing and supply professionals must be conversant on a diverse body of subjects. One of the more complex of these is law. This summary gives only some key elements of many of the laws with which purchasing professionals must deal in their profession. As new philosophies and new technologies bring new processes and best practices, the laws affecting purchasing and supply will likely change as well. While staying abreast of new topics in many fields is important, staying well informed on issues such as electronic commerce law, licensing agreements, and global sourcing issues will serve the purchasing and supply professional well.

Martin J. Carrara, J.D., C.P.M., is director of contract management in global procurement at Pharmacia & Upjohn Company. He is former president of NAPM—New York. He is an instructor of C.P.M. review and contract law seminars for various NAPM affiliates. He has authored several "Legal Briefs" columns for Purchasing Today®.

Ernest G. Gabbard, J.D., C.P.M., CPCM, is director of procurement and contracting for Allegheny Teledyne Inc. He is a frequent speaker on purchasing and contract law and management for NAPM and the National Contract Management Association and has taught these subjects for the University of California and California State University system.

Legal Briefs: Practical Tips on Purchasing Law

Purchasing Today®

> The NAPM's Purchasing Today® includes the monthly feature "Legal Briefs," short articles that provide practical insights and practices to make the legal aspects of the purchasing and supply process go smoothly and to help you avoid problems that others may have encountered. This part of the yearbook includes a selection of some of the most current of these pieces. You'll find the following:
>
> - Playing It Safe, Dan J. Ricketts
> - Defining Damages, Leslie S. Marell
> - Keep the Cards Stacked in Your Favor, Sara L. Vinas
> - The Statute of Frauds in Cyberspace, Karen L. Manos
> - Keeping Pace with the Times, Helen M. Pohlig
> - You Can't Always Take It with You, Mark A. McLean
> - "Do You, Purchaser, Take This Contract…," Stefanie London
> - Your Project's Contract, Mark Grieco
> - Are They or Aren't They? Henry F. Garcia

Playing It Safe
Dan J. Ricketts, J.D.

Employee welfare can never be overemphasized, and purchasing and supply can ensure safety by implementing proper clauses in contracts.

Purchasing and supply managers, as well as end users, often overlook an important area of the purchasing contract: safety clauses. Most lump safety clauses into either the "boilerplate" category—along with "assignment," "forum," and other similar clauses—or they are lumped into those "non-changeable" clauses such as "limitation of liability" and "indemnity," which are allowed to be modified only in the halls of the corporate legal department. However, overlooking these clauses in the event of a job site accident or product use problem can prove disastrous not only for the purchasing organization but also for the purchasing manager's continued employment. Therefore, for everyone's safety, safety clauses should be taken seriously.

Critical safety clauses generally fall into two types. The first type deals with safety notification and labeling requirements. The second type—and the type that might best be described as "critical" critical safety clauses—deals with job or product-specific safety requirements.

Safety Notification and Labeling Requirements

Safety clauses in this category are often mandated by local, state, and/or federal law and/or regulation. They may be mandated by local ordinance—especially in case of a city or county with a history of toxic waste dumping, that is the site of a facility such as a nuclear power plant, or is on a major transportation route, be it water, road or rail, over which hazardous materials may be transported. The use and language of these clauses may also be required by state regulatory agencies. State regulations and requirements frequently vary depending on the proactive nature of the state governor and legislature. (Some states have more of a regulatory reputation than do others.) Most likely, critical safety notification and labeling requirements, and their corresponding contractual clauses, are mandated by the federal government through such agencies as the U.S. Environmental Protection Agency (EPA), Occupational Safety and Health Administration (OSHA), and the like. Frequently, requirements imposed by local, state, and federal governments will both overlap and contradict.

This, of course, brings to the forefront the problem the purchasing manager faces: Which law prevails and which safety clause or clauses should be used in the purchasing contract? While the general rule is that federal laws and regulations prevail, it's prudent to seek the advice of knowledgeable counsel to ensure proper adherence to law and safety issues.

As all states and product/job categories require different types of safety notification and labeling, generalities are hard to come by in this area. California, which has enacted some of the strictest safety requirements, is illustrative. In California, companies should generally have contractual clauses requiring, at a minimum:

Material safety data sheets. These explain the potential hazards associated with a given product or component. These data sheets should comport with both federal and state (if applicable) OSHA Hazard Communications Standards. The federal standards can be found at www.osha.gov/.

Container labeling. This clause would require the supplier to label, with specificity, all containers of hazardous materials shipped to the job site.

California Toxic Enforcement Act Requirements. Many people have become accustomed to seeing notices warning that a building or product may contain chemicals known to cause birth defects, cancer, or otherwise be harmful. While these warnings are required by statute in California, prudent purchasing managers in all states should require suppliers to furnish similar warnings if hazardous chemicals are expected to be present in products furnished by the supplier.

Asbestos notification. This informs the supplier that the purchaser's facilities may contain asbestos. The notification here is clearly meant to protect the supplier.

Job- or Product-Specific Safety Requirements

These are frequently the most important in terms of protecting persons and property. They are also the hardest to set out in an article such as this as these clauses must be, by their nature, written to address specific job or product safety issues. The purchasing and supply manager should keep the following factors in mind when drafting clauses in this area:

Inspection rights. Specific to the job being performed, this clause allows the purchasing manager to inspect the job site (or have it inspected) for specific hazards related to the product or service being performed by the supplier.

Site access requirements. These clauses will set forth the hazards that may be encountered by the supplier on the job site as well as the type of employees and the rules governing those employees that the supplier may have on the job site. This could also pertain to personnel that should have access, for example, to certain machinery or equipment. A contract can stipulate that all operators must be licensed to operate such equipment, for example.

Non-qualified suppliers. On especially critical jobs, such as in a nuclear facility, or on government-related projects, a list of nonqualified subcontractors may be inserted into the contract to ensure that the prime contractor acknowledges that these subcontractors are not to be used on the project.

Acceptance certificates. Certification that specific parts or services meet certain contractually-defined safety measures may be required from the supplier.

In the end, there is no better measure of how well a particular safety clause was written than if the disaster it was meant to prevent never happens.

Dan J. Ricketts, J.D., is general counsel for Wareforce, Inc., in El Segundo, California.

Defining Damages
Leslie S. Marell, J.D.

An effective supply contract will use liquidated damages clauses to set the stage for consequences of nonperformance.

You've written up a contract for services to be performed by a given supplier. Unfortunately, a contract is no guarantee of performance. Ideally, the payment to a supplier is reason enough to perform, but in some cases, a purchasing and supply professional needs more protection in the contract. What compensation should you receive if a supplier fails to perform? How much is a particular service worth? These issues are often addressed through liquidated damages clauses.

Liquidated means "agreed upon." The concept is that before you and your supplier sign the contract, you both fix the damages (or "penalty") that the supplier will incur if he or she fails to perform his or her obligations according to the contract.

Liquidated damages clauses can serve as a good incentive for the supplier to perform services on time. In maintenance contracts, these types of clauses often are structured such that the purchaser deducts a certain amount of money from the monthly maintenance fee depending on the equipment downtime.

One cautionary note: damages in contract law are intended to compensate the injured party and not penalize the breaching party. A clause which fixes unreasonably large liquidated damages will be viewed as a penalty and considered void. You should justify (and keep on file) how you arrived at these amounts of money. Also, avoid using the word "penalty" in your contract.

Tips for Negotiating Clauses

You will have a difficult, if not impossible time convincing your supplier to agree to penalties of an extensive magnitude. For example, if a piece of equipment fails due to a supplier's failure to perform maintenance, your organization may incur revenue losses of $10,000 per hour. However, it is fair to say that no supplier would agree to a contract that contains liquidated damages clauses requiring him or her to pay that amount for every hour that the equipment is not running. Also, in the unlikely event that you actually ended up in court over such a dispute, that amount of money might be considered excessive, designed to penalize, and, therefore, void.

It's more realistic to fix liquidated damages to be an amount proportionate to the service fee you will pay. Other analogous concepts include (a) an extended period of maintenance at no charge, (b) rebate of a certain portion of fees previously paid, or (c) termination of the maintenance agreement. See the sidebar for more information on sample clauses.

Where you end up, of course, will depend on your leverage. In that regard, don't forget to negotiate when your leverage is the highest. If you are purchasing the equipment from the supplier who will maintain it, make sure you negotiate the maintenance contract at the same time that you negotiate the acquisition of the equipment.

The Best Offense...

Given the option of resorting to the liquidated damages clauses in the contract, or never having to refer to them in the first place, most purchasing and supply professionals would choose the latter. While liquidated damages clauses can serve as incentives to timely performance, your real goal is not to deduct for late service; rather, your goal is to receive good maintenance and eliminate downtime. Whether you need a core piece of capital equipment repaired, the copier down the hall serviced, or the plumbing leak fixed on the spot, a supplier's failure to perform can be costly but avoided. To that end, you should understand and address the following "up front" issues in your contract:

Preventative Maintenance: What type will be performed, how often, by whom, and when (during or after business hours)?

Spare Parts: What are the critical units of equipment and what are their mean times between failure (MTBF)? What is the minimum type and quantity of spare parts that should be maintained? Where should they be stored (at the purchaser's facility on a consignment basis or at the supplier's facility)? Have you predetermined the price of these parts?

Preventative and Remedial Maintenance: Have these terms been clearly defined in the contract? Does the contract specifically state the responsibilities of the maintenance provider and the purchaser?

Response Times: What is the MTBF and the mean time to repair (MTTR) key equipment? Response time, while important, is only a means to an end. What you want is a short downtime. The MTBF and MTTR figures can be used in the liquidated damages clause if the number of repairs is greater than would be predicted by the MTBF or if the equipment is down for more than a specified time.

Back-Up System: Is it possible or realistic to require the maintenance provider to provide a back-up system if the equipment exceeds a certain downtime?

These terms and conditions, when agreed upon during the initial contract negotiations, can ease the road to satisfactory performance by suppliers, and hopefully reduce the need to act upon liquidated damages clauses.

Check Out Some Sample Clauses

If a contract stipulates the following:

Maintainor will respond to all requests for Services within twenty-four (24) hours of each request by Customer. Maintainor will remedy any defect in the Software or Equipment within forty-eight (48) hours after the initial request for Services by Customer and, if necessary and within such time frame, either replace any defective module or swap the entire defective unit.

The following liquidated damages might be appropriate to include as well: Either ...

If Maintainor fails to remedy any such defect within forty-eight (48) hours of the Customer request, Customer shall be entitled to a one (1) month maintenance credit for each additional twenty-four (24) hour period during which any such defect remains unresolved. In the event any such defect remains unresolved for more than one (1) week, Customer may, in its sole discretion, elect to terminate this Agreement and receive a refund of any fees that were paid in advance by the Customer.

Or...

> If Maintainor does not respond and remedy the failure, malfunction, defect or non-conformity within forty-eight (48) hours of receipt of Customer's request, Customer shall be entitled to a credit against future maintenance costs of (dollar amount) for every hour or part thereof that Maintainor fails to remedy the failure, malfunction, defect or non-conformity. Monies becoming due to the Customer shall be applied as a credit against future maintenance invoices submitted by Maintainor hereunder.

Leslie S. Marell is an attorney at law in Hermosa Beach, California.

Keep the Cards Stacked in Your Favor
Sara L. Vinas, J.D.

Protect your organization against employee misuse of a procurement card.

It's an issue that is in the forefront of every person in management, audit, and finance when a procurement card program is proposed—what if an employee misuses the procurement card? What can you and your organization do to protect yourself against this type of fraud?

The Potential Problem

Every employee in your organization, and, to a certain extent, contractors are considered agents of the organization. "Agency" is defined in *Black's Law Dictionary* as "a relation in which one person acts for or represents another by latter's authority, either in the relationship of principal and agent, master and servant or employer and proprietor and independent contractor." More specifically, "general agency" is defined as "that which exists when there is a delegation to do all acts connected with a particular trade, business or employment. It implies authority on the part of the agent to act without restriction or qualification in all matters relating to the business of his or her principal."

Consequently, there is an implied limit as to what an employee, as agent, may lawfully transact on behalf of his or her organization. The agent has certain rights to act on behalf of the organization, but with those rights come obligations, duties to act within the scope of the agent's (employee's) employment. Acting outside that scope of employment may void the rights that the agent has to act on behalf of the organization and provide grounds for the employer to deny liability for its employee's actions.

For example, if an employee is a driver for an organization, that employee may, as an agent, drive a vehicle owned by that organization. If that employee subsequently has an accident while driving to his or her specified delivery destination, that would most likely be in the scope of his or her employment and the organization's insurance would cover that accident. However, if the employee is driving the truck and intentionally detours from his or her route to drive over his or her neighbor's prize roses, that would be considered outside the scope of his or her employment and the organization could argue that point to avoid liability for the property damage incurred while the employee was operating outside his or her scope of employment/agency.

Apply It to Procurement Cards

Similarly, a procurement card used to furnish an employee's house with all new furniture and a state-of-the-art sound system is outside that scope. Unless, of course, that employee was a music critic and had been given specific authority to use the procurement card for those purposes. Now armed with this understanding, what steps can you take to limit your organization's liability?

- Draft a corporate policy that clearly states the intent for the usage of the procurement card and ensure its adoption and distribution—part of the policy should require reimbursement by and/or termination of an employee who intentionally misuses the card.
- Use terms and conditions within the agreement with the card issuer that clearly define the commodities by category and merchant code, consistent with your organization's policy, that may be procured by your organization.
- Contractually cap the dollar amount of liability that your organization will incur in the event of misuse.
- Clearly define misuse of the card in the agreement with the card issuer and your organization's employees, i.e., "misuse" shall be defined as any purchase utilizing a procurement card which is inconsistent with or in violation of the organization's policies and procedures. Misuse of the procurement card should void any further liability of the organization for payment of those purchases.
- Establish checks and balances within your organization so that the purchases are subject to random audit to avoid any manager/subordinate fraud schemes.
- Expressly state in the agreement with the card issuer that only employees may use the card and that the employees will be identified through PIN numbers or pass codes to avoid third-party misuse.
- Have each employee who is issued a card sign a separate agreement in which he or she assumes personal liability to reimburse your organization for purchases made that are not in compliance with your organization's policy. The agreement could also detail other possible disciplinary action.
- Provide for exception reporting at a senior management level for those purchases that exceed set budgets and/or minimums.

Use It Wisely

Be aware that there is no silver bullet solution that will ensure that a procurement card will always be used properly by your organization's employees. The good news is that the reporting on procurement cards is improving and that while a procurement card may be considered opening a door to fraudulent acts by its employees, it's also an opportunity for your organization to gain more information and management reporting on how your organization spends its money. In addition, a procurement card program may, to a certain extent, prevent fraud through the restrictions that your organization places upon the card expenditures, thus limiting the suppliers with whom the money is spent and limiting the amount of money that may be spent per day.

Sara L. Vinas, J.D., is senior manager, global procurement group for Ryder Transportation Services in Miami, Florida.

The Statute of Frauds in Cyberspace
Karen L. Manos, J.D., CPCM

Can a paperless, electronic contract satisfy Statute of Frauds requirements?

Every state in the United States has adopted some form of the Uniform Commercial Code (UCC). Section 2-201 of the UCC codifies the common law Statute of Frauds, which provides in pertinent part that "a contract for the sale of goods for the price of $500 or more is not enforceable by way of action or defense unless there is some writing sufficient to indicate that a contract for sale has been made between the parties and signed by the party against whom enforcement is sought or by his authorized agent." Hence, for such a contract to be enforceable, there must be a writing (1) that serves as evidence, but need not itself constitute a contract for the sale of goods, (2) that specifies a quantity, and (3) that is signed by the party against whom enforcement is sought. A similar rule pertains to contracts for the sale of intangible goods, such as royalty rights, for the price of $5,000 or more.

There are a number of recognized exceptions to the Statute of Frauds. For example, an oral contract for the sale of goods between merchants is enforceable if, within a reasonable period of time, one party sends a writing confirming the contract and the other party receives the confirmation and does not object—in writing—within 10 days of receipt. See UCC §2-201(2). Additionally, oral contracts for the sale of goods are enforceable if:

- the goods are specially made for the purchaser and are not suitable for sale to others in the ordinary course of business, and, before the purchaser gives notice of repudiation, the seller has made either a substantial beginning of the goods' manufacture or commitments for their procurement;
- the party against whom enforcement is sought admits that a contract for sale was made;
- payment has been made and accepted; or
- the goods have been received and accepted.

In Cyberspace

In the absence of one of these exceptions, however, the question arises whether a paperless electronic contract can satisfy the Statute of Frauds.

Electronic contracts are frequently preceded by a Trading Partner Agreement (TPA), which is used to establish the terms and conditions under which the parties will conduct their electronic commerce transactions. The standard Department of Defense (DoD) electronic data interchange (EDI) TPA, for example, states that the purpose of the agreement "is to create an obligation between the parties using EDI and to ensure that (1) use of any electronic equivalent of documents (transactions) referenced or exchanged under this agreement shall be deemed an acceptable practice in the ordinary course of business, and (2) such transactions shall be admissible as evidence on the same basis as customary paper documents." TPAs, such as the standard DoD agreement, are typically paper-based documents that have physically been signed by both parties. The agreements, therefore, satisfy at least two of the three requirements for the Statute of Frauds: They are a writing that evidences a contract for the sale of goods and are signed by the party against whom enforcement is sought. However, TPAs typically do not specify a quantity, and, therefore, do not satisfy the third requirement. Nonetheless, the electronic contracts and EDI transactions may themselves satisfy the Statute of Frauds.

In December 1991, the Comptroller General of the United States issued an advisory opinion, in response to an inquiry by the National Institute of Standards and Technology, that concluded that federal agencies could use EDI technologies, including message authentication codes and digital signatures, to create valid contractual obligations. See B-245714, 71 Comp. Gen. 109, 96-2 CPD 225 (Dec. 13, 1991).

In reaching this result, the Comptroller General made two particularly important observations:

- A digital signature "embodies all of the attributes of a valid, acceptable signature," because it is unique, capable of verification, and under the sole control of the signatory; and
- Electronic contracts, while "stored in a different manner than those of paper and ink contracts... ultimately take the form of visual symbols," and, therefore, fall within the statutory definition of a "writing."

Consistently, the Federal Acquisition Regulation was amended in January 1997 to expressly include electronic systems within the definition of signature. See 48 C.F.R. § 2.101.

Within the last two years, many states have similarly enacted legislation designed to facilitate electronic contracting. See, e.g., Alaska Stat. § 09.25.510(a); Arizona Rev. Stat. § 41-132; Florida Stat. § 282.73; Official Code of Georgia § 10-12-4; Rev. Stat. Nebraska § 86-1701; 15 Oklahoma Stat. § 963-965; Virginia Code § 59.1-468. The National Conference of Commissioners of Uniform State Law and the American Law Institute are working to adapt the UCC to cyberspace: for example, the proposed changes attempt to define "writing" broadly enough to encompass electronic contracts. However, most of the state laws do not provide a blanket amendment to the UCC for electronic contracts and signatures. Rather, most provide that the parties *may*, but need not, agree to be bound by an electronic record, and that *if they have agreed to be bound*, the electronic record and signature will satisfy the requirement for a writing and signature. Accordingly, it's important to review your own state law carefully before relying on an electronic contract.

Karen L. Manos, J.D., CPCM, is a partner in the law firm of Howrey & Simon in Washington, D.C.

Keeping Pace with the Times
Helen M. Pohlig, J.D.

Statute of frauds, statute of limitations, remedies, and shipping terms—just some of the areas addressed in UCC Article 2 revisions.

After nearly 10 years of work, the National Conference of Commissioners on Uniform State Laws (NCCUSL) is poised to give final approval at the end of this month to the redraft of Article 2 of the Uniform Commercial Code (UCC).* The following proposed changes are some of the most significant for purchasing and supply professionals.

Statute of Frauds

Currently, UCC §2-201 requires written evidence of contracts for the sale of goods of $500 or more (with some exceptions). After extensive discussion the threshold level has been increased to $5,000. In addition, the requirement of a writing signed by the party against whom the contract is to be enforced has been replaced with language calling for a "record authenticated" by that party. This change recognizes the increasingly common practice of electronic contracting.

What Do You Have to Offer?

Where the parties exchange offer and acceptance in the formation of a contract, there is a general legal principle that the offeror is the "master of the offer," and, thus, courts tend to honor "my terms only" provisions when they appear in offers. Revised Article 2 includes a new requirement that such a provision be conspicuous (boldface or larger type—anything that makes it stand out from the rest of the document language) if it is included in a written offer. The other party must then specifically agree to that provision. If there is no specific agreement and the parties go forward with their deal, the offeror, in effect, waives his or her "my way or the highway" condition.

The revisions also change the way additional or different terms in the offer and acceptance are handled. The revised language provides in part:

> If a contract is formed by offer and acceptance and the acceptance is by a record containing terms additional to or different from the offer..., the terms of the contract include:
> (1) terms in the records of the parties to the extent that they agree;
> (2) non-standard terms, whether or not in a record, to which the parties have otherwise agreed;

*Revisions are still in the discussion stage as of the printing of this book.

(3) standard terms in a record supplied by a party to which the other party has expressly agreed; and

(4) terms supplied or incorporated under any provision of the UCC.

Shipping Terms

Currently, Article 2 defines a variety of terms, but these definitions are replaced by §2-309, which simply provides:

> The effect of a party's use of shipment terms such as "FOB," "CIF," or the like, must be interpreted in light of applicable usage of trade and any course of performance or course of dealing between the parties.

In other words, the UCC is getting out of the business of defining shipping terms. Purchasing and supply professionals would be well served to develop a working knowledge of the INCOterms published by the International Chamber of Commerce since these shipping terms are likely to become more broadly used than those currently found in the UCC.

Remedies

The final segment of Article 2, Part 8, deals with available remedies. Several significant changes appear here. For example, consequential damages and the remedy of specific performance, both of which are available only to the purchaser under current law, are made available to the seller. Consequential damages typically cover damage to property (other than the goods sold) and injury to persons resulting from the breach of contract. A court would use the remedy of specific performance to order the parties to perform the contract as it is written as an alternative to awarding money damages.

Statute of Limitations

Perhaps the most significant change in Part 8 deals with the statute of limitations, specifying the outside time period allowed for initiating a lawsuit resulting from the breach of a sale of goods contract. Existing law allows four years for the commencement of a legal action, and the clock starts to run from the time of the actual breach, whether or not the aggrieved party knew about the breach. The revisions contain an additional period of one year from the time the breach was discovered, not to exceed five years from the time of the breach.

Plan into Action

The current and proposed drafts of Article 2 are available on the Internet at www.law.upenn.edu/library/ulc/ulc.htm. After the NCCUSL annual meeting, check this Web site for results. A word of caution: NCCUSL is NOT a law-making body; it can only make recommendations. Assuming NCCUSL gives its approval at the end of the month, individual states could be expected to begin adopting the revisions beginning in January 2000.

Helen M. Pohlig is an attorney and NAPM seminar instructor based in Phoenix, Arizona.

You Can't Always Take It with You
Mark A. McLean, J.D.

Going to work for a new employer means knowing what knowledge can legally travel with you.

Employees are valuable assets, perhaps the most valuable assets of an organization, typically because of their knowledge. Sometimes a purchasing and supply professional's knowledge value can be general, such as his or her creative sourcing strategies or top negotiation skills. But sometimes this knowledge is unique and specific to an employer, such as the knowledge of how a particular supplier conducts business, or specifics about prices, processes, and preferences. For example, through a strategic alliance experience with a supplier, you may have been privy to sensitive financial figures, but that information was not intended for the general public and is generally kept confidential. If you go to work for a new organization and consequently have dealings with that same supplier, sharing that financial information may violate the legal rights of your former employer, new employer, and other parties involved.

Many state courts recognize a general right of employees to be free from restraint in seeking employment. While this general rule alone should not give complete comfort to you and your new employer, it does mean that in most cases the former employer will be facing an uphill battle if they are trying to find some basis on which to assert a claim against you or your new employer.

Breach of Contract

One possible area of legal concern for you as a new employee (and subsequently your new employer) is breach of contract. Did you sign any agreements when you went to work for your former employer? Many organizations require all employees to sign a confidentiality and non-disclosure agreement which identifies the intangible personal property the employer considers trade secrets or confidential. An employee who is subject to a confidentiality agreement and who discloses confidential information in violation of that agreement may be held liable for breach of contract. The new employer could also be held liable if it was found to have conspired with the new employee to breach the agreement, or if it induced the new employee to commit the breach. Therefore, if employees sign such an agreement, they should read it carefully and make a copy available to their new employer.

Breach of Loyalty

Even in the absence of a contract prohibiting an employers from using or disclosing trade secrets, or from soliciting other employees or customers of the former employer, a cause of action may be brought under a breach of loyalty theory. However, courts have held that former employers as well as competitors may solicit another's employees so long as they do not use unlawful means or engage in acts of unfair competition. The same is generally true with respect to customers, so long as the identity of the customers is not a trade secret and no other trade secrets are used in the solicitation (such as confidential pricing information of the former employer).

Violation of UTSA

Many states have adopted a version of the Uniform Trade Secrets Act (UTSA) which authorizes a court to enjoin any actual or threatened misappropriation of a trade secret, and provides for the recovery of substantial damages for any such misappropriation. Thus, even without a confidentiality agreement, both you and your new employer could face liability under the UTSA for the improper disclosure and use of a former employer's trade secrets. The definition of a trade secret remains elusive and can differ from state to state and even from court to court within the jurisdiction. While confidential customer data, such as product specifications, and even preferences, are generally considered trade secrets of a supplier, you should understand that even customer identities and contact personnel can, under certain situations, fall within the definition of trade secret.

In most states, a trade secret may consist of any formula, pattern, physical device, idea, process, compilation of information, or other information that provides an organization with a competitive advantage which the owner has taken measures to keep secret, and is not generally known or readily ascertainable by the public.

Inevitable Disclosure Doctrine

Under the inevitable disclosure doctrine, an employer can prevent a former employee from working for a competitor if the new position is comparable to the old one and the steps taken by the new employer to prevent the misappropriation of trade secrets are deemed inadequate. The theory gained a strong foothold several years ago when the Seventh Circuit Court of Appeals discussed it in upholding an injunction prohibiting a former PepsiCo executive from taking a job with a PepsiCo competitor for six months because, the court reasoned, it was inevitable that PepsiCo's confidential marketing plans would be used by the employee in his new position since he had extensive knowledge of the plans [*Pepsi Co. Inc. v. Redmond*, 54 F3d 1262 (7th Cir. 1995)].

Protective Measures

Given the very real possibility of litigation by a former employer, what can you do to reduce the risk of adverse judgments? Following is a list of steps that should be considered.

- Conduct careful due diligence to determine if any agreements were signed with former employers that could affect the new employment, such as confidentiality agreements. Bring those to the attention of the new employer and have them reviewed by legal counsel. If there are no such agreements, a new employer might require you to sign documentation confirming that fact.

- When leaving the former employer, return all property and copies of proprietary information to that employer *before* beginning new employment.
- Make yourself familiar with the laws concerning the confidentiality of your former employer's trade secrets. For its own protection, a new employer may want to document the fact that you have been instructed to avoid disclosing your former employer's trade secrets or proprietary information.
- If, in your new position, you intend to contact suppliers or partners of your former employer, send out only a neutral announcement of your new position. Keep a record of all contact with such people, including who initiated the contact, how the contact was made (for example, in person, by telephone, by mail), and the substance of the communication.
- Keep *dated* records of supplier information (including contacts and preferences), as well as proprietary business plans and details regarding new product lines or contemplated technological improvements, that were in place at your new employer, prior to your transfer there. Your new employer will want to do this as well, to establish business efforts that existed prior to your hire date.

Who's Responsible?

Keep in mind that if a suit is brought, the costs of defense may be covered by insurance. In a recent appellate case, the court held that a general liability carrier had an obligation to defend an employer sued by a competitor after hiring one of the competitor's employees under the "advertising injury" portion of the policy. Of course, policy provisions will vary from carrier to carrier, and policy to policy. As is advisable in any litigation, all insurance policies should be forwarded to legal counsel for review at the first indication of any threatened legal action.

Going to work for another organization can sometimes involve sensitive and legal issues for both you and your new employer. Understanding the risks and what steps can be taken to minimize them can mean the difference between creating a successful new employment relationship without liability, and losing an expensive battle in court.

Mark A. McLean, Esq., is an attorney with Arter & Hadden in Woodland Hills, California.

"Do You, Purchaser, Take This Contract..."
Stefanie London, J.D.

Signifying the marriage of purchaser and supplier, contract acceptance hinges on many factors.

Riddle: What do acceptance and marriage have in common? Just as marriage is one of the most significant events in our lives, the most important event in the life of a contract is the point in time when a purchaser *accepts* the goods. One hopes that both events go smoothly and as planned. But after marriage and after acceptance, sometimes the only way to unwind both relationships is to file a lawsuit—an unpleasant and costly experience.

Because most transactions involve the exchange of standard boilerplate terms and conditions, rather than specifically drafted acceptance clauses, it's important to know what the Uniform Commercial Code (UCC) §§ 2-602(1), 2-605(1), and 2-606(1) have to say about properly rejecting nonconforming goods.

Delivery of nonconforming goods requires the purchaser to notify the supplier, within a reasonable period of time, that the goods are being rejected on the basis of nonconformance. (See §2-602.) Although the initial notice may be informal, if the defect is curable, or if the supplier requests a more detailed expression of the defects, then the purchaser is obliged to provide a more formal notice of rejection. (See §2-605.) Acceptance will be deemed to have occurred when the purchaser, after having the opportunity to inspect, takes the goods as his or her own, whether he or she does so by words, action, or silence, when it is otherwise time to speak. (See §2-606.)

Has This Happened to You?

Here are some examples demonstrating how these sections of the UCC operate in real life.

Example 1: Ten boxes arrive at your dock. The dock worker signs the carrier's receipt in agreement that 10 boxes were received. Have you, the purchaser, accepted the contents? *No.* Receipt does not equal acceptance. You have a reasonable amount of time to inspect the contents of the boxes. It's wise to have that dock worker sign "received, subject to inspection" just in case the supplier's receipt contains terms stating that receipt constitutes acceptance.

Example 2: The invoice for the boxes arrives before delivery and you pay because you receive a good discount for early payment. Upon inspection, which should occur within a reasonable amount of time, you find that the goods are defective. Have you waived your rights by paying early? *No.* Payment does not equal acceptance.

Example 3: The boxes are received and set aside for 45 days before they are inspected. Once inspected, the goods are found to be defective. Have you accepted the goods? *Probably.* The UCC gives you a reasonable period of time to inspect goods, but unless you can demonstrate that 45 days is within that reasonable time period, you will have to redress the problem through an action for breach.

Example 4: Upon receipt of the boxes, you inspected the goods carefully and found no defects. Six months later, when incorporating the goods into your organization's product, the goods fail to perform as specified. Can you still reject the goods? *Probably.* It depends on whether a reasonable inspection should have uncovered that particular defect. Defects that should have been discovered upon reasonable inspection ("patent defects") cannot be relied upon as a basis for rejection, but "latent" or hidden defects may serve as a basis for rejection.

Once Accepted, Always Accepted?

UCC §2-608 allows a purchaser to revoke acceptance of nonconforming goods within a reasonable period of time after the purchaser discovers a problem that *substantially impairs* the value of the goods, and if the initial acceptance was based upon a reasonable assumption that the nonconformity would be cured and, in fact, has not been cured.

Clearly, if the goods turn out to be nonconforming after acceptance, the purchaser has an action for breach of warranty. So what's the benefit of revoking acceptance? First, rejected goods don't have to be paid for. Second, a purchaser has the burden of proving breach with respect to goods accepted. [See §2-607(4).] Third, the measure of damages for breach of warranty is the difference between value of goods as received and the value of the goods had they not been defective. Because most goods at least have some salvage value, that is likely to be less than the full purchase price. Finally, once goods have been accepted, UCC §2-607(3) requires the purchaser to notify the supplier of any breach or nonconformance of goods within a reasonable period of time after the discovery, or be barred from *any* remedy.

Warranty Period Begins upon Acceptance

You don't want acceptance to occur at delivery or a reasonable time after delivery if you are purchasing equipment that needs to be integrated before it can be tested or a system that is supposed to operate in a certain manner for a specified period of time before it is considered accepted. You should work with your legal advisor to assure that these acceptance clauses are very specifically tailored to the particular equipment or system and cover:

- How supplier will notify purchaser that equipment/system is ready for final testing.
- Define standard of performance—what do you want the system to do and for how long?
- What are specific levels of acceptable "downtime"?
- Who will test?
- How long does the supplier have to fix problem if it fails inspection?
- Final payment will not be made unless/until acceptance.

Rejection

What if a purchaser effectively rejects a shipment, but the supplier refuses to take back the nonconforming goods? Assuming the nonconformity was the supplier's fault (rather than the carrier's), the purchaser is only obligated to use reasonable care while holding the rejected goods and waiting for supplier's reasonable instructions, the cost of such storage to be borne by the supplier. Although written notice is always a good idea, it's important that purchaser's attempt to return the goods to supplier, its refusal to take them back and the resulting necessity to store them be well documented. Storage costs are more easily substantiated if done by a third-party warehouseman.

Inspection Procedures

Does a purchaser have to inspect every item of every box with a magnifying glass? Can a purchaser randomly sample goods received? In *Integrated Circuits Unlimited v. E.F.*

Johnson Co., 691 F. Supp. 630 (E.D.N.Y. 1988), the court upheld the rejection of an entire shipment of microprocessors based on a testing of a reasonable number of parts selected in a manner that assured a reasonable and random sampling technique. The court did not require the purchaser to hire a statistician to develop a mathematical testing method, but if a purchaser wants to reject an entire shipment based on an audit, the sampling methods should be randomized, unbiased and test a sufficient number of items.

Notice

This notice of breach requirement has caused problems for purchasers. This is one section of the UCC that courts universally interpret very strictly. Notice has to be given promptly after discovery of the breach. For example in *White v. Mississippi Order Buyers, Inc.*, 33 U.C.C. Rep. Serv. 1303 (Colo. Ct. App. 1982) the purchaser in a hurry to resell some unquestionably defective livestock at reduced rates in an effort to mitigate his losses didn't notify the supplier until after he resold the cattle. The purchaser clearly had a case for breach, but because he failed to give notice of the breach promptly after he discovered or should have discovered the defect, he is barred from relief. What may seem arbitrary at first blush does serve a logical purpose. The notice requirement provides the supplier an opportunity to cure a defect, to prepare for negotiation and/or litigation and to protect itself against stale claims after it is too late to investigate them meaningfully.

Consider these facts. Your organization purchased a computer system from a supplier. The system failed to operate as expected and the parties tried for six months to make the system work, but they could not. The supplier convinced you to try another system and it too failed. Finally, one year after the initial purchase you decided to revoke your acceptance of the replacement system. Certainly a system that doesn't work at all substantially impairs its value to the purchaser. Could the purchaser sue for a refund of its entire purchase price? This is obviously a fact question, but clearly the purchaser expected a correction of the nonconformity.

Contract Drafting

What can you do to improve your odds of success in the game of acceptance? First, you can train those who receive goods and pay invoices to avoid the use of the word "acceptance." Train them instead to write "received, subject to inspection."

You can also make sure that you have a solid acceptance clause on the back of your purchase order so if you find yourself in a battle of the forms, you won't be fighting without full armor. For a standard purchase of goods, the following clause works well:

> Payment for goods delivered hereunder shall not constitute acceptance thereof. Buyer shall have the right to inspect such goods and to reject and/or all of said goods which are defective in Buyer's judgment. Goods so rejected and goods supplied in excess of quantities called for herein may be returned to the seller at its expense and, in addition to Buyer's other rights, Buyer may charge the seller all

expenses of unpacking, examining, repacking and reshipping such goods. In the event Buyer receives goods whose defects or nonconformities are not apparent on examination, upon discovery of the defect, Buyer reserves the right to revoke its acceptance, require the replacement, as well as payment of damages.

Acceptance, like marriage, is filled with hopes and expectations. Speak now or forever hold your peace. Don't say "I do" or "I accept" unless you are ready. The legal consequences are significant.

Sample Acceptance Clauses

1. Capital Equipment—Right to Reject; Specifications.

(a) All equipment and/or services furnished will be subject to inspection and testing by buyer and buyer's agents upon arrival and after installation. Any equipment and/or services found by buyer in its sole discretion to be not in accordance with the specifications, drawings, plans, instructions, performance criteria, samples or other description furnished or adopted by buyer for the order or otherwise not in conformance with the terms of this order shall be subject to rejection, return and back charge as appropriate, together with the necessary costs of handling and shipping. Buyer's payment of all or any part of the purchase price prior to such inspection, testing and non-acceptance of the equipment and/or services involved shall not constitute a waiver of any of buyer's rights hereunder.

(b) When supplier believes that the work and equipment are "finally completed," it shall notify buyer in writing and upon receipt of said notice, buyer shall inspect the work and either accept such work as being "finally completed" or identify in writing to supplier that the work is not finally completed in the opinion of buyer and state specifically why buyer believes the work is not finally completed. The work and equipment shall be considered finally completed following successful start-up of the equipment and full operation of such equipment for a reasonable number of days or for such period of time set forth in the applicable Purchase Order, and at that time supplier shall submit a final payment application for all amounts remaining due and owing to supplier under this Agreement and the applicable Purchase Order. Following buyer's acceptance of the equipment as finally completed, final payment shall not be made to supplier unless and until supplier submits to buyer: (1) an affidavit that all payrolls, bill for materials and equipment and other indebtedness connected with all work performed pursuant to this order, for which buyer or its property might in any way be responsible, have been paid or otherwise satisfied; (2) executed lien waivers (subject to receipt of final payment) signed by all subcontractors who have performed work pursuant to this order in an amount equal to or greater than $10,000 and who may be entitled to a lien against buyer's property (final and unconditional lien waivers from each such subcontractor shall be provided to buyer by supplier within seven (7) days of supplier's receipt of final payment); and (3) an executed lien waiver signed by supplier discharging and waiving all liens and lien rights which supplier may have against buyer's property, effective upon receipt of final payment.

2. Data Processing Equipment—Acceptance of Equipment.

(a) The intent of this clause is to establish a standard of performance which must be met before any equipment is accepted by buyer and before which any obligation for buyer to pay hereunder arises. This section applies to all equipment ordered hereunder, including, without limitation, replacement and substitute equipment, equipment which is added and equipment which is field modified after the completion of a successful performance period.

(b) The performance period shall begin on the date seller certifies that the equipment has been installed and is ready for operational use and shall end when the equipment operated by buyer's personnel has met buyer's Standard of Performance for a period of 30 consecutive calendar days.

(c) In the event the equipment is unable to meet the standard of performance within 60 days after the completion of installation, the equipment will be deemed unacceptable and unable to achieve the standard of performance required hereunder and buyer may elect one of the following options and so notify seller in writing of such election.

(d) Buyer may terminate the order, reject the equipment and request the removal of the equipment with no charges or penalties.

(e) Buyer may demand, and seller agrees to install a direct replacement of equipment causing the failure to meet the standard of performance. Such direct replacement shall also be subject to acceptance as provided in this section.

(f) Buyer may demand, and seller agrees to install, additional equipment as necessary to meet the standard of performance. Such additional equipment shall be added at no cost to buyer and shall be subject to acceptance as provided in this section.

(g) The standard of performance is a percentage determined by dividing the total productive operational use time by the total productive operational use time plus equipment failure time. Equipment failure time is the sum of each incident of failure which shall be all those incidents during the performance period when any equipment or any part thereof is rendered inoperable due to the failure of equipment or software provided by seller. The interval of time of each incident of failure shall be the hours and minutes between the time that seller was notified of equipment failure and the time such equipment is returned to buyer in proper operating condition.

(h) Equipment which is added, modified, substituted or mechanically replaced shall be deemed to have met buyer's standard of performance if this equipment operates in conformance with seller's published specifications and buyer's specifications if any, and operates at an average effectiveness level of ninety-nine percent (99%) or more during the standard of performance period as provided for herein.

(i) Buyer shall maintain appropriate daily records to satisfy all requirements of this section.

(j) The equipment shall not be accepted nor shall any obligations for payment exist unless and until the foregoing standard of performance is met. Seller shall be notified in writing of buyer's acceptance or rejection of the equipment.

Stefanie London is a partner in the law firm of Paule, Camazine & Blumenthal in St. Louis, Missouri.

Your Project's Contract
Mark Grieco

Adapt your contract to a project management environment using custom clauses.

The contracting process in a project management environment will be very similar to many other contract situations. The difference will be that the contract must adapt to the specific problems which arise in the various situations. With that in mind, a few factors exist that are especially relevant, as they will likely be a part of every project management contract.

Amendments to Agreements

First, your agreement should contain an amendment clause, such as, "This Agreement may be modified only by a writing signed by both parties."

That sounds easy, but the hard part is actually practicing what is in the contract. As contract managers know, a contract can be modified by several things, such as the actions of the parties under the existing contract. There is the law of waiver which states that if someone breaches a contract and you do nothing about it then you may be waiving your rights to object if there is a subsequent breach. You will need to put an additional clause in your contract which protects you from this occurrence. For example, if you were using a contractor the clause could read, "Any breach by Contractor which Company does not object to shall not operate as a waiver of Company to seek remedies available to it for any subsequent breach."

Throughout the life of the project and contract, get into the habit of putting things in writing. If there is a breach during the course of the project you should notify the other party immediately pursuant to the notice provisions contained in the agreement.

If any part of the agreement changes, you need an amendment. That may include place of delivery, price, inspection criteria, and so forth. In construction agreements it takes on greater importance. For example, if your project calls for change orders, they must be in writing. You should also designate who must sign them. One important thing about amendments: you must identify in the contract who is authorized to make amendments. You don't want everyone in the organization being able to amend the agreement. A sample clause might read, "Change orders may only be accepted with written signature of the following person(s): John Doe (President). The parties agree that any change orders by any person other than those mentioned above shall have no weight or effect."

Close-out Provisions

All good projects must come to an end. And your project contract must also include some specific clauses addressing this stage.

There are certain elements of the contract which will actually survive the length of the contract and should be stated as such. For example, "The clauses contained in this Agreement which, by their nature, should survive termination of this Agreement shall, in fact, survive its termination. Specifically clauses which shall survive termination of this Agreement for any reason shall include, but not be limited to, warranties, payments, quality, or non-competition." Include the appropriate paragraph numbers in this section, referencing the specific clauses.

One element mentioned in this clause is payments. Payments, especially if they are periodic payments, are tied to some type of performance. Final payments are most likely tied to final acceptance. You test a product and it passes, you pay. You get a certificate of occupancy, your contractor will want the balance of his money. In the end, your payment provision must contain a close-out of its own. For final payments, a clause might read: "Final Payment may only issue upon the occurrence of the following events: all equipment must pass inspection; final acceptance must occur which shall be testing with a demo database."

One more point: after a contract is complete and you know you will never use it again you may want to think about executing a release. A release is a document wherein one party releases another party from any obligations and responsibilities arising out of the contract. That way you cannot be sued due to some past action. Generally, the other party will want a release as well.

Contracts, like people, need to adopt to a variety of situations, and this is particularly true in the project management environment. Paying close attention to amendment clauses and close-out provisions are just a couple of ways to help ensure a successful project.

Mark Grieco is an attorney with Grieco and Scalera, P.A., in West Palm Beach, Florida.

Are They or Aren't They?
Henry F. Garcia, C.P.M.

How do you distinguish between employees and independent contractors, and why is it legally important to do so?

Purchasing and supply management professionals, from both public and private sector organizations, engage the services of various individuals to provide independent advice, methods, services, and practices for the resolution of specific business issues or problems. These independent contractors (ICs) support and/or complement the organizations' core staff (full-time employees) by applying their specialized knowledge. However, it's important to clearly differentiate between individuals classified as employees and those classified as ICs, and understand criteria for classifying ICs, laws, and regulations affecting the engagement of ICs, and the creation of effective contracts that can withstand federal, state, or internal audits.

Criteria for Classifying ICs

Independent contractors, as defined by the Internal Revenue Service (IRS), are individuals who contract to perform services for others but do not have the legal status of employees. As "independent" businesspersons, ICs do not depend on any one organization (employer) for their sole source of income. They retain control over how the work will be accomplished, where the work will be performed, and when work-related deadlines and milestones will be met. Generally, the salient criterion for classifying individuals as independent contractors is the degree of control exercised by the organizations contracting for their services.

Although no single and inclusive test exists for the classification of individuals as ICs, different legal tests are used by various government agencies, including:

- the Internal Revenue Service
- State unemployment compensation insurance agencies
- State workers' compensation insurance agencies
- State tax departments
- the U.S. Department of Labor
- the National Labor Relations Board

Each of these agencies establishes classification criteria for different reasons and makes classification decisions independent of the others. The IRS employs 20 factors to measure control under the common law test. State unemployment, workers' compensation, and tax agencies use various tests to define the status of ICs. These tests include:

- Common Law Right of Control Test
- Economic Reality Test
- Special Statutory Test (also called ABC)

Moreover, the Fair Labor Standards Act offers its own test for ICs. The Independent Contractor Tax Simplification Act of 1996 challenges the IRS 20-factor common law test, and the Independent Contractor Simplification and Relief Act of 1999 will clarify the "safe harbors" for determining that certain individuals are not employees but actually ICs.

Laws and Regulations Affecting ICs

Obviously, several laws and regulations will have an effect on an organization's treatment of ICs versus employees, as well as the repercussions of misclassification. Organizations that hire ICs can avoid the responsibilities associated with the following acts:

- Federal Insurance Contribution Act (FICA)
- Federal Unemployment Tax Act (FUTA)

- Consolidated Omnibus Budget Reconciliation Act (COBRA)

However, organizations will not be covered by some of the following:

- Americans with Disabilities Act
- Family and Medical Leave Act
- Title VII of the Civil Rights Act
- Age Discrimination in Employment Act

Improper classification of individuals can have severe financial implications or lead to lawsuits. For example, for an IC, an employer may not be responsible for payroll taxes, employee benefits, unemployment and workers' compensation premiums, or overtime pay. However, if it turns out an employee was erroneously classified as an IC, those charges would be incurred, possibly in addition to severe penalties.

Hiring ICs reduces the organizations' exposure to certain types of lawsuits, including those alleging job discrimination or wrongful termination, but again, if it's later determined an IC should have been classified as an employee, the employer faces those lawsuits.

Other legal factors include The Federal Acquisition Regulation (Part 37, Service Contracting), which distinguishes between personal services contracts and service contracts and encourages the use of performance-based contracting in the acquisition of consultants as ICs. In addition to the Service Contract Act of 1965, the Privacy Act and Contract Work Hours and Safety Standards Act affect the award of contracts to ICs. Numerous and varied state laws will complement or conflict with federal laws and regulations requiring legal interpretation and reconciliation to avoid costly penalties or repercussions.

Creation of Contracts for Independent Contractors

Purchasing and supply management professionals should craft language in these contracts, either directly or by reference, that supports and/or complements their organizations' core competencies. These contracts should provide for delivery of services that use the IC's specialized knowledge skill sets to resolve specific issues or problems within a defined and relatively short length of time. Contracts with the "right" language and structure also can evidence that organizations intend to create a purchaser-supplier relationship, not an employer-employee contract. The following pre- and post-award practices will help mitigate audit challenges to the status of ICs.

- Submit requests for proposals (RFPs) with well-defined statements of work (SOWs).
- Ensure all contracts and paperwork are consistent in identifying and individual as an IC.
- Allow the selection of where and when ICs will accomplish the SOW.
- Request that they use their own tools, supplies, and equipment consistent with the RFP.
- Insist ICs compensate associates either as employees or additional independent contractors.

- Prefer the use of fixed-price contracts, whenever feasible, over cost-type contracts.
- Require monthly invoices, if possible, to corroborate independent contractor status.
- Avoid direct and separate reimbursement for travel and entertainment expenses.
- Place explicit termination, renewal, and cost/fee escalation clauses in the contract.

Be in the Know

Independent contractors can be an effective strategy for obtaining knowledge, competencies, and experience without the commitment and expense associated with permanent staffing. You should be aware of the classification criteria for ICs and the legal ramifications of treating ICs as employees.

Henry F. Garcia, C.P.M., is director of administration for the Center for Nuclear Waste Regulatory Analyses, in San Antonio, Texas.

Part Six

Industry Practices

Part Six is designed to give you a review of current industry practices in the form of how-to articles and case studies. Thus we've selected 13 articles dealing with several different practices that we think you'll find useful in understanding what the best companies are doing today in purchasing and supply chain management.

We begin with an original article by Carla Lallatin on "Key Considerations in Buying Services." What are the best ways to assure that your organization will find the services it's looking for at the price and quality you require? The answer to this question for a variety of different services is found in Lallatin's article.

How can you proactively contribute to the profitability of your company? In the article "Unchained Profits," learn how different companies have turned purchasing and supply into a profit center. It includes three case studies of companies that have done this.

Apple Computer's recovery has been widely covered in the press. However, its innovative products are only part of the story. An equally important part has been its ability to substantially reduce inventory costs. In the article "What's Really Driving Apple's Recovery?" you'll learn how an aggressive approach to supply chain management has made a big difference at Apple, with a dramatic decrease in inventory costs.

Another modern practice some firms are trying is described in the article "Spinning-off Procurement: Establishing an Independent Procurement Company" by Wolfgang Buchholz and Lutz Kaufmann. This explains how different companies have outsourced purchasing to third-party companies. These are companies that specialize in purchasing and potentially can more efficiently and effectively procure the goods and services an organzation requires.

Two case studies by Joe Mazel, "Cintas Corp. Builds Supplier Management from the Ground Up" and "Caterpillar Gains Big Inventory Cuts by Improving Supply Chain" provide additional documentation on the important role of purchasing/supply chain management in helping companies achieve their strategic goals. In the Cintas article, we learn how this company views its suppliers similarly to how they view employees and seek to develop them in the same way. The Caterpillar piece documents the steps the company took to substantially reduce inventory costs.

In "The Logistics of Success" by Oren Harari, we learn how Fujitsu, through the strategic use of outside suppliers, specifically Federal Express, turned its laptop computer business from moribund to hot in a very competitive marketplace.

This is a sampling of what you'll find in Part Six. Our goal here has been to provide you with the tactical information you need to make purchasing reach its full potential in any company.

Key Considerations in Buying Services

Carla S. Lallatin, C.P.M., CPPO

Besides tangible goods, purchasing and supply managers are often also responsible for the procurement of the services the organization needs to function properly. This original article, prepared especially for this yearbook, provides you some sound practices when purchasing services. It includes a review of the different types of services you may be seeking, the differences among them, and how to successfully contract for these services.

Introduction

Contracting for services, on or off the owner's premises, is one of the fastest growing segments of purchasing responsibility. In 1995, a study by the Center for Advanced Purchasing Studies (CAPS), jointly sponsored by the National Association of Purchasing Management and Arizona State University, showed that across all sectors (manufacturing, nonmanufacturing and government), purchasing and supply professionals were involved in only 20 to 40 percent of purchased services (*Purchasing of Nontraditional Goods and Services,* Bales and Fearon). This study also reported that the ratio of goods to services total spend across the various industries was 46 percent for goods and 54 percent for services. And, the study noted that most organizations under-report service expenditures.

Organizations cite lots of reasons for buying services. Saving money is one, but certainly not the only one nor necessarily the most important. Quality, streamlining and leveraging resources (downsizing has cut into the amount of work that can be done) are among the top reasons. Another is that organizations are purchasing those services that are not directly related to their core business activities.

Services Are Unique

In making the transition from purchasing goods to purchasing services, we immediately see dissimilarities. The bidding, negotiating and contracting phases of service purchasing are more complex than similar features of materials procurement. We have to clearly define levels of acceptable performance and give specific meaning to commonly used terms.

For example, telling our janitorial services contractor that our premises must be "clean" only sets the stage for future problems. Our interpretation of "clean" and that of our contractor may be entirely different. We need to define the intangible words ("clean facilities," "maintain equipment," and "professional manner") often used to describe services in finite, measurable terms. In a cleaning contract, we should describe a "mopped surface" as a "floor free of dirt, dust, debris, streaks, or standing water, and without splash marks or water stains on baseboards." This is the only way to ensure we will receive the quality our organization requires.

While performance on supply contracts usually is the delivery of tangible property, on service contracts, it is the delivery of documents, completed projects and human resources. This gives rise to the question of how we, our internal client and the contractor can agree on what constitutes acceptable performance. We must describe all obligations and liabilities clearly in the contract documents.

Categories

When it comes to service categories, there are as many opinions as authorities—perhaps, even more. Basically, all are saying the same thing in different ways. Logically, we can group services into five major types: personal, professional, support, personnel and construction services. With clear grouping of our service purchases, we can distinguish unique issues within each area of service and identify ways to address the foregoing concerns.

Personal Services

Examples of personal services are technical editing, translation, and appraisals. Such services are unique and technical; i.e., we can describe specific requirements for a particular project, but the next project will probably be different so we cannot "reuse" the same statement of work. In describing requirements, we need to be specific about the exact amount of work to be done, the format to be used, the results to be achieved, and the time for project completion.

Because we can be specific, we can use a firm, fixed-price contract. When seeking suppliers, we usually are looking for independent entrepreneurs that are individuals, not partnerships, firms or corporations. We can minimize risk in supplier selection by requiring that the individual provide evidence of past, similar work. We should be specific about how we will determine whether or not performance is acceptable. For example, if a technical editing contractor delivers an edited document slightly past the specified deadline, is that acceptable? Or, will we have a person or panel review the work for acceptability? If so, what will they use as a basis to determine acceptability?

Professional Services

Examples of professional services are management and systems consultants, engineers, legal services, and medical research. Unlike personal services, the results to be achieved with professional services are more difficult to describe. We may or may not be able to be specific about the amount of work to be done and the time in which it is to be completed. For example, if we are contracting for legal services to help our organization develop hazardous waste disposal policies, we can be specific about our requirements and use a firm, fixed-price contract. However, if we are contracting for legal services to help our organization defend itself in a hazardous waste violation dispute, we can be specific only about a certain portion of the work to be done. The other party(ies) and the court(s) involved in the case leave too many unknowns to be specific about the entire contract.

Therefore, we should define as much as we can and identify ways to work with our contractor to define and pay for additional requirements during the term of the contract as these requirements become apparent. Often, professional services contracts are a combination of firm, fixed-price (for the portion of the contract that is specific at the outset) and cost (for the additional work that may occur during the contract term). On the cost portion of the contract, we want to identify and monitor the types of personnel used to perform the work, be specific about the types of costs we will reimburse and have a ceiling on the total amount we will pay. We do not want to pay an attorney's hourly rate for work performed by a legal aide, nor do we want to pay first-class travel expenses if our organization's policy is for economy rates.

When seeking suppliers, we are looking for independent contractors whose occupation is the rendering of such services. These may be individuals, partnerships, firms and corporations. We want our contractor to have a track record in the specific area of our requirements. We also must identify how we will determine acceptable performance.

Support Services

Examples of support services are janitorial, landscaping, protection, and security. These types of services support the operation of the purchasing and supply organization and the requirement for them is usually ongoing. Most often, they are not unique or technical. When describing requirements, purchasers tend to focus on the process and frequency of tasks rather than the results to be achieved. While it is acceptable to identify process and frequency of tasks, we should also describe the results we are seeking in finite, measurable terms. For example, we might require that throughout the term of a contract for mowing services the grass always be two to four inches high, regardless of how many or how few times the contractor has to mow. In this way, we put the responsibility for assigning resources and accounting for weather and growing conditions on the contractor.

While most support service contracts can include a firm, fixed-price, we may need to build some alternatives into our contracts to accommodate seasonal or workload variations should they occur. Most support services are provided by independent contractors, usually partnerships, firms or corporations rather than individuals. We should check to make sure the contractor is financially sound, has the proper business license and a good safety record, and has sufficient resources (people and equipment) to perform to our standards. As with other types of service contracts, we need to identify how we will determine acceptable performance. Oftentimes, purchasers use a combination of follow-up monitoring (checking completed work) and customer feedback and/or complaints.

Personnel Services

Examples of personnel services are temporary personnel, counseling, and rehabilitation. Such services may or may not be unique or technical. Likewise, the requirement for such services may or may not be ongoing. For example, our organization may need laborers for a short-term project. In this case, our requirements are nontechnical and infrequent. On the other hand, our organization may contract for an employee counseling program. Here, our requirements are technical and ongoing.

When describing our requirements for personnel services, we want to be as specific as possible about the work to be done, requisite skills of personnel, results to be achieved and timing needs. When we can specifically identify and describe our requirements, we can use firm, fixed-price contracts. Frequently, such specificity is not possible with personnel services contracts and we have to use cost contracts. With this option, we must be prepared to carefully monitor results against predefined measurements to ensure we receive adequate service at the agreed-upon price. Such measurements can include types of personnel used to perform the work, estimated number of hours and expenditures we will reimburse.

When looking for suppliers of personnel services, we find partnerships, firms and corporations as the major types of suppliers. Occasionally, we may encounter individuals that can meet our requirements. With personnel services, our suppliers may include nonprofit organizations for rehabilitation or counseling programs. The government requires licensing in some areas of personnel services. As part of the qualification process, we should look at experience, qualifications, skills and proper licensing of both the company and the individuals that will be involved in service delivery.

In identifying how we will determine acceptable performance, we should again focus on results. For example, in a rehabilitation program, we not only want to know how many employees entered the program, but how long they were in it and what were the long-term effects. Were they rehabilitated? Did the rehabilitation have lasting results?

Construction Services

Examples of construction services include architects, general contractors, painters, carpenters, and electricians. These types of services can be either technical, such as architects, or nontechnical, such as painters. We frequently can be very specific about our requirements for construction services and, therefore, can use firm, fixed-price contracts. The exception may be architectural services. In these cases, pricing methods include lump-sum, cost plus fixed fee or cost reimbursement with a not-to-exceed price limit. To keep final construction costs within projected budget, we can require the estimated construction costs when design is 25 percent complete to be equal to or less than the estimated cost when design is 90 percent complete.

Usually, we find that suppliers of construction services are independent contractors.

As a rule, they are partnerships, firms or corporations rather than individuals, but we may find individuals from the trades (carpenters, painters, electricians).

Phases of Service Contracting

Buying services is divided into three general phases: planning, supplier selection and contract administration. Planning may or may not begin with the "make-or-buy" decision, but whether or not this process occurs, planning must.

Planning

Developing the Statement of Work (SOW) is part of the planning process. We can describe the service in performance or technical terms, or both, but we must keep in mind that we are seeking results that we can measure. In defining the service, we should address all required tasks, functions, activities, performance levels (what is acceptable and what is not), and deliverables. Comments from different organizations regarding what they have learned about service contracting reveal that most have learned—through a negative experience—that you have to spend the time up front to define all this detail—or pay the price later.

A well-written SOW can do more for the success of a service contract than any other part of the contracting process. Because the SOW and the related terms and conditions of service delivery are the point of reference for resolving problems throughout the contract term, it must be clear, specific and appropriate to the audience.

The service should achieve pre-defined standards of performance. Therefore, one or more indicators of performance (performance indicators), standards and acceptable quality levels must be defined for each activity. A performance indicator is a measurable characteristic that is used to determine the acceptability of a product or service. A standard is the quantitative value that defines the expected performance level for the selected characteristics. The acceptable quality level is the allowable deviation from that standard. For example, an office supplies contract stipulates that all supplies must be delivered the next business day after receipt of order. That is the delivery standard. The contract further indicates that over a year's time, delivery requirements must be met 90% of the time. The 10% variable is the allowable deviation from the stipulated standard and is the acceptable quality level for delivery on the contract. The definition of result-oriented performance is the basis for determination, through competent contract administration, that we are receiving the quality for which we are paying.

Another part of planning is identifying risk—technical, schedule and cost—and deciding how much of that risk a contractor might assume. We should look at risk in these areas as high, medium and low and identify the risk drivers in the high and medium areas so that we can include language in the SOW to preclude problems. For example, if we contract for food service in the employees' cafeteria and the contractor fails to have sufficient quantities, what happens? Or, what if the food is substandard? What happens? It is essential to select the appropriate contract type. This helps ensure performance and understanding and minimizes risk.

Cost estimates are especially important in service contracts because there is no "off-the-shelf" competitor's product that we can use for price comparison. We can develop a cost estimate using internal and external data or by comparing the planned acquisition to past experience. Cost projections related to specific service activities are needed as a basis for: price and cost analysis of offers, negotiation and determination of deductions for non-performance.

Supplier Selection and Contract Administration

The supplier selection phase of buying services entails locating suppliers, evaluating suppliers, identifying a contractor, negotiation and contract development. We must pay attention to this phase because the service industry is a relatively unstable market. Companies manufacturing or selling supplies must make a capital investment to be in business; however, many service suppliers become service suppliers merely by obtaining the proper business license. We want to make sure the supplier we select has experience and will still be in business at the end of our contract.

Purchasing services does not end with the contract. The purchasing organization needs to monitor and have a realistic degree of control over both its own and the supplier's performance. Contract administration includes meetings, monitoring, resolving disputes, documenting, reporting and lots of internal and external communication. Proactively managing the relationship ensures success.

In all service contracts, we should tie our payments to deliverables. It is all too common to see payments made just because a certain amount of time has passed. Another error made in the payment process is that we pay the full amount regardless of the level of service received. If the acceptable level of service is 95 percent and we receive 90 percent performance, why do we neglect to take deductions? We probably would never make these mistakes on supply contracts. We cannot make services an exception if we expect to obtain full performance from our suppliers.

Carla S. Lallatin, C.P.M., CPPO, directs a consulting firm, Lallatin & Associates, whose mission is to promote the understanding and improvement of purchasers and suppliers. Previously vice president of Dun & Bradstreet's BidNet, Lallatin has over 25 years experience in all phases of purchasing and materials management. Her background in executive purchasing management includes D&B, United Computing Systems, the City of New York, and the State of Wyoming, giving her unique insights into both commercial and public sector procurement.

Unchained Profits:
The Role of Suppliers

Libby Estell

> *Customers are making more and more demands on your company. As a manager of the supply chain, you can make a difference in the quality of products and services your company delivers and help the company increase its profits. This article discusses these points in more detail and provides three case studies of companies like Herman Miller where effective supply chain management is successfully supporting the efforts of sales and marketing.*

Your product is no longer good enough. Customers want more than a great product; they want a product that meets their exact specifications and is delivered just in time. They want a twelve-course meal with fast-food efficiency. With an efficient supply chain, you just might be able to give it to them.

First, a quick definition for the uninitiated: A supply chain is the series of business processes that moves products from raw materials to end users. In an inefficient supply chain, every link adds extra production time and cost to the finished product, compromising the sales force's ability to meet customer needs. "Salespeople often either promise too little or too much, and the company may not be able to actually deliver on those promises" says Beth Enslow, a senior analyst at the Gartner Group, a technology consulting firm in Stamford, Connecticut. But high-tech solutions aimed at improving supply chains are helping to make sure that a salesperson can deliver to that customer on time and in a way that's profitable.

Indeed, salespeople and marketers can now compete by communicating as closely with suppliers and distributors as they do with customers. "The ability to promise fast, accurate delivery times is becoming a real sales tool," Enslow says. "The truth is that when a salesperson goes out and promises an order they aren't sure the company can deliver, they're at a distinct disadvantage to a sales rep from a company that has the ability to deliver an informed promise."

Originally adopted by the high-tech and consumer packaged goods industries, supply chain management is spreading to include aerospace, oil, and utility companies among others, all looking to achieve the same result: improved customer service. "The number-one reason companies are conducting supply chain activities is to be more responsive to customers and to serve those customers at a lower cost," Enslow says. Even when supply chain optimization is an effort to cut costs and improve customer service, it almost always boosts sales. "If a company's able to be more responsive to the changing needs of its customers, then it's going to be more successful at capturing repeat business and upselling those customers."

The three companies described here run the gamut from big to small, consumer to industrial, but they all have one thing in common: Their supply chain initiatives are helping to increase profitability, boost customer service, and fuel skyrocketing sales.

Herman Miller Inc.—The Promise Keepers

Herman Miller Inc. processes more than 3,000 orders each week for its build-to-order line of office furniture and accessories. Approximately 80 percent of the office systems manufacturer's business is project-based, requiring extensive coordination among its five plants and other operations so that an entire order can be shipped together and on time. "Synchronization is key to fulfilling customer demand," says Mark Douglas, project manager for the Zeeland, Michigan-based company's supply chain efforts. "We call it the 99 percent effect. If only one piece of a multipart order is missing, the entire order becomes late—[damaging] delivery performance."

Herman Miller wanted to improve its delivery performance by enabling its sales force to make reliable promises. "Lead times are extremely competitive in this industry, and so is cost—even more so is reliability," Douglas says. "Being able to deliver what the customer wants when they want it is key."

The manufacturer got a jump on industry competitors when it began a supply chain optimization program four years ago. Supply chain management software from i2 Technologies and a Baan enterprise resource planning system identify and manage the company's business constraints. This enables Herman Miller to maintain customer identity throughout the manufacturing process, ensuring that entire orders are completed simultaneously and shipped according to client specifications. The company has also improved on-time delivery from 76 to 99 percent and decreased factory lead time from six weeks to four. A $56 million cut in the cost of goods sold has allowed the Herman Miller sales force to pass along the savings in the form of deeper customer discounts.

And for Herman Miller, a happier customer means healthier sales. The company's sales volume has increased by four times the industry average since synchronizing its supply chain—something it attributes to improved customer satisfaction among new and repeat buyers alike. "Our sales force can use the fact that we're more reliable as a competitive advantage," Douglas says. "It helps them to form relationships with the end user. It's a hit against us if we aren't reliable."

Herman Miller, now the country's second largest office systems manufacturer, wants to see its startling sales growth lead to increased market share. Since industry-leader Steelcase and number-three Hayworth have recently begun supply chain management initiatives of their own, Douglas says Herman Miller is far from finished with its supply chain. "We're a long way from being as reliable as we need to be," he says, adding that the manufacturer wants to boost direct shipping from 30 percent to 80 percent of orders. "As we continue to make improvements, we're going to continue to find things we can improve."

Tum Yeto Inc.—Ramping Up Sales

Tum Yeto Inc., the world's third largest maker of skateboards and accessories, knows its business boils down to the simple law of supply and demand: When a 13-year-old skater demands a new board, you'd better have a supply on hand. So two years ago, when Tum Yeto realized its production was falling far short of consumer demand, the San Diego-based company overhauled its supply chain and saw its sales soar.

Using what operations manager Rob Valerio calls the "basic 1980s Japanese business model" of just-in-time delivery and a forecast incorporating 50 economic factors, Tum Yeto brought raw materials delivery in phase with production of its boards and other products, allowing the company to pay suppliers with the receipts from the finished order. "We schedule materials at the time it takes to turn them around," Valerio says. "It takes about five weeks to build a skateboard, but things like hats and T-shirts take just a couple of days." The just-in-time schedule allowed Tum Yeto to shrink cycle times and reduce inventory while improving the cash flow so critical to a small business.

The just-in-time business model and the 12-month supply-and-demand forecasts that drive it may not be revolutionary, but the results have been nothing short of remarkable. In a market that showed 15 to 20 percent growth during the past two years, Tum Yeto, which declined to reveal its annual revenues, increased its sales volume by 50 percent each of the past two years. The company has also enlarged its stable of domestic retailers to 1,000, up 50 percent from two years ago.

But the benefits of Tum Yeto's improved supply chain stretch beyond its walls to include subcontractors and retailers alike. Suppliers, Valerio says, now devote a larger portion of their production to Tum Yeto because its orders and payments are more reliable. And retailers are carrying a deeper Tum Yeto product line—something Valerio attributes to the 44 percent improvement in the manufacturer's level of in-stock merchandise. "Supply of product from us to them had been their number-one complaint," Valerio says. "Now they're able to get a reliable monthly supply with a larger selection because we have more in stock and more on the way than ever before. It's made them order from us over the competition."

Tum Yeto's improved reliability and selection have helped make it one of the largest accounts at Blades, a chain of 18 skate shops in Boston, Chicago, New Jersey, and New York, says Shawn Zappo, the retailer's skateboard buyer and merchandiser. "It's nice to work with a company that's this organized," Zappo says. "They have a huge selection and it's pretty much always available when you want it. They have everything covered."

Reggie Barnes couldn't agree more. As president of Wilmington, North Carolina-based Eastern Skate Supply, the exclusive U.S. distributor of Tum Yeto products, Barnes will do close to $1 million in business with the manufacturer this year. "As a company they've increased by leaps and bounds," he says. "And it's been great for us. It's an edge for us that we sell Tum Yeto products and our competitors can't get their hands on them."

Tum Yeto made other changes in its supply chain to better serve the 13-year-old skate rat anxious to replace his broken board. Last year the company began selling its entire 600-item product line direct to consumers over the Internet. Now skate enthusiasts can view the Tum Yeto catalog, order merchandise, and track delivery status via UPS online. As a result, Internet sales have grown to account for 10 percent of the company's business. Thanks to the tracking component, which adds value for a buyer who could have just as easily gone to a retail outlet, Valerio says, "In the last year, e-commerce has gone from being a revenue taker to being a revenue generator."

Pinacor—Demystifying Distribution

"To some extent distributors have been kind of quiet and discreet, but we formed Pinacor to put more focus on distribution and supply chain," says Robert O'Malley, CEO of Pinacor, the third largest distributor of high-tech goods in the United States. A spin-off of global-technology solutions giant MicroAge, Pinacor moves 300 tons of product a day. To further complicate matters, those 30,000 different products from more than 200 manufacturers are shipped to more than 25,000 computer resellers. So to make sure each of those customers gets what they ordered, the Tempe, Arizona-based distributor has made supply chain visibility a priority.

Pinacor has placed e-commerce at the center of its supply chain initiative. Resellers can visit Pinacor's EC Worksite to manage their complete order cycle. They can check pricing and availability, create price quotes for end users, order products, and track their order as it travels from Pinacor's system configuration center to their doorstep via a link to UPS's Web site. "This gives us the light to see down the end of the tunnel and effectively communicate with our customers," says Joe Ippolito, sales opportunity specialist at GreenPages, a computer reseller in Kittery, Maine. GreenPages, which does more than $100 million in sales and has grown by more than 100 percent in each of the past four years, does not own or operate from a warehouse. "We drop ship directly from distributor warehouses to the end user," Ippolito says. "Since we don't have our hands on the product, we depend on our distributors to give us the tracking capabilities our customers need."

The Pinacor field sales force depends on EC Worksite as well. In the first six months after splitting from MicroAge, Pinacor sales grew 20 percent. "I'm quickly ramping up all my customers to be on EC Worksite," says Joe Barnes, Pinacor's account development director. "It's a remarkable sales tool. I can go into a reseller and help make all these people's roles easier. There's a tremendous demand among their customers to have information in minutes or seconds, and because EC Worksite provides that, it helps me to win more business."

Based on the success of EC Worksite, Pinacor decided to further improve customer visibility along the supply chain. In October the distributor partnered with Descartes Systems

Group Inc., an Ontario-based provider of supply chain execution software, to design and implement a Web-based delivery management system capable of tracking products throughout the entire supply chain, from Pinacor's suppliers to the customer's doorstep.

The system, which went live at the end of 1998, is expected to bolster both customer service and sales. "A customer is only going to buy what they can see on the Web site that Pinacor has in stock, even if a huge shipment of exactly what they need is arriving three hours later," says Art Mesher, executive vice president at Descartes. "By connecting to the supplier and [allowing customers to see] when the supplier ships the goods, Pinacor is able to promise customers delivery on products they don't even have in inventory yet."

Through the Web interface, users will have access to the real-time status of shipments, and receive instant notification about any exceptions to their orders and delivery schedules. Users will be able to tailor the notification system to meet their needs, such as an option that alerts the reseller only when the product is delivered. The system will also generate alert messages to Pinacor when follow-up action is necessary. "We've really seen a shift from [supplier-driven] to customer-driven business," O'Malley says. "The supply chain has taken on a brand dimension wherein we ask ourselves, 'What is the experience you want the customer to get?'"

According to O'Malley, an effective supply chain empowers the Pinacor front office to make promises the back office can consistently meet. "You can drop the prices, but you can't sustain that," he says. "An efficient supply chain is something you can sustain."

Libby Estell is a writer for Sales & Marketing Management *magazine.*

What's Really Driving Apple's Recovery?

Doug Bartholomew

If you think iMac is the answer to that question, you're only part right. As important as neat products to Apple's current success is the fact that it has found supply chain religion. The article details how Apple has reduced internal inventory from $437 million in 1997 to $25 million by December 1998. Purchasing and supply plays an important role in all this. Timothy Cook, the former Compaq executive who is leading this initiative, says, "I consider internal inventory to be a defect." His job is to eliminate that.

If you believe the common wisdom in the business press, Apple Computer Inc. was saved from being turned into cider by the return of cofounder Steve Jobs and the advent of a new product, the hot-selling iMac. Truth be told, that's only half the story.

It's a fact that in 1996-97, the Cupertino, Calif.-based computer maker lost nearly $1.9 billion. It's also true that last year a 40% smaller Apple—a pared-down core of its 1996 self—earned $309 million, with the iMac representing about one-third of total Macintosh sales during the latest quarter. But beneath all of the iMac's new colors, what's really driving Apple's resurgence is a whole new strategy for manufacturing and supply-chain management conceived by a former Compaq Computer Corp. executive.

That's not to say that Jobs, the legendary industry visionary, doesn't deserve his share of the credit for Apple turning in five consecutive profitable quarters. Having taken over in mid-1997, Jobs accelerated the company's restructuring. On his watch, the company shed 15 of 19 products including printers and the slow-selling Newton personal digital assistant, closed plants, and laid off thousands of employees. Jobs instilled new confidence among investors, with Apple shares rebounding from a low of $12.75 a year ago to $39 in February. He even had the audacity to sell Apple stock to archenemy Microsoft Corp. in exchange for a cash infusion of $150 million.

Finally, Jobs enlisted a new executive team, paying signing bonuses where needed to get the best people to keep an already tarnished Apple from spoiling altogether. Of the seven-person executive team, only CFO Fred Anderson joined the company before 1997. Perhaps the most important of those executives Jobs brought on board was Timothy D. Cook, whom Jobs lured away from industry leader Compaq with a $500,000 signing bonus and a $400,000 base salary to become Apple's senior vice president for worldwide operations. At Compaq, Cook was vice president in charge of corporate materials. A computer-industry veteran, Cook also worked for a major computer reseller and spent a dozen years at IBM Corp., where he was head of North American fulfillment. Cook has been religious in his fervor and dedication to remake Apple's lazy, bloated supply chain and wring out inefficiencies in its production processes.

Aiming at twin goals of slashing inventories to the bone and cutting order-to-delivery times, Cook has pushed Apple as if there were no floor under the accelerator pedal. "I'm really big on asset velocity," he says, referring to how fast a company can turn its inventory. "For a PC manufacturer, that's perhaps the most key metric. In the business we're in, the product gets stale as fast as milk."

Historically, one of Apple's greatest weaknesses has been its supply chain. Managers did a poor job of matching production to demand. One reason for the mismatch was that sales forecasts often were way off. "Apple's problem was a supply-chain management problem," says Tom Grace, senior manufacturing analyst at AMR Research Inc., an IT research firm in Boston. "They always had shaky forecasting ability."

As a result, the company either missed potential sales because it couldn't fulfill demand or piled up huge excess inventory that later had to be written off at a crippling cost. For years the company struggled with the twin demons of insufficient supply and excess inventory.

Most of Apple's huge losses, in fact, can be attributed to sloppy inventory management, Cook says. "The company lost $1 billion in 1997 mainly as a result of asset problems, such as being too long on inventory," he says. "We had five weeks of inventory in the plants, and we were turning inventory 10 times a year." In general, other manufacturers in the industry were turning inventory about 10 to 12 times, although Dell Computer Corp. was at 40 and Gateway Inc. somewhere in the middle. "We set our eyes on beating Dell," Cook says. "We're looking at how to leapfrog them and be better."

Cook contends that Apple not only has caught Dell in the last year, but bettered the direct-sales PC leader in inventory speed in the latest quarter. The company, whose latest marketing slogan is "Think Different," finished December with just two days' worth of inventory in its plants, compared with seven days' worth for Dell.

"We've gone from 10 turns to 180 turns," Cook says. "That's a direct metric of your supply chain. We've now gone past Dell. In a year or two, I'd prefer to be able to talk inventories in terms of hours, not days." A spokesperson at Austin-based Dell confirmed that the PC giant currently is turning inventory 52 times a year, or roughly every seven days.

The numbers bear out Apple's steady improvement in this area. In fiscal 1997 Apple had $437 million tied up in inventory, or a full month's supply on the books. But by the close of fiscal 1998 last Sept. 25, the company had slashed inventory levels to just six days, or $78 million worth—an 80% reduction. A further reduction down to $25 million worth—for a total reduction of 94%—was achieved in the quarter ended in December. "And we're not letting up," Cook promises. "I consider any internal inventory to be a defect."

Since Christmas, Apple has begun using SAP AG's R/3 system, which has helped speed the filling of custom orders. Cook is pushing to chop the custom-order-to-delivery time from 10 to five days.

Yet another essential link in Cook's supply-chain scheme is the shift of most manufacturing and assembly work to contract manufacturers, which tend to be more efficient at various steps in the process than Apple. "There are many very good companies with economies of scale in the board-manufacturing business," Cook says. "We're going to leverage outside partners for that."

Last summer, Apple formed a partnership with a Singapore firm to build computer boards at sites closer to each of Apple's assembly plants, a move other PC manufacturers are making. "A lot of suppliers in the PC industry are building replenishment plants right next to the OEMs' plants," observes AMR's Grace.

To further streamline its supply network, Apple announced on Feb. 1 plans to discontinue building the iMac at its Elk Grove, Calif., plant, shifting production to LG Electronics, a Korean contract manufacturer that has plants in Seoul and Mexico. As a result, Apple will shed up to 350 workers, including 25 permanent employees and 300 temps at the California plant, which will continue to produce custom-order iMacs and the higher-end G3 computers. LG also will take over production of iMac units from Apple's plants in Ireland and Singapore, according to a company spokesperson. The reason? "We are trying to improve our inventory management."

Representing one of Apple's most egregious supply-chain anomalies, parts produced at an Apple supplier in Asia were shipped to the Apple plant in Ireland and later shipped back to Asia. "It was not a bright supply chain," Cook admits. Now, with a partner in Taiwan, the assembly is fully handled in Asia. "We've achieved a dramatic reduction in cycle time and a corresponding reduction in cost, plus we're able to get to market faster," he adds.

Apple also has outsourced much of its logistics and transportation planning. "I don't want to own an airplane or a truck," Cook says. "We've let someone else negotiate rates and execute the warehousing portion of the business for us."

After looking at different supply-chain-planning software packages, Apple began using i2 Technologies Inc.'s Rhythm about six months ago. The PC maker is using several Rhythm advanced planning modules and plans to install more during the next year. "SAP is the cornerstone, but i2 is a key piece of what we do," says Cook. "We've separated planning and execution." Several computer manufacturers use i2, including Compaq, Dell, Gateway, Acer, Hewlett-Packard, IBM, and Silicon Graphics.

Now, instead of building hundreds of thousands of computers in advance to meet a sales forecast, Apple projects sales each week and adjusts production schedules daily. "We plan weekly and execute daily," says Cook. "I'm relentless on that."

Indeed, in PC manufacturing, the ability to respond swiftly to changing market conditions is critical, industry experts say. "You cannot win with just quality and product design," says Sanjiv Sidhu, Chairman and CEO at i2 Technologies in Dallas. "You have to be able to react quickly. The profitability of making computers depends on the velocity of your organization."

Careful management of suppliers is increasingly critical to Apple's success. The company lets its suppliers keep in inventory certain "industry standard" parts and components,

Cook says. With the company's powerful G3 computer, for instance, the main options for customers are different microprocessors, various storage options, a CD/ROM or digital-video-disc-player choice, and different modems. "Some of these are industry standards, and we have our suppliers hold these in inventory for us," Cook explains. "There's a limited number of parts, but you can put them together in different ways."

Apple also overhauled its distribution channels. In mid-1997 the company began reducing the number of its national reseller chains from five to the current one—CompUSA Inc. Although the PC manufacturer won't release sales figures, Phil Schiller, vice president for worldwide product marketing, says Apple is doing "extremely well" selling iMacs, Powerbook laptop computers, and G3 computers direct to consumers and small businesses via the Apple Store, which opened in late 1997 on its Web site at www.apple.com. Certainly, online sales offer Apple a tremendous opportunity—Dell, for example, does an estimated $2 billion annually in online sales.

Of course, even the new Apple under Cook's supply-chain mastery has struggled at times. Look at what happened to the company last August and September, when the iMac was first being shipped. The colorful blue computers were selling faster than the PC maker was able to crank them out. According to Jobs, it took the company a few weeks' production to eliminate its order backlog for both the iMac and the G3.

Cook says last autumn's experience was only natural for the debut of a popular product, and it also was an indicator of the company's return to being an industry leader. "Anytime you have a new product as popular as the iMac, you'll never be able to fill all those orders the first day," he says. "And if you can, you don't have a hot product. You try to fill those orders within a reasonable time. We got a significant supply of iMacs out very fast."

Apple sold 800,000 iMacs in the first four and a half months. "It is the No. 1-selling computer model in America," Jobs boasted at the MacWorld show in San Francisco in January.

In addition to the order backlog, Apple has had other hurdles to clear. During the darkest months when the company was fighting to survive, Apple began charging consumers $35 for access to product support. The only problem was, doing so meant breaking an earlier promise of free technical support for life for consumers who bought its products from 1992 to 1996.

After customers complained, the Federal Trade Commission stepped in, forcing Apple to make good on its commitment. The company agreed to reinstate the "Apple Assurance" program, offering free support to purchasers. Furthermore, Apple agreed to reimburse consumers who had paid the fee since the company began charging for the service in October 1997.

Perhaps one of the most damaging endeavors—from an internal standpoint—that Apple launched was its botched first attempt to install SAP's enterprise-resource-planning software. The company spent years and tens of millions of dollars on software licenses and consultants in an attempt to adapt its business processes to fit the complex SAP R/3 software, with minimal success.

"The project was not managed very tightly," Cook says. The initial consultant on the project, Andersen Consulting, was replaced by another major firm. Ultimately, though, the project stalled. "The company wrote off a bunch of it," Cook says. Following the SAP debacle, CIO Joe Riera left the company to join DHL Airways Inc. as CIO. Apple elected not to replace him.

Instead, when Jobs returned, he smartly took a page from one of the PC industry's leaders, hiring Cook from Compaq. The SAP effort was resurrected and refocused to support the slimmed-down operations that remained following the company's enterprise-wide restructuring. Unlike what happened to the earlier effort, when managers and employees reportedly resisted changing their ways of doing work to fit R/3, this time around the company took the project seriously, marching faithfully to the SAP tune.

"We changed our business processes to map to the SAP system," Cook says bluntly. "The SAP installation is a really big deal for us." In addition to the accounting package, the main pieces of R/3 Apple is employing are for manufacturing, order management, and order fulfillment.

In another potentially more embarrassing misstep, Jobs announced at the January MacWorld show that the new Macs with the powerful G3 microprocessor, when equipped with a $49 third-party software package, Virtual Game Station from Connectix Corp. of San Mateo, Calif., are capable of running Sony game CDs. "This turns the Mac into a Sony game station," Jobs said.

Unfortunately, no one bothered to check to see what Sony thought about the idea. Sony Computer Entertainment Inc. remains mum on what, if any, action it plans to take. "It's a sensitive situation," says a spokesperson for Sony, which makes its own proprietary Play-Station machines and the CD games that run on them.

Finally, there is the question of leadership. Many in and outside the computer industry wonder if Jobs can effectively run Apple indefinitely as "interim" CEO, given his simultaneous responsibilities as CEO of Pixar, the animation firm. If anything, his entrenched role with Pixar appears to have affected his steerage of Apple, since the company appears to be evolving into a manufacturer of computers primarily aimed at multimedia and graphics applications.

In fact, many of the new features of the upgraded G3 model are graphical or multimedia-related, such as video editing, 3-D graphics, and computer games. "We are totally committed to making the Macintosh the best game platform in the world," says Jobs, noting that Macs now run several popular titles, including SimCity 3000, Fly!, Rainbow Six, Starcraft, and Tomb Raider II.

Ironically, it's in the multimedia world—not operating systems, where Apple continues to offer one of the few alternatives to Windows—that Apple has its biggest tiff with Microsoft. "Our relationship with Microsoft is like a marriage—99% of the time it's great," Jobs says. "But 1% of the time we argue about stuff—usually multimedia."

Asked if Apple is turning its back on the computing needs of business, marketing chief Schiller responds, "Everybody else in the computer industry wants to be like IBM. We do have enterprise business customers, but that's not our primary focus. We are a great consumer company, but we also have a unique specialty professional business in publishing."

One favorable sign for Apple—besides stringing together five quarters of profits—is that it's no longer merely selling to its existing base of Macintosh followers. Nearly one-third of the 800,000 iMacs sold were purchased by first-time computer buyers. Another 13% of iMac buyers were what Jobs refers to as "Wintel converts." The remaining 55% were purchased by Mac owners either adding new machines or replacing older ones. "That means 45% are new to the Mac platform," says Jobs.

Admittedly, the January launch of the new multicolored iMac, with its five striking hues, adds a sudden layer of complexity that gives supply-chain guru Cook reason to pause. "I've lost a little hair over it," he says. "But we've figured out a way to manage the color detail."

Doug Bartholomew is a senior editor with Industry Week *magazine.*

Spinning-off Procurement—Establishing an Independent Procurement Company

Wolfgang Buchholz, Ph.D. and Lutz Kaufmann, Ph.D.

Have you heard about spinning-off procurement and using third-party companies to purchase goods and services for your company? You can learn more about what this is all about in this article. You'll learn about how this works and the three phases in its implementation. Of course, the reason to do this is that it can make your company more efficient and effective using the services of such third-party experts rather than doing it all in-house.

Introduction

"**M**aster contracts for non-core-products will be negotiated by consortiums and third-party-companies that have leverage and buying expertise."

This statement is one of the major findings of a recent five- and ten-year forecast by the Center for Advanced Purchasing Studies (CAPS) about "The Future of Purchasing and Supply."[1] This best practice article highlights the spinning-off of such a unit, let's call it High Performance Procurement (HPP), from a large chemical company.

A formerly centralized cost center was first transformed to a purchasing unit offering its services to decentralized business units within the firm (closed procurement network). As such, it not only helps the decentralized parts of the firm to concentrate on their core competencies, but represents a core competency in itself. The closed procurement network is being further developed to an open network where HPP is also doing business with external companies. The final step of the Procurement Spin-Off (PSO) will be a completely independent company.

Background: Realigning the Company's Organization (Phase 1)

The roots of HPP lie in a large chemical/pharmaceutical company—let's call it ChemLife. In Europe, ChemLife is a true example of the term "change management." Since 1994 the company has been changing from a massive, diversified chemical firm to a company with a clear focus on life science activities. Legally, ChemLife is a strategic management holding company. ChemLife no longer undertakes its own business but rather concentrates on the strategic management of a portfolio of businesses from fields such as pharmaceuticals, health care products, and agriculture. Under the roof of the holding company, all businesses are legally independent subsidiaries, which offer a maximum amount of flexibility for acquisitions, alliances, or if necessary, to restructure the portfolio through divestitures.

However, the process of decentralization refers not only to the operational businesses but also to the supporting areas, which were formerly centralized departments. For service functions such as materials management, intelligent solutions had to be found that would not cause a loss of the advantages gained from size and specialization.

In the past, the service center materials management was responsible for all procurement activities of ChemLife with approximately 800 employees and a purchase volume of $15 billion. Its task was the centralized purchasing of raw materials, technical equipment and services, packaging materials, and distribution services. This lack of focus had its price. The central buyers were over-burdened with placing orders and as a result did not have enough time for true strategic procurement planning. Consequently, it was decided that there was a need to distinguish between strategic and transactional procurement.

In addition to the central service center in Germany there were numerous purchasing departments in ChemLife's locations all over the world. Do-it-yourself activities of the decentralized procurement departments often jeopardized the advantages of pooling demand to the maximum extent possible. Because purchasing in the past was acting within the boundaries of its defined functional area, another main objective of the realignment was implementing process orientation within and across departments and functions.

In order to reestablish and optimize procurement within ChemLife Holding Group, the following questions were addressed:

- How can a formerly centralized purchasing unit be efficiently transformed under the roof of a strategic management holding organization?
- Should a solution be sought that strives for a complete decentralization of procurement, or can a strategic procurement center create synergies and pool the group's purchasing power?
- Should procurement become a profit center and a stand-alone enterprise that can compete effectively on the market generating its own profit (Procurement Spin-Off)?

Establishing a Procurement Network (Phase 2)

The direction that was decided upon was to combine the advantages of centralized and decentralized purchasing through cooperative purchasing activities. The subsidiaries of ChemLife are viewed as a purchasing network, in which the legally independent company HPP, formed on the 1st of January 1998, has taken the role of a network-catalyst. HPP has about 150 employees and an annual purchase volume of $4 billion (1997). The 100 percent shareholder of HPP is ChemLife. The other players in the network are the decentralized businesses or site procurement departments—the suppliers and customers, which at that time were subsidiaries and companies where ChemLife held a minority stake.

The next step was for HPP to also serve ChemLife external customers. In any case the customers are the drivers of the network; their main task is to set clear goals, e.g., sayings targets, for the other participants.

HPP now is responsible for the strategic procurement process, while the decentralized units are in charge of the transactional procurement process. Only through this clear focus can both processes be effective. Strategic procurement deals with cross-business materials and services. Specific business or site needs, from which no bundling or know-how advantages can be expected, are passed on further and dealt with by the decentralized subsidiaries. All transactional duties, such as placing orders or checking bills, are carried out directly by the subsidiaries themselves. Therefore the task of HPP does not correspond to that of a traditional purchaser or dealer—HPP sees itself as a procurement service provider or a procurement consulting firm.

Examples of strategic procurement services offered by HPP are the investigation and development of new supply markets; ABC analyses of products and suppliers; and developing new ideas for overall quality improvement. Other services offered include professional contract management (including the negotiation of general agreements with strategic suppliers); keeping customers informed about selected sources and conditions of supply; and offering advice on legal questions. An innovative service being offered in the field of business procurement consulting is the Procurement Enhancement Program (PEP). This is a standardized team-oriented, cross-functional approach to implement cooperative procurement of strategic buyers and representatives from the business units. The goal of the PEP-initiative is to systematically investigate all material groups and implement new ways of reducing Total-Cost-of-Ownership (TCO). It is not only the procurement activities that are analyzed, but also internal cost areas such as storage and transport. The identified savings potential for many materials groups lies beyond the mark of 10 percent.

Teamwork within a network is promoted if mechanisms of integration are employed that speed up and foster cooperation. Only if all the network participants commit to cooperation and joint action can the network be maintained. This requires an integration of style and culture. The rules of the game must be agreed upon and adhered to by all participants. It is absolutely necessary to trust one's partners and to commit yourself to not only your own targets but also to the overall targets of the system. A structural integration is carried out by an operating board, in which representatives of the network participants guide common action. Furthermore, coordinating human resource activities is very important, as it enables the exchange of people within the network. Job rotation is key in this regard, providing integration of skills. Finally, the integration of information systems is especially important in a decentralized holding structure. If the flow of information across units, countries, or even continents is possible, the network works.

HPP had (and still struggles with) the problem of diverse information requirements from various information systems in the subsidiaries, as well as from external sources.

Since there is no single standard information system in the network, a "translation key" is needed in order to bring all data to the same level (common denominator). This process is carried out through a data warehouse, which collects the relevant procurement data, prepares it, and molds it to provide useable information for the strategic buyers. Ideally, the decentralized network participants should have the access rights to the information, but because of the need for data security and confidentiality, this critical issue has yet to be resolved.

Opening the Procurement Network (Phase 3)

The strategic direction of HPP aims specifically at continuous expansion of its activities. HPP also strives to develop new services (product development), as well as to open up new customer segments (market development). Due to the dividing of the ChemLife group it is imperative for HPP to acquire customers from outside the existing network. Building systems, information technology, and telecommunications are industries where HPP has developed outside customers. In purchases of materials and services that are not of strategic relevance to these customers' processes, HPP has been able to create added value. Typically, a client company does not have enough resources to pay close attention to those products, or to look at them through "strategic spectacles." HPP can also offer its customers best practice solutions in market investigation or supplier development for those non-strategic purchases.

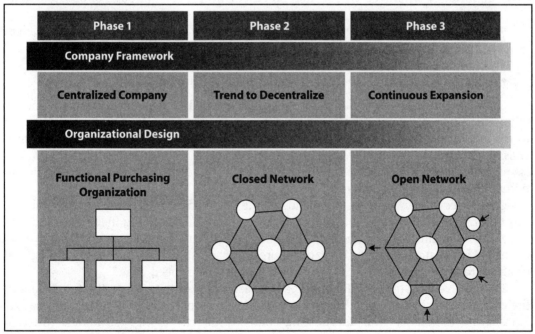

Figure 1. The phases in procurement spin-off

The HPP-marketing strategy defines three strategic business areas for its activities. Besides the traditional areas of strategic purchasing the two other business areas include procurement consulting and training, and procurement information management.

"Impact on procurement" is the slogan of the HPP Consulting Team that offers the following products to its customers:

- Identification of savings potentials
- Measurement of procurement performance
- Procurement via Internet (E-commerce, electronic bidding)
- Auditing of management systems
- Consulting and design of supply chain management
- Training in innovative procurement tools

The core product in the area information management is data warehousing. HPP supports its clients in identifying and processing business-related data and helps them implement their own data warehouse.

Working with HPP offers internal and external customers many advantages, summarized as follows:

- Optimal procurement conditions and the lowest costs through pooling purchasing power
- Availability of professional procurement know-how
- Continuous improvement of the procurement process through cross-functional sourcing teams
- Advantages of cooperative purchasing while safeguarding autonomy and confidentiality
- Access to global supply markets
- Regular exchange of experience and technical consulting.

Since January 1998, HPP has been working as a legally independent company mostly within the ChemLife group. The basic conditions and requirements of a business exposed to the market forces are considerably more complicated than those of a centralized purchasing department operating within a large company. A difficult transformation process is still underway but HPP is learning and adapting very quickly and is well on the way to becoming a stand-alone purchasing company.

Challenges remain for HPP and include the necessity to develop marketing capabilities. The task of HPP employees is not only the buying of products but also the pricing and selling of procurement services. The change requires several internal initiatives: an innovative offensive, internationalization, human resource management, and business planning—all designed to move HPP from a "sturdy tanker" to an "agile speed boat."

The involvement of all HPP employees is needed in order to shape the future fate of the company. In this context, the structure of the shareholders is also subject to change. Transferring the shares from the holding company directly to HPP customers (internal and/or external) is one idea, but from a motivational angle, a management buy-out is also an idea still under discussion.

There is a growing market for purchasing services following the HPP model. In the process of developing "core competency with outsourcing" strategies, many companies face the issue of whether they continue to carry out purchasing on their own. If somebody offering procurement services has a core competency and can provide added value for the customer, a successful relationship may be established. Identifying the value and successfully marketing it is, and will continue to be a challenge for the "central buyers of the good old days." The slogan, "Buy smart use HPP" sends this message to the customers.

Note

1. *The Future of Purchasing and Supply, A Five- and Ten-Year Forecast* is available by contacting CAPS, 800 888-6276 ext. 3059.

Wolfgang Buchholz, Ph.D., is with Hoechst Procurement International.

Lutz Kaufmann, Ph.D., is at the University of Giessen, Germany.

Cintas Corp. Builds Supplier Management from Ground Up

Joe Mazel

In this case study, you'll learn about a company where the central role of purchasing and supply management is to develop and nurture relationships with suppliers. Cintas Corp. views suppliers in the same way it views employees and uses the same careful selection procedures in qualifying new suppliers.

Consider a corporate purchasing department that doesn't place purchase orders or approve invoices. Instead, the purchasing team's primary responsibilities include developing and maintaining supplier relationships, sourcing and qualifying suppliers from a commercial standpoint, and establishing a core supplier base for key purchases.

In a nutshell, that's the philosophy and policy of purchasing/supplier management at Cintas Corporation (Cincinnati; www.cintas-corp.com). But there's more. The truly remarkable aspect of the Cintas story is that a corporate purchasing function did not exist seven years ago. What they've created is a textbook example of innovation, well worth the consideration of other purchasing professionals.

Strong corporate culture manifests itself in purchasing. Robert J. Kohlhepp, CEO, Cintas declares, "Our corporate purchasing department's role is to contribute to our operations' goals and to satisfy our customers." Specifically, purchasing's goals must align with Cintas' corporate objectives. Therefore, purchasing must:

- Contribute to customer service;
- Accommodate growth;
- Ensure all suppliers and products are available; and
- Contribute to overall total cost management.

At Cintas, the leader in the corporate identity uniform industry, its dominant culture impacts its purchasing philosophy. "We have a spartan attitude about business," maintains Kohlhepp. "We spend our company's money very sparingly; we act with a sense of urgency; we have the air of positive discontent; and we are never satisfied with the status quo."

Uniform culture sets tone and values for supplier relationships. "Our suppliers are a key factor in our ability to successfully service our customers," Kohlhepp explained at the 84th Annual International Purchasing Conference of the National Association of Purchasing

Management. "As business partners, we expect our suppliers to have the same ideals and passion for success as we do.

"We look at our suppliers just as our working partners (employees), for whom we have the highest standards of performance," he details. "We strive for excellence in our partners, and we don't settle for less from our suppliers."

Supplier selection process is stringent. "Procurement focus at Cintas is important because we buy value from our suppliers, so we can sell value to our customers," Kohlhepp emphasizes. Therefore, the purchasing team identifies and defines requirements from the standpoint of cost and use.

"We assess supplier qualifications, not only to find the best-in-class, but to find the one that fits our company from a culture standpoint," he explains. "Once we have chosen a supplier, we work with them to keep them competitive." This is accomplished by setting performance objectives, measuring the suppliers' performance, and improving suppliers' performance by working with Cintas field locations.

Loyalty to 'established' suppliers laudable. "We rarely fire an established supplier who's doing a good job," Kohlhepp remarks. If there's a problem with a supplier, or if a "significantly lower" price is received from another source, the incumbent supplier "is always given the opportunity to try to work things out with us," he maintains. "For a new supplier to uproot an established, high performance supplier, it must offer significant and distinguishable advantage to us," according to Kohlhepp. "And we usually give the incumbent a second time at bat."

Even when another supplier is given serious consideration, Cintas takes a series of "necessary precautions." These include:

- Confirmation of their resources, capabilities, and commitment;
- Conducting pilot programs first; and
- Communication of Cintas objectives "very carefully and completely" to the potential new supplier.

Scrutiny of supplier performance measurement. The Cintas process is unique in that it performs certain evaluations and the supplier measures the balance. "Our measures are mostly subjective," he explains. "We survey our field locations (there are 200) to determine their levels of satisfaction."

"The objective is to help the supplier improve their performance; it's not punitive," Kohlhepp insists. "The components we measure are weighted according to their importance to us," he explains. Factors affecting importance are leadtimes, availability, and whether the product is where it's supposed to be when it's needed. "We rarely, if ever, provide space for inventory for any of our suppliers," he mentions.

Meanwhile, the supplier also performs certain measurements. "We have found that a supplier can measure certain elements more precisely than we can," Kohlhepp notes. These tend to be quantitative in nature and contain data that is more readily available to the supplier rather than to Cintas.

"We also have found that when there's a problem, the supplier will know about it a lot faster and take action, if they're keeping score," he maintains.

The information Cintas gathers and the supplier compiles is discussed at a joint business review meeting held quarterly. The suppliers are also evaluated on an annual basis.

"When necessary, we ask the supplier to consult with our field operation," says Kohlhepp. "Sometimes the supplier believes they're doing a good job, but the field location doesn't." The suppliers are asked to present an action plan.

Aftermath of review: Development of new objectives. Based on the action plan, and other inputs, Cintas and the supplier jointly decide on new objectives. The supplier implements the action plan, and Cintas "selectively secures feedback in the interim."

"Our suppliers' response to this process has been extremely positive," says Kohlhepp. "They take the feedback seriously as they become immersed in the details and institute improvement recommendations."

The Cintas CEO declares the entire process extremely positive. "We are seeing significant improvements in our suppliers," he explains. "The bottom line objective is the better our suppliers service our field locations, the higher the performance they can give to our customers."

Future purchasing goals and their alignment with corporate and customer objectives. The fundamental requirements to provide adequate supply of purchased items at low cost consistent with the needs of Cintas operations remain firm. But future goals reflect continuous change and improvement. For example:

- Purchasing excellence remains a near-term goal. For the future, it will shift to achieving logistics excellence. "We'll be focusing on the integration of suppliers, manufacturing, distribution, and transportation to provide even faster service, better products, and lower costs," he explains.
- Cost reduction and the continuing scrutiny of costs is another near-term goal. Revenue improvement is the focus for the future. "Our intent is to source more accurately and directly to our customer needs, introduce new products and services, and broaden the scope of purchasing beyond conventional boundaries."
- Supplier performance improvement continues as a near-term goal. "We'll continue to intensify supply management education, cost optimization efforts, and supplier excellence recognition," Kohlhepp describes. "That will be an on-going effort for the future also."
- Streamlining and removing unnecessary functions is a near-term and future incentive. "We'll be investigating technology such as EDI and P-cards in our efforts to improve our processes," he explains. "We are convinced that e-commerce has and will continue to offer greater efficiency, faster delivery, and lower cost."

Joe Mazel is editor of Supplier Selection and Management Report.

Caterpillar Gains Big Inventory Cuts by Improving Supply Chain

Joe Mazel

High inventory equals high costs for companies in heavy manufacturing. This was a problem for Caterpillar, and it looked at supply chain management as a potential solution to this problem. This article provides an overview of the steps Caterpillar's managers took to solve this problem. Understanding the approach of this company may provide valuable lessons for your company as well—whether you're a large or not-so-large manufacturer.

Supply chain and logistics problems, typical to heavy manufacturing industries, were straining Caterpillar's North American track production and assembly operations. With their facilities being widely dispersed and lacking close coordination and cohesion, the organization came to realize:

- Component inventory levels were much higher than acceptable;
- Material flow from Caterpillar plants and suppliers were not well managed;
- Manufacturing lot sizes and buffers were not tied to assembly levels; and
- Lead times for component parts were not coordinated with assembly schedules.

"The multiple assembly locations plus the high inventories resulted in excessive logistics costs without a smooth, sequenced flow," according to Andrew D. Nicoll, C.P.M., CFPIM, CIRM, procurement manager, Caterpillar, Inc. (Peoria, Ill.). To solve these problems, a project team was formed to review the operations and provide improvement recommendations.

The blueprint for sound logistics, inventory management practice. An early decision by the team was to consolidate the total assembly process at one facility in Peoria for all North American customers of tractors, excavators, replacement parts, and OEM products.

While the consolidation was taking place, a detailed review of the logistics and inventory management practices was taking place.

"One of the previous shortcomings was in the area of forecasting," according to Nicoll. "Without a long-term forecast of demand, it was difficult to plan resources for assembly, develop scheduling plans, or establish inventory levels and manufacturing orders for components," he explained at the APICS 41st Annual International Conference.

A group was assigned to do demand planning for track groups by reviewing past history, using data from machine users and dealers to determine replacement parts and evaluate needs for "customized" track groups for OEM customers.

"The forecasts were extended a full year with the next two months fairly solid and the next three weeks firm," Nicoll detailed. These forecasting techniques also facilitated the use of fixed lot size work orders for manufactured components.

The lot sizes are based on forecasted average usage for the next six months. This technique allows the component manufacturing processes (primarily for links, shoes, pins, and bushings) to anticipate needed resources and minimize large fluctuations in process quantities.

Establishing an inventory bank for parts with frequent demand. A "sequencer" or inventory bank was established for the majority of parts that had ongoing usage. The inventory levels for each part are based on past observations of peaks in usage over the lead time required to replace these parts, he explained.

If the usage varies significantly from one monthly period to the next, the inventory level in the sequencer is allowed to fluctuate with the short-term changes in demand. Then fixed lot size orders replenish materials at a constant rate.

"This technique is also beneficial in minimizing the inventory levels stored at the supplier's track group assembly lines," Nicoll maintained. As an aside, the storage of most components for assembly is consolidated at the supplier location, to "save space and extra material handling."

An addition to the supplier's main building was constructed specifically for component material receiving and storage. The inventory transactions are recorded at the supplier and at Caterpillar to reflect available parts and to satisfy track group demand.

Developing a flow to deliver components on a JIT basis. "With a consolidated assembly operation, good requirements forecasts, and weekly schedules for track group build, the logistics flow was established to deliver components Just-in-Time," Nicoll noted.

The finished track group volume averages 150 pieces per day, which requires about 15 truckloads of the tractor plants' needs and replacement parts. Supplying that volume of finished groups likewise requires over 10 truckloads each day of the major components (links, shoes, pins, and bushings), plus several truckloads per week for smaller parts like nuts and bolts.

Links and shoes are now delivered several times each day based on the build schedule sequence. Pins and bushings are delivered weekly.

"The overseas sources ship two to four times each month, with deliveries about twice a month to the assembly operation," he said. "Deliveries to tractor plant customers are made each shift, arriving about eight hours before needed to be assembled on a tractor or excavator. Replacement parts deliveries are sent as built to cover weekly schedules."

Resolving the problems caused by the consolidation process. "As with any new process, there were many problems encountered with the movement of the assembly functions, the startup at a new supplier facility, and different people involved in the operations at Caterpillar," according to Nicoll. Among them:

- *Storage location at new track assembly supplier sized on previous assumptions.* "It was sized based on assumptions for component delivery and storage similar to those for the previous operations," Nicoll said.

  In the past, much of the overflow material was stored in various Caterpillar locations, but this was not considered at the new facility. Likewise, the major component delivery schedules were based on past experiences.

  At the startup, the new supplier had far too many loads of links and track shoes from Caterpillar. "Gradually the logistics team established a JIT delivery process based on assembly schedules and sequences which did limit the bulky and large usage component parts to less than one day," Nicoll describes.

  Then the flow of material from the receiving dock through storage and to assembly lines was rearranged to avoid building congestion in aisles and reduce total material handling time.

- *Too much backup inventory at old track group suppliers.* When the new supplier operation opened, the old suppliers began shipping material to the new location. Some of it was required for startup.

  However, the shipment of surplus material quickly filled the available space and had to be slowed until a plan could be established that would send the parts into the new facility based on demand.

  "The previous suppliers wanted to vacate their storage space as soon as possible," he acknowledged, but "this delay caused some concern about the new supplier's ability to manage the track assembly process." Eventually all excess inventory was absorbed. Inventory levels at the new supplier are now maintained at 30% of the volume held at the previous suppliers.

- *Scheduling began with the techniques used at the previous suppliers.* "This caused some difficulties in combining the schedules from three previous operations into one facility and subsequent shipment to five major customer facilities in the U.S., and to a consolidation point for shipment overseas," he explained.

  "Gradually, working with the customer locations and the link, track shoe, and pin and bushing components suppliers, a new scheduling routine was developed to overcome capacity and time constraints," according to Nicoll.

  The demand forecasting routines also were changed to add OEM customer forecasts. "Their volume is a relatively small percent of the total, but they impact assembly schedules because many short-dated orders are received, especially for 'customized' track groups with very low and sporadic usage," he explains. "By combining all requirements for similar track groups, the new assembly facility reduces the number of setups for these small volume orders."

Significant inventory reductions achieved. The inventory of steel to manufacture track shoes was reduced $6 million due to consistent ordering and assembly processes. Further, the component inventory at the assembly supplier was slashed by more than 30%.

As a result of consistent on-time delivery and quick response to short-dated orders, the inventory levels in the replacement parts operations have been reduced by over $22 million. Meanwhile service to dealers and customers has been maintained worldwide above 95%, even for old, noncurrent models. Likewise, deliveries to the tractor and excavator plants have been 100% on time since early in the startup.

Joe Mazel is editor of Inventory Reduction Report.

Purchasing for Profit

Elizabeth Baatz

This article reminds us that the function of the procurement division in many companies is not just reducing costs but making money. *Purchasing and supply managers are now figuring out ways to make what they do a profit-making service both in the company and in dealing with the company's customers. This article explains how this is happening at three companies: Delta Air Lines, IBM, and American Express.*

Have you ever thought that running a cost center isn't your cup of tea anymore? Think you have to jump ship from the procurement profession to something a bit higher profile—sales and marketing, for example? Well, think again.

Today, leading purchasing departments are spinning off products and services and generating revenue from it. Gone is the procurement profession's single-minded goal of simply saving money. The end game tomorrow for purchasing departments may be tougher: making money.

As business units question the overhead fee being paid for procurement services, says Donavon Favre, senior manager of Andersen Consulting Company's supply chain practice in Cleveland, purchasing departments are looking for ways to earn their keep. So not only are progressive purchasing pros working to save more money, they're also searching for ways to add value to the company's external customers or, in some cases, to actually turn a profit. "I see this trend accelerating, especially in the financial services industry," says Favre.

Paul Matthews, Andersen Consulting's partner who leads the global procurement practice in Cambridge, Mass., says at least four factors are driving the profit-motive thinking of procurement today.

- Mergers between global giants like Mobil and Exxon add fuel to the reengineering of procurement which then often leads to profit-seeking activities.
- Speedier cycle times force companies to rethink the role of procurement.
- New technologies from the World Wide Web and friendly order software also push purchasing to exploit its strengths and make money.
- Most important, another driver helps to shift the focus from saving to making money: Some super-efficient procurement departments already have saved all the money they possibly can.

For example, Matthews cites the story of General Electric's engine division. "GE Engine realized they had reduced costs in every way possible. So how else could purchasing add value to the company?" They decided to offer an entirely new service to their customers called "power by the hour."

As Matthews explains, GE now rents airplane engines by the hour instead of selling engines outright. For a fee, GE then maintains the engine and manages spare parts. Launched about three years ago, the company's procurement group broadened their service and started generating revenue. "That's the next generation of the procurement enterprise," says Matthews.

The jury remains out, however, on whether or not innovative, profit-hungry procurement groups will make much money. Many are just getting started. And companies that are trying to make money via procurement operations are not releasing sales or profit data yet.

Also, simply because a purchasing group is on the forefront of turning a cost center into a revenue engine does not guarantee survival. For example, three years ago *Fortune* magazine wrote about groundbreaking procurement operations being led by a new generation of chief purchasing officers. One story was about a purchasing subsidiary of Tenneco called TennEcon Services. Marketing everything from telephone services to computers at low, bulk prices to small companies, TennEcon earned $30 million in 1994, not counting the savings earned for the parent company.

But the parent company underwent extensive restructuring and the TennEcon group was eventually disbanded, says a Tenneco spokeswoman. Thus, even a profit-making procurement organization is at risk of falling victim to the vagaries of repeated reorganizations and downsizing.

Here are three stories from procurement operations at American Express, IBM Corp., and Delta Air Lines that are spinning off products or services for a profit.

Delta Air Lines: Ringing Up Strategic Gains

At Delta Air Lines in Atlanta, transforming a strategic purchasing activity into a revenue-generating service is not a new idea. Indeed, way back in 1981 Delta Air Lines formed a wholly owned subsidiary called Epsilon to buy and sell jet fuel. "United Airlines was the first company to get a distributor's license; we just followed suit," says Tom Shell, general manager for fuel purchasing at Delta. "We sell $40 to $50 million of jet fuel, mostly in Cincinnati, where we operate that facility's fuel system. DHL is our largest customer.

"We don't pursue this activity to make a lot of revenue," says Shell. "We make comfortable returns, but Epsilon meets our strategic objectives more than it meets any profit objective." (Airlines garner some tax advantages by owning a fuel-trading arm.) As a result, Delta Air Lines and Epsilon share the same fuel-purchasing staff.

Meanwhile, another Delta Air Lines subsidiary was formed in April 1995. This one is called DeltaTel and meets an entirely different set of strategic objectives. Like Epsilon, DeltaTel generates revenue and is profitable. However, Delta's general manager of technical purchasing and the president of DeltaTel, Mike McHale, says the venture meets two other paramount objectives. One, becoming a certified telecommunications carrier allows

Delta to lower its own costs. Two, McHale's staff has the opportunity to provide higher-quality services to Delta's airline passengers as well as his internal clients.

After negotiating telecom costs to the lowest possible price, "we felt we had gone as far as we could go using normal supply chain management fundamentals," says McHale. "So we brainstormed with a clean sheet of paper. The telecommunications industry was changing and lots of upstart companies were putting pressure on the big telecom companies. So we thought, 'why can't we do the same?'"

A huge buyer of telecom services from AT&T and MCI, as a reseller, DeltaTel can negotiate lower rates than Delta Air Lines. Then DeltaTel markets its long-distance, 800-number, calling-card, and pager services to its airline passengers in the Delta Air Lines magazine, to internal employees, and to its connection carriers like SkyWest. As an added bonus, Delta Air Lines also distributes telephone debit cards to distressed airline passengers.

Only three people in the procurement organization work with Delta Air Lines' telecom subsidiary, as marketing and order fulfillment functions are outsourced. Revenues from DeltaTel have grown 15% to 20% each year since 1995. "Most important, DeltaTel helps illustrate that we have moved from being a tactical, reactionary procurement organization to being a strategic resource for the company," says McHale.

For more information, see DeltaTel's Web page at www.deltatel.com.

IBM: Reengineering Procurement for Profit

IBM Vice President Theresa M. Metty heads up the 800-strong Customer Solutions Procurement group that was created two-and-a-half years ago in an effort to make IBM's consulting engagements more profitable. Unlike a commodity-oriented procurement organization (a model which is still deployed among another 800 IBM buyers and sourcing specialists), Metty's group is organized to provide purchasing support for the global consulting practice's end customer.

"We actively participate with the consultant at the customer site and we are structured by client groups," says Metty. For example, if IBM has a sales team focused on the travel industry, then Metty has a team focused on the travel industry too. Industry-focused buyers understand what is unique to customers in a particular industry and this understanding informs their purchases of software, computer and telecommunication equipment, and technical services.

In some cases, when the deal is big enough, Metty's buyer might sit in with the consultant and the customer before the deal is signed. In the biggest accounts, the IBM procurement professional may relocate to sit at the customer site.

One result of this customer-based focus is that the lines between purchasing and sales have been blurred. "We actively recruit buyers from the sales organization and several people from Customer Solutions Procurement have been recruited into sales," says Metty. With global consulting services growing 22% to 28% each year and purchases in support of the service growing even faster, there's plenty of room for cross-pollination.

Success in its customer-focused procurement process has led IBM to improve the profitability of its information-technology consulting jobs. "We absolutely know that we had a lot to do with the increase in profitability," says Metty. Profit numbers are not available.

Now IBM is taking the concept of purchasing for profit one step further by establishing a strictly for-profit procurement outsourcing organization. The service is called Business Process Management for Procurement and Sourcing. Begun less than a year ago with one client—United Technologies—signed up so far, the service replicates the processes that Metty's group uses and manages non-production purchasing for clients.

"The decision my customers face is this: Do you start down the reengineering road for your non-production sourcing yourself, or do you team up with a partner that can get you there faster?" says Bill Schaefer, vice president of procurement services for the new outsourcing service in White Plains, N.Y. The biggest hurdle in selling his service, says Schaefer, is becoming accustomed to another company's culture and building a long-term alliance.

Established as a separate entity from IBM's procurement group, suppliers are not asked to extend IBM's prices to Schaefer's customers. Instead, "we work to do the same things for United Technologies and other customers that we already have done with IBM's non-production purchases," says Schaefer. So for example, where IBM was able to get the escape rate (percentage of spending in which employees went outside the approved procurement system and purchased from non-approved suppliers) from 30% to 1%, Schaefer aims to do the same for his customers.

For more information, see IBM's Web site at www.ibm.com/services/bpm.

American Express: Making Marketing Music

With a degree in musical composition and a career in operations and procurement, Joseph A. Yacura, senior vice president of global procurement for American Express, has never thought of himself as an entrepreneur. Then again, he's not boxed in by labels either.

That's why when the opportunity arose to pitch a new idea to leverage his group's procurement skills to external customers, he leapt. In late 1997, Yacura and his team were bouncing around ideas on how to use their unique skills to help the company and keep the procurement group employed.

"I knew the service establishment group [who sells credit card services to restaurant chains] is always looking for new ideas on how to add value for their clients," says Yacura. So in early 1998, when a member of his team attended a service establishment marketing meeting, Yacura's group introduced a new entrepreneurial idea.

"We had a large restaurant chain that spent more than $1 million a year in printing things like guest checks and cash register paper rolls," Yacura explains. "We went to our printer and asked if they would allow a third party to buy printed forms at our rate. The answer was yes."

Would the service establishment marketing people approach the restaurant chain to propose a unique extension of American Express's procurement prowess? The answer: yes again.

"Now, we pass on a 16% reduction in printing costs to the customer," says Yacura. "In exchange, we get the American Express logo printed on the bottom of their restaurant checks for free, a service for which we used to pay."

American Express has launched a marketing program to pitch the "partner supply program" for printed forms to the top restaurant chains in North America. With one person in his 220 person global procurement group dedicated to the service establishment program, Yacura admits he feels like the program is forcing his group to be more entrepreneurial.

The procurement group has to answer lots of start-up questions: "How do we standardize the service? How do we track the queries? How do we track the value returned? How do we determine what service to offer after printed forms?" asks Yacura.

The venture is forcing procurement to address another question too. Chiefly, how does one become a better listener? "We have to be more attuned to the different needs of different customers," says Yacura.

For Yacura, who also is exploring a pilot program to sell procurement consulting services, the procurement-for-profit trend is exciting. Like any good entrepreneur, "we had to think outside the box," says Yacura. "But there were no massive studies. The economics just sounded right."

Elizabeth Baatz is economics editor for Modern Materials Handling *and previously worked as senior editor for* CIO Magazine *and staff writer for* WebMaster.

The Logistics of Success

Oren Harari, Ph.D.

Here's a story of a major Japanese company—Fujitsu—that wasn't doing very well in the U.S. market until it teamed up with its suppliers in some pretty unique ways. Fujitsu actually gave its suppliers some of the authority for strategic decision making and logistics development. With the help of its suppliers, it was able to develop and successfully exploit a market for custom-made laptop computers delivered in the exact configuration the customer requests in less than a week.

As you survey your business, do you find yourself complaining about having to operate in "mature" or "flat" markets? Or, do you feel distressed that your company is "stuck" at a mediocre performance level, unable to break away from its past? Then consider this story as one way to pull yourself out of either morass.

In 1996, 70 percent of Fujitsu's business was in Japan. But its profits had declined during the previous few years in that fiercely competitive, glutted domestic environment. Therefore, in an attempt to jump-start the business, Fujitsu's PC division entered the lucrative laptop computer market in the United States. Overall sales inched up a bit in 1996, but as Fujitsu learned, the American PC market is as saturated as Japan's.

Clearly, it was time to do something different—from the company's own traditions and from the actions of its myriad competitors. Fujitsu began by taking serious stock of its performance. The results of the self-analysis revealed that one of the company's main problems centered around logistics.

The laptops were being fully manufactured in the Tokyo area. For the sake of scale and cost-efficiencies, the company would wait until a sufficient volume of orders justified the use of a cargo ship to transport the product from Japan to its PC warehouses in Milpitas, California, and Hillsboro, Oregon. When all was said and done, it usually took a month to get an ordered product to retailers and end users. The delay was creating dissatisfaction among customers, and the yen's slide was exacerbating the financial impact.

Consequently, Fujitsu PC decided to transfer its warehousing and distribution functions to Federal Express. Instead of shipping product in large bulk by sea, Fujitsu could now fly small batches to the United States via FedEx—which immediately meant significantly less transportation time and opportunity cost. Once the products were in the United

States, FedEx's core warehousing and distribution competencies meant the laptops would reach their final destinations quickly and efficiently.

Closed-Loop Alliance

These changes alone would have had a significant impact, but collaborative discussions between the two firms unearthed some additional opportunities. In October 1997, Fujitsu PC opened a customer support center in Memphis, Tennessee, not only to be close to the FedEx superhub but to offer customers faster service benefits. The company cut more costs by closing the Hillsboro facility (admittedly an unfortunate move for Oregon employees).

The close physical proximity allowed further discussions among members of the two companies, which led to the next leap in innovation. In March 1998, Fujitsu PC announced that it would expand the support center to include built-to-order configuration on its laptops. The configuration would be done by CTI, an American company with an established history of subassembly work with many of FedEx's customers.

The closed-loop alliance including Fujitsu PC, FedEx and CTI now allows Fujitsu PC a four-day distribution-to-market cycle on customized products, as opposed to a four-week cycle on an undifferentiated product. The design, development and basic manufacturing are still done by Fujitsu in Japan, but once the product reaches Osaka airport and FedEx takes over, the remaining functions are performed by FedEx and CTI. The result is that a customer who places an order on Monday at 4 P.M. can take possession of a tailored Fujitsu "Built to Human" notebook computer by Thursday at 10:30 A.M.

Fujitsu doesn't release financials by subsidiary, but it is clear to industry observers that the PC division's market visibility, sales and margins (the product is not cheap) have gone up sharply. Just as important, Fujitsu is at the forefront of the next wave of PC manufacturing and distribution: built-to-order products. A recent posting on the *Electronic Buyers News* Web site noted: "As build-to-order and configure-to-order programs revolutionize the PC supply chain, old rules that have governed the business no longer apply."

Rather than waiting until the 11th hour and then adopting an uphill catch-up strategy, Fujitsu is ahead of most competitors in reconfiguring its systems to allow customers to order à la carte.

I believe this case study illustrates several important lessons for all of us:

The Maddening Crowd

First, you can't escape the reality that every *existing* market is, or shortly will be, crowded. Fujitsu had hoped to escape a glutted domestic market in Japan by penetrating the United States.

I'm all in favor of expanding globally; in fact, too many companies are myopically concerned with protectionist strategies, clinging to small domestic turfs rather than looking at the entire planet as the potential market. I often advise clients (especially smaller companies) that with the advances in technology which eliminate time and distance as we understand them, they should view their enterprise as a global phenomenon.

That said, we need to recognize an important caveat. If your product or service is undifferentiated from the competition, and if it's not particularly interesting to customers, then "going global" will only buy you a little bit of time. Free markets inevitably mean crowded markets—if not now in Place X, then very shortly. Why? Because if Place X has the potential for business growth, you can bet that, like vultures, your competitors will sniff it out the same way you did.

Fujitsu learned an important lesson in its domestic market. Because its product (albeit reliable) and service (albeit solid) were not much different from competitors', the company inevitably (note that word: inevitably) experienced shrinking share and financials. It looked to the United States for salvation, but soon realized that the situation was just as bad, if not worse, there. The problem was not that Fujitsu came to the United States (it should have); the problem was the assumption that an undifferentiated product in Japan would become a killer product in America.

The bottom line is that unless you lead your market—or even better, create a new market—every market you enter will be crowded. To Fujitsu's credit, its managers realized that the ultimate growth solution was to expand globally—*and* to do something different, unique, special and exciting.

Days of Reckoning

Fujitsu's leaders also realized that they couldn't do a turnaround on their own. In theory, of course, they could have. Their own designers and engineers could have developed an eye-popping, revolutionary laptop product—one so special it would have immediately zoomed ahead of the pack. 3Com did just that with its Palm device, for example, which blew away competitors in the handheld market and generated a 6 percent increase in 3Com's revenue stream.

But that's a low-probability strategy if you're hurting right now and don't have anything hot in the pipeline and ready to go. Had Fujitsu decided to solve the problem on its own, it is likely that it would have engaged in more immediate, conventional tactics, like throwing lots of dollars and yen into advertising or shrinking every department's budget to shave the product's price a bit.

At best, those tactics would have delayed the day of reckoning even as they sliced further into the company's margins. The basic problem, after all, was that customers perceived Fujitsu's laptops to be fundamentally the same as those of its competitors. That's what creates "saturated" or "flat" markets in the first place. Besides, Fujitsu recognized that competitors like IBM and Compaq are monsters when it comes to aggressive advertising and price cutting. The real solution, as Fujitsu correctly surmised, was to look beyond the four walls of the company to the special talents and resources of other players.

Above and Beyond

Fujitsu's arrangement with FedEx went far beyond simple "outsourcing." Everyone does outsourcing these days—and not just with minor activities. A study by the American Management Association, summarized in the April 1998 issue of *Management Review,* showed that 94 percent of surveyed firms currently outsource at least one *major* business activity.

The fastest-growing candidates for outsourcing are traditional in-house functions, such as accounting and finance (where outsourcing has doubled over the past three years), information systems (up 40 percent) and marketing (up 35 percent). And as manufacturers from IBM to General Motors will tell you, even core functions like manufacturing and shop maintenance are being sourced to outsiders, whenever appropriate.

So the outsourcing of traditional in-house functions to achieve cost-efficiencies, speed and marketing muscle is no longer big news. It's a survival strategy. What Fujitsu did was something well above and beyond that. It chose a company from outside its country—and, for that matter, its industry—to provide it with a new capacity and a new approach to its business.

In fact, Fujitsu selected a company that could provide it with the capability to do something outrageous and unconventional. It chose a "strategic partner" in the purest sense of the word—that is, a close-knit partner who could help redefine and reinvent a strategy.

Think about it. How could Fujitsu possibly have gone in one year from providing U.S. customers with a uniform, mass-produced product in 30 days to providing a customized, built-to-order product in four days—without the involvement of FedEx and CTI? No way. Fujitsu didn't try to become a quickie in-house expert in transportation and subassembly by hiring a bunch of new people, building new facilities or, heaven forbid, doing a slam-bang acquisition. The time and cost needed to even attempt the necessary resource absorption and corporate reinvention would have been catastrophic.

Instead, Fujitsu scanned the world for cutting-edge players that were doing exceptional things in the arenas it needed but did not excel in itself and didn't necessarily want to develop as a core competency. Since the initial problem was one of logistics, it made sense to contact FedEx to see if some strategic compatibilities could be developed. Ultimately, the key is that Fujitsu, in a very fast and cost-effective way, was able to *access* (even *"borrow")* the talent, resources and brains of a superior transportation and logistics provider.

A Customized Partnership

Fujitsu entered the relationship with a spirit of true *strategic alliance.* The company didn't choose FedEx because it was the cheapest provider. Nor did it reward its purchasing managers for jerking around and lying to FedEx to save a few yen. Nor did it enter the "partnership" with an arm's-length, quasi-adversarial, hyper-legalistic, super-secretive, no-trust, lowest-cost-at-all-cost, dump-them-tomorrow-if-we-get-a-better-deal mind-set.

Instead, it enlisted FedEx as a full, active, intimate partner. Fujitsu and FedEx people tackled Fujitsu's operational problems together—openly and cooperatively—and developed a revamped logistics package. Even more profound, it was FedEx that came up with the breakthrough idea of laptop customization.

As FedEx international manager Colleen Faryabi explains, the ongoing logistics and warehousing history that FedEx has shared with Dell Computer provided the seeds for this new intervention: "Our FedEx people knew that Dell Computer was basically bringing their unfinished parts and materials for subassembly in order to make customized product in a rapid just-in-time cycle. Dell does that on its own, and it does a great job. So we said, 'Why couldn't we do the same thing for Fujitsu?'"

Why not, indeed? This wasn't part of Fujitsu's original strategic plan. From its perspective, it was unanticipated. But because the company had entered into a genuine relationship with FedEx, it turned out that the partner was able to conceptualize and initiate the next-wave strategy for Fujitsu. That's a helluva lot more than "outsourcing," isn't it? Moreover, it was FedEx that brought subassembler CTI into the picture, and it is FedEx that takes operational responsibility for that entire subassembly and customization process.

Further, FedEx is again taking the lead in developing Fujitsu's next strategic wave. The company is introducing Fujitsu to its "International Priority Distribution" system—which allows Fujitsu to quickly, efficiently and simultaneously send product to different locales around the world using one simple entry in the FedEx system.

This distribution concept will open up new global avenues for Fujitsu. What will they be? Will they affect product development, marketing, after-sale? Who knows? At this point, the only thing for certain is that the two companies will capitalize on opportunities *together.*

Lesson Redux

So let's review. A good Japanese company faces saturated, flat markets and realizes that it's stuck. It does an honest self-appraisal and recognizes that logistics are a huge problem. Rather than try to fix things in-house—incrementally, in bits and pieces—the Japanese company enlists the help of a good American company to do something sweeping and different.

The U.S. partner does so, and ultimately takes the lead in developing an even more dramatic approach to the Japanese company's business. The Japanese company is receptive to these radical ideas and works collaboratively with its American partner to forge some new strategic directions that help the company break out of its market funk. A shared mind-set and open, cooperative cultures allow the two firms to bring together their mutual talents and resources to plan more pathbreaking avenues for the future.

In *Leapfrogging the Competition,* I show that effective organizations like Fujitsu and FedEx literally transform themselves into a "web of relationships." They understand that nowadays, networking capabilities are growing exponentially. In fact, Netscape co-founder Marc Andreessen sees the next wave of business as "the networking of the world, or the interconnecting of all businesses and a growing number of individuals in a seamless electronic web."

Leapfrogging organizations don't wait for this trend to come to them. They initiate the webs, guide them and orchestrate them. By embracing truly collaborative relationships with the cream of the crop—not necessarily the cheapest of the crop—they can sharply accelerate product development and market penetration and significantly reduce operational and distribution costs. Ultimately, that's the logistical and logical lesson offered by the Fujitsu/FedEx/CTI alliance.

Oren Harari, a professor of management at the University of San Francisco, works with both Fortune 500 and new venture companies worldwide, advising them on competitive advantage and organizational change. He also speaks to business groups around the world. Harari's latest book is the newly revised Leapfrogging the Competition: Five Giant Steps to Market Leadership *(Prima Press, 1999). E-mail: oren@harari.com.*

Anatomy of a Purchasing Revolution: Wellman's Story

Erv Lewis, C.P.M.

On December 31, 1998, Wellman, Inc. purchasing ended a five-year strategic plan intended to transform and optimize the way purchasing is conducted within the Wellman organization. This article is intended to overview that process with specific emphasis on the state of Wellman purchasing at the beginning, the major change initiatives, methods of approach, difficulties encountered, and the benefits derived.

The Starting Point

From 1987 to 1994, Wellman, Inc. grew by 600% through acquisition and expansion. Each site had a purchasing staff of seasoned professionals that reported to site management and pursued a site-specific optimization strategy. From a single site perspective, this was very effective. However, no single site, acting alone, had sufficient volume in any commodity to realize the value that could be delivered under a larger volume, company-wide agreement. So, from a corporate perspective, there was little economy of scale and, consequently, little volume-related leverage with suppliers. This meant comparatively higher prices, duplicated effort, and generally lower purchasing position strength. In short, given that Wellman was then a multi-site organization, the existing purchasing organization did not optimally serve the bottom line. While the need for change was obvious to some, others did not realize the potential value of aggregating volume among sites and negotiating large-volume national agreements. Given those pockets of skepticism and the fact that sites operated with a high level of autonomy, purchasing moved cautiously to identify a few areas in which to prove the strategy. That began in 1991 and, by 1993, the increase in purchasing contribution was so dramatic that a proposal for reorganization of purchasing was submitted and approved.

The Strategy

The overall strategy was to organize site purchasing departments into a single national team, aggregate requirements among sites, reduce the supplier base to a smaller, more manageable size and, where practical, use the larger volume to negotiate highly leveraged national contracts in each commodity area. The strongest suppliers in each commodity area were identified and evaluated through comprehensive selection criteria. The top two were then selected for negotiation of a single-source contract under which the supplier would serve all Wellman sites in the nation. Where a national supplier was not available, we focused on a region. Where a regional supplier was not available, we selected a local supplier. Obviously, the larger the geographic coverage, the greater the volume and the more beneficial the contract terms. Each contract was negotiated as a mutually beneficial alliance. Wellman enjoyed significantly lower pricing, higher service levels, and a wide range of "peripheral benefits" such as warranty extensions, technical support, better terms, etc. Each supplier enjoyed significantly more business volume which, even with a lower margin on sales, permitted him to bank significantly more profit dollars. The target purchasing environment was one in which:

- Routine purchasing practice is standardized.
- Goods and services are standardized among sites to the fullest practical extent.
- Requirements among sites are aggregated for purchasing economies of scale.
- Purchases are covered by highly leveraged, large volume contracts.
- There is a focus on administrative simplicity.
- Electronic interfaces, internally and with suppliers, are optimized.

Successful pursuit of the strategy required:

- A well-coordinated team effort involving all site purchasing players.
- An integrated system linking purchasing, manufacturing, inventory control, and payables.
- Consensus on key suppliers and support for national/regional contracts.
- A much smaller, optimized supplier base.
- Focused participation and support by a core of key suppliers.

Organizational Structure

Some felt purchasing should be fully centralized, with all players operating from a single point. Purchasing players wanted the benefits of centralization while avoiding the downsides, which usually involve loss of sensitivity to site-specific needs. The decision was made to leave purchasing departments at the sites and form a council of site purchasing managers, chaired by the director of purchasing. Council members met in late 1993, agreed to aggregate and leverage volumes, and began the process of shaping the function into a single purchasing "team".

Difficulties Encountered

Initially, the difficulties appeared to lie in the areas of getting consensus among site players on selection of key suppliers and negotiating contracts that, in some cases, were much more deeply leveraged than the suppliers were already experiencing with Wellman. Actually, the greater difficulties encountered were more centered in maintaining common focus and involvement in pursuit of a target end state that was, at best, 5 years away. More specifically, the greater challenges involved (1) satisfying the motivational needs of those less comfortable with long-term planning periods, (2) maintaining awareness, enthusiasm and motivation while pursuing objectives that required several years to accomplish, (3) skepticism on the part of some key managers about the value of the strategy, and, of course, (4) the usual resistance to change and perceived loss of autonomy.

Keys to Success

The Strategic Development Plan. As the kind of change needed would present strong challenges, some of which would require several years to accomplish, there was need for a planning methodology that would facilitate innovation and keep everyone focused on the end state. We selected a five-year period and used the model shown in Figure 1 to guide the development process.

The model requires a mission statement and a "warts and all" analysis of the purchasing function, to a point where purchasing is profiled in terms of strengths and weaknesses, inside and outside of the function. Then, over several meetings, purchasing players were asked to define a purchasing function in its most ideal state; the function they would design if they had total control. After some refinement, that definition became the vision towards which we would work over the five-year period. We called it the "idealized end state." Differences between that end state and the then current purchasing environment, as defined in the internal and external profiles, were recognized as "barriers" to the end state and objectives were designed to eliminate or minimize the effect of those barriers.

Note that the improvement plan was not aimed at improving the status quo. Instead, the plan was to start at the idealized end state and work backwards to the present, establishing whatever objectives were necessary to bridge the gap between the current environment and the idealized end state. Those broad five-year objectives formed the basis for annual objectives which, year by year, moved us closer to the end state. Each site purchasing department supported accomplishment by ensuring that their part of the objectives found their way into individual employee objective sets.

Note that the development model was designed so that each part could be pursued as a "stand alone" project and completed in relatively short time. These easily identifiable starting and ending points provided comfort to players who are less comfortable with long-term planning time frames. Yet, each part led into the next so that, over time, the whole model was completed. As a reference, the purchasing council met once a month for a few hours to summarize work done at the sites and each part was completed in one to two months, depending on the requirement. Over about seven months, the team worked through the whole model to establish the idealized end state, five-year objectives, and first year annual objectives. At the end of this period, each player knew a lot about purchasing's strengths, weaknesses, and the long-term vision for the function. While this may seem long to some, keep in mind that the team was newly formed and consisted of play-

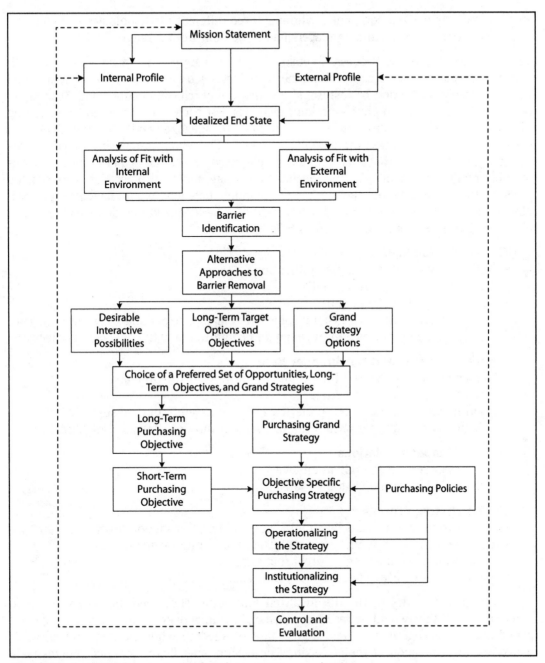

Figure 1. A model for strategic development in purchasing

ers from recently merged companies who employed different methodologies and cultures. In that environment, trust among players had to be built from scratch.

Shared Ownership of the Process. To ensure buy-in and support by those who would ultimately be responsible for accomplishing the objectives, each part of the development model was discussed in detail and brainstormed by, first, the purchasing council and, second, all purchasing department employees in joint meetings. For each part of the model, including the mission statement, internal and external profiles, the idealized end state, objectives, etc., the end product represented the combined input of the whole purchasing function. Our objective was to ensure that each purchasing player could see his or her input in each of the final products. In that way, the idealized end state and final objectives were not the product of the managers, but the product of the individuals who would have key responsibility for accomplishing them on a day-to-day basis. The Idealized End State leading to the five-year objectives was characterized as follows.

The Purchasing Staff
- Confident, well trained, highly professional.
- High levels of interpersonal skills.
- Will challenge the status quo.
- Focused on total cost and long-term value rather than price per unit and short-term gain.
- Dedicated to continuous improvement and comfortable with challenging objectives.

Supplier Relations and the Supplier Base
- Core commodities sourced from a minimum number of suppliers.
- Common suppliers among sites.
- Broad national contracts and preferred agreements with all core suppliers.
- Continuous supplier performance improvement through statistical methods.

Internal Customer Relations
- A customer service attitude at all levels.
- High levels of internal customer satisfaction.

The Purchasing Process
- An effective, administratively simple, value adding transaction process.
- A focus on continuous process simplification and improvement.
- All sites linked into a single purchasing system.
- Optimal use of electronic interfaces, EDI, etc.

These characteristics define the Idealized End State. They were purposely broad in scope so that (1) they would represent an unchanging target over the five-year development period and (2) players would retain a great deal of freedom when crafting strategies that would lead to realization of the end state. The level of specificity increased progressively with five-year objectives, annual objectives, and, then, site-specific objectives which supported the whole. While this may appear simple on the surface, making the characteristics listed above a reality entailed a large number of long and tremendously complex lists of things to accomplish. As examples:

- The first point under *The Purchasing Staff* which calls for "confident, well trained, highly professional" purchasing players led to adoption of core competency training requirements containing 15 different training events including statistical methods, negotiation skills, basic and advanced contract law, basic and advanced problem solving, NAPM certification, etc. The objective was for all purchasing professionals to complete core competency training during the five-year period ending in 1998. About 96% was completed. A key and ongoing part of this training involved improving skills to communicate, motivate, and persuade when presenting and selling ideas.
- The bullets under *Supplier Relations and Supplier Base* required purchasing consensus on key suppliers, qualification of and agreement on the "best" supplier from lists of site preferences, and strategies to sell operations players at all sites on the value of single-source relationships with suppliers other than their "favorites". Then came negotiating contracts, implementing at each site, and dealing with inevitable resistance that arises when implementing such a strategy.

While space does not permit the level of detail that would more thoroughly define specific objectives, suffice it to say that all other characteristics were attacked in similar fashion. All in all, it made for a busy, challenging five years.

You will note that the development model includes "operationalizing" and "institutionalizing" the strategy. A strategy is "operationalized" when the actions and activities through which it will be accomplished are a part of each individual's personal annual objectives. It is "institutionalized" when the process of strategic development becomes so much a part of day-to-day work that it is pursued routinely rather than as a special event from time to time.

Maintaining Awareness, Enthusiasm, and Motivation. It is critically important to routinely reiterate the strategy, note accomplishments to date, and review remaining challenges. Wellman purchasing rarely opened a meeting without covering those points in an effort to ensure continuing awareness. Enthusiasm and motivation are typically a function of involvement and the level of success. Accordingly, every purchasing manager assumed a responsibility to keep each of his or her staff members actively involved in the transformation process by ensuring that each individual's personal objectives were challenging and that they supported functional objectives aimed at realizing the idealized end state. Then, through coaching and assistance, the managers ensured successful accomplishment by each individual and recognized it when it occurred. It is important to note that, when a player begins making routine decisions in ways that solve the here-and-now problem and, at the same time, move the function closer to the targeted end state, he or she will have turned the corner from "reactive" to "proactive".

A Continuous Process Improvement Program

As many of the objectives under pursuit involved improving processes, it was obvious at the outset that our players would need problem solving and process improvement skills and techniques that would really facilitate improvement rather than just report data. The term "continuous improvement" implies a continual closing of the gap between current results and desired results and, the fact is, true ongoing improvement of processes is not very likely unless measuring variation in results and trends, and comparing them to desired results. This kind of measurement requires the use of statistical techniques, so we adopted the W. Edwards Deming statistical measurement and improvement techniques as primary tools for process improvement and made their use a part of core competency requirements.

Dealing with Skepticism

Our plan for dealing with skepticism was to sell the value of our strategy to the operations players who would reap the benefits. We made little attempt to sell the strategy itself as that could be viewed as the ideas of only one function among many. However, measurable value was much more salable and we gradually won over most of the skeptics. Use of the Deming statistical tools enabled us to more rapidly improve some processes to a point where that improvement was both obvious and measurable in terms of real value. In dealing with those who resisted change and perceived a loss of autonomy, we found that keeping them in the loop and, where practical, involving them in the decision process tended to raise their comfort levels.

Value Delivered

As raw materials are under long-term contracts, the strategy defined in this article was aimed initially at purchases other than raw materials. Of those purchases, about 35% are proprietary in nature, are specific to a site or business unit, and do not provide the economies of scale required for leveraging. Of the remaining 65%, about half have been leveraged according to the strategy. For the five-year period, average hard-dollar reduction on total purchases, from all sources, was 3.1%, though only about 32.5% of these purchases are currently leveraged.

Though obviously important, the Wellman purchasing strategy considers hard-dollar reductions in the price of goods as a secondary target. The primary target is soft-dollar savings, as they represent larger value. Soft-dollar savings include improved supplier engineering and technical service, warranty extensions, free technical training that would otherwise cost Wellman, improved terms, consigned inventories, supplier solutions to on-the-plant-floor problems, less engineering and maintenance effort due to the effect of standardized goods, etc. These soft-dollar impacts positively influence the manufacturing environment which, in turn, can lead to improved productivity, higher quality of manufactured product, lower waste levels, etc. Further, through the aggregate effect of process improvements and elimination of much of the effort associated with supplier selection, qualification, and the bid process, the inventory control and purchasing staffs are operating successfully with 25% fewer employees.

By now you will have determined that the transformation in Wellman purchasing was more internal than external. Individual site purchasing departments were doing an excellent job for their respective sites. However, no individual site represented sufficient volume to significantly leverage service up and prices down. So, from a whole company perspective, purchasing was fragmented and, even though, as it was structured, could not maximize contribution to company profitability, the need to change it was not obvious to those outside of purchasing. Wellman purchasing is now a well organized, forward thinking team of professionals who work together towards a common, always evolving vision. Individual players have a high level of reciprocal trust, function well together, and create synergy among sites that otherwise would not exist. Though I am writing this article, credit for this transformation belongs to the team. Due to the aggressive nature with which they implemented this strategy, and the results achieved, the function is now regarded as proactive and value adding, and enjoys a higher level of respect in the company.

Where We Go from Here

With a view towards process improvement, Wellman purchasing conducts informal brainstorming all during the year and a formal brainstorming session involving all purchasing players each year. Every other year that session is devoted to updating the five-year strategic development plan. Accordingly, the function is always targeting an idealized end state that is three to five years in the future, based on our best information on how the field is changing and where the opportunities live. In all cases we follow the development model presented here. Year 2000 objectives include, among others, further staff development, leveraging the balance of purchases that reasonably could and should be leveraged, and further definition and refinement of systems.

　　It is an ongoing challenge… a shot that is still being heard.

Erv Lewis, C.P.M., is director of purchasing, Wellman, Inc., Johnsonville, SC 29555, 843 386-8036, erv.lewis@wellmaninc.com.

"How May I Help You?"

Ray E. Biddle

Have you considered purchasing third-party customer service representation? That's a direction companies are taking these days, and purchasing and supply can certainly play a key role in the selection and management of such outside service providers. This article provides the basics of purchasing customer service representation, including what to look for in a potential supplier, contract issues, and the challenges such a relationship may pose.

Who you gonna call? If your external customer has a request, question, or concern for your organization, his or her first contact might be a customer service representative. Giving a first impression, that customer service representative has the ability to make or break a sale or relationship. For such an important role, some purchasing organizations are considering third-party organizations that specialize in customer service.

However, for customers to receive the full benefit of your organization, those third-party representatives must be trained as though they were your own employees and they must represent your organization's philosophies. Customer service representatives will be on the front lines as your organization grows, not only in the number of customers, but also the products and services you offer to them. This job title holds weight with every phone call. If you're outsourcing customer service, consider some key issues about the benefits of third-party providers, selecting a provider, and managing the operation.

Benefits: World-Class Capabilities

One benefit often associated with outsourcing relationships is cost reduction. When outsourcing the customer service function, however, the key benefit may not be related to cost. Timothy Larson, C.P.M., CPIM, CPP, assistant vice president-supply at H&R Block, says that it should not be considered as a cost reduction initiative, "but rather as a means of gaining access to the world-class capabilities necessary to effectively manage a difficult function." The Outsourcing Institute says this is one of the top reasons for outsourcing in that it provides organizations a competitive advantage while avoiding the cost of training and chasing technology. Customers essentially gain the expertise of the provider's previous investments in methodologies, technology, and people.

Qualities to Look for in a Provider

When developing the outsourced customer service relationship, the goal is a seamless mesh between the provider's employees and your own organization. These individuals represent their image of your organization to your customers. As with any supplier selection decision, you must discover if they have the capabilities to meet your customer demand. Do they have sufficient personnel to handle your flow of calls? Can they meet the demand of calls that come in across geographic areas and time zones? Do they have the capability to receive and transfer calls as need be?

The third-party provider will need to be measured for responsiveness, not only as a whole, but at an individual level. For example, how well is an individual representative able to accommodate any given customer request? Are the individuals courteous? Does the level of courtesy coincide with how you want your organization to be represented?

Other than meeting these basic requirements, a third-party customer service provider should also meet your visions for future activities. Today you may have that provider merely fielding telephone calls, while your own staff is developing new strategic activities. But tomorrow, those strategic activities can become standard operating procedure which the third party will now handle while you develop another level of innovative practices. If you've arranged for a third-party provider to handle some of the basic tasks, make sure the provider is equipped to handle those tasks, even as those tasks evolve in the future.

When shopping for an outsourcing provider for customer service, an important area to examine is the potential provider's strategic development in customer service methodologies. In what types of technology, relative to customer service, is the provider investing? In regard to customer service, the provider should be researching voice response capabilities, interactive switching capabilities, and other cutting-edge technologies. Does the provider have the technology to keep up with the region that needs to be serviced and the region where its employees are located? For example, is the provider able to capitalize on new technologies and able to adopt these technologies for employees working in hi-tech fields, as well as those in more remote areas of the country?

Because high turnover equals more training, a low turnover rate of third-party employees is desirable. To meet this goal, determine whether or not your provider is making wise economic choices in terms of where it is located, how it has scaled its pay ranges, and how that relates to other organizations in the area. For example, if the provider has chosen to locate a call center in an area that is desirable in terms of environment and cost of living, the turnover rate will probably be lower.

Consider the provider's global potential. If you are currently operating globally, then you might be using the provider's outsourcing services immediately. However, if you are not currently operating globally, you will want to examine the provider's global potential because if your operations do expand, it's much easier to simply expand your customer service operation with a provider already familiar with your products, procedures, and philosophies. This saves time and money for both you and the provider. Obviously, cultural issues and specific training issues unique to each country will still need to be addressed.

Tips for Success

William K. Pollock, president of Strategies for Growth^{SM}, a firm specializing in business planning and customer service consulting says the most important thing to remember when choosing to outsource the customer service function, is to have "all the workers that represent the organization in the marketplace put on a cohesive and consistent front when they deal with customers and prospects." In his article, "Maintaining Customer Service in an Outsourcing Environment," he cites these tips from Alan D. Simpson, national service manager of electronic imaging and equipment service for Fuji Medical Systems:

1. Train your outsourced personnel as if they were your own.
2. Take any outsourced customer contract workers on a short field trip, showing them how the customer support center works.
3. Ensure that the manager or supervisor of the outsourced operation always has a fail-safe "back door" to a fulltime contact in your organization. Let that individual know he or she is not alone when help is needed.
4. Get daily reports in a standard reporting format (such as faxed activity, problem, or exception reports) every morning to ensure everything is in order.
5. Give the outsourced employees "gifts" of your organization's products, product pictures, or service marketing brochures. Not only does this help educate them about your products, but it can make them feel "connected" to your organization.
6. Problems should be confronted immediately, head on, with the outsource manager.

Source: The Association for Services Management International, *The Professional Journal* (March 1998)

Contract Issues

Your specific contract issues and clauses will depend on how your organization decides to measure customer service. It might include increased services or products purchased through customer service agents, or might be based on time efficiency of phone calls. Regardless which areas are measured, the contract for an outsourced customer service provider should always be incentive-based. In customer service, a highly enthusiastic, motivated staff will secure the greatest customer loyalty. One way you can always provide for that is through compensation, which is easy to adopt in incentive-based contracts. In other words, because the performance is tied directly to an individual's actions, the contract should be worded so that it will motivate and appeal to the individuals. To foster that relationship even further, the more cooperative the management between the organizations and the more interest you can take in showing appreciation to those third-party employees, the more responsive they will be to the relationship.

Constant Communication

When using a third-party provider for customer service, the two organizations should be communicating on a weekly, if not daily basis. The content of the communication is not just for operational reasons, but also for teaming purposes. Because customer service performance is tied primarily to individuals' performance, the communication is vital to provide them with accolades or critiques.

Progress meetings or review meetings, on a monthly basis, ensure the right focus and provide the right amount of receptivity. These meetings should involve key management of both organizations. It's important that the employees of both organizations recognize that upper management is directly involved, allowing them to see the level of importance of this outsourced relationship.

Challenges

In order for a third party to provide effective customer service, the employees who will actually be performing tasks must be thoroughly familiar with the purchasing organization's practices, policies, and products. It's different than other outsourcing relationships, because in, for example, an outsourced finance or maintenance contract, the third-party employees may not have any contact with the purchasing organization's external customers. But with customer service, these people will not only have direct contact with your external customers, they will be questioned, tested, and judged by those customers, possibly being the deciding factor in a customer's decision on whether or not to patronize your organization.

To achieve a seamless relationship, training is vital. This includes the fundamentals of your products and services, as well as how you would prefer they handle customer comments, requests, and concerns. Other actions that can ensure this integration include having the third-party provider employees participate in planning meetings or in the development of campaigns and service platforms. These activities may involve the outsourced employees spending more time on-site with the purchasing organization than in other outsourced relationships, but can also include members of the purchasing organization spending a fair amount of time at the customer service site. This visibility allows the purchasing organization management to acknowledge and celebrate successes with the employees, showing their loyalty. A good example might be if a particular milestone has been achieved, an on-site visit would be in order.

One of the toughest challenges for managing an outsourced customer service function is in measuring performance. It's easy to measure how many telephone calls representatives field, duration of calls, or new product or service orders, but much of customer service is subjective. How do you measure whether a representative was courteous? How do you determine if a customer was completely satisfied with the service they received? One common method of measurement is call monitoring, where a supervisor or manager listens to phone calls on a random basis. However, if this tool is used, it needs to be presented to the third party as a means of improving customer service, rather than as a watchdog for poor performance. Keep in mind, however, a call monitoring system is like taking a "snapshot" of performance. To obtain a more objective, complete picture, sufficient data must be collected to determine trends; the more calls actually monitored, the truer the picture. Response cards or calls are other tools of measurement for customer service. These cards or calls go out to external customers that have had interaction with the third-party provider and ask their opinion of the service they received.

According to Larson, when deciding whether or not outsourcing customer service is the appropriate decision, the first thing to do is examine your current situation. "If your organization's current ability to provide customer care provides clear strategic advantage, outsourcing should not be considered," he says. "However, if your organization is at an extreme customer care disadvantage relative to your competition and you have had significant success with other outsourcing relationships, or you see a critical need and improvement opportunity associated with outsourcing, then outsourcing is something to seriously consider." There can be many benefits to outsourcing the customer service function, but each organization will need to evaluate its present resources and decide which course of action offers the best value.

Ray E. Biddle is vice president of global procurement for the Americas at American Express in New York.

Integrated Supply Successes

James V. Veronesi, Rodney A. MacLea, and Robert P. Zigas, Ph.D., C.P.M.

Earlier in this book we included an article on integrated supply basics. Now we include an article that looks at how three firms and one hospital have applied the principles of integrated supply successfully. You'll learn how PPG Industries, Tekelec, and Rhône-Poulenc along with St. Luke's Hospital in New York have developed long-term relationships with their suppliers to reduce costs and better serve customers.

You need goods and services. Your supplier has them. What are the most efficient ways to bridge the gap? The days of huge warehouses holding idle inventory are long gone. With the advent of Just-In-Time (JIT) inventory models, purchasing organizations discovered the advantage of not holding inventory until it was needed. But the evolution continues. Many organizations are now taking things one step further and improving on these models. For some, it means a supplier is actually on-site. For others, a supplier is close by and inventory is handled fewer times, stored more efficiently, and transported in strategic amounts. Whatever the specifics, these organizations are all involved in integrated supply strategies. NAPM's *Glossary of Key Purchasing Terms* (second edition) defines integrated supply as "A special type of partnering arrangement usually developed between a purchaser and a distributor on an intermediate to long-term basis. The objective of an integrated supply relationship is to minimize, for both the purchaser and the supplier, the labor and expense involved in the acquisition and possession of items that are repetitive, generic, high transaction, and have a low unit cost." The results of integrated supply models? Cost savings is a major result. Other benefits include inventory reductions, improved supplier relations, and improved production efficiencies. The following profiles illustrate how three organizations have successfully taken supply models to new heights. In their own words, practitioners share their experiences based on their specific environment and needs.

PPG Industries: Improving Their Ways

At PPG Industries' chemical complex near Lake Charles, Louisiana, customer shipments of more than 7,000 tons a day of basic chemicals make the 1,600-employee plant the largest of nearly 100 PPG plants worldwide. We have taken a 10-year-old JIT concept and improved it. Vendor City consists of 11 maintenance, repair, and operating (MRO) suppliers located less than a half mile from our complex. These suppliers supply a variety of MRO items such as gaskets, safety equipment, pipe, valves, and fittings. Our facility spends in excess of $12 million annually with these 11 suppliers. Using one common carrier, Vendor City suppliers provide PPG with MRO supplies, just in time. This 10-year-old program includes four scheduled daily deliveries plus emergency service. The system has allowed PPG to reduce our inventory of MRO parts by more than $5 million, or in excess of 30 percent.

Using Technology

In the past, all the materials were unloaded at our main warehouse from the common carrier then moved cross dock to be reloaded on our delivery wagon. While the physical movement of materials was taking place, receiving clerks were busy key punching receipts into our receiving system. Using up-to-date electronic tools such as EDI, bar-coding, and radio frequency, PPG employees now pick up our materials at the suppliers' location. The materials are placed strategically on our delivery wagons, which means a "one-time handling" until they are delivered at the appropriate delivery stations within the plant. Using bar-code readers, the materials are being received real time off site. The system uses standard bar-code readers that scan the purchase order number. The only time a manual entry is necessary is when the quantity shipped is different than the quantity ordered, which occurs less than 5 percent of the time. Under these conditions, the entry is merely a simple key stroke. Using radio frequency, which is a system of antennas, base radios, and a wireless bridge, the data is transferred from the scanners real time to our client server, which in turn transfers the data into our mainframe materials management system. The results: More accurate receiving, improved service, plus annual costs savings of approximately $500,000.

Taking Things a Step Farther

Like other organizations, at PPG Procurement we are always striving to reduce our costs while providing equal or better service to our internal customers. The Vendor City system has served us well, but we wanted to take another bite out of our inventory costs. Our challenge was to analyze our existing inventory by looking at what other MRO supplies could be moved to our supplier base. We looked at items that did not require the intense service requirements of the MRO suppliers that were a part of Vendor City but still required deliveries of more than once-a-day plus emergency services of two hours or less. These items include things such as filters, insulation, paint, and paint-related products.

Next, we looked at our supplier base to see if we could identify suppliers that could meet our daily delivery requirements for the items identified. These suppliers needed to be located within 10 miles of our plant. We have been successful in developing five suppliers that meet our needs. Again, we use EDI and bar-coding to make the system efficient. Through this effort, PPG has eliminated an additional $1 million in inventory. The program is known as our Satellite Stocking Partners. In both Vendor City and Satellite Stocking Partners arrangements, each supplier must provide the best total value package to PPG in order to maintain 100 percent of our requirements.

These efforts, and a conscious step to take a 10-year-old JIT program to the next level, have added value to the processes at PPG. In the true spirit of integrated supply, we have made the purchase and delivery of targeted MRO items easier, and improved on previous models. Through technology, including the bar-coding capabilities of suppliers and the radio transmitted inventory information, we've saved money and reduced inventories.

—*James V. Veronesi, manager of procurement at the Lake Charles Complex, PPG Industries, in Lake Charles, Louisiana.*

Tekelec: Pooling Efforts with Suppliers

At Tekelec, a Calabasas, California-based organization of over 500 employees, which provides switching solutions and advanced diagnostic systems that deliver advanced communication products and services for the global marketplace, we have integrated a supplier managed inventory (SMI) program into our manufacturing process. By linking the SMI program to our manufacturing information system, we created a fully integrated, closed loop, transactionally error-free, and highly auditable process that stretches from customer shipment to supplier inventory replenishment. At Tekelec, we are replenishing completed circuit packs shipped to customers and our suppliers are replenishing all the electronics required to manufacture those circuit packs. The components range from passives and miscellaneous hardware on the low end, to Pentium® processors and memory modules on the high end. Over 75 percent of our product costs are managed through this process.

The factory was ready for the migration to this new process since we had already reduced our supplier base by 70 percent and had contracts in place for over 80 percent of our components. In addition, we had just completed a review of the factory floor layout and made major changes to leverage the efficiencies of a pull process. The pull concept, derived from JIT, refers to the fact that we pull product all the way through the process. Completed assemblies are shipped to customers; untested assemblies are pulled through the test department to replenish finished goods; our contract manufacturer is pulling components from the supplier's inventory to backfill the untested board inventory; and our component suppliers are replenishing their bins of raw material from their central warehouse. The key here is that we do not build, buy, or stock any products unless demand by our customers warrants the activity. We do not push work-orders based on manufacturing resource planning (MRP) outputs.

Before implementing the SMI process, Tekelec differed from many organizations in using a two-bin system with an auto-replenishment package furnished by one of our suppliers. In short, the two-bin system is a process by which there are two bins containing equal amounts of a product and the operator pulls material from the front bin until it's empty. Prior to pulling the back bin forward and consuming material from it, the operator triggers the replenishment flag, which in our case is a laminated card with a bar code detailing the part number, quantity, and location. The bar code is scanned and a replenishment order is sent via EDI to the appropriate supplier. When the replenishment inventory arrives, it's placed in the empty bin and that bin becomes the back bin. Although our two-week cycle time was already close to best in class, we were not comfortable with the level of redundancy and waste in this process. In addition, we recognized that our growth rate demanded either a more efficient process or more manpower.

Project Objectives

The primary project objective was to reduce the cycle time required for replenishing the manufacturing inventories and to better support the pull manufacturing method. The goal to reduce our cycle time also included the support functions within the organization such as accounts payable, stores, receiving, and quality. Our second objective was not to add any liabilities typically associated with increased inventories (i.e., delayed implementation of engineering change orders, increased scrap risks, increased carrying charges). Our aggressive schedule for design enhancements and the need to maintain maximum flexibility eliminated going turn-key, that is, having our contract manufacturer procure material on our behalf.

How It Works

In short, our suppliers manage their inventory warehoused at our contract manufacturer. When the factory needs to be replenished, the contract manufacturer pulls material from the consigned location and assembles the printed circuit boards (PCBs), sometimes referred to as a printed circuit pack, identified by our pull flag. Upon delivery of completed PCB assemblies to Tekelec, the system automatically generates purchase orders for all components, receives the components to inventory, and issues them to the work order. The work order is then closed to inventory. The system goes on to generate our supplier invoices, match them to the receipts, and generate payment. All records are sent via EDI to our suppliers to update their systems.

Internal Benefits

We have operated the switching division's printed circuit board requirements under this program for the last several months with the following results:

- Inventory turns for the division have increased an average of 40 percent from the preceding year to a current high of 7.8 percent annualized.
- Inventory levels for the division have been reduced by 30 percent, and on-time shipments are up 1 percent to over 98 percent year-to-date.
- Several months' supply of inventory based on forecast was reduced 30 percent from what it was in January 1998, and we have not had a single stock-out.

The resulting increased efficiencies, from the combined efforts and process changes for us and our suppliers, has proven that integrated supply strategies can be successful and add to the bottomline.

—*Rodney A. MacLea, assistant vice president, materials, at Tekelec in Calabasas, California.*

Rhône-Poulenc Ag Company: Integrating with Suppliers and Through the Organization

Rhône-Poulenc Ag Company is one of seven entities that make up the RP family of companies in the United States and Canada. Rhône-Poulenc Ag Company is in life science products and operates a research facility in Research Triangle Park, North Carolina, as well as research farms and formulation facilities. Being one of seven organizations results in a unique challenge for integrated supply opportunities. Through a strong supply chain management council, we've managed to gain the leverage of seven combined without centralization. Each organization is represented on the council, with input from various functions, such as purchasing, transportation, and warehousing. From there, purchasing teams, representing the seven, work with suppliers to negotiate better contracts and develop integrated supply processes.

Gaining Leverage

For us, the key to making our integrated supplier relationships work has been the ability for us to approach suppliers as a more powerful buying unit. For example, at Rhône-Poulenc Ag alone, we may buy about $1.2 million worth of certain items per year, but when we put the family of seven together, we may buy over $12 million. So we get a supplier to recognize us as a $12 million customer. We get tremendous leverage this way.

There are agreements like this in place for laboratory supplies and consumables, but also for various services such as telecommunications and leased fleet vehicles. What is also interesting is how we work together. For example, in my team we have a number of procurement people, but, in fact, I have some seven times more working on my behalf. Each of the individuals is trained to work for their company, but also to the benefit of the family. The result of this leveraged purchasing skill has been agreements with suppliers that offer superior services and processes, not to mention better pricing.

Integrated Benefits

Each of the seven entities benefit from these leveraged relationships with the supplier of lab supplies and consumables—for example, each, if they choose, has supplier on-site representatives that can work directly with internal users. So the scientists that are doing the ordering can speak directly with the supplier representative to make decisions, ask questions, or resolve problems. This supplier agreement has also taken us out of the storeroom business. We used to maintain our own storeroom, which housed laboratory supplies. First, our supplier buys and holds all that inventory and now provides Just-In-Time (JIT) delivery to us twice a day. We maintain no inventory of laboratory consumables. They're delivered to us from a distribution center, operated by the supplier, which is just 6 miles away.

The role of the supplier of laboratory consumables does not stop at the back door, however. All deliveries are made to the labtop, directly to the requisitioner. The supplier also takes away any packaging materials and even handles the recycling, so that Rhône-Poulenc

Healthy Welfare for People and Suppliers

St. Luke's Roosevelt Hospital Center (STLR), a university hospital of Columbia University College of Physicians and Surgeons located in New York City, faces the same challenges as many other hospitals.

In addition to caring for their patients, they must order, manage, and store all the supplies and materials needed to provide healthcare services. Previously, STLR had general supply and central stores, which were only handling about 30 percent of STLR's supplies. The remainder of orders for some 11,000 items were being placed by individual nursing units and handled by 23 logistics unit managers who juggled requisition paperwork. The result was numerous negative side effects: $600,000 of unaccounted for inventory each year, supply hoarding, fewer bulk discounts, more deliveries, higher freight bills, and overcrowding at the facility's loading docks. So, STLR began exploring alternatives that would ultimately lead to their Hospital Support Center, which houses the combination of a distributor and logistics provider to maintain an efficient continuous replenishment system.

One of the first steps to this integrated supply solution was to move the facility from the pricey Manhattan area to Bronx, New York. Just as dramatic was the renovation of STLR's ordering and replenishment process.

To regain control of the decentralized ordering function, they now use a "two bin" inventory and bar-coding method, which is a fully paperless replenishment system that enables STLR's nursing units and various other cost centers to keep the inventory on hand at all times. Each morning, nursing units and other departments scan their supply bins with hand-held, bar-code scanners. These replenishment needs are then transmitted to the Hospital Support Center, where computer software then calculates the number of "totes" that will be needed to replenish supplies. A bar code is attached at the Hospital Supply Center, by the supplier, that provides specific order and product information. The software then transmits order picking instructions to radio frequency devices used by the supplier pick line employees who assemble orders into the totes. Once the orders are complete, the Hospital Support Center loads orders onto one of the four or five trucks that travel to STLR (approximately eight miles) each day. The system then creates electronic debits and posts them to the general ledger, which completes the order cycle.

STLR's distributor actually has title of the supplies and took the initiative to retain the logistics provider. Besides trimming $1 million in STLR's inventory carrying costs, this model has also saved an estimated $1.3 million in operating expenses, and maintained delivery fill rates at an average 99.5 percent. Moving this supply process offsite and staffing it with suppliers has had other benefits. The nurses are happy because it's simplified their lives; the financial stakeholders are happy because it saves the hospital money; and the administration is happy because the hospital was able to add so much square footage to the available space for patient care.

Information provided by Manny Losada, vice president of Caligor Hospital Supply in Pelham Manor, New York.

stays environmentally friendly. This is the type of integrated service that we have negotiated, through the purchasing teams of the supply chain management council, for each of our seven entities.

By definition, integrated supply also means reducing expenses, which we've been able to do through consolidated billing. For example, with one particular supplier, prior to this arrangement, we averaged 4,500 invoices each year. Now we have 24—that's twice-a-month summary bills. We pay them electronically, with varying payment terms, lowering administrative costs drastically.

Third-party products are also handled in a unique manner. If our supplier doesn't carry something we need, there are provisions in the contract that require them to procure those products, and supply them to Rhône-Poulenc with no additional cost. The benefit for suppliers is that they gain a better understanding of our needs, and, because they're working directly with the requisitioner, can offer other available options.

In the future, we see our suppliers playing an even more integrated role. We are introducing our key suppliers to our customers. Not only would that further increase our leverage with the supplier, but the customer and the supplier get the benefit of working directly with each other within our agreement terms.

Lessons Learned

Probably the biggest challenge to developing this type of supply model is finding the right supplier. You will need someone that can meet your geographic, as well as product and service, needs. We have some facilities in remote areas and our suppliers need to meet their product needs, as well as be available for service. Not all suppliers could accommodate that. Suppliers will need to meet other needs, too, such as Internet ordering—or whatever is specific to your organization.

For us, another challenge that we met was in getting our seven companies aligned to approach suppliers. Each of the supply chain management council representatives works on a volunteer basis. We have no centralized corporate management and we come from a wide range of corporate cultures, so it was a great achievement to pull together and realize leverage opportunities.

For organizations looking to implement integrated supply strategies, a shift from a traditional, transactional purchasing focus to a more strategic vision is key. Not only is this a step to a best-in-class role for purchasing specifically, but also in your organization's goals of servicing customers. Speak and benchmark with other organizations that have been successful and learn from them. The development of such a model will take time—time to find the right supplier, but also time to work on their strengths as well as your own.

—*Robert P. Zigas, Ph.D., C.P.M., director of customer satisfaction and supply at Rhône-Poulenc Ag Company in Research Triangle Park, North Carolina.*

The Goods Are at the Supplier's: Do You Feel Lucky?

J. A. (Andy) Watkins, Jr., J.D., C.P.M.

It happens. You have your goods at a supplier for processing, and the goods are damaged or destroyed. What do you do to recover your investment in those goods? Better yet, what steps can you take to prevent such events from happening? It is questions like these that this article addresses. If you can't recover a loss from insurance, you may have to take legal action. You'll learn here under which legal theories you can take such actions with a reasonable expectation of being reimbursed.

Just imagine, you've sent $50,000 worth of goods (property) to a supplier for additional tooling. While at the supplier's, several gallons of caustic soda is accidentally spilled on your property, rendering the goods useless. Your organization is left to handle a $50,000 property loss.

In this real-life situation, no damages were recovered because neither the buying organization or the supplier carried liability insurance.

Beyond liability insurance, difficult legal issues can arise when you send goods to a supplier for work, also known as outside processing. What happens if the supplier damages your goods? What happens if you provide a supplier with tooling to work on the goods you send them and your tooling is damaged in addition to the goods you sent them? What are your rights if you provide a supplier with money to purchase special test equipment instead of sending them the equipment yourself and the equipment is damaged in addition to your goods that the supplier was recalibrating?

These are some of the problems that your purchasing and supply department should address in advance of the inevitable (and hopefully only occasional) loss, damage, or destruction to your property. Put effective measures in place to allow for financial recovery. Proactive protections exist for a purchaser before placing the purchase order. Additionally, specific legal rights that provide the basis for legal recovery are available.

Proactive Protection

Purchasers must remember that once damage occurs to their property at a supplier's location, the choices to collect can come from the supplier's insurance company, the buying organization's own insurance company, or the supplier by negotiation or lawsuit. The buying organization may also choose to forgo collection and absorb the loss.

Since the last choice is usually unacceptable, the purchasing and supply manager's first choice should be to deal with suppliers who can show proof of general business insurance in an amount that will protect the purchaser's property from damage or total loss. If the supplier does not have general business insurance that covers damage to another's property while at the supplier's location, the next request should be for the supplier to post a bond covering the full value of the property. This should be less expensive for the supplier because it's more limited in dollar amount than general insurance, more limited in what is insured (your property only, not the supplier's), and more limited in the length of time the bond is in effect.

One "trick of the trade" that helps the supplier is for the purchaser to allow the supplier to have a fairly large deductible (e.g., $5,000) which the purchaser can agree to pay. This will keep the premiums much lower, but will still provide coverage against total loss.

In addition to these measures, a purchaser can reserve the right of "offset" (or some form of "debit memorandum") that allows the purchaser the right to withhold payment pending conclusion of negotiations with the supplier.

Common Legal Theories for Recovery

Remember that assuming you did "feel lucky" and did not use any of the measures for protection just discussed, and $50,000 worth of your property has caustic soda spilled on it, you may have to file (or threaten to file) a lawsuit to get the supplier in a negotiating mood. Also keep in mind that your supplier could borrow the money to replace your property.

Going through litigation to recover damages is not the end of the world for your supplier, and you must be aware of what legal theory to sue for in order to prevail in an action to recover your losses.

Many instances arise in which the owner of personal property entrusts it to another. A person checks his or her coat at a restaurant or loans his or her car to a friend. He or she delivers a watch to a jeweler for repairs or personal property to a supplier for modification or repairs, takes furniture to a warehouse for storage, or delivers goods to an airline for shipment. The delivery of property under such circumstances is a bailment. The bailment is a common transaction, and frequently a bailment exists even when the parties to the transaction are not aware of its existence. In business situations where you are paying a supplier to perform a service (mutual-benefit bailments), for instance you loan your lawn mower to your neighbor, a bailment exists.

As a general rule, a bailment is created by contract. Whether or not a bailment exists can be determined from all the facts and circumstances of the case. The test generally applied is whether possession has been delivered and whether the person into whose possession the article has been delivered intended to assume custody and control over the object or to dispose of it as directed by the owner. Usually, if one goes into a restaurant, a barber's shop, or a similar place, and hangs his or her hat and coat on a rack provided for that purpose, no bailment will arise. But, if the circumstances are such that the owner expressly (purchase order) or impliedly assumes control over the hat and coat (or purchaser's parts), a bailment will arise. The owner (purchaser's company) is called the bailor, and the person or company who has possession and control of the goods (the supplier) is called the bailee.

Bailee's Duty of Care—To determine the liability of the bailee for damage to or loss of the bailed property, bailments have been divided into three classes: (1) mutual-benefit bailments, (2) bailments for the sole benefit of the bailor, and (3) bailments for the sole benefit of the bailee.

All commercial bailments are mutual-benefit bailments, that is, both the bailee and the bailor receive benefits from the relationship. For example, if goods are being reworked at a supplier, the supplier (bailee) is compensated for his or her services, and the owner of the goods (the purchaser-bailor) has his or her goods stored and/or modified during the period of the purchase order. The mutual-benefit bailee owes a duty of ordinary care and is liable for damage to or loss of the goods only if such damage or loss is the result of his or her negligence. Ordinary care has been defined as that care which a person of ordinary prudence would take of his or her goods of like nature under the same or similar circumstances.

Alteration of Liability by Contract—The bailee's liability may be either increased or decreased by the purchase order between the parties. An attempt by a bailee to relieve him- or herself of liability for intentional or reckless wrongdoing is against public policy. The extent to which a bailee may relieve him- or herself from the liability for his or her own negligence is limited. Under the law of contracts, a contract (purchase order) whereby a person relieves him- or herself of liability for his or her own negligence may be against public policy and considered void. The courts have, as a general rule, enforced provisions in contracts of bailment whereby the bailee is relieved from specific perils; but the courts have been reluctant to enforce provisions in such contracts whereby the bailee is relieved from all liability for his or her negligent acts. If the bailment is based upon contract (and therefore the lawsuit is for breach of contract), then any defensive language based upon "negligence" would not help the supplier because he or she would not be sued for negligence.

Preventative Maintenance: The Best Medicine

When considering all the legal issues just presented, attempting to prevent legal action is always the best path to take. With key suppliers, most strategic purchasing and supply professionals have taken positive steps to address such property damage occurrences so legal action can be avoided.

In the case of the caustic soda spill, if both parties would simply have evaluated proof of general business insurance in an amount that would have protected the purchaser's property from damage or total loss, then monetary disaster could have been averted. If, during the evaluation, the supplier was shown to not have adequate business insurance, the next step should have been for the supplier to post a bond covering the full value of the property. Helping with the cost of insurance via the deductible would have also been a preventative maintenance approach to this situation.

Unfortunately, disasters cannot always be predicted. However, they can be planned for. The purchaser/supplier relationship is where the positive planning can take place.

J.A. (Andy) Watkins, Jr., J.D., C.P.M., is manager of subcontracts for Logicon Inc. (a Northrop Grumman company) in Los Angeles, California.

Clean Up Your Act:
Purchasing Janitorial Services

Michelle B. Knepper, C.P.M., A.P.P.
and Mark K. Lindsey

How do you go about hiring janitorial services? Like most such questions, the answer is both simple and complicated. There are plenty of such services available, but how do you make sure you get the quality and reliability of service you want and expect for a reasonable price? This article provides an overview of the things you should consider, including industry trends, cost containment, facility distinctions, contractual issues, and more.

Are you wondering how much organizations spend in purchasing janitorial and maintenance services? Although janitorial services do not top purchasing and supply managers' purchasing agenda, they form major operating expenses for organizations. Statistics from the Building Owners and Managers Association (BOMA), an international organization headquartered in Washington, D.C., confirm that organizations spend a considerable amount of resources on janitorial services. According to the latest figures released by BOMA (1998 annual report), office cleaning expenditures account for almost $14 billion a year, which translates to nearly 15 percent of building operating costs. An expenditure of $1.30 per square foot is typical for cleaning and janitorial services in an office building environment.

Hiring janitorial services is a very important function of the purchasing and supply department according to "Purchasing of Nontraditional Goods and Services." According to this 1995 research initiative, conducted by NAPM and the Center for Advanced Purchasing Studies (CAPS), a program jointly sponsored by Arizona State University and NAPM, 94 percent of total dollars spent on janitorial services in the 116 organizations surveyed in the study were handled by the purchasing and supply department. Compared to other services, such as temporary help (10 percent) and market research (28 percent), the purchasing department's control of dollars spent on janitorial services was quite high. Given that the purchasing and supply department in most organizations is already highly involved in the purchase of these services, how can purchasing managers leverage their influence and expertise to bring even greater benefits?

Industry Trends

Mergers and Acquisitions: The janitorial services industry has experienced a great deal of consolidation among the major players in recent years. Several larger firms have been in acquisition mode, pulling in smaller suppliers to add to their growing business.

Recently, a consultant in the process of sourcing janitorial firms for a client in Pennsylvania telephoned a contact in a large janitorial service organization. The consultant indicated that he was having trouble locating a good firm in the client's region and asked who the janitorial organization considered to be competitive in this particular market. The contact was quick with a name and gave a little background as well, but soon realized that his organization had just taken over the organization he was recommending.

Over the past year, this scenario has developed into a pattern. Purchasing and property managers report that they have fewer and fewer regional providers and are doing more business with large, multinational, multiservice firms. According to *Hoover's 1998 Organization Profiles*, the largest services average over $2 billion in annual sales and have an average of almost 53,000 employees.

Expanding Service Lines: Along with the expansion in size and/or geography gained through consolidation in the industry, janitorial service providers are also expanding in scope. Over time, as these suppliers have repeatedly complied with client needs to provide additional services, their menu of commonly provided services has grown to include a variety of facilities management tasks—from furniture relocation to engineering and mechanical services. The opportunity to work with a supplier who can more completely understand your facilities and grow with your needs is now more common. When selecting a janitorial services provider, be sure to assess your current and future needs within the facilities management arena.

"It's Just a Rental": As organizations transform their work places and offer more flexible work arrangements which do not require employees to be in the office, the demand for maintenance, security, janitorial, and other facilities' services continues to change and become more critical.

Hoteling is one such practice adopted by organizations where work space is assigned to employees on a day-to-day and/or as-needed basis. Rather than hold permanent offices, employees reserve space ahead of arrival by calling, faxing, or e-mailing their individual space requests. While this has become a popular concept in several industries, it places an added burden on janitorial services.

The idea of temporary ownership is often interpreted by the user as low or no maintenance. There are places you would not drive your four-wheel drive truck, but would willingly venture into in a rental car. People will mistreat rental items or temporary things, and in a hoteling environment, they often do not treat their workspace as if it were their own. Organizations may find hoteling to be more economical than the traditional office environment but often do not properly estimate the ongoing maintenance costs.

Key Issues

There are certain key issues that organizations must consider when seeking to hire janitorial service providers.

Cost Containment: Janitorial services can be an area of cost containment, but you must remember that this is a labor-intensive service and a decrease in headcount or hourly wages will quickly be reflected in service quality. It should be noted, however, that supply and material contracts through the janitorial firm could provide savings opportunities.

Materials and Supplies: As with any material purchase that is to be installed, consumed, or used by a service provider, a decision must be made as to who will specify and negotiate the janitorial materials. Should your organization provide the materials? Should the service provider place orders against your corporate contracts? Alternatively, should you allow the service provider to acquire the materials based on their own purchasing leverage and industry expertise, and then bill you along with their services?

A janitorial contract should be specific about the materials and supplies to be provided by the janitorial services provider. Unless your organization performs studies on cleaning materials and supplies, listen to the supplier's suggestions in these specialty areas. This is the key to maintaining pricing, volume discounts, liability, and shrinkage. The premise is very simple: economies of scale. One individual found that he had paid $530 for a single box of hand soap, while the typical cost to his janitorial supplier was less than $100. He had fallen into the trap—common among professionals in all areas— of believing that he could negotiate and maintain better agreements than his suppliers. If you still feel uncomfortable handing over the purchasing authority and losing control over material purchases, specify in your contract with the janitorial provider how you will oversee or monitor material usage for reasonableness.

Facility Distinctions: As facilities vary so do the types of janitorial services needed to maintain them. These distinctions may be the result of something as apparent as the materials used on walls and flooring, to the various types of facilities—whether office, distribution, or manufacturing.

To prevent misunderstandings and to clearly outline the requirements, you should try to incorporate a formal supplier walk-through with several bidding firms. This will better define the scope of work, quality standards, and, most importantly, a solid provider buy-in so as to eliminate unforeseen, out-of-scope costs.

You should verify the dimensions of the areas by measuring them on a square footage basis as opposed to rentable space. For example, a janitorial request for proposal (RFP) was distributed to a series of suppliers detailing square footage based on rentable figures from the lease agreements. One of the suppliers caught the error, reduced his quote by 15 percent, and won the bid. Vacant or storage space does not require daily maintenance, though periodic attention may be needed.

Management of Supplier and Personnel: Stabilizing the janitorial work force is critical in building maintenance. A janitorial firm should identify key positions within an account and be willing to commit designated personnel as a key portion of the contract. Service quality for one purchaser suffered when the supplier's labor pool became a labor stream as turnover escalated. This issue then created a major barrier in the purchaser/supplier relationship. To prevent this type of situation from occurring, clearly state in your contract that the supplier shall not change or reassign the designated key personnel without the prior approval of a designated representative from your organization.

A purchaser of janitorial services, as with any other service, will also want to specify the skill sets required to perform the services to be purchased. The training schedule may also include any necessary instruction on security protocol and safety precautions specific to your type of business and the particular facility.

Are you the biggest player in your supplier's game? A senior executive of a local janitorial firm maintained a philosophy that no more than 37 percent of his gross revenue would come from any one client. This way he could aggressively manage his business and not be dictated by a major client. Additionally, the possible loss of the largest account would not severely impact his organization.

You should note this mindset, and apply a corresponding strategy based on the same principles. Being your supplier's smallest account may not get you the attention and support you need, and the loss or change of the supplier's other accounts may severely impact his economic stability—leaving you in a bind.

This does not necessarily mean that you want to be a supplier's only account. While you would have the supplier's attention in this case, you would also be solely responsible for the supplier's financial stability, a responsibility you may not want to take on. An extremely small provider may not have the resources to expand as you grow, and eventually will not meet your needs. The key is to understand your position in the market and strike a balance with a service provider who can be both responsive to your needs and whose attention you can command when necessary.

Supplier Transitioning: A lower janitorial services bid can be very appealing, but there are many additional factors to be considered prior to making such a change of service providers. The cost of replacing or transitioning to a new janitorial firm is often underestimated. The purchaser should take the time to understand these transitional costs—from start up to implementation—and consider them in the bid process. Depending on the magnitude of the account, a 5 percent transitioning factor should be added in such bid situations.

If a change in janitorial firms is forthcoming, however, the transition should be swift and seamless. A 30-day termination clause may provide too long of a transition period, because commitment to service levels often becomes a secondary priority during these times.

Contractual Issues

The RFP: The RFP and other contracts for janitorial services should provide a basic framework for the janitorial services contract. The purchasing and supply manager should outline the facility, the standards, and existing conditions, and then a more detailed scope should be jointly authored by the provider(s) and edited by the purchaser (see sidebar below). Be aware of specialty materials that may be included in the scope of cleaning such as exotic wood desks, patterned carpets, or art objects. Additionally, buildings that operate multiple shifts require special service efforts so as not to disrupt business production. The final leg to the RFP should be a physical site walk-through conducted individually with each bidder. Multiple bidders will serve to further clarify the janitorial needs of an area.

Squeaky Clean Specifics

Scope elements to include in a janitorial services contract:

- Description of premises to be cleaned (include space maps if necessary)
- Specific description of services to be provided (for example, uncarpeted floors shall be wet mopped, dried, and spray buffed. All wax marks shall be removed from baseboards.)
- Frequency of services (nightly, weekly, monthly, quarterly)
- Outlined by area (for example, lobby, kitchen areas, elevators)
- Specification of any materials to be used (such as cleaning agents or polishes) and how they are to be purchased
- Reports or other required periodic documentation
- Insurance requirements (for example, automobile liability, commercial general liability, workers' compensation) and liability

---

Service Levels: Of particular importance is the service level agreement (SLA) for the cooperation and quality between all involved parties. This document should include a description of the means, methods, organization, and processes along with material requirements. The foundation for the SLA is then based on the relationship between the service provider and the purchaser, and the requirements made by the end users or occupying parties.

Flexibility: A word of caution when detailing janitorial services: Maintain flexibility. Provide enough leeway in an agreement to expand or contract the required service levels—always leave something on the plate. One particular organization was very proud of the cleaning and janitorial RFP they had designed. It was extremely thorough and numbered almost 200 pages. After distributing the document to a large supplier segment, they were surprised by the minimal response. When contacted for follow-up, these firms indicated that they were not interested because such a contract was too constrictive and micro-managed the most basic janitorial functions.

> ### *Defining Specifications*
>
> As with any purchase, the needs of the end user should be considered. You should keep the following questions in mind:
>
> - Who in my organization will be directly affected by this service?
> - Who in my organization will interact with the service provider and with what frequency?
> - Are my organization's customers directly affected by this service? (i.e., do my customers visit my facility?)
> - How do I distinguish needs from wants?

Operational Performance Measures

Bonus Systems: A system of rewarding for cost savings and performance enhancements is becoming commonplace in today's janitorial contracts. Organizations need to communicate their goals and expectations of the service provider and reward appropriately.

Checks and Balances: A majority of janitorial services are performed at night when there is minimal personal contact with the client. Security sign-in sheets and access systems can be designed and maintained to verify work patterns or area activity.

Take a Walk: A proactive approach to services management is always more desirable than receiving a telephone call from one of your less-than-pleased internal customers. Facility services in particular often call for a "management by walking around" (MBWA) approach. Periodic site visits with the provider enhance communications and provide a show of interest to your client groups. Gathering a feel for general customer satisfaction within your organization several days before the site visit is often helpful and offsets major surprises for both you and the provider.

Benchmarking: Benchmarking is an effective way to measure suppliers against other suppliers and industry standards. In the janitorial services arena, such benchmarks might include a measure of total cost of service per square foot.

As in all areas of business, no single measure can provide a clear performance target. You may find that a balanced scorecard approach, which goes beyond financial accounting measures, works well with janitorial services. Components of the scorecard might include both quantitative measures of time and cost, and qualitative measures of the quality of supervision, timeliness and appropriateness of response to customer requests, ease of contact, and rate of improvements.

Performance measures are only good if progress against them is communicated on a regular basis so that action can be taken to correct problems and reinforce positives. Detailed weekly evaluations may be necessary in some instances, but as improvements are made you may decide that you can perform walk-throughs less frequently. Over time, you and your con-

Purchasing Security Services

- Training is typically provided by the security firm but often additional organization training or orientation is also provided. Note that state requirements are often much lower than you'd expect (as low as eight hours of training!) and be sure that your security provider meets not only the legal minimums but your expectations as well.
- Background checks are typically provided by the security firm though guidelines should be established jointly between the security firm and your organization.
- As a customer of a security firm you should not be responsible for paying overtime, since you are essentially employing a labor pool, and the security organization should be adequately staffed so that overtime is not necessary. Your contract may specify, however, a limited number of total hours provided, with any requests for hours above this amount being considered overtime.
- Due to the skilled nature of security services, wage fluctuations by labor market may be significant. Allow for local pricing if you are pursuing a regional or national contract. Also be aware of composite or blended rates and what they represent. Some clients of security firms prefer custom rates because of the visibility and control it provides them with respect to particular skill levels and the corresponding pay rates.
- While the customer typically specifies the standards for uniforms and pays for them, they can usually be purchased through the security firm or their account, taking advantage of their purchasing expertise and leverage.
- Security is a very personal service which requires trust, much more so than janitorial or other facility maintenance services. Be aware of the sensitivity of your internal customers when selecting a security provider or making a change in suppliers.

tact at the janitorial firm may decide that monthly lunch meetings are sufficient. Along with passing feedback to your suppliers, be open to feedback from your internal clients.

Strategic Approaches

As in any supplier relationship, ongoing communication is key. As your business changes, so will your need for services. Oftentimes, involving your janitorial service provider when planning facility changes can save you time, money, and trouble in the long run. High end fixtures or materials that are costly at initial purchase may also require specialty equipment or personnel to maintain. Often, your service provider can be the best source of ideas on how to cope with your changing needs.

Michelle B. Knepper, C.P.M., A.P.P., is a manager with Ernst & Young LLP's management consulting practice in Cincinnati, Ohio.

Mark K. Lindsey is manager of corporate real estate for Ernst & Young Kenneth Leventhal Real Estate Group in Los Angeles, California.

Part Seven

Purchasing and Supply Management References and Resources

W e have created *The Purchasing & Supply Yearbook* as an anthology to keep you current with what's going on in your field. However, we also want to provide you with additional resources for improving your own performance. Parts One to Six of this book are the anthology. Part Seven includes resources. All the materia in this section of the yearbook is as current as we could make it up to press time. Here's what you'll find:

- **Directory of Magazines, Journals, and Newsletters Dealing with Supply Management.** Here we provide an annotated directory of magazines, journals, and newsletters that cover purchasing and supply management issues. We've briefly explained the focus of each publication and provide information on how to get in touch with the publishers and how to subscribe.
- **Purchasing and Supply Management Resources Online.** The Internet has become a tremendous repository of information on every subject as well as a communication medium. It has certainly taken hold in the purchasing and supply management field in a major way. There are hundreds of Web sites that deal in one way or another with purchasing issues. To help you identify those that may be useful to you, we include this annotated directory that provides a representative sampling of what's available on the World Wide Web as well as e-mail discussion groups, newsletters, and newsgroups. We have sought to make this the most comprehensive and current directory of such resources you'll find anywhere in print.

- **Directory of Purchasing and Supply Management Associations and Organizations.** This directory provides a descriptive listing of professional organizations and associations that people in purchasing and supply management may need to know about. This directory includes annotations describing each organization. We've sought to make this as complete as possible including both U.S. and international organizations.
- **Calendar of Major Events, Meetings, and Conferences, 2000.** This is a listing of meetings of interest to those in purchasing and supply management for 2000, including dates, locations, and how to find out more information on the Web.

Directory of Magazines, Journals, and Newsletters Dealing with Purchasing and Supply Management

T his section presents a comprehensive but not exhaustive list of magazines, journals, and newsletters that will be of interest to those involved in purchasing and supply management. Many organizations offer newsletters that are not listed here because they are only sent to members. Check the Directory of Purchasing and Supply Management Associations and Organizations to find out more about those.

For each listing, you'll find addresses, phone numbers, fax numbers, e-mail addresses, and World Wide Web URLs. (Many of the Web sites provide resources that go beyond the periodicals.) You'll also find information on how to subscribe (prices are in U.S. dollars, unless indicated otherwise) and a brief description. Often with specialized journals and newsletters you can get a sample copy by contacting the publisher. For those in which you have an interest but not enough to subscribe, use this directory as a guide to what you might find at your local college or university library. If you have any recommendations for publications we should list in the next edition of this annual, or to update our information, please contact us through McGraw-Hill or e-mail jwoods@execpc.com.

ADC News & Solutions
Published monthly by Cahners Business Information. Editorial: ADC News & Solutions, Gary R. Forger, Editor, 275 Washington Street, Newton, MA 02158, phone: (617) 558-4234 or (617) 964-3030, fax: (617) 558-4327, e-mail: gforger@cahners.com, Web: http://www.manufacturing.net/magazine/adc/. Subscriptions: Cahners Business Information, 8773 S. Ridgeline Boulevard, Highlands Ranch, CO 80126, phone: (800) 662-7776 or (303) 470-4000, fax: (303) 470-4546, e-mail: cahners.subs@denver.cahners.com.
Subscriptions: Free to qualified applicants.

Dedicated to "Automatic Data Capture applications in manufacturing, warehousing, and distribution," this magazine covers industrial applications of automatic data capture (ADC) technologies and related information systems in manufacturing, warehousing, and distribution operations.

Advanced Planning and Scheduling Magazine (APS Magazine)
Published quarterly by Penton Media, Inc., 9 West Street, Beverly, MA 01915-2225, phone: (978) 922-1075, fax: (978) 921-1255, e-mail editor@apsmagazine.com or subscriptions@apsmagazine.com, Web: http://www.apsmagazine.com/.
Subscriptions: U.S., $40; Canada and Mexico, $60; other countries, $96.

This magazine is the only publication that focuses exclusively on the theory, use, implementation, benefits, and challenges of the use of Advanced Planning and Scheduling systems. It's aimed at executives and managers in manufacturing companies that are interested in the characteristics, uses, and benefits of APS systems.

APICS—The Performance Advantage
Published monthly by the American Production and Inventory Control Society (APICS), The Educational Society for Resource Management, 5301 Shawnee Road, Alexandria, VA 22312-2317, phone: (800) 444-2742 or (703) 354-8851, fax: (703) 354-8106 or (703) 354-8794 (editorial), e-mail: editorial@apics-hq.org, Web: http://www.apics.org/magazine.
Subscriptions: Free to APICS members. For nonmembers, $47 in the U.S., $59 in Canada and Mexico, and $75 elsewhere.

The editorial focus is on real-life applications/case studies of supply chain management, electronic commerce, scheduling, systems integration and data collection, inventory management, manufacturing technology, and integrated resource management.

The Australian Purchasing and Supply
Published monthly (11 issues) by the Australian Institute of Purchasing and Materials Management Ltd., Suite 3, 21 Ringwood Street, Ringwood, VIC 3134, Australia, phone: (03) 9876 9713, fax: (03) 9876 9714, e-mail: info@aipmm.com.au, Web: http://www.aipmm.com.au.
Subscriptions: Free to members; AUS$48.00 for nonmembers.

This journal has regular features on new and developing issues covering all aspects of the supply chain from raw materials to finished product. It provides information on current trends, theories, techniques, procedures, new products, legislation, and services.

Better Buys for Business
Published 10 times a year by Better Buys for Business, 370 Technology Drive, Malvern, PA 19355, phone: (800) 247-2185 or (610) 296-4031, fax: (610) 296-4967, e-mail: info@betterbuys.com, Web: http://www.betterbuys.com.
Subscriptions: U.S., $145; Canada, $152; other countries, $245.

This magazine—previously known as *What to Buy for Business*—specializes in publishing guides to the major types of office equipment relating to the printing, copying, transmission, and storage of documents. The series of 10 annual guides covers copiers, fax machines, multifunctional equipment, color devices, printers, duplicators, and electronic filing systems. The Web site provides information about the guides and an electronic order form. It also provides bulletins that update the guides.

The Business Consumer's Advisor
Published monthly by Buyer's Laboratory, Inc., 20 Railroad Avenue, Hackensack, NJ 07601-3309, phone: (201) 488-0404, Fax: (201) 488-0461, e-mail: info@buyers-lab.com, Web: http://www.buyers-lab.com.
Subscriptions: $175.
　　This 16-page newsletter covers office products and services, as well as many other business topics, with articles that are thorough and easy to read.

Buyer's Guide to Electronic Commerce
Published annually by Electronic Commerce Strategies, Inc., 2627 Sandy Plains Road, Suite 202, Marietta, GA 30066, phone: (770) 565-4010, fax: *(770) 565-4062*, e-mail: order@e-com.com, Web: http://www.e-com.com/buyersguide.
Subscriptions: $15.95.
　　This publication features suppliers of electronic commerce products and services.

Buying Strategy Forecast (Purchasing Magazine)
Published semi-monthly by Cahners Business Information. Editorial: Kevin Fitzgerald, Editor-in-Chief, 275 Washington Street, 3rd Floor, Newton, MA 02158-1630, phone: (617) 964-3030, fax: (617) 558-4327, e-mail: kevinf@cahners.com, Web: http://www.manufac-turing.net/magazine/purchasing/stores/pricing/bsf/bsfhome.html. Subscriptions: Cahners Business Information, 8773 S. Ridgeline Boulevard, Highlands Ranch, CO 80126, phone: (800) 446-6551 or (800) 662-7776 or (303) 470-4000, fax: (303) 470-4546, e-mail: cahn-ers.subs@denver.cahners.com.
Subscriptions: $275 (print or online).
　　This newsletter is a compilation of market intelligence for industrial buyers. It reports on developments in metals, chemicals, electronics, and a wide variety of other manufac-turing markets. Each issue contains the industry snapshot reports and forecasts, pricing changes and trends, macroeconomic analysis and forecasts, capacity actions, and "at a glance" data files.

Canadian Logistics Journal
Published quarterly by the Canadian Professional Logistics Institute, 10 King Street East, 4th Floor, Toronto, ON M5C 1C3, Canada, phone: (416) 363-3005, fax: (416) 363-5698, e-mail: loginfo@loginstitute.ca, Web: http://www.loginstitute.ca.
Subscriptions: $34.24 CDN for members; otherwise, $38.52 CDN.
　　The official publication of this national educational organization.

Caveat Emptor
Published quarterly by the Ontario Public Buyers Association Inc., 111 Fourth Avenue, Suite 361, Ridley Square, St. Catharines, ON, L2S 3P5, Canada, phone: (905) 682-2644, fax: (905) 682-2644, e-mail: opbasup@vaxxine.com, Web: http://www.vaxxine.com/opba.

Subscriptions: Individual $25 CDN.

This newsletter aims to further excellence in and promote awareness of the public procurement profession.

Chain Store Age

Published monthly by Lebhar-Friedman, Murray Forseter, Associate Publisher/Editor, 425 Park Avenue, New York, NY 10022, phone: (212) 756-5257 or (800) 453-2427, fax: NA, e-mail: mforseter@chainstoreage.com, Web: http://www.chainstoreage.com/The_Publication/about.htm.

Subscriptions: $105.

This is a news magazine for corporate executives at headquarters in all the major segments of retailing: home centers, supermarkets, drug chains, specialty stores, discount, convenience, and department stores. It reports on retailing trends and the forces behind them, with regular sections covering retail technology, merchandising, marketing, physical support systems, finance, legislative affairs, security, store design and display, strategic planning and human resources, distribution, and transportation.

Contract Management

Published monthly by the National Contract Management Association, 1912 Woodford Road, MS-P5, Vienna, VA 22182, phone: (800) 344-8096 or (703) 448-9231, fax: (703) 448-0939, e-mail: hoskins@ncmahq.org, Web: http://www.ncmahq.org/pubs/cm/cm.html.

Subscriptions: $75.

This magazine reports on contract matters for people who do acquisition or procurement of goods and services through contracting.

Electrical Construction & Maintenance (EC&M)

Published monthly by Intertec Publishing, John DeDad, Editorial Director, 9800 Metcalf Avenue, Overland Park, KS 66212-2215, phone: (913) 967-1818 or (800) 441-0294 (subscriptions), fax: (913) 967-1903, e-mail: jdedad@compuserve.com, Web: http://www.ecmweb.com.

Subscriptions: Free to qualified applicants.

This magazine covers the electrical industry, informing electrical contractors, engineers, and electrical personnel in manufacturing plants and non-manufacturing facilities.

Electronic Business

Published monthly by Cahners Business Information. Editorial: Kathleen Doler, Editor-in-Chief, Electronic Business, Cahners Business Information, 1101 South Winchester Boulevard, Building N, San Jose, CA 95128-3901, phone: (408) 345-4427, fax: (408) 345-4400, e-mail: kdolen@cahners.com, Web: http://www.eb-mag.com. Subscriptions: Cahners Business Information, 8773 S. Ridgeline Boulevard, Highlands Ranch, CO 80126, phone: (800) 662-7776 or (303) 470-4466, fax: (303) 470-4693, e-mail: cahners.subs@denver.cahners.com.

Subscriptions: Free to qualified applicants in U.S. and Canada. Otherwise, check Web site for rates.

This publication is designed exclusively to meet the information needs of the senior electronics executive. It focuses on electronic original equipment manufacturers and related markets for electronics manufacturing and the organizations that supply and distribute electronics. Recipients are corporate, purchasing, engineering management, purchasing, engineering personnel, manufacturing management, sales and marketing management.

Electronic Buyers' News

Published weekly by CMP Media, Inc., 600 Community Drive, Manhasset, NY 11030, phone: (516) 562-5000, fax: (516) 562-7830, e-mail: msheerin@cmp.com, Web: http://www.cmp.com/domesticpubs/elecbuyfiles/elecbuy2.htm.
Subscriptions: Free to qualified applicants in U.S. and Canada.

Subtitled "The Industry Newspaper for Purchasing and Business Management," this publication covers the electronics industry for members of the electronics supply chain—including OEM executives, procurement professionals, distributors, contract manufacturers, and component makers.

Electronic Commerce News

Published weekly (50 issues) by Phillips International, Inc., 7811 Montrose Road, Potomac, MD 20854, phone: (301) 340-2100, fax: NA, e-mail: info@phillips.com, Web: http://www.ectoday.com/. Subscriptions: Client Services, 1201 Seven Locks Road, Suite 300, Potomac, MD 20854, phone: (800) 777-5006 or (301) 424-3338, fax: (301) 309-3847, e-mail: clientservices.pbi@phillips.com.
Subscriptions: $697.

This newsletter, which incorporates *EDI News*, provides news and analysis of electronic commerce technologies and components, such as EDI, E-forms, groupware, integrated messaging, workflow, Internet applications, and security.

Electronic Commerce World

Published monthly by Electronic Commerce Publishing Group, Faulkner & Gray. Editorial: Richard D'Alessandro, Publisher, 300 S. Wacker Drive, Floor 18, Chicago, IL 60606, phone: (954) 925-5900 x 115 or (312) 913-1334, fax: (954) 925-7533 or (312) 913-1365, e-mail: rdallessandro@ecresources.com or ecweditor@ecresources.com (editorial), Web: http://www.ecomworld.com.
Subscriptions: U.S., $34.95 for one year, $59.95 for two years, $74.95 for three years; Canada and Mexico, add $18 per year; other countries, add $50 per year.

This magazine integrates comprehensive editorial and advertising content on electronic commerce implementations, financial EDI, electronic messaging, workflow automation, and shipping to bring management and technology together to provide common ground for executives and middle- to upper-level managers.

EM—Electronic Markets: The International Journal of Electronic Markets
Published quarterly by the Institute for Media and Communications Management and Routledge Publishers. Editorial: Beat F. Schmid, Editor-in-Chief, Institute for Media and Communications Management MCM-HSG, University of St. Gallen, Müller-Friedberg-Strasse 8, CH-9000 St. Gallen, Switzerland, phone: + +41 71 2242297, fax: +41 71 224 2771, e-mail: Beat.Schmid@unisg.ch, Web: http://www.electronicmarkets.com/. Subscriptions: Routledge, 29 West 35th Street, New York, NY 10001, phone: (212) 216-7800, fax: (212) 564-7854, e-mail: journals@taylorandfrancis.com, Web: http://www.routledge-ny.com.
Subscriptions: U.S. and Canada: $75 (individual) and $330 (institutional). Rest of world: £45 sterling (individual) and £200 sterling (institutional).

The journal reports on the principal developments and latest trends in electronic commerce and markets.

European Journal of Purchasing & Supply Management
Published quarterly by Elsevier Science, Inc., Regional Sales Office, Customer Support Department, P.O. Box 945, New York, NY 10159-0945, phone: (212) 633 3730 or (888) 4ES-INFO (437-4636), fax: (212) 633-3680, e-mail: usinfo-f@elsevier.com, Web: http://www. elsevier.com/inca/publications/store/3/0/4/1/6/.
Subscriptions: Europe and Japan: Euro 242.77. Other countries: $271.00.

This journal, for researchers and practitioners, covers every aspect of the purchasing of goods and services in all sectors, including industry and commerce, government, health, and transportation.

European Purchasing and Logistics Strategies
Published irregularly by the International Federation of Purchasing and Materials Management in cooperation with World Markets Research Centre. IFPMM, Secretariat, Rockhgasse 6, P.O. Box 131, A-1014 Vienna, Austria, phone: +43 (1) 533 86 38 78, fax: +43 (1) 533 86 36 79, e-mail: secretariat@ifpmm.co.at, Web: http://www.ifpmm.co.at/ifpmm. WMRC, Academic House, 24-28 Oval Road, London NW1 7DP, England, phone: +44 171 428 3030 (editorial) and +44 171 526 2400 (sales), fax: +44 171 428 3035 (editorial) and +44 171 526 2350 (sales), e-mail: world.markets@wmrc.com, Web: http://www.wmrc.com.
Subscriptions: Free to members of the IFPMM member associations.

The Federation is the union of more than 40 national purchasing associations worldwide, representing about 200,000 purchasing professionals. This journal covers strategic procurement, purchasing management, supply chain management, outsourcing, supplier relationships, logistics, transportation, environment and ethics, and the European context for procurement.

Federal Acquisition Practitioner
Published monthly by Federal Publications Inc.—A West Group Company, 1120 Twentieth Street, NW, Suite 500 South, Washington, DC 20036, phone: (202) 337-7000 or (800) 922-

4330, fax: (202) 659-2233 or (800) 292-4330, e-mail: support@fedpub.com, Web: http://www.
fedpub.com/govtcontracting/fap.html.
Subscriptions: $296.

This is a practical guide for "working-level professionals," to pick up where the policy announcements, the directives, the regulations, and the decisions on contract disputes
and protests leave off."

Federal Buyers Guide
Published semiannually by Federal Buyers Guide, Inc., Peter R Hemming, Publisher, 104
West Anapamu Street, Suite I, Santa Barbara, CA 93101, phone: (805) 963-7470, fax: (805)
963-7483, e-mail: petersb@gte.net, Web: http://www.online-info.com/fbg.html.
Subscriptions: NA.

This magazine is used by government procurement facilities for vendor, product, and
service sourcing. It's intended specifically for government buyers who need to add vendors to their bid lists.

Food Logistics
Published bimonthly by Bill Communications, 355 Park Avenue South, New York, NY 10010-
1789, phone: (212) 592-6200, fax: (212) 592-6619. Editorial: Katherine Doherty, Editor-in-
Chief, phone: (917) 256-2443 or (201) 833-1900, fax: NA, e-mail: kdoherty@ foodlogis-
tics.com, Web: http://www.foodlogistics.com.
Subscriptions: Free to qualified applicants.

This magazine focuses on logistics strategies and practices, particularly those that pertain to managing the movement and storage of materials, products, and related information from any point in the manufacturing process to the point of sale—and beyond.

Forecast
Published monthly by American Demographics, P.O. Box 10580, Riverton NJ 08076-0580,
phone: (800)529-7502 or (203) 358-9900, fax: (203) 358-5833, e-mail: subs@demograph-
ics.com, Web: http://www.demographics.com/publications/fc/index.htm.
Subscriptions: $199.

The editorial focus is predicting trends in demographics—"What's New and What's
Next."

Freight E-Commerce News
Published biweekly by Transport Technology Publishing, 270 Lafayette Street, Suite 700,
New York, NY 10012, phone: (212) 925-1714, fax: (212) 925-7585, e-mail: info@ttp-
news.com, Web: http://www.ttpnews.com.
Subscriptions: North and South America, $545; Europe, £345; elsewhere, £375.

This newsletter, resulting from a merger of *Logistics Technology News* and *Logistics
Technology Europe,* is devoted to covering the issues affecting development and growth of

e-commerce usage in the freight transportation market. Coverage includes detailed accounts of issues including automated customs clearance, the evolution of EDI, initiatives on electronic bills of lading, the latest in on-line shipment tracking, and emerging standards for Internet-based e-commerce.

Global Import-Export Weekly Newsletter
Published weekly by the Golden Bridge Trade Center, 1426 Fisher Avenue, Suite B, Ottawa, ON K2C 1X2, Canada, phone: (613) 228-2950, fax: (613) 228-8987, e-mail: info@goldenbridge.ca, Web: http://www.goldenbridge.ca/letter.html.
Subscriptions: CDN$15 a month.

This newsletter provides import-export information worldwide by connecting buyers with sellers and importers with exporters. There's also an electronic version.

Global Logistics & Supply Chain Strategies
Published 11 times yearly by Keller International Publishing Corporation, 150 Great Neck Road # 4, Great Neck, NY 11021-3309, phone: (516) 829-9210, fax: (516) 829-5414, e-mail: kellpub@worldnet.att.net, Web: NA.
Subscriptions: NA.

This publication, formerly *Global Sites & Logistics*, provides case studies and in-depth reports that offer integrated solutions for managing the flow of materials, information, and funds across all channels, from the supplier's supplier to the customer's customer.

Global Purchasing and Supply Chain Management
Published irregularly by the International Federation of Purchasing and Materials Management in cooperation with World Markets Research Centre. IFPMM, Secretariat, Rockhgasse 6, P.O. Box 131, A-1014 Vienna, Austria, phone: +43 (1) 533 86 38 78, fax: +43 (1) 533 86 36 79, e-mail: secretariat@ifpmm.co.at, Web: http://www.ifpmm.co.at /ifpmm. WMRC, Academic House, 24-28 Oval Road, London NW1 7DP, England, phone: +44 171 428 3030 (editorial) and +44 171 526 2400 (sales), fax: +44 171 428 3035 (editorial) and +44 171 526 2350 (sales), e-mail: world.markets@wmrc.com, Web: http:// www.wmrc.com.
Subscriptions: Free to members of the IFPMM member associations.

The Federation is the union of more than 40 national purchasing associations worldwide, representing about 200,000 purchasing professionals. This journal provides an in-depth analysis of the issues facing global purchasing professionals at the start of the new millennium. The editorial focuses on commentary and research from leading practitioners and academics providing a global information exchange platform. Reports and case studies focus on globalization strategies, electronic procurement, reverse logistics, and other key areas.

Government Procurement

Published bimonthly by Penton Media, Inc., 1100 Superior Avenue, Cleveland, OH 44114-2543, phone: (216) 696-7000, fax: (216) 696-7658, e-mail: sbergen@penton.com, Web: http://www.govpro.com/index.html.
Subscriptions: Free to qualified applicants in U.S. and Canada. Otherwise, $24.

This magazine targets upper-level, public-sector purchasing officials through articles that cover best practices, projects, and methodology, as well as opportunities for professional growth.

Government Purchasing Guide

Published monthly by Moorshead Magazines, Ltd., 10 Gateway Boulevard, North York, ON M3C3T4, Canada, phone: (416) 696-5488, fax: (416) 696-7395, e-mail: gpg@moorshead.com, Web: http://www.moorshead.com/gpg.
Subscriptions: Free to all qualified personnel.

This tabloid is a new products guide for government officials at the municipal, provincial, county, and federal levels of government. Each issue describes about 100 new products, covering industrial, office, maintenance, computer, medical, engineering, safety, and manufacturing products available in Canada.

Health Care Buyers Guide

Published semiannually (January and July), by Federal Buyers Guide, Inc., Peter R. Hemming, Publisher, 104 W. Anapamu Street, Suite I, Santa Barbara, CA 93101, phone: (805) 963-7470, fax: (805) 963-7483, e-mail: petersb@gte.net, Web: http://www.online-info.com.
Subscriptions: $19.95.

This is a directory that helps buyers procure medical supplies, services, and equipment for municipal, county, state, and federal health care facilities.

Healthcare Purchasing News

Published monthly by McKnight Medical Communications, 2 Northfield Plaza, Suite 300, Northfield IL 60093-1219, phone: (800) 451-7838 or (847) 441-3700, **fax:** (847) 441-3701, e-mail: hpn@medec.com, Web: http://www.medec.com/hpn
Subscriptions: Free to qualified applicants.

This tabloid covers the acquisition, management, and disposal of medical products and equipment within health care facilities. It focuses on news and trends affecting the purchase of supplies, capital equipment, and services. It's aimed at directors of hospital purchasing and/or materials management, infection control practitioners, or directors and central supply supervisors.

Hospital Material Management Quarterly

Published quarterly by Aspen Publishers, Inc., 200 Orchard Ridge Drive, Gaithersburg, MD 20878, phone: (800) 562-1973 or (301) 417-7500, fax: (301) 695-7931, e-mail: customer.service@aspenpubl.com, Web: http://www.aspenpub.com.

Subscriptions: NA.

This journal focuses on effective strategies for inventory control, purchasing, staff management, receiving, warehousing, automation, material utilization, and other areas of concern to hospital material managers.

Hospital Materials Management

Published monthly by The Business Word Inc., 5350 S. Roslyn St., Suite 400, Englewood, CO 80111, phone: (303) 290-8500 or (800) 328-3211, fax: (303) 290-9025, e-mail: cassandra.simmons@businessword.com, Web: http://www.businessword.com.
Subscriptions: $279.60.

This newsletter covers materials management and group purchasing. It's aimed at hospital materials managers, purchasing managers, group purchasing organizations, and multi-hospital systems.

ID Systems

Published monthly by Helmers Publishing, Inc., 174 Concord Street, P.O. Box 874, Peterborough, NH 03458, phone: (603) 924-9631, fax: (603) 924-7408, e-mail: editors@idsystems.com or ids-circ@helmers.com, Web: http://www.idsystems.com.
Subscriptions: Free to qualified applicants in U.S. Canada and Mexico, $55. Other countries, $110 (airmail).

This magazine covers trends, best practices, and technologies in Automatic Data Capture, Enterprise Resource Planning, Advanced Planning and Scheduling, e-commerce, Warehouse Management Systems, and other supply chain solutions.

Inbound Logistics

Published monthly by Thomas Publishing Co., 5 Penn Plaza, New York, NY 10001, phone: (212) 629-1560, fax: (212) 629-1565, e-mail: editor@inboundlogistics.com or subscriptions@inboundlogistics.com, Web: http://www.inboundlogistics.com/.
Subscriptions: Free to qualified subscribers in the U.S., Canada, and Mexico. Outside North America, check the Web site.

"The Magazine for Demand-Driven Logistics," this periodical focuses on presenting "new ideas, new technologies, new services, and the best that today's leading carriers and providers can offer to build the logistics system of the future."

Industrial Paint & Powder

Published monthly by Cahners Business Information. Editorial: Jane Bailey, Editor, 2000 Clearwater Drive, Oak Brook, IL 60523, phone: (630) 320-7000, fax: (630) 320-7373, e-mail: jbailey@cahners.com, Web: http://www.ippmagazine.com. Subscriptions: Cahners Business Information, 8773 S. Ridgeline Boulevard, Highlands Ranch, CO 80126, phone: (800) 662-7776 or (303) 470-4000, fax: (303) 470-4546, e-mail: cahners.subs@denver.cahners.com.

Subscriptions: Free to qualified applicants in the U.S. For rates elsewhere, check Web site.

This magazine is intended for buyers and specifiers of paint and powder coatings, coatings application equipment, raw materials and environmental control equipment and services.

Industrial Product Bulletin

Published monthly by Cahners Business Information, Industrial Product Bulletin, Anita LaFond, Editor, 301 Gibraltar Drive, Morris Plains, NJ 07950, phone: (973) 292-5100, fax: (973) 539-3476, e-mail: alafond@cahners.com, Web: http://www.ipb.com.
Subscriptions: Free to qualified applicants.

This magazine is a guide to new products, systems, and equipment service for manufacturing industry professionals.

Industry Week

Published weekly by Penton Media, Inc., 1100 Superior Avenue, Cleveland, OH 44114-2543, phone: (216) 696-7000, fax: (216) 696-7670, e-mail: iwinfo@industryweek.com, Web: http://www.industryweek.com.
Subscriptions: Free to qualified applicants.

This magazine covers manufacturing, mining, contract construction, transportation, communication, utilities, wholesale trade, business services, educational services, engineering, accounting, research, management, and public administration.

International Journal of Electronic Commerce

Published quarterly by M.E. Sharpe. Editorial: Vladimir Zwass, Editor-in-Chief, Journal of Electronic Commerce, 19 Warewoods Road, Saddle River, NJ 07458, phone: (201) 327-9239, fax: (201) 327-3682, e-mail: zwass@alpha.fdu.edu, Web: http://www.cba.bgsu.edu/ijec/. Subscriptions: M.E. Sharpe, Inc., 80 Business Park Drive, Armonk, NY 10504, phone: (800) 541-6563 or (914) 273-1800, fax: (914) 273-2106, e-mail: mesinfo@usa.net.
Subscriptions: U.S., $66 (individual) and $315 (institutional); outside U.S., $79 (individual) and $349 (institution)

This refereed journal is devoted to advancing the understanding and practice of electronic commerce. Launched in summer 1996 as the first scholarly journal devoted exclusively to advancing the understanding and practice of electronic commerce, it serves the needs of researchers as well as practitioners and executives involved in electronic commerce. The journal aims to offer an integrated view of the field by presenting approaches of multiple disciplines.

International Journal of Logistics: Research and Applications

Published three times a year (April, July, and November) by Carfax Publishing, Taylor & Francis Ltd., Customer Services Department, 47 Runway Road, Suite G, Levittown PA

19057-4700, phone: (215) 269-0400, fax: (215) 269-0363, e-mail: enquiry@tandf.co.uk, Web: http://www.carfax.co.uk/jol-ad.htm.
Subscriptions: North America, $70 (individual) and $262 (institutional); elsewhere, £42 (individual) and £156 (institutional).

This journal publishes original and challenging work that has a clear applicability to the business world. As a result the journal concentrates on articles of an academic journal standard but aimed at the practitioner as much as the academic. The term "logistics" is taken in its broadest context with articles crossing the various traditional functional boundaries of the complete supply-chain.

International Journal of Logistics Management
Published semiannually (August and December) by The International Logistics Research Institute, Inc., Marian Kuhn, Program Manager, P.O. Box 2166, Ponte Vedra Beach, FL 32004-2166, phone: (904) 880-8653 fax: (904) 880-8654, e-mail: mkuhn@gw.unf.edu, Web: http://www.unf.edu/dept/logistics/journal.html.
Subscriptions: U.S., $75. Other countries: $85.

This journal aims to be "the global publication that bridges the gap between logistics theory and logistics practice."

International Journal of Physical Distribution and Logistics Management
Published in 10 issue (five dispatches) by MCB University Press Ltd., 60/62 Toller Lane, Bradford, West Yorkshire, England BD8 9BY, phone: +44 (0) 1274 777700, fax: +44 (0) 1274 785200, e-mail: customerservices@mcb.co.uk, Web: http://www.mcb.co.uk/cgi-bin/journal1/ijpdlm.
Subscriptions: North and South America, US$7299.00; Australasia, AUS$9199.00; elsewhere, £4699.00 plus VAT £448.54 or Euro 7059.00 plus VAT Euro 673.81.

This journal covers areas including channel management and relationships, distribution planning and costing, information technology, materials and purchasing management, order processing systems, transport and inventory management, service logistics, and outsourcing.

International Journal of Retail and Distribution Management
Published in 11 issues (six dispatches) by MCB University Press Ltd., 60/62 Toller Lane, Bradford, West Yorkshire, England BD8 9BY, phone: +44 (0) 1274 777700, fax: +44 (0) 1274 785200, e-mail: customerservices@mcb.co.uk, Web: http://www.mcb.co.uk/cgi-bin/journal1/ijrdm.
Subscriptions: North and South America, US$5499.00; Australasia, AUS$6999.00; elsewhere, £3599.00 plus VAT £636.36 or Euro 5399.00 plus VAT Euro 545.09.

This journal covers areas including quality initiatives in retailing and distribution, competitive strategies, lifestyle and store patronage factors, e-commerce, international joint ventures in retailing, store locations, new technology, alternative retail formats, and human resource issues.

International Trade
Published quarterly by the International Trade Association, 1224 North Nokomis NE, Alexandria, MN 56308, phone: (320) 763-5101, fax: (320) 763-9290, e-mail: ita@iami.org, Web: http://www.iami.org/ita.html.
Subscriptions: Free to ITA members. Available for $29.50.
   This newsletter covers developments affecting global trade and provides advice for improving international business.

Internet Public Purchasing Review
Published online by the National Purchasing Institute Inc., 100 N. Arlington Ave., Suite 105, Reno, NV 89501 or P.O. Box 2777, Reno, NV 89505, phone: (702) 332-1NPI or (755) 332-1674, fax: (702) 323-0648, e-mail: triddle@purchasing.co.harris.tx.us, Web: http://npi.purchasing.co.harris.tx.us.
Subscriptions: Free.
   NPI is a national public purchasing affiliate of NAPM serving government, educational, and institutional purchasing professionals.

Inventory Reduction Report
Published monthly by the Institute of Management and Administration, Inc., 29 West 35th Street, 5th Floor, New York, NY 10001-2200, phone: (212) 244-0360, fax: (212) 564-0465, e-mail: subserve@ioma.com, Web: http://www.ioma.com/newsletters/irr/index.shtml.
Subscriptions: $249.
   This newsletter shows how to reduce inventory and cost, better manage materials handling, and improve the company's cash flow and increase its profitability through better inventory management. It includes benchmark information on fill rates, customer service, cycle counting, reducing lead time, improving warehouse and distribution management. Provides hundreds of cost-cutting tactics, evaluations of the latest automation equipment, and exclusive salary data for managers and staff.

Journal for Strategic Outsourcing Information
Published online by InfoServer LLC, 660 Preston Forest Center #388, Dallas, TX 75230-2718, phone: (972) 239-5614, fax: (972) 980-1503, e-mail: info@outsourcing-center.com, Web: http://www.outsourcing-journal.com/.
Subscriptions: Free.
   This online magazine, formerly known as *Infoserver*, presents timely trends in the worldwide outsourcing market from at least three distinct perspectives: the customer, the supplier, and the analyst.

Journal of Business Logistics
Published semiannually (spring and fall) by the Council of Logistics Management, 2805 Butterfield Road, Suite 200, Oak Brook, IL 60523, phone: (630) 574-0985, fax: (630) 574-0989, e-mail: clmadmin@clm1.org, Web: http://www.clm1.org.

Subscriptions: $35.

The journal has an editorial thrust toward applied, real-life articles with a blend of theoretical material.

Journal of Internet Purchasing

Published online bimonthly by ARRAY Development, Inc., 2285 St. Laurent Boulevard, Ottawa, ON K1G 5A2, Canada, phone: (613) 733-4464, fax: (613) 733-5691, e-mail: communications@ARRAYdev.com, Web: http://www.arraydev.com/commerce/JIP.
Subscriptions: Free.

This publication informs purchasing professionals and executives on principal developments, benchmark practices, and future trends in the Internet-based purchasing practices of governments and industry. Through a mailing list, this online journal provides an interactive way to keep in touch, to share information, and to establish business contacts (networking) for purchasing professionals around the world who specialize in electronic commerce solutions.

The Journal of Supply Chain Management: A Global Review of Purchasing and Supply

Published quarterly by the National Association of Purchasing Management, 2055 East Centennial Circle, P.O. Box 22160, Tempe AZ 85285-2160, phone: (800) 888-6276 or (480) 752-6276, fax: (480) 752-7890, e-mail: pcarter@napm.org, Web: http://www.napm.org/.
Subscriptions: Members: in U.S., Canada, and Mexico, $59 for one year, $94 for two years, and $136 for three years; elsewhere, $69 for one year, $109 for two years, and $159 for three years. Nonmembers: add $20 to appropriate member rates.

This journal, which continues the journal formerly known as the *International Journal of Purchasing and Materials Management*, is written specifically for and by purchasing professionals and academicians. It provides in-depth coverage and analysis of management issues, leading-edge research, long-term strategic developments, supplier relationships, and applications.

Logistics and Materials Handling

Published bimonthly by Publishing Services Australia Pty. Ltd., 244 St. Paul's Terrace, Spring Hill, QLD, 4006, Australia, phone: +61 7 3854 1286, fax: +61 7 3252 4829, e-mail: lmh@pubserv.com.au, Web: http://www.pubserv.com.au.
Subscriptions: Australia $45 AUS for one year, $90 AUS for two years; New Zealand, $55 AUS for one year, $110 AUS for two years; elsewhere, $65 AUS for one year, $120 AUS for two years.

This magazine is intended for decision makers throughout the logistics chain, from purchasing materials management and handling to distribution and sea and air cargo.

Logistics Europe

Published monthly by Haymarket Business Publications, Ltd., Nick Allen, Editor, 174 Hammersmith Road, London, W6 7JP, England, phone: +44 0171 413 4176, fax: +44 0171

413 4138, e-mail: Nick.Allen@haynet.com, Web: http://www.logisticseurope.haynet.com. **Subscriptions:** Free to qualified applicants in Europe. Otherwise, £100.

This magazine covers supply chain issues across the continent, presenting management strategies that can create a competitive advantage and cut costs by reducing inventory, controlling purchasing, selecting fewer suppliers, creating partnerships, using efficient handling practices, and applying IT solutions.

Logistics Information Management

Published in six issues (four dispatches) by MCB University Press Ltd., 60/62 Toller Lane, Bradford, West Yorkshire, England BD8 9BY, phone: +44 (0) 1274 777700, fax: +44 (0) 1274 785200, e-mail: customerservices@mcb.co.uk, Web: http://www.mcb.co.uk/cgi-bin/journal1/lim.

Subscriptions: North and South America, US $3369.00; Australasia, AUS$4269.00; elsewhere, £2169.00 plus VAT £216.90 or Euro 3259.00 plus VAT Euro 325.90.

Logistics Information Management covers a broad range of issues, with an emphasis on practical applications. The areas include electronic data interchange (EDI), inventory management, just-in-time (JIT), loading, MRP II, resource allocation, scheduling, supply chain management, through lite-costs (TLC), electronic point of sale (EPOS), and outsourcing.

Logistics Management and Distribution Report

Published monthly by Cahners Business Information. Editorial: Logistics, 275 Washington Street, Newton, MA 02158, phone: (617) 558-4473, fax: (617) 558-4327, e-mail: LM@cahners.com, Web: http://www.logisticmgmt.com/. Subscriptions: Cahners Business Information, 8773 S. Ridgeline Boulevard, Highlands Ranch, CO 80126, phone: (800) 662-7776 or (303) 470-4000, fax: (303) 470-4546, e-mail: cahners.subs@denver.cahners.com.

Subscriptions: Free to qualified readers. For others, check the Web site for rates.

This publication was formed in January 1998 by the merger of *Logistics Management* and *Distribution* magazines.

Material Handling Engineering

Published monthly (13 issues) by Penton Publishing, Dave Gibson, 1100 Superior Avenue, Cleveland, OH 44114-2543, phone: (216) 931-9728, fax: (216) 696-7658, e-mail: dgibson@penton.com, Web: http://www.mhesource.com.

Subscriptions: Free to qualified applicants in U.S. and Canada. Otherwise, $55 in U.S., $70 in Canada (add 7% GST), and $95 in other countries. (10% discount on orders through the Web site.)

This magazine covers products, services, and issues of interest to people involved in engineering and supervision of material handling and packaging in manufacturing and non-manufacturing industries.

Material Handling Product News

Published monthly by Cahners Business Information. Editorial: Joseph Pagnotta, Editor, Material Handling Product News, 301 Gibraltar Drive, Box 650, Morris Plains, NJ 07950-0650, phone: (973) 292-5100 x 272, fax: (973) 539-3476, e-mail: jpagnotta@cahners.com, Web: http://www.mhpn.com/. Subscriptions: Cahners Business Information, 8773 S. Ridgeline Boulevard, Highlands Ranch, CO 80126, phone: (800) 662-7776 or (303) 470-4000, fax: (303) 470-4546, e-mail: cahners.subs@denver.cahners.com.

Subscriptions: Free to qualified applicants.

This tabloid covers the entire range of material handling products—from the loading dock through the manufacturing process to storage and distribution.

Materials Handling and Distribution Magazine

Published bimonthly by The Intermedia Group Pty. Ltd., 747 Darling Street, Rozelle NSW 2039, Australia, phone: 61-2 9818 4111, fax 61-2 9818 4089, e-mail: subscriptions@inter-media.com.au, Web: http://www.intermedia.com.au.

Subscriptions: Australia, $55 AUS; U.S. and Canada, $80 AUS; other areas, check the Web site for rates.

This magazine gives management up-to-date information about leading-edge technology for logistics and supply chain applications.

Materials Management & Distribution

Published monthly by Maclean Hunter Publishing Ltd., 777 Bay Street, Toronto, ON, Canada M5W 1A7, phone: (416) 596-5709 (editorial) or (416) 596-5743 (subscriptions), fax: (416) 596-5554 (editorial) or (416) 596-5905 (subscriptions), e-mail: rrobertson@mhpublishing.com (editorial) or vdesroche@mhpublishing.com (subscriptions), Web: http://www.mhbizlink.com/mmd.

Subscriptions: $46.95 CDN.

Subtitled "Canada's Total Logistics Magazine," this is a supply chain management magazine with an editorial mandate to inform, educate, and help readers involved in the dynamics of integrated logistics do their jobs more cost-effectively.

Materials Management in Health Care

Published monthly by Health Forum, American Hospital Association, Jaime Shimkus, Editor, 737 N. Michigan Avenue, Suite 700, Chicago, IL 60611, phone: (312) 893-6887, fax: (312) 951-8491 or (312) 422-4516, e-mail: shimkus@aha.org, Web: http://www.matman-mag.com/.

Subscriptions: U.S., $35; other countries, $65.

This publication is for health care executives responsible for purchasing, managing, and using supplies, equipment, and resources. It provides news, features, and articles on finance and cost containment, regulatory developments, legal issues, accreditation standards, total quality management, and new technology.

Messaging Magazine
Published bimonthly by the Electronic Messaging Association, 1655 North Fort Myer Drive, Suite 500, Arlington, VA 22209, phone: (703) 524-5550, fax: (703) 524-5558, e-mail: info@ema.org, Web: http://www.ema.org/
Subscriptions: Free to EMA members; U.S., $180; other countries, $225.

This magazine addresses a broad range of subjects concerning messaging, electronic commerce, privacy, security, Internet, directories, public policy, messaging management, the future of messaging, information on EMA events, and similar issues.

Metal Construction News
Published monthly by Modern Trade Communications Inc. Editorial: 109 Portage Street, Woodville, OH 43469, phone: (419) 849-3109, fax: (419) 849-3367, e-mail: mtci@moderntrade.com, Web: http://www.moderntrade.com/mtcinc/mcn.htm. Subscriptions: 7450 N. Skokie Boulevard, Skokie, IL 60077, phone: (847) 674-2200, fax: (847) 674-3676.
Subscriptions: Free to qualified applicants in U.S. Canada and Mexico, $45. Other countries, $125.

This magazine serves the building systems and metal roofing/wall segments of the construction industry. Coverage is devoted to building systems contractors, general contractors, suppliers, manufacturers, metal roofing/wall contractors, building designers, developers, and building owners who provide the world with a lower-cost alternative of energy-efficient commercial, institutional, industrial, residential, and agricultural buildings.

Midrange ERP
Published 10 times a year by Penton Media, Inc., 9 West Street Beverly, MA 01915-2225, phone: (978) 922-1075, fax: (978) 921-1255, e-mail editor@mfg-erp.com, Web: http://www.mfg-erp.com/.
Subscriptions: Free to qualified applicants. Otherwise, $50 for U.S., $80 for Canada and Mexico, and $205 for other countries.

This magazine is for managers in mid-sized manufacturing companies that use or intend to use commercially packaged Enterprise Resource Planning (ERP) software to manage their business information. The focus is on management issues—production and planning, materials and procurement, finance and accounting, sales and marketing, and engineering.

The Minority Supplier News
Published quarterly by the National Minority Supplier Development Council, 1040 Avenue of the Americas, 2nd Floor, New York, NY 10018, phone: (212) 944-2430, fax: (212) 719-9611, e-mail: nseaberr@nmsdcus.org, Web: http://www.nmsdcus.org.
Subscriptions: Check Web site.

This is the official publication of the National Minority Supplier Development Council, distributed to corporate members of the NMSDC and 15,000 certified minority-owned businesses.

Modern Materials Handling

Published 14 times a year by Cahners Business Information. Editorial: Gary R. Forger, Executive Editor, 275 Washington Street, Newton, MA 02458, phone: (617) 558-4234 or (617) 964-3030, fax: (617) 558-4327, e-mail: gforger@cahners.com, Web: http://www. manufacturing.net/magazine/mmh/. Subscriptions: Cahners Business Information, 8773 S. Ridgeline Boulevard, Highlands Ranch, CO 80126, phone: (800) 446-6551 or (303) 470-4000, fax: (303) 470-4546, e-mail: cahners.subs@denver.cahners.com.

Subscriptions: Free to qualified applicants.

This magazine is written for managers and engineers who recommend, select, or buy materials handling systems and equipment for manufacturing and distribution operations. It covers system planning, equipment selection, and operation management for movement, storage, control, and protection of materials and products throughout manufacturing and distribution. It also provides the basic information needed to integrate manufacturing, handling, and information-processing systems under computer control.

Modern Purchasing

Published 10 times a year by Maclean Hunter Publishing Ltd., 777 Bay Street, Toronto, ON, Canada M5W 1A7, phone: (416) 596-5704 (editorial) or (416) 596-5743 (subscriptions), fax: (416) 596-5866 (editorial) or (416) 596-5905 (subscriptions), e-mail: andrewbrooks@mhpublishing.com (editorial) or vdesroche@mhpublishing.com (subscriptions), Web: http://www.mhbizlink.com/purchasing/.

Subscriptions: $47 CDN. In Canada, add 7% GST (GST#R103439444).

This is the national magazine for purchasing and materials managers in private and public sectors. It provides reports on key management issues and business trends and information on management strategies that purchasers need for effective performance. The coverage includes articles on professional development, management techniques, office technology, industrial concerns, transportation (and logistic issues), fleet management, plus new products and services. It's supplemented by a quarterly directory, *Office Products Sourcing Guide.*

MRO Marketplace

Published quarterly by Putman Publishing, 555 West Pierce Road, Suite 301, Itasca, IL 60143, phone: (630) 467-1300, fax: (630) 467-1108, e-mail: pspeer@putmanpublishing.com (editorial) or einselberger@putmanpublishing.com (subscriptions), Web: http://putmanpublishing.com/.

Subscriptions: NA

This magazine delivers the latest products and literature available quarterly to the MRO market.

National Contract Management Journal

Published semiannually by the National Contract Management Association, 1912 Woodford Road, MS-P5, Vienna, VA 22182, phone: (800) 344-8096 or (703) 448-9231, fax:

(703) 448-0939, e-mail: hoskins@ncmahq.org, Web: http://www.ncmahq.org/pubs/journal/journal.html.
Subscriptions: $35.

This is a refereed journal that showcases the research of NCMA members and nonmembers who belong to the procurement community. It has presented articles that run the gamut of policy, legal, and management issues intended to meet the needs of its diverse readers.

NIGP Technical Bulletin

Published bimonthly by the National Institute of Governmental Purchasing, Inc., 151 Spring Street, Suite 300, Herndon, VA 20170-5223, phone: (703) 736-8900 or (800) 367-6447, fax: (703) 736-9644, e-mail: droper@nigp.org, Web: http://www.nigp.org.
Subscriptions: Free with membership.

This newsletter provides information on standards, specifications, procurement methodology, and other technical issues, including cooperative purchasing and technological solutions to purchasing issues.

New Equipment Digest

Published monthly by Penton Media, Inc., Robert F. King, Editor, 1100 Superior Avenue, Cleveland, OH 44114-2543, phone: (216) 931-9269 or (216) 696-7000, fax: (216) 696-7658, e-mail: bking@penton.com, Web: http://www.newequipment.com.
Subscriptions: Free to qualified applicants. Others: U.S., $55; Canada, $80 (plus 7% GST); elsewhere, $106.

This magazine presents concise descriptions and photos of new and/or improved industrial products, materials, components, equipment, and services announced by established companies in the U.S. and by international concerns marketing in the U.S.

Plant Services

Published monthly by Putman Publishing, 555 West Pierce Road, Suite 301, Itasca, IL 60143, phone: (630) 467-1300, fax: (630) 467-1108, e-mail: pspeer@putmanpublishing.com (editorial) or einselberger@putmanpublishing.com (subscriptions), Web: http://www.plantservices.com.
Subscriptions: U.S., $95; other countries, $140 (surface mail) or $250 (airmail).

"Dedicated to maintenance, repair, and operations in manufacturing," this magazine addresses the problems of plant engineers at mid-to-large manufacturing plants, from automating equipment and systems to upgrading equipment and facilities during production shutdowns.

PRACTIX: Best Practices in Purchasing and Supply Chain Management

Published quarterly by the Center for Advanced Purchasing Studies, National Association of Purchasing Management, P.O. Box 22160, 2055 E. Centennial Circle, Tempe, AZ 85285-

2160, phone: (480) 752-2277, fax: (480) 491-7885, e-mail: reports@capsresearch.org, Web: http://www.capsresearch.org.
Subscriptions: $25 each issue, available individually or by subscription, electronic and hard copy.

This publication—named *Praxis* until March 1999—presents "policies, procedures, and programs, referred to as the critical success factors, that top performers are using that lead to superior performance."

Procurement Law Advisor

Published monthly by Management Concepts, Inc., 8230 Leesburg Pike, Suite 800, Vienna, VA 22182, phone: (703) 790-9595, fax: (703) 790-1371, e-mail: info@ManagementConcepts.com, Web: http://www.mgmtconcepts.com/publications /pubacp.htm.
Subscriptions: $249.

This newsletter tracks, reports, and analyzes court, board, and GAO cases that constitute emerging law on procurement issues, providing guidance to both contractors and government personnel.

Producer Price Indexes

Published monthly by the Superintendent of Documents, U.S. Government Printing Office. Order from New Orders, Superintendent of Documents, P.O. Box 371954, Pittsburgh, PA 15250-7954, phone: (202) 512-1800, fax: (202) 512-2250, e-mail: blsdata_staff@bls.gov, Web: http://stats.bls.gov.
Subscriptions: $34.

This publication presents a comprehensive report of price movements at the producer or wholesale level, arranged by stage-of-processing and by industry.

Professional Purchasing

Published monthly by the American Purchasing Society, 430 W. Downer Place, Aurora, IL 60506, phone: (630) 859-0250, fax: (630) 859-0270, e-mail: Propurch@aol.com, Web: http://www.american-purchasing.com.
Subscriptions: Free with APS membership. For nonmembers, $89 (individual) or $99 (corporate).

This newsletter provides information on buying and on managing purchasing departments, news about benefits of membership, discounts on books, and announcements of positions available.

Progressive Purchasing

Published quarterly by the Purchasing Management Association of Canada, 2 Carlton St., Suite 1414, Toronto, ON M5B 1J3 Canada, phone: (416) 977-7111, fax: (416) 977-8886, e-mail: info@pmac.ca, Web: http://www.pmac.ca.
Subscriptions: Free with PMAC membership.

This magazine covers techniques, news, and trends and Purchasing Management Association news. Text is in English and French.

The Public Purchaser
Published bimonthly by Governing Magazine in affiliation with the National Institute of Governmental Purchasing. Penelope Lemov, Editor, 1100 Connecticut Avenue, NW, Suite 1300, Washington, DC 20036, phone: (202) 862-8802, fax: (202) 862-0032, e-mail: plemov@governing.com, Web: http://www.governing.com/tpp.htm.
Subscriptions: $19.95 for one year, $34.95 for two years, $49.95 for three years.

This magazine for government purchasing professionals tracks new practices, emerging trends, and changing roles in government procurement systems in the United States and Canada.

Purchaser's Legal Adviser
Published monthly by Business Laws, Inc., 11630 Chillicothe Road, P.O. 185, Chesterland, OH 44026, phone: (440) 729-7996 or (800) 759-0929, fax: (440) 729-0645, e-mail: inquiry@businesslaws.com, Web: http://www.businesslaws.com/comm.htm#purlegadv.
Subscriptions: $177.

This newsletter covers legal developments affecting purchasing. It discusses recent cases and applies them to the issues at hand, addressing the legal aspects of contracting, particularly Article 2 of the UCC, writing purchase orders, and negotiating better terms and conditions.

Purchasing Magazine
Published 19 times a year by Cahners Business Information. Editorial: Kevin Fitzgerald, Editor-in-Chief, 275 Washington Street, 3rd Floor, Newton, MA 02158-1630, phone: (617) 964-3030, fax: (617) 558-4327, e-mail: kevinf@cahners.com, Web: http://www.purchasing.com. Subscriptions: Cahners Business Information, 8773 S. Ridgeline Boulevard, Highlands Ranch, CO 80126, phone: (800) 446-6551 or (800) 662-7776 or (303) 470-4000, fax: (303) 470-4546, e-mail: cahners.subs@denver.cahners.com.
Subscriptions: U.S., $99.90; Canada, $147.90 (includes 7% GST); Mexico, $138.90; elsewhere, $197.90 (surface mail) or $273.90 (air expedited).

The "Magazine of Total Supply Chain Management" for purchasing professionals in all manufacturing, *Purchasing* reports and interprets news, forecast prices and market conditions, and generates proprietary information on transaction prices, lead times, and overall buying conditions.

Purchasing Management Bulletin
Published semi-monthly by Bureau of Business Practice, 24 Rope Ferry Road, Waterford, CT 06386, phone: (800) 243-0876 or (860) 442-4365, **fax:** (860) 437-3150, e-*mail:* deborah_cottrill@prenhall.com, Web: http://www.bbpnews.com.
Subscriptions: $139.80.

This newsletter identifies trends and developments that are making efficient purchasing essential to success in the industry. It details techniques used by the most successful purchasing organizations.

Purchasing Today

Published monthly by the National Association of Purchasing Management, Julie Murphree, Editor, 2055 East Centennial Circle, P.O. Box 22160, Tempe, AZ 85285-2160, phone: (800) 888-6276 or (480) 752-6276, fax: (480) 752-7890, e-mail: jmurphree@napm.org, Web: http:// www.napm.org/.
Subscriptions: Free to NAPM members.

The mission of the magazine is to create and distribute purchasing-related business news and forecasts, as well as innovative, educational, technical, and practical information to purchasing and supply professionals. It now includes *InfoEdge*, formerly a monthly publication, as a supplement, to focus on a single topic, with tactical, ready-to-use tips and applications for purchasing and supply management professionals.

The Source

Published quarterly by The Outsourcing Institute, 500 North Broadway, Suite 141, Jericho, NY 11753, phone: (800) 421-6767 or (516) 681-0066, fax: (516) 938-1839, e-mail: editor@outsourcing.com, Web: http://www.outsourcing.com.
Subscriptions: Complimentary to Institute members. Available for $29.95 per issue. For shipping and handling, add $4.95 in the U.S. and $6.95 outside the U.S.

This review features articles and insight from industry leaders and experts in the area of outsourcing, lessons learned, and marketplace information and executive events. It tracks trends and issues in the outsourcing marketplace as they impact both buyer and seller, such as managing the outsourcing relationship, privatization, negotiating successful contracts, and the economics of outsourcing.

Southern Purchasor

Published quarterly by the Purchasing Management Association of Carolinas-Virginia, Inc., Editorial and Business Office, 5601 Roanne Way, Suite 312, Greensboro, NC 27409-2932, phone: (336) 292-9228, fax: (336) 292-8415, e-mail: speditor@napm-cv.org, Web: http://www.napm-cv.org/southern_purchasor1.htm.
Subscriptions: Free.

This magazine focuses on chain supply management education and related topics.

State & County Government Vendors Registry

Published quarterly by Federal Buyers Guide, Inc., Peter R Hemming, Publisher, 104 W. Anapamu Street, Suite I, Santa Barbara, CA 93101, phone: (805) 963-7470, fax: (805) 963-7483, e-mail: petersb@gte.net, Web: http://www.online-info.com.
Subscriptions: $19.95.

This directory is used by government procurement facilities for vendor, product, and service sourcing. It's intended specifically for government buyers who need to add vendors to their bid lists.

State, County & Municipal Government Purchasing Guide
Published quarterly by Federal Buyers Guide, Inc., Peter R Hemming, Publisher, 104 W. Anapamu Street, Suite I, Santa Barbara, CA 93101, phone: (805) 963-7470, fax: (805) 963-7483, e-mail: petersb@gte.net, Web: http://www.online-info.com/state.html.
Subscriptions: NA.
This directory helps procurement officers across the United States find reliable sources for all types of equipment, supplies, and services.

Supplier Selection and Management Report
Published monthly by the Institute of Management and Administration, 29 West 35th Street, 5th Floor, New York, NY 10010-2299, phone: (212) 244-0360 or (800) 401-5937 (subscriptions), fax: (212) 564-0465, e-mail: kmandal@ioma.com or subserve@ioma.com, Web: http://www.ioma.com/nls/.
Subscriptions: $269.
This newsletter shows purchasing and materials managers how to choose suppliers with confidence and ensure consistent quality and timeliness.

Supply Chain & Logistics Journal
Published quarterly for the Canadian Association of Logistics Management by Naylor Publications Co. Editorial: CALM, J. David Long, President, 610 Alden Road, Suite 201, Markham, ON, L3R 9Z1 Canada, phone: (905) 513-7300, fax: (905) 513-1248, e-mail: journal@calm.org, Web: http://www.calm.org/calm/quarterly/aalq0.html. Subscriptions: Naylor Publications Co. (Canada), 920 Yonge Street, Suite 600, Toronto, ON M4W 3C7 Canada, phone: (416) 961-1028, fax: (416) 924-4408, e-mail: journal@calm.org or kristin@toro.naylor.com.
Subscriptions: For members only.
This is the official publication of the Canadian Association of Logistics Management, titled *Logistics & Supply Chain Journal* until the summer 1999 issue.

Supply Chain Management: An International Journal
Published in five issues (four dispatches) by MCB University Press Ltd., 60/62 Toller Lane, Bradford, West Yorkshire, England BD8 9BY, phone: +44 (0) 1274 777700, fax: +44 (0) 1274 785200, e-mail: customerservices@mcb.co.uk, Web: http://www.mcb.co.uk/cgi-bin/journal1/scm.
Subscriptions: North and South America, US$399.00; Australasia, AUS$479.00; elsewhere, £239.00 plus VAT £20.31 or Euro 359.00 plus VAT Euro 31.41.
This journal is broad based, but with a strategic focus, covering aspects of marketing, logistics and information technology, economics, management, and organizational behavior in relation to the operation of supply chains in all sectors.

Supply Chain Management Review
Published quarterly by Cahners Business Information. Editorial: Supply Chain Management Review, 275 Washington Street, Newton, MA 02458, phone: (888) 240-7324 or (617) 558-4474, fax: (617) 558-4327, e-mail: scmr@cahners.com, Web: http://www.manufacturing.net/scl/. Subscriptions: SCMR, P.O. Box 15565, N. Hollywood, CA 91615-9655, phone: (888) 343-5567 or (818) 487-4558, fax: NA, e-mail: custserv@espcomp.com.
Subscriptions: U.S., $179; outside the U.S., $207.

This journal is dedicated to the art and science of moving goods to market. It covers a wide range of supply chain management issues, with in-depth feature articles, exclusive columnists, professional development opportunities, and reviews of current books and other information resources.

Supply Chain Technology News
Published monthly by Penton Media, Inc., 1100 Superior Avenue, Cleveland, OH 44114-2543, phone: (216) 931-9673, fax: (216) 696-7658, e-mail: info@penton.com, Web: NA.
Subscriptions: Free to qualified applicants.

Launched in September 1999 and scheduled to be published monthly starting in January 2000, this magazine focuses on the practical application of technology in supply chain operations such as purchasing, transportation logistics, information systems, manufacturing, warehousing, sales and marketing, and customer service. It provides news and brief "best practice" features for using technology to improve efficiency and reduce costs.

Supply Management
Published biweekly by the Chartered Institute of Purchasing and Supply, Easton House, Easton on the Hill, Stamford, Lincolnshire, PE9 3NZ, England, phone: 44 (0)1780 756777, fax: 44 (0)1780 751610, e-mail: info@cips.org, Web: http://www.cips.org/bookshop/journals.asp
Subscriptions: Complimentary for members.

This magazine combines international and UK news coverage, features, regular columns on the law and academic research, book and video reviews, Institute news, and a special section on key prices and economic indicators. (This publication has subsumed *Procurement Weekly*, *Purchasing and Supply Management*, *Logistics*, and *Pactum Serva*.)

Traffic World
Published weekly by Traffic World Magazine. Editorial: Clayton Boyce, Editor, 1230 National Press Building, Washington, DC 20045, phone: (202) 661-3372 or (202) 783-1101, fax: (202) 661-3383, e-mail: clayton_boyce@trafficworld.com, Web: http://www.trafficworld.com. Subscriptions: 445 Marshall Street, Phillipsburg, NJ 08865, phone: (800) 331-1341 or (908) 859-1300, fax: (908) 454-6192, e-mail: circulation@trafficworld.com.
Subscriptions: $174.

This magazine provides industry news for the transportation and logistics community.

Transportation & Distribution

Published monthly by Penton Media, Inc., Perry A. Trunick, Editor, 1100 Superior Avenue, Cleveland, OH 44114-2543, phone: (216) 931-9274 or (216) 931-9547 (editorial) or (216) 931-9188 (subscriptions), fax: (216) 696-6413 (subscriptions), e-mail: ptrunick@penton.com, Web: http://www.penton.com/td.

Subscriptions: Free to qualified applicants in U.S. and Canada. Otherwise, $50 in U.S., $70 plus 7% GST in Canada, and $90 in other countries.

This magazine is directed to people who guide the efficient flow of material and information from original sources, through a series of integrated logistics processes, to meet the requirements of their customers. It incorporates integrated warehousing and distribution, global logistics, and bimonthly supply chain flow supplements, targeting readers with special interest in these segments of supply chain management.

Transportation Research Part E: Logistics and Transportation Review

Published quarterly by Elsevier Science, Inc., Regional Sales Office, Customer Support Department, P.O. Box 945, New York, NY 10159-0945, phone: (212) 633 3730 or (888) 4ES-INFO (437-4636), fax: (212) 633-3680, e-mail: usinfo-f@elsevier.com, Web: http://www.elsevier.com/inca/publications/store/6/0/0/2/4/4/index.htt.

Subscriptions: Europe and Japan: Euro 382.08. Other countries: $428.

This journal publishes articles from across the spectrum of logistics and transportation research. The aims and scope of Part E of *Transportation Research* are complementary to Part A (Policy and Practice), Part B (Methodological), Part C (Emerging Technologies), and Part D (Transport and Environment).

Warehousing Forum

Published monthly by The K.B. Ackerman Company, 1328 Dublin Rd., Columbus, OH 43215, phone: (614) 488-3165 or (614) 488-3166, fax: (614) 488-9243, e-mail: sales@warehousing-forum.com, Web: http://www.warehousing-forum.com.

Subscriptions: $96.

This newsletter covers everything related to warehouses.

Warehousing Management

Published monthly by Cahners Business Information. Editorial: Michael Lear-Olimpi, Editor-in-Chief, 201 King of Prussia Road, Radnor, PA 19089, phone: (610) 964-4385 or (610) 964-4310, fax: (610) 964-4381, e-mail: mlearolimpi@cahners.com, Web: http://www.warehousemag.com. Subscriptions: Cahners Business Information, 8773 S. Ridgeline Boulevard, Highlands Ranch, CO 80126, phone: (800) 662-7776 or (303) 470-4000, fax: (303) 470-4546, e-mail: cahners.subs@denver.cahners.com.

Subscriptions: Free to qualified applicants.

The mission of this magazine is to optimize distribution and warehouse performance.

World Trade Magazine

Published monthly by Business News Publishing Company, World Trade Magazine, 17692 Cowan, Suite 100, Irvine, CA 92614, phone: (949) 798-3500, fax: (949) 798-3501, e-mail: tims@link.freedom.com, Web: http://www.worldtrademag.com.

Subscriptions: $24 for one year, $39 for two years.

This magazine is targeted to the senior management of mid-sized American manufacturers actively involved in exporting and importing, as well as the service industries supporting their efforts.

Purchasing and Supply Management Resources Online

The Internet is an excellent source of information resources on virtually everything, including any part of the supply chain. The purpose of this part of our yearbook is to provide a good sampling of what's out there on the 'Net that can help you do your job more effectively and efficiently.

Since most World Wide Web sites have links to other sites, with the sites listed below you're just a few clicks away from many more sites. The same is true of discussion lists: you're often just a query away from other lists, through suggestions by cyber colleagues. At the end of these lists, in "Going Beyond These Resources," we provide more help so you can find other discussion lists, newsgroups, and Web sites so you can get what you need from the 'Net.

What You'll Find Here

Our directory consists of four categories of online resources:

- **Internet Discussion Lists**. These are free mailing lists that allow members (subscribers) to send e-mail messages to a central location, which then copies the messages to all members of that group. Some mailing lists are for distribution only: they send members information (usually publications or other resources), but don't allow members to post messages.
- **Internet Newsgroups**. These are informally managed, open forums, unlike discussion lists, which are by membership. Each is like a bulletin board, where anybody can post a message of any sort for anybody else to read. Although the term is "*news*groups," the content is often ads and chatty conversations, but the groups allow you to connect with people who can provide information and opinions about virtually anything in the world.
- **World Wide Web Sites**. These are sites hosted by associations, companies, and other organizations. You access these sites (pages) using a Web browser such Netscape Navigator or Microsoft Internet Explorer.
- **Going Beyond These Resources**. This is a list of Web sites that can help you find more discussion lists, newsgroups, and Web sites.

The Internet has grown and expanded in the last few years. There's something for everybody and information to meet every need—if you can find it. Some of the discussion groups bring together experts and we can gain a lot from their exchanges; others are more like discussions around the water cooler. There are many Web sites that are treasures, while others are basically infomercials or more glitter than gold. Also, discussion groups and Web sites are time-sensitive. The groups are like any other types of association: the value to any member depends on what the other members are contributing at any given time. Many of the sites suffer from inadequate maintenance as they age; some move to other addresses or just disappear.

We can't list every site, of course. We're simply offering some suggestions for you to explore the opportunities out there ... and wish you good luck. It's also impossible to be comprehensive with any listing of 'Net resources. We've simply tried to mention some of the best lists and sites and to show the variety out there.

If you'd like to recommend a list or a site that we haven't included here, please e-mail us at jwoods@execpc.com.

Discussion Lists and E-Mail Newsletters

To join a discussion list or subscribe to an e-mail newsletter, you simply send an e-mail message to the computer that maintains the list (usually known as listserv, listproc, majordomo, or mailbase). This is called *subscribing*. Since you're just giving a command to a computer, you usually leave your subject line blank and your message consists of only the command (usually "subscribe"), the name of the list, and generally your first and last names.

This may seem confusing if you're new to discussion lists, so for each of the groups below, we give you the e-mail address and specify the message to send.

When you subscribe to a list, you should receive an introductory message that describes the purpose of the group, what you can expect, and how to participate. This message will also tell you how to stop your subscription ("unsubscribe") if you don't find it of value. Save this list: it takes up very little space on your hard drive or printed out, but it can help you avoid embarrassment and frustration.

Complex Industries Special Interest Group (CISIG)
Discussion forum for professionals in complex industries focusing on the integrated resource tools of project management, configuration control, product data management, regulatory affairs, and systems engineering
Subscribe through the Web site: **http://www.apics.org/joinlists.htm**

E.surplus
Distribution lists announcing bids, contracts, and items appearing in *Commerce Business Daily*, the federal government's central clearinghouse for bid requests, contract notifications, and notices of surplus equipment
Subscribe through the Web site: **http://www.esurplus.com/signup.htm**

Forest Sector Logistics Research
Address: logistics-forest-subscribe@egroups.com
Message: (blank)

GBOT Trade Leads
Global Board of Trade distribution list of postings: international trade contacts, products, and services—offers and requests—in any industries chosen by subscriber
Subscribe through the Web site (fee): **http://www.tradenet.org**

GTON—Global Trade Opportunities Newsletter
Distribution list for product advertisements and demands among exporters, importers, and other firms
Address: majordomo@esosoft.com
Message: subscribe GTON

Logistics
For people involved in the logistics or distribution industry at management level
Address: Logistics-subscribe@onelist.com
Message: (blank)

Logistics Automation
Monthly newsletter on automating logistics: Willett International, Ltd.
Address: logistics-automation-subscribe@onelist.com
Message: (blank)

Logistics Research Network
Research ideas and developments in logistics and supply chain management
Address: mailbase@mailbase.ac.uk
Message: join logistics-research-network firstname lastname

NOFOMA Network (Nordic Research in Materials Management)
Address: nofoma-subscribe@eGroups.com
Message: (blank)

Procurement
Distribution and discussion list that addresses all matters relating to government procurement
Subscribe through the Web site: **http://www.financenet.gov/financenet/start/sub/procure.htm**

Purchasing Pros
Address: Purchasingpros-subscribe@onelist.com
Message: (blank)

Purchasing Supply Chain
All aspects of purchasing and supply chain management, and interorganizational theory: International Purchasing and Supply Education and Research Association
Address: mailbase@mailbase.ac.uk
Message: join purchasing-supply-chain firstname lastname

SCM-Food
Address: mailbase@mailbase.ac.uk
Message: join scm-food firstname lastname

Supply Management
Address: mailbase@mailbase.ac.uk
Message: join supply-management firstname lastname

Trade
Daily distribution of commercial advertising exclusively for businesses engaged in wholesale buying/selling of large-lot merchandise and commodities internationally
Address: trade@intl-trade.com
Subject: subscribe

Trade-News
Distribution list for two weekly bulletins: Trade Week in Review and NAFTA Monitor, with a list of articles, books, videos, and upcoming conferences
Address: kmander@igc.apc.org
Message: subscribe Trade-News e-mail address

World Trade Zone
Posting of buy/sell/seek/company profile announcements for products and services in international trade
Address: requests@lists.worldtradezone.com
Message: subscribe WTZ-INTRADELEADS

Newsgroups

To access a newsgroup, simply use your Web browser and enter "news://" followed by the address, e.g., news://alt.hypertext.

alt.business.import-export (business aspects of international trade)

alt.business.import-export.only (import-export trade, moderated)

alt.business.import-export.computer (international trade in computers) alt.business.import-export.food (international trade in food)

alt.business.import-export.raw-material (international trade in raw materials)

alt.business.import-export.services (international trade in services)

World Wide Web (WWW) Sites

What follows is our directory of Web sites, organized alphabetically. The addresses can sometimes be confusing, even overwhelming. We'll just mention that sites in the U.S. contain a suffix—usually "com," "edu," "org," or "gov." Sites in other countries end in a two-digit code, such as "ca" for Canada, "uk" for the United Kingdom, and "au" for Australia. Also, remember that Web addresses may be case-sensitive.

Access Global Trade Exchange, Inc.
http://www.access-trade.com
This site features the Global Business Toolkit, an "easy, fast, and affordable" way to market products and services internationally, source foreign products and services, and find critical business, economic, and trade information.

Aluminium Industry WWW-Server
http://www.aluminium.net
This is a resource site for anybody in aluminum.

American Export Register
http://www.aernet.com
This is a multilingual sourcing directory (six languages) containing more than 45,000 American suppliers in over 5,500 product and service categories. The focus is on exports.

AMM Online: The World Metals Information Network
http://www.amm.com
AMM Online is the international news service of *American Metal Market*, the daily newspaper of the metals and recycling industries published by Cahners. Subscribers can access the entire site; other visitors get only limited access. The site presents news, a reference desk, and a prices menu.

APICS Online
http://www.apics.org
This site by APICS—The Educational Society for Resource Management. The site primarily promotes the association, but there are also links to other Web resources.

Asian Sources Online
http://www.asiansources.com
This site features "product and trade information for volume buyers." Search for suppliers or products or by country.

BidCast
http://www.bidcast.com
This site features government contract opportunities: subscribers can search the database or receive announcements by e-mail.

BidMatch Buyer's Assistant
http://www.bidmatch.com/assistant.html
Purchasers complete a request form for products or services and the information is posted within 24 hours and e-mailed to vendors.

BioAPI Consortium
http://www.bioapi.org
The BioAPI Consortium was formed to develop a widely available and widely accepted application programming interface (API) that will serve for various biometric technologies. This site provides information on this organization.

Biometric Consortium
http://www.biometrics.org/html/testcenter.html
The Biometric Consortium serves as the U.S. government's focal point for research, development, test, evaluation, and application of biometric-based personal identification/verification technology. This site provides information and links to articles, associations, and other Web resources.

BioSpace.com
http://www.biospace.com
If you need to purchase anything in the areas of biotechnology and phramaceuticals, visit "The Hubsite for The World's Most Exciting Industry." Visitors can also sign up to receive BioSpace News daily e-mail reports.

BizWeb
http://www.bizweb.com
BizWeb searches the Internet for company and product information. Companies are categorized and listed by the goods or services they provide.

Business World
http://www.dks.com/dks/businessworld
This is a commercial Internet mall with a global focus.

Buyer's Guide to Electronic Commerce
http://www.e-com.com/buyersguide
This site provides information and resources on e-commerce.

Buyer's Zone
http://www.buyerszone.com
BuyersZone provides purchasing advice and online shopping for small to mid-sized business, helping with purchasing decisions on products and services.

BuyLines2000
http://www.innovativepurchasing.com/
This site was established by Innovative Purchasing Resources, Inc., to serve as a tool for purchasing and supply management organizations that want to use the Internet to more effectively manage the supply chain.

Center for Advanced Purchasing Studies
http://www.capsresearch.org
The Center produces research reports and hosts International Executive Roundtables. This is the place to find out more about the center and order reports.

Centre for International Trade
http://www.centretrade.com
Centre for International Trade (CIT) is a member organization established to improve, facilitate, and expand international trade. It has 3,500 members around the world, including embassies, government agencies, trade associations, companies, firms, and individuals. The members network and offer courtesy discounts to each other. The site provides information on national rules, regulations, procedures, and trade opportunities, as well as industry news. There are also products, services, training, publications, links, and a discussion forum. CIT publishes a free newsletter, *International Trader*, and the site provides access to back issues.

The Chartered Institute of Purchasing and Supply
http://www.cips.org
CIPS is an international non-profit organization representing purchasing and supply chain professionals. This site has a good resources area that links to many of the purchasing and supply organizations around the world, particularly in Europe.

China External Trade Development Council (CETRA)
http://www.tptaiwan.org.tw
CETRA, a non-profit government-sponsored professional trade promotion association based in Taiwan, helps with sourcing in the Asia-Pacific Region. It offers a wide range of

474 **Part Seven. Purchasing and Supply Management References and Resources**

trade-related periodicals, directories, and market reports in Chinese and English. The Web site is maintained in collaboration with Taipei World Trade Center, a non-profit trade promotion organization in Taiwan.

CIO Magazine's Government Resource Center
http://www.cio.com/CIO/rc_govt.html

This site provides information on government issues, such as EC/EDI, procurement reform, and more.

CommerceNet
http://www.commerce.net

This is the site of a non-profit consortium of about 150 organizations that want to stimulate e-commerce on the Internet.

Computer Information Center
http://www.compinfo-center.com/tpedi-t.htm

"These pages provide links to sites and resources concerned with the burgeoning cashless society. These include Electronic Commerce, Electronic Data Interchange (EDI), Digital Cash, Secure Credit Card Transactions, Digital Signatures and other related subjects."

Consumer World
http://www.consumerworld.com

Consumer World®—which purports to be "*The* Consumer Resource Guide"—is a public service, non-commercial site that presents more than 1800 of the most useful consumer resources on the Internet, categorized for easy access. Visitors can find buying advice and read product reviews and comparisons.

Council of Logistics Management Online Logistics Bibliography
http://www.clm1.org/Bibliography/index.asp

This is a database of over 10,000 abstracts of logistics-related articles. It replaces CLM's annual *Bibliography of Logistics Management*, which will no longer be printed. The bibliography includes abstracts and full bibliographic citations of articles from current periodicals and journals from 1997 to the present and abstracts that appeared in the printed versions for 1993, 1994, 1995, and 1996. The bibliography is updated weekly.

DeveloPages
http://www.developages.com/

DeveloPages brings together corporations that have specific needs with companies that meet their product development requirements, using a database of more than 15,000 companies involved in the design and manufacturing industries.

e-Chemicals
http://www.e-chemicals.com
This site sells chemicals, but it also features industry news and industry events.

EcomWorld
http://www.ecomworld.com
EcomWorld is "the Online Magazine for EC Professionals." This site is centered on the print publication, *Electronic Commerce World*, but there are other resources, including news, an events calendar, and discussions.

ElectroNet
http://www.electronet.com
This site features three databases for electronics: manufacturers, distributors, and sales representatives—factory-authorized sources for over 1,500 component manufacturers. Visitors can do online requests for quotes.

Electronic Buyers' News Online
http://techweb.cmp.com/ebn/942/index.html
This is an online magazine for electronics purchasers.

Electronic Commerce Association (ECA)
http://www.eca.org.uk
This is the home page of the ECA, an association that promotes electronic commerce.

Electronic Commerce and the European Union
http://www.ispo.cec.be/ecommerce/Welcome.html
This is the official site of the European Commission for supporting and promoting electronic commerce in member countries of the European Union.

Electronic Commerce Europe
http://www.ec-europe.org
ECE, an international non-profit association, was founded in March 1997 to promote, coordinate, and assist in the development of electronic commerce in Europe.

Electronic Commerce Guide
http://ecommerce.internet.com
To get up to speed on electronic commerce and to keep up with developments, this could be a good site to bookmark. It provides news, product reviews, a library (articles, journals, white papers), a Link Vault, and a "webopedia" of the most up-to-date terms, definitions, and acronyms in electronic commerce. There are also a free weekly electronic newsletter, discussion forums, and an electronic discussion list.

Electronic Commerce Research Center
http://www.cio.com/forums/ec
"From small business to multinational, Electronic Commerce will change the way you do business. This Research Center examines the current state and future directions of conducting commerce on the Net."

Electronic Commerce Resource Center
http://www.ecrc.ctc.com
The ECRC Program is sponsored by the Department of Defense's Joint Electronic Commerce Program Office. There are 17 regional offices, which "serve as a catalyst for a vast network of small- and medium-sized enterprises to adopt electronic commerce."

Electronic Commerce Resource Center
http://www.becrc.org
This site promises "comprehensive e-commerce and Internet business and government resources for beginners to experts, help in becoming better cheaper faster." It offers a good variety of links, categorized for convenience, and a free quarterly newsletter. Since this is a regional site located in Bremerton, WA, the focus of the events listings is on the Northwest, but most of the resources are of value to all visitors.

Electronic Commerce Resource Guide
http://www.premenos.com/frames/home.html
This guide from Premenos Software includes an overview of EDI standards and links to interesting Web sites for EDI users.

Electronic Commerce Today
http://www.ectoday.com
This electronic commerce information site requires a site license.

ERP Supersite
http://www.erpsupersite.com
This site devoted to Enterprise Resource Planning provides news, forums, books, and information related to ERP and ERP products.

ERP/Supply Chain Research Center
http://www.cio.com/forums/erp
This site provides articles, links, and information about events and vendors.

E.surplus
http://www.esurplus.com
If you're interested in government contracts and/or surplus property, this is the place. Visitors can search through recent back issues of *Commerce Business Daily*, the federal

government's central clearinghouse for bid requests, contract notifications, and notices of surplus equipment, covering federal agencies and offices domestic and abroad. There are also distribution lists to inform subscribers of bids, contracts, and items appearing in each issue of CBD. There are fees for some services.

ETA Forum
http://www.webcom.com/legaled/ETAForum
This site is a public forum on the Uniform Electronic Transactions Act.

Europages: The European Business Directory
http://www.europages.com
This site indexes 500,000 companies in 30 countries. Visitors can search by product/service or company name.

Federal Acquisition Reform Network
http://www.arnet.gov
This site focuses on providing information on acquisition reform and federal regulations.

Federal Electronic Commerce Program Office
http://www.ec.fed.gov
This is the resource for information on what the federal government is doing about conducting business electronically.

Federation of International Trade Associations (FITA)
http://www.fita.org
This site provides links to 1000 annotated and indexed Web resources. It also features a global book store, trade leads posted daily from around the world, and a searchable list of seminars, conferences, and trade shows relating to international trade. Trade Hub identifies a few hundred systems that list offers to buy and sell on a wholesale basis internationally.

FreeMarkets OnLine Inc.
http://www.freemarkets.com/
FreeMarkets® creates business-to-business online markets for *Fortune* 1000 and Global 1000 companies. These online markets are real-time interactive bidding events between pre-qualified suppliers that enable buyers to purchase industrial materials and components at true market prices. This type of market interaction is a fundamentally new way for buyers to negotiate prices and for suppliers to generate low-cost sales.

GE Trading Process Network
http://tpn.geis.com
GE TPN Post is an Internet-based trading network that enables buyers and sellers to do business-to-business electronic commerce, including transactions. It started in early 1995 as an

internal GE corporate initiative, but it's now a commercial offering from GE Information Services. Visitors can join the network as buyers or as sellers.

Global Board of Trade
http:// www.tradenet.org
The slogan for this site says it all—"Broadcasting Trade Leads to the World." Visitors can select an industry and check trade leads, then go to the "Trade Floor" to exchange trade information "in a secured and confidential manner."

Golden Bridge Trade Center
http://www.goldenbridge.ca
This site is billed as "The Most Comprehensive and Efficient Source for International Trade Leads." Golden Bridge publishes (in paper and electronic versions) the *Global Import-Export Weekly Newsletter,* which provides import-export information worldwide by connecting buyers with sellers and importers with exporters. There's a registration fee for accessing the on-line trade center, $15CDN/month.

Global Contact Online
http://www.globalcontact.com
This Web site was developed to offer free information to help companies locate products and services worldwide. There's also news and information related to the world of international trade and transportation and import/export legal information. Global Contact also allows searches of *The Directory of U.S. Companies* and *The NAFTA Register.*

The Global Forum for Marketing & Logistics
http://www.mcb.co.uk/mlf/
This forum is hosted by MCB, publisher of *Logistics Information Management* and *Supply Chain Management.* This arena provides "current awareness," including interactive services and a comprehensive resources archive, intended for "practitioners, academics, authors, and anyone interested in developing their knowledge of this area." The focus is primarily on marketing and distribution.

Global Information Network
http://www.ginfo.net
It's easier to keep up with what's affecting business around the world with a resource like this, "The Search Engine for Global Business." It's a well-organized source of sources.

The Global Procurement & Supply Chain Benchmarking Initiative
http://gebn.bus.msu.edu/
The primary mission of this initiative is to study the best procurement and supply chain strategies, practices, and processes used by companies worldwide. The site features the Strategic Self-Assessment System, an on-line, real-time benchmarking application launched in July 1996. Companies that are members of the Benchmarking Initiative can

complete strategic self-assessments about their procurement and supply chain strategies and practices, submit data, and receive immediate comparison feedback.

Global Procurement Group
http://www.globalpg.com
This site features a short list of international procurement resources on the Internet.

GlobalSpec.com
http://www.globalspec.com
This site provides a free service: engineers or technical buyers can plug in their specs to do a 'parametric search' through a database of products from hundreds of suppliers.

Global Trade Center
http://www.tradezone.com
Global Trade Center provides many international trade services for manufacturers, importers, exporters, trade service businesses, and opportunity seekers. This site features international trade business opportunities, free import-export trade leads, a trade bulletin board, and links to traders' Web sites. The focus is more on export than on import.

Grainger Business Catalog
http://www.grainger.com
W.W. Grainger, Inc.'s online catalog featuring more than 90,000 MRO supplies from the leading business-to-business distributor of MRO supplies and related information.

Health Care Buyers Expo
http://www.healthcarebuyers.com
This site is intended to give health care purchasers a comprehensive and immediate search facility for locating products and services.

i2 Fans Club
http://www.i2fans.com/
The goal of this site is to serve users of i2 Technologies products. It provides information on supply chain management, access to user forums on i2 products, chat rooms, articles, and books.

IBC-Forum
http://www.arraydev.com/commerce/JIBC/forum.htm
The forum is an electronic discussion on Internet banking and commerce sponsored by the publisher of *The Journal of Internet Purchasing*.

Import Export Bulletin Board
http://www.iebb.com

The IEBB is inteded to be the premier international trade lead site on the Internet, to serve as a one-stop shop for trade leads and other import-export resources, "The Home on the Internet for Professional International Trade."

Incoterms
http://www.iccwbo.org/home/incoterms/menu_incoterms.asp
"Incoterms," standard trade definitions for use throughout the world, are established periodically by the International Chamber of Commerce. This site provides information and copies of *Incoterms 2000* are available through the Business Bookstore (**http://www.iccbooks.com**).

The Industrial Purchasing Guide
http://key.cyberg8t.com/qry/pglst.html
The purpose of the purchasing guide is to provide a single location where purchasers of industrial products can go to find the materials and services they need in their business. There are 18 categories: Automotive, Chemicals, Coatings, Construction, Consultants, Distributors, Electronics, Financial, Food, Machinery, Metals, Office Equipment, Packaging, Printing, Retail, Tools, Travel and Recreation, and Other.

Industry Link
http://www.industrylink.com
This site provides links to suppliers and resources in 20 industries.

Industry Net
http://www.industry.net
Featuring "the Web's largest collection of online product catalogs" and information on companies and products, this site offers one-stop shopping.

Industry Network Canada Inc.(INCAN)
http://www.incan.net
Industry Network Canada Inc. is a full-feature business tool to help members of Canada's industrial community in promoting their products and services. Visitors can search the database by company, product, or province.

Industry Search
http://industrysearch.com
This site provides access to a database of over 350,000 U.S. manufacturing companies and free searches for suppliers and manufacturers by state and keyword.

Institut du Management de l'Achat Industriel (MAI)
http://www.mai-purchasing.com

This site, hosted by a postgraduate purchasing program, features a very good collection of links for sourcing in Europe and the Americas, with some coverage of the rest of the world.

International Business Resource Center
http://www.ibrc.bschool.ukans.edu/
The International Business Resource Center in the University of Kansas School of Business helps small and medium-sized companies broaden their international business skills and explore available international trade opportunities through this collection of international business and trade resources.

International Purchasing and Supply Education and Research Association (IPSERA)
http://www.ipsera.org
This site provides information about IPSERA, access to a discussion forum and a discussion groups, and links to other sites of interest.

International Purchasing Associates
http://www.intpur.com/
International Purchasing Associates is a sourcing service. For over 25 years the goal has been to provide companies with top-quality service and products at lower prices. IPA claims to be able to find anything—and at prices lower than the competition. It allows comparison shopping with office supplies stores.

International Purchasing Service
http://ipserv.com/links.html
The Page of Links for Purchasing Agents and Buyers—"Places to Find and Buy and Do Stuff," directories and search engines, and professional resources.

InternationalWorkz
http://www.internationalworkz.com/
This site is the "global eBusiness toolkit." There are resources for building a global business online, managing an international businmess, and promoting and marketing worldwide, as well as news and references.

Internet Purchasing
http://www.informational.com/purchase.htm
This site offers an assortment of links to resources—information, supplier directories, and categories of suppliers.

Inventory Depot
http://www.inventorydepot.com
This is an industrial and commercial "auction" trading center for surplus inventories of materials, supplies, products, and equipment.

The Journal of Commerce Online
http://www.joc.com

The JOC—"The Daily Journal of Trade Logistics"—provides news on global trade and transportation as well as information and insights about companies, markets, products, and issues, and a collection of links organized in categories.

Journal of Internet Purchasing
http://www.arraydev.com/commerce/jip

This online magazine for purchasing over the Internet focuses on developments and trends in Internet-based purchasing practices. There's also a free quarterly email edition. This publication informs purchasing professionals and executives on principal developments, benchmark practices, and future trends in the Internet-based purchasing practices of governments and industry.

Kompass
http://www.kompass.com

Kompass is a worldwide network of companies specialized in business-to-business information databases of products and services. This site boasts access to 1.5 million companies and 23 million products and services in more than 60 countries. It allows free extensive regional specific searches by allowing multiple searches of numerous country-specific industrial directories. The site allows for easy currency conversion calculations. The site can be accessed in five languages—English, French, German, Spanish, and Italian.

Krislyn's Favorite Purchasing Sites
http://www.krislyn.com/sites/purchase.htm

This page offers a collection of links selected by the Krislyn Corporation.

Logistics Management & Distribution Report Online
http://www.manufacturing.net/magazine/logistic/default.html

This site for supply chain professionals provides news items, several articles from *Logistics Management & Distribution Report,* and links to trade associations of interest to logistics managers.

The Logistics Network
http://www.logisticsnetwork.com

This is the "Gateway to Business Logistics on the Internet." It offers some lists of links and a logistics discussion forum.

LogisticsWorld
http://www.logisticsworld.com/logistics/

A guide to logistics, freight, transportation, warehousing, distribution, supply, maintenance, manufacturing, management, reliability, mathematics, business, and quality sites on the Web. Maintained by Matthew Cox, this is an overwhelming accumulation of links—for organizations, publications, news, projects, colleges and universities, and more.

LogLink: Transportation and Logistics Links
http://www.loglink.net
This site categorizes links of interest and allows for searches.

Manufacturer's Information Net
http://www.mfginfo.com/
This site provides information for manufacturers and services related to manufacturing. There's a search engine to locate information on manufacturers, suppliers, professional services, and many more resources on and off this site.

Material Control: Purchasing and Material Management Resources
http://www.materialcontrol.com/links.html
This is an eclectic collection of sites, with an emphasis on electronic commerce.

Materials Management & Distribution Online
http://www.mmdonline.com/
This is the site of a supply chain management magazine, but it's not just an on-line version of the magazine: it's a separate entity, with logistics news, features, and links Internet resources. There's a directory of suppliers throughout Canada.

Materials Management in Health Care
http://www.matmanmag.com/mat-home.html
This site features *Materials Management in Health Care*. It allows access to current issues as well as an archive search.

Mectronic.net
http://mectronic.net
This is a one-stop source for electronic, electrical, and mechanical products and services. There's a database of manufacturers, distributors, and service providers.

Mercado Magazine
http://www.mercadousa.com
Mercado Magazine is a commercial information publication that reaches the Latin American business audience interested in establishing commercial ties with wholesalers, exporters, importers, and manufacturers in the U.S. *Mercado Magazine* is distributed internationally in U.S. embassies, to business associations, and at trade shows and conferences. It has a monthly circulation of 40,000.

Metal Suppliers Online
http://www.suppliersonline.com
This is a good place to visit for sourcing metals.

MexPlaza
http://mexplaza.com.mx/mexplaza/english/
This is a directory to various businesses in Mexico, arranged by category.

The Mining Company: Purchasing Site
http://purchasing.miningco.com/
This page offers a variety of links to organizations, publications, products, and other resources related to purchasing, provided by a cyber company that produces Web sites with specialized links.

MLTWEB: Resources for Purchasing Professionals
http://www.mltweb.com/mltweb.htm
This site "is assembled and maintained by Michael L. Taylor, C.P.M., for the benefit and enjoyment of his friends and fellow purchasing professionals."

Modern Purchasing
http://www.mhbizlink.com/purchasing/
This site, which promotes the magazine *Modern Purchasing*, allows archives searches, hosts an online discussion group, and provides a calendar of trade shows and some basic links.

MRO Central: Plant Services on the Web
http://198.110.248.107
The focus of this site is the magazine *Plant Services*, but there are other resources, including directories and discussion groups.

MRO Explorer
http://www.mro-explorer.com
This site provides a search engine that looks for industrial organizations. It has considerable potential, but it's fairly new, so listings are limited.

MSU-CIBER
http://ciber.bus.msu.edu/busres.htm
This is an index to international business resources on the Web and at the Michigan State University Center for International Business Education and Research (MSU-CIBER). The index can be browsed by category or searched by words.

NAFTA Net
http://www.nafta.net
This site is maintained by NAFTAnet, Inc., a provider of information, telecommunications, implementation, and consultative services in electronic commerce/electronic data interchange (EDI), international trade, and NAFTA. It also maintains the Centro Electrónico de Negocios NAFTAnet.

National Association of Purchasing Management (NAPM)
http://www.napm.org
This site provides information about NAPM and qualified access to "News and Resources."

NAPM Silicon Valley
http://www.catalog.com/napmsv/
This site is maintained by the Silicon Valley chapter of the National Association of Purchasing Management as "The Information Resource for the Purchasing & Supply Management Professional." It features an online reference library for purchasing supply base managers.

National Conference of Commissioners on Uniform State Laws (NCCUSL)
http://www.nccusl.org/
The National Conference of Commissioners on Uniform State Laws was formed in 1892. NCCUSL is composed of more than 300 lawyers, judges, and law professors, appointed by the states as well as the District of Columbia, Puerto Rico, and the U.S. Virgin Islands, to draft proposals for uniform and model laws and work toward their enactment in legislatures. NCCUSL is jointly responsible with the American Law Institute for drafting, updating, and promulgating the Uniform Commercial Code (UCC). The site provides information about the organization and its activities.

National Initiative for Supply Chain Integration, Ltd. (NISCI)
http://www.nisci.org
This non-profit organization was founded to develop the most effective solutions to optimize the performance of supply chains composed of three or more links. Visitors can enter click the NICSI Intranet (password: Demo100) and take a tour of the NISCI Process.

Oanda
http://www.oanda.com/converter/classic
This site features perhaps the best conversion utility on the Web. It allows conversions among 164 currencies and displays history for any day since 1 January 1990. It also allows a choice of various conversion rates and displays median, minimum, and maximum prices.

Outsourcing Center
http://www.outsourcing-center.com

The Outsourcing Center presents information about the outsourcing industry—books, articles, research, events, a database of outsourcing suppliers, events of interest, and other resources.

Outsourcing Interactive
http://www.outsourcing.com

Visitors to this site by the Outsourcing Institute can read news, check out events, join the outsourcing network, and participate in the discussion forum.

Outsourcing Journal
http://www.infoserver.com

This is an online journal with many features and resources. Visitors to this site can register to be notified by e-mail whenever a new issue is posted and/or to receive an electronic version of the journal.

Outsourcing Research Center
http://www.cio.com/forums/outsourcing

This page features articles from *CIO* magazine and an events calendar.

PANGAEA.NET: Interactive Global Marketplace
http://www.pangaea.net/igm/articles.htm

PANGAEA.NET is the online service of PANGAEA, a global marketing and strategic business development consulting. The Interactive Global Marketplace section of the site features articles and insights from experienced businesspeople regarding international business and trade issues, including country-specific observations, brand- or industry-related issues, and legal challenges.

PartnerBase
http://www.partnerbase.com

This is a dedicated resource for companies seeking international trade partners.

PartNET
http://part.net

This is a directory of electronic, electromechanical, and mechanical parts—with a difference. Purchasers can bring together information from multiple suppliers to form a "virtual catalog" that fits their buying needs.

ProcureNet
http://www.procurenet.com/

"The Electronic Mall of the future for buyers, suppliers and distributors," ProcureNet has been designed to help buyers simplify the purchasing process and to help suppliers and distributors by grouping them with other vendors who market to the same customers.

Pronet Global Interactive Business Centre
http://pronet.ca
This site features searches of a business database by topic, by city or nation, or by word. There are also at least 50 forums.

Purchasing A2Z
http://www.purchasinga2z.com
This site features links to purchasing and electronic commerce resources.

Purchasing Guide
http://www.purchasingguide.com
This "buyer-supplier network" allows visitors access to 130,000 suppliers throughout U.S. Buyers can further select GSA suppliers, 8A suppliers, or minority- and woman-owned small business suppliers, as well as suppliers accepting credit cards.

Purchasing Home Page
http://members.aol.com/DennisKQV/purch.htm
This page offers links and other resources of interest to purchasing professionals.

Purchasing Manager's Forum
http://www.execforum.com/
This is an online community of purchasing professionals, serving a global community of purchasing managers, supply management executives, and buyers. Registration is free, but limited to purchasing professionals. Registered members have access to *A Buyer's Guide to the Internet* ("the top 1,000 internet sites and services to rely on for valuable information about suppliers, markets, prices, and purchasing best practices"), purchasing discussion groups, and a purchasing resource library (articles, documents, web sites, and useful templates from around the world).

Purchasing Online
http://www.manufacturing.net/magazine/purchasing/
This site offers news, a few articles from *Purchasing Magazine,* a bookstore (books by *Purchasing*), a reference desk, and a software mart.

Purchasing Resources: Purchasing Office of The University of Texas at Austin
http://www.utexas.edu/ftp/depts/purchasing/list.html
Here are links of interest to college and university procurement staff.

The Purchasing Station
http://management.bus.okstate.edu/faculty/christensen/index.htm
This site, maintained by William Christensen, of Christensen Consulting & Training, specialists in international purchasing and global sourcing, offers a great variety of links.

Purchasing Web
http://www.catalog.com/napmsv/pwhead.htm
This site consists of links to articles for the supply management professional. Unfortunately, the articles are primarily from 1994 through 1997.

RFQ Data, Inc.
http://www.rfqdata.com
Companies can use this site to enter their requests for quote and make them accessible to vendors throughout the world. There's a monthly fee.

Stanford University Global Supply Chain Forum
http://www.stanford.edu/group/scforum
This forum was established to identify, document, research, develop, and disseminate the best practices, as well as innovations in supply chain management in order to advance teaching and research in global supply chain management. Some sections of this site are for members only.

The Supply-Chain Council, Inc.
http://www.supply-chain.org
This site is devoted to supply chain management and more specifically to the Supply-Chain Process Reference Model, which helps companies evaluate their supply-chain performance, identify weak areas, develop solutions for improvement, and compare the costs of improvements against the expected returns.

Supply Chain Link
http://www.manufacturing.net/scl/
This Cahners Business Information site features news from Lexis-Nexis and the Cahners "supply chain magazines."

Supply Chain Management Resource Web Page
http://www.createcom.8m.com/
This page lists links to a wide variety of sites of interest to practitioners, researchers, and consultants.

The Supply Chain Organisation
http://www.supply-chain.org.uk
This is the web site gateway to many valuable resources available to managers and researchers in the field of supply chain management.

Supply Chain Super Links
http://www.goldata.com.au
This site claims to be "the most comprehensive internet link to the world's best Supply Chain resources." Some of these resources are accessible at no charge, but others are available by paid subscription only.

Telephone Directories on the Web
http://teldir.com
This is the Internet's most comprehensive index of online directories, with links to yellow pages, white pages, business directories, e-mail addresses, and fax listings from all around the world.

Thomas Register of American Manufacturers
http://www2.thomasregister.com/
This site features a search by company or product in U.S. or Canada. Registration is required, but it's free.

Thomas Register of European Manufacturers
http://tipcoeurope.com
This site is a buying guide that provides immediate access to 155,000 industrial suppliers in 17 European countries.

TIPS (Trade and Technological Information and Promotion System)
http://www.redtips.org
TIPS is touted as "the largest integral and informative e-commerce network available for doing business." This service was designed specifically for small and medium-sized enterprises. TIPS processes and disseminates offers and demands gathered directly from companies—particularly SMEs.

TradeBook
http://www.tradebook.com
TradeBook is a business directory of products and inquiries for on-line trade all over the world. Any company can search all products and inquiries and register its products and inquiries free of charge.

Trade Compass
http://www.tradecompass.com
This site provides an impressive array of international business information and tools including: news feeds, shipping schedules, trade leads, trade statistics, market reports, cargo tracking, trade show database, company directories, company intelligence, and country trade statistics.

TradePort
http://tradeport.org
This is proclaimed to be "the premier international trade web site on the Internet." That may be true if you want to sell, but if you need to buy, this site offers little of interest.

TradeWinds
http://www.intl-trade.com
TradeWinds Publishing, a company that focuses on the electronic publication of information to promote International Trade, hosts this site that provides trade leads and access to an international trade law library.

Trade Winds Online
http://www.trade-winds.net
This is a library of magazines and directories from the Far East.

Uniform Code Council, Inc.
http://www.uc-council.org
This site provides information and news about on bar codes and electronic commerce. There's also a glossary.

Universal Currency Converter
http://xe.net/currency or www.xe.net/currency
This site gives exchange rates of all foreign currency. It's updated daily.

VerticalNet
http://www.verticalnet.com
VerticalNet leverages the interactive features and global reach of the Internet to create multi-national, targeted business-to-business communities. These narrowly focused Web sites attract buyers and sellers from around the world by with similar professional interests. This site provides links to Web sites that feature industry-specific directories, news, listings, trade leads, and job postings.

Virtual Logistics Directory
http://www.logisticdirectory.com
The Virtual Logistics Directory provides an open, objective and comprehensive directory of logistics resources on the Web, compiled by Craig T. Hall.

Website Formerly Known as The 2BGuide
http://www.webcom.com/legaled
This site provides information and news about the Uniform Computer Information Transactions Act, adopted by the National Conference of Commissioners on Uniform State Laws, July 29, 1999.

WIZnet eCommerce Portal
http:// www.wiznet.net/
Formerly known as "The Purchasing Extranet," this portal consists of a portal for buyers and a portal for suppliers. It provides potential purchasers with access to supplier information, secure negotiation, and commerce capabilities for a price. Users pay a one-time fee and then a rate per hour of usage to access the portal with passwords and conduct natural language searches across a database of 100,000 catalogs from more than 90,000 suppliers. Purchasing pros can designate their preferred suppliers, with contractual pricing, and can limit lower-level buyers' access to these pre-arranged relationships.

WLW Online
http://web.wlwonline.de/
This site—accessible in nine languages, including English—allows searches for suppliers in Europe. (The WLW comes from "Wer liefert was?"—Who Supplies What?) Visitors can search among 238,500 companies in 10 countries, by product/service or company name.

World Access Network Directory
http://wand.com
WAND claims to be "the world's largest directory of products and services." It's an interactive multi-language global sourcing tool that matches buyers and sellers.

WorldBid.com
http://www.worldbid.com
WorldBid claims to be "the World's Largest Source of Free Business-to-Business Trade Leads." Purchasers can search among offers to sell by word or phrase, category, or codes—SIC, Harmonizing, and NAICS—or sign up to receive by e-mail offers in any categories they select. There's no cost and the interface is neat and efficient.

World Trade Centers Association
http://iserve.wtca.org
The World Trade Centers Association is an organization of over 300 world trade centers in more than 100 countries, connected to expand global business. Registered visitors can search through the Trade Opportunities Bulletin Board.

World Trade Organization
http://www.wto.org
This site features information about the WTO and events of importance to global trade.

WorldTradeZone
http://www.worldtradezone.com/wtzlist.html
WorldTradeZone sponsors 28 lists: one general (WTZ-INTRADELEADS) and 27 market sector lists. The Web site provides information on participating in the lists and a searchable archive.

World Wide Yellow Pages
http://www.yellowpages.com
This site provides a convenient means of finding any business in the United States.

WWW Virtual Library: Logistics
http://209.51.193.25/logistics
This is a good place to begin any search for resources related to logistics.

X-Rates
http://www.x-rates.com
Visitors to this site can calculate currency exchange rates (updated daily), buy currencies, and check histories (7, 30, 90, and 120 days) of exchange rate fluctuations for each currency listed.

Going Beyond These Resources

The 'Net is a huge universe and growing at an amazing speed. Even the most comprehensive directory would be inadequate as soon as it's compiled. Any listing of Internet resources in a yearbook should include some instructions so you can find other discussion lists, and Web sites to meet your specific needs.

To find other *discussion lists*, you can use the search functions of the following Web sites:

http://www.liszt.com
Through this site you can search among over 90,000 mailing lists by word or by category.

http://www.neosoft.com/internet/paml
This site allows searches for publicly accessible mailing lists.

http://catalog.com/vivian/interest-group-search.html
This site is operated by Vivian Neou, author of the book, *Internet Mailing Lists Navigator*.

http://tile.net/lists
This site allows searching for discussion lists and ftp sites and Usenet newsgroups.

http://www.lsoft.com/lists/listref.html
CataList is "the *official* catalog of listserv lists," with information on about 27,000 public lists, out of more than 132,000.

To find other *newsgroups*, we recommend the following Web sites:

http://tile.net/lists
This site allows searching for Usenet newsgroups, discussion lists, and ftp sites.

http://deja.com
This site allows for several types of searches. You can find groups according to interest,

you can search through the thousands of messages by keyword, and you can browse the groups systematically, by hierarchy. (You'll probably find "biz" to be the best top-level hierarchy, "misc" might provide something of interest, and "alt" and "rec" and "talk" might be the least productive.)

To find other *Web sites*, you can use any of dozens of search engines. The following are among the best at this time:

http://www.alltheweb.com
http://www.hotbot.com
http://www.altavista.com
http://www.google.com
http://www.yahoo.com
http://metasearch.com
http://www.dogpile.com
http://www.all4one.com
http://www.search.cnet.com
http://www.infoseek.go.com
http://go.excite.com
http://www.lycos.com
http://www.webcrawler.com
http://www.thebighub.com

Search engines use varying protocols, but the procedures are fairly easy if you read the instructions on each site.

Also check out these two sites:

http://www.searchenginewatch.com
This site presents everything you might like to know about search engines and a lot more.

http://www.seekhelp.com
This is "the one-stop source for all the information you'll ever need to search the Internet."

Directory of Purchasing and Supply Management Associations and Organizations

What follows is a reasonably comprehensive directory of associations and organizations in areas of relevance to purchasing and supply management. What you'll find here is the association or organization name, contact (if known), address, phone and fax numbers, e-mail (if available), and Web page (if available), along with a brief description of what the organization does, to give you an idea of its potential value to you with regard to purchasing and supply management.

If there are organizations that you think we should include here, please let us know about them. Just e-mail us at jwoods@execpc.com and then we'll get more information about the organization to include in future editions of this yearbook.

AFT-IFTIM
Bernard Prolongeau, Président délégué
  général
46, avenue de Villiers
75 847 Paris cedex 17
France
Phone: +33 1 42 12 50 50
Fax: +33 1 42 12 50 10
E-mail: webmaster@aft-iftim.asso.fr
Centre de Ressources
60290 Monchy Saint-Eloi
France
Phone: 03 44 66 36 36
Fax: 03 44 74 06 69
E-mail : cdr@aft-iftim.asso.fr
Web: http://www.aft-iftim.asso.fr
AFT-IFTIM aims to be the leader in professional training in the areas of transportation, logistics, and tourism.

AIM, Inc.
634 Alpha Drive
Pittsburgh, PA 15238-2802
Phone: (412) 963-8588
Fax: (412) 963-8753
E-mail: aidc@aimglobal.org
Web: http://www.aimi.org
AIM (Automatic Identification Manufacturers) is the worldwide authority on automatic identification, data collection, and networking in a mobile environment. AIM is the global trade association of providers and users of components, networks, systems, and services that manage the collection and integration of data with information management systems.

**American Association of Exporters and
  Importers**
11 West 42nd Street, 30th Floor
New York, NY 10036
Phone: (212) 944-2230
Fax (212) 382-2606

E-mail: AAEICLZ@aol.com

Web: http://www.aaei.org/

The American Association of Exporters and Importers, with over 1,000 U.S. member firms, is the only national association specifically representing U.S. corporations involved in both importing and exporting before the Executive Branch, Congress, and the regulatory agencies. AAEI maintains a liaison with the U.S. Customs Service, the Commerce Department, the Food and Drug Administration, USDA, USTR, ITC and other agencies that impact the importing and exporting community.

American National Standards Institute (ANSI)

11 West 42nd Street, 13th Floor

New York, NY 10036

Phone: (212) 642-4900

Fax: (212) 398-0023

E-mail: ansionline@ansi.org

Web: http://www.ansi.org

The American National Standards Institute is a private, nonprofit membership organization that administers and coordinates the U.S. private sector voluntary standardization system. Its primary goal is to help U.S. business be more competitive globally and to improve the quality of life by promoting and facilitating voluntary consensus standards and conformity assessment systems and promoting their integrity.

American Production and Inventory Control Society (see APICS)

American Productivity and Quality Center

123 North Post Oak Lane, 3rd Floor

Houston, TX 77024

Phone: (800) 776-9676 or (713) 681-4020

Fax: (713) 681-8578

E-mail: apqcinfo@apqc.org

Web: http://www.apqc.org

APQC is a nonprofit education and research organization that helps companies and the public sector improve. It runs the International Benchmarking Clearinghouse, focusing on benchmarking and the development of best practices, and offers training and other resources in many areas. It publishes a magazine, *Continuous Journey*, and books.

The American Purchasing Society

Harry Hough, President

American Purchasing Society, Inc.

430 W. Downer Place

Aurora, IL 60506

Phone: (630) 859-0250

Fax: (630) 859-0270

E-mail: propurch@aol.com

Web: http://www.american-purchasing.com

The American Purchasing Society is an organization of buyers, purchasing managers, executives, and others interested in the purchasing profession. It was founded in 1969 and has members from every state and 28 countries worldwide. Its objective is to improve the business purchasing function through education and its certification program. The APS publishes the *Directory of Buyers and Purchasing Executives*, and *Professional Purchasing* (monthly newsletter), as well as reports (including an annual salary survey report and an annual benchmarking report), booklets, manuals, and training guides for APS members.

American Society for Quality, Inc.

611 E. Wisconsin Avenue

Milwaukee, WI 53202

Phone: (800) 248-1946 or (414) 272-8575

Fax: (414) 272-1734

E-mail: cs@asq.org

Web: http://www.asq.org

ASQ is a society of individual and organizational members dedicated to the ongoing, development, advancement, and promotion of quality concepts, principles, and techniques. Its vision is to advance individual and organizational performance excellence worldwide by providing opportunities for learning, quality improvement, and knowledge exchange.

American Society for Testing and Materials

100 Barr Harbor Drive

West Conshohocken, PA 19428-2959

Phone: (610) 832-9585 or (610) 832-9500

Fax: (610) 832-9555

E-mail: infoctr@astm.org

Web: http://www.astm.org

The mission of this organization is "to be the foremost developer and provider of voluntary consensus standards, related technical information, and services having internationally recognized quality and applicability that promote public health and safety, and the overall quality of life; contribute to the reliability of materials, products, systems and services; and facilitate national, regional, and international commerce."

American Society of Transportation and Logistics, Inc.

320 East Water Street
Lock Haven, PA 17745
Phone: (570) 748-8515
Fax: (570) 748-9118
E-mail: info@astl.org
Web: http://www.astl.org
AST&L is a professional organization founded in 1946 by a group of industry leaders to ensure a high level of professionalism and promote continuing education in the field of transportation and logistics. It publishes *Transportation Journal*, a quarterly.

American Warehouse Association (AWA)

Michael Jenkins, President & CEO
1300 W. Higgins Road, Suite 111
Park Ridge, IL 60068-5764
Phone: (847) 292-1891
Fax: (847) 292-1896
E-mail: logistx@aol.com
Web: http://logistx.dartgc.com/
The American Warehouse Association is a 106-year-old international trade association representing companies involved in public and contract warehousing and third-party logistics. It promotes the growth and success of third-party warehousing and related logistics services and works to promote a high standard of business ethics within the industry and keep its members informed on trends, technology, research, legislation, and regulations impacting the logistics industry.

APICS—The Educational Society for Resource Management

5301 Shawnee Road
Alexandria, VA 22312-2317
Phone: (800) 444-2742 or (703) 354-8851

Fax: (703) 354-8106
E-mail: j_battin@apics-hq.org or international@apics-hq.org
Web: http://www.apics.org
Founded in 1957 as the American Production and Inventory Control Society, this organization has since expanded its focus to include a full range of programs and materials on individual and organizational education, standards of excellence, and integrated resource management. It's a not-for-profit international organization with more than 70,000 individual and corporate members in 20,000 companies worldwide. APICS publishes *APICS—The Performance Advantage* and holds an annual international conference and exposition.

APICS Region VIII

3 Church Street, Suite 604
Toronto, ON M5E 1M2
Canada
Phone: (416) 366-5388 or (800) 567-8207
Fax: (416) 862-0315
E-mail: apicstor@inforamp.net
Web: http://www.apics8.org/
Region VIII of APICS, formerly known as the Canadian Association for Production and Inventory Control (CAPIC), is a society of over 3,500 professionals engaged in materials and operations management.

Arbeitsgemeinschaft Einkauf Forum für Beschaffung, Materialwirtschaft und Logistik OPWZ

Bibiane Sibera, Sekretariat
Postfach 131
Rockhgasse 6
A-1014 Wien
Austria
Phone: 43 1 533 86 36 - 56
Fax: 43 1 533 86 36 - 72
E-mail: bibiane.sibera@opwz.com
Web: http://www.opwz.com/Einkauf/index.htm
The primary goal of this organization is the development of the professional areas of purchasing, materials management, and logistics.

**Associação Portuguêsa de Compras e
Aprovisionamento (APCADEC)
(Portuguese Purchasing and Supply
Management Association)**
Alameda das Linhas de Torres, 201 – 3° dto.
P-1700 Lisboa
Portugal
Phone/Fax: +351 1 758 5348
E-mail: NA
Web: NA
APCADEC is a sponsor of the European Council of
Purchasing and Supply Eurodiploma.

**Associação Portuguêsa de Logistica
(APLOG) (Portuguese Logistics
Association)**
Reboleira
Praça Felix Correia no 2
P-2720 Amadora/Lisboa
Portugal
Phone: (351 1) 496 20 64 or (351 1) 496 20 65
Fax: (351 1) 495 44 04
E-mail: NA
Web: NA

**Asociación Española de Responsables de
Compras y Existencias (AERCE)
(Spanish Association of Purchasing and
Supply)**
Rosellón, 184, 7°. 4°.
E-08008 Barcelona
Spain
Phone: +34 93 4532580
Fax: +34 93 4534567
E-mail: info@aerce.org
Web: http://www.aerce.org
AERCE is a nonprofit association that serves per-
sons who are primarily involved with purchasing
(procurement), logistics, transportation, and ware-
housing and who are interested in these areas.
AERCE provides its members free of charge
Gestión de Compras, a quarterly publication on
purchasing and materials management in Spain.
AERCE also publishes *Estudio de Coyuntura de
Materiales y Productos de Compra e Índices de
Precios de Compras,* a quarterly report that features

original research data from a survey of purchasing
managers working in all sectors of commerce,
industry, and public service in Spain. AERCE is a
sponsor of the European Council of Purchasing
and Supply Eurodiploma.

**Association Belge des Cadres d'Achat et de
Logistique (ABCA) (Belgian Association
of Purchasing and Logistics Executives)**
Jean-Paul Trum, secretary
c/o CIBE
Rue aux Laines 68-70
B-1000 Bruxelles
Belgium
Phone: +32 2 518 82 30
Fax: +32 2 518 82 20
E-mail: NA
Web: NA
ABCA is a sponsor of the European Council of
Purchasing and Supply Eurodiploma.

**Association for EC Professionals
International (AECPI)**
15153 Kittrell Drive
Spring Hill, FL 34610
Phone: (727) 862-0108
Fax: NA
E-mail: aecpii@aecpii.com
Web: http://www.aecpii.com
AECPI is a professional association focused on the
professional well-being of its members. Formed by
EC professionals for EC professionals, AECPI sup-
ports and advances the careers of EC/EDI profes-
sionals.

**Association for Healthcare Resource and
Materials Management**
AHRMM/AHA
1 North Franklin
Chicago, IL 60606
Phone: (312) 422-3840
Fax: (312) 422-4573
E-mail: ahrmm@aha.org
Web: http://www.ahrmm.org/
This association, known as American Society for
Healthcare Materials Management until August
1998, is dedicated to education and promotion of

resource management in support of cost-effective, quality healthcare and committed to providing its members with information and resources to help them in their current jobs and to prepare them for the upcoming challenges and opportunities of the evolving delivery system.

Association for Standards and Practices in Electronic Trade—EAN UK Ltd.

e Centre
10 Maltravers Street
London WC2R 3BX
England
Phone: 020 7655 9000
Fax: 020 7681 2290
E-mail: info@e-centre.org.uk
Web: http://www.eca.org.uk

This organization was formed by the merger of the Electronic Commerce Association and the Article Number Association in October 1998. It provides help and advice on electronic commerce to UK organizations at large and provides a comprehensive suite of services to its members to help them to adopt best practice in doing business electronically across the extended enterprise. It supports and publicizes the EAN/UCC (International Article Numbering Association/Uniform Code Council) standards and electronic commerce standards as required by members.

Association Française pour la Logistique (ASLOG) (French Association for Logistics)

119, rue Cardinet
F-75017 Paris
France
Phone: (33) 1 40 53 85 59
Fax: (33) 1 47 66 27 08
E-mail: aslog@wanadoo.fr
Web: http://www.aslog.org/

ASLOG promotes logistics in companies through such activities as meetings, symposia, and special studies.

Association of Professional Material Handling Consultants, Inc. (APMHC)

8720 Red Oak Boulevard, Suite 201
Charlotte, NC 28217-3992

Phone: (704) 676-1184
Fax: (704) 676-1199
E-mail: bcurtis@mhia.org
Web: http://www.mhia.org/apmhc/

APMHC was organized in 1959 by several leaders who saw the need for more reliable, capable, and professional services in the material handling consulting field. A professional society composed of individual consultants in the material handling field, it promotes and coordinates the exchange of ideas and information among members; encourages the improvement of analysis, synthesis, installation, and training; advances the profession through the development of standards of performance; and helps other groups promote material handling generally and the consulting profession specifically.

Associazione Italiana di Logistica (AILOG) (Italian Logistics Association)

Segretaria AILOG Servizi
Via Cornalia 19
I-20124 Milano
Italy
Phone: +39 2 667 10 622
Fax +39 2 670 14 83
E-mail: NA
Web: http://www.logisticscity.com/ailog.it

Associazione Italiana di Management degli Approvvigionamenti (ADACI) (Italian Association of Supply Management)

Viale Ranzoni 17
I-20149 Milano
Italy
Phone: +39 02/40072474 or
    +39 02/40090362
Fax: +39 02/40090246
E-mail: informazione@adaci.it
Web: http://www.adaci.it

ADACI (formerly Associazione degli Approvvigionatori e Compratori Italiani) is a sponsor of the European Council of Purchasing and Supply Eurodiploma.

Australasian Production and Inventory Control Society (APICS)

P.O. Box 249

Parramatta NSW 2124
Australia
Phone: (02) 9891 1411
Fax: (02) 9891 1220
E-mail: apics@ozemail.com.au
Web: http://www.apics.org.au/html/home.htm
The Australasian Production and Inventory Control Society covers Australia, New Zealand, and Southeast Asia, helping industry professionals advance their abilities, expand their knowledge and skills, and increase their productivity in the changing global marketplace. The organization fosters professionalism in manufacturing, wholesaling, distribution, and service industries, through the services it provides both to its members and to Australasian industry in general. It publishes *Enterprise Resource Management*, a bimonthly magazine.

Australian Institute of Purchasing and Materials Management, Ltd. (AIPMM)

3/21 Ringwood Street
Ringwood, Vic 3134
Australia
Phone: (61) (03) 9876 9713
Fax: (61) (03) 9876 9714
E-mail: info@aipmm.com.au
Web: http://www.aipmm.com.au
AIPMM is the primary professional organization fulfilling the needs of purchasing and materials management in Australia. A member of the International Federation of Purchasing and Materials Management, AIPMM is committed to the advancement of the professional interests of its membership and improving the quality of purchasing and materials management across industry and government. The Institute publishes a monthly journal, *The Australian Purchasing and Supply*.

BioAPI Consortium

c/o Compaq Computer Corporation
20555 SH 249
Houston, TX 77070
Phone: NA
Fax: NA
E-mail: bioAPI@compaq.com
Web: http://www.bioapi.org
The BioAPI Consortium was formed in April 1998 to develop a widely available and widely accepted application programming interface (API) that will serve for various biometric technologies.

Bundesverband Materialwirtschaft, Einkauf und Logistik, e.V. (BME)

Dr. Friedrich von Heyl
Bolongarostrasse 82
D-65929 Frankfurt am Main
Germany
Phone: +49 69 308 38-100
Fax: +49 69 308 38-199
E-mail: friedrich.vonheyl@bme.de
Web: http://www.bme.de
BME is a sponsor of the European Council of Purchasing and Supply Eurodiploma.

Bundesvereinigung Logistik e.V. (BVL)

Schlachte 31
D-28195 Bremen
Germany
Phone: (0421) 17 38 40
Fax: (0421) 16 78 00
E-mail: bvl@bvl.de
Web: http://www.bvl.de
The BVL is the largest logistics association in Germany. It is divided in 20 active regional logistics groups. The BVL holds the yearly Deutsche Logistik-Kongress and operates a logistics data bank and a logistics education institute, Deutsche Logistik Akademie.

Bundesvereinigung Logistik Österreich, (BVL)

Birostrasse 12
A-1230 Wien
Austria
Phone: (43 1) 615 70 55
Fax: (43 1) 615 70 50 33
E-mail: bvl@bvl.at
Web: http://www.bvl.at/
This organization works to advance and develop logistics in Austria.

Business Products Industry Association

301 North Fairfax Street
Alexandria, VA 22314-2696

Phone: (703) 549-9040
Fax: (703) 683-7552
E-mail: info@bpia.org
Web: http://www.bpia.org
Formerly the National Office Products Association, BPIA is committed to delivering information and services that help the business products industry better serve the changing needs of people at work.

Buyers Laboratory, Inc.
20 Railroad Avenue
Hackensack, NJ 07601-3309
Phone: (201) 488-0404
Fax: (201) 488-0461
E-mail: info@buyers-lab.com
Web: http://www.buyers-lab.com
"The Nation's Leading Independent Office Products Testing Lab," BLI tests office products and provides comprehensive reports on their reliability, ease of use, efficiency, cost factors, and features. Its Buyers Alliance division allows organizations to outsource their equipment acquisitions.

Canadian Association of Logistics Management (CALM) / L'Association Canadienne de Gestion de la Logistique
610 Alden Road, Suite 201
Markham, ON L3R 9Z1
Canada
Phone: (905) 513-7300
Fax: (905) 513-1248
E-mail: admin@calm.org
Web: http://www.calm.org/
CALM is a non-profit organization of business professionals interested in improving their logistics and distribution management skills. Its mission is to serve its members by advancing the logistics and supply chain profession in Canada through communication and networking, education and training, and knowledge leadership. CALM publishes *Logistics & Supply Chain Journal* (quarterly) and *Logistics Canada/Logistique Canada* (for members only)

Canadian Professional Logistics Institute
Victor Deyglio, President
10 King Street East, 4th Floor

Toronto, ON M5C 1C3
Canada
Phone: (416) 363-3005
Fax: (416) 363-5698
E-mail: loginfo@loginstitute.ca
Web: http://www.loginstitute.ca
The Institute was established in 1992 to develop and provide a national education program in logistics, leading to professional status. Education leading to Professional Logistician (P.Log.) designation includes formal assessment and certification process that recognizes previous experience. The Institute publishes *Canadian Logistics Journal* (quarterly).

Canadian Association of Warehousing and Distribution Services
Michael Jenkins, President & CEO
1300 W. Higgins Road, Suite 111
Park Ridge, IL 60068-5764
Phone: (847) 292-1891
Fax: (847) 292-1896
E-mail: logistx@aol.com
Web: http://logistx.dartgc.com/
The Canadian Association of Warehousing and Distribution Services is an 80-year-old national association representing companies involved in public and contract warehousing and related logistics services. Its provides marketing, education, and a buying cooperative service.

Center for Advanced Purchasing Studies
Sheri Rhine, Department Secretary
2055 E. Centennial Circle
P.O. Box 22160
Tempe, AZ 85285-2160
Phone: (602) 752-6276 x 3003
Fax: (602) 491-7885
E-mail: srhine@capsresearch.org
Web: http://www.capsresearch.org
CAPS is a non-profit independent research organization affiliated with the National Association of Purchasing Management and the Arizona State University College of Business. Its mission is to help organizations achieve competitive advantage by providing them with leading-edge research to support the evolution of strategic purchasing and supply management.

Center for Logistics Research, Penn State
The Smeal College of Business
  Administration
The Pennsylvania State University
509 Business Administration Building
University Park, PA 16802-3005
Phone: (814) 865-0585
Fax: (814) 863-7067
E-mail: sek15@psu.edu
Web: http://www.smeal.psu.edu/clr/index.
  shtml
The mission of the Center for Logistics Research is to be the world leader in the creation and dissemination of new knowledge in business logistics. CLR helps companies find a competitive edge through effective business logistics strategy. The center strives to be a world leader in the development of new knowledge and, through its internationally recognized faculty, provides expertise in supply chain integration, procurement, information systems, import and export issues, and more.

Centre for International Trade
General Maritime Services
76 Mamaroneck Avenue, Suite 6
White Plains, NY 10601
Phone: (914) 946-2734
Fax: (914) 946-3093
E-mail: mail@centretrade.com
Web: http://www.centretrade.com
Centre for International Trade (CIT) is a member organization established to improve, facilitate, and expand international trade. It has 3,500 members around the world, including embassies, government agencies, trade associations, companies, firms, and individuals. The members network and offer courtesy discounts to each other. CIT publishes a free newsletter, *International Trader*.

Centro Español de Logística (Spanish Center for Logistics)
Paseo de la Castellana, 114
28046 Madrid
Spain
Phone: (91) 411 67 53 or (91) 562 42 67
Fax: (91) 564 09 10
E-mail: cel@cel-logistica.org

Web: http://www.cel-logistica.org
CEL is a national not-for-profit organization of companies, academics, and others interested in the logistics field. By offering training courses, journeys, roundtables, visits, and publications, it seeks to improve the standard of individual and corporate skills in the area of logistics management.

The Chartered Institute of Purchasing and Supply (CIPS)
Easton House
Easton on the Hill
Stamford
Lincolnshire PE9 3NZ
United Kingdom
Phone: 44 (0)1780 756777
Fax: 44 (0)1780 751610
E-mail: info@cips.org
Web: http://www.cips.org
CIPS is an international non-profit organization representing purchasing and supply chain professionals. This education and qualification body is a central reference point worldwide on matters relating to purchasing and supply chain management. CIPS provides a wide range of services for the benefit of members and the wider business community. CIPS provides a program of continuous improvement in professional standards and raises awareness of the contribution that purchasing and supply makes to corporate, national, and international prosperity. It publishes a biweekly magazine, *Supply Management* and is a sponsor of the European Council of Purchasing and Supply Eurodiploma.

China External Trade Development Council (CETRA)
6th floor, 333 Keelung Road, Sec. 1
Taipei 110
Taiwan, Republic of China
Phone: NA
Fax: NA
E-mail: cetra@cetra.org.tw
Web: http://www.cetra.org.tw
CETRA, a non-profit government-sponsored professional trade promotion association based in Taiwan, assists with sourcing in the Asia-Pacific Region. It offers a wide range of trade-related periodicals, directories, and market reports in Chinese and English.

The Web site is maintained in collaboration with Taipei World Trade Center, a non-profit trade promotion organization in Taiwan.

CommerceNet
Business Development Team
10050 N. Wolfe Road, Suite SW2-255
Cupertino, CA 95014
Phone: (408) 446-1260 x 505
Fax: (408) 446-1268
E-mail: bizdev@commerce.net
Web: http://www.commerce.net/
This organization—"The premier global industry consortium for companies using, promoting, and building electronic commerce solutions on the Internet"—was founded in April 1994. Membership consists of more than 500 companies and organizations worldwide, including banks, telecommunications companies, VANs, ISPs, online services, software and services companies, and end users.

Compagnie des Dirigeants d'Approvisionnement et Acheteurs de France (CDAF) (Society of Purchasing Managers and Buyers of France)
Cécile Masseron, secretary
2, rue Paul Cézanne
F-93364 Neuilly-Plaisance Cedex
France
Phone: (33) 1 43 08 20 20
Fax: (33) 1 1 43 08 53 89
E-mail: cdaf@cdaf.asso.fr
Web: http://www.cdaf.asso.fr
CDAF has three objectives: to promote purchasing in business and government, to help purchasers become more efficient, and to unite purchasers and gain respect for purchasing as a profession. This organization is a sponsor of the European Council of Purchasing and Supply Eurodiploma.

Consortium for Supplier Training
Ray Laughter, Associate Vice Chancellor for Community and Economic Development
Center for Business & Economic Development
North Harris Montgomery Community College
250 N. Sam Houston Parkway East
Houston, TX 77060
Phone: (281) 260-3121
Fax: NA
E-mail: cst@nhmccd.edu
Web: http://www.cst-stc.org
The Consortium is an industry-wide group of leading quality-focused companies that have come together with their partner Supplier Training Centers to provide world-class total quality training to all businesses on an affordable and accessible ongoing basis.

Council for Continuous Improvement
Peter E. Hamm, President and CEO
1777 Barcelona Street
Livermore, CA 94550
Phone: (925) 960-8740
Fax: (925) 960-8745
E-mail: tellcci@aol.com
Web: http://157.226.110.30/default.htm
CCI is a consortium of organizations sharing best practices and lessons learned with each other and collectively developing training material and other resources for use by the entire membership. It was formed in 1989 to address the need for a cooperative approach to quality improvement. The Council's charter sought to develop a documented system, called the Continuous Improvement Implementation System, that builds on the real-world experience of member organizations and includes their most successful quality improvement techniques. Individuals participating in CCI activities represent all facets of management and operations, and all kinds of organizations.

Council of Logistics Management
2805 Butterfield Road, Suite 200
Oak Brook, IL 60523
Phone: (630) 574-0985
Fax: (630) 574-0989
E-mail: clmadmin@clm1.org
Web: http://www.clm1.org
The Council of Logistics Management is a not-for-profit organization of business personnel who are interested in improving their logistics management skills. CLM works in cooperation with private industry and various organizations to further the understanding and development of the logistics

concept. CLM seeks to enhance the development of the logistics profession, aiming all the while to provide logistics professionals with educational opportunities and relevant information. CLM publishes *Journal of Business Logistics.*

Cranfield Centre for Logistics and Transportation

Lynne Hudston
Cranfield Centre for Logistics and
  Transportation
Cranfield School of Management
Cranfield
Bedford MK43 OAL
England
Phone: +44 (0)1234 754183 (direct line),
  751122 (switchboard)
Fax: +44 (0)1234 752158
E-mail: l.hudston@cranfield.ac.uk
Web: http://www.cranfield.ac.uk/som/cclt/
The Cranfield Centre for Logistics and Transportation provides an international focal point for advanced teaching and research in the field of logistics and transportation. Its mission is to develop an understanding of opportunities for improving the efficiency and effectiveness of systems for managing the movement of materials, products, and people, and to foster skills that enable the exploitation of these opportunities. Much of its work has an international dimension, with links to leading centers in North America, Europe, and Asia-Pacific.

Dansk Indkøbs- og Logistikforum (DILF) (Danish Purchasing and Logistics Forum)

Dannebrogsgade 1
DK-1660 København
Denmark
Phone: +45 31 21 16 66
Fax: +45 31 21 15 66
E-mail: mail@dilf.dk
Web: http://www.dilf.dk
DILF is a sponsor of the European Council of Purchasing and Supply Eurodiploma.

Data Interchange Standards Association, Inc. (DISA)

Jennifer Alcazar, Executive Assistant
333 John Carlyle Street, Suite 600
Alexandria, VA 22314
Phone: (703) 548-7005 x 180
Fax: (703) 548-5738
E-mail: jalcazar@disa.org
Web: http://www.disa.org
Data Interchange Standards Association, a not-for-profit association, is the leading provider of educational and networking forums on e-business. Representing e-commerce professionals from around the world, DISA's affiliation with EC User Groups, the Accredited Standards Committee (ASC) X12, and many others facilitates an interchange of e-commerce topics. DISA and ASC X12 serve as the entry point for the United States into the United Nations/Electronic Data Interchange for Administration, Commerce and Transport (UN/EDIFACT), an international standard relating to the exchange of trade goods and services.

Deutsche Gesellschaft für Logistik e.v. (German Society of Logistics)

Joseph-von-Fraunhofer-Strasse 20
D-44227 Dortmund
Germany
Phone: + 44 231 9700-121
Fax: + 44 231 9700-464
E-mail: dgflev@t-online.de
Web: http://www.dgfl.de
The purpose of the organization is the promotion of scientific and practical research and development in the field of logistics, with particular consideration of industry, commerce and services, and educational programming.

EAN International

rue Royale 145
B-1000 Bruxelles
Belgium
Phone: + 32 2 227 10 20
Fax: + 32 2 227 10 21
E-mail: info@ean.be
Web: http://www.ean.be/
EAN International is a voluntary, not-for-profit association founded in 1977 as the European Article Numbering Association, as a result of the initiative of European manufacturers and distributors; it has

expanded to cover the world. The organization has a decentralized structure with a membership of 92 numbering organizations covering 94 countries. The EAN-UCC system is used by more than 800,000 companies around the world.

E&I

P.O. Box 18027
Hauppauge, NY 11788-8827
Phone: (800) 283-2634 or (516) 273-7900
Fax: (516) 273-2305
E-mail: membership@eandi.org
Web: http://www.eandi.org
The Educational and Institutional Cooperative Service, Inc. is "The Buying Cooperative for Higher Education & Health Care."

Electronic Commerce Canada

582 Somerset Street West,
Ottawa, ON K1R 5K2
Canada
Phone: (613) 237-2324
Fax: (613) 237-9900
E-mail: office@ecc.ca
Web: http://www.ecc.ca
Electronic Commerce Canada is a voluntary organization composed of executives from the public and private sectors. ECC provides a forum for sharing information, discussing ideas and initiatives, and networking. Among the electronic commerce technologies addressed by ECC are streamlining processes, interconnectivity, Internet, electronic data interchange (EDI), electronic funds transfer, e-mail, security, electronic document management, workflow processing, middleware, bar coding, imaging, smart cards, voice response, and networking.

Electronic Commerce Council of Canada

885 Don Mills Road, Suite 301
Don Mills, ON M3C 1V9
Canada
Phone: (416) 510-8039 or (800) 567-7084
Fax: (416) 510-8043
E-mail: info@eccc.org
Web: http://www.eccc.org/
The Electronic Commerce Council of Canada is a not-for-profit voluntary standards organization that works with industry sectors to enhance the efficien-

cy and effectiveness of their supply chains. The ECCC provides education and standards documentation. It maintains international barcode registration for an annual fee, as part of an international system with the United States represented by the Uniform Code Council and EAN International in Brussels representing 89 countries outside North America. A company in Canada that now registers or secures a manufacturer's ID number is guaranteed acceptance of that number around the world.

Electronic Commerce Resource Center

4312 Kitsap Way, Suite 104
Bremerton, WA 98312
Phone: (800) 478-3933 or (360) 478-0333
Fax: (360) 478-0225
E-mail: band@ctc.com
Web: http://www.becrc.org
The Electronic Commerce Resource Centers are a national network of 17 centers in the United States. The ECRC is a small business advocate performing in an interpreter role between industry and government. The program is sponsored by the Department of Defense's Joint Electronic Commerce Program Office. The mission of the National ECRC program is to improve the global competitiveness of U.S. industry and government by promoting awareness and implementation of Electronic Commerce technologies and practices.

Electronic Messaging Association

1655 North Fort Myer Drive, Suite 500
Arlington, VA 22209
Phone: (703) 524-5550
Fax: (703) 524-5558
E-mail: info@ema.org
Web: http://www.ema.org/
The Electronic Messaging Association is the forum that enables the evolution of e-business through the application of universal messaging, directory, security, web services, and other related technologies. The association operates for the benefit of large and medium enterprises through education, industry coalitions, and industry awareness.

Equipment Leasing Association of America

4301 N. Fairfax Drive, Suite 550
Arlington, VA 22203-1627
Phone: (703) 527-8655

Fax: (703) 527-2649 or (703) 522-7099
E-mail: membership@elamail.com
Web: http://elaonline.com
ELA is a national organization composed of more than 700 member companies within the equipment leasing and finance industry.

European Council of Purchasing and Supply
Brussels
Belgium
Phone: NA
Fax: NA
E-mail: NA
Web: http://www.eurodiploma.org/
The European Council of Purchasing and Supply (ECPS) is a regional group of the International Federation of Purchasing and Materials Management that serves the European Community. ECPS has 20 member associations, which are also the European members of the IFPMM. Recently the ECPS developed the Eurodiploma, the highest qualification in the field offered through the purchasing associations of Europe.

European Institute of Purchasing Management
Bernard Gracia, Director
French Geneva Campus
International Business Park
Le Centre Universitaire et de Recherche
Archamps
Haute-Savoie
France
Phone: 33 4 50 31 56 78
Fax: 33 4 50 31 56 80
E-mail: eipm@eipm.org
Web: http://www.eipm.org/
EIPM was founded in 1990 by 10 top European multinational companies to meet the growing needs of the purchasing function. A team of multinational professionals provides training programs and networking activities in the areas of purchasing, supply chain management, and materials management.

European Logistics Association (ELA)
Laetitia Hoste
rue Archimède 5/11

B-1000 Brussels
Belgium
Phone: +32 2 230 02 11
Fax: +32 2 230 81 23
E-mail: ela@elalog.org
Web: http://www.elalog.org
ELA is a federation of 36 national organizations, covering almost every country in western Europe. Its goal is to provide a link and an open forum for any individual or society concerned with logistics within Europe and to serve industry and trade. ELA formulates European Logistics Education Standards and encourages the acceptance of these standards in each member nation.

European Forum on Global Supply Chain Management
ir. P. den Hamer
c/o Eindhoven University of Technology
Tema 1.18
P.O. Box 513
5600 MB Eindhoven
Netherlands
Phone: +31-40-2473983
Fax: +31-40-2450258
E-mail: efgscm@tm.tue.nl
Web: http://www.tm.tue.nl/efgscm/
The European Forum on Global Supply Chain Management offers an opportunity to share problems and solutions in the fields of supply chain management and design. Through its alliance with the Stanford Forum on Global Supply Chain Management in the U.S. and the Asian-Pacific Forum on Global Supply Management at Hong Kong University of Science and Technology, the European Forum is the access to contacts with leading global players in various industrial sectors.

Federal Acquisition Institute
Office of Acquisition Policy
General Services Administration
1800 F Street, NW, Room 4017
Washington, DC 20405
Phone: (202) 501-2980
Fax: (202) 501-3341
E-mail: gayle.messick@gsa.gov
Web: http://www.gsa.gov/staff/v/training.htm

FAI provides training on US Federal Acquisition Regulations, including online training. Pursuant to the Office of Federal Procurement Policy Act, as amended, the FAI has worked for more than a decade to foster and promote government-wide career management programs for a professional procurement work force.

Federation of International Trade Associations (FITA)

11800 Sunrise Valley Drive, Suite 210
Reston, VA 20191
Phone: (800) 969-FITA (3482)
Fax: (703) 620-4922
E-mail: info@fita.org
Web: http://www.fita.org
The federation is a network of 300,000 companies belonging to 300 trade international associations in the U.S., Canada, and Mexico.

First American Group Purchasing Association

1001 Howard Avenue
Plaza Tower, 35th Floor
New Orleans, LA 70113-2002
Phone: (504) 529-2030
Fax: (504) 558-0929
E-mail: lenn@firstgpa.com
Web: http://www.firstgpa.com/index1.html
FAGPA is a buying cooperative that provides over 285,000 small businesses with savings of 5% to 70% on virtually any product and service. By combining the purchasing power of thousands of small businesses across America, FAGPA has assembled a network of national suppliers that offer substantial savings and benefits to FAGPA members.

Fritz Institute of Global Logistics

Richard Dawe, Executive Coordinator
4415 Cowell Road, Suite 200 C
Concord, CA 94518-1945
Phone: (510) 939-7391
Fax: NA
E-mail: rdawe@fritzinstitute.org
Web: http://www.fritzinstitute.org
The Fritz Institute of Global Logistics is a non-prof-

it institution committed to the creation, acquisition, dissemination, promotion, and application of knowledge in global supply chain logistics to help enterprises attain the performance improvement and management development required to meet complex current and future needs. The Institute will form partnerships with knowledge creators and knowledge users from academic, consulting, industry, professional development, service provider, and publishing organizations.

The Global Procurement & Supply Chain Benchmarking Initiative

Dr. Robert Monczka
Professor of Strategic Sourcing Management
N505 North Business Complex
The Eli Broad School of Management
Michigan State University
East Lansing, MI 48824-1122
Phone: 517-432-2086
Fax: 517-432-2094
E-mail: sourcres@msu.edu
Web: http://gebn.bus.msu.edu/
The Initiative is a third-party procurement and supply chain benchmarking effort to collect and disseminate information concerning the best procurement and supply chain strategies, practices, and processes used by companies across industries worldwide.

Health Industry Manufacturers Association

1200 G Street, NW, Suite 400
Washington, DC 20005-3814
Phone: (202) 783-8700
Fax: (202) 783-8750
E-mail: hima@himanet.com
Web: http://www.himanet.com
HIMA is the largest medical technology trade association in the world, supported by more than 800 medical device, diagnostic products, and health information systems manufacturers of all sizes. HIMA is the only medical device association that operates globally to promote a legal, regulatory, and economic climate that advances health care by assuring worldwide patient access to the benefits of medical technology.

Hellenic Institute of Logistics Management (HILM)

Constantinos C. Sifniotis, Chair
36, Posidonos Avenue
GR-17561 P. Faliro/Athens
Greece
Phone: +30 1 988 28 44
Fax: +30 1 988 08 36
E-mail: NA
Web: NA

Hellenic Purchasing Institute (EIN)

Vicky Galani, Secretary
36 Aristotelous St.
GR-104 33 Athens
Greece
Phone: +30 1 620 9726
Fax: +30 1 620 9776
E-mail: NA
Web: NA
The Institute is a sponsor of the European Council of Purchasing and Supply Eurodiploma.

Holland International Distribution Council

25, Koninginngracht
2514 AB The Hague
P.O. Box 85599
2508 CG The Hague
Netherlands
Phone: (31 70) 346 7272
Fax: (31 70) 360 3698
E-mail: info@hidc.nl
Web: http://www.hidc.nl
HIDC is a private, non-profit organization founded in 1987 by the Dutch Transport and Distribution Industry. All of its services to the industry are provided entirely free of charge, without bias and without obligation. HIDC now has more than 600 member companies or organizations, all of which provide a service relevant to companies studying or implementing a pan-European physical distribution solution.

Hong Kong Trade Development Council

38th Floor, Office Tower
Convention Plaza
1 Harbour Road
Wanchai
Hong Kong
Phone: (852) 2584 4333
Fax: (852) 2824 0249
E-mail: hktdc@tdc.org.hk
Web: http://www.tdc.org.hk
The HKTDC is the statutory organization set up to promote Hong Kong's trade in goods and services. It helps to develop Hong Kong's role as an information hub, a sourcing and business center in Asia-Pacific, and the gateway to China. It has a global network of 50 branch offices. The Hong Kong Trade Development Council publishes 13 English product magazines, one trade directory, and four trade services magazines.

Human Factors and Ergonomics Society

P.O. Box 1369
Santa Monica, CA 90406-1369
Phone: (310) 394-1811
Fax: (310) 394-2410
E-mail: hfes@compuserve.com
Web: http://www.hfes.org/
The Society's mission is to promote the discovery and exchange of knowledge concerning the characteristics of human beings that are applicable to the design of systems and devices of all kinds. The Soci-ety furthers serious consideration of knowledge about the assignment of appropriate functions for humans and machines, whether people serve as operators, maintainers, or users in the system. It advocates systematic use of such knowledge to achieve compatibility in the design of interactive systems of people, machines, and environments to ensure their effectiveness, safety, and ease of performance.

Hungarian Association of Logistics, Purchasing, and Inventory Management (HALPIM)

Veres Pálné
H-1053 Budapest
Hungary
Phone: NA
Fax: + +36 1 117 2959
E-mail: NA
Web: NA

The main objective of HALPIM is to contribute to the increase of economic efficiency in logistics, purchasing, and inventory management and develop the professional standard of the profession in Hungarian trade, industry, and public administration. HALPIM helps establish contact between professionals in the field, supports the spread of new ideas, keeps in contact with other organizations at the international level, and publishes a logistics newsletter.

Indian Institute of Materials Management
405, Kaliandas Udyog Bhavan
Century Bazar Lane, Prabhadevi
Mumbai 400 025
India
Phone: 91 022 437 2820
Fax: 91 022 430 9564
E-mail: iimm@commercenetindia.com
Web:http://www.commercenetindia.com/am
 /iimm/index.htm
IIMM was formed in 1975 with the merger of three professional associations—The National Associa-tion of Materials Management (formerly the Na-tional Association of Purchasing Executives), the Materials Management Association of India (formerly known as the Purchasing Officers' Association), and the Materials Management Association of Hyderabad.

Institut International de Management pour la Logistique (International Institute for Logistics Management)
Unité Logistique, Economie, Management
Institut des Transports et de Planification
Ecole Polytechnique Fédérale de Lausanne
CH-1015 Lausanne
Switzerland
Phone: (41) 21 693 24 65
Fax: (41) 21 693 50 60
E-mail: direction.iml@epfl.ch
Web: http://imlwww.epfl.ch/iml
The institute is a non-profit-making association founded to promote the development and use of logistical organization methods through education and research., participate in the development of procedures concerning international trade, train high-level managers in the field of logistics, and introduce young people to the methodological, instrumental, and practical foundations of the field of logistics.

Institut du Management de l'Achat Industriel (MAI)
Claude Garrabos
MAI / Groupe ESC Bordeaux
Domaine de Raba
680, cours de la Libération
33 405 Talence Cédex
France
Phone: (33) 05.56.84.55.75
Fax: (33) 05.56.84.55.80
E-mail: claude.garrabos@esc-bordeaux.fr
Web: http://www.mai-purchasing.com
This is postgraduate purchasing program that hosts a Web site with a good collection of links for sourcing in Europe and the Americas.

Institute for Purchasing and Supply Development
Prof. Arjan J. van Weele
NEVI-Chair Purchasing and Supply Management
Eindhoven University of Technology
 P.O. Box 513
5600 MB Eindhoven
Netherlands
Phone: +31 40-2473841
Fax: +31 40-2465949
E-mail: ipsd@tm.tue.nl
Web: http://www.tm.tue.nl/ipsd/
The Institute is working to be a center of excellence in the field of purchasing and supply management, to connect and help researchers and practitioners around the world.

Institute of Logistics and Transport
Supply-Chain Centre
Earlstrees Court
Earlstrees Road
P.O. Box 5787
Corby
Northants NN17 4XQ
United Kingdom
Phone: +44 (0) 1536 740100
Fax: +44 (0) 1536 740101
E-mail: enquiry@iolt.org.uk
Web: http://www.iolt.org.uk/
The Institute of Logistics and Transport was formed

in June 1999, after the integration of the Institute of Logistics and The Chartered Institute of Transport in the UK. It publishes a journal, *Logistics & Transport Focus*, and a variety of books and provides training and development opportunities.

Institute of Management and Administration

29 West 35th Street
New York, NY 10001
Phone: (212) 244-0360
Fax: (212) 629-9479
E-mail: kmandal@ioma.com
Web: http://www.ioma.com/nls
The Institute publishes several newsletters of interest, including *The Supplier & Management Report*, *Managing Logistics*, and *Inventory Reduction Report*.

Institute of Purchasing and Supply of Hong Kong

Dr. Patrick Fung
P.O. Box K72241
Kowloon Central Post Office
Kowloon
Hong Kong
China
Phone: (852) 27667392
Fax: (852) 27743679
E-mail: mspfung@hkpucc.polyu.edu.hk
Web: NA

Institute of Purchasing and Supply South Africa

P.O.Box 319
Auckland Park
2006
South Africa
Phone: (011) 482 1419
Fax: (011) 726 6540
E-mail: ipsa@mweb.co.za
Web: http://www.ipsa.co.za/index.html
The mission of IPSA is to provide a recognized institution that can promote and maintain the interests of organized purchasing in Southern Africa. IPSA has recently joined with the Bureau for Economic Research at Stellenbosch to produce a new economic indicator, the Purchasing Manager's Index.

Instytut Logistyki i Magazynowania (Institute of Logistics and Warehousing)

ul. E. Estkowskiego 6
61-755 Poznan
Poland
Phone: +48 61 8527681 or +48 61 8529898
Fax: +48 61 8526376
E-mail: office@ilim.poznan.pl
Web: http://www.ilim.poznan.pl/

Integrated Business Communications Alliance

Kelley M. Tracy
24 Far View Road
Chalfont, PA 18914
Phone: (215) 822-6880
Fax: (215) 822-8109
E-mail: kelleyt@quadii.com
Web: http://www.isit.com/ibca/
This organization, until 1996 the Industry Bar Code Alliance, serves as a clearinghouse of information and education supporting the use of bar code and e-Commerce, a forum for discussion of the mutual needs of technology providers and users, and a unified voice on technology issues.

International Air Cargo Association (TIACA)

Secretariat
P.O. Box 330669
Miami, FL
Phone: (305) 443-9696
Fax: (305) 443-9698
E-mail: info@tiaca.org
Web: http://www.tiaca.org
The International Air Cargo Association is a worldwide organization that brings together all elements of the air logistics industry to work for progress and growth in world trade and economic development. Its members include all major components of the industry—air and surface carriers, forwarders, shippers, vendors, manufacturers, airports, countries, financial institutions and consultants. TIACA also represents international, national, regional, and city air cargo associations and their students involved in air cargo training.

International Association of Purchasing Managers

45 W. Woodside Avenue
Patchogue, NY 11772-0115
P.O. Box 508
Bayport, NY 11705-0508
Phone: (516) 654-2384
Fax: (516) 475-2754
E-mail: IntlPur@worldnet.att.net
Web: http://www.globalpurchasing.org/
IAPM is a non-profit New York State professional organization dedicated to the advancement of world trade. Membership is open to buyers, purchasing managers, importers, and all individuals who may be involved in or have an interest in the important functions of buying goods and services on the global market. IAPM is an educational organization to help make world trade easier for the new buyer. It publishes a monthly newsletter and offers a program for certification.

International Chamber of Commerce

38, cours Albert 1er
75008 Paris
France
Phone: +33 (1) 49. 53. 28. 28
Fax: +33 (1) 49. 53. 29. 42
E-mail: icc@iccwbo.org
Web: http://www.iccwbo.org
ICC is the world business organization, the only representative body that speaks with authority on behalf of enterprises from all sectors in every part of the world. Its purpose is to promote international trade, investment, and the market economy system. It makes rules that govern the conduct of business across borders and enforces them through the ICC International Court of Arbitration, the world's leading institution of its kind. Members from 63 national committees and over 7000 member companies and associations from over 130 countries throughout the world present ICC views to their governments and coordinate with their membership to address the concerns of the business community. ICC also establishes "incoterms," standard trade definitions for use throughout the world.

International Chamber of Commerce Asia

ICC Asia

Suite 7B
Shun Ho Tower
24-30 Ice House Street
Central
Hong Kong
Phone: +852 2973 0006
Fax: +852 2869 0360
E-mail: 100443.2325@compuserve.com
Web: http://www.iccwbo.org/ICC_Asia/
  home_iccasia.htm
The International Chamber of Commerce opened this regional office in January 1997.

International Federation of Public Warehousing Associations

1300 W. Higgins Road, Suite 111
Park Ridge, IL 60068-5764
Phone: (847) 292-1891
Fax: (847) 292-1896
E-mail: logistx@aol.com
Web: http://logistx.dartgc.com/
The International Federation of Public Warehous-ing Associations is composed of warehouse associations from all over the world. The fifteen member countries are Brazil, China, Cyprus, France, Greece, Iran, Israel, Italy, Japan, Mexico, Spain, Switzerland, United Kingdom, United States, and Canada. IFPWA is committed to providing education and networking opportunities for warehouse companies and associations on a global level.

International Federation of Purchasing and Materials Management

Secretariat
Rockhgasse 6
P.O.Box 131
A-1014 Wien
Austria
Phone: + +43 (1) 533 86 38 78
Fax: + +43 (1) 533 86 36 79
E-mail: secretariat@ifpmm.co.at
Web: http://members.eunet.at/ifpmm/
IFPMM is an international nonprofit federation that facilitates the development and distribution of knowledge to elevate and advance the procurement profession, thus favorably impacting the standard of living worldwide through improved business prac-

tices. IFPMM brings together more than 40 national purchasing associations worldwide, comprising about 200,000 purchasing professionals. The federation publishes *European Purchasing & Logistics Strategies* (in cooperation with World Market Research Centre, London) and the *IFPMM Newsletter*.

International Organization for Standardization (ISO)
ISO/IEC Information Centre
1, rue de Varembé
Case postale 56
CH-1211 Genève 20
Switzerland
Phone: +41 22 749 01 11
Fax: + 41 22 733 34 30
E-mail: mbinfo@iso.ch
Web: http://www.iso.ch
ISO is a worldwide federation of national standards bodies from some 130 countries, one from each country. Established in 1947, its mission is to promote the development of standardization and related activities in the world, in order to facilitate the international exchange of goods and services and to develop cooperation in the spheres of intellectual, scientific, technological, and economic activity. ISO establishes international standards.

International Purchasing and Supply Education and Research Association
Dr. Simon Croom
Warwick Business School
University of Warwick
Coventry CV4 7AL
United Kingdom
Phone: +44 1203 528222
Fax: +44 1203 404175 or +44 1203 572583
E-mail: simon.croom@warwick.ac.uk
Web: http://www.ipsera.org
IPSERA is intended to be an active international network of academics and practitioners committed to the development of the greater understanding of matters and issues affecting the future of purchasing and supply chain management. IPSERA has two prime objectives: to provide a research network and to encourage development in education. IPSERA also hosts two electronic discussion lists—purchasing-

supply-chain and supply-management, a discussion forum for academics and professionals.

International Trade Association
1224 North Nokomis NE
Alexandria, MN 56308
Phone: (320) 763-5101
Fax: (320) 763-9290
E-mail: ita@iami.org
Web: http://www.iami.org/ita.html.
ITA is a worldwide organization providing recognition and membership services to qualified individuals who specialize in world trade. ITA has members in over 90 nations of the world, providing a global network of government, corporation, and industry professionals.

International Warehouse Logistics Association
1300 W. Higgins Road, Suite 111
Park Ridge, IL 60068-5764
Phone: (847) 292-1891
Fax: (847) 292-1896
E-mail: logistx@aol.com
Web: http://logistx.dartgc.com/

Irish Institute of Purchasing and Materials Management
5 Belvedere Place
Dublin 1
Ireland
Phone: 01 8559257 or 01 8559258
Fax: 01 8559259
E-mail: iipmm@iol.ie
Web: http://www.iipmm.ie
IIPMM is the main reference point for purchasing and supply chain professionals in the Republic of Ireland and a sponsor of the European Council of Purchasing and Supply Eurodiploma. The Institute offers a comprehensive suite of education and training programs for industry and government and meets the continuing professional development needs of members and nonmembers.

Irish Production and Inventory Control Society (IPICS)
51 Grand Parade

Cork City
Ireland
Phone: Int + 353 + 21-251505
Fax: Int + 353 + 21-251510
E-mail: peter.black@ipics.ie
Web: http://www.ipics.ie
IPICS is a voluntary not-for-profit professional and educational organization dedicated to providing leading edge educational and training programs to manufacturing industry personnel throughout the island of Ireland. It is the professional and educational society for production, operations, logistics, and supply chain resource management professionals in Ireland.

Israeli Purchasing and Logistics Management Association (IPLMA)

12 Kaplan Street
P.O. Box 7128
Tel Aviv 61071
Israel
Phone: +972 3 696 6944
Fax: +972 3 691 9047
E-mail: iplma@doryanet.co.il
Web: http://www.iplma.org.il
IPLMA is a not-for-profit educational association for purchasing and supply chain management professionals, focusing on education, professional development, certification, and research. It is a sponsor of the European Council of Purchasing and Supply Eurodiploma.

Japan Institute of Logistics Systems (JILS)

Headquarters
Sumitomo Higashi Shinbashi Bldg.3goukan
1-10-14 Hamamatsu-cho
Minato-ku
Tokyo 105-0013
Japan
Phone: NA
Fax: NA
E-mail: support@logistics.or.jp
Web: http://www1.mesh.ne.jp/jils/
JILS is a nonprofit national organization specializing in logistics with cooperation from governmental, industrial, and academic fields. It was formed in 1992 with the merger of the Japan Logistics Management Association and the Japanese Council of Logistics Management.

Logistics Association of Australia

New South Wales Office
P.O. Box 943
Auburn NSW 1835
Australia
Phone: 1300 651 911
Fax: 02-9649 3794
E-mail: logadmin@logassoc.asn.au
Web: http://logassoc.asn.au/
The Logistics Association of Australia represents the interests of logistics professionals. Its mission is "to provide a forum for Australian management to expand and develop their understanding and skills in the practical implementation of operational and strategic aspects of logistics." The Logistics Association, formed in 1998 by a merger of the Logistics Management Association (LMA) and the Australian Institute of Materials Management (AIMM), exists primarily as an educational forum.

The Logistics Institute, Georgia Tech

Dr. H. Donald Ratliff, Executive Director
Room 109, ISyE Building
School of Industrial and Systems Engineering
Georgia Tech
765 Ferst Drive, NW
Atlanta, GA 30332-0205
Phone: (404) 894-2343
Fax: (404) 894-6527
E-mail: don.ratliff@isye.gatech.edu
Web: http://tli.isye.gatech.edu/
The Institute was established to provide education and research in logistics. The corporate sponsors are supporting industrial organizations that provide financial and/or advisory guidance. The mission of the Institute is to provide a comprehensive research and educational program focused on total optimization of the logistics value chain.

Logistics Institute of New Zealand (LINZ)

Michael Grace, Executive Secretary
P.O. Box 345
Manurewa
New Zealand
Phone: +64-9267-1106

Fax: +64-9267-9075

E-mail: geenzprolink.co.nz

Web: http://www.log-inz.org.nz/

LINZ is the national body representing businesses and business people involved in supply chain management. This includes all the processes in the chain from purchasing to the delivery to customers. LINZ aims to provide a forum to tackle the unique logistics challenges facing New Zealand business: a high dependency on international trade, geographic isolation, and a small widely spread consumer base.

Logistics Management Institute

2000 Corporate Ridge

McLean, VA 22102-7805

Phone: (703) 917-9800

Fax: NA

E-mail: library@lmi.org

Web: http://www.lmi.org

LMI is a private, nonprofit corporation that provides management consulting, research, and analysis to governments and other nonprofit organizations. Founded in 1961 to serve the U.S. Department of Defense, LMI began expanding in 1994 to serve other clients and to go beyond logistics.

LogistikSelskabet IDA

Ingeniørforeningen i Danmark

Att.: Mette Holck

Kalvebod Brygge 31-33

DK-1780 København

Denmark

Phone: +45 33 18 48 48 or +45 33 18 46 53

Fax: +45 33 18 48 87

E-mail: log_fts@ida.dk

Web: http://www.logistikselskabet.dk

This association was established in 1987 to promote the importance of logistics in Denmark and help logistics professionals develop.

Magyar Logisztikai Egyesület (MLE)
(Hungarian Logistics Association)

Rózsa utca 4-6

1077 Budapest

Hungary

Phone: +36 1 342-0500

Fax: +36 1 352-7056

E-mail: mlebp@elender.hu

Web: http://www.flatline.hu/MLE

Malaysian Institute of Purchasing and
Materials Management

Room 2.23, YMCA Building

211 Jalan Macalister

10450 Penang

Malaysia

Phone: 603-2272188

Fax: 603-2270188

E-mail: mipmm@tm.net.my

Web: http://www.mipmm.org.my

MIPMM is a non-profit organization that actively promotes professional development of purchasing, materials, and logistics management. One of the Institute's objectives is to secure a wider recognition and promote the importance of efficient materials management in commercial and industrial undertakings. The MIPMM Web site features an online sourcing center.

Manufacturing Extension Partnership
(MEP)

Kevin Carr, Director

National Institute of Standards and
Technology

100 Bureau Drive, Stop 4800

Gaithersburg, MD 20899-48000

Phone: (800) MEP 4 MFG (637-4634), (301)
975-5020, or (301) 975-5454

Fax: (301) 963-6556

E-mail: MEPinfo@mep.nist.gov or
kevin.carr@nist.gov

Web: http://www.mep.nist.gov/

MEP is a nationwide network of not-for-profit centers in over 400 locations nationwide, whose sole purpose is to provide small and medium-sized manufacturers with the help they need to succeed. The centers, serving all 50 states, the District of Columbia, and Puerto Rico, are linked together through the Department of Commerce's National Institute of Standards and Technology, to make available the expertise of knowledgeable manufacturing and business specialists all over the U.S. The Web site provides contact information for the centers by location.

Material Handling Equipment Distributors Association

201 U.S. Highway 45
Vernon Hills, IL 60061-2398
Phone: (847) 680-3500
Fax: (847) 362-6989
E-mail: connect@mheda.org
Web: http://www.mheda.org
MHEDA is a not-for-profit trade association composed of member companies that are involved in selling, installing, and servicing material handling equipment. Products and services available through MHEDA include regional educational seminars, a quarterly trade journal, annual membership directory, statistical comparison surveys, resource materials, and discounted endorsed products.

Material Handling Industry of America

8720 Red Oak Boulevard, Suite 201
Charlotte, NC 28217-3992
Phone: (704) 676-1190
Fax: (704) 676-1199
E-mail: bcurtis@mhia.org
Web: http://www.mhia.org/
MHIA is a non-profit organization for manufacturers of industrial material handling equipment and systems or user-specified components for such equipment.

National Association of Education Buyers, Inc. (NAEB)

450 Wireless Boulevard
Hauppauge, NY 11788
Phone: (516) 273-2600
Fax: (516) 273-2305
E-mail: mservices@naeb.org
Web: http://www.naeb.org
NAEB was organized in 1922 and is the professional association serving colleges and universities nationwide. Its mission is to promote the development and use of ethical and effective purchasing management techniques among member institutions. It provides workshops and publications and it promotes communications through networks of members.

National Association of Black Procurement Professionals

Elliot L. Warley, President
P.O. Box 70738
Washington, DC 20024-0738
Phone: NA
Fax: (202) 554-3146
E-mail: NA
Web: http://www.nabpp.org
NABPP provides resources and support services necessary to enhance the professionalism of its members and provides career development and training in the field of procurement to the public and private sectors.

National Association of Procurement Professionals (NAPP)

Dave Elko, Chairman
Phone: (215) 751-3379
Fax: (215) 751-7084
E-mail: David.Elko@sb.com
Sal Grillo, Co-Chairman
Phone: (212) 236-0930
Fax: (212) 236-1083
E-mail: Sgrillo@exchange.ml.com
Web: http://www.nappconference.com
The National Association of Procurement Professionals provides an annual forum for the exchange of new and innovative ideas for improving the procurement process. Conference speakers are selected from a broad spectrum of companies that are known for being leaders in introducing new business practices, procedures, and technology. Workshops are designed to be informative, interactive, and fun. NAPP conferences are certified by the National Association of Purchasing Management for C.P.M. credits.

National Association of Purchasing Management, Inc. (NAPM)

Christine Hudgins, Supervisor, Customer Relations
2055 East Centennial Circle
P.O. Box 22160
Tempe, AZ 85285-2160
Phone: (800) 888-6276 x 3070 or (480) 752-6276 x 3070

Fax: (480) 752-7890, fax-on-demand: (800) 444-6276
E-mail: chudgins@napm.org
Web: http://www.napm.org
NAPM is a not-for-profit association that provides national and international leadership in purchasing and supply management research and education. NAPM provides its 180 affiliated associations and its more than 46,000 members with opportunities to expand their professional skills and knowledge. Founded in 1915, NAPM is a communication link with more than 44,000 purchasing and supply management professionals. NAPM publishes *Purchasing Today, International Journal of Purchasing and Materials Management,* and *The Journal of Supply Chain Management* (quarterly).

National Association of Purchasing Management, Inc. Advanced Technology Center

Terri Tracey
P.O. Box 22160
Tempe, AZ 85285-2160
Phone: (800) 888-6276 x 3071 or (480) 752-6276 x 3071
Fax: (480) 752-7890
E-mail: ttracey@napm.org
Web: http://www.napm.org/Education/atc.cfm
Sponsors of the ATC form a consortium dedicated to underwriting the costs of creating complex, computer-based learning systems, Electronic Performance Support Systems, and information, education, and training resources. The consortium provides an affordable means of participating in the design and development of interactive, multimedia, computer-based learning tools that will be used throughout sponsors' internal purchasing and supply management functions to facilitate continuing education and professional development. Members gain additional value by receiving many NAPM products and services.

National Association of State Procurement Officials

Chris Walls
167 West Main Street, Suite 600
Lexington, KY 40507

Phone: (606) 231-1963 or (606) 231-1877
Fax: (606) 231-1928
E-mail: cwalls@amrinc.net
Web: http://www.naspo.org
NASPO, formerly the National Association of State Purchasing Officials, is a professional organization made up of the directors of the central purchasing offices in each of the 50 states, the District of Columbia, and the territories of the United States. Through NASPO the member purchasing officials provide leadership in professional public purchasing, improve the quality of purchasing and procurement, exchange information, and cooperate to attain greater efficiency and economy.

National Association of Wholesaler-Distributors

1725 K Street, NW, 3rd Floor
Washington, DC 20006-0140
Phone: (202) 872-0885
Fax: (202) 785-0586
E-mail: membership@nawd.org
Web: http://www.nawpubs.org
This organization represents the needs and interests of wholesale distribution professionals.

National Conference of Commissioners on Uniform State Laws (NCCUSL)

211 E. Ontario Street, Suite 1300
Chicago, IL 60611
Phone: (312) 915-0195
Fax: (312) 915-0187
E-mail: nccusl@nccusl.org
Web: http://www.nccusl.org/
The National Conference of Commissioners on Uniform State Laws is jointly responsible with the American Law Institute for drafting, updating, and promulgating the Uniform Commercial Code (UCC).

National Contract Management Association

1912 Woodford Road
Vienna, VA 22182
Phone: (800) 344-8096 (toll-free outside of Virginia) or (703) 448/9231 (direct in Washington DC metropolitan area)
Fax: (703) 448-0939,

fax-on-demand (888) 592-NCMA
E-mail: info@ncmahq.org
Web: http://www.ncmahq.org
NCMA is an individual-membership, professional society dedicated to the professional growth and educational advancement of its members and others in the contract management/procurement field. It publishes a monthly magazine, *Contract Management.*

National Initiative for Supply Chain Integration, Ltd. (NISCI)

Bob Parker, Executive Director
551 Roosevelt Road M/D 123
Glen Ellyn IL 60137
Phone: (888) AT NISCI or (630) 469-2600
Fax: (630) 469-1216
E-mail: BobParker@NISCI.org
Web: http://www.nisci.org
This non-profit organization was founded in September 1997 to research and develop the most effective solutions to optimize the performance of supply chains composed of three or more links, to "integrate the best thinking of all public and private efforts into the design and development of improved chainwide business processes with the goal of making U.S.-based operations increasingly competitive in the global market."

National Institute for Transport and Logistics

Dr. Stefan Bungart, Director General
Dublin Institute of Technology
Aungier Street
Dublin 2
Ireland
Phone.: +353 1 402 3115
Fax: +353 1 402 3022
E-mail: Stefan.Bungart@dit.ie
Web: http://www.nitl.ie
NITL was founded to provide expertise in transport and logistics (total supply chain integration and management) to firms operating in and from Ireland both nationally and in overseas markets. The Institute provides tailored services to every kind and size of business. NITL is supported by the European Regional Development Fund managed by the Department of Enterprise, Trade & Employment.

National Institute of Governmental Purchasing, Inc.

Joanne Cheves, Administrative Assistant
151 Spring Street, Suite 300
Herndon, VA 20170-5223
Phone: (703) 736-8900 or (800) 367-6447
Fax: (703) 736-9644 (main), (703) 736-9639 (education/membership/enhanced services)
E-mail: jcheves@nigp.org
Web: http://www.nigp.org
The Institute was established in 1944 to provide education, research, technical assistance, and networking opportunities in public purchasing. Its membership is composed of purchasing agencies in the federal government, cities, states, provinces, counties, colleges, libraries, hospitals, and other public bodies. The Institute works to help members do their jobs more effectively and efficiently, to raise their level of professionalism, and to ensure that their processes and methods will stand up under the strictest scrutiny and meet the highest ethical and professional standards.

National Minority Supplier Development Council, Inc.

1040 Avenue of the Americas, 2nd Floor
New York, NY 10018
Phone: (212) 944-2430
Fax: (212) 719-9611
E-mail: nseaberr@nmsdcus.org
Web: http://www.nmsdcus.org
The primary objective of the Council is to provide a direct link between corporate America and minority-owned businesses and increase procurement and other opportunities for minority businesses of all sizes. It publishes a quarterly, *The Minority Supplier News.* The NMSDC network includes a National Office in New York and 38 regional councils across the country.

National Purchasing Institute (NPI), Inc.

Richard Schlegel, Executive Director
P.O. Box 2777
Reno, NV 89505-2777
Physical Address:
100 N. Arlington Ave., Suite 105

Reno, NV 89501
Phone: (702) 332-1NPI or (755) 332-1674
Fax: (702) 323-0648
E-mail: schlegelra@aol.com
Web: http://npi.purchasing.co.harris.tx.us.
NPI is a national public purchasing affiliate of
NAPM, serving government, educational, and institutional purchasing professionals. NPI holds an annual conference and products exposition, publishes a newsletter called the *Public Purchasing Review*, and maintains a specifications library available to members.

**Nederlandse Vereniging voor
  Inkoopmanagement (NEVI) (Netherlands
  Association for Purchasing Management)**
Orfeoschouw 2
Postbus 198
NL-2700 AD Zoetermeer
Netherlands
Phone: (31 79) 330 0766
Fax: (31 79) 330 0760
E-mail: ver@nevi.nl
Web: http:// www.nevi.nl
NEVI is a sponsor of the European Council of
Purchasing and Supply Eurodiploma.

New Zealand Industrial Supplies Office
1st Floor, NGC House
22 The Terrace
Wellington
New Zealand
Phone: (64 4) 472-0030
Fax: (64 4) 472-0880
E-mail: general@nziso.govt.nz
Web: http://www.nziso.govt.nz
The NZISO is a government-funded organization
facilitating contact between government and industry in New Zealand and Australia. It promotes the government purchasing policy by providing information on competitive local producers of goods and services for government purchasers.

**Norsk Forbund for Innkjøp og Logistikk
  (NIMA) (Norwegian Association of
  Purchasing and Logistics)**
General Secretary

Postboks 2602
St Hanshaugen
Akersbakken 12
N-0131 Oslo
Norway
Phone: +47 22 20 14 00
Fax: +47 22 20 06 50
E-mail: gudrun@nima.no
Web: http://www.nima.no
NIMA is a sponsor of the European Council of
Purchasing and Supply Eurodiploma.

**North American Logistics Association
  (NALA)**
Michael Jenkins, President
1300 W. Higgins Road, Suite 111
Park Ridge, IL 60068-5764
Phone: (847) 292-1891
Fax: (847) 292-1896
E-mail: logistx@aol.com
Web: http://logistx.dartgc.com/

Ontario Public Buyers Association, Inc.
111 Fourth Avenue, Suite 361
Ridley Square
St. Catharines, ON L2S 3P5
Canada
Phone/Fax: (905) 682-2644
E-mail: opbasup@vaxxine.com
Web: http://www.vaxxine.com/opba
OPBA is a not-for-profit volunteer-driven professional association, whose mission is to further excellence in and promote awareness of the public procurement profession. Members have the opportunity to post tender offers (IFBs) to the site.

**Organisationen för Inköp och Logisitik
  (I&L) (Swedish National Association of
  Purchasing and Logistics)**
Box 1278
164 29 Kista
Sweden
Phone: 08-752 16 90
Fax: 08-750 64 10
E-mail: il@silf.se
Web: http://www.iolservice.se

I&L, an organization with about 3000 members, is dedicated to helping purchasing and logistics professionals be more effective and help make their organizations more competitive.

Österreichisches Produktivitäts- und Wirtschaftlichkeits-Zentrum (ÖPWZ) (Austrian Productivity and Economy Center)

Rockhgasse 6
1014 Wien
Austria
Phone: (01) 533 86 36-0
Fax: (01) 533 86 36 36
E-mail: office@opwz.com
Web: http://www.opwz.com
OPWZ is a sponsor of the European Council of Purchasing and Supply Eurodiploma.

The Outsourcing Institute

Frank Casale, President
500 North Broadway, Suite 141
Jericho, NY 11753
Phone: (800) 421-6767 or (516) 681-0066
Fax: (516) 938-1839
E-mail: info@outsourcing.com
Web: http://www.outsourcing.com
The Institute is a professional association and executive network with a mission to provide timely information exchange and services on outsourcing and related sourcing strategies. The Institute's network, consisting of over 16,000 individuals worldwide, includes senior professionals, consultants, legal experts, and industry observers. The Institute provides its members with forums and other opportunities to exchange information and network, including regional and national events and a quarterly management brief, *The Source*. It provides advisory and referral assistance for those tasked with assessing or managing outsourcing for their enterprise.

Philippine Exporters' Confederation, Inc. (PHILEXPORT)

PHILEXPORT Building
ITC Complex
Roxas Boulevard
Pasay City
Philippines
Phone: 63 2 833 2531, 63 2 833 2532, 63 2 833 2533, 63 2 833 2534, or 63 2 833 2550
Fax: 63 2 831 2132, 63 2 831 3707, or 63 2 831 0231
E-mail: philxprt@I-next.net
Web: http://www.philippines1.com/philexport
PHILEXPORT is committed to work for the continuing development of the Philippines and the prosperity of the Filipinos through exports.

Plan: Föreningen för Produktionslogistik (Swedish Production and Inventory Management Society)

Blekholmsterassen 3
Box 553
103 31 Stockholm
Sweden
Phone: (46 8) 24 12 90
Fax: (46 8) 24 12 05
E-mail: kansli@plan.se
Web: http://www.plan.se
PLAN, founded in 1963, has more than 1900 members.

Purchasing and Materials Management Association of the Philippines, Inc. (PMMAP)

Unit 1706-A Philippine Stock Exchange Center Exchange Road
Ortigas Center
Pasig
Metro Manila
Philippines
Phone: 63 2 634-6632, 63 2 634-5955, or 63 2 634-5942
Fax: 63 2 634-6348
E-mail: pmmap@mnl.sequel.net
Web: http://www.sequel.net/ ~ pmmap
PMMAP, formerly Purchasing Association of the Philippines, is a non-profit organization founded in 1968 to bring together purchasing and materials management practitioners to advance the profession. It is a C.P.M. allied member of the National Association of Purchasing Management and a charter member of the International Federation of Purchasing and Materials Management.

Purchasing Management Association of Thailand
54 BB Building, Suite #1509
Asoke Road,
Wattana, Bangkok
10110 Thailand
Phone: (+662) 260-7326~8
Fax: (+662) 260-7328
E-mail: pmat@thai.org
Web: http://thai.org/pmat/
This organization began as the Thai Purchaser Club, formed in Bangkok in November 1988. It attained association status in 1996 as the Purchasing Management Association of Thailand. It numbers more than 4,000 members. Its objectives are to bring professionalism into purchasing and inventory management, to serve its members and organizations, and to develop and encourage more effective methods in the field of purchasing and material management.

Purchasing & Supply Institute of Pakistan
Lahore
Pakistan
Phone: +92 (42) 5868440
Fax: +92 (42) 5868451
E-mail: NA
Web: http://www.purchasing.org.pk/
PIP exists to promote and develop high standards of professional ability and integrity among all those engaged in purchasing and supply chain management in Pakistan.

Resource Management Institute
6212 Samuell Boulevard
Dallas, TX 75228-0711
Phone/Fax: (214) 388-9057
E-mail: dmaples@resource-mgt-institute.org
Web: http://www.resource-mgt-institute.org/
This consulting organization has two goals: to provide high-quality, low-cost training in purchasing, inventory management, operations management, logistics, and conservation, and to research training needs in the business community.

Schweizerischer Verband für Materialwirtschaft und Einkauf (SVME) (Swiss Association for Supply and Purchasing)
Zentralsekretariat
Laurenzenvorstadt 90
CH-5001 Aarau
Switzerland
Phone: +41 062 824 71 31
Fax: +41 62 824 60 45
E-mail: svme@box.echo.ch
Web: http://www.svme.ch/
SVME is a sponsor of the European Council of Purchasing and Supply Eurodiploma.

Schweizerische Gesellschaft für Logistik/ Association Suisse de Logistique/ Associazione Svizzera di Logistica (SGL/ASL) (Swiss Logistics Association)
Egelbergstrasse 33
Postfach
CH-3000 Bern 32
Switzerland
Phone: (41 31) 350 43 43
Fax: (41 31) 350 43 50
E-mail: info@sgl.ch
Web: http://www.sgl.ch

Singapore Institute of Materials Management (SIMM)
Level 5, Pico Creative Centre
20 Kallang Avenue
Singapore 339411
Phone: 65 2954427
Fax: 65 2984012
E-mail: simmsg@www.simm.com.sg
Web: http://www.simm.com.sg
The Institute was incorporated in 1980 as a non-profit and self-supporting independent educational institution, with quality as its corporate emphasis and committed to the principle of "buying right." The Institute publishes *SIMMER*, a bimonthly publication covering various aspects of logistics and materials management that includes the modern trends and research activities of the industry.

Small Business Alliance Group Purchasing Network
Small Business Alliance National Headquarters

301 North Water Street
Milwaukee, WI 53202
Phone: (414) 270-9510
Fax: NA
E-mail: aboldin@smallbizalliance.com
Web: http://www.smallbizalliance.com/
index.htm
This organization offers savings on a wide variety
of products and services.

SOLE—The International Society of Logistics

8100 Professional Place, Suite 211
Hyattsville, MD 20785
Phone: (301) 459-8446
Fax: (301) 459-1522
E-mail: hq@sole.org
Web: http://www.sole.org/
SOLE is a non-profit international society composed
of individual and corporate members. The members
include technical and management personnel working in the logistics fields of planning, operations, and
training. The primary purpose of SOLE is to engage
in scientific, educational, and literary endeavors to
enhance the art of logistics technology, education,
and management. SOLE activities are directed to the
in-depth development of logistics as a system of scientific disciplines. There are over 100 chapters in
more than 50 countries, including chapters in Saudi
Arabia, United Kingdom, Italy, Luxembourg, France,
Russia, Japan, Australia, and Taiwan.

SOLEUROPE (Society of Logistics Europe)

c/o NATO Maintenance and Supply Agency
(NAMSA)
11 Rue de la Gare
L-8302 Capellen
Luxembourg
Phone: +47 22 20 14 00
Fax: +47 22 20 06 50
E-mail: NA
Web: NA

South African Production and Inventory Control Society (SAPICS)

Postal Address: P.O. Box 1403
Kempton Park

1620 South Africa
Physical Address:
2 Forum Building
Thistle Street
Kempton Park
South Africa
Phone: (011) 975-1389
Fax: (011) 975-1856
E-mail: sapics@mweb.co.za
Web: http://www.sapics.org.za
The SAPICS vision statement is to be the leading
provider of knowledge and continuous improvement
in production, operations, and supply chain manage-
ment in South Africa.

Stanford Global Supply Chain Management Forum

Deborah Nobel Newman, Assistant Director
Thornton Center, Room 207
Stanford University
Stanford, CA 94305-4022
Phone: (650) 723-4289
Fax: (650) 723-7349
E-mail: newman@cdr.stanford.edu
Web: http://www.stanford.edu/group/
scforum/
The Forum is a program in partnership with industry and the School of Engineering and the Graduate
School of Business at Stanford University that
advances the theory and practice of excellence in
global supply chain management. The Forum aims
to identify, document, research, develop, and disseminate best practices and innovations in this area
in order to advance teaching and research in global
supply chain management. The Forum also publishes a quarterly newsletter.

Suomen Logistiikkayhdistys r.y. (Finnish Logistics Association)

Katajanokankatu 5D14
FIN-00160 Helsinki
Finland
Phone: +358 9 179 545
Fax: +358 9 177 675
E-mail: logistiikka@clarinet.fi
Web: http://www.logy.fi

The purpose of the Finnish Logistics Association is to develop procedures for purchasing materials and services and to promote physical logistics (transportation, storage, handling) and the professional skills of employees in logistics for the benefit of the Finnish economy and society. The objectives are to improve logistics and increase the internal and external integration of logistics, to develop the use of computer processing and data interchange in logistics, and to provide Finnish logistics services.

Suomen Tuotannonohjausyhdistys (STO) (Production Management Society of Finland)

Anne-Maj Viio
Tuija Tiihonen
PL 62
FIN-02601 Espoo
Finland
Phone: +358 9 560 75 40
Fax: +358 9 561 70 033
E-mail: anne.tuija@megabaud.fi
Web: http://pe.tut.fi/sto
STO is an international society of logistics, production, and operations management founded in 1978. The society consists of professionals who work in industry, software companies, universities, and research centers.

Supply America Corporation

Edward Kwiatkowski, President
102 Spring Drive
Chagrin Falls, OH 44022
Phone: (440) 338-3622
Fax: (440)338-3603
E-mail: ehksupam@aol.com
Web: http://www.supplyamerica.org/
Supply America is a not-for-profit corporation whose mission is to improve the competitiveness of small and medium-sized U.S. manufacturers by improving their supply chain performance. The organization helps American industry develop and implement successful supply chain management strategies. It coordinates supply chain management assistance of the Manufacturing Extension Partnership (MEP) program, a nationwide network of manufacturing and business experts.

Supply-Chain Council, Inc.

303 Freeport Road
Pittsburgh, PA 15215
Phone: (412) 781-4101
Fax: (412) 781-2871
E-mail: info@supply-chain.org
Web: http://www.supply-chain.org
Launched in April 1996, the Supply-Chain Council is a global, not-for-profit trade association with membership open to all companies interested in improving supply-chain efficiencies through the use of the SCOR-model, a supply-chain diagnostic tool.

Supply Chain Management Research Group

Bernard J. La Londe, Emeritus Professor of Transportation and Logistics
Max M. Fisher College of Business
The Ohio State University
351 Fisher Hall
2100 Neil Avenue
Columbus OH 43210
Phone: (614) 292-5233
Fax: (614) 688-3955
E-mail: Lalonde.3@osu.edu
Web: http://www2.cob.ohio-state.edu/~scmrg
The purpose of the Research Group is to conduct relevant business research in the area of supply chain management that will be valuable to supporting organizations, students, and faculty. Research will focus on increasing knowledge in the public domain in the form of working papers, presentations, and publications.

Supply Chain Planning Limited

Building 32
University Campus
Cranfield
Bedford, MK43 0AL
England
Phone: +44 (0)1234 750323
Fax: +44 (0)1234 752040
E-mail: scp@cranfield.ac.uk
Web: http://www.ila.co.uk/main.html
Set up as the National Materials Handling Centre in 1970 jointly by the Institute of Materials Handling,

the Ministry of Technology, the Federation of Mechanical Handling Equipment Manufacturers, and the Cranfield Institute of Technology (now Cranfield University), Supply Chain Planning Limited serves as the focal point for information and advice for industry.

Svensk Indkøbs och Logistik Forbund (SILF) (Swedish National Association of Purchasing and Logistics)

Silf Utbildning AB
Box 1278
164 29 Kista
Sweden
Phone: +46 8 752 1670
Fax: +46 8 750 6410
E-mail: silf@silf.se
Web: http://www.silf.se
SILF is a sponsor of the European Council of Purchasing and Supply Eurodiploma.

Uniform Code Council, Inc. (UCC)

Customer Service Center
7887 Washington Village Drive, Suite 300
Dayton, OH 45459
Phone (937) 435-3870
Fax: (937) 435-7317
E-mail: info@uc-council.org
Web: http://www.uc-council.org
The mission of the Uniform Code Council, Inc., is to take a global leadership role in establishing and promoting multi-industry standards for product identification and related electronic communication. The UCC establishes and promotes multi-industry standards for product identification and related electronic communications. The UCC, in partnership with EAN International, is committed to the development, establishment, and promotion of global, open standards for identification and communication throughout the supply chain.

United States Council for International Business

1212 Avenue of the Americas, 21st Floor
New York, NY 10276
Phone: (212) 354-4480
Fax: NA
E-mail: info@uscib.org

Web: http://www.uscib.org/
The purpose of the USCIB is "Giving business a seat at the table in promoting an open system of world trade, finance, and investment." The USCIB advances the global interests of American business both at home and abroad. It is the U.S. affiliate of the International Chamber of Commerce, the Business and Industry Advisory Committee to the OECD, and the International Organisation of Employers (IOE). As such, it officially represents U.S. business positions both in the main intergovernmental bodies and with foreign business communities and their governments. The USCIB addresses a broad range of policy issues with the objective of promoting an open system of world trade, finance, and investment in which business can flourish and contribute to economic growth, human welfare, and protection of the environment.

Vereniging Logistiek Management

P.O. Box 23207
NL-3001 KE Rotterdam
Netherlands
Phone: (31 10) 436 41 55 or (31 10) 440 85 81
Fax: (31 10) 436 46 25
E-mail: vlm@worldonline.nl
Web: http://www.vlmnet.nl/
VLM works to improve the practice of logistics, particularly through developing its network of regional offices, awarding the Netherlands Logistics Award, and promoting education.

Vereniging voor Inkoop en Bedrijfslogistiek (VIB) (The Belgian Association of Purchasing Management)

VIB-Centrale Administratie
Langemarkstraat 42
B-2600 Berchem/Antwerp
Belgium
Phone: 32 3 286 80 90
Fax: 32 3 286 80 98
E-mail: vib@bevib.be
Web: http://www.bevib.be/VIB
The VIB serves people involved in purchasing and logistics in all areas of industry, trade, and services in the Flemish area of Belgium. It is a sponsor of the European Council of Purchasing and Supply Eurodiploma.

Warehousing Education and Research Council
1100 Jorie Boulevard, Suite 170
Oak Brook, IL 60523-4413
Phone: (630) 990-0001
Fax: (630) 990-0256
E-mail: wercoffice@werc.org
Web: http://www.werc.org
WERC is an international professional association, based in the U.S., dedicated to the advancement and education of people involved in the management of warehouses and distribution facilities. WERC provides its members with the latest information available on warehousing and distribution trends, issues, and potential concerns.

World Trade Organization (WTO)
154 rue de Lausanne
1211 Geneva 21
Switzerland
Phone: (41 22) 739 5111
Fax: (41 22) 739 5458
E-mail: enquiries@wto.org
Web: http://www.wto.org
WTO is the only international organization dealing with the global rules of trade among nations. Its main function is to ensure that trade flows as smoothly, predictably, and freely as possible, so that consumers and producers know that they can enjoy secure supplies and greater choice of finished products, components, raw materials, and services. And that producers and exporters know that foreign markets will remain open to them.

Calendar of Major Events, Meetings, and Conferences, 2000

To help you plan for 2000, the following list provides information about some events of interest to professionals in areas of purchasing and supply management, with Web sites that you can check for details. Since we cannot include every event, you might also want to visit the Web sites listed in the Directory of Purchasing and Supply Management Associations and Organizations.

January 2000

World Trade Group
Supply Chain Expo
January 11-12, 2000
London, United Kingdom
http://www.globalsupplychain.com

Institute for International Research
Global Sourcing Conference
January 12-14, 2000
Atlanta, GA
http://www.iir-ny.com/

Material Handling Industry of America
2000 MHIA Annual Meeting & Executive Conference
January 13-15, 2000
Naples, FL
http://www.mhia.org/

National Retail Federation
89th Annual Convention & EXPO
January 16-19, 2000
New York, NY
http://www.uc-council.org/events/ev_ucc_events_calendar.html

**RAMS 2000: The Annual Reliability and Maintainability Symposium
(The International Symposium on Product Quality & Integrity)**
January 24-27, 2000
Los Angeles, CA
http://www.rams.org
Sponsored by 10 technical societies:
    American Institute of Aeronautics and Astronautics
    ASQ Electronics Division
    ASQ Reliability Division
    IEEE Reliability Society
    IEST Quality Control, Evaluation and Product Reliability Divisions
    IIE Quality Control and Reliability Engineering Division
    Society of Automotive Engineers
    Society of Logistics Engineers
    Society of Reliability Engineers
    Systems Safety Society

Worldwide Business Research
eTail 2000 (online retail)
January 25-26, 2000
San Francisco, CA
http://www.wbresearch.com

Mercer Management Consulting
The 2000 Logistics Conference: Integrating Supply and Demand Chains
January 27-28, 2000
Chicago, IL
http://www.conference-board.org/logistics.htm

February 2000

Worldwide Business Research
LOGICON2000: Executive Summit for the Supply Chain
February 2-3, 2000
New Orleans, LA
http://www.wbresearch.com

National Association of Purchasing Management and Florida State University
Developing Excellence in Purchasing and Supply Management Program
February 2-6, 2000
Tallahassee, FL
http://www.napm.org

Electronic Commerce Canada, Inc.
6th Annual Symposium: Symposium 2000—"We Are Connected: Now What?"
February 9-10, 2000
Ottawa, ON, Canada
http://www.ecc.ca/Events/Upcoming/Symposium2000/Index.html

International Warehouse Logistics Association
109th Annual Convention
February 13-16, 2000
Tampa, FL
http://www.warehouselogistics.org/IWLA_Site/index.htm?id = AnnualConventionHome

SOLE—The International Society of Logistics
1st World Symposium on Logistics in Forest Sector
February 14-15, 2000
Helsinki, Finland
http://www.sole.org/news.asp?article = 26

The Conference Board
2000 Strategic Outsourcing Conference
February 15-16, 2000
San Diego, CA
http://www.conference-board.org/search/dconference.cfm?conferenceid = 2000890

March 2000

Workgroup for Electronic Data Interchange
WEDI 2000
March 2000 (dates and location to be announced)
http://www.wedi.org

National Association of Purchasing Management
Arizona State University
The Changing Nature of the Supply Process
March 6-10, 2000
Tempe, AZ
http://www.napm.org

Stanford Supply Chain Management Forum and Eindhoven Forum
Annual Symposium
March 15-16, 2000
Eindhoven, Netherlands
http://www.stanford.edu/group/scforum/

National Association of Purchasing Management
Executive Forum
March 20-21, 2000
Tempe, AZ
http://www.napm.org

American Society for Quality
7th Annual ISO 9000 Conference: Moving From Conformance to Performance
March 20-21, 2000
Dallas, TX
http://www.asq.org

The Conference Board
2000 Strategic Outsourcing Conference
March 21-22, 2000
New York, NY
http://www.conference-board.org/search/dconference.cfm?conferenceid = 2000867

IDG
Internet Commerce Expo
March 27-30, 2000
Boston, MA
http://www.iceexpo.com/

April 2000

National Association of Procurement Professionals
2000 National Conference
April 2-5, 2000
Marco Island (Naples), FL
http://www.solcon.com/NAPP

National Association of Purchasing Management
Arizona State University
Global Supply Chain Management Program
April 3-6, 2000
Tempe, AZ
http://www.napm.org

Electronic Messaging Association
EMA 2000/Boston, Annual Conference and Exposition
April 6-8, 2000

Boston, MA
http://www.ema.org

National Contract Management Association
World Congress 2000: "The Acquisition Professional in the New Millennium"
April 9-12, 2000
Washington, DC
http://www.ncmahq.org/congress2000/index.html

National Association of Purchasing Management
Arizona State University
Strategy Development and Executive Leadership in Supply Management
April 10-13, 2000
Tempe, AZ
http://www.napm.org

Supply Chain Council
2000 Supply-Chain World Conference and Exposition: "SCOR: The SCM Tool for the 21st Century"
April 10-12, 2000
Chicago, IL
http://www.supplychainworld.com

Material Handling Industry of America
NA 2000: The North American Material Handling Show and Forum
April 10-13, 2000
Detroit, MI
http://www.mhia.org/na2000/default.htm

Aspect Development
North American Summit 2000 (inbound supply chain management)
April 17-19, 2000
Scottsdale, AZ
http://www.aspectdv.com

National Association of Educational Buyers, Inc. (NAEB)
79th Annual Meeting & Product Exhibit
April 26-29, 2000
San Diego, CA
http://www.naeb.org/AM2000/2000index.htm

National Association of Purchasing Management
85th Annual International Purchasing Conference and Educational Exhibit
April 30-May 3, 2000
New Orleans, LA
http://www.napm.org

May 2000

American Society for Quality
54th Annual Quality Congress and Exhibition
May 8-10, 2000
Indianapolis, IN
http://www.asq.org

3rd IMRL/RIRL Conference (International Meeting for Research in Logistics / Rencontres Internationales de la Recherche en Logistique)
May 9-11, 2000
Trois-Rivières, QC, Canada
http://www.uqtr.uquebec.ca/RIRL2000

Purchasing Management Association of Canada
National Association of Purchasing Management
Chartered Institute of Purchasing and Supply
International Purchasing and Supply Education and Research Association
Conference 2000:
3rd Worldwide Research Symposium on Purchasing and Supply Chain Management
9th International IPSERA Conference
3rd Annual North American Research Symposium on Purchasing and Supply
May 24-27, 2000
London, ON, Canada
http://www.ivey.uwo.ca/conference2000

Canadian Association of Logistics Management
2000 Annual Conference: "Supply Chain Emergence"
May 28-30, 2000
Toronto, ON, Canada
http://www.calm.org

June 2000

National Association of Purchasing Management
Electronic Commerce and Supply Chain Management Conferences
June 7-9, 2000

Scottsdale, AZ
http://www.napm.org

Purchasing Management Association of Canada
Annual Conference
June 7-9, 2000
Ottawa, ON, Canada
http://www.pmac.ca/Annual%20Conference.htm

Institute of Logistics and Transport
Logistics Conference and Exhibition 2000
June 13-15, 2000
Birmingham, United Kingdom
http://www.iolt.org.uk

NOFOMA Network (Nordic Research in Materials Management)
12th Annual International Conference on Nordic Logistics Research
June 14-15, 2000
Århus, Denmark
http://www.egroups.com/group/nofoma/fullinfo.html

Management Centre Europe (European Headquarters, American Management Association International)
International Logistics Conference
June 15-16, 2000
Brussels, Belgium
http://www.mce.be/management/conferen.htm

National Association of Purchasing Management
Arizona State University
Executive Program
June 20-24, 2000
Phoenix, AZ
http://www.napm.org

July 2000

National Contract Management Association
West Coast National Conference
July 2000
Los Angeles, CA
http://www.ncmahq.org

Summit Online
Summit 2000
July 31-August 4, 2000
Santa Clara, CA
http://www.summitonline.com

August 2000

SOLE—The International Society of Logistics
35th Annual International Symposium (SOLE 2000): "Logistics In the 21st Century"
August 8-10, 2000
New Orleans, LA
http://www.sole.org

National Institute of Governmental Purchasing
55th Annual Forum and Products Exposition
August 18-24, 2000
Baltimore, MD
http://www.nigp.org/forum/forum.htm

September 2000

Uniform Code Council
Global Supply Chain Conference
September 19-21, 2000
Tampa, FL
http://www.uc-council.org/events/ev_ucc_events_calendar.html

Council of Logistics Management
Annual Conference
September 24-27, 2000
New Orleans, LA
http://www.clm1.org

October 2000

APICS—The Educational Society for Resource Management
2000 APICS International Conference and Exposition
October 16-20, 2000
Orlando, FL
http://www.apics.org

Association for Enterprise Integration (AFEI)
21st Century Commerce 2000

October 20-27, 2000
Albuquerque, NM
http://www.afei.org/events.htm

November 2000

Workgroup for Electronic Data Interchange
Forum 2000
November 2000 (date and location to be announced)
http://www.wedi.org

National Association of Purchasing Management
Electronic Commerce, Supply Chain Management, and Global Supply Management
Conferences
November 5-8, 2000
Nashville, TN
http://www.napm.org

Canadian Association of Logistics Management
2000 Fall Logistics Symposium
November 8-9, 2000
Toronto, ON, Canada
http://www.calm.org

National Association of Purchasing Management
Arizona State University
Purchasing Management Program
November 13-17, 2000
Tempe, AZ
http://www.napm.org

American Society of Naval Engineers
Naval Logistics Conference 2000
November 14-16, 2000
Norfolk, VA
http://www.navalengineers.org/nlc/default.htm

December 2000

National Association of Purchasing Management
Annual Economic Summit
December 12, 2000
New York, NY
http://www.napm.org

Index